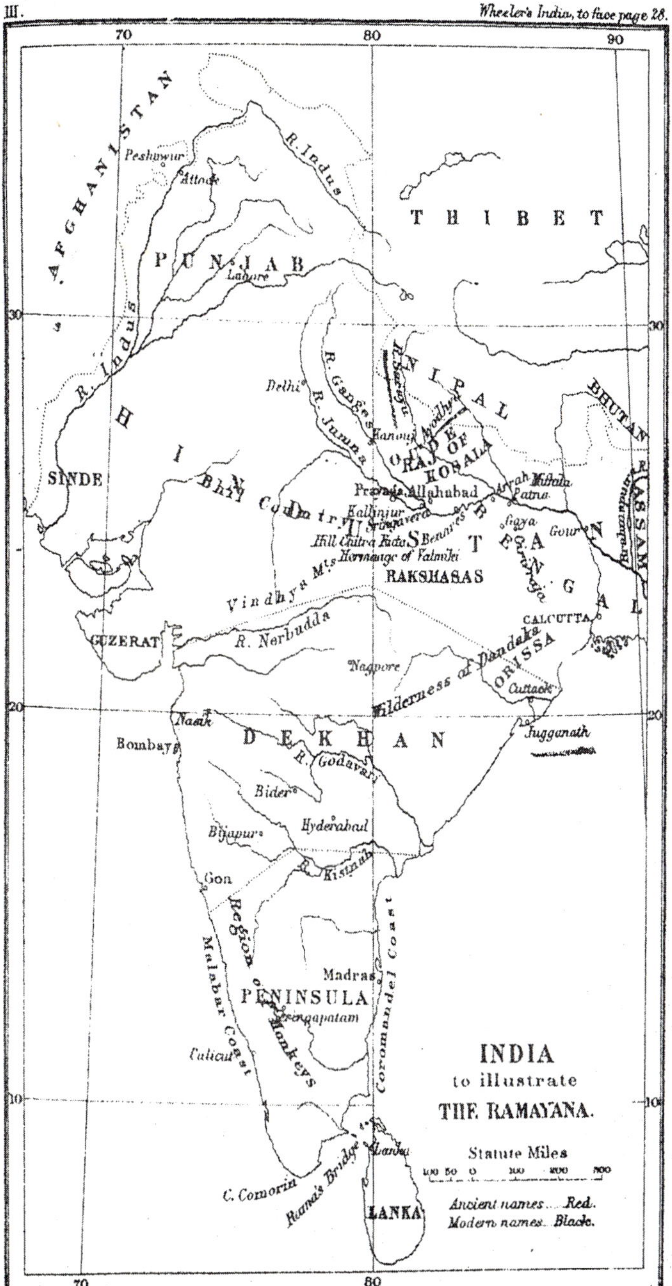

London; Macmillan & Co. Stanford's Geog! Estab!

HISTORY OF INDIA AND OF THE FRONTIER STATES OF AFGHANISTAN, NEPAL, AND BURMA,

HISTORY OF INDIA

AND OF THE FRONTIER STATES
OF
AFGHANISTAN, NEPAL,
AND BURMA,

By

J. TALBOYS WHEELER

GYAN

ISBN : 978-81-212-0115-5

Published, 2018

Published by

Gyan Publishing House
5, Ansari Road
Daryaganj, New Delhi-110002
Phone: 011-47034999, 9811692060
www.gyanbooks.com
E-mail: books@gyanbooks.com

Printed at: G. Print Process, Delhi.

PREFACE.

It is a common complaint that whilst the annals of India are of paramount importance to the people of England, there is no history which they seem less inclined to study. Greece and Rome, Egypt and Palestine, Assyria and Babylon—countries which have long ceased to play a part in the drama of humanity—are the subjects of text-books in our schools and universities; whilst India, which is literally a modern reflex of the ancient world, and has moreover become a part and parcel of the British empire, is to this day a sealed book to the masses. The essays of Lord Macaulay on Robert Clive and Warren Hastings are perhaps known to every English household; but they refer to mere episodes in the history, and are wanting in that familiarity with native character and forms of thought, which is essential to a right appreciation of the great collision between Europe and Asia that has been going on in India for the last two centuries.

The truth is that the preparation of a history of India, political and religious, is a far more difficult and laborious task than is generally imagined. Twenty-two years ago the author began such a work at Madras under every possible advantage. There were libraries at Madras containing almost unique collections of books appertaining to India. To these were added the government records at Madras, which were freely opened to the author by Sir Charles Trevelyan, who was at that time Governor. The author completed a History of Madras, compiled from the government records, and he taught Indian history in the Madras Presidency College; but he was unable to complete a real history of India from a consciousness of want of knowledge. After four years he proceeded to Calcutta as Assistant Secretary to the Government of India in the Foreign or Political Department, and was soon astounded at his own ignorance. He had learnt something of Clive and Hastings, of the Moghuls, Mahrattas, and the Marquis of Wellesley; but of the history of India and its civilisation, and especially of the conflicts between opposite lines of policy laid down by different Anglo-Indian statesmen during the eighteenth and nineteenth centuries, he found that he knew literally nothing.

The writer has no desire to carry the reader into his workshop, or to dwell on the extent of his labours. It will suffice to say that having sounded the depths of his ignorance, he has since then lost no opportunity, official or literary, to perfect his knowledge of Indian history. Some samples have already appeared in his large *History of India from the Earliest Ages*, which deals with the Hindu and Muhammadan periods, and of which four volumes have already been published. His history of British India is now given for the first time in the present volume. It has been an entirely independent work, drawn direct from the fountain head, after a study of the records of the Government of India, official reports and parliamentary blue books, and of such current annals, memoirs, travels, or correspondence, as have been found to yield historical materials. Thus it is only after the unremitting application of many years, during which official duties have often helped him as much as literary studies, that the author has been able to complete the history of India, from the earliest dawning of legend to the breaking out of the present Afghan war: and to reduce the whole to a compact form which, it is hoped, will render it both interesting and useful to general readers, as well as to students in the religion and politics of our Indian empire.

In conclusion, attention may be drawn to the series of maps which illustrate the successive changes in the history. They have been constructed on a plan originally suggested by Mr. Macmillan, but which has been somewhat modified to meet the requirements of the present volume.

WITHAM, ESSEX,
Jan. 22, 1880.

CONTENTS.

PART I.

HINDU INDIA.

CHAPTER I.

CHAPTER II.

CHAPTER III.

CHAPTER IV.

PART II.

MUHAMMADAN INDIA.

CHAPTER I.

CHAPTER II.

CHAPTER III.

CHAPTER IV.

CHAPTER V.

CHAPTER VI.

CHAPTER VII.

CHAPTER VIII.

PART III.

BRITISH INDIA.

CHAPTER I.

CHAPTER II.

CHAPTER III.

CHAPTER IV.

CHAPTER V.

CHAPTER VI.

CHAPTER VII.

CHAPTER VIII.

CHAPTER IX.

CHAPTER X.

CHAPTER XI.

CHAPTER XII.

CHAPTER XIII.

CHAPTER XIV.

CHAPTER XV.

CHAPTER XVI.

CHAPTER XVII.

CHAPTER XVIII.

CHAPTER XIX.

CHAPTER XX.

CHAPTER XXI.

CHAPTER XXII.

CHAPTER XXIII.

CHAPTER XXIV.

CHAPTER XXV.

CHAPTER XXVI.

LIST OF MAPS.

Wheeler's India, to face page

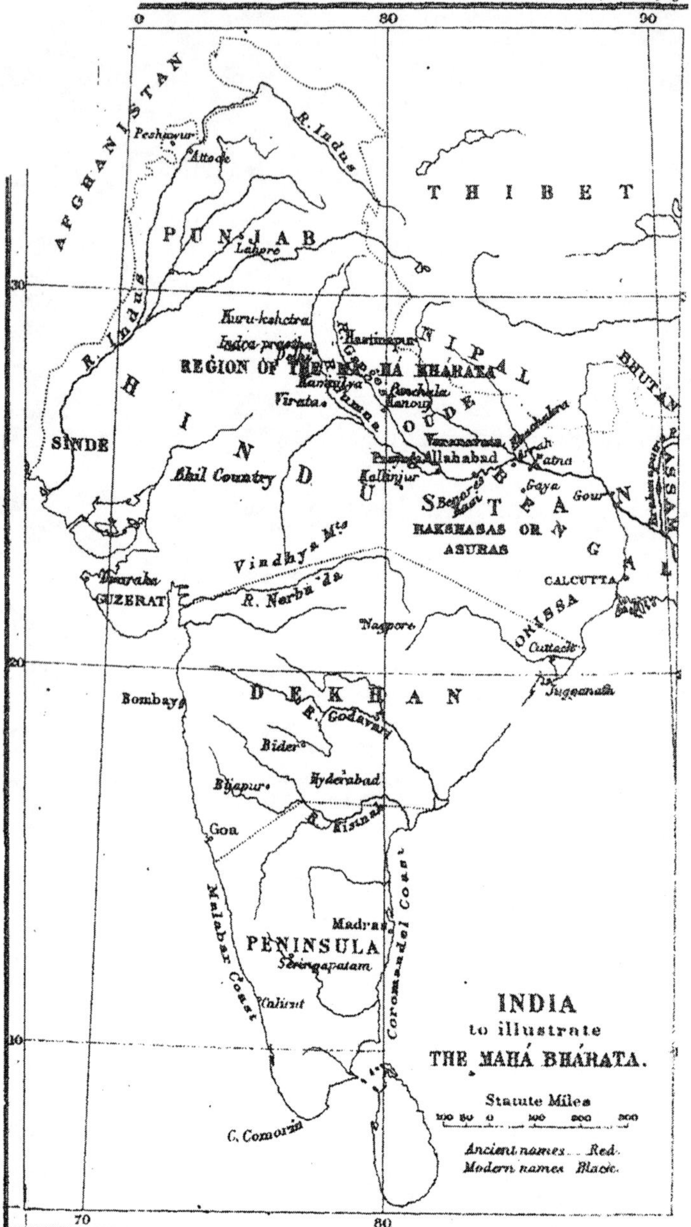

London: Macmillan & Co.

Stanford's Geogl. Estab.

PART I

HINDU INDIA.

CHAPTER I.

MAHÁ BHÁRATA: PUNJAB AND NORTH-WEST.

ABOUT B.C. 1500-1400.

B.C. 1500-1400

India under the Rajas.

INDIA in ancient times was parcelled out, like Palestine and Greece, into a number of small kingdoms, each under the government of its own Raja. Every Raja had a council of elders, including chiefs and kinsmen, who were collectively known as the Durbar. Sometimes there was a minister or ministry. Sometimes a Raja might be under the influence of a queen or Rání, or of a queen mother or dowager Rání. Sometimes a Raja conquered other Rajas, and became known as a Mahárája, or "great Raja." At a remote period the life at Hindu courts was modified by the rise of priests or Brahmans. The working of these various elements finds full expression in Hindu legends, and constitutes what may be called Hindu history.

Earliest traditions: the Punjab and North west of Hindustan.

The earliest traditions of India are recorded in the Mahá Bhárata, an ancient Hindu epic, written in the Sanskrit language. It tells of a great war between Kauravas and Pándavas, just as Homer's Iliad tells of a war between Greece and Troy. The scene is laid partly in the Punjab, and partly in the north-west of Hindustan. The Kauravas and Pándavas were rival kinsmen of the royal house of Hastinápur. The city of Hastinápur was situated about sixty-five miles to the north-east of Delhi, and is still represented by

B.C. 1500 1400

a group of shapeless mounds on the upper course of the Ganges. The extent of the Raj is unknown; but it included a certain area round Hastinápur on the river Ganges. It probably consisted of arable and pasture lands, occupied by Rajpúts, and bordering on uncleared jungle and forest, which were inhabited by aboriginal populations; but in the Sanskrit epic the Raja is always known as a Maháraja, or "great Raja."[1]

Hastinápur, an Aryan colony.

Hastinápur was to all appearance an Aryan colony, having other Aryan or Rajpút colonies in its neighbourhood, each forming a kingdom under its own Raja. But all these colonies were struggling more or less against aboriginal or non-Aryan populations. The Aryans were immigrants from High Asia; they had established kingdoms in Central Asia, the Punjab, and the north-west quarter of Hindustan, as far as Kanouj on the Ganges, and probably in Ayodhyá or Oude to the northward of the Ganges. They regarded the aborigines as demons and cannibals, and called them Rákshasas and Asuras. Some aboriginal tribes were treated rather as subject races; such as the Bhíls or Bheels, who occupied the hills and jungles to the south, and the Nágas, or snake worshippers, who appear to have migrated from Kashmír towards the banks of the Ganges.

Bharata, the hero ancestor.

The Maháraja of Hastinápur was named Santanu. He claimed descent from the hero Bharata, who was said to have conquered all India. The name of Bharata was famous in the days of yore. All India was called the land of Bharata. Even the war of the descendants of Santanu, which forms the main tradition of the epic, has always been known as the Mahá Bhárata, or "great war of Bharata."

Marriage of an old Maháraja: the dreadful vow.

Maháraja Santanu was an old man with a grown-up son. He wanted to marry a young damsel; but her parents would not consent to the marriage unless he disinherited his present son, and reserved the Raj for any other son he might have by their daughter. Moreover, to prevent any future disputes, the parents insisted that the son already living should pledge himself never to marry. The Maháraja was thus at the mercy of his son. But the son was a model of filial obedience; he resigned all claim to the Raj; and he vowed never to marry, and never to become a father. The

[1] General Cunningham, on the strength of certain astronomical data, fixes the date of the war of the Mahá Bhárata in 1426 B.C.

parents then gave their daughter in marriage to the Maháraja; but the son became known by the name of Bhíshma, or "dreadful," because of his dreadful vow.

B.C. 1500-1400

Bhíshma, the faithful guardian.

The old Maháraja became the father of a second son, and then died. Bhíshma kept his vow, and proved a faithful guardian of the widow and her infant son. He placed the son upon the throne, instructed him in the use of arms, and conducted the affairs of the Raj for him as minister or manager. When the prince was grown, Bhíshma provided him with two wives; he fought and conquered the Raja of Benares, and carried off his two daughters to become the brides of his young half-brother.[1] This capture of daughters was in accordance with the old customs of the Kshatriyas or Rajas; but the captor was always obliged to fight and conquer the father before he could carry off a daughter, either to marry her or to give her in marriage.[2] The man who stole away a daughter without fighting the father was a coward and a Rákshasa.[3]

Dhritaráshtra, the "blind," and Pándu the "pale-complexioned."

After a while the young Maháraja sickened and died, leaving two infants to inherit the Raj,—Dhritaráshtra the "blind," and Pándu the "pale-complexioned."[4] Again Bhíshma proved a faithful minister and instructor; he managed the Raj, educated the two boys, and in due time procured wives for both. Dhritaráshtra the blind was married to a daughter of the Raja of the Gándhára country.[5] The bride was named Gándhárí; and when she knew that her husband was blind, she tied a handkerchief over her eyes, so that she might have no advantage over him. Pándu

[1] Attock, on the river Indus, was anciently known as Benares. It is a question whether the princesses belonged to Benares on the Indus, or to Benares on the Ganges.

[2] *Manu*, iii. 26, 32, 41. For further explanation, see *History of India*, vol. i.: Mahá Bhárata.

[3] Rákshasa was a name of reproach applied to the aborigines of India.

[4] The legend has been slightly modified to suit modern tastes. The details are given in the larger *History of India*, vol. i.

[5] The name of Gándhára still lingers in that of Kandahar in Central Asia. The country, however, is said to be identical with the lower Cábul valley, including Peshawur. The Gandarians fought in the army of Xerxes, armed, like the Baktrians with bows of cane and short spears. (*Herodotus*, vii. 64, 66.) Rawlinson locates them on the lower Indus, and makes them migrate to Kandahar.

B.C. 1500-1400

the pale-complexioned was married to two wives, Kuntí and Madrí.[1]

Exclusion of the blind prince.

The council of elders at Hastinápur would not accept a blind prince as their Maháraja. Dhritaráshtra was set aside notwithstanding he was the elder of the two; and Pándu the pale-complexioned was installed on the throne of Hastinápur.

Maháraja Pándu; death and satí.

The reign of Pándu is obscure, and of no moment. After a while he abdicated the throne, and went into the jungle, and spent his time in hunting. Subsequently he died in the jungle, leaving three sons by Kuntí and two sons by Madrí. There was a contest between his two widows as to who should burn herself with his remains. Madrí pleaded that she was the youngest and most beloved, and therefore the most likely to comfort the dead Maháraja in the world of shades.[2] Accordingly Madrí perished on the funeral pile, and Kuntí returned with the five sons of Pándu to the palace of Hastinápur. The three sons of Kuntí were named Yudhishthira, Bhíma, and Arjuna. The two sons of Madrí were named Nakula and Sahadava.

Maháraja Dhritaráshtra: Kauravas and Pándavas.

Meanwhile Dhritaráshtra the blind became Maháraja of Hastinápur. Indeed after the abdication of Pándu there was no alternative; for there was no one left but the blind prince. Bhíshma, however. was still minister or manager of the Raj. Dhritaráshtra had several sons, but only two of any note, namely, Duryodhana the eldest, and his brother Duhsásana. The sons of Dhritaráshtra were called the Kauravas, after a remote ancestor called Kuru. They were thus distinguished from their cousins, the five sons of Pándu, who were known as the Pándavas.

Drona the preceptor: his feud with Drupada.

The Kauravas and Pándavas were brought up in the old palace at Hastinápur. Bhíshma, the patriarch of the family, was by this time too old to teach the rising generation. A tutor or preceptor was engaged named Drona. He was an exiled prince from Pancháia, who had taken refuge at the court of Hastinápur. Pancháia lay to the south-east; it was a Raj situated on the lower Doab

[1] The birth of Kuntí is obscured by a religious myth. Madrí is said to have been bought with money.

[2] This story was current amongst the Greeks. It is retold in the history of Didorus Siculus.

between the Ganges and the Jumna.[1] The Raja of Panchála was named Drupada. Drona had a feud with Drupada, and became an exile. He married a daughter of the house of Hastinápur, and had a son, named Aswattháma. He became preceptor of the young princes of Hastinápur, on the condition that when they were fully versed in the use of arms, they should help him to be revenged on Raja Drupada.

B.C. 1500–1400

Jealousy between Kauravas and Pándavas.

There was soon a jealousy between the Kauravas and the Pándavas. It was a question who should succeed to the Raj; Duryodhana, the eldest of the Kauravas, or Yudhishthira, the eldest of the Pándavas. Yudhishthira was not given to fighting, and never proved himself a warrior. But Duryodhana was jealous of the strength of Bhíma, the second Pándava, who was the giant of the family. He mixed drugs in Bhíma's food; and when the giant was in a deep sleep, he threw him into the Ganges. Bhíma was rescued by some of the Nága people, and returned to Hastinápur; but the strife between Duryodhana and the Pándavas still remained.

Instructions of Drona.

Drona took great pains in teaching all the young men, but he had a special leaning towards the Pándavas. He taught Yudhishthira the use of the spear, but nothing would make that young man a warrior. Bhíma, however, learnt to use his club; whilst Arjuna became the most famous archer of his time. Nakula learned to tame horses, and Sahadava to calculate the stars. The Kauravas were taught the use of arms, like their cousins the Pándavas, and so was Aswatthám̃a, the son of Drona; but there was no one to equal Arjuna; and Duryodhana began to hate Arjuna as much as he hated Bhíma.

Fame of Drona.

The fame of Drona as a teacher of archery was soon noised abroad. Sons of Rajas flocked to Hastinápur to learn the use of the bow. Amongst others came a son of a Bhíl Raja from the southern hills; but Drona refused to instruct him. Drona declared that the Bhíls were a race of highwaymen and cattle lifters, and that it would be a sin to

[1] The frontiers of a Hindu Raj, in ancient times, are often obscure. According to the Mahá Bhárata the kingdom of Panchála extended from the Himalayas to the Chambal river. Manu again indentifies Panchála with Kanouj. The city of Kanouj, on the Ganges, was about two hundred miles to the south of Hastinápur.

B.C. 1500-1400

teach them the use of the bow. The Bhíl prince was much abashed by this refusal, and went away very sorrowful to his own country.

Superstition of a Bhíl prince.

The Bhíls in those days were as superstitious as they are now. The Bhíl prince adored Drona as a god. He made a clay image of Drona, worshipped it, and practised with his bow and arrows before it; and he became so skilful an archer that his fame reached to Hastinápur. Drona was angry with the Bhíl prince; he was alarmed lest the Bhíls should become dangerous archers. He went to the Bhíl country, accompanied by all the young men at Hastinápur, and resolved to spoil the archery of his worshipper. He called the Bhíl prince before him, and commanded him to cut off the forefinger of his right hand. The prince fell down and worshipped him, and prepared to do his bidding. But Drona's heart was touched. He ordered the Bhíl to stay his hand, but made him swear that he would never shoot the bow with his forefinger, but with his middle fingers only.[1]

Exhibition of arms.

After the return from the Bhíl country a day was appointed for an exhibition of arms at Hastinápur. An area was set apart without the city, and marked round with barriers. Galleries were built round about for the accommodation of chieftains and ladies, and were adorned with flags and garlands. When the day began to dawn, the people gathered round the barriers, and between the galleries, to witness the exercises of the Kauravas and Pándavas. The blind Mahá-raja was led to the galleries, and took his seat amongst his chieftains, with Bhíshma sitting on his right hand. All the ladies of the court also took their seats in the galleries; and the chief amongst them were Gándhárí, the mother of the Kauravas, and Kuntí, the mother of the Pándavas.

Public exercises.

Drona and his son Aswatthána then entered the arena in white garments, and chanted the praises of Indra and the gods. The princes followed with their weapons in their hands, and kissed the feet of their preceptor. They began by shooting arrows at a butt, first on foot, and afterwards from horses, elephants, and chariots. Next followed mock fights with swords and bucklers, and afterwards they fought with clubs, to prove their strength as well as their skill.

[1] The legend is remembered in Malwa to this day, but the modern Bhíls have forgotten the oath, and use their forefingers in shooting, as they say their fathers had done before them.

B.C. 1500-1400

Rivalry between Duryodhana and Bhíma.

During the club fighting, the old jealousy broke out. Duryodhana and Bhíma engaged in combat at the other end of the arena, and soon fought in downright earnest. They rushed upon one another like wild elephants, whilst the multitude ran to and fro, and shouted some for Bhíma and others for Duryodhana. The air was filled with noise and dust, and the whole plain was in an uproar. Drona sent his son Aswatthámа to stop the combat, but no one heeded him. At last Drona went himself in all haste, parted the young men by sheer force, and thus put an end to the turmoil.

Arjuna's splendid archery.

When quiet was restored, Drona ordered Arjuna to show his skill at archery. The young prince entered the arena clothed in golden mail, with his bow inlaid with many colours. The multitude hailed him as another Indra; and the heart of Kuntí thrilled with pride and exultation as she beheld her youngest son. Arjuna set up an iron boar and shot five arrows into its mouth. He tied a cow's horn to the top of a pole, and shot twenty-one arrows into the hollow of the horn. He mounted his chariot, and was driven swiftly along, whilst shooting arrows right and left with the utmost skill and dexterity. Next he played with the sword, and the blade flashed like lightning. He whirled his sharp-edged quoit or chakra wherever he would, and never missed his mark. Lastly, he armed himself with a noose, and threw it at horses and deer, and drew every one to the ground. When he had finished, he kissed the feet of his preceptor, and was embraced by Drona before all the assembly.

Rebuff of Karna.

At this moment a young warrior entered the arena, and challenged Arjuna. His name was Karna. He was a close friend of Duryodhana, for he was as skilled an archer as Arjuna; but his birth was low, for his father was a charioteer. Arjuna would have fought Karna, but a kinsman prevented the combat. Duryodhana made him a Raja on the spot, but the Pándavas treated him as an upstart. Bhíma asked him what he had to do with bows and arrows, and told him to take a whip and drive a bullock-cart after his father. Karna was very angry, but said nothing; and night coming on soon dispersed the assembly.

Drona revenged on Drupada.

After this Drona claimed the reward of his instructions. His pupils were skilled in arms, and he was longing to be

B.C. 1500-1400

revenged on the Raja of Panchála. Neither the Maháraja nor his council objected to the war against Drupada. Drona marched against Drupada, accompanied by the Kauravas and Pándavas, and defeated the Panchála Raja, and carried him off prisoner to Hastinápur. Drona now obliged Drupada to give him half the Raj of Panchála; and Drupada returned to his reduced dominion, and swore to be revenged on Drona.

Appointment of Yuva-raja, or "little Raja."

Meanwhile the time arrived for appointing a Yuva-raja, or "little Raja." The Yuva-raja was to help the Maháraja, or "great Raja," in his old age, and to inherit the Raj after his death. A Yuva-raja was appointed whilst the Maháraja was alive, in order to secure the succession, and to accustom the young prince to the duties of government.[1]

First exile of the Pándavas.

In the first instance, Maháraja Dhritaráshtra appointed Yudhishthira to be Yuva-raja. Duryodhana and the Kauravas raised a great outcry. They asked the Maháraja why he promoted his nephews at the expense of his sons. The blind old sovereign became sorely troubled. The sons of Pándu had a rightful claim, but his own sons had a natural claim. The Maháraja was afraid that war and bloodshed would break out in Hastinápur. After much hesitation he ordered Yudhishthira and his brethren to go to the city of Váranávata, the modern Allahabad, there to abide until he should recall them to Hastinápur. The Pándavas obeyed the words of the Maháraja, and went with their mother Kuntí to the city of Váranávata. When they had departed out of Hastinápur, the Maháraja appointed Duryodhana to be Yuva-raja.

Aryan pale.

The exile of the Pándavas carried them to the frontier of the Aryan pale. The city of Váranávata, the ancient Prayág and modern Allahabad, was situated at the junction of the Ganges and Jumna. On the north was the famous Raj of Ayodhyá, or Oude. To the south and east was the country of Rákshasas and Asuras, demons and cannibals.[2]

[1] The custom of appointing a Yuva-raja, or Joobraj, still prevails in Hindu courts. A similar custom prevailed amongst the later kings of Judah and Israel.

[2] Further particulars respecting the region outside the Aryan pale will be furnished in dealing with the Rámáyana. The region to the eastward of Allahabad, which is said to have been occupied by Rákshasas and Asuras, corresponds with Magadha, the modern Behar, the cradle of Buddhism.

B.C. 1500–1400

Narrow escape of the Pándavas.

The Kauravas had already sent a trusty retainer to Váranávata to compass the destruction of the Pándavas. On reaching the city, the Pándavas were met by this retainer, who led them to a college of holy men, and then conducted them to a house which he had prepared for their reception. At night-time the Pándavas discovered that this house was built of combustibles, and that it was locked and barred on the outside. They escaped through a subterranean passage, which is shown to this day in the fortress of Allahabad. The house was burnt down with all that it contained, including a Bhíl woman and five of her sons, who had got drunk after the manner of their race, and fallen asleep inside the building. The discovery of their blackened remains led all men to believe that Kuntí and her five sons had perished in the conflagration.

Adventures amongst the Rákshasas.

The Pándavas next disguised themselves as Brahman mendicants, and journeyed eastward through the land of Rákshasas and Asuras. The sacred garb ensured them respect, whilst they collected enough alms for their daily needs. In this manner they journeyed to the city of Ekachakra, the modern Arrah. On the way Bhíma is said to have conquered and slain a cannibal Asura, named Hidimba, and then to have married his sister Hidimbí.

Battle between Bhíma and an Asura.

At Ekachakra, the Pándavas and their mother lodged in the house of a Brahman. There Bhíma had an adventure with another cannibal Asura, named Vaka. According to the story, Vaka lived in the outskirts of the city, and required the inhabitants to supply him with a stock of provisions and a human victim every day. The household of the Brahman where the Pándavas lodged were in great grief, for it was the Brahman's turn to supply a human victim. The infant son of the Brahman broke off a pointed blade of grass, and wanted to go and kill the Asura. Kuntí and her sons were moved to tears. Bhíma went out to meet the Asura. He tore up a tree by the roots to serve as a club; and then fought the cannibal and slew him, and dragged his body to the gate of the city.[1]

[1] The stories of Hidimbí and Vaka are apparently allegorical fictions, coined by the Brahmanical compilers of the Mahá Bhárata, as an expression of their hatred against the Buddhists. The country, as already seen, was the hot-bed of Buddhism; consequently it is peopled by Rákshasas and Asuras. In Burma and other Buddhist countries, the ladies, though

B.C. 1500-1400

Swayamvara of Draupadí.

At this crisis heralds were proclaiming in all lands that Raja Drupada of Panchála was about to celebrate the Swayamvara of his daughter Draupadí at his city of Kámpilya.[1] The Swayamvara was a marriage festival. Young men of the noble race of Kshatriyas contended in feats of strength and skill for the hand of a daughter of a Raja. It was called a Swayamvara, or "self choice," because the damsel was supposed to have some choice in the matter.[2] Accordingly the Pándavas laid aside their old hostility against Drupada, and went to the Swayamvara of his daughter, who was said to be the fairest maiden in all the world.

The golden fish.

The Swayamvara of Draupadí is a Rajpút romance. All the Rajas of India are said to have been present, including Duryodhána and the other Kauravas, as well as Karna, their low-born ally. A large plain was set apart with barriers and galleries, like the area of the exhibition of arms at Hastinápur. At one end of the plain a golden fish was set up on the top of a pole. Beneath, or before, the fish, a chakra or quoit was hung, and kept constantly whirling round. Near the same spot was a heavy bow of enormous size. The man who strung the bow, and shot an arrow through the chakra, which should strike the eye of the fish, was to be the winner of the daughter of the Raja.

Draupadí and her brother Dhrishtadyumna.

When the Pándavas reached the city of Kámpilya they found a number of Rajas encamped round about. There were soldiers and elephants, merchants and showmen, and multitudes of spectators. After many days of sports and feasting, the morning of the Swayamvara began to dawn. The city was awakened with drums and trumpets, and the

perfectly modest, are more free and unreserved than in a Brahmanical country like India. This fact is exaggerated in the story of Hidimbi, who is represented as asking Bhíma to take her as his wife. Vaka is nothing more than an allegorical personification of a Buddhist monastery, situated in the outskirts of a city, and receiving a daily supply of provisions from the inhabitants. The Buddhist monks had no objection to flesh meat, which was opposed to Brahmanical laws; accordingly they figure as cannibals. Bhíma, the hero of the Pándavas, is described as destroying the monster or monastery.

[1] General Cunningham identifies Kámpilya with the modern Kampil, between Budaon and Farukhabad.

[2] At later Swayamvaras there were no preliminary games, but a princess simply chose her own bridegroom.

plain was hung with flags and garlands. The multitude crowded round the barriers; the Rajas filled the galleries; the Brahmans chanted the Vedic hymns in praise of Indra and the gods. The princess Draupadí appeared with a garland in her hand, and her brother Dhrishta-dyumna stood at her side. The prince stepped forward and proclaimed that his sister would be the bride of the man who shot an arrow through the chakra and struck the eye of the golden fish. He then turned to his sister and said, "If a Kshatriya[1] performs this feat, you must throw your garland round his neck, and accept him for your lord and bridegroom." B.C. 1500-1400

Failure of the Rajas.

Then the Rajas arose from their seats and entered the area. They gathered round the golden fish and looked wistfully at the bow; but every man was afraid to lift it lest he should fail to bend it, and excite laughter and scorn. Presently one tried to bend the bow and failed. Then many tried and shared his fate. At last Karna entered the lists; he bent the bow and fitted an arrow to the string. At this moment Draupadí stepped forth. She cried aloud, "I wed not with the base-born!" So Karna was abashed and walked away; but his heart was burning with rage and mortification.

Triumph of Arjuna.

Other Rajas came up, but not one could bend the bow. The Pándavas looked on, still disguised as Brahmans. Suddenly Arjuna stept forth and strung the bow, and fitted an arrow to the string. The Brahmans looked on with wild surprise to see a Brahman contend at a Swayamvara. The Brahmans in the crowd were sore afraid lest the Rajas should be offended and withhold their alms; they implored Arjuna to withdraw. But Arjuna, nothing daunted, drew his bow with all his might; he shot the arrow through the centre of the whirling chakra into the eye of the golden fish. A roar of acclamations rose like the crash and roll of thunder. The Brahmans forgot their fears and waved their scarfs with delight. The beautiful Draupadí came forth, as her brother had commanded her, and threw the garland round the neck of Arjuna, and allowed him to lead her away as her lord and bridegroom.

[1] The Aryans included at least two castes, the Kshatriyas, or military caste, and the Brahmans, or priests and sages. The Rajpúts claim to be Kshatriyas.

B.C. 1500-1400

Wrath of the Rajas.

The sight drove the Rajas into a fury. They cried out, "Could not a Kshatriya win the damsel?" "Are we to be humbled by a Brahman?" "The life of a Brahman is sacred, but down with the guilty race of Drupada!" They gathered round Raja Drupada with angry faces and naked swords; they threatened to burn his daughter on a pile unless she chose a Kshatriya for her husband. At this moment the Pándavas threw off their disguise. Arjuna stood forth and proclaimed his birth and lineage. The children of Bharata were the noblest Kshatriyas in the land, and none could doubt the right of Arjuna to contend at a Swayamvara. So the Rajas sheathed their swords in sullen anger, and went away to their own homes; whilst Arjuna led away his bride, and placed her in the charge of his mother Kuntí, until the marriage rites could be performed, according to the law.[1]

Alliance between the Pándavas and Drupada.

The marriage of Draupadí broke up the league between the Pándavas and Drona against Drupada. The Kauravas remained on the side of Drona. The Pándavas went over to Drupada and formed a close alliance with him. Both Drupada and the Pándavas prepared to make war upon Drona and the Kauravas. Drupada was anxious to recover the lost half of his Raj of Panchála; whilst the Pándavas were anxious to secure the Raj they had inherited from their father Pándu.

Division of the Raj.

This alliance caused much alarm at Hastinápur. The younger men were clamorous for war, but the blind Maháraja was averse to bloodshed. At last Bhíshma proposed that the Raj of Hastinápur should be divided between the Kauravas and Pándavas. After many debates the Maháraja followed the counsel of Bhíshma. The Raj was divided, but it was not a fair division. The uncleared jungle of Khándava-prastha was made over to the Pándavas; whilst the Maháraja and the Kauravas remained in possession of Hastinápur.[2]

1 The marriage of Draupadí has a dark side, which is best left in obscurity. According to a barbarous law, which prevailed in times when female infanticide was a general rule, a woman was married to the eldest brother, but became the wife of all the brothers of a family. Thus Draupadí was married to Yudhishthira, but became the wife of all five Pándavas. The subject is sufficiently discussed in the larger history. See vol. i. Mahá Bhárata.

2 The old jungle or forest of Khándava-prastha covered the site of modern Delhi and the surrounding country.

The jungle of Khándava-prastha was occupied by a Scythic tribe, known as Nágas, or serpent-worshippers. They were driven out by the simple process of burning the forest. The Pándavas built a fortress, and called it Indra-prastha.[1]

B.C. 1500-1400

Raj of Khándava-prastha.

Status of the Kshatriyas.

The tradition of the new Raj tells something of the social status of the ancient Kshatriyas. They were at once a soldier and a ruling caste. They were all Rajpúts, or the sons of Rajas; and so long as they protected their people, so long they exercised the rights of sovereignty. They did not trade like the Vaisyas, nor cultivate the lands like the Súdras. Their duty was to fight with the bow and arrows, the sword and spear.[2]

Growth of the Raj.

The Pándavas ruled their Raj like true Kshatriyas. For a while they supported themselves by hunting in the jungles. But cultivators soon flocked to the cleared lands, and sowed the seed, and gave the Raja's share of the harvests to Yudhishthira. In return the Pándavas protected them from every enemy, and drove out all robbers and cattle-lifters.

Exile of Arjuna.

After a while there was a misunderstanding amongst the Pándavas. Arjuna left the Raj, and went into exile for twelve years. His adventures during this period are so marvellous that they may be treated as romance rather than as history. He married Ulúpí, a daughter of the Raja of the Nágas; but she is described as a serpent rather than as a mortal woman. He is said to have received weapons from the gods. He went to Manipura in eastern Bengal, and married the daughter of a Raja, and had a son. He went to Dwáraká in Guzerat, and married Subhadrá, the sister of Krishna. At the end of twelve years he returned to Hastinápur, accompanied by Subhadrá.

[1] There are said to have been five districts corresponding to the five Pándavas. The point is of small moment, except to archæologists. Every traveller to Delhi who has visited the Kútab tower, will remember the desolate heaps, the *débris* of thousands of years, that are scattered along the road. To this day there is a broken mound, called the "Old Fort," which tradition would identify with the fortress built by the Pándavas.

[2] The Hindus are divided into four great castes, namely Brahmans or priests, Kshatriyas or soldiers, Vaisyas or merchants, and Súdras or cultivators. These again are distributed into a number of subdivisions, which are also called families, tribes, or castes.

B.C. 1500-1400

The Rajasúya, or royal sacrifice.

By this time the Pándavas were established in their Raj. Accordingly they celebrated a great feast or sacrifice, known as the Rajasúya, or royal sacrifice. It was a royal banquet given to all the neighbouring Rajas as an assertion of their independent sovereignty over their new Raj. All the Rajas were there, and amongst them was Duryodhana and his brethren. The Rajasúya was extolled by all the guests, but it made the Kauravas more jealous than ever, and they began to plot amongst themselves for the destruction of the Pándavas.

Plot against the Pándavas.

The ancient Kshatriyas were all given to gambling. Sákuni, a brother of Gándhárí, the mother of the Kauravas, was a noted gambler, and had an evil reputation for using loaded dice. He was dwelling at Hastinápur, and the Kauravas asked him how they could ruin the Pándavas. Sákuni counselled his nephews to invite the Pándavas to a gambling match at Hastinápur. Duryodhana was to challenge Yudhishthira to play, but Sákuni was to throw the dice; and Yudhishthira was to be egged on until he had lost the Raj, and the whole of his possessions.

Gambling match.

The invitation was sent and accepted. The Pándavas went to Hastinápur, accompanied by Draupadí. The gambling match was held in a pavilion set up near the palace. Duryodhana challenged Yudhishthira to a game. The play began, and Sákuni threw the dice for his nephew. Yudhishthira protested against the game. He complained that Sákuni ought not to throw the dice; but still he continued to play. He laid stake after stake, wildly, madly, and without regard to consequences. He was the elder brother; the other Pándavas reverenced him as their father, and would not venture to interfere.

Yudhishthira's losses.

It is needless to lengthen out the story. Yudhishthira lost all the wealth and cattle of himself and his brethren. Then he gambled away the Raj of Khándava-prastha. Next he staked his brethren, one after the other, beginning with the youngest, and lost every one. Then he staked himself and lost. Finally he staked Draupadí, and lost her with all the rest to the wicked Duryodhana.[1]

Terrible scene.

The scene which followed is perhaps the most sensational in Hindu history. The Pándavas and Draupadí had

[1] Similar cases of such reckless gambling are to be found to this day in Burma and Nipal.

become the slaves of Duryodhana. The assembly was in a state of consternation; the chieftains looked from one to the other, but no man spoke a word. Duryodhana sent a messenger to bring Draupadí from the palace. The princess was filled with wrath when she was told that she had been gambled away as a slave-girl to Duryodhana. She asked whether Yudhishthira had not gambled away himself before he had staked his wife; for if he had become a slave he could not stake a free woman. She refused to go to the gambling pavilion until she received an answer. But reason and arguments were thrown away. Duhsásana went to the palace, seized Draupadí by her long black hair, and dragged her into the pavilion. He told her to take a broom and sweep the rooms. She appealed to all the chieftains in the pavilion; she called upon them as husbands and fathers, to protect her from Duryodhana; but not a man would stir hand or foot in her defence. Yudhishthira was paralyzed with fear; he refused to interfere, and he ordered his brethren to be silent. Duryodhana then dragged Draupadí to his knee. Bhíma could hold out no longer: he gnashed his teeth, and swore that the day should come when he would smash the knee of Duryodhana, and drink the blood of Duhsásana.

B.C. 1500-1400

Blind Maháraja.

At this moment the blind Maháraja was led into the pavilion. He had been told all that had occurred, and was anxious to stop bloodshed. He decided that the Pándavas had lost their Raj; but he would not permit the Pándavas and Draupadí to become the slaves of Duryodhana. He ordered them to go into the jungles as exiles for a period of twelve years. At the end of that time they were to secrete themselves in any city they pleased for one more year. If the Kauravas failed to find them, they were to recover their Raj. If the Kauravas discovered them before the year was up, they were to lose their Raj for ever.[1]

Second exile of the Pándavas.

The Pándavas went forth, followed by Draupadí. Bhíma repeated his oath that a day would come, when he would smash the knee of Duryodhana, and drink the blood of Duhsásana. Draupadí untied her long black hair, and swore that it should never be tied again until Bhíma had fulfilled his vow.

[1] The story of this exile is probably a myth, which had no place in the original tradition, but was inserted at a later period in the Sanskrit poem of the Mahá Bhárata.

B.C. 1500-1400

Twelve years.

The adventures of the Pándavas, during the twelve years' exile in the jungle, are either trivial or supernatural. There is nothing that illustrates real life. The main interest centres in the thirteenth year, during which the Pándavas were to conceal themselves in some city without being discovered by the Kauravas. Even this story is so artificially constructed, that it might be rejected as a palpable fiction; an episode of a game of "hide and seek" between Kauravas and Pándavas, to fill up the interval between the expulsion of the Pándavas and the beginning of the great war.

Belief in ghosts or demons.

But the story of the thirteenth year, artificial as it is, presents a picture of Hindu courts in primitive simplicity. Moreover, it is a satire on the belief in ghosts or demons, as lovers of fair women. This belief in "spirit lovers" was common enough in the ancient world, and finds full expression in the book of Tobit. Sara, the daughter of Raguel, married seven husbands in succession, but each one was murdered in turn by a demon lover named Asmodeus.[1] The same belief still lingers in all parts of India. The Hindu story of the thirteenth year is contrived to ridicule such a belief; it is a relic of an age of Hindu civilization, which has died out of the world.

Pándavas at Viráta.

According to the Sanskrit epic the Pándavas proceeded to a city, named Viráta, just before the beginning of the thirteenth year.[2] They were disguised in various ways, in the hope of entering the service of the Raja, who was also named Viráta. They found the Raja sitting at the entrance-hall to his palace, surrounded by his council of chiefs or elders, after ancient Hindu fashion. After a long preliminary conversation all the five Pándavas were taken into the service of the Raja. Yudhishthira was engaged to teach the Raja how to gamble. Bhíma, the giant, was appointed head cook, as his strength would enable him to prevent the under cooks from wasting or stealing the victuals. Arjuna was disguised as a eunuch, and engaged to teach music and dancing to the daughter of the Raja. The two younger brothers were employed, one as master of the horse, and the other as master of the cattle.

[1] Tobit, chaps. iii. to viii.

[2] General Cunningham identifies this city with the modern Bairat, about 105 miles to the south of Delhi.

B.C. 1500-1400

Draupadí, a lady's-maid.

There was some difficulty about Draupadí. She had vowed not to tie up her hair; this was evaded by twisting it into a string like the tail of a serpent. Her beauty excited the jealousy of the Rání; this was overcome by her telling the Rání that she was beloved by five ghosts, called Gandharvas, who would murder any mortal man who paid her the slightest attention. Accordingly she was engaged as lady's-maid to the Rání.

Bhíma's strength.

Bhíma soon gained the favour of Raja Viráta. A foreign wrestler, named Jimúta, had put all the warriors of the Raja to shame, so that none dared to encounter him. Bhíma came forward, and vanquished Jimúta, and put him to death amidst the acclamations of the multitude. The Raja leaped from his seat with joy, and bestowed many gifts on Bhíma. From that time he took a great liking to Bhíma, and made him fight with lions, tigers, or bears, in the presence of his ladies.

Kicháka, the brother of the Rání.

In those days a prince, named Kicháka, was dwelling at Viráta. He was brother of the Rání, and commander-in-chief of the army of the Raj. He did what he pleased at Viráta, according to the old saying, "The brother of the Rání is always to be feared by the Raja."

Fight in the music-room.

Kicháka became enamoured of Draupadí, and asked her to become his wife. She replied that she could not marry him because of her five Gandharva lovers. Kicháka would not be refused; he told her she must marry him, and treated her with rudeness. She complained to the Raja, but he would do nothing; he was too much afraid of the Rání's brother. She next complained to Bhíma, and he promised that she should be revenged. One night Kicháka went to the palace to see Draupadí, but met Bhíma in her stead. A desperate battle was fought in the music-room. At last Bhíma killed Kicháka and left him dead on the floor. He then went off to sleep in the kitchen, without saying a word to any one.

Gandharva lovers.

Next morning the dead body of Kicháka was found in the music-room. Every bone was broken; those who saw the body said that Kicháka had not been murdered by men, but by demons. The story was soon told in the streets and bazars, that the commander-in-chief had been killed by Gandharvas, because of his love for the Rání's waiting-maid. The whole city was in an uproar. The brothers of

B.C. 1500-1400

Kicháka came to the palace to bring away the dead body to the place of burning. They saw Draupadí and carried her off likewise to burn with Kicháka, and compel her to join him in the world of shades. Bhíma heard her screams. He drew his hair over his face, so that no man should know him. He tore up a tree by its roots to serve as a club. He fell upon the brothers of Kicháka and slew every one, and returned to the palace by a secret way.

General panic.

The general consternation was now greater than ever. The city was seized with a panic. The Raja and the council of chieftains were in mortal fear of Draupadí and her Gandharvas. The Raja was afraid to speak to her. The Rání told her to leave the city; but the thirteenth year of concealment was nearly over, and Draupadí remained in the palace in spite of them all.

Viráta invaded.

Meanwhile the death of Kicháka had been noised abroad. The Rajas round about said, "Kicháka is dead; let us invade the Raj of Viráta and carry off the cattle." One Raja invaded the northern quarter, and carried off cows and buffaloes; and the herdsmen ran to the city to tell Raja Viráta. The troops were called out, and Raja Viráta mounted his chariot, and drove off to recover the cattle.

Dancing-master turns warrior.

Whilst Viráta was gone to the northern quarter of the Raj, Duryodhana and the other Kauravas invaded the southern quarter, and carried off more cattle. The herdsmen came to the city complaining and lamenting, but there was no Raja to protect them. Arjuna called for a chariot, put on his armour, and appeared before the court, with his weapons in his hands. The princess and her damsels laughed merrily to see the dancing-master in armour; they all cried to him to bring back a rich spoil of silks and jewels. In this manner Arjuna drove off to recover the cattle from the Kauravas.

Difficulties in the story.

At this point the story loses its interest. Arjuna was discovered by the Kauravas, and it was a question whether the discovery was made before or after the completion of the fourteenth year. The question was never settled. Negotiations were opened which might have been begun immediately after the expulsion of the Pándavas; although, according to the Mahá Bhárata, they were not begun until after the completion of the thirteenth year of exile.

Raja Drupada, the father-in-law of the Pándavas, sent a

Brahman, as envoy from the Pándavas to the Maháraja of Hastinápur. The Maháraja called the council together to receive the envoy. The Brahman spoke thus to the council: "An envoy is the tongue of the party by whom he is sent: If he fails to discharge his trust, and does not faithfully repeat his master's words, he is guilty of treachery: Have I therefore your permission to repeat the message sent by the Pándavas?" The whole council exclaimed, "Speak the words of the Pándavas without extenuation and without exaggeration." Then the Brahman spoke as follows: "The Pándavas send their salutations and speak these words: 'Dhritaráshtra and Pándu were brothers, as all men know; why then should the sons of Dhritaráshtra inherit the whole Raj, whilst the sons of Pándu are shut out? It is true that the Pándavas have lost their Raj of Khándava-prastha in a game of dice; but it was by loaded dice and false play; and unless you restore their inheritance they must declare war, and the blood of the slain will be upon your heads.'"

B.C. 1500-1400

Pándavas send an envoy to Hastinápur.

The speech of the Brahman threw the council into a turmoil. The Kauravas wrangled like angry kinsmen. The points of the debate were very simple. Was there, or was there not, foul play at the gambling match? Were the Pándavas discovered by the Kauravas before or after the close of the thirteenth year? Bhíshma praised Arjuna to the disgust of Karna. The debate was ended by the Maháraja, who sent his charioteer, Sanjaya, with a reply to the Pándavas.[1]

Debate in council.

The real object of the mission of Sanjaya was to induce the Pándavas to return to Hastinápur, without giving them any pledge that their Raj would be restored. Maháraja Dhritaráshtra sent a message which was duly repeated to the Pándavas and their allies. He poured out praises upon the Pándavas; he said that enemies and friends were equally loud in extolling them; some of the Kauravas might have used harsh language, but he would make peace

Mission of Sanjaya to the Pándavas.

[1] Sanjaya is said to have been the minister and charioteer of Maháraja Dhritaráshtra. He thus held an important post in the court of Hastinápur. Karna is accounted low-born, because he was the son of a charioteer. The origin of this discrepancy is discussed in the larger history. The Brahmanical compilers of the Mahá Bhárata were jealous of the important part played by charioteers in the original version of the tradition, and therefore represented them in the poem as a low-born race of carters and waggoners.

B.C. 1500-1400 between all parties, if the Pándavas would only return to Hastinápur.

Its failure. The Pándavas, however, were not to be entrapped. Yudhishthira replied that neither he nor his brethren would return to Hastinápur, unless a pledge was given that their half of the Raj would be restored. Accordingly both parties prepared for war.

Character of the war. There is little in the war of the Mahá Bhárata to render it memorable in after generations, beyond the horrible tale of slaughter. In its original form it was not associated with any sentiment of patriotism or religion, such as animated the children of Israel during the conquest of the promised land. Neither was it a war in which men fought to wipe out dishonour, as the Greeks fought the Trojans during the siege of Troy. Nor was it a war between men of different blood like that between Greece and Persia. It was nothing but a battle between kinsmen for the possession of land.

Plain of Kuru-kshetra. The Kauravas and Pándavas assembled their respective allies on a famous plain round a lake or tank, known as Kuru-kshetra. It was situated about fifty or sixty miles from modern Delhi. The warriors were arrayed against each other, and stirred up every angry passion by abusing and railing at each other. At last when they had lashed each other into fury by taunts and gibes, they rushed against each other like ferocious beasts or madmen. Some threw stones; others fought with their fists, teeth, and nails, or kicked and wrestled till one or other was killed. Others fought with clubs, knives, swords, spears, javelins, chakras, or bows and arrows. Whenever a conqueror had overthrown his adversary he severed his head from the body, and carried it off as a trophy.

Single combats The story of revenge and slaughter was one which fathers might tell their sons from generation to generation, as a ghastly moral against feuds and wars. It is not so much a description of a general battle, as of a series of single combats between distinguished warriors, which would be sung in ballads for ages afterwards. Bhíshma, the patriarch of the royal house of Hastinápur, was slain by Arjuna. Drona engaged in mortal combat with Drupada to settle the old feud which had driven him into exile. Drupada was slain by Drona; but his son Dhrishta-dyumna revenged his death by fighting against Drona until he slew him. Bhíma engaged in mortal combat with Duhsásana, the man who dragged Draupadí by her hair into the gambling pavilion. Bhíma overthrew his enemy, cut off his head, and drank his blood in accordance with his vow, and then tied up the dishevelled hair of Draupadí whilst his fingers were dripping with the blood of the evil doer. Lastly there was the crowning contest between Arjuna and Karna. They fought in war-chariots with their bows and arrows in their hands. Arjuna was almost overcome by the arrows of Karna, when the wheel of Karna's charriot sank into the earth, and would not move. Karna called out to his adversary to hold his hand until he recovered the wheel; but Arjuna saw his opportunity, and shot Karna dead with an arrow.

B.C. 1500-1400

Slaughter of the Kauravas.

The details of the battle are interminable, and occupy volumes. One dreadful night the warriors fought through the darkness with a weapon in one hand and a torch in the other. The battle was really over on the seventeenth day, when Bhíma slew Duhsásana, and Arjuna slew Karna. On the eighteenth day Duryodhana rallied his forces for a general engagement, but all the Kauravas excepting himself were slain upon the field, and he fled away to the lake in the centre of the plain. Bhíma ran after Duryodhana, and mocked and reviled him until the ghastly warrior came out and engaged in a final combat. The two men fought with clubs, until Bhíma struck a foul blow, which smashed the knee of Duryodhana, and then left him to die where he lay.[1]

Revenge of Aswattháma.

The Pándavas had got the mastery, but the bloodshed was not over. There was yet to be a slaughter of sleeping men in the camp of the Pándavas; it is known as "the revenge of Aswatthàma." Drona, the father of Aswatthàma, had slain Drupada, and had then been killed by Drupada's son Dhrishta-dyumna. Aswatthàma lived to carry on the feud, and swore to be revenged on Dhrishta-dyumna and the Pándavas.

Omen of the owl and crows.

At evening time Aswatthàma and two surviving warriors stood by the side of the wounded Duryodhana. They cheered his dying agonies by pledging themselves to avenge

[1] The foul blow of Bhíma consisted in his striking Duryodhana below the waist. The blow was given in accordance with the vow which Bhíma had made in the gambling pavilion.

B.C. 1500-1400

his death. They left him on the field, and sat under a tree to consider what to do. Suddenly Aswatthám̆a learnt a lesson from an omen. Crows were roosting in the tree; an owl approached them warily; he killed them one at a time without awakening them. "Thus," cried Aswattháma, "we will revenge ourselves on the sleeping Pándavas; we will kill them one at a time, as the owl has killed the crows."

Camp of the Pándavas.

The camp of the Pándavas was on one side of the lake, and the camp of the Kauravas on the other. The Pándavas had left Draupadí and her sons in charge of, allies and servants, and had gone to the camp of the Kauravas to take possession of the spoil, and pass the night there.

Slaughter of Dhrishta-dyumna.

At midnight Aswattháma and his two comrades approached the camp of the Pándavas. It was surrounded by a deep trench, and had but one entrance. Aswattháma posted his two comrades at the entrance, and stole off to the quarters of Dhrishta-dyumna. The son of Drupada was sleeping on the ground. Aswattháma awoke him by kicking his head. The doomed warrior saw his enemy standing over him with a drawn sword. He cried out "Treachery!" Aswattháma broke his skull with the back of the sword, and silenced him for ever. He then rushed out of the tent to be revenged on the Pándavas.

General massacre.

The Pándavas were away at the camp of the Kauravas, but Draupadí and her sons were sleeping at their quarters. The young men were awakened by the turmoil in the quarters of Dhrishta-dyumna. They ran out one after the other, and were cut down and killed by Aswattháma. By this time the whole camp was in disorder. Friends and kinsmen were shouting and fighting against each other. The women filled the air with shrieks and screams. Numbers were killed and wounded on all sides. Some tried to escape from the camp, but were cut down by the two men at the entrance. Aswattháma lost his way in the darkness, but set alight to a great pile of firewood. The camp was filled with a sudden glare of fire and flame. Aswattháma escaped amidst the uproar, gained the entrance, and disappeared with his comrades into the outer world.

Death of Duryodhana.

The day was just dawning as the three men walked across the plain of Kuru-kshetra. Wolves and jackals had begun to attack the dead corpses, but were scared away by

B.C. 1500-1400

the light of morning. The three warriors took a last farewell of the dying Duryodhana; they gladdened his last moments with the story of their revenge; and then, as he gave up the ghost, they fled away into the jungle and were heard of no more.

Funeral rites.

The final scene in the great war is told with much pathos. The agony of Draupadí and the woe of the Pándavas may be passed over in silence. The sympathies of the reader are not with the victors, but with the mourners for the dead. As the day began to dawn, the widows, daughters, and mothers of the slain came on the field of Kuru-kshetra weeping and wailing, to perform the last rites of their dead kinsmen. The funeral piles were burning, but no widow threw herself into the flames. The imagination rests upon the weeping women, without the additional horror of female sacrifices, which characterised a later period of Hindu history.[1]

Submission of the blind Maháraja.

Next followed another painful scene. The blind old Maháraja Dhritaráshtra, and his wretched wife Gándhárí, were borne down with grief for the loss of their sons; yet both came out of Hastinápur, with the touching submission of Hindus, to bend to the decrees of fate, and pay their homage to the victors. This done, they went off to the jungle to take up their abode on the bank of the Ganges, and spend their last years in devotion and prayer.

Triumph of the Pándavas.

Amidst these scenes of mourning the conquerors were exulting in their victory. Drums were beaten, trumpets were sounded, flags were flying, whilst Yudhishthira and his brethren went in joyful procession to take possession of the Raj of Hastinápur. But the songs of triumph must have jarred upon ears that were filled with the cries of the mourners for the dead and dying.

Close of the story of the Pándavas.

The end of the story may be told in a few words. Yudhishthira and his brethren became great conquerors; they are said to have subdued every Raja throughout the length and breadth of India. When they had brought their

[1] It is difficult to reconcile the fact that no widow performed a Satí after the war of the Mahá Bhárata with the statement that Madrí, the younger wife of Pándu, perished on his funeral pile. There was evidently some conflict of authority as regards the rite of Satí; possibly the story of Madrí is an interpolation, and the rite of Satí originated in a later age.

B.C. 1500-1400

conquests to a close, they celebrated a horse feast or sacrifice, known as an Aswamedha; it was an assertion of their sovereignty over the empire of India. All the Rajas whom they conquered were summoned to Indra-prastha to pay their homage to the conquerors, and to feast on horse-flesh after the manner of the ancient Kshatriyas. But before describing the Aswamedha, it will be as well to review the scope and subject matter of the whole poem of the Mahá Bhárata.

Composition of the Mahá Bhárata.

The foregoing narrative is a bare outline of the original tradition of the Mahá Bhárata. It records events which are referred to the fifteenth century before the Christian era; when the Israelites were delivered out of Egypt, and conducted by Moses to the promised land. After an apparent interval of unrecorded centuries, the story of the great war was retold in the Sanskrit poem as a religious parable, replete with spiritual meanings and pious teachings. The poem of the Mahá Bhárata is of such inordinate length, that it may have been composed by a variety of bards; but the work is referred to one particular Brahman sage, who is known by the name of Vyása, or "the arranger."

Part played by Vyása.

Vyása is represented as playing an important part in the events recorded in the Mahá Bhárata; but everything which is told about him is improbable or supernatural. He is said to have been an illegitimate son of the damsel who afterwards married Maháraja Santanu; to have been the real father of Dhritaráshtra and Pándu; to have caused Gándhári to have a hundred sons at a birth. Sometimes he appears in an abrupt and supernatural manner to impart religious instruction to the Pándavas. He directed Arjuna to perform penance on the Himalayas, and ordered Yudhishthira to celebrate the Aswamedha as an atonement for sin. Sometimes he appears to explain away something that is opposed to Brahmanical ideas, such as the marriage of Draupadí to Yudhishthira and his brethren.

Religious teaching of the Mahá Bhárata.

The religious teaching of the Mahá Bhárata is evidently the product of a later age than that in which the great war was fought. The Kauravas and Pándavas sacrificed to Indra, the king of gods, and appear to have worshipped the gods of fire, water, wind, and other Vedic deities. But the compilers of the Mahá Bhárata resolved all these gods into one Supreme Spirit, under the name of Vishnu, and taught the worship of Krishna as an incarnation of Vishnu.

Thus Krishna appears in the Mahá Bhárata as a mortal hero, and as the Supreme Being. Like Vyasa he plays an important part in the history of the great war, but generally in an improbable and supernatural manner. He is a mediator in times of feud, and a consoler in times of affliction. He was present at the Swayamvara of Draupadí to mediate between the Pándavas and the angry Rajas. He suddenly appeared in the gambling pavilion to prevent Duryodhana from insulting Draupadí. He was mixed up in the negotiations which preceded the great war, flying vast distances through the air in a moment of time. The Kauravas plotted to seize him at Hastinápur, but he became manifest as the Supreme Being; all the gods issued from his body, flames of fire fell from his eyes, and his form was as radiant with golden beams as the sun at noonday. He appeared to Arjuna on the morning of the first day of the war. Arjuna was shrinking from the slaughter of friends and kinsmen; he would rather die, he said, than fight against such good men as Bhíshma and Drona. Krishna consoled him with the doctrine that death was but the transmigration of the soul from one body to another. He stirred Arjuna into action by assuring him that fighting was the duty of all Kshatriyas; and that if he proved himself a coward, and failed to fight, he could never hope to enter the heaven of Indra.

B.C. 1500-1400

Part played by Krishna.

The story of the great war has been reduced in the foregoing pages to a simple narrative of life and manners. But it is told in the Mahá Bhárata with all the exuberance and exaggeration of Oriental imaginations revelling in an ideal world. Every Raja in India is said to have been present at the Swayamvara of Draupadí and the Raja-súya of Yudhishthira. Every Raja is said to have fought in the great war of the Mahá Bhárata, on the side of the Kauravas, or on that of the Pándavas. The armies at Kuru-kshetra were thus reckoned by millions of millions; elephants and chariots by tens of millions. The battle is described with a grandeur greater than that of the war of Zeus against the Titans. Drums were beaten, trumpets and war-shells were sounded, and gorgeous banners were waving in the air. Gigantic Rajas, arrayed in golden mail, and armed with supernatural weapons, appeared in chariots radiant with strings of jewels and bracelets of gold and pearls. Vast

Grandeur and exaggerations.

B.C. 1500-1400

masses of elephants and chariots, horse and foot, were swayed to and fro like the waves of the sea. The air was darkened by darts and arrows, or illuminated with the flashing of swords and spears. Rivers of blood issued from mountains of slain. Lastly, frantic widows, with dishevelled hair, shrieked over the slaughtered bodies of husbands and sons, not by tens or hundreds, but by millions.

Aswamedha, or horse sacrifice.

The Aswamedha, or horse sacrifice of Yudhishthira, is described on an equally grand scale. The primitive idea of an Aswamedha was to let a horse loose for a year as a challenge to all the neighbouring Rajas. Whenever the horse wandered into the territory of another Raja, there was a battle for the supremacy. It was a rude sport adapted to a warlike race like the ancient Kshatriyas. If a warrior gained a succession of victories, he slaughtered the horse, and served it up at a great feast to all the conquered Rajas. In this manner Arjuna is said to have followed the horse of Yudhishthira, and conquered all the Rajas in India. He then summoned all the Rajas to attend the Aswamedha, to pay their homage to Yudhishthira, and to feast on the horse which was roasted for the occasion. Whether Arjuna did or did not conquer all the Rajas in India is a question which the reader must decide for himself. If he did, the horse must have travelled immense distances. How the horse-feast became converted in after times into an atonement for sin is a religious question which may be left to conjecture.[1]

Final scene at the Ganges.

The story of the great war concludes with a grand creation of Hindu imagination. It has already been seen that the blind Maháraja of Hastinápur went away with his wife Gándhárí to dwell in retirement on the bank of the Ganges. Fifteen years after the great war, the widows and mothers of those who had been slain went to the same spot to mourn for the loss of their husbands and sons. Vyása, the Brahman sage, appeared amongst the women to console them. He stood on the bank of the Ganges and invoked the dead warriors by their various names. Presently the river began to foam and boil, and a great noise rose out of the waters. The ghosts of the departed heroes appeared

[1] Some information on this point will be found in Chapter IV. on the "Religion and Literature" of the Hindus.

above the surface in all the glory and magnificence which they displayed on the plain of Kuru-kshetra. Bhíshma and Drona, seated in their chariots in full armour, ascended out of the waters with all their armies, arrayed as they were on the first day of the Mahá Bhárata. Next came Karna and Duryodhana, together with Sákuni and Duhsásana, and many other warriors and Rajas. There too were the sons of Draupadí, and her brother Dhrishta-dyumna, and all the men who had been slain in the revenge of Aswatthàma. All appeared in great beauty and splendour, with horses, chariots, banners, and arms. But all enmity had departed from them, and they were all in perfect friendship with one another. Then the widows and other women were overjoyed; not a trace of grief remained amongst them. Widows went to their husbands, daughters to their fathers, and mothers to their sons; and all the fifteen years of sorrow were forgotten in the ecstasy of meeting. The night passed away in the fulness of joy; but when the morning dawned all the dead mounted their horses and chariots, and disappeared in the waters. Then Vyása gave the widows leave to follow their husbands; and having paid their devotions they plunged into the Ganges and joined their husbands in the heaven of Indra.[1]

B.C. 1500-1400

[1] All Kshatriyas who perished on the field of battle were supposed to go to Swarga, the heaven of Indra; but when their merits were sufficiently rewarded they returned to the world, and entered upon a new chain of existences in successive transmigrations. (See Chap. IV.)

CHAPTER II.

RÁMÁYANA : OUDE.

ABOUT B.C. 1000.

B.C. 1000

Raj of Ayodhyá, or Oude.

THE Rámáyana is a Sanskrit epic like the Mahá Bhárata, but the main tradition reveals a higher stage of civilization.[1] The principal scenes are laid in Ayodhyá, or Oude, a large territory on the northern bank of the Ganges; and north of the land of Rákshasas and Asuras, described in the Mahá Bhárata. The Raj of Ayodhyá thus occupied the centre of Hindustan.[2] Its capital was also named Ayodhyá, and was situated on the river Sarayu;[3] it was hundreds of miles to the south-east of Hastinápur and Delhi. The Maháraja of Ayodhyá was married to three wives or Ránís. He had eight chosen ministers; two Brahman priests as his advisers; and a great council of state for the exercise of certain constitutional powers.

[1] An approximate date of the reign of Ráma is fixed by the following data. General Cunningham has fixed the war of the Mahá Bhárata in the fifteenth century before the Christian era. Mention is made in the Mahá Bhárata of a certain Rituparna, as Raja of Ayodhyá. Rituparna reigned in the fifteenth generation before Ráma, as shown in the genealogical lists. (See Tod's *Rajasthan*, vol. i.) Reckoning a generation at thirty years there would be an interval of 450 years between the war of the Mahá Bhárata and the reign of Ráma. The date of the composition of the Rámáyana is a very different matter; perhaps the poem was composed more than a thousand years after the actual exile of Ráma.

[2] The Raj is known in the Rámáyana as the Raj of Kosala; and the name of Ayodhyá, or Oude, is only applied to the city. The name of Kosala is important in dealing with Buddhist legends.

[3] The river Sarayu is now known as the Gogra. The site of the ancient city of Ayodhyá is still to be traced amongst the mounds in the neighbourhood of Fyzabad.

III. *Wheeler's India, to face page 28.*

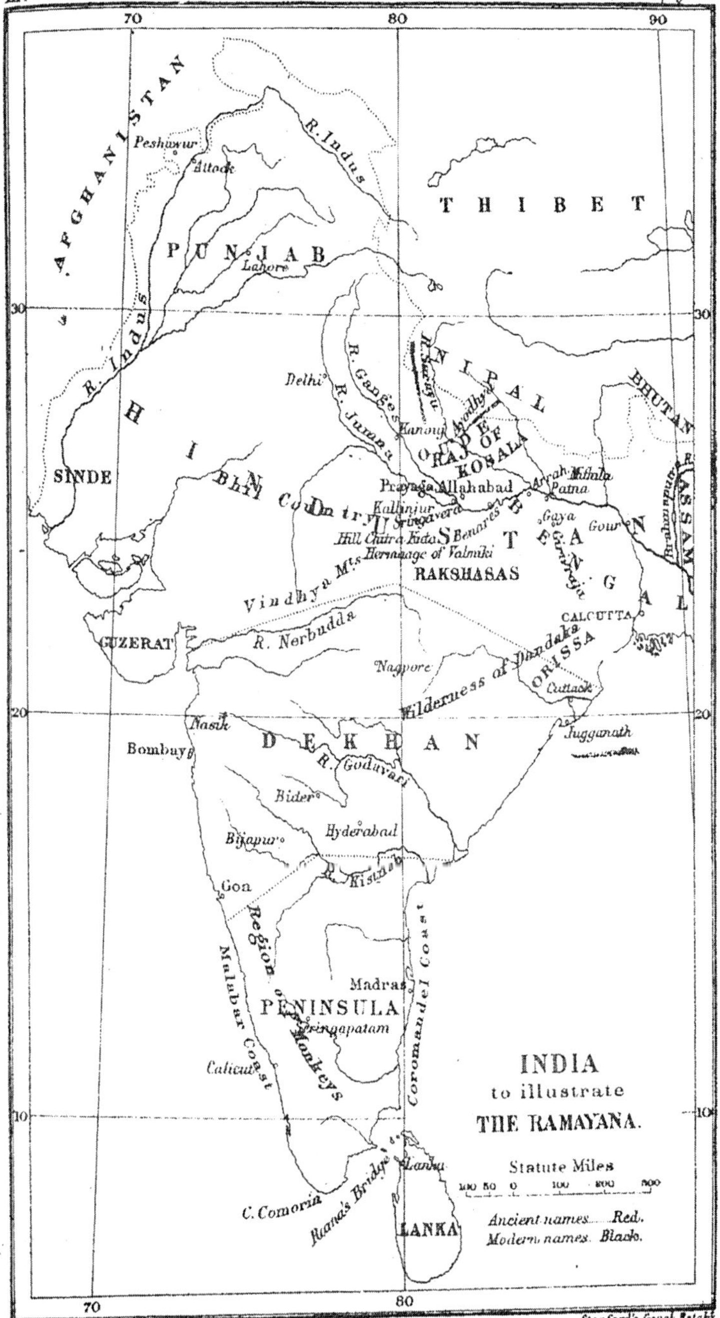

London; Macmillan & Co. Stanford's Geogl Estabt

B.C. 1000

Maháraja Dasaratha: his four sons.

Dasaratha, Maháraja of Ayodhyá, had four sons by his three Ránís, namely, Ráma, Lakshmana, Satrughna, and Bharata. Ráma was the son of Kausalyá, the first and chief wife. Lakshmana and Satrughna were the sons of the middle wife. Bharata was the son of the last wife, the reigning favourite, the young and beautiful Kaikeyí. The plot of the Rámáyana turns upon the jealousy between Kausalyá and Kaikeyí, and the rival claims of Ráma and Bharata.

Ramá, the eldest, married Sítá.

Ráma, the eldest son by Kausalyá, had been fortunate and happy. The Raja of Mithilá, to the eastward of Oude,[1] proclaimed the Swayamvara of his daughter Sítá. There was a huge bow, and Sítá was to be given in marriage to the Raja who could bend the bow. The Swayamvara was held, but not a Raja could lift the bow from the ground. At last Ráma took up the bow, and bent it until it broke in twain; and in due course he became the husband of the beautiful Sítá.

Ráma appointed Yuva-raja.

At last the time arrived for the appointment of a Yuva-raja or "little Raja." According to the story, Ráma was the universal favourite. Ministers, chieftains, and the people were all loud in their praises of Ráma. The Maháraja resolved on appointing Ráma to the post of Yuva-raja. He got rid of Bharata by sending him with his half-brother Satrughna on a visit to Kaikeyí's father, the Raja of Giri-vraja, seven days' journey from Ayodhyá.[2] The Maháraja summoned Ráma to the palace, and told him that on the morrow he would be installed as Yuva-raja. Meanwhile Ráma was to keep a careful watch throughout the night, lest Bharata should suspect what was going on, and return to Ayodhyá and upset the arrangement.[3]

According to the Rámáyana, the whole city of Ayodhyá

[1] The Raj of Mithilá corresponded to the modern Tirhút.

[2] Giri-vraja was the old name of Rajagriha, the modern Rajgír, in Behar. In ancient times it was a centre of Buddhism, and suggests the idea of a religious element in the antagonism between Ráma and Bharata. Ráma was certainly a champion of the Brahmans. Bharata may have been a representative of a Buddhist faction.

[3] The jealousy between the first wife and the youngest is as old as polygamy. Did not Jacob prefer Rachel to Leah, and Joseph or Benjamin to his eldest son Reuben? The reader must judge for himself whether the Maháraja did not in his heart prefer Bharata to Ráma, although he made a show of favouring Ráma.

B.C. 1000

Rejoicings in the city of Ayodhyá.

was in a blaze of joy and exultation at the approaching installation of Ráma. The houses were illuminated throughout the night with endless clusters of lamps. At early dawn the people watered the streets, strewed the roads with flowers, and set up gay banners in all directions. The news of the installation spread far and wide. Crowds of country people flocked into Ayodhyá. Singers, musicians, and dancing-girls delighted the hearts of young and old. Even the little children, who were playing in the court-yards and under the porticoes, kept on saying to one another, "This day Ráma is to be anointed Yuva-raja."

Discovery of the intrigue.

All this while a very different scene was being enacted in the palace. On the previous day Kaikeyí, the youngest wife, was unaware that Ráma was to be installed. The Maháraja had promised to see her in the evening, and purposed coaxing her to agree to the appointment of Ráma. But his intentions were thwarted. A slave-girl belonging to Kaikeyí, named Manthará, had gone to the roof of the palace, and discovered that the whole city was illuminated for the coming installation of Ráma. She ran to the apartments of her mistress, and told her that Bharata was excluded from the throne; that the Maháraja had sent Bharata to his grandfather, in order to instal Ráma as Yuva-rajá.

Wrath of Kaikeyí.

Kaikeyí saw through the whole intrigue. She threw off her jewels and scattered them over the floor of her room. She untied her hair, and dishevelled it over her shoulders. She threw herself upon the ground, and covered her face with the darkness of anger.

Elevation of Bharata, the youngest son.

At this crisis the Maháraja entered the apartments of Kaikeyí. It is needless to dwell upon what followed. The doting old Maháraja was in sore distress; for a long time Kaikeyí would not speak to him; then she stormed at him; finally she befooled him. She insisted that Bharata should be installed as Yuva-raja; and that Ráma should be sent into exile for fourteen years. The Maháraja was a helpless slave in the hands of Kaikeyí; he could not resist her, and at last was compelled to yield to her imperious will.

Ráma condemned to exile.

At early morning, whilst the city was preparing for the installation, Ráma was summoned to the palace, and ushered into the presence of his father. The Maháraja

B.C. 1000

was speechless from grief.[1] Kaikeyí was exulting in her triumph over the first wife. She told Ráma his fate in words of steel. Ráma received the news like a model prince who had been trained by Brahmans. He showed neither anger nor sorrow; his face was an unruffled calm. He prepared to obey the commands of his father without a murmur. He was bent on going into exile with as much tranquillity as if he had been ordered to ascend the throne.

Agony of the mother of Ráma.

Ráma left the presence of the Maháraja and Kaikeyí to carry the news to his mother Kausalyá. The princess had been spending the night in offering sacrifices to Vishnu in behalf of her beloved son. She had gloried in the thought that the machinations of Kaikeyí had been defeated, and that Ráma was to be appointed Yuva-raja. In one moment the cup of happiness was dashed to the ground. Instead of reigning as Maháraja in the city of Ayodhyá, her son was to go as an exile into the jungle. His place upon the throne was to be filled by the son of her detested rival. She herself, deprived of the protection of Ráma, was to be exposed to the caprices and domination of Kaikeví, as the mother of the future Maháraja. In agony of soul, Kausalyá implored Ráma to resist the commands of his father; to assume the government of the Raj; and, if opposed, to slay the royal dotard who had become the slave to Kaikeyí. She was his mother, and her commands, she said, were as binding upon him as those of his father Dasaratha.

Obedience of Ráma.

Ráma was not to be moved from his high resolve. He was deaf to all suggestions of disobedience, rebellion, or parricide. He told his mother that the Maháraja was her husband and her god, and that she was bound to obey him whatever might be his commands.

Remonstrances.

Kausalyá next entreated Ráma to take her with him into the jungle. She could not live in the palace to endure the insults of Kaikeyí and the contempt of the slave-girls. But Ráma was inexorable. By taking his mother into the jungle he would make her a widow whilst her husband was alive. She would violate her duty as a wife, and he would violate his duty as a son.

Ráma's wife, Sítá.

Ráma left his mother, to return to his own palace, and break the news to his wife Sítá. The young wife was not

[1] The exaggerated accounts of the Maháraja's sorrowing over the exile of Ráma give rise to the suspicion that his grief was all a sham.

B.C. 1000

cast down by her husband's doom; but she was angry when he proposed going alone into exile, and leaving her behind at Ayodhyá. She declared that a wife must share the fortunes of her husband, and that she must accompany him into the jungle. Ráma dwelt upon the dangers and privations of jungle life; but his words were thrown away. She prayed and wept until he allowed her to share his exile. He also permitted his half-brother Lakshmana to accompany them into the jungle.

Historical significance of the exile.

The story of the exile of Ráma is suggestive. The first and second exiles of the Pándavas, as told in the Mahá Bhárata, are somewhat mythical; they might be omitted altogether without interfering with the current of the tradition of the great war. The exile of Ráma is historical; it forms an essential portion of the main tradition. The inference follows that the horrible slaughter of kinsmen in the war of the Mahá Bhárata left a lasting impression upon history. It taught a wholesome lesson to the ancient world that fratricidal wars were the ruin of empires. After the war of the Maha Bharata, a sentence of exile became the rule in cases of domestic feuds, as the only safeguard against fratricidal war.

Contradictions in the story.

The story of the exile of Ráma is however contradictory. In modern times the sentence of exile amongst the princes of Rajputana has been carried out with funereal pomp. The offender was clothed in black, invested with a black sword and buckler, mounted on a black horse, and solemnly commanded to depart out of the limits of the Raj.[1] Henceforth the exiled prince either entered into foreign service, like Drona, or led the life of a bandit and outlaw.[2]

Political exiles, not religious devotees.

According to the Rámáyana, Ráma and Lakshmana led the life of religious devotees. They were supposed to live on roots and vegetables, and to pass their time in religious austerities, abstracted from the outer world. But traces of the funereal ceremonial are still to be found in the poem. Ráma, accompanied by his wife Sítá, and his brother Lakshmana, walked on bare feet through the streets of Ayodhyá to the palace of the Maháraja, amidst the tears and lamenta-

[1] See the larger *History of India*, vol. iii. chap. 8.

[2] The exile of Drona differed altogether from that of Ráma. It only lasted until he had procured the means of revenge. Ráma was bound over not to return to Ayodhyá for a period of fourteen years.

tions of the people. They took their leave of the Maháraja and Kaikeyí, like doomed exiles. They were clothed in dresses made of the bark of trees, and despatched to the frontier in the Maháraja's own chariot. The Rámáyana also tells how the exiles shot deer in the jungle, and lived on flesh meat, like other Kshatriyas. Moreover, they were soon engaged in wars against Rákshasas and demons. Such a mode of life was certainly more fitted for Rajpúts than for Brahmans, for political exiles than for religious devotees.

B.C. 1000

Journey to the frontier.

The journey in the royal chariot from the capital at Ayodhyá to the frontier town of Sringavera occupied some days.[1] At night the chariot halted beneath trees, and the royal exiles slept on beds of leaves. At Sringavera the charioteer left the exiles, and returned to the city of Ayodhyá, carrying loving messages from Ráma to his father Dasaratha.

Aryans and Bhíls.

The town of Sringavera, the modern Sungroor, was situated on the northern bank of the Ganges, about twenty miles from Allahabad. It was the frontier town of Ayodhyá against the Bhíls. It thus forms a land-mark between the Aryan dominion of Oude and the non-Aryan aborigines. The Raja of the Bhíls, named Guha, was most respectful and attentive to the royal strangers. He entertained them with much hospitality, and provided them with a boat for crossing the Ganges.

Worship of the Ganges

During this voyage across the Ganges, Sítá offered up her prayers to the goddess of the river, and vowed to present her with an offering of wine and flesh, whenever Ráma should return and take possession of his kingdom.

Prayága, or Allahabad.

The exiles next proceeded to the city of Prayága, the modern Allahabad, at the junction of the Ganges and Jumna.[2] The site is of much importance in Hindu history. The union of the river deities rendered it a holy spot in the eyes of Vedic worshippers. At Prayága, Bharadwája the

[1] There were at least two rivers to be crossed between the city of Ayodhyá on the river Sarayu, the modern Gogra, and the town of Sringavera, on the northern bank of the Ganges. The reader may conjecture that the chariot was carried across in some primitive fashion; or he may adopt the interpretation of learned Pundits that the chariot flew through the air.

[2] This locality has already been noticed in connection with the first exile of the Pándavas, under the name of Váranávata.

B.C. 1000 — Brahman had already established a hermitage. Further south, in the jungle of Dándaka, were other Brahman hermitages, which will be presently brought under review.[1]

Hermitage of Bharadwája: worship of the Jumna and sacred tree. At Prayága the exiles were hospitably entertained by Bharadwája. They crossed the Jumna on a raft, and Sítá offered up the same prayers to the goddess of the Jumna as she had previously offered up to the goddess of the Ganges. After they had landed on the opposite bank, Sítá paid her adorations to a sacred fig-tree, walking humbly round the tree, and propitiating the god with joined hands.

Hermitage of Valmíki. The exiles next proceeded towards the hermitage of Valmíki the sage, on the hill Chitra-kúta in the country of Bundelkund. The spot was surrounded by the hermitages of other Brahmans. Valmíki was celebrated in after years as the author of the Rámáyana, just as Vyása was celebrated as the author of the Mahá Bhárata. The exiles built a hut of wood and leaves near this hermitage, and sojourned there many days, subsisting on honey and game.

Death of Maháraja Dasaratha. Meanwhile the charioteer returned to the city of Ayodhyá, and delivered to the Maháraja the filial messages which had been sent by Ráma. That same night the Maháraja died in the chamber of Kausalyá; but no one knew of it outside the chamber, for the Rání had fallen into a deep swoon.

Palace life at early morning. Next morning at early dawn the palace-life began as though the Maháraja was still sleeping. The bards and eulogists were chanting his praises, in order that he might waken to pleasant words. The Brahmans sang their Vedic hymns. The servants began their daily business; the men brought in jars of water, and the handmaidens were ready with food and flowers. The sun began to rise in the heavens, yet nothing was seen of the Maháraja.

Weeping and wailing. Suddenly the screams of women rang through the morning air. The Ránís had gone to the royal chamber; they found that the Maháraja was a corpse, and that Kausalyá had fallen into a swoon. Then the cry went forth that the Maháraja was dead.

Council of State. The Ministers hastened to the chamber of death. They called together a great council of Brahmans and chieftains. The Maháraja was dead, and all his sons were absent from

[1] The area of the forest of Dándaka is somewhat confused. The whole country seems to have been a jungle or wilderness from the Ganges at Sringavera to the remote south.

Ayodhyá. There was no son present at Ayodhyá to conduct the funeral ceremony. Ráma and Lakshmana were in exile; Bharata and Satrughna were gone to Giri-vraja. So the body of the Maháraja was placed in a bath of oil; and swift messengers were sent to Giri-vraja to bring back Bharata to the city of Ayodhyá. B.C. 1000

Return of Bharata.

When the messengers arrived at Giri-vraja, they would not tell Bharata that his father was dead. They said that all was well, but that he must return with all speed to the city of Ayodhyá. So Bharata took leave of his grandfather, and returned with the messengers, accompanied by his brother Satrughna. When he heard at Ayodhyá that his father was dead he was in sore distress; and when he heard that Ráma had been sent into exile, he declared that he would not reign in the room of his elder brother Ráma. He said that when the days of mourning were over, he would go into the jungle and bring back his brother Ráma.

Funeral preparations.

Meanwhile all preparations had been made for the burning. Bharata and his brother Satrughna placed the royal body on a litter, and covered it with garlands, and strewed it round about with incense. All this while they cried aloud with mournful voices, "O Maháraja, whither art thou gone?"

Procession to the river Sarayu.

The sad procession then moved from the royal palace to the place of burning without the city. The bards and eulogists marched in front, chanting the praises of the dead Maháraja, whilst musicians filled the air with doleful strains. Next the widows appeared on foot, screaming and wailing, with their long black hair dishevelled on their shoulders. Then came the litter borne up by the royal servants; Bharata and Satrughna holding on to the back of the litter. All round the ensigns of royalty were carried as though the Maháraja were still alive. The white umbrella was held over the body; the jewelled fans of white hair were moved to and fro to sweep away the flies; the sacred fire was carried constantly burning. Other royal servants followed in chariots, and scattered alms amongst the multitude as funeral gifts of the Maháraja.[1]

The burning.

In this way the procession reached the banks of the river Sarayu. The funeral pile of fragrant woods was already

[1] It is worthy of note that none of the widows of the Maháraja were burnt alive on the funeral pile.

B.C. 1000 prepared. The body of the Maháraja was placed upon the pile. Animals were sacrificed and placed round about the dead body together with heaps of boiled rice. Oil and clarified butter were poured upon the wood together with incense and perfumes of various kinds. Then Bharata brought a lighted torch and set the pile on fire. The flames blazed up on high, and consumed the dead body, and all the sacrifices. The widows shrieked louder than ever; and the multitude lamented aloud, "O Maháraja, O sovereign protector, why hast thou departed and left us helpless here?"

Rite of water.

When the mourners had performed the rite of fire, they began to perform the rite of water. Bharata and Satrughna bathed in the river with all their friends; they poured water out of the palms of their hands to refresh the soul of the Maháraja. This done, the mourners returned to the city of Ayodhyá.

Days of mourning: the Sráddha.

For ten days Bharata mourned for his father, lying upon a mat of kusa grass, according to the custom which still prevails amongst the Hindus. On the tenth day he purified himself. On the twelfth day he performed the Sráddha, or feast of the dead, by offering funeral cakes to the soul of his deceased father.[1] On the thirteenth day, Bharata proceeded to the river Sarayu, and collected the relics of the funeral pile, and threw them into the sacred stream.

Bharata refuses the Raj.

On the fourteenth day of the mourning a great council of state was held at Ayodhyá. The Raj was tendered to Bharata, according to the will of the dead Maháraja. But Bharata refused to supplant his elder brother; he declared that he would journey through the jungle to the hill Chitra-kúta, and offer the Raj to Ráma.

March to Chitra-kúta.

The march of Bharata from Ayodhyá to Chitra-kúta is described at length in the Rámáyana; but it can scarcely

[1] The Sráddha is one of the most important ceremonies amongst the Hindus. It is performed by the mourner within a certain period after the death, or on hearing of the death, of a near kinsman. A Sráddha is also celebrated every month in propitiation of paternal ancestors. Special Sráddhas are likewise performed on great occasions, and notably at the celebration of any marriage ceremony. The funeral cakes are eaten by cows or Brahmans, or cast into water or fire. The ceremony is accompanied by a feast to the Brahmans, which is sometimes conducted on the most extensive and costly scale. See the larger *History of India*, vol. ii. Brahmanic period, chap. ix.

B.C. 1000

be regarded as historical.[1] He was accompanied by an army; and it was therefore necessary to repair the road from Ayodhyá to the frontier. The hills were levelled, and chasms were filled with earth.[2] Pavilions were set up at the several halting-places; and Bharata and his army moved along the route which had already been traversed by Ráma and his fellow-exiles.

Action of Guha, the Bhíl Raja.

The first station of any note was the frontier town of Sringavera. There Guha, Raja of the Bhíls, appeared as before in the character of a respectful neighbour. At first Guha was under the impression that Bharata was about to make war on Ráma; and he made preparations for resisting the advance of the army. When, however, he heard that Bharata was about to offer the Raj to Ráma, he carried large presents of fish, honey, and flesh to the camp, and entertained the whole army. He also provided five hundred boats to carry the women and leading personages over the river Ganges.

Passage of the Ganges.

The passage of the army of Bharata over the Ganges is exactly in accordance with the ways of Hindu soldiers and their endless followers. The men set their booths on fire on leaving the encampment. They made a great uproar during embarkation. The boats, adorned with gay streamers, crossed the river with ease amidst the sing-song of the rowers; some were filled with women, some carried horses, and others were filled with carriages, cattle, and treasure. The elephants swam through the waters like winged mountains. The multitude went over on rafts or empty jars, or breasted the stream with their hands and arms.

Miraculous feast of Bharadwája.

Next followed the march to the hermitage of Bharadwája. The holy Brahman gave a great feast to the whole army.

[1] Great stress is laid in the Rámáyana on the reluctance of Bharata to accept the throne of Ayodhyá at the expense of his elder brother Ráma. The reluctance is improbable; it is contrary to human nature; it may, however, have been feigned to strengthen his claim to the throne in the absence of Ráma. But whether real or feigned, it has little to do with the progress of the history.

[2] The preparation of a road through the jungle for the passage of an army is not unfrequent in Oriental life. It finds full expression in the prophecies of Isaiah: "Prepare ye the way of the Lord, make straight in the desert a highway for our God. Every valley shall be exalted, and every mountain and hill shall be made low; and the crooked shall be made straight, and the rough places plain."

B.C. 1000 By virtue of his many austerities, he prevailed on the gods to supply all that was necessary from the heaven of Indra. Viswakarma, the architect of the gods, levelled the ground, covered it with green turf, and built up magnificent pavilions. Tanks were filled with sacred food—milk, rice, and sugar. Metal dishes, loaded with cooked meats, were supplied in abundance. Rivers flowed with wine and sweet liquors; the banks were covered with sweetmeats and delicacies; the trees dropped honey. The beautiful Apsaras, nymphs from Swarga, danced on the grass; the Kinnaras filled the air with their songs; the Gandharvas played sweet music. Thousands of beautiful damsels, with garlands round their necks, served up viands and drinks to the exhilarated warriors.[1]

Meeting of the two brothers: Ráma performs the Sráddha.

The army of Bharata next crossed the river Jumna in the same way that it had crossed the Ganges; and in due course it marched through the jungle of Dándaka to the hill Chitrakúta. In the first instance Bharata told Ráma that his father Dasaratha was dead. Ráma gave way to grief and performed the funeral rites. He bathed in the neighbouring river, and filled his two joined palms with water. He then turned his face towards the south quarter, sacred to Yáma, the judge of the dead, and said, "O Maháraja, may this water always quench your thirst in the region of spirits!"

[1] The miracle of Bharadwája will serve as a specimen of the mode in which the original traditions of the Mahá Bhárata and Rámáyana have been embellished when retold in the form of Sanskrit epics. The deities of fire, water, the winds, the snn and moon, the gods of wealth and war, and a host of other deities, were supposed to dwell on high in the heaven of Indra; and Indra reigned as sovereign of the gods, just as Zeus reigned as sovereign over the gods on Mount Olympus. But Brahman sages, by the force of austerities and other religious merits, could force the gods to work their will.

The dancers, singers, and musicians call for some explanation. The Apsaras were dancing-girls in the service of Indra. The Kinnaras were a people fabled to have horses' heads; and Herodotus describes a people, whom he calls Eastern Ethiopians, who fought in the army of Xerxes, and wore the scalps of horses on their heads, with the ears and mane attached. (*Herodotus*, vii. 70.) They were equipped like the Indians. How they came to serve as singers in the heaven of Indra is a mystery. The Gandharvas were a hill tribe dwelling on the Himalayas, and famous for the beauty of their women. They appear in the story of the adventures of the Pándavas at Viráta, as ghostly lovers of women. In the Rámáyana they appear as musicians in the heaven of Indra.

He afterwards prepared funeral cakes, and offered them to the spirit of his departed father.

B.C. 1000

Ráma refuses the Raj.

The meeting between Bharata and Ráma is told at great length in the Rámáyana. They discussed the question of the succession to the Raj; Bharata offering it to his elder brother, and Ráma refusing to take it until he had completed his exile. In the end it was resolved that Bharata should return to Ayodhyá, and rule over the Raj in the name of Ráma; and that when the fourteen years of exile were accomplished, Ráma should leave the jungle and take possession of the throne.

Rákshasas persecute the Brahmans.

After the departure of Ráma, the Brahman hermitages at Chitra-kúta were sorely troubled by the Rákshasas. These people are described as demons, monsters, and cannibals, like those encountered by Bhíma in the Magadha country. They were especially hostile to the Brahmans and their sacrifices, and enemies to the worship of the gods. Accordingly the Brahmans abandoned their hermitages at Chitra-kúta, and went away to another country.

Wanderings of Ráma: wars with Rákshasas.

When Chitra-kúta was deserted by the Brahmans, Ráma went away further south, accompanied by Sítá and Lakshmana. The royal exiles wandered over the jungle of Dándaka towards the sources of the river Godavari in the Vindhya mountains. They visited the hermitages of many holy Brahmans, and Ráma carried on war against many Rákshasas. In this manner thirteen years of the exile passed away.[1]

Pictures of Rákshasas.

The Rákshasas of the Rámáyana are creations of Hindu imagination. They are not gigantic men like those who were slain by Bhíma, but huge misshapen monsters. One cannibal, named Virádha, was tall as a mountain, with a deep voice, hollow eyes, a monstrous mouth, and a tun belly; he was smeared with fat and blood; before him, on a huge iron spit ready cooked for a meal, were three lions, four tigers, two wolves, ten deer, and the head of an

[1] One famous locality visited by Ráma was Nasik, near the sources of the Godavari, about ninety miles to the north-east of Bombay. The name may be familiar to English readers, as some years back a distinguished Indian official recommended the transfer of the capital of British India from Calcutta to Nasik. In the present day Nasik is a holy place, a centre of Brahmanism. But a number of Buddhist ruins are in the neighbourhood, and prove that Buddhism once flourished there.

B.C. 1000

elephant. Another demon, named Kabandha, was a mountain of flesh, without head or neck; his face was in his belly; he had one eye and huge teeth; he had two arms of interminable length, with which he swept up his prey. Of course both Virádha and Kabandha, as well as other demons, were all slain by Ráma. Indeed Ráma is always the victor, whether encountering a single monster, or assailed by a whole army of Rákshasas.

Ráma, an incarnation of Vishnu.

The remainder of the Rámáyana may be described as a romance converted into a religious parable. Ráma is represented as an incarnation of Vishnu, born upon earth for the destruction of the Rákshasas, who are the enemies of gods and Brahmans.

Rávana, the oppressor of the gods.

Rávana, the Raja of the Rákshasas, was reigning in the island of Lanká, the modern Ceylon. His empire extended over the greater part of southern India; his power was felt on the river Godavari and hill Chitra-kúta. He was said to have made the gods his slaves. He had delivered his subjects from the fear of Yáma, judge of the dead, and had compelled Yáma to cut grass for his steeds. The sun was obliged to smile gently at Lanká, and the moon to be always at the full. Agni, the god of fire, burnt not in his presence. Vayu, the god of wind, blew gently at Lanká. No one dared to perform sacrifice out of fear of Rávana.[1]

Abduction of Sítá: Ráma prepares for war.

Rávana had heard of the beauty of Sítá, the wife of Ráma. He disguised himself as a Hindu devotee, and paid a visit to Sítá whilst Ráma and Lakshmana were absent in the jungle. He was smitten with her charms, and forcibly carried her off in a chariot, which flew through the air like chariots in fairy tales. Ráma was much distressed when he returned to the hut and found that Sítá had vanished. At last he discovered that Sítá had been carried off by Rávana, the mighty Raja of Lanká. Accordingly he formed alliances for waging war against so potent an enemy. He is said to have secured the services of armies of monkeys and bears, who had been born on earth as incarnations of the gods, in order to help in the holy war against Rávana.

The monkey Raja.

According to the Rámáyana there was a great Raja of monkeys reigning in the western mountains.[2] His name

[1] See larger *History of India*, vol. ii.: Rámáyana.

[2] The region corresponded generally to the Mysore country, but may have extended over a larger area, including the Mahratta country. The

B.C. 1000

was Báli. He had a younger brother, named Sugríva, whom he had driven out of the Raj, and was still anxious to capture and murder. Ráma visited Sugríva in his secret retreat in a hill-fortress, and made a league with him. Ráma fought against Báli, slew him, and placed Sugríva on the throne. In return, Sugríva joined Ráma with an army of monkeys to carry on the war against Rávana.[1]

Exploits of Hanuman, the monkey hero.

A famous monkey, named Hanuman, was commander-in-chief of the army of monkeys. The exploits of Hanuman have been the delight of the people of India for unrecorded centuries.[2] He could swell himself to the size of a mountain, or dwarf himself to the size of a man's thumb. He was bent on discovering the retreat of Sítá. He marched to the sea shore, where a strait, sixty miles across, separates India from Ceylon. He took a gigantic spring and leapt across the strait. He climbed the vast fortifications which surrounded the city of Lanká, and entered the palace of Rávana. He found Sítá in the palace garden secluded in a grove, and gave her a ring he had received from Ráma. He saw that Rávana was anxious to make Sítá his chief Rání, but that nothing would induce her to break her marriage vows. Sítá was glad to see Hanuman and gave him a jewel as a token for Ráma.

Hanuman's burning tail.

When Hanuman left Sítá, he was so enraged against Rávana that he began to tear up all the trees and flowers in the palace garden. The Rákshasas fell upon him with overwhelming forces, but he withstood them all. At last he was entrapped by a noose which had belonged to the god Brahma. He was dragged into the palace hall, where Rávana was sitting surrounded by his council. His tail was dipped in butter and set on fire; but he whisked the tail

wife of the monkey Raja was named Tara, a name which is frequently given to Mahratta women.

[1] This strange legend illustrates the feuds which prevailed in ancient India. The confusion between monkeys and men is inexplicable. The bears played a less important part in the war, and may be ignored.

[2] Hanuman is worshipped as a god in all parts of India. His image is carved in numerous pagodas. Della Valle, who travelled in India in the seventeenth century, describes a festival in which the image of Hanuman was carried in procession from a temple in the western Gháts to the eastern coast of Coromandel, the scene of Ráma's later exploits.

B.C. 1000

over the city of Lanká, and set all the houses in flames.[1] He then went off to the sea shore, and leaped over the strait as before; and told Ráma that he had seen Sítá, and gave him the token.

Marvels of the war against Rávana.

The rest of the Rámáyana is a string of marvels. The army of monkeys brought rocks from the Himalaya mountains, and built a bridge over the sea between India and Lanká.[2] The war was carried on with supernatural weapons and mystic sacrifices. It was diversified by single combats, like the war of the Mahá Bhárata; but they are devoid of all human interest. They are the combats of gods and demons armed with weapons that worked impossible marvels. At last Rávana was slain by Ráma, and Sítá was restored to her husband's arms.

Sítá's ordeal.

Here the story might have been brought to a close; but Sítá had been captured by an enemy, and was yet to pass through a terrible ordeal. A pile of wood was built up and set on fire. Sítá invoked Agni, the god of fire, to testify to her purity. She threw herself into the midst of the flames, relying upon the god to protect her. For a while she disappeared from mortal eyes. Presently the earth opened, and Agni rose up, and revealed himself in human form. He

[1] The burning of Hanuman's tail is a favourite scene in dramatic representations, and is always hailed by a Hindu audience with a storm of delight. The false tail of the representative of Hanuman is of course stuffed with combustibles, and flares away with a display of fireworks, until the flimsy properties which indicate the streets and houses of Lanká are destroyed by the devouring flames. See larger *History of India*, vol. ii. chap. xx.: Rámáyana.

[2] The origin of the conception of Ráma's bridge forms a curious subject of inquiry. The famous bridge of boats by which the army of Xerxes passed over the Hellespont is commonplace in comparison with a bridge of stone, sixty miles long, extending over a deep sea. Strangely enough a rocky causeway runs out from the Indian side of the channel, and terminates at the island of Ramisseram; and although it is at present covered by the sea, it is said to have formerly been above the waves. A similar causeway runs out from the opposite shore of Ceylon, and terminates in the island of Manaar; whilst a sandy ridge, known as Adam's Bridge, connects Manaar with Ramisseram. There can, therefore, be little doubt that the Hindu bard formed the idea of a bridge from a contemplation of the physical geography of the locality; and the conception once formed was readily believed and widely disseminated. To this day the huge blocks or boulders which are to be found in various parts of India are said to have been dropped by the monkeys in attempts to carry them southwards for the purpose of building the bridge.

carried Sítá on his knee as a father carries a child, and delivered her to Ráma as pure as the undriven snow. B.C 1000

Triumphant return to Ayodhyá.

The fourteenth year of exile was now accomplished. Ráma and Sítá returned to Ayodhyá, and reigned in great happiness and splendour. Ráma became a mighty conqueror; his empire is said to have covered all India. Like Yudhishthira he performed the Aswamedha, or horse-sacrifice; and every Raja in India, if not in all the world, attended the sacrifice and paid homage to Ráma.

Cruelty of Ráma.

The conclusion of the Rámáyana is a painful episode. There was a famine in the land; it was said that the gods were angry with Ráma for having taken back Sítá. Ráma was in sore distress, for Sítá was about to become a mother; nevertheless he ordered his brother Lakshmana to conduct her to the wilderness of Dándaka and leave her alone in the jungle.

Fate of Sítá.

Lakshmana was obliged to obey the cruel commands of the Maháraja. He drove Sítá to the hill Chitra-kúta; told her that Valmíki the sage had returned to the hermitage accompanied by his wife; and counselled her to seek for refuge at the hermitage. It is needless to dwell on the agony of Sítá at finding herself abandoned by her husband. It will suffice to say that she found her way to the hermitage. and was kindly entertained by Valmíki and his wife, and became the mother of twin sons, Lava and Kusa.

Valmíki composes the Rámáyana.

Sixteen years passed away. Valmíki composed the poem of the Rámáyana, from the birth of Ráma to the triumphant return of Ráma and Sítá to the Raj of Ayodhyá. He taught the poem to the two sons of Ráma.

Discovery and reconciliation.

At this time it came to pass that Ráma made an excursion into the jungle of Dándaka. He heard Lava and Kusa chanting the Rámáyana at the hermitage. His heart yearned towards his two sons, and their mother Sítá. He entered the hermitage, and was reconciled by Valmíki to his wife Sítá. Ráma and Sítá then returned to the city of Ayodhyá with their two sons, and lived in happiness until death.[1]

The poem of the Rámáyana was composed for a religious purpose similar to that which pervades the Mahá Bhárata.

[1] The story of the reconciliation of Ráma and Sítá has been slightly modified to escape details which are of no moment, and which would only involve lengthy explanations. The correct version will be found in the larger *History of India*, vol. ii.

B.C. 1000

Religious significance of the Rámáyana.

Ancient legends are retold in the form of religious parables to represent Ráma as an incarnation of the Supreme Spirit—Vishnu, in the same way that the Mahá Bhárata represents Krishna, as an incarnation of the same deity. In the original poem the character of Ráma is wildly distorted, and his moral actions are exaggerated, in order to exhalt him into a Brahmanical hero of a supernatural type.[1] It should also be remarked that in the Rámáyana two separate legends appear to have been linked into one. The exile of Ráma from Ayodhyá is apparently the original tradition which has been referred to B.C. 1000; it is the backbone of the epic, and complete in itself, irrespective of the wars in the Dekkan. On the other hand, the conquest of the Dekkan and capture of Lanká are additions of a mythical character, belonging to a later period of perhaps many centuries. They are relics, fantastic and grotesque, of the religious wars and antagonisms which prevailed for centuries in southern India between the Brahmans, or worshippers of the gods, and the Buddhists and Jains, who denied the existence of the gods, and were denounced as atheists and Rákshasas.[2]

[1] Such stories please oriental imaginations, but are repulsive to practical morality as understood by Europeans. Similar supernatural myths are told of Gótama Buddha, such as giving his own flesh to a hungry tiger. Fables of this extreme character are more calculated to excite ridicule than to enforce moral rules.

[2] This question is treated at length in the larger *History of India*, vol. ii. Further evidence is furnished in the second part of vol. iv. chap. viii.

IV. Wheeler's India, to face page 45

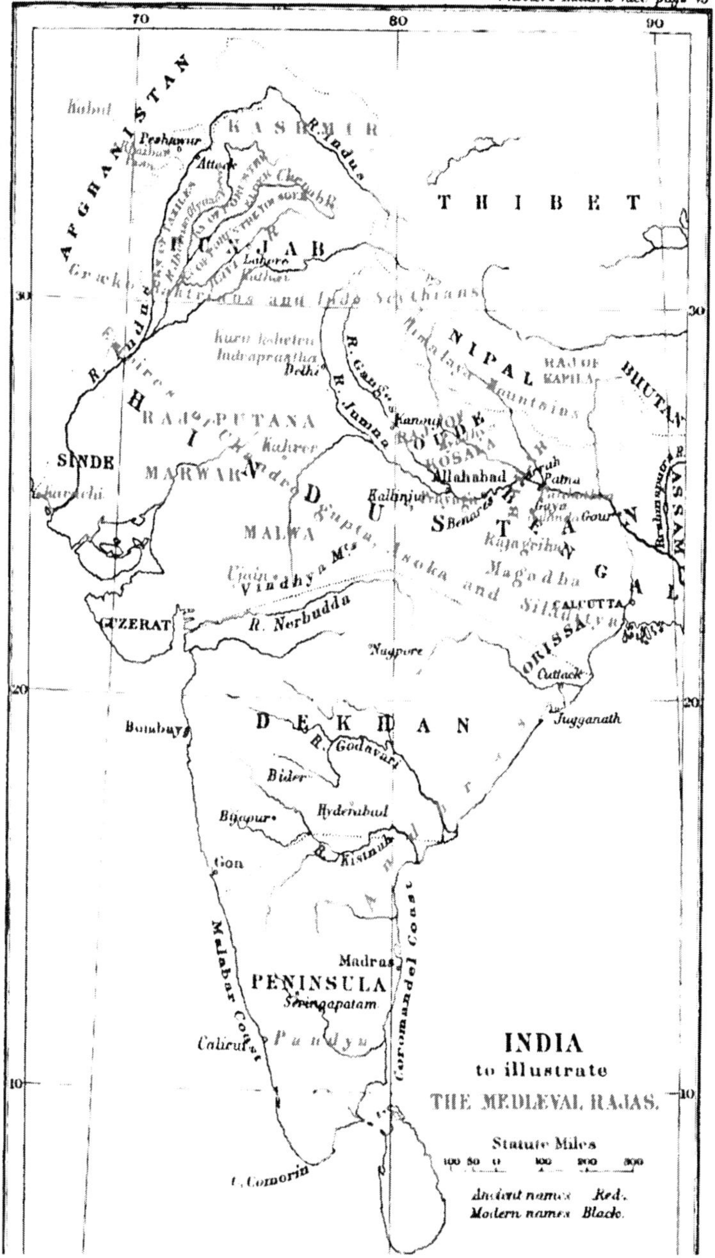

CHAPTER III.

MEDIÆVAL RAJAS.

B.C. 500 TO A.D. 1000.

B.C. 500 TO A.D. 1000

Belief in the transmigrations of the soul.

THE belief that there is but one God, and that the soul is immortal, has done much towards elevating the barbarian into a civilized and responsible being. But there is another belief that has extended widely over the eastern world: it is known as the dogma of the metempsychosis, or belief in the transmigrations of the soul.

Sákya Muni: old age, disease, and death.

Sákya Muni,[1] afterwards known as Gótama Buddha, was the son of a Raja of Kapila, a country seated on the southern slopes of the Himalayas.[2] Sákya Muni was brought up in every luxury, married a loving wife, and was the father of a son. But he was wearied or surfeited with pleasure, and felt a loathing for life. According to the legend, he saw an old man, a diseased man, and a dead man; and his eyes were opened to the woes of humanity. In the agony of his soul he is said to have exclaimed, "Youth, health, and life itself are but transitory dreams; they lead to age and disease; they end in death and corruption." This feeling was intensified, and magnified, by the belief in the transmigrations of the soul. He saw the evils, not only of an individual life, but of an endless

[1] The era of Sákya Muni is still uncertain; opinions are divided as to whether he flourished in the fifth or sixth century before the Christian era. Perhaps B.C. 500 is good as an approximate date.

[2] The locality is somewhere on the frontier between Nipal and Sikhim, and has sometimes been a bone of contention between the two powers.

B.C. 500 TO A.D. 1000

chain of successive existences, beginning in an unknown past and running on to eternity.

The religious mendicant.

Sákya Muni next saw one of those religious mendicants who have abounded in India from the remotest antiquity. The man had no cares or sorrows, no wife or family, no earthly ties of affection or kinship. He lived on the daily alms of food which are given to such mendicants by the masses. Sákya Muni resolved to become a religious mendicant in like manner; to abandon his father's palace, his wife and son, and his expectation of a throne, and to lead a life cut off from all the ties that bind men to the world.

Sákya becomes a mendicant, a recluse, and a Buddha.

Sákya Muni carried out his resolve. He went from his father's palace at Kapila to the country of Magadha on the southern bank of the Ganges. He carried his alms-bowl round the city of Rajagriha.[1] He next led a life of solitude and meditation in the jungle of Gaya, where he became a Buddha, or apostle, to deliver humanity from the miseries and evils of existence. Finally, he proceeded to the deer forest near Benares, and began to preach what he termed the law.

Teaching of Sákya Muni.

The essence of Sákya Muni's teaching was that every one should strive to be good in thought, word, and deed; that by so doing he would be born to a better and happier life in the next birth. But he taught that those who were truly wise would also seek to attain a higher object, namely, the deliverance of the soul from the chain of transmigrations. This he maintained could only be effected by leading the life of a religious mendicant; by rooting out every affection, passion, or desire; by severing every tie that bound the soul to the universe of being. When that end was accomplished, the soul would be detached from all life and being; it would be delivered or emancipated from the endless chain of transmigrations, and would finally sink into an eternal sleep or annihilation known as Nirvána.

War and parricide.

Sákya Muni appeared in a world of Rajas and Brahmans, not unlike that which is depicted in the Sanskrit epics. The reigning Maháraja of Magadha was at war with the Maháraja of Kosala. Peace was made and cemented by intermarriages. The Maháraja of Magadha was subsequently put to death by his own son, who succeeded

[1] Rajagriha is the same as Gira-vraja, the capital of Magadha, the city of the father of Kaikeyí. See *ante*, page 29.

to the throne and conquered Kosala. Sákya Muni was thus preaching in troubled times. His success is proved by the after history. To this day the whole region of Magadha, on the southern bank of the lower Ganges, is known by the name of Bihar or Vihára, the land of Viháras or monasteries.

Alexander the Great invades the Punjab, B.C. 327.

In B.C. 327, a century or more after the preaching of Sákya Muni in Magadha, Alexander the Great crossed the river Indus for the invasion of the Punjab, or "land of the five rivers." The Punjab was distributed amongst kings or Rajas, who were more or less at war with each other. After crossing the Indus there were three kingdoms to be conquered: that of Taxiles, between the Indus and the Jhelum; that of Porus the elder, between the Jhelum and the Chenab; and that of Porus the younger, between the Chenab and the Ravi. There were also other Rajas to the north and south. Porus the elder, however, seems to have been the ruling suzerain, whilst the others were his refractory vassals.

Submission of Taxiles.

Alexander called upon all the Rajas to tender their submission. Many flocked to his camp and paid their homage. Possibly they were anxious to secure his help against Porus the elder. Amongst others came Taxiles, who placed his kingdom at the disposal of Alexander. This opened the way for the advance of the Macedonian army to the banks of the Jhelum, the frontier of the kingdom of Porus the elder.

Passage of the river Jhelum.

The passage of the Jhelum or Hydaspes is famous in history. Porus was encamped on the opposite bank with a large force of horse and foot, as well as of chariots and elephants. Alexander had to cross the river, not only in the face of the enemy, but exposed to the wind and rain of the south-west monsoon. One dark and stormy night he reached a small island in the river; he and his troops then waded through the remainder of the stream breast high. The Hindu scouts saw him coming, and ran off to tell Porus. A force of horse and chariots was sent to repel the invaders. The Hindu chariots stuck in the wet clay, and were nearly all captured by the Macedonians. Alexander lost his horse Bucephalus, but the son of Porus was amongst the slain.

Porus moved the greater part of his army to retrieve the

B.C. 500 TO A.D. 1000

Defeat of Porus the elder.

disaster, and took up a position on firm ground. His front was formed by a line of elephants, supported from behind by masses of infantry. His two flanks were formed of chariots and horsemen. Alexander was strong in cavalry. He did not attack the elephants, but charged the two flanks, and drove the Indian horse upon the elephants. Porus tried in vain to bring his elephants into action; the unwieldy animals could not keep pace with the Macedonian horse. At last the elephants turned tail, and trampled down the masses of Indian infantry. Porus was wounded and compelled to fly; but afterwards tendered his submission, and Alexander treated him as a friend.

Flotilla on the Jhelum.

The victory on the Jhelum was the salvation of the Macedonian army. Had Alexander been defeated, he must have retreated towards Kábul, and his army might have been cut to pieces in the Khaibar pass. As it was he resolved on marching to the Ganges, but he provided for a retreat by building a flotilla on the Jhelum. It was better to float down the Jhelum and Indus, and dare the danger of the Indian ocean, than to cut a way to Persia through the hardy mountaineers of Kábul.

Flight of Porus the younger.

Alexander crossed the Chenab, and entered the territory of Porus the younger. This prince had wanted Alexander to help him against his uncle Porus the elder. When he heard that his uncle and Alexander were friends, he was seized with a panic, and fled into exile. Accordingly Alexander made over the kingdom to Porus the elder, and nothing more was heard of Porus the younger.

Macedonian retreat.

Alexander next crossed the Ravi, but a tribe, known as the Kathæi, revolted in his rear. He turned back and reduced the Kathæi to obedience by the capture of their capital. By this time the Macedonians had grown weary of their Punjab campaign. Their spirits were broken by the storms of the south-west monsoon. They refused to advance to the Ganges, and clamoured to be led back to Greece. Alexander tried to re-assure them, but his efforts were in vain. He returned to the Jhelum, and embarked on board the fleet with a portion of his troops, whilst the remainder marched along the banks on either side.

Alexander's vengeance on the Brahmans.

During the retreat down the Jhelum and the Indus, the Macedonian army was harassed by tribes who were encouraged by the Brahmans. Alexander wreaked his vengeance by slaughtering every Brahman that came in his way. At last he reached the ocean, and beheld, for the first time, the phenomena of the tides. He landed his army near Karáchi, and marched through Beluchistan to Susa, whilst Nearchos conducted the fleet to the Persian Gulf.

Flourishing state of the Punjab.

The Greeks, who accompanied Alexander, described the Punjab as a flourishing country. There were numerous towns and villages, abundant harvests, a variety of fruits and vegetables, cotton growing on shrubs, sugar canes, banyan trees, alligators, elephants, monkeys, serpents, scorpions, lizards, and ants.

Marriage customs.

The marriage customs were various. In some tribes damsels were offered as marriage prizes in boxing, wrestling, running, and archery. In other tribes a wife might be bought with a pair of kine. At Taxila the poor people sold their daughters in the bazar.

Brahman philosophers.

The Brahmans were called wise men and philosophers. Some attended the Raja as counsellors. Others practised religious austerities by standing in one position for days, or exposing themselves to the burning sun. Others imparted instruction to their disciples. Others prognosticated respecting rain, drought, and diseases. But all were held in honour, and went where they pleased, and took what they pleased from the shops. They wore no clothing, and affected to be indifferent to pleasure or pain. They were known to the Greeks as Gymnosophists, or "naked philosophers."

Customs of the Kathæi.

The Kathæi chose the handsomest man to be their king. They reared no children that were not handsome. Every child was publicly examined when it was two months old, and the magistrate decided whether it was to live, or die. Marriages were made by the mutual choice of the bride and bridegroom. The widows burnt themselves alive with their dead husbands.

Murder of Philip and Porus.

When Alexander left the Punjab, he appointed a lieutenant at Taxila, named Philip, with a garrison of Hindu mercenaries and a body-guard of Macedonians. Philip was murdered by the mercenaries, who in their turn were nearly all murdered by the Macedonian body-guard. Alexander heard of the murder in Beluchistan, and appointed Eudemos in the room of Philip, to carry on the government in conjunction with Taxiles. Three years afterwards news reached India that Alexander was dead. Eudemos murdered Porus, possibly

B.C. 500 TO A.D. 1000

in the hope of founding an empire in the Punjab; but he was subsequently driven out of the country by a prince, who was known to the Greeks as Sandrokottos and to the Hindus as Chandra-gupta.

Adventures of Sandrokottos.

Sandrokottos was a type of the Hindu princes of ancient times. He was at Taxila when Alexander was there. He was at that time an exile; an off-shoot of the royal house of Magadha. He wanted Alexander to conquer Magadha, which he said was eleven days' journey from the Punjab; but he offended the Macedonian by some impertinence, and was obliged to fly for his life. Subsequently he procured the help of banditti, and captured the city of Pali-bothra, the modern Patna. He then ascended the throne of Magadha, and drove the Greeks out of India. He thus established an empire which extended over the Punjab and Hindustan.

Megasthenes, the Greek ambassador.

Sandrokottos is an important personage in ancient Hindu history. He formed an alliance with Seleukos, the Greek sovereign of Persia and Baktria. He married a daughter of Seleukos, and received a Greek ambassador at his court, named Megasthenes. The marriage of a Hindu Mahárajа with a Greek princess is one of the most remarkable events of the time. The description which Megasthenes wrote of Patna and its people, comprises nearly all that is known of ancient Hindustan.[1]

Description of Pali-bothra, the modern Patna.

Megasthenes says that the ancient city of Pali-bothra extended ten miles along the bank of the river, and two miles inland.[2] It was surrounded by wooden walls, pierced with holes through which the archers shot their arrows. Megasthenes describes the streets and bazars; the elephants, chariots, and horsemen, followed by large retinues; the soldiers armed with bows and arrows, swords, bucklers, and javelins. Sometimes there were festival processions of elephants and chariots. Men in rich apparel carried vases and drinking-bowls of gold and silver; whilst others led strange animals in the procession, such as hump-backed oxen, panthers, lions, and various kinds of birds.

[1] See *Ancient India as described by Megasthenes and Arrian*, translated into English by Professor McCrindle, Principal of the Government College at Patna. London: Trübner and Co.

[2] The Sanskrit name is Patali-putra. Some excavations made at Patna during the cold season of 1876 revealed a low brick wall of remote antiquity, supporting a stout wooden palisading.

The people of India were divided into castes, and hereditary trades and professions. The cultivators were servants of the Maháraja. The produce was stored up every year in the royal granaries; some was sold to the traders and artisans, whilst the remainder was devoted to the maintenance of the soldiers and officials. The cultivators were a most mild and gentle people. They never resorted to the cities or joined in tumults; and they were all exempted from military service. Thus when an army was fighting an enemy, the husbandmen were ploughing and sowing close by in the utmost security.

B.C. 500 TO A.D. 1000

Hindus of Magadhá.

The magistrates in the city of Pali-bothra exercised a strict supervision. Some overlooked the working of arts and manufactures, to prevent negligence; others overlooked all sales and exchanges, to prevent cheating. Some collected a tax for the Maháraja of one-tenth on the price of every thing sold. Others registered all births and deaths in order to tax the people. Others were appointed to entertain all strangers and foreigners, and reported all they said and did to the Maháraja.

Magistrates at Pali-bothra.

The palace of Sandrokottos was stately and secluded. No one dwelt within the walls but the Maháraja and his queens; even the body-guard was posted at the gate. Sometimes the Maháraja left the palace to take command of his army, which numbered 400,000 men. Sometimes he took his seat in the court of justice, or offered sacrifices to the gods. Sometimes he went into the jungle on a hunting expedition, accompanied by his queens; the ladies rode in chariots, or on horses and elephants, surrounded by spearmen to keep off intruders.

Sandrokottos.

Some years after the mission of Megasthenes, another Maháraja was reigning over Magadha, named Asoka.[1] The adventures of Asoka were very like those of Sandrokottos. He quarrelled with his father, and went away to Rajpútana and the Punjab. He returned to the capital at the moment of his father's death, and massacred all his brethren, and obtained the throne. He then became a great conqueror, and established an empire over Hindustan, the Punjab, and Afghanistan.

Reign of Asoka.

[1] The capital of Asoka was also at Pali-bothra, Patali-putra, or Patna.

B.C. 500 TO A.D. 1000

Asoka converted to Buddhism.

Asoka was a man of blood. Apart from his wars and massacres, he sacrificed thousands of animals and birds to the gods of the Brahmans. Afterwards he changed his religion and became a follower of Buddha. He promulgated a religion of moral duty; and his edicts, sculptured on rocks and pillars, remain to this day in all parts of his empire.

Edicts of Asoka.

The edicts of Asoka taught the merits of goodness, virtue, loving-kindness, and religion, as summed up in the one word, Dharma. They taught that all people should render dutiful service to father and mother; kindness and help to kinsfolk, neighbours, and acquaintance; filial veneration to spiritual pastors; reverence and almsgiving to Brahman priests and Buddhist monks; respect and obedience to masters; frugality and temperance; abstinence from evil-speaking and slandering; kindness towards servants and dependants; and kindness towards all living creatures.

Acts of Asoka.

Asoka abolished the slaughter of animals throughout his dominions, whether for food or sacrifice. He established public hospitals for sick people, and also for sick animals. He appointed public teachers to instruct the people in moral conduct. The memory of Asoka has died out of India, but his teachings bear fruit to this day; for the Hindus are more tender to living creatures than any other nation, and are ever kind to kinsfolk and neighbours.

Græko-Baktrian kings in Central Asia.

About the time when Asoka was reigning in India, the independent Græko-Baktrian kingdom in Central Asia became an empire. Subsequently, under successive kings, the Græko-Baktrians extended their supremacy over the Punjab and the upper course of the Ganges. About a hundred years before Christ, they were driven out of Central Asia by the Indo-Scythians; but they left their mark in art and religion which remains to this day. Greek sculptures are found amidst the ruins of Buddhist temples. Greek gods and Greek inscriptions are stamped on the coins of old Hindu Rajas.

Indo-Scythian kings.

The history of the Indo-Scythian kings is unknown. They were doubtless of the class which ancient writers placed under the Greek name of Scythian. They came from the eastward to the banks of the Oxus. Later on they were pressed towards the east and south by other hordes of the same character. They swept in successive waves through

B.C. 500 TO A.D. 1000

Afghanistan and the Punjab. One branch appears to have gone southwards down the valley of the Indus; another went eastward down the valley of the Ganges. From this time they are no longer spectres floating in an age of darkness, but appear upon the stage of history in substantive forms. Their features are revealed upon their coins. Their faces show that they were men of bright intelligence and high resolve. Their annals have yet to be discovered, but the process has begun. Their names and dates are either decyphered, or being decyphered. Already it is possible to tell something of the part played by the Indo-Scythian kings in the bygone history of India.

Reign of Kanishka, about B.C. 56.

The latest dynasty of the Indo-Scythian kings stands out more prominently than all the others. It seems to have been founded by a sovereign, whose name was Kanishka; but this name appears on his coins in the Greek form of Kanerke. He probably ascended the throne of the Indo-Scythians about B.C. 56 or 57; or about the time that Julius Cæsar first landed on the shores of Albion.

Mixed religions.

From the banks of the Oxus, Kanishka brought the Persian worship of Mithra or the sun, which his tribe had added to their ancestral worship of fire, water, and the firmament. Even Syrian and Egyptian gods are found in the Pantheon of the Indo-Scythians. Their latest conquests brought them into contact with the mythology of Greece and India; also with the religion of Gótama Buddha. Kanishka seems to have been a liberal patron of the Buddhists. His dynasty lasted about a century, and the latest king bore a Hindu name.

Guptas: possibly children of the Græko-Baktrians.

Meanwhile, a mysterious people, known as the Guptas, were making a name and home in India. The Hindus called them Mlechhas, or barbarians. According to tradition they were strangers in the land. Possibly, they were children of the Greeks; immigrants from the old Græko-Baktrian empire, who had half-forgotten their Hellenic instincts and become Hinduised. They succeeded to the dynasty of Kanishka. From what follows, they appear to have made common cause with Hindu Rajas against the Indo-Scythian invaders.

Contest between Indo-Scythians and Rajpúts.

It has been said that one branch of the Indo-Scythians moved down the valley of the Indus; thence they passed through the desert of Scinde, Guzerat, and Marwar, towards

B.C. 500 TO A.D. 1000

Ujain or Oojein. The kingdom of Ujain was seated on the table-land of Malwa in southern Rajpútana. In ancient times the city of Ujain was a centre of Rajpút sovereignty and Brahmanical literature; and to this day it is haunted by memories of Rajpút bards and Sanskrit dramatists.

Final defeat of the Indo-Scythians at Kahror, A.D. 78.

History sheds but faint gleams of light on this distracted period. The western Indo-Scythians from the Indus seem to have been men of nerve and resolution, who pushed on towards Central India to restore the failing fortunes of their race. They were met by a general league of Hindu princes. The Guptas shared in the league; possibly they led it. A great battle was fought at Kahror, near the eastern confines of the great desert of Marwar. It was one of the decisive battles of the world; a mortal struggle between Indo-Scythian invaders and long-established Rajpút sovereignties. The Rajpúts and Guptas gained the victory. The Indo-Scythians were utterly defeated; they lost their place in history. Future discoveries may bring to light some further details respecting the children of the Indo-Scythian kings, but at present nothing further of them is known.

Era of Salivahana.

The battle of Kahror was fought probably about A.D. 78. It is said that the year 78 has become known as the Saka or Salivahana era in consequence of this battle.[1]

Disappearance of the Guptas, about A.D. 319.

The further history of the Guptas is nearly as obscure. They were supplanted by the Vallabhi Rajas about A.D. 319. The supposed children of the Greek invaders passed away, after exercising dominion, in some shape or other, in Baktria or in India, for nearly 600 years.

Greek and Roman knowledge of India.

The historians and geographers of Greece and Rome tell but little of ancient India. From the overthrow of the Græko-Baktrian kingdom by the Indo-Scythians to the downfall of the Gupta dynasty, India was nearly cut off from the outer world. Greek and Roman writers discoursed about India; they likened it to Egypt, and sometimes even confounded it with Egypt, mixing up the alligators in the Indus with the crocodiles in the Nile. Roman merchants brought back stories of the Malabar pirates on the western coast,

[1] There is an earlier era known as that of Vikramaditya. It corresponds to B.C. 55 or 56. The legends of Vikramaditya and Salivahana are so mixed up with fable as to be unreliable and unmeaning. It is said that Vikramaditya reigned over the whole world for a thousand years,—a statement which sets history and chronology at defiance.

B.C. 500 TO A.D. 1000

but they had nothing to say about Bengal or Coromandel. Indeed there was little in the current of events in India to interest men accustomed to the political life of Greece and Italy. India was still divided into a number of little kingdoms; as it had been in the war of the Mahá Bhárata. Sometimes congeries of kingdoms were formed into empires under sovereigns like the kings of Magadha and Kosala, of Andhra and Pandya.[1] The story of their wars told of battles between armies with lines of elephants, but it taught nothing about the people. The religious controversies between Brahmans and Buddhists were unheeded or unknown to the philosophers of Greece and Rome.

Buddhist pilgrims from China.

History never stands still. Ideas spread and seethe beneath the surface of humanity, and their outbreak takes the world by surprise. In the third century before the Christian era, Asoka had sent forth Buddhist missionaries to preach the law of Sákya Muni in Upper Asia. Orders of Buddhist monks were established in China. Six or seven centuries passed away, and then Chinese monks began to appear in India. They made pilgrimages to the sacred spots that were associated with the life of the Buddhist apostle :—Kapila, his birthplace; Rajagriha, where he first carried his alms-bowl; the jungle of Gaya, where he became Buddha; and the deer-forest near Benares where he first preached the law.

Pilgrimage of Fah Hian. A.D. 400.

About A.D. 400, a Chinese monk, named Fah Hian, travelled through the Punjab into Hindustan. He was pious and humble, but zealous for the law. He saw many Brahmans and idol temples, but rejoiced also to see that Buddhism was flourishing. Buddhist monks were maintained at the public expense, and foreign monks were hospitably entertained in the monasteries.

Residence at Patali-putra.

Fah Hian visited all the sacred spots, but the main object of his pilgrimage was to carry back revised copies of the Buddhist scriptures for the benefit of his brethren in China. Accordingly he dwelt for three years at Patali-putra, the centre of Buddhism; he learnt the Pali language in which

[1] The empire of Andhra had a long existence; it is supposed to correspond with the Telinga, or Telugu country. The Andhras are mentioned by name in the edicts of Asoka. Pandya has been identified with Madura, or the Tamil country in the remote south. The king of Pandya, or Pandion, sent an embassy to Augustus Cæsar.

B.C. 500 TO A.D. 1000

the Buddhist scriptures are written; and he secured copies of all the sacred books. He describes a few features of Buddhist life; the ruins of the once famous palace of Asoka; the religious processions of images of Sákya Muni and other Buddhist saints; and the public hospitals where the destitute, the crippled, and the diseased were attended by physicians, and supplied with food and medicines until they were sufficiently relieved.

Pilgrimage of Hiouen-Thsang, A.D. 629-645; Buddhist rule in India.

Two centuries afterwards, about A.D. 629-645, another Chinese monk travelled in India, named Hiouen-Thsang. He was a zealous Buddhist like Fah Hian, but he was more observant and more highly cultured. He describes the people of India as easy and gentle, volatile in their manners, honest in their dealings, and restrained by fear of punishment after death. The administration in Buddhist India was very mild. There were no capital punishments. Most offences were punished by fines; but injustice, lying, or disobedience to parents were punished by mutilation or exile.

Memories of the Mahá-Bhárata.

Hiouen-Thsang did not go to the city of Indraprastha, but he knew something of the Mahá Bhárata. He was told that the bones of the warriors that fell in the great war were still lying on the field of Kuru-kshetra, and that they were as big as the bones of giants. He went to the city of Kanouj on the river Ganges, which at this time was the metropolis of an empire that covered Hindustan and the Punjab.

Empire of Síláditya in Hindustan.

The empire of Kanouj included a number of tributary Rajas stretching from Kashmir to Assam, and from the Himalayas to the Nerbudda river. The reigning emperor or Maháraja was named Síláditya, and was known as a Maháraja Adhiraj, or "lord paramount." He tried to conquer the Dekhan, but failed. He was a patron of Buddhism, but he also favoured the Brahmans, and was tolerant of all religions. Probably he sought to keep the religious orders in peace by showing a friendly countenance to all.

Field of happiness at Prayága

Síláditya held a great festival at Prayága, the modern Allahabad, which reveals the connection between the Maháraja and the religious orders. This locality had been regarded as sacred from a very remote period, because of the union of the Ganges and Jumna. Under the vast systems of almsgiving advocated by Brahmanism and Budd hism, Prayága had continued to be regarded as holy ground. It was called "the field of happiness;" and the merit of almsgiving was enhanced a thousand-fold by the alms being bestowed at Prayága.

B.C. 500 TO A.D. 1000

Imperial alms-giving.

Every five years Maháraja Síláditya distributed all the treasures of his empire as alms. Hiouen-Thsang was present at one of these extraordinary gatherings, and describes it at length. All the Rajas of the empire were there, together with half a million of people, and all were feasted by the Maháraja for seventy-five days. Meanwhile the alms were distributed without distinction of person or religion. The whole of the accumulated treasures of the empire were given away to Buddhist monks, Brahman priests, heretical teachers, and mendicants of every grade and degree. The poor, the lame, and the orphan, received alms in like manner. The Maháraja was supposed to expiate all his sins by this unlimited almsgiving. At the close of the festival Síláditya stripped himself of all the robes and jewels he had worn during the seventy-five days, and distributed them amongst the multitude. He appeared in tattered garments like a beggar. "All my wealth," he cried, "has been spent in the field of happiness, and I have gained an everlasting reward: I trust that in all future existences I may continue to amass riches and bestow them in alms, until I have attained every divine faculty that a creature can desire."[1]

University of Nalanda.

Hiouen-Thsang dwelt for a long time in a huge monastery at Nalanda, near Rajagriha, where the ruins are still to be seen. The monastery was a vast university, where ten thousand Buddhist monks and novices were lodged and supplied with every necessary. Towers, domes, and pavilions stood amidst a paradise of trees, gardens, and fountains. There were six large ranges of buildings, four stories high, as well as a hundred lecture-rooms. All the inmates were lodged, boarded, taught, and supplied with vestments without charge. They were thus enabled to devote their whole lives to the acquisition of learning. They studied the sacred books of

[1] By profuse almsgiving the Maháraja hoped to acquire genius and wisdom; but he could not expect to obtain final deliverance or emancipation of his soul from the endless chain of transmigrations; that could only be acquired by leading a life of abstraction from all affections and desires. See the next chapter.

B.C. 500 TO A.D. 1000

all religions. In like manner they studied all the sciences, especially arithmetic and medicine.

India between the seventh and eleventh centuries.

India before the Muhammadan conquest must thus have resembled Europe during the dark ages. The Hindu people were in the background; ignorant and superstitious, but wanting no poor-laws, and maintaining their sick and aged as part of their religious duties. Rajas and chieftains were at frequent war. Principalities and powers sprung into ephemeral existence and then perished. Porus and Alexander, Asoka and Síláditya, and all the armies of Baktrians, Scythians, and Guptas, have passed away like the ghosts of the warriors of the Mahá Bhárata beneath the waters of the Ganges, without leaving a ripple on the surface of humanity.

Religious revolutions.

All this while a religious life was illuminating colleges, monasteries, and pagodas. Brahmans were rehabilitating ancient superstitions in metaphysical forms. Buddhists were ignoring the existence of the gods, and denying the efficacy of priests, sacrifices, and prayers. Religious books were composed in secluded universities and revolutionised the Indian world. Cities and courts were drawn into theological controversies. Hence arose quarrels between the old religion and the new; between Brahmans and Buddhists; between the men who worshipped the gods of the Hindu Pantheon, and the men who worshipped no gods whatever, beyond the goodness incarnate in Gótama Buddha and his disciples.

CHAPTER IV.

RELIGION AND LITERATURE.

THE Hindu people of historical times are divided into four great castes; namely, Brahmans or priests; Kshatriyas or soldiers; Vaisyas or merchants;[1] and Súdras or cultivators. But there is a remarkable distinction between the three first castes and the Súdras, which is recognised throughout the whole of India. The Brahmans, Kshatriyas and Vaisyas are known as the "twice born," because they are invested at an early age with a mysterious thread, which marks their entrance into civil life. The Súdras have no such thread, and consequently are separated from the "twice born" as an inferior race. It may therefore be inferred that the three first castes, or "wearers of the thread," are descendants of the Aryan invaders of India, who conquered the Punjab and Hindustan in a remote antiquity. The Súdras, on the other hand, who are not "wearers of the thread," may be descendants of the non-Aryan, or so-called Turanian race, who were the dominant people in India at the time of the Aryan invasion, and were subsequently treated as a conquered and servile population.

Four castes: the twice-born and the Súdras.

Besides the four castes, there is a large population known as Pariahs or outcastes. They are altogether inferior to the Súdras, and were probably the Helots of India when the Súdras were masters. They include menial servants of various grades and artisans of all descriptions; and are divided in

Pariahs, or outcastes.

[1] The Vaisyas correspond to the Banians, so often mentioned by old English travellers in Western India. The Bunniahs of Bengal are of the same caste, but from some unknown cause they have ceased to wear the thread of the "twice-born."

their turn into numerous other so-called castes, according to their hereditary trades or occupations. These Pariahs call themselves Hindus, and make up the lower strata of the Hindu social system.

Hill-tribes non-Hindus.

In all parts of India, however, there are certain barbarous tribes, who are altogether outside the pale of Hindu civilization. They are primitive communities, the so-called aborigines of India, who were driven by the conquerors out of the culturable plains into the hills and jungles, and have never as yet been Brahmanised into castes or otherwise absorbed into the Hindu social system. The Bhíls and Nágas mentioned in the Mahá Bhárata are existing types of the so-called aboriginal races. To these may be added the Mhairs and Mínas of Rajpútana; the Kóls, Ghonds, and Khonds of the Dekhan; the Kalars of the Peninsula, and a host of other tribes under a variety of names.

Relics of ancient Turanians and Aryans.

The bulk of these hill and jungle tribes are probably Turanians, without any political organisation, excepting of the patriarchal type. Others, however, are distinctly Aryan, with a rude town-hall in the centre of a village, and crude remains of a feudal system. These last are probably relics of the Aryan invaders, who had either penetrated into remote regions beyond the van of Aryan civilization; or had lagged behind in the hills and jungles as worn-out invalids or cripples who had dropped off from the rear of the conquering army.

Religion of the Turanians: mysteries of death and birth.

The religious ideas of Turanians and Aryans have been so closely interwoven in the course of ages, that it is perhaps impossible to treat them as race distinctions. It may, however, be broadly stated that the religion and literature of the Turanians were derived from the mysteries of death and birth, of which Siva or Mahádeva, and his wife Kálí or Durgá, were originally personifications. The Turanians of India also worshipped certain wrathful or avenging deities, such as the goddesses of cholera and small-pox, and the angry ghosts of men or women who had died violent deaths. The religious ceremonial was made up of bloody sacrifices, orgiastic dances, and deafening music. Other strange rites were enjoined in a mystic literature known as the Tantras; but these have died out together with human sacrifices, self immolation, and other abominations. A few revolting forms of worship and propitiation may still linger in secluded localities; but the sacrifice of goats to the goddess Kálí is, perhaps, one of the last relics of the old Turanian religion which is still practised by the civilized caste people of India.

Religion of the Aryans: worship of genii or spirits.

The religion and literature of the Aryans were associated with the worship of genii or spirits, which were supposed to dwell in all material forms as well as in the outward manifestations of nature. The Aryan people worshipped the genii of swords and ploughshares; of trees, hills, fountains, and rivers; of the sun, the firmament, the rain and the winds. They also worshipped the manes of departed heroes and ancestors; and the titular deity or guardian spirit of a township, village, tribe, family, or household. These spiritual existences were often personified as gods and goddesses, and shapened into idols. Civilized Hindus propitiate these deities with offerings of boiled rice, milk, sugar, and butter; and sometimes with meat and wine. Hill tribes offer up delicacies of their own, such as fowls and pigs, and a strong fermented liquor resembling beer. In return both classes of worshippers hope to be rewarded with brimming harvests, prolific cattle, health, wealth, long life, and other temporal blessings.

Vaidik hymns: poetical and ethical.

The earliest religious utterances which have been preserved in Aryan literature are known as the Vaidik hymns. They are songs or invocations addressed to different Aryan deities in the language of praise and prayer. These hymns are not the outcome of a single generation, but the growth of centuries. The earlier hymns were the ejaculations of a childlike people. The worshippers praised each god in turn as if he had been a great sovereign; and then implored him for material blessings, in the simple language in which children might be expected to entreat a patriarch or father. The later hymns were of higher and more thoughtful import. The ideas of children or savages were expressed in the language of sages and divines. The original invocations were interlarded with poetical feelings and imagery which belonged to a more advanced civilization, and with spiritual and moral sentiments which were the outcome of later Brahmanical teaching.

Vaidik gods: Agni, Varuna, Vayu, and Indra.

Fire was personified as Agni, the god who cooked the food, warmed the dwelling, and frightened away beasts of prey. Agni thus became the divinity of the homestead, whose presence was as dear as that of a wife or mother. Agni was also the sacrificial flame, the divine messenger, who licked up the sacrifice and carried it to the gods.

Water was personified as Varuna, the god of the sea; and Varuna was gradually invested with divine attributes as a deity powerful to destroy, but mighty to save; who engulfed the wicked man in the drowning depths, or mercifully bore the repentant sinner over the surging billows in safety to the shore. The wind and breezes were personified as Vayu and the Maruts. Vayu roared amongst the trees; whilst the Maruts blew up the clouds for showers. The firmament was personified as Indra, and the Maruts were his followers. He was king of the Vaidik gods; he struck the sky with his thunderbolt, pierced the black clouds with his spear and brought down the earth-refreshing showers. He went forth to battle riding on his elephant, attended by the Maruts bearing their lances on their shoulders in the forms of youthful warriors. He was the national deity of the Aryan invaders; who slew his enemies by thousands and destroyed their cities by hundreds; who brought back the spoil and recovered the cows that were carried away. He was the sovereign of the gods, enthroned in his heaven of Swarga on the Himalayas, like Zeus among the deities of Olympus.[1]

Worship of the sun: Vishnu and his incarnations.

Súrya, or the sun god, the Persian Mithra, was originally the deity who journeyed through the sky and measured the days and nights, but he was eventually invested with attributes still more divine than those of Indra. Indeed the worship of the supreme all-seeing orb of day was always more spiritual than that of Indra, and at a later period superseded it. He was personified as the ideal of manly beauty; the deity of light, the Hindu Apollo. He was also represented in myth and legend, as the remote ancestor of the solar race of Rajpúts, who to this day are known as the children of the sun. In later Vaidik literature he was elevated to the godhead as the creator of the universe, and the divine soul that illuminated the universe. Eventually the worship of the sun developed into that of Vishnu, the Supreme Spirit, whose incarnations as Krishna and Ráma were glorified in the Mahá Bhárata and Rámáyana.

The Vaidik hymns contain no distinct reference to a future state of rewards and punishments; but there are numerous

[1] Professor Max Müller's editions of the text to the Rik Vaidha, and his eloquent translations of the Vaidik hymns into English, have opened up new fields of religious thought and philosophical research to English readers.

allusions to a judge of the dead, who is personified as the god Yáma, and who consequently may be regarded as presiding over the entrance to a world of departed souls.

Yáma, judge of the dead.

The Vaidik Aryan was thus constantly surrounded by the unseen gods of a visible universe; and his daily life and conduct were more or less influenced by the presence of such deities. In one Sanskrit drama a wicked prince endeavours to persuade a parasite to commit murder, by assuring him that there was no one to witness the act. The parasite replies in indignant language :—

Moral influence of Vaidik gods.

> "All nature would behold the crime,
> The genii of the grove, the sun, the moon,
> The winds, the vault of heaven, the firm-set earth,
> Yáma, the mighty judge of all who die,
> Aye, and the inner conscience of the soul."[1]

In addition to the Vaidik gods above mentioned, there are a host of minor personifications in the Vaidik Pantheon, such as earth, day, night, the four seasons, the gods of the air, the gods of the brooks and streams, and many others, all of whom are clothed in forms at once human and divine. Thus Ushas, the dawn, the Eos of the Greeks, is imaged as a white-robed maiden, awakening a sleeping world as a mother awakens her children, to kindle the morning sacrifice, and invoke the gods with praise and prayer.

Minor personifications: Ushas the dawn.

In Vaidik literature all the more prominent gods are extolled in turn as the Supreme Being; but in the modern belief of the Hindus three different deities stand out as representatives of the One God, under the names of Brahma, Vishnu, and Siva. Each of these gods is worshipped in different localities as the creator and ruler of the universe, the Divine Spirit who is above all and in all. One important sect of Hindus worships Brahma as the creator, Vishnu as the preserver, and Siva as the destroyer of the universe; but more frequently all these attributes of creation, preservation, and dissolution are assigned to one Supreme Being, who permeates the universe and is the universe; and all the endless emblems, incarnations, and idols are reverenced as so many vehicles through which the Supreme Spirit receives the adorations and offerings of his worshippers.

Brahma, Vishnu, and Siva.

[1] The *Toy-Cart*, by Raja Sudraka, translated by H. H. Wilson in the *Theatre of the Hindus*. The passage has been slightly modified, and is remarkable as showing how the law of merits and demerits blended with the old nature-worship of the Vaidik hymns.

Popular deifications of good luck, prosperity, learning, wealth, love, and war.

There are other and popular deities amongst the Hindus, which cannot be referred distinctly to an Aryan or a Turanian origin. Their worship has been rooted in the hearts of the people of India from a remote antiquity; and has become associated with that of Aryan and Túranian gods by numberless supernatural myths and fables. Foremost amongst these is Ganesh, the god of good luck; Lakshmí, the goddess of prosperity; Saraswatí, the goddess of learning; Kuvera, the god of wealth; Káma, the god of love; and Kartikeia, the god of war.

Astrological origin.

The propitiation of the more important of these deities is so much a matter of everyday life with the Hindus, as to appear like a national instinct. No Hindu will undertake a journey, nor engage in any business or transaction, without a visit to the temple of Ganesh. No Hindu will begin a literary composition without an invocation to Ganesh. The idol meets the eye all over India, with the head of an elephant and the prominent stomach of a Chinese deity; but whilst he is represented in Brahmanical myths as a son of Siva and Durgá, the real origin of his worship continues to be a mystery. Lakshmí, the goddess of prosperity, is propitiated in like manner on every possible occasion. She is represented in Brahmanical myths as the goddess of beauty, who rose out of the foam of the ocean, like a Hindu Aphrodite, to become the bride of Vishnu. Saraswatí, the goddess of learning, was originally the divinity or spirit of the river Indus;[1] but was converted into the mythical wife of Brahma, and as such appears as the goddess of literature and science of every kind. Kuvera, Káma, and Kartakeia, are apparently the outcome of astrological ideas, and may possibly be the personification and deification of supposed planetary influences.

Worship of the serpent, the bull, and the cow.

Besides the foregoing, the serpent, the bull, and the cow are worshipped all over India. They are apparently the incarnations of mysterious deities associated with ideas of sex. The serpent is propitiated with bread and milk as the guardian of the household. The bull is a masculine deity associated with the worship of Siva or Mahadeva. The cow is a feminine divinity, and is worshipped and reverenced

[1] The river Indus is often invoked as the goddess Saraswatí in the Vaidik hymns.

by all Hindus, as the universal mother, the personification of earth, the incarnation of the goddess Lakshmí.

Rise of the Brahmans.

The rise of the Brahmans is as obscure as that of the Druids. They appeared amongst the people of India,—Aryans and Turanians, barbarous and civilised,—as priests, divines, and holy men. They ingratiated themselves with Rajas and warriors by worshipping the old gods, but after new and mystic forms; interpreting the present and the future by the bubbling of the boiling milk and rice in the daily sacrifices, the marks on sacrificial victims, or the manifestations of the sacrificial smoke and flame. They pronounced the lower gods of the aboriginal races to be incarnations or avatars of the great gods of the conquerors; and they associated the higher gods of the aboriginal races with new and more spiritual teachings, and raised them to the highest rank of deity. Thus even Siva or Mahadeva, the god of death, was resolved into a Supreme Being; and Kálí, the black goddess, who revelled in intoxication and slaughter, was worshipped as a divine mother, under the names of Parvatí and Durgá.

Growth of Brahmanical power: Purohitas, Gurus, and Swamis.

The growth of the Brahmans in power and influence is one of the most important elements in Indian history. Every Raja or great man had his own Brahman priest, preceptor, or purohita. So had every family, or group of families, or village community. But priests and laymen were subject to inquisitorial forms of Brahmanical government, of which traces are still to be found in all directions. Religious teachers of a superior order, known as Gurus, undertook regular ecclesiastical tours, confirming neophytes, and excommunicating heretics and caste offenders. Above all there were Brahmans of still higher sanctity, who were worshipped as gods under the name of Náths and Swamis, and exercised a vast spiritual authority over courts and Rajas, whilst extending secret ramifications to remote quarters of India. Meanwhile religious centres were established at convenient spots in the shape of temples, colleges, and places of pilgrimage; and Brahmanical hermitages were set up in the countries inhabited by aboriginal races outside the Aryan pale. Thus in the course of ages, the Brahmans have spread abroad a religious faith and worship, which notwithstanding the number and variety of divinities, are essentially the same throughout the length and breadth of India.

Laws of Manu. A further development of the religious teaching of the Hindus is to be found in the Brahmanical code, known as the laws of Manu. The life of Manu is unknown; he has no personality whatever; he is a mythical being, a reputed son of Brahma, and lord of all living creatures. But the sacred character of the code of Manu is acknowledged and reverenced throughout India.

Transmigrations of the soul. Manu taught the belief in the endless transmigrations of the soul; that the soul of every individual being, whether of man or of animal, passed at every successive death into a newly born body; rising or falling in the scale of being at every successive birth according to the sum of its merits or demerits in all past lives. Thus the belief in a future state of rewards and punishments was associated by Manu with a chain of existences without beginning or ending; running up and down the scale of animal being from the meanest vermin to the highest order of intellectual man.[1]

Merits and demerits. The code of Manu itself was the source of all merits and demerits. It demanded the observance of caste laws, the worship of the gods, and the offerings of cakes and water to departed ancestors. Obedience to its enactments constituted the only merits which were rewarded in future lives; and disobedience constituted the only demerits which were punished by future pains and miseries. Rajasúyas and Aswamedhas were treated as arch merits, and converted into sacrifices for the atonement of sin.

Heaven and hell. The religion of the Brahmans also recognised the existence of different heavens and hells. Thus the souls of warriors who died in battle went to the heaven of Indra; whilst the spirits of departed ancestors went to a world of shades where they could only be consoled by the cakes and water offered in the Sráddhas. But this spirit life in heaven or hell only lasted for a limited period, until merits had been sufficiently rewarded and demerits sufficiently punished. At the expiration of the appointed term the soul returned to earth and re-entered on a fresh course of successive existences in the endless chain of transmigrations.

Divine Spirit. Whilst the code of Manu enforced the worship of the gods, it further developed those conceptions of the Supreme Spirit, which find expression in the Vaidik hymns. "All

[1] It is a question whether vegetable life was not also included in the transmigrations of the soul.

gods," says Manu, "are in the divine spirit, all worlds are in the divine spirit; and the divine spirit produces the connected series of acts which are performed by embodied souls. Him some adore as present in the element of fire; others as present in Manu lord of creatures; some as present in Indra; others as present in pure ether; and others as present in the most high Eternal Spirit. It is He who, pervading all beings in five elementary forms, causes them by the gradations of birth, growth, and dissolution to revolve in this world like the wheels of a car."

Deliverance of the soul in absorption.

But Manu pointed out that there was a way of deliverance or emancipation of the soul from the endless chain of transmigrations, whether on earth or in heaven or hell. He taught that a term of austerities would quench the fires of affection, passion, and desire, and break every tie which bound the soul to the universe of being. The soul would then enter upon a term of pure contemplation, during which it would behold the Supreme Soul present in all things, and would finally be absorbed in the Divine Spirit.[1]

Four terms of life.

Manu thus fashioned out a universe of being, driven by an artificial law of merits and demerits along a chain of endless transmigrations. He also showed how the individual soul might be delivered or emancipated from this chain of existences, and become absorbed in the Divine Essence. He next mapped out the life of man into the four terms of student, householder, hermit, and devotee, with the view of enabling each individual to work out his own deliverance or emancipation. As a student each individual of the twice born castes would learn the divine law; as a householder he would marry a wife and collect merits as a husband and a father; as a hermit he would perform religious austerities; and as a devotee he would contemplate the Supreme Soul until his own soul was absorbed in the Divine Spirit. The duties which each individual must fulfil within the four terms are duly set forth in the code of Manu, and still make up the ideal of the Hindu.

Buddhism a revolt against Brahmanism.

Buddhism was practically a revolt against the Brahmanical system of Manu. It ignored the existence of

1 "The man who perceives in his own soul the Supreme Soul present in all creatures, and regards them all with equal benevolence, will be absorbed at last in the highest Essence, even of that of the Almighty Himself."—Manu, xii. 126.

deity; denied the efficacy of prayers and sacrifices; broke up the bondage of caste; and declared that goodness and loving-kindness were the only merits by which the soul could rise in successive transmigrations. It laid down five great commandments against the five deadly sins of murder, theft, adultery, drunkenness, and falsehood; and it taught that the slightest infringement of any one of these commandments in thought, word, or deed, constituted a demerit which would detract from the happiness of the soul in a future state of being.

Deliverance of the soul in annihilation.

But as regards the deliverance or emancipation of the soul, the teaching of Gótama Buddha coincided, with one important exception, to that of Manu. Gótama Buddha taught that a life of goodness and divine contemplation would quench the fires of affection, passion, and desire, which bound the soul to the universe of being. But he denied the existence of a Divine Spirit, and was thus driven to accept the dogma of annihilation. Consequently he taught that when the soul was delivered from the chain of existences, it sank into the eternal sleep or annihilation known as Nirvána.

Modern Brahmanism.

Modern Brahmanism, as expounded in the Mahá Bhárata and Rámáyana, introduced a new element in religious teaching, a shorter way of effecting the emancipation of the soul. Without ignoring the efficacy of good works, it taught that by faith alone, in Krishna or in Ráma, as an incarnation of Vishnu, the soul might be delivered from the vortex of successive existences, and would either be raised to an everlasting heaven of the highest beatitude, or be absorbed in the Supreme Spirit,—Vishnu.

Hindu literature: non-historical.

HINDU LITERATURE comprises numerous works on metaphysics, logic, rhetoric, poetry, arithmetic, musical science, and other like compositions, which were all more or less treated in connection with religion. But nothing has been discovered that merits the name of history, or warrants the hope that authentic annals exist in any of the Indian languages.[1] Relics of traditions are however to be found in

1. Grant Duff, in his *History of the Mahrattas*, speaks with favour of native annals; but later researches have proved that such annals are nearly worthless for purposes of history. The author wasted much time and labour before he was driven to this conclusion, which has

poetry and the drama, which may serve to illustrate Hindu life and manners before Muhammadans or Europeans appeared upon the scene. But Hindu poets devoted so much time to the arbitrary conceits of composition, fanciful descriptions of scenery and the four seasons, and endless myths and marvels, that vast accumulations of poetical overgrowth have to be cleared away before it is possible to arrive at the kernel of matter of fact history.[1]

Sakúntalá.

The drama of "Sakúntalá" was written by a poet named Kálidása, and was probably composed at a late period in the history of the mediæval Rajas; but the plot refers to the oldest period in Hindu legend, namely, the birth of Bharata, the conqueror of India. It opens with a Brahmanical hermitage; one of those secluded groves where Brahmans dwelt with their wives and families, and were supposed to spend their lives in sacred studies, religious worship, and divine contemplations.

Marriage of a Raja with a Brahman's daughter.

A Raja, named Dushyanta, was hunting in the jungle, and chased an antelope which took refuge in the hermitage. He was drawing his bow to shoot the animal, when the Brahmans rushed out and implored him not to pollute their sanctuary by shedding blood. The Raja piously refrained, but at this moment he saw the daughter of a Brahman, the beautiful Sakúntalá, walking in the garden of the hermitage with other girl companions. The Raja soon fell in love with her, and induced her to marry him by one of those

since been confirmed by Professor Bühler of Bombay. See larger *History of India*, vol. iv. chap. ii. and Appendix. Also Bühler's *Introduction to the Vikramánkakávya*, Bombay, 1875.

[1] The court life of Hindu authors was unfavourable to historical accuracy. They depended for their existence on the bounty of reigning Rajas, and the first object of their compositions was to please their royal patrons. Every principality, small and great, had its own hereditary bards and Pundits, who were supported by allowances from the palace. Young students, fresh from their preceptors, betook themselves to a wandering life, and visited one court after another, holding disputations, showing off their learning, and composing poetry for the delectation of princes, who cared only to be amused. Such wandering bards and Pundits are still to be encountered all over India; but the greater number appear to be travelling from the Punjab and Oude through Rajputana towards Baroda and Bombay. The tour often lasts five or six years, and includes places of pilgrimage as well as courts of princes. Professor Bühler, in the Introduction already quoted, dwells on the jealousies displayed by the hereditary bards and Pundits towards these foreign wanderers.

irregular ceremonies which were discountenanced by Manu. Subsequently Sakúntalá gave birth to the infant Bharata, but the Raja refused to recognize his marriage, and even denied all knowledge of Sakúntalá, until by some supernatural incident his eyes were opened, and he accepted her as his wife and Bharata as his son. Bharata grew up to be the conqueror of India, and was the ancestor of the Pándavas and Kauravas who fought in the great war.

Super-natural incidents.

The drama of "Sakúntalá" is based upon incidents which are foreign to European works of imagination. The Raja had given a ring to Sakúntalá as the pledge of his troth; and she had lost the ring whilst bathing in a pool; and so long as the ring was missing the Raja could not recognize his wife. Subsequently the ring was found in the body of a fish and recovered by the Raja. From that day he remembered his lost Sakúntalá; and going out into the jungle he saw a young lad playing with lions, who proved to be his own son Bharata.

Characteristics of the drama.

The beauty of the play of "Sakúntalá" lies not in the strong individuality of the leading characters, but in the general appreciation of external nature, the love of flowers, the girl-like talk of the damsels, and the variety of emotions which stir the heart of Sakúntalá. Indeed the language is so sweet and touching that to this day no Sanskrit drama is more admired by the people of India than "Sakúntalá; or, the lost ring."[1]

Nala and Damayantí: the royal charioteer.

The poem of "Nala and Damayantí" is more romantic. Nala, Raja of Malwa, was a famous archer, but especially renowned as a charioteer. The tramp of his horses was heard from afar, like the roll of distant thunder; and the noise of his chariot wheels was like the rushing of many waters.

Princess of Vidarbha.

Damayantí was a princess of Vidarbha.[2] She was the pearl of maidens as Nala was the tiger amongst Rajas. She had given her heart to Nala, and vowed that no one but Nala should be her lord and husband.

The poem opens with the Swayamvara of Damayantí.

[1] The drama of "Sakúntalá" is best known to European readers through the elegant translation of Professor Monier Williams.

[2] The old city of Vidarbha in the Dekhan corresponds to the city of Bíder. The magnificent remains of the fortress and palace are still to be seen at Bíder.

Swayamvara of Damayantí: descent of the Vaidik gods.

The fame of her beauty had reached the skies; and Indra and the other gods came down from the heaven of Swarga to be candidates for her hand. They appeared in the assembly hall in the forms of Rajas, but Damayantí knew that they were gods, for there was no winking of their eyes, no perspiration on their brows, no dust on their garments, and no faded leaf in their wreaths of flowers. But she was reckless in her love; she cared not for the anger of the gods; she threw the garland round the neck of Nala, and chose him for her husband in the presence of them all.[1]

Happy marriage.

Nala and Damayantí were married at Vidarbha, and the Raja returned with his loving wife to his city in Malwa.[2] Beautiful children were born to them, and they were rich in every blessing.

Ruin of a royal gambler.

But Nala was a gambler, and the dice box was his ruin. In an evil hour he sat down to play, and lost stake after stake, like Yudhishthira in the gambling booth at Hastinápur. The chieftains of the Raj assembled at the palace, and implored him to stay his hand; but he was deaf to all their prayers, and hotly continued the game. At last he lost all his treasures, his kingdom, and his home; and then went out in the jungle to live on fruits and roots.

Jungle exile: flight of Nala.

Meanwhile Damayantí never deserted her husband. She sent her children to the palace of her father at Vidarbha, and went with Nala into the jungle. But Nala was driven wild by the sufferings of his wife, and fell into a melancholy madness. At last he left her sleeping in the jungle, and fled to the city of Ayodhyá, and entered the service of the Raja of Kosala as his charioteer.

Agony of Damayantí.

The poem next dwells on the anguish of Damayantí at discovering that her husband has deserted her. She wandered on in a distracted state, calling in vain for Nala. She was threatened with death in a variety of ways; by a jungle fire, a stampede of elephants, and the coils of a deadly serpent. At length she found refuge in the city of Chedipur, and eventually returned to the palace of her father. But her heart still yearned after her husband Nala, and she

[1] The appearance of the Vaidik gods at the Swayamvara of Damayantí is a poetical episode. It had nothing to do with the after story.

[2] The region known as Malwa lies in Hindustan, between the Nerbuddha and Chandal rivers. It is impossible to identify the site of Nala's capital.

sent Brahmans in all directions to find out whither he had gone.

Reconciliation and conclusion.

At this crisis the Raja of Kosala had occasion to go to the city of Vidarbha, and was driven by Nala as his charioteer. Damayantí was aroused from her despair by the well-remembered sounds of her husband's driving. The peacocks in the palace gardens clamoured at the tramp of the horses and rolling of the chariot wheels, whilst the royal elephants roared tumultuously. The wife was thus restored to her husband, and Nala recovered possession of his children and his Raj.

Characteristics of the poem.

The story of "Nala and Damayantí," like the drama of "Sakúntalá," owes its chief charm to the play upon the emotions and affections. It does not carry the reader back to the wild tumults of a barbarous age, like Shakespeare's tragedies of "Macbeth" and "King Lear;" but it points to an age of Arcadian simplicity, when the chieftains of a Raj endeavour to induce the Raja to put a stop to his gambling match. In other respects the story was calculated to excite warm sympathies in a palace or zenana, but tells nothing of the old world of the Hindus which has passed away.

The Toy-cart.

A Sanskrit drama, known as the "Toy-cart," deals with a wider range of characters. The scene is laid in Ujain or Oojein, one of the oldest cities in Rajputana. A vicious prince, the brother of the Raja of Ujain, falls in love with a lady of the city; she resists his advances, and he leaves her for dead in a public garden. He tries to throw the guilt of the murder on an innocent Brahman. The case is investigated by a Hindu court of justice; and the judges, whilst anxious to shield the Brahman, are compelled by the force of the circumstantial evidence to find him guilty. The sentence is referred to the Raja of Ujain, who orders the Brahman to be executed.

A popular revolution.

The unfortunate man is led away to the scaffold. At this crisis, the lady who is supposed to have been murdered suddenly makes her appearance. The multitude exult in the escape of the Brahman, and rush off to tell the Raja of his innocence; but at that moment a revolution breaks out in another quarter of the city, the Raja is deposed and slain, his wicked brother escapes into exile, and a cow-keeper sprung from the dregs of the people is raised to the throne of Ujain.

Out of this simple plot the Sanskrit bard has constructed a drama, which may have been drawn from actual life, but the incidents are artificial, the sentiments are devoid of all romance, and the characters are exaggerated in themselves and move about like automata. Characteristics of the drama.

The innocent Brahman, the hero of the story, is named Charudatta, and is said to have spent his patrimony in giving entertainments to his friends, acquaintances, and dependants; and in building temples and monasteries, laying out gardens and digging fountains of water. He continues, however, to reside in the ruined mansion, and maintains his family by the sale of his wife's jewels, and by such gifts as the people of India are accustomed to give to Brahmans out of respect for their sacred character. The heroine of the drama is not the wife of Charudatta, but a courtesan, who is in love with him; and this is the lady who is supposed to have been murdered by the brother of the Raja. The hero and heroine.

The foregoing incidents will suffice to show that the story is out of the pale of European sympathies, which would have been given to the wife alone. But the Sanskrit dramatist goes further, and introduces an incident which is an outrage on all morality and good manners. He winds up the plot by giving the courtesan as a second wife to Charudatta, and by representing the first wife as slavishly submitting to the arrangement, and addressing her rival as her sister. Such an ending could only have been constructed for the amusement of Hindu Rajas; it could never have satisfied the moral sense of the Hindu people, or have been regarded as a contribution to the national drama. Unsatisfactory *dénouement.*

It is difficult out of the disjointed and inconsistent materials collected in the foregoing chapters, to realise the actual condition of India under the ancient Hindu Rajas. It is, however, evident that the whole Indian continent was a chaos of conflicting elements, evolving large ideas of God and the universe, but utterly wanting in political life and cohesion. The after history will show the results of Muhammadan and British rule, and how much remains to be effected before the people of India can expect to take their place amongst the independent empires of the world. Historical results.

PART II.

MUHAMMADAN INDIA.

CHAPTER I.

TURKS AND AFGHANS.

A.D. 1000 TO 1525.

A.D. 1000-1200

Muhammad, or Mahomet, 570-632; his teachings.

MUHAMMAD, the prophet of Arabia, commonly called Mahomet, was born A.D. 570, and died in 632. He was still living when Hiouen-Thsang began his pilgrimage to India. He taught that there was but one God, and that he himself was the prophet of God. All who believed in God and his prophet were to be rewarded with eternal bliss in heaven; all who refused to believe were to punished with eternal torment in hell. Moreover, all believers were regarded as equals in the eyes of God, without distinction of caste or tribe; they were all bound together in the brotherhood of Islam. Every man who accepted Islam was also allowed to marry more than one wife; he might be content with one, but if he chose he might marry others, not exceeding four.

The Khalifs, or successors of Muhammad, 632-1258.

After the death of Muhammad, four Khalifs reigned in succession at Medina from A.D. 633 to 660; their names were Abubakr, Omar, Othman, and Ali.[1] They were followed by a line of Khalifs who reigned at Damascus from A.D. 660 to 750; and these again by a line of Khalifs

[1] The importance of these names will be seen in the sequel.

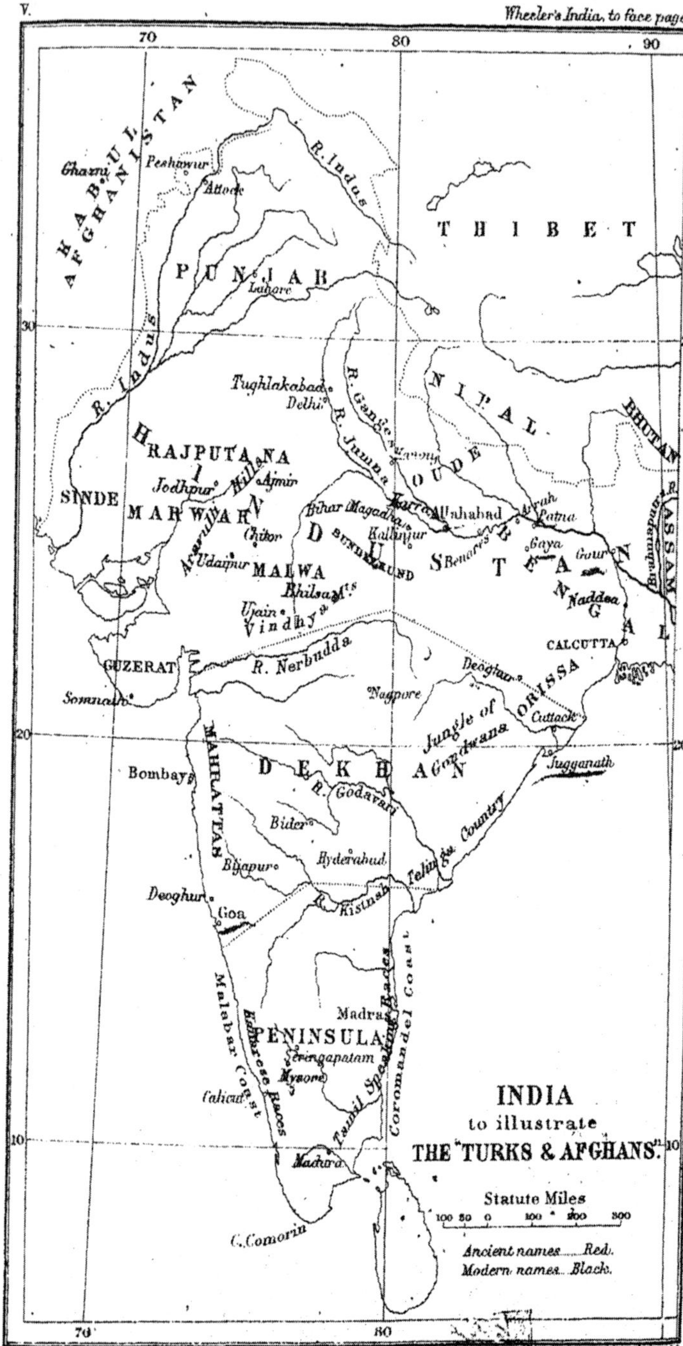

London; Macmillan & Co. Stanford's Geogl Estabt

A.D. 1000-1200

who reigned at Bagdad from A.D. 750 to 1258. These Khalifs were not prophets or founders of a new religion like Muhammad, but sovereign pontiffs who were supposed to be supreme in all spiritual and temporal affairs.

Revolt of Turk and Afghan against the Arab.

The death of Muhammad was followed by the Arab conquest of all Asia as far as the Indus and Oxus; but there the tide of invasion began to turn. Persians, Turks, and Afghans accepted the religion of the Koran, but rebelled against the domination of the Arabs. The Turks especially founded independent kingdoms in Central Asia. They acknowledged the reigning Khalif as their spiritual head, but refused to obey him as a temporal sovereign.

Arab invasion of Sinde.

The Arabs began to invade India when the Khalifs were reigning at Damascus. They ravaged Sinde on the lower course of the Indus, destroying temples, slaughtering Brahmans, and carrying off the people into slavery. But the Hindus would not become Muhammadans. At last they agreed to pay tribute, and were permitted to rebuild their temples and worship their gods after their own fashion.

Mahmúd of Ghazní, 997-1030.

The first conqueror of India of any renown was a Turk named Mahmúd. In 997 Mahmúd succeeded to the throne of Ghazní, a small territory in Kábul. Before he died he conquered all Persia on one side, and a great part of India on the other; but he never removed his court from Ghazní, and consequently he is only known to history as Mahmúd of Ghazní.

Defeats the Rajpúts at Peshawar, 1001.

In 1001 Mahmúd marched an army of Turkish horsemen from Ghazní to Peshawar. Jaipal, Raja of the Punjab, came out to meet him with a host of elephants and foot soldiers, but was beaten by the Turkish horsemen, and taken prisoner. Jaipal promised to pay tribute, and was set at liberty, but he would not survive his disgrace. He returned to Lahore, gave his kingdom to his son Anandpal, and burnt himself alive on a funeral pile.

Rajpút league against the Turks.

For some years Raja Anandpal paid the tribute regularly. He then began to grow refractory, and prevailed on the Rajas of Western Hindustan to come to his help. Vast armies of elephants and Hindu foot soldiers moved up from Delhi and Kanouj, Ajmír and Ujain, and marched through the Punjab to Peshawar. The Hindu women joined in the enthusiasm against the Turks, and sold their jewels, or spun cotton, to keep the armies in the field.

A.D. 1000-1200

Conquest of the Punjab.

Mahmúd marched an army of horsemen and archers to the plain of Peshawar. He placed his archers in front and his horsemen behind. The archers began the battle; but some wild hill tribes, known as the Gakkars, crept through the archers, and began to cut down the horsemen with sharp knives. Meanwhile the elephants of the Hindus were blinded by arrows and maddened by fire-balls, and turned round and trampled down the Hindu infantry. At that moment the Turkish horsemen raised their swords and maces, and galloped furiously upon the Hindus with loud cries of "Allah Akbar!" The army of the Rajpút league wavered and fled. The Turkish horsemen pursued the fugitives for two days, and plundered temples and destroyed idols. At last Anandpal sued for peace, and sent tribute and war elephants. The peace lasted till the death of Anandpal, when Mahmúd annexed the Punjab, and made it a province of his empire of Ghazní.

Twelve invasions of Hindustan.

Subsequently Mahmúd began to invade Hindustan. He is said to have made twelve expeditions into that country, plundering temples, breaking down idols, and carrying off vast treasures to Ghazní, as well as multitudes of slaves, male and female.

Great temple of Somnáth.

When Mahmúd was growing old he resolved on destroying the great temple of Somnáth in Guzerat. Somnáth was a thousand miles from Ghazní, but was reputed to contain immense treasures. There was an idol pillar in the temple, the symbol of the Supreme Spirit, known as Siva, or Mahadeva. A thousand Brahmans dwelt at Somnáth to offer the daily sacrifices, and five hundred damsels were engaged in the temple to dance before the idol.

Desperate battles at Somnáth, 1026-27.

The route to Somnáth lay through the desert of Sinde. Mahmúd marched 30,000 horsemen through western Rajpútana to escape the burning sands. The Rajpúts made no attempt to oppose him, but abandoned their cities at his approach. When, however, Mahmúd reached Somnáth the Rajpúts were assembled in great strength to defend their god. The temple was built on a peninsula out at sea; it was approached by a narrow isthmus, which was strongly fortified with walls and battlements, manned with Rajpúts. For two days there was desperate fighting and great slaughter. The Turkish archers sought to drive the Rajpúts from the battlements, whilst the Turkish swordsmen planted their ladders and climbed the walls. At last the Rajpúts saw that all was lost, and fled to their boats, and put out to sea. A.D. 1000-1200

Idol pillar.

When the battle was over Mahmúd entered the temple. It was a large gloomy building supported by fifty-six columns. The idol pillar was in an inner chamber. The Brahmans implored Mahmúd to spare the idol pillar, and offered to pay an enormous ransom. But Mahmúd said, "I come to destroy idols, not to sell them." He struck the pillar with his mace and broke it to pieces, whilst piles of diamonds and rubies, which had been hidden in the pillar, fell scattered upon the floor.

Death and madness in the Sinde desert.

Mahmúd returned from Guzerat to Ghazní, but lost nearly all his army on the way. The Rajpúts of Ajmír came out in such force that he was compelled to march through the desert. His guides led him astray through sandy wastes in order to avenge the destruction of Somnáth. Many of his soldiers died of thirst, whilst others went mad from the burning sun. Water was found at last; the guides were put to death; but only a remnant of the army reached Ghazní.

Rise of the Afghans, 1180.

Mahmúd died in 1030, aged sixty-three. The annals of the century and a half which followed tell of wars and revolutions in Central Asia, but say nothing of India. The Afghans supplanted the Turks. They became masters of a mountain fortress named Ghor, between Ghazní and Herát; they next drove the dynasty of Mahmúd out of Ghazní, and became lords of Kábul and the Punjab. The next conqueror after Mahmúd, who made a name in India, was Muhammad Ghori, the Afghan.

Muhammad Ghori defeated at Delhi, 1191.

Muhammad Ghori resolved on the conquest of Hindustan, In 1191 he marched an army against the Raja of Delhi. He tried to throw the Rajas into confusion by repeated charges with cavalry, but found himself surrounded by the enemy, and had a narrow escape with his life. But the Rajpút dominion was weakened by feuds. There was a feud between Delhi and Kanouj, which soon opened a way for the Afghans into Hindustan.

Maháraja of Kanouj lord paramount.

The Maháraja of Kanouj on the Ganges claimed to be a lord paramount amongst the Rajpúts. He gave a great feast and summoned all the Rajas of Hindustan to appear as his vassals, and play their parts as servants in his household. At the same time he celebrated the Swayamvara of his daughter.

A.D. 1000-1200

Swayamvara of the princess of Kanouj.

The Raja of Delhi loved the daughter of the Mahárája of Kanouj, but he scorned to serve as doorkeeper at the feast, and he refused to come. The Mahárája was wroth at the affront, and ordered an image to be made of the Delhi Raja and placed it at the door of the hall. The feast was held and the Swayamvara began. The princess entered the hall with the marriage garland in her hand. She threw one look on the assembly, and then turned to the door and cast the garland round the neck of the image. The whole assembly was in commotion. Before a man could speak, the Raja of Delhi appeared in the hall and led away the princess. In another moment the bridegroom galloped off with his bride along the road to Delhi.

Afghans capture Delhi.

The Mahárája of Kanouj brought the Afghans down upon his son-in-law. He invited Muhammad Ghori to march another army to Delhi, and the Afghan horsemen were soon on their way to the famous city. The Raja of Delhi heard that his enemy had again taken the field; he took no heed, for he cared only for his bride. At last the Muhammadans were thundering at the gates of Delhi. The Raja put on his mail and went out against the invaders; but it was too late. He perished sword in hand, and his widow burned herself upon his funeral pile.

Overthrow of the Mahárája of Kanouj, 1194.

The Mahárája of Kanouj soon had bitter cause to rue his treachery; he shared the fate of his son-in-law. In 1094 he was defeated by Muhammad Ghori, and he and his army were driven into the Ganges. His remains were known by his false teeth, which were fastened by golden wire; the relic of an age of Rajpút civilisation which has passed away.

Mussulmans advance from Delhi to Benares; flight of the Rajas.

The defeat and death of the Mahárája of Kanouj advanced the dominion of the Muhammadans from Delhi to Benares. Temples were plundered and idols were destroyed along the valleys of the Jumna and Ganges. Meanwhile the Rajpút princes left their ancestral homes to carve out new empires with their swords in the jungles and hills of the south; and they preserved their old laws and usages in the region which to this day is called Rajpútana or Rajasthan, "the land of the Rajpúts or Rajas."[1]

Muhammad Ghori conquered a larger territory in India

[1] The region extends on the south and west of the Jumna, between the river Indus and the river Chambal.

A.D. 1200-1300

than Mahmúd; but he too kept his court at Ghazní. When absent from India he appointed a favourite named Kútub-ud-dín to be his Viceroy over the Punjab and Hindustan. In 1206, whilst returning from India to Ghazní, he was assassinated by some men of the Gakkar tribes—the same race who had slaughtered Mahmúd's horsemen at Peshawar. They had vowed revenge for the slaughter of some kinsmen, and they stabbed Muhammed Ghori to death as he lay sleeping in his tent on the banks of the Indus.

Assassination of Muhammad Ghor by the Gakkars, 1206.

The death of Muhammad Ghori was followed by the dismemberment of the Afghan empire. Kútub-ud-dín ceased to be a Viceroy, and was proclaimed Sultan of Delhi. He was originally a slave, who rose to power under Muhammad Ghori as Joseph had risen in the court of the Pharaohs. He was the first of a dynasty which is known in history as that of the slave kings. His reign was a career of conquest. His tower of triumph still stands amongst the ruins of old Delhi, and is one of the tallest in the world. It is known as the Kútub Minar. It proclaims the victory of Islam over the idol-worshippers of Hindustan.

Kútub-ud-dín, Sultan of Delhi, the slave-king, 1206-1210.

Under Kútub-ud-dín the dominion of the Muhammadans was extended to the Brahma-putra river. The intervening country of Bihar and Bengal was conquered with the utmost ease. A Muhammadan adventurer named Bakhtiyár was famous for the length of his arms. He was a man of valour and audacity, but so ill-favoured that he could not obtain military service at Delhi, and went away to the eastern frontier near Benares. Here he became the leader of a band of horsemen, and began to make plundering raids into Bihar, the holy land of Magadha. He captured the city of Bihar and plundered it. He destroyed a college of Brahmans with shaven heads, and put them all to the sword. He advanced eastward to Nuddea, the old capital of Bengal,[1] and entered the city with only eighteen troopers disguised as horse-dealers. Nobody stopped him, and he and his men reached the palace, cutting down and murdering all who stood in their way.

Conquest of Bihar and Bengal.

The Raja of Nuddea was eating his dinner, when he heard an outbreak in the court-yard; Bakhtiyár and his horsemen

Flight of the Raja of Nuddea.

[1] Nuddea is about sixty miles due north of the modern city of Calcutta.

A.D. 1200-1300

had broken into the palace. The Raja was so frightened that he ran out at the back of the palace, reached the bank of a river, and took a boat and sailed away to Jagganath, leaving his family and treasures at the mercy of the Muhammadans. He never returned to Nuddea, but passed the remainder of his days at Jagganath as a religious devotee.

Gour, the capital of Bengal.

Bihar and Bengal were then formed into a province of the Delhi empire, and Bakhtiyár was the first Viceroy. The capital was fixed at Gour, at the elbow of the Ganges, where the river turns towards the south. It thus commanded the whole water communication of the country. Since then the river has changed its course, and Gour has become a heap of ruins.

Moghul invasions.

Kútub-ud-dín died in 1210. The history of his immediate successors is of no interest or moment. The Sultans of Delhi had nothing to fear from Hindus. Their chief enemies were Tartar hordes known as Moghuls;—the men who overran Asia and part of Europe under Chenghiz Khan in the thirteenth century. They entered the Punjab and Hindustan under different leaders, and were a terror wherever they went. They are described as ugly nomades with yellow complexions, high cheek-bones, flat noses, small eyes, and large mouths. They were covered with vermin, and their smell was detestable. They plundered towns and villages, and carried off women and children to serve as slaves.

Fall of the slave kings, 1290.

In 1290 the last Sultan of the Afghan slave dynasty was assassinated, and a Sultan ascended the throne at Delhi under the name of Jelál-ud-dín. He was an old man of seventy, and made no mark in history; but he had a nephew, named Alá-ud-dín, who became a man of renown.

Adventures of Alá-ud-dín: plunder of Buddhist temples at Bhilsa.

Alá-ud-dín was appointed governor of the fortress of Karra, near Allahabad. His first exploit was the plunder of the Buddhist temples at Bhilsa. This involved an expedition more than 300 miles to the south through the jungles of Bundelkund; for Bhilsa is seated on the slopes of the Vindhyá range of mountains, which separate Hindustan from the Dekhan. The Sultan was so pleased with this adventure, and especially with the treasure brought away from Bhilsa, that he appointed Alá-ud-dín to be Viceroy of Oude.

Expedition to Deoghur.

Alá-ud-dín next planned another expedition, still more venturesome. At Bhilsa he had heard of a Mahratta kingdom extending southwards of the Nerbudda river over the

Western Dekhan. The capital was Deoghur, but it was as far from Bhilsa as Bhilsa was from Karra. Indeed, the distance from Karra to Deoghur was not less than 700 miles.

A.D. 1200-1300

March into the Dekhan.

Alá-ud-dín kept his scheme a profound secret from his uncle the Sultan. He levied a force of 8,000 horsemen, and disappeared quietly from Karra. His way led through much of the scene of Ráma's wanderings; through the jungles of Bundelkund, the table-land of Malwa, and over the Vindhyá mountains and river Nerbudda. He gave out that he had quarrelled with his uncle the Sultan, and was going to enter the service of some Hindu Raja. No one doubted the truth of the story; indeed, as already seen, princes in India had been going into exile from the remotest antiquity, as the natural result of some feud or quarrel that could not be promptly avenged.

Fortress provisioned with salt.

Alá-ud-dín and his horsemen at last approached the walls of Deoghur. The Mahratta Raja was taken by surprise; he could not believe his eyes when the Muhammadan horsemen galloped into the city. He fled to a hill fortress, and found to his discomfiture that it was provisioned with salt instead of grain. He hoped, however, that the strangers would force the city to pay a ransom, and speedily go away, after the manner of predatory brigands.

Plunder of Deoghur.

Meanwhile Alá-ud-dín plundered the city, and tortured the merchants and bankers to deliver up their hidden hoards. He attacked the fortress where the Raja had taken refuge, and found it to be very strong. He gave out that he only came as the commander of an advanced guard of the army of the Sultan of Delhi; and that the Sultan was coming up with the main army, and would soon starve out the Raja. This threat and the want of grain soon brought the Raja to terms. He paid over a large hoard of money and jewels, and pledged himself to send a yearly tribute to Delhi.

Trickery and assassination.

Alá-ud-dín carried the plunder in safety to Karra, but there he had another game to play. His uncle the Sultan would certainly march an army to Karra, and demand the surrender of the plunder; and Alá-ud-dín was resolved to keep the spoil. He tried to cajole the Sultan; expressed himself afraid of the Sultan; declared that if the Sultan came alone he would make over the plunder, but that if the Sultan came with an army he would escape with the plunder

A.D. 1200-1300

into Bengal. The Sultan was deceived; he believed that his nephew was really afraid of him. He went to Karra with an army, but halted the troops on the western bank of the Ganges, whilst he crossed the river in a small boat to meet his nephew on the opposite side. Alá-ud-dín greeted his uncle affectionately, when the Sultan was struck by an assassin. The old uncle cried out "treachery," and ran back to the boat; but he was thrown down and beheaded on the spot, and Alá-ud-dín was proclaimed Sultan of Delhi.

Wholesale scattering of money.

Alá-ud-dín made no attempt to excuse the murder. He silenced the army by distributing money, and silenced the people by the same means. He went to Delhi, scattering money the whole way. At Delhi booths were set up, and victuals and liquors were given to all comers. The two sons of the murdered Sultan were thrown into prison, deprived of their eyesight, and then murdered. Meanwhile the multitude were amused with money and feasting. Such liberality proclaimed the accession of a new sovereign. At the same time almsgiving and feeding the poor are regarded throughout the east as atonements for sin. Thus, even those who knew that the new Sultan had murdered his uncle were inclined to believe that his charities expiated the crime.

Conquest of Guzerat.

When Alá-ud-dín was established on the throne at Delhi, he sent an army to conquer Guzerat. The Raja was a Rajpút; he was defeated by the Muhammadans, and fled away south into the Mahratta country. His queen was carried off to Delhi, and became the wife of Alá-ud-dín. The Rajpút princess, in the palace of her Muhammadan conqueror, was sad and lonely; she pined for the company of a little daughter, whom she had left in Guzerat, named Dewal Deví; and the Sultan sent messengers to bring the girl to Delhi.

Story of a Rajpút princess.

This girl had a strange fate. She was only eight years old. Her father had taken her with him to the Mahratta country, and the Mahratta Raja wanted to marry her to his son; but the Rajpút Raja, even in exile, was too proud to give his daughter in marriage to a Mahratta. Presently messengers came from Alá-ud-dín to bring away the girl to her mother at Delhi. Such a fate was considered to be worse than a Mahratta marriage; so the Raja of Guzerat changed his mind and agreed to marry his daughter to the Mahratta. But whilst the bride was going in the marriage procession, a

A.D. 1300-1350

body of Muhammadans fell upon the party, and carried her off to Delhi. In the end she was married to a son of Alá-ud-dín.

Projected conquest of Rajpútana, 1300.

The Sultan next planned the conquest of Rajpútana. A century had passed away since the Muhammadan conquest of Hindustan. A Rajpút prince of Kanouj had founded a kingdom in Marwar, or Jodhpore. Another Rajpút prince of Ayodhyá, a descendant of the famous Ráma, had founded a kingdom at Chitór. The sovereign of Chitór was renowned far and wide under the name of the Rana. The suzerainty of the Rana of Chitór, the descendant of Ráma, the representative of the children of the Sun, was acknowledged by every prince in Rajpútana.[1] In the present day the suzerainty is represented by the Rana of Udaipur or Oodeypore.

Siege of Chitór: human sacrifice.

Chitór was the heart of Rajpútana. Alá-ud-dín had invaded the country round about, apparently to strike at the heart. Already he had marched through Bundelkund on the east; conquered the Mahrattas on the south; and subdued Guzerat on the west. He now lay siege to Chitór. The siege is remarkable on account of the self-devotion of the Rajpúts; they preferred to die rather than surrender themselves or their wives to the Muhammadans. Accordingly, when all was lost, they performed the terrible rite known as the Johur. Huge piles of timber were built up and set on fire. The women threw themselves into the flames. The men then rushed out of the city and perished sword in hand. A few cut their way through the Muhammadan army, and found a refuge in the Aravulli hills.

Rebellions of Muhammadans.

The siege of Chitór lasted several months. Meanwhile there was more than one rebellion amongst the Muhammadans. The nephew of the Sultan tried to assassinate him, just as Alá-ud-dín had tried to assassinate his own uncle; but on this occasion the uncle escaped, and the nephew was beheaded. Afterwards there was an outbreak at Delhi, where a rebel seized the throne and held it for seven days, when the city was retaken by a party of horse. The rebel Sultan had opened the public treasury and scattered the

[1] The Rajpúts are divided into two families, the children of the Sun and the children of the Moon; the former have a blazing sun as their ensign, the latter have a crescent. The children of the Sun were sovereigns of Ayodhyá and Kanouj. The children of the Moon were sovereigns of Delhi and Patali-putra, or Patna.

A.D. 1300-1350

money amongst the people. When the ringleaders were slain, and the head of the rebel Sultan was paraded on a spear, the people were so frightened that they carried back to the treasury all the money they had picked up.

Stern measures of suppression.

After the capture of Chitór, the Muhammadan army returned to Delhi, and Alá-ud-dín took strong measures for keeping the city under subjection. He kept a host of spies to report all that was said and done in the streets and bazars. He prohibited all wine-drinking and entertainments. All who imported wine, sold it, or drank it, were flogged and sent to prison. The prisons were soon overflowing, and great pits were dug outside Delhi for the reception of offenders. The Sultan found, however, that it was impossible to prevent drinking; he therefore proclaimed that when liquor was distilled privately, and drunk in private houses without any drinking parties, the informers were not to interfere.

Massacre of Moghuls.

Meanwhile the Moghuls were very troublesome. In the previous reign the uncle of Alá-ud-dín had enlisted 3,000, and settled them near Delhi; but they were turbulent, refractory, and mixed up with every rebellion. Alá-ud-dín ordered them to be disbanded, and then they tried to murder him. Alá-ud-dín then ordered a general massacre. Thousands are said to have been put to death, and their wives and children were sold into slavery.

Dekhan and Peninsula.

Alá-ud-dín was the first Muhammadan sovereign who conquered Hindu Rajas in the Dekhan and Peninsula. Here it may be explained that India is divided into three great belts or zones, namely: Hindustan in the north, with the Punjab at one end and Bengal at the other; the Dekhan in the centre; and the Peninsula in the south. The line of the Nerbudda river separates the Dekhan from Hindustan. The line of the Kistna or Krishna river separates the Dekhan from the Peninsula.

Telinga, Tamil, and Kanarese countries.

Alá-ud-dín had already conquered the Mahratta country in the Western Dekhan. The Eastern Dekhan was covered with the jungles of Gondwana, but towards the south was the Telinga country,[1] where the Telugu language is spoken. The Peninsula, generally speaking, is divided between the

[1] The Telinga or Telugu country was the seat of an ancient empire, known as that of the Andhras.—See *ante*, p. 55.

A.D. 1300-1350

Kanarese-speaking people in the west, and the Tamil-speaking people in the east.[1]

Plunder of Hindu temples in the south.

Alá-ud-dín sent his general Malik Kafúr to invade these southern countries, ransack temples, and carry off treasure and tribute. The story is a dreary narrative of raid and rapine. The Hindus were powerless against the Muhammadans. Occasionally they shut the gates of a city against the invaders, and tried to defend their walls, but were soon overpowered or starved out. Temples were stripped of gold and jewels, idols were thrown down and spoiled of all precious stones, and scenes of bloodshed and outrage were enacted by Muhammadan troopers. The Hindus could make little resistance: they apparently yielded to their fate in abject despair.

Chain of posts from the camp to Delhi.

It is certain that Malik Kafúr plundered the temples of Madura to the south of Madras, and those of Mysore in the western Peninsula; a distance of fifteen hundred miles from Delhi. Yet Muhammadan historians say that the army of Malik Kafúr was always connected with Delhi by a chain of posts, with relays of horsemen and runners. Every day news reached Delhi of the progress of the army, whilst news reached the army of the health of the Sultan. This constant flow of intelligence between the camp and the capital was necessary to prevent rebellion. A false rumour that the army was cut off might have caused an outbreak at Delhi; whilst reports that the Sultan was sick or dying might have driven the army to mutiny or rebellion.

Hindu revolt at Delhi.

Alá-ud-dín died in 1316. His death was followed by a Hindu revolt; indeed Hindu influences must have been at work at Delhi for many years previously. Alá-ud-dín had married a Hindu queen; his son had married her daughter. Malik Kafúr was a Hindu converted to Islam. The leader of the revolt at Delhi in 1316 was another Hindu convert to Islam. The proceedings of the latter rebel, however, were of a mixed character. He was proclaimed Sultan under a Muhammadan name, and slaughtered every male of the royal house. Meanwhile his Hindu followers

[1] There are other languages, such as Malayalim; but further details will appear hereafter. Telugu is spoken between Hyderabad and the coast of Coromandel. The Tamil language is spoken in the Madras Presidency from Pulicat to Comorin. Kanarese is spoken in Mysore.

A.D. 1300-1350

set up idols in the mosques, and seated themselves on Korans. The rebels held possession of Delhi for five months. At the end of that time the city was captured by the Turkish governor of the Punjab, named Tughlak. The conqueror then ascended the throne of Delhi, and founded the dynasty of Tughlak Sultans.[1]

Tughlakabad.

The Tughlak Sultans would not live at Delhi; they probably regarded it as a Hindu volcano. They held their court at Tughlakabad, a strong fortress about an hour's drive from old Delhi. The transfer of the capital from Delhi to Tughlakabad is a standpoint in history. It shows that a time had come when the Turk began to fear the Hindu.

Reign of Muhammad Tughlak, 1325-1350.

The conqueror of Delhi died in 1325. He was succeeded by a son who has left his mark in history. Muhammad Tughlak was a Sultan of grand ideas, but blind to all experiences, and deaf to all counsels. He sent his armies into the south to restore the Muhammadan supremacy which had been shaken by the Hindu revolt. Meanwhile the Moghuls invaded the Punjab, and Muhammad Tughlak bribed them to go away with gold and jewels. Thus the imperial treasury was emptied of all the wealth which had been accumulated by Alá-ud-dín.

Taxation and famine.

The new Sultan tried to improve his finances, but only ruined the country by his exactions. The rich people were driven into rebellion, whilst the poor people were driven to beggary. To make matters worse, there was a failure of the rains, and consequently a dreadful famine. The whole of the Punjab and a great part of Hindustan are said to have become a desolation. Villages were broken up, and thousands of families were starving.

Fatal removal of the capital.

The Sultan was so horrified at the famine that he tried to escape it. He ordered the whole population of Delhi to remove to Deoghur in the Dekhan. Thousands died on this cruel journey. It was a march of more than seven hundred miles through jungles, over mountains, and across rivers like the Nerbudda. When the survivors reached Deoghur, they were reduced to such misery, and died away so rapidly, that the Sultan ordered them to go back to Delhi.

[1] There is a curious likeness between the quasi-religious revolt in the fourteenth century, and the Sepoy mutiny in the nineteenth. The facts are set forth at greater length in the larger *History of India*, vol. iv.

A.D. 1300-1350

The Sultan next committed another act of madness. He had heard that the Chinese used paper money, bearing the stamp of the emperor, and payable at the imperial treasury. Accordingly he struck a number of copper counters, and ordered his subjects to receive them as gold money. At first this measure was successful. People could buy all they wanted with copper counters. Merchants bought the products of India with copper counters, and sold them in foreign countries for gold money. Muhammad Tughlak, by means of his copper counters, raised a large army for the conquest of China, and sent it over the Himalayas, where it perished miserably. He raised another large army for the conquest of Persia. By this time the state was bankrupt; no one would take copper money, and gold rose to four times its value. The army intended for Persia was disbanded for want of pay; and the reign of anarchy began.

Copper counters.

Copper counters were brought to Tughlakabad in vast heaps, but there was no gold or silver in the treasury to give in exchange. The Hindus had coined copper money for their own use; they had turned their houses into mints, and flooded the country with copper counters. They paid their tribute in copper. Trade flourished when merchants bought Indian goods for copper and sold them for foreign gold; but no merchants would bring their goods to India and sell them for copper. Consequently trade was stopped, and the country was ruined.

Financial anarchy.

Then followed rebellions and revolutions. Bengal revolted, and became a separate kingdom under an independent Sultan. The Rajas of the Dekhan and Peninsula withheld their tribute. The Muhammadan army of the Dekhan broke out into mutiny, and set up a Sultan of their own. Muhammad Tughlak saw that all men turned against him. He died in 1350, after a reign of twenty-five years.

Rebellions and revolutions.

The history of Delhi fades away after the death of Muhammad Tughlak. A Sultan reigned from 1350 to 1388, named Firuz Shah. He is said to have submitted to the dismemberment of the empire, and done his best to promote the welfare of the subjects left to him; but it is also said that he destroyed temples and idols, and burnt a Brahman alive for perverting Muhammadan women.

Decline of Muhammadan rule.

In 1398-99, ten years after the death of Firuz Shah,

A.D. 1350-1525 — Invasions of Timúr and Baber, 1398-1525.

Timúr Shah invaded the Punjab and Hindustan. The horrors of the Tartar invasion are indescribable; they teach nothing to the world, and the tale of atrocities may well be dropped into oblivion. It will suffice to say that Timúr came and plundered, and then went away. He left officers to rule in his name, or to collect tribute in his name. In 1450 they were put aside by Afghans;—turbulent Muhammadan fanatics whose presence must have been hateful to Hindus. At last, in 1525, a descendant of Timúr, named the Baber, invaded India, and conquered the Punjab and Hindustan.

Review of Muhammadan rule in India.

The history of Muhammadan rule in India may be summed up in a few words. About 1000 Mahmúd of Ghazní conquered the Punjab and Western Hindustan; but before 1200 his empire had died out, and the Afghans of Ghor had become the dominant power from the Punjab to Bengal. India was next exposed to inroads of Moghuls; the same men who overthrew the Khalifs of Bagdad in 1258. About 1300 the Muhammadan Sultans of Delhi extended their conquests into the Dekhan and Peninsula; but then followed the reaction. A Hindu revolt broke out at Delhi, which had ramifications extending into the remote south. The Muhammadan empire in India was dismembered into petty kingdoms, but the Hindus could not throw off the Muhammadan yoke. Different Muhammadan dynasties were founded in Hindustan and Bengal, but their history is meagre and confused. For two centuries, from 1350 to 1550, the Dekhan and Peninsula were the theatre of wars between Muhammadans and Hindus; whilst the Portuguese established a Christian power at Goa, on the coast of Malabar. Meanwhile the once famous Moghul empire was founded in Hindustan, and for a period of two centuries was respected as the paramount power in India.[1]

[1] The history of the Muhammadan empire in the Dekhan will be told in the next chapter. The history of the Portuguese power in India is told in Chapter III. The history of the Moghul empire begins in Chapter IV., and is continued in the following chapters.

VI. *Wheeler's India, to face page 89.*

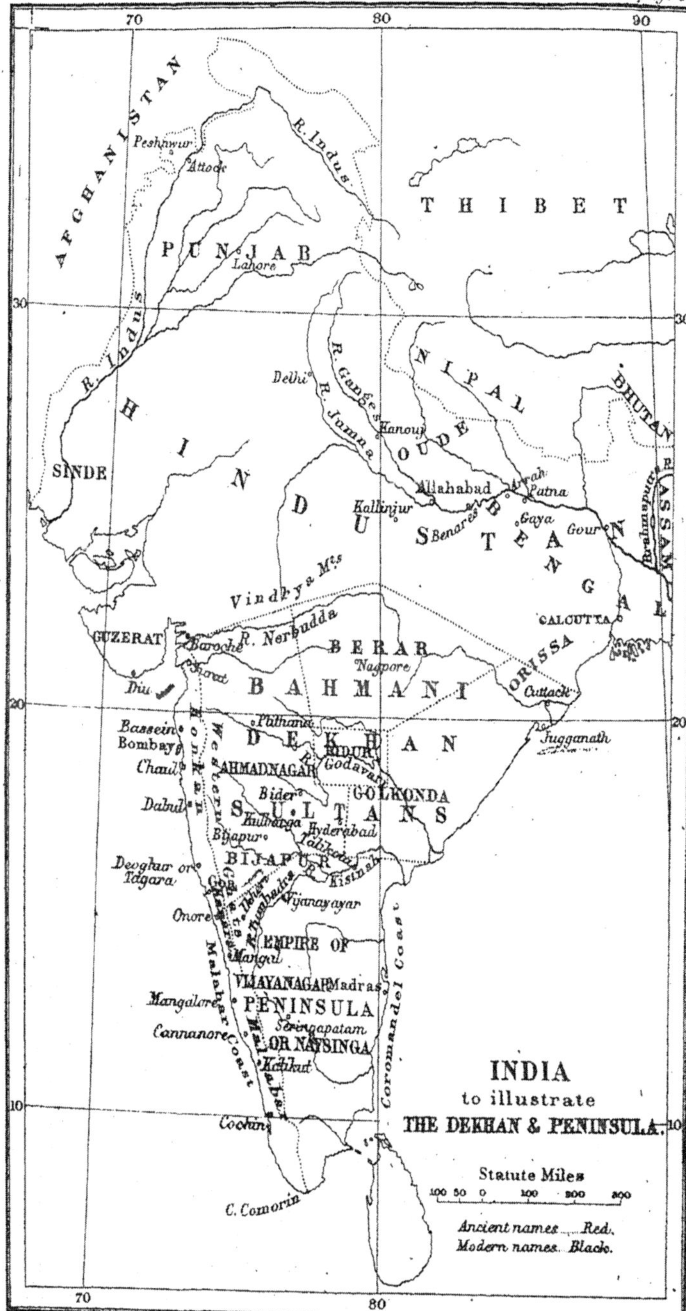

London; Macmillan & Co. Stanford's Geog! Estab!

CHAPTER II.

DEKHAN AND PENINSULA.

A.D. 1350 TO 1565.

A.D. 1350-1400

Rajas of Coromandel and Malabar.

WHEN Alá-ud-dín sent his army into the Dekhan and Peninsula, he opened up new territories. The whole of the region to the south of the Nerbudda river was distributed into a number of kingdoms, each having its own Raja, like the Punjab and Hindustan. Marco Polo was coasting round the country between 1260 and 1295, and describes some of these Rajas. Those of the Tamil country on the coast of Coromandel were black barbarians, wearing nothing but a cloth about their loins, but adorned with massive gold bracelets, and strings of rare and precious stones. They worshipped the bull and cow, and had temples, idols, priests, and dancing girls. The Rajas of the Malabar country were much of the same stamp, but were also famous for their piracies, as they had been in the days of the Greeks and Romans.[1]

Hindu traditions: Buddhists and Jains.

Hindu traditions tell of different Hindu empires which were founded at intervals, and were associated with differences of religion. There were Brahman kingdoms and Jain kingdoms; there were sages expounding rival faiths; Jain Rajas were converted to the religion of the Brahmans, and Brahmanical Rajas were brought over to the religion of the Jains. These controversies were often accompanied by cruel persecutions and religious wars, but the traditions are dying out of the memory of the people of the land.

The religion of the Jains is the outcome of the same forms

[1] Marco Polo seems to have visited the coast before the expeditions of Malik Kafúr, as he says nothing whatever about them.

A.D. 1350-1400

Religion of the Jains.

of thought as Buddhism. It expresses the same distaste for life, the same yearning for the deliverance of the soul from the vortex of endless transmigrations. But the Jains reject the doctrine of annihilation or Nirvána. They be[illegible] that when the soul has been liberated from the trammels of successive existences it begins a spiritual life in some indefinable mansion of the blessed. The Jains worship the saints who have attained this spiritual life, and they hold twenty-four particular saints in the profoundest veneration. The Jains are divided, like the Buddhists, into monks and laymen. Originally some of the sects abandoned all clothing, like the Gymnosophists of old; but the Jain monks, in general, are not only clothed, but distinguished as the "white-robed."

Modern Brahmanism.

The lower orders of the people of India are slaves to idolatry and supersitition, but modern Brahmanism, as understood by the more enlightened classes, is of a more intellectual character. It teaches the transmigrations of the soul after death, but it also teaches the deliverance of the soul from the chain of transmigrations by good works or by faith. Deliverance by good works is generally associated with the worship of Síva. Deliverance by faith is associated with the worship of Vishnu. It is said that by faith in Ráma or Krishna, as incarnations of Vishnu, the soul may be delivered from the vortex of transmigrations. These differences of belief have originated numerous sects and controversies; yet all seem to be agreed that the deliverance of the soul from transmigrations is the beginning of a new spiritual life, and that the emancipated soul is either absorbed in the Godhead, or received in the heaven of the Supreme Spirit.

Hindu empire of Narsinga, or Vijayanagar, about 1300.

Hindu traditions tell of an empire named Vijayanagar, which was associated with the worship of Vishnu. It extended over the whole of the Peninsula from the river Kistna to Cape Comorin, and from the coast of Coromandel to that of Malabar. Some traditions say that it also included the Dekhan and Hindustan. European travellers speak of the same empire under the name of Narsinga; they describe it as spreading over the Peninsula, whilst the Dekhan was held by the Muhammadans.

City of Vijayanagar.

The metropolis of this empire was founded about the fourteenth century, or some earlier date, on the banks of the

Tumbadra river, an affluent of the river Kistna. It was known as the city of Vijayanagar. It was built of stone and granite, and the temples, palaces, and fortifications are to be seen to this day.

A.D. 1350-1400

Wars between the Muhammadans of the Dekhan and the Hindus of Peninsula.

The Muhammadan army of the Dekhan revolted, as already stated, in the year 1350, and raised up a line of Sultans of their own, who are known as Bahmani Sultans. These Sultans reigned at Kulbarga,[1] and soon came in conflict with the Hindu empire of Vijayanagar. The wars which ensued between Muhammadans and Hindus are the most horrible on record, and were often waged to gratify the paltry passions of jealousy or revenge.

Insolence of a Sultan.

Krishna Rai, Maháraja of Narsinga, was proud and overbearing, corresponding closely to Southey's conception of Kehama. He was said to have been the great conqueror who subdued all peninsular India, from Malabar to Coromandel. One day he received an insulting document from the Sultan of the Dekhan. The Sultan had been drinking wine in his palace, and listening to flattering songs in praise of kings. In the pride of his heart he gave the musicians an order for the payment of money on the Hindu treasury at Vijayanagar.

Wrath of the Maháraja.

In due course the order reached the Maháraja. It amounted to a demand that the Maháraja should pay the musicians out of his own treasury in obedience to the orders of the Sultan. Krishna Rai was enraged at the insult. He ordered the messenger to be led through the streets of Vijayanagar with every mark of contempt. He resolved to wipe out the insult with blood and slaughter. He crossed the river Tumbadra with his army, captured one of the frontier fortresses belonging to the Sultan, and slaughtered the garrison almost to a man.

Vow of the Sultan.

The Sultan was enraged in his turn. He entered the mosque in his city of Kulbarga, and swore upon the Koran that he would not sheathe his sword until he had slain a hundred thousand idolaters. He crossed the river Tumbadra with his army, and began a horrible massacre of men, women, and children, until, it is said, he had completed the tale of slaughter. At last the Brahmans declared that Krishna Rai had offended the gods, and they compelled him to sue for

[1] The city is situated in the Nizam's territories, about 150 miles west of Hyderabad. It is now a railway station.

A.D. 1400-1500

terms. The Sultan demanded that the Maháraja should pay the musicians, and Krishna Rai was bound to obey. This simple concession brought the war to a close. But the Sultan and the Maháraja were alike horror-stricken at the bloodshed, and it was agreed that for the future none should be slain in war except the soldiers that were fighting in the field.

Assassins disguised as dancing girls.

In 1400 there was a Maháraja named Deva Rai; he invaded the Sultan's territories and encamped his army on the bank of the Kistna. The Sultan was afraid to cross the river in the face of the Hindu host. At this crisis eight men offered to go and assassinate either Deva Rai or his eldest son. The Sultan gave his consent to the proposed assassination. The men crossed the river and made friends with some dancing-girls who were going that night to perform before the eldest son of Deva Rai.

War dances in the Dekhan.

The dances in Southern India often represent battles. The performers appear with sticks or weapons in their hands, and sing and dance, strike their sticks or brandish their weapons, whilst leaping, fencing, and indulging in other mad gestures. Della Valle describes a performance in which the master of the troop appeared amongst the girls with a naked poniard, and pretended to slaughter them.

Drinking, dancing, and assassination.

The son of Deva Rai entertained his officers in a large pavilion. There was feasting and drinking, whilst the dancers began to perform in their usual fashion. After a while the men from the Sultan's camp appeared amongst the girls in the guise of dancers, with naked daggers in their hands. The revelry was at its height; the prince and his guests were drunk with wine, when suddenly the prince was stabbed to the heart, with many of his chief men. The lights were put out, and the assassins escaped in the uproar.

Massacre of Hindus.

The Hindu camp was thrown into a panic, which lasted all night; every man was afraid of his neighbour. Amidst the darkness the Sultan crossed the river and fell upon the terror-stricken army. The massacre which followed may be left to the imagination. Deva Rai was paralysed. At last he made over large treasures to the Sultan, and pledged himself to send a yearly tribute to Kulbarga.

Marriage of a Sultan to a Hindu princess.

Years passed away, and the same Sultan and same Maháraja engaged in another war; but this time it was brought to a close by a marriage. The Sultan married the daughter of Deva Rai. The marriage feast continued forty days, and was the great event of the time. The Muhammadan army was encamped four miles from the city of Vijayanagar. The road between the city and the camp was converted into a street, and lined on either side with shops and booths. All comers took what they pleased as a free gift. Provisions and sweetmeats, flowers and perfumes, fruits and choice drinks, were open to all. Meanwhile conjurers, play-actors, snake-charmers, dancing-girls and performers, performed before the multitude from day to day.

A.D. 1400-1500

Processions.

When the marriage rites were over, the street was covered with carpets, and the princess was carried with great pomp from the palace of the Maháraja to the pavilion of the Sultan. After some days the bridegroom and bride paid a visit to the Maháraja. All the chief officers of the Sultan went in procession in gorgeous array; music was playing, banners were flying, and beautiful children were scattering flowers of gold and silver. The Sultan was feasted for three days by the Maháraja, and then took his leave.

Unpropitious parting.

The parting was unpropitious between the Sultan and his father-in-law. The Maháraja accompanied his son-in-law half-way to the camp, but then returned to the city. The Sultan was offended because the Maháraja had not gone the whole way to the camp; and he nursed up the secret in his heart. Ten years afterwards he renewed the war to avenge the affront. In this war he was utterly defeated by the Maháraja, and died of grief and mortification.

Bahmani empire split into five kingdoms.

About 1500 the Bahmani empire was dismembered, and formed into five separate kingdoms, under different Sultans. The Dekhan at this period might be described as a square, having a little kingdom in the centre, and a large kingdom at each of the four angles. Bídur was the centre. Northward of Bídur was Ahmadnagar and Berar; southward of Bídur was Bíjápur and Golkonda.

Muhammadan weakness and dissension.

The division of the Bahmani empire weakened the Muhammadan dominion in the Dekhan. Ahmadnagar, Berar, and Bídur were far away to the north, and had little to fear from the Hindu power of Vijayanagar. But Bíjápur and Golkonda were on the border, and not strong enough of themselves to withstand the collected force of the Hindu empire. To make matters worse, the Sultans of the Dekhan quarrelled amongst themselves, and were at war with each other, when

A.D. 1500-1565

they ought to have united their forces against their southern neighbour.

Distractions at Vijayanagar.

But for some years there was nothing to fear from Vijayanagar. The Hindu court was distracted by a series of treacheries, assassinations, and butcheries, equally revolting and bewildering. It would be tedious to unravel the story. A plain narrative of the progress of events will suffice to show why the Hindus of the Peninsula were forced to keep the peace towards the Muhammadans of the Dekhan.

Ambitious minister.

The atrocities at the court of Vijayanagar began with an intrigue, which has always been common in Oriental courts. It was an intrigue for the transfer of the sovereignty of the Raj from the family of the Maháraja to the family of the minister. It has been generally carried out by the removal of the males of the reigning family, and the marriage of the minister's son to one or more of the princesses, in order to give to the son of the minister a show of right to the throne.

Murder of infant Mahárajas.

Deva Rai, Maháraja of Narsinga, died, leaving an infant son. The infant was placed upon the throne, while the minister conducted the government in the capacity of regent or guardian. When the infant reached his majority, he was murdered, and another infant was placed upon the throne. Three infants reigned in succession, and were murdered in like manner.

Ram Rai, Maháraja.

Meanwhile the minister, Timma, brought about a marriage between his son Ram Rai and a grand-daughter of Deva Rai. When the third infant was murdered, Ram Rai was proclaimed Maháraja, and all the males of the royal family were put to death, with two exceptions. One was a half-witted man named Termal Rai; the other was an infant belonging to the female branch of the family.

Revolt and assassination.

Ram Rai was accepted as Maháraja without opposition; but his pride and arrogance soon created enemies. The old nobles of the empire refused to submit to the insolence of a usurper, and proceeded to the provinces and raised a rebellion. Ram Rai took the field against the rebels, leaving his treasures in the charge of a trusted slave. The slave was a favourite who had risen to high offices, but his head was turned by the treasures. The sight of the gold is said to have driven him mad, and stirred him up to desperate actions. He plotted a conspiracy with the half-witted Termal Rai. He placed the infant of the female line on the throne of Vijayanagar, and assumed the post of minister. The rebel nobles rallied round the infant representative of the royal house. They marched on to the capital. Ram Rai saw that his cause was lost, and retired to his own estates for security.

A.D. 1500-1565

But Termal Rai was infected with the same madness as the slave. He murdered the infant and the slave, and seized the throne as Maháraja. He was akin to the old dynasty, and so far was preferred to the usurper, Ram Rai. Notwithstanding his fits of madness he was acknowledged sovereign by all the nobles at Vijayanagar.

Termal Rai, Maháraja.

The madness of Termal Rai soon began to show itself in intolerable ways. He exasperated the nobles by his insolence; and they appealed to Ram Rai for deliverance, and joined him with their retainers. An overwhelming army was soon marching to the capital with Ram Rai at its head. Termal Rai was seized with terror. In sheer desperation he called in the help of the Muhammadans. He sent messengers to Bíjápur, promising to become the vassal of the Sultan, if the Sultan would only protect him against his revolted subjects. The Sultan, nothing loth, marched an army to Vijayanagar; he was admitted into the city, conducted to the palace, and placed upon the throne. To crown all, Termal Rai did homage before the Sultan, and acknowledged him as his suzerain and protector.

General rebellion: Termal Rai calls in the Muhammadans.

This sudden revolution sent a thrill through the Peninsula. The Hindus were horror-stricken. They saw to their dismay that a mad Maháraja had made over his throne and empire to the Muhammadans; that their metropolis was occupied by an army of Turks and other foreigners, who had desolated their country in days gone by, destroyed temples, broken down their idols, and filled the land with bloodshed and terror.

Horror of the Hindus.

Meanwhile Ram Rai and the nobles had recourse to guile. They promised to become reconciled to Termal Rai if he would only send away the Muhammadans. They swore to become his faithful subjects for life, if he would only get rid of the intruders. They declared that the presence of the Muhammadans polluted the temples and angered the gods; and that prayers and worship were of no avail so long as the enemies of the gods remained in the land.

Action of Ram Rai.

A.D. 1500-1565

Termal Rai betrayed.

By this time Termal Rai had grown weary of his new allies; he was, in fact, heartily sick of the sight of the Muhammadans. He tried to persuade the Sultan to leave Vijayanagar, and return to Bíjápur. At last he succeeded, but not until he had bribed the Sultan with money and jewels to the value of two millions sterling.

Despair and suicide.

No sooner had the Muhammadans crossed the Kistna river, than Termal Rai found that he was betrayed. Ram Rai and the nobles were on the march for Vijayanagar to deprive him of his throne, and take possession of his empire. Termal Rai played out the remainder of his part like a desperate lunatic. He put out the eyes of the horses and elephants in the royal stables, and cut off their tails. He began to destroy the precious stones in the treasury by crushing them with heavy millstones. At last he heard his enemies breaking into the palace, and fell on his sword and perished on the spot.

Ram Rai allies with the Sultans.

Ram Rai was once again Maháraja of Narsinga. He found the Sultans of the Dekhan at war against each other, and soon began to interfere in their dissensions. The Sultans of Bíjápur and Golkonda entreated him to help them in a war against the Sultan of Ahmadnagar, and Ram Rai was only too ready to interfere. Thus an alliance was formed by two Sultans with a Hindu Maháraja for the overthrow of another Sultan; and Ram Rai took the field in Muhammadan territory in concert with Muhammadan allies.

Repentance of the Sultans.

The Sultans of Bíjápur and Golkonda soon repented of their unholy league. The Muhammadans of India were horrified at hearing that Muhammadan Sultans were helped by an idolatrous Maháraja in a war against a brother Muhammadan. Moreover, the Hindu soldiery had committed enormous sacrilege in Muhammadan territory; they stabled their horses in mosques, and offered sacrifices to their idol gods in the shrines of holy men, whilst the recreant Sultans made no attempt to prevent them.

Muhammadan league against Ram Rai.

When the war was over, the Sultans found that the alliance with the Hindu Maháraja was not to be endured. Ram Rai was puffed up with pride and vain-glory; he treated the Sultans as his vassals, and put their envoys to shame. At last, four of the Sultans banded together to throw off the yoke of the infidel Maháraja. They laid aside all quarrels; they leagued together as brother Muhammadans, to be avenged once and for all on the Mahárája of Vijayanagar.

A.D. 1550-1565

The decisive battle was fought in 1565; it is known as the battle of Talikota, and is famous alike in Muhammadan history and Hindu legend. The four Sultans assembled their armies on the banks of the Kistna. Ram Rai was filled with wrath, and collected together all his horse, foot, and elephants to overwhelm the Muhammadans. Both armies had cannon, but the Muhammadans had the better. The confederate Sultans guarded their front with a line of cannon fastened together with ropes and chains. The Hindus guarded their front with war elephants as well as cannon; and through these elephants they lost the day.

Battle of Talikota, 1565.

The Hindus advanced bravely to battle, with songs and dances after the old Telinga fashion. They began the battle with shot and rockets, and drove back the Muhammadan wings. But the Muhammadan centre was unbroken, and began to open fire. The Muhammadan gunners had loaded their cannon with bags of copper money. The Hindus were slaughtered in heaps by the fiery storm. At this moment a war elephant ran madly about, and overturned the litter of Ram Rai. The Muhammadan gunners seized the Mahárája as their prisoner, and beheaded him on the spot; and then fixed the bleeding head upon a spear, and paraded it before the contending armies.

Fall of Ram Rai.

The death of the Mahárája brought the battle to a close. The Hindus fled like sheep when they beheld his head upon a spear. The Muhammadans pursued them to the gates of Vijayanagar; they took possession of the city, and found none to oppose them. The metropolis of the last of the great Hindu empires was at their mercy; and six months are said to have been spent in the work of plunder.

Pursuit and plunder.

Two years afterwards a European traveller, named Cæsar Frederic, visited the city of Vijayanagar; he found the houses standing, but the inhabitants had vanished from the spot. The whole country round about was infested with thieves. He stayed six months at Vijayanagar out of fear of the thieves; and when at last he set out for Goa he was every day attacked by robbers, and nearly every day compelled to pay a ransom.

Ruin of Vijayanagar.

The empire of Vijayanagar was broken up by the battle of Talikota, but it was not conquered by the Sultans. The

A.D. 1550-1565

Dismemberment of the Hindu empire.

court removed to Pennakonda, eight days' journey to the south; but the successor of Ram Rai was little better than an exile, and his sovereignty soon dwindled away. The provinces became kingdoms. The Naiks, or deputies of the Maháraja, who had ruled as Viceroys, soon began to reign as Rajas; they ceased to pay tribute to the exiled Maháraja, and in the course of two or three generations the descendants of Ram Rai possessed nothing but an empty name.

Religious revolutions.

The Hindu empire of Vijayanagar was of the same type as that of Magadha, but in both there was a religious antagonism in the background. Under Asoka the Brahmanical worship of the gods faded away from Hindustan, and Buddhism became a state religion. Under Krishna Rai, Deva Rai, and Ram Rai, the teachings of Buddhist and Jain were denied or ignored, and the Brahmanical worship of the gods was restored from the Kistna river to Cape Comorin. The story of these religious revolutions has yet to be decyphered from withering palm-leaves and mouldering inscriptions; but enough has been revealed to show that amidst the jars and conflicts of rival creeds, sparks of divine truth have not been altogether wanting; and the day may yet dawn when Brahmans will confess that without goodness and purity of the heart the worship of the gods is of no avail, whilst Jains may learn that the true spirit of holiness to which they aspire is the outcome of Deity alone.

CHAPTER III.

PORTUGUESE EMPIRE: MALABAR.

A.D. 1498 TO 1625.

In 1498, sixty-seven years before the battle of Talikota, ships from Portugal made their first appearance in the Indian seas, and anchored off the coast of Malabar. The whole Indian continent was in a state of unrest. Afghan chiefs were invading the Punjab, and devastating Hindustan from the banks of the Indus to the mouths of the Ganges. The Bahmani empire of the Dekhan was divided against itself, and splitting into five kingdoms under five independent Sultans. The empire of Vijayanagar, in the Peninsula, was distracted with revolts, treacheries, and assassinations, which accompanied the transfer of the sovereignty from the family of the Maháraja to the family of the minister. But the Portuguese knew nothing of these revolutions. They saw only the coast of Malabar and the purple heights of the Western Gháts. As far as they were concerned, the region beyond the mountains was an unknown world.

A.D. 1498-1520

First arrival of the Portuguese, 1498.

Malabar, or western coast of India.

The western coast, commonly called the coast of Malabar, must always have been the first land in India which met the eyes of European discoverers. Pliny tells of the voyages of Roman merchants from Egypt to Malabar, which occupied seventy days. The Roman ships were manned with archers to keep off the Malabar pirates. In the fifteenth century the pirates were equally troublesome, although few probably would have dared to encounter the cannon of the Portuguese.[1]

[1] Pliny does not call the western coast by the name of Malabar; but there is no question about its identity. He speaks of Barace, the

A.D. 1498-1520

Western Gháts, the Indian Apennines.

Whilst the western coast of India has been open to the Indian Ocean, it has been more or less shut out from the empires of the Dekhan and Peninsula. A mountain chain runs southward from the Vindhyá mountains to Cape Comorin, enclosing a long and narrow strip of territory towards the sea, and walling it off from the eastern plains. This chain is known in India as the Western Gháts; it might be better described to European readers as the Indian Apennines.

Malabar proper.

The term Malabar is properly restricted to the southern portion of this coast territory. The region between the sea and the Gháts, from the Nerbudda river to Cape Comorin, is properly divided into three sections, namely: Konkan on the north; Kanara in the centre; and Malabar on the south. It will be seen hereafter that each of these sections has a history of its own.

Twelve kings of Malabar.

Malabar proper extended from Cape Comorin northward to the port of Cannanore.[1] It was the first Indian country reached by the Portuguese. It was distributed among a number of petty Rajas, known in tradition as the twelve kings of Malabar.[2] They were black barbarians more or less under the influence of Brahmans, and ready to share the profits of freebooters, pirates, or traders. They and their dependents formed a military class, devoted to arms, and living amongst an agricultural people of an inferior race. They were in fact a hereditary caste known as Nairs; and may be described as Rajpúts in the rough. They wore cloths hanging from their girdles, and carried swords and bucklers; but the Rajas decorated themselves with gold and jewels. The twelve Rajas of Malabar owed allegiance

modern Baroche, as the most convenient port; and a glance at a map of India will show that the port of Baroche, at the mouth of the Nerbudda river, would be the most convenient shelter for ships coming from Egypt. Again, the pepper of Cochin, towards the southern extremity of the coast, has been famous for ages; and Pliny tells us that the pepper of Cothinara was brought to Barace in canoes.

Two important marts on the western coast are mentioned by Ptolemy, namely, Plithana and Tagara. Plithana has been identified with Paitan, the capital of Salivahana on the river Godavari. The name of Tagara still lingers in that of Deoghur, whither Muhammad Tughlak sought to remove his capital.

[1] Sometimes it was advanced as far north as Mangalore; but the matter is of no moment.

[2] There were thirteen in all, including the Zamorin of Calicut.

to an emperor, who reigned at Calicut, and was known as the Zamorin. At times they may have paid tribute to the Mahâraja of Vijayanagar;[1] but otherwise they maintained a political independence. A.D. 1498-1520

Malabar has always been famous for pepper and spices. The different Rajas held a monopoly of these commodities. They either supplied cargoes, or levied duties on all sales. The trade was in the hands of Arab Muhammadans who were called Moors, and had carried it on for centuries. They shipped Indian commodities and Indian pilgrims to the Red Sea. The pilgrims were landed at Jedda, and proceeded through the desert to the holy places at Mecca and Medina. The goods were landed at Suez and carried on the backs of camels through Egypt to Alexandria, where they were again shipped by the merchants of Venice and Genoa, and conveyed to the different ports of the Mediterranean. Pepper and pilgrims.

The first Portuguese fleet that reached India consisted of three ships under the command of Vasco de Gama. The voyagers left Lisbon on the 8th of July, 1497, like an army of martyrs. Every man went to confession and received absolution. The monks of Our Lady of Bethlehem walked to the ships in solemn procession, and offered up prayers for the success of the voyage. Departure of the fleet from Lisbon, 1497.

It is needless to dwell on the perils and privations of the expedition. The voyagers rounded the Cape of Good Hope, and steered boldly across the Indian Ocean towards the coast of Malabar. On the 28th of May, 1498, the fleet anchored off Calicut, the residence of the Zamorin;[2] and Vasco de Gama sent a message on shore, announcing his arrival as an ambassador from the King of Portugal, with a letter and presents for the Zamorin. Anchorage off Calicut.

The Portuguese ambassador was soon invited to an audience. Vasco de Gama landed at Calicut with twelve of his officers. In the first instance the party were carried in palanquins to a pagoda, to be purified and perfumed. They were received by four Malabar Brahmans, naked to the waist, who Portuguese ambassador worships an idol.

[1] In this little empire of Malabar there are traces of a constitution. Each state is said to have sent a representative to the court of the Zamorin at Calicut; and their representatives formed a council, and caused much turmoil by their jealousies and rivalries.

[2] Calicut is about 250 miles to the northward of Cape Comorin, and about 100 miles to the north of Cochin.

A.D. 1498-1520

sprinkled them with scented water, and presented them with a sweet-smelling paste made of sandal-wood. The temple was dedicated to the goddess Mariamma. The Portuguese saw the statue of a woman, and asked the name of the goddess; the Malabars cried out "Mari, Mari." The Portuguese confounded the name with that of the Virgin Mary; and prostrated themselves at the feet of the goddess before they discovered their folly.

Audience in the palace of the Zamorin.

Vasco de Gama and his retinue were next conducted to the palace of the Zamorin. It was built of mud, but was pleasantly situated amidst trees and gardens. The chief Brahman led the ambassador into the audience-hall. The Zamorin was seated on a couch of silk, while a grave official stood by his side holding a golden plate filled with betel. The Zamorin was arrayed in white cotton flowered with gold.[1] He wore jewels in his ears, bracelets on his arms, bangles on his legs, and was crowned with a diadem of pearls. He assumed the grave, stolid demeanour which eastern princes display under like circumstances; but the letter and presents were received, and the ambassador was promised a speedy answer.

Muhammadan traders intrigue against the Portuguese.

The Muhammadan traders at Calicut soon learnt all that was going on. They knew that the Portuguese were their enemies in religion, and likely to be their rivals in trade. They bribed the officials of the Zamorin. They whispered that the Portuguese were not ambassadors; that the presents were not such as a king would send, or the Zamorin could receive; that the so-called ambassadors were dangerous pirates and kidnappers, who had already committed outrages on the coast of Africa.

Threatened mischief.

Vasco de Gama soon saw that the Moors were bent on mischief. He had landed his goods, and the Zamorin gave him a house; but the factor placed in the house could neither sell nor buy, and was soon treated as a prisoner.

Return of Vasco de Gama.

Vasco de Gama seized some fishermen by way of reprisals. The Zamorin was alarmed, and the factor was released. The ambassador then released most of the fishermen, but kept back a few in order to carry them to

[1] This simple fact has a significance. It shows that the audience was regarded as a great State ceremony. On such occasions the Zamorin wore a white vestment, but never otherwise. None of his Nairs were allowed to wear a vestment at any time.

A.D. 1498-1520

Portugal. This last proceeding awakened the suspicions of the natives. They believed the story of the Moors that the Portuguese were pirates and slave-dealers. The alarm spread along the coast, and ships began to assemble at the neighbouring ports for the destruction of the strangers. Vasco de Gama found that the country was against him. He left Calicut with his ships, steered out in the Indian Ocean, and returned to Portugal by the way he came.

Expedition of Alvarez Cabral.

The King of Portugal next sent a fleet of thirteen ships with the fishermen on board, under the command of Alvarez Cabral. More than half the ships foundered during the voyage, and only six anchored off Calicut. The fishermen were put on shore, and left to tell their own story. The Zamorin became better disposed towards the Portuguese. He again made over a house at Calicut; and a factor was placed in the house with goods and money under the protection of sixty chosen Portuguese.

Violence of the Portuguese admiral.

But the Moors were soon at their old tricks. The Portuguese could not obtain a cargo; and the few goods they were permitted to buy, were purchased at very advanced rates. All this while they saw that the Moors were procuring cargoes with the utmost ease, and loading their own ships very rapidly. The Portuguese admiral was so exasperated that he boarded a Moorish vessel, and transferred the cargo to his own ship.

Slaughter of the Portuguese: cannonading of Calicut.

This violent proceeding stirred up the Nairs. The cry went forth that the Portuguese were pirates. All the Nairs in Calicut gathered round the factory, and assailed the inmates with darts and javelins. The Portuguese fought for their lives, but were overwhelmed by numbers. At last a portion of the wall was broken down, and the Nairs rushed in. Forty Portuguese were slaughtered on the spot; the survivors escaped to the shore and swam to the ships. The factory was plundered by the Nairs, and Cabral was told that the Zamorin shared the plunder. The admiral was so angry that he burnt fifteen native ships that were lying in the harbour, and cannonaded the city of Calicut for two days.

Alliance with the Raja of Cochin.

The cannon worked a great change. It inspired the Rajas round about with respect for the Portuguese, and the hopes of revenge against the Zamorin. The Raja of Cochin, further south, had a special feud against the

A.D. 1498-1520

Zamorin, and was anxious for the friendship of the powerful strangers. The Raja concluded a treaty with the Portuguese, supplied them with cargoes, and permitted them to build a fort within his territory.

Portuguese atrocities on Muhammadan traders.

But nothing could allay the bitter opposition of the Moors. Hostilities broke out between Christians and Muhammadans which might be described as war to the knife. Cruelties were perpetrated which are too horrible to contemplate. One atrocity may serve as a type of the whole. A Muhammadan ship was captured by the Portuguese, whilst carrying two hundred and sixty Mecca pilgrims to the Red Sea. Twenty children were saved and baptized; the remainder, to the number of two hundred and forty souls, were thrust into the hold without mercy, and the ship was scuttled and set on fire.[1]

Interference of the Sultan of Egypt.

After some years the Sultan of Egypt raised a turmoil. The Portuguese had absorbed the Indian trade, and diverted it from Egypt round the Cape of Good Hope. The Sultan was angry at the loss of transit duties in Egypt, and he was driven to fury by the atrocities of the Portuguese, the capture of Muhammadan ships and drowning of Mecca pilgrims. He sent letters to the Pope threatening to destroy all the holy places in Palestine unless the Portuguese abandoned the eastern seas. After great preparations he sent a fleet down the Red Sea; but it was defeated by the Portuguese off Guzerat, and the shipping was plundered and destroyed.

Foundation of Goa by Albuquerque.

The real founder of the Portuguese empire in the east was Alfonso de Albuquerque, the Viceroy of the Portuguese possessions in India from 1509 to 1515. He selected the island of Goa, nearly half way down the western coast of India, between Konkan and Kanara, to be the metropolis of the Portuguese empire, and the emporium of eastern trade. This island had been originally a nest of pirates, but had been captured and cleared by a Muhammadan Sultan of the Dekhan. Albuquerque seized and conquered the island, and founded the city of Goa, which was destined to become the Venice of the east. In like manner he founded the city of Malacca on the Malay peninsula opposite the island of Sumatra. Albuquerque died at the bar of Goa in December

[1] This story, and many other tales of horror, are told by the Portuguese historian, Faria y Sousa, who was Secretary for India to the King of Spain and Portugal.

A.D. 1520-1550

1519, at the age of sixty-three, just as he was about to return to his native land.

Policy of the Portuguese: forts at Diu, Bassein, Chaul, Dabul, Onore, Mangalore, and Cochin.

Meanwhile the policy pursued by the Portuguese at Cochin was repeated by the Viceroy of Goa. Permission was obtained to build forts at various points along the coast; and when a fort was defended by cannon, and manned by Europeans, it was impregnable to Asiatics. A Raja or a Sultan might repent of his alliance with the strangers, and try to turn them out of the fort, but the task was beyond his power. In this manner the Portuguese built one fort at Diu in an island off the southern coast of Guzerat; another at Bassein in Konkan to the north of Bombay;[1] others at Chaul and Dabul in Konkan to the south of Bombay; others at Onore and Mangalore in Kanara; whilst another, as already seen, was built at Cochin, in Malabar. Churches and houses were built within these forts; priests were appointed, and monasteries were often endowed; and Roman Catholic Christianity began to make a stir in Western India.

Mission to Bengal, 1538.

In 1538 the Viceroy of Goa proposed to open up a trade with Bengal, and sent a Portuguese mission to Chittagong. At that time the Sultan of Bengal was an Arab in mortal fear of his life; and he ordered the strangers to be sent as prisoners to Gour. The orders were obeyed, and the Portu guese would probably have been murdered; but the Sultan was slain by an Afghan, and the prisoners were released and permitted to return to Goa.

Muhammadan rule in Bengal.

According to the Portuguese historian, the government at Bengal was at this period of the worst possible kind. A series of low-born adventurers, favourites or slaves, arose in turn, murdered the reigning Sultan, and obtained the kingdom. Sultan after Sultan cut his way to the throne by treachery and assassination, and after a brief reign of self-indulgence and terror, was slaughtered in his turn. The new comer might be an Arab, or an Afghan, or even a black Abyssinian slave; but the people of Bengal were too timid and effeminate to throw off the yoke, or even to interfere. If the intruder held the throne for three days, the population accepted him as their sovereign.

[1] The Portuguese ultimately built a fort at Bombay, but it was a weak affair; and Bombay played no part in history until it was ceded by Spain to the English in 1661, as the dowry of the Infanta who married Charles the Second.

A.D. 1520-1550

Sultan of Turkey makes war on the Portuguese, 1538.

About this time the Sultan of Turkey once again played a part in the affairs of India. The Sultan of Guzerat sent messengers to implore the Porte to help him to drive the Portuguese out of Diu. The Porte sent an armament from Egypt,[1] to capture Diu, but the expedition proved a failure. No Muhammadan prince would join the Turks except the Sultan of Guzerat, and he was soon tired of his new allies. The Portuguese garrison at Diu fought with the utmost bravery and repelled every assault. At last the Muhammadan forces united in a general charge, and were repulsed with great slaughter. But the Portuguese were nearly starved out, and suffered the most horrible privations. They were on the point of surrendering, when the Turkish fleet sailed away and was never seen again in the eastern seas. The Sultan of Guzerat had got rid of his Turkish allies, by telling them that a great fleet was coming out from Portugal and would destroy them all.

Repulse of the Great Turk.

The news of the repulse of the Great Turk was hailed by the Portuguese nation with enthusiastic joy. The commandant of Diu returned to Lisbon, and was received with acclamation. All the nobles thronged to the Tagus to welcome him. All the foreign ambassadors strove to do him honour. The French ambassador ordered a painting to be made of the brave man who had defeated the Great Turk in the Indian seas.

Triumphant procession at Goa.

In 1545 there was another war about Diu. The Portuguese Viceroy relieved the fort in person, and on his return to Goa was received with the honours of a Roman triumph. His head was crowned with laurel, and he was accompanied through the streets of Goa by a procession of prisoners and captured guns and arms. Salutes were fired, bands of music were playing, the houses were adorned with silks, and fair women threw flowers and perfumes from the verandahs. When the Queen of Portugal heard the story she declared that the Viceroy had conquered like a Christian and triumphed like a pagan.

Goa in the sixteenth century.

A picture of Goa during the latter half of the sixteenth century, is furnished by a Dutch traveller named Linschoten. Goa was situated on the northern side of the island, facing an arm of the sea. The shore was covered with country-

[1] The Sultan of Turkey conquered Egypt in 1517.

houses and gardens, and adorned with forts and churches. The Viceroy's palace was built over the city gate. It was a splendid building, and portraits of every Viceroy of India were hung in the Council-hall. Passing through the gateway, the visitor entered a fine broad street, half a mile long, leading from the palace to a church. In front of this church was the Exchange.

A.D. 1550-1600

The Exchange.

Every morning, except Sundays and Saints days, the Exchange at Goa was the great centre of attraction. It began at sunrise, and was generally over by nine o'clock. It resembled the old Fairs of Europe, except that gentlemen of noble birth bought and speculated like common dealers. It was a kind of auction at which goods were sold at public outcry by men specially appointed. Some criers ran about, hung with costly chains, jewels, pearls, rings, and precious stones, which were thus offered for sale. Others disposed of bales of damasks, velvets, silks, satins, spices, drugs, pepper, and porcelain. Others sold the goods of deceased persons; for according to the law of Goa, whenever a man died, from the Viceroy downwards, his goods were sold at the Exchange for the benefit of his heirs. Slaves were also sold, male and female. Men were bought to serve as menial servants; others to be hired out to different masters. Women slaves were taught to make sweetmeats and confections, or to embroider pocket-handkerchiefs; and the youngest and fairest were sent into the streets to offer such commodities for sale.

Social life at Goa.

The social life at Goa was not healthy. The city was often overrun by Portuguese adventurers, who came out to India under the name of soldiers, and affected to be nobles and gentlemen. These men were often required to garrison forts, or to serve as soldiers on board the ships in different expeditions; but when not on service their presence was an intolerable evil. They were often reduced to poverty, living ten or twelve in one house, with perhaps only one or two suits of silk clothes amongst them, which they wore in turns. At the same time they were so touchy as regards etiquette, the return of salutations, and other points of honour, that they often filled the city with brawls and bloodshed. Their dissolute lives led to other disorders. Portuguese householders shut up their wives and daughters in Oriental seclusion; but this only aggravated the evil. The

A.D. 1550-1600 — ladies became demoralised by their female slaves, and often intrigued with the soldiers, causing more jealousies and bloodshed, as well as poisonings, assassinations, and other secret crimes.

Great wealth. Meanwhile there was no lack of wealth at Goa. Trade was the main business of the city; and the arrival and departure of ships in the river added to the excitement of the daily exchange. Ventures on board ships were exposed to the risks of capture or wreck, but the profits of a successful voyage were often three or four hundred per cent. Again, profits from thirty to forty per cent. were often to be made by money-changing alone, without any risk whatever. Every September, Portuguese ships arrived at Goa, and sought to exchange their reals for Persian money for the purchase of pepper and spices at Cochin. Every April the ships went to China, and were glad to give Persian money for reals, which were required for the purchase of silks and porcelain.

Expenditure in Goa. During the sixteenth century the Portuguese monopolised the whole trade between Europe and the east; and a large share of the accumulated wealth was spent in Goa. The Viceroy returned to Portugal every three years with a splendid fortune; leaving a successor to amass riches in like manner. The commandants of forts, and a few disappointed soldiers, may in like manner have returned to their native country after a term of years. But gentlemen traders married and settled in Goa, and adopted it as their home. They built country-houses with secluded gardens. They made splendid shows of gold and silver plate. They adorned their wives and daughters with rings, chains, bracelets, and jewels of every description. They endowed churches, monasteries, colleges, and schools. Missionaries from Goa, chiefly Jesuits, were sent out to convert, not only the natives of the surrounding country, but the people of remote regions, such as those of China and Japan.

Government, civil and ecclesiastical. The Viceroy and Council were at the supreme head of affairs. There were also Secretariats, a Court of Chancery, and other public officers. A large ecclesiastical authority was exercised by the Archbishop and his Secretaries. There was an Inquisition with authority superior to that of the Archbishop; and religious offenders were arrested, imprisoned, condemned, tortured or executed, by this tribunal, without any control whatever, beyond what might be involved in its correspondence with Rome. No Hindu rite was permitted within the island of Goa. No Muhammadan was allowed to perform his devotions in public, or to call believers to prayers. But otherwise the Inquisition rarely interfered with Hindu or Muhammadan, and generally confined its attention to Portuguese and native converts. If once a native, Hindu or Muhammadan, embraced Christianity, he was a slave to the Inquisition, and was punished for acts of apostacy as if he had committed the gravest crimes.

A.D. 1623-1625

Between the years 1623 and 1625, a Roman Catholic gentleman, named Pietro della Valle, visited Goa. He has left graphic descriptions of the country, when the fortunes of Goa were on the turn. The surroundings were still as imposing as ever. As Della Valle entered the arm of the sea, known as the river of Goa, he saw a beautiful city stretched out on his right hand. The churches were the finest buildings in Goa. Many belonged to religious orders, such as the Augustines, Dominicans, Franciscans, Carmelites, and Jesuits. Already, however, there were too many priests in Goa, and half the number would have sufficed for a much larger city.

Visit of Della Valle, 1623-25.

The native inhabitants formed the bulk of the population. They were a black generation, mostly slaves. The Portuguese were few in number, and had lost their wealth through the invasions of the Dutch and English. But they were very proud, and made what show they could, for all wished to be accounted gentlemen and soldiers.

Inhabitants, Kanarese and Portuguese.

The religious processions at Goa were very remarkable. Della Valle saw a procession of the Holy Sacrament made by the whole clergy, with a greater show of green boughs than clothes. Mysteries were represented by persons in disguise, accompanied by fictitious animals, dances, and masquerades. Della Valle remarked that in Italy such scenes would be confined to villages, and would not have been witnessed in great cities.

Strange religious procession.

Subsequently the order of Carmelites celebrated the canonisation of Saint Teresa. Two boys, clad as couriers, announced the canonisation to the Viceroy of Goa in appropriate verses, and then proclaimed it with the sound of a trumpet through the streets of Goa. At night there were

Canonisation of St. Teresa

A.D. 1623-1625

displays of fireworks throughout the city; and all the Portuguese gentlemen of note paraded the city in various disguises, after the manner of a masquerade.

Kanarese Christian soldiers.

At the feast of John the Baptist, the Viceroy and other Portuguese gentlemen rode through the streets in masquerading habits, but without masks. They next attended Mass, and then went to the large street of St. Paul. Many companies of Kanarese Christian soldiers went through their exercises in this street, marching past with ensigns, drums, and arms, and then leaping and playing along the street with drawn swords.

Splendid religious shows.

Shortly afterwards the canonisation of Ignatius and Xavier was celebrated by the Jesuits of the college of St. Paul. All the collegians came forth in a great cavalcade, divided into three squadrons, under three banners. One squadron represented Europe, the second Asia, and the third Africa. The men of each squadron were dressed in the costumes of the nations of their respective continents. Before the cavalcade went a chariot of clouds, with Fame on the top, who sounded her trumpet to the accompaniment of other music, and proclaimed the canonisation of the two saints. Two other chariots followed; one represented Faith, or the Church; the other was a Mount Parnassus, carrying Apollo and the Muses as representatives of the sciences taught in the college. Five great pyramids, covered with pictures, were also drawn along the streets on wheels by men on foot. The first was painted with all the martyrs of the order of the Jesuits. The second was painted with doctors and authors belonging to the same order. The third was painted with figures of every nation to whom the Jesuits had sent missions, and thus represented the various languages in which the Jesuits preached and taught. The fourth pyramid was painted with devices showing the provinces of the said religion. The fifth displayed all the miracles which had been performed by the two saints, Ignatius and Xavier. These pyramids were drawn through the principal streets, and then placed as monuments in different parts of the city.

Ecclesiastical influences.

There was no city in the world where there were so many religious processions as in Goa. Della Valle remarked that such shows were right and proper when kept within bounds, but in Goa they were much too frequent. The crowds of monks and ecclesiastics were burdensome to the state and prejudicial to the military. Goa was a city bordering on enemies; the metropolis of a kingdom lying in the midst of barbarians. Under such circumstances the utmost attention should have been given to fleets and armies. A.D. 1623-1625

Mission to the Raja of Kanara.

Della Valle accompanied a Portuguese ambassador on a mission to the so-called king of Kanara, named Venk-tapa Naik. Sixty years had passed away, since the battle of Talikota was fought in 1565. The predecessors of Venk-tapa had been Naiks or governors of the province of Kanara under the old Mahárajas of Vijayanagar; and Venk-tapa still retained the name of Naik, although he ruled Kanara as an independent Raja, and added to his dominions by the conquest of less powerful neighbours.

Pepper dealings of the Portuguese.

There had been some difficulty between the Viceroy of Goa and Venk-tapa Naik, which the embassy was intended to clear up. The Naik had been drawn into hostilities with the Portuguese, but was anxious for peace. His country produced much pepper, and the Portuguese were accustomed to buy it, but they had not come for the pepper of the current year, and they had not paid for the pepper of the previous year. The Portuguese were equally anxious to keep on good terms with the Naik, for their cash was low, and they were afraid lest the Naik should sell his pepper to the English or Dutch.

Voyage from Goa to Onore.

The capital of Venk-tapa Naik was at Ikkeri, a city in the interior, about fifty miles from Onore. The journey might have been made by land, but the Sultan of Bíjápur was in possession of the intervening territory, and his officers were not always courteous towards the Portuguese. Accordingly it was determined to go by sea to the Portuguese port at Onore,[1] and then to proceed by land to the city of Ikkeri.

Onore, a type of a Portuguese fort.

Onore was a type of a Portuguese settlement. A few of the Portuguese dwelt outside the fort, where there was a native bazar. But the commandant and all the married Portuguese dwelt inside the fort, which was laid out in streets of houses with wells and gardens. There was also a piazza within the fort, which would contain all the inhabitants in the event of a siege.

[1] Onore appears in modern maps under the name of Honahwar.

A.D. 1623-1625

Kanara, a type of a Hindu Raj.

The kingdom of Kanara was in like manner a type of a Hindu Raj in Southern India. In the journey to Ikkeri Della Valle climbed the Ghát.[1] The mountain in that place was not so high as the Apennines, and the ascent was easier, but the woods were more dense. On the top of the mountain was a fortress belonging to Venk-tapa Naik, and a temple to the god Hanuman, the famous monkey who helped Ráma.

City of Ikkeri.

The city of Ikkeri was surrounded by three lines of defences. The two outer ones were mere fences of bamboo, intended to keep out horse and foot. The third enclosure was a wall, but weak and inconsiderable. The houses were scattered and ill-built, especially outside the wall, where they were diversified with groves of trees and ponds of water.

Public audience at the palace of Venk-tapa Naik.

After a day or two's delay, the Portuguese ambassador obtained an audience with Venk-tapa Naik. The party rode to the palace in procession, accompanied with drums and music. The palace stood in a large fortress, environed with a ditch and some badly built bastions. Venk-tapa Naik received the Portuguese ambassador and party in a small court. He was seated on a raised pavement at the upper end of the court, under a wooden canopy covered with gilding. Several courtiers stood at his right hand, and one of them fanned him to drive away the flies. He chewed betel leaves throughout the audience. He asked the ambassador why the Portuguese ships were so late this year. The ambassador replied in a long rhodomontade. A Portuguese fleet was coming to India with a great army. The King of Spain and Portugal had formed an alliance with England. Prince Charles of England was on a visit to the court of Madrid. To this he added other bits of news which could have but little interest for the Hindu prince, and were only intended to glorify the Portuguese.

Scenes in a Hindu city.

Della Valle saw other sights at Ikkeri which are common to Hindu cities in the south. There were companies of young girls in figured silks and linen jackets, with diadems of white and yellow flowers, who danced in circles with painted sticks in their hands, and sang songs in honour of

[1] The ruins of Ikkeri are still to be seen in Western Mysore, about eighteen miles to the north of Bednore. The Raj of Kanara appears to have occupied a considerable area in Western Mysore.

A.D. 1623-1625

their goddess. There were wooden beams set up with ropes and hooks on which devotees were accustomed to swing themselves at certain festivals. There were large chariots in which, on certain days, the gods were carried in grand processions. There were Indian friars smeared with ashes, known as Jangamas, who led the lives of mendicants, and were worshipped as holy men.

Procession of a Hindu widow.

One night Della Valle met a procession which is no longer to be seen in India. A woman had lost her husband and was bent on burning herself. She rode on horseback with open face, holding a looking-glass in one hand and a lemon in the other. She went along singing and chanting her farewell to the world with such passionate language as moved all who heard her. She was followed by many men and women, and some carried an umbrella or canopy over her to do her honour. Drums were sounded before her, and she never ceased to accompany the noise with her sad songs. Della Valle was told that she would ride in procession through the streets for a certain number of days, and then go out of the city and be burned with great solemnities.

Hindu worship at Ikkeri.

At Ikkeri Della Valle was a close observer of Hindu worship. There were several temples in the city, but the greatest of all was dedicated to the god Aghoresvara.[1] The idol was in the form of a man with one head and sixteen arms.

Procession of Brahmans and dancing girls.

One evening tapers were lit in all the temples in Ikkeri. A great noise was made with drums and pipes, whilst priests began to dance before the gates of the temples. Della Valle went off to the temple of Aghoresvara. The people were called together by the sound of trumpets. The priests formed a procession, carrying two idols in a palanquin decked with flowers and ornaments. The procession was accompanied by music, torches, lances, streamers, and umbrellas. There was a long train of dancing-girls two by two, decked in gold and jewels. There were other women, marching on either side of the palanquin, carrying little staves with long white horse-tails with which they fanned away the flies from the idols. Many priests accompanied the idols. In this

[1] The ruins of this temple are still to be seen. The god was a form of Esvara or Siva; also known as Mahadeva, or the "great god." The idol was a representative of the Supreme Being. See *ante*, pages 63 and 65.

A.D. 1623-1625

manner the procession entered the piazza of the temple, and made a large ring or circle, and the dancing began.

Saluting the idols.

Two women, from either side of the circle, advanced three steps forward and then fell three steps backward, but always with their faces towards the idols; and this they did several times by way of saluting the idols. Two others then joined them, and after that two others.

Concluding ceremonies.

After the salutations were over, the dancing began with leaping, fencing, and many mad gestures. When the dancing was over, the procession moved outside the temple round the outer enclosure, halting at intervals to repeat the salutations and dancing. At last the procession re-entered the temple and the ceremonies were brought to a close.

Celebration of the New Moon.

The next night was the new moon. All the temples in Ikkeri were illuminated with candles and torches; so were all the streets, houses, and shops. Every temple had its idol, and in some temples the idol was a serpent. The outer porches were illuminated with lights, and adorned with transparencies of painted horsemen, elephants, people fighting, and other odd figures. A great concourse of men and women went about the city visiting all the temples in Ikkeri. Late at night Venk-tapa came to the temple of Aghoresvara with his two nephews,[1] attended by a large train of soldiers and servants. He stayed in the temple for about an hour, during which he was entertained with music and dancing, and then returned to his palace.

Della Valle's views on Hindu worship.

Della Valle remarked that the Hindu worship of the gods chiefly consisted in music, songs, and dances; and in serving the idols as though they were living beings. Thus the priests presented the idols with things to eat, washed them, perfumed them, gave them betel leaves, dyed them with sandal, and carried them abroad in processions. Della Valle was undoubtedly correct. To this day the temple

[1] Throughout the countries of Kanara and Malabar, nephews of Nairs, when born of sisters, were treated as sons, and inherited the property to the exclusion of sons. The causes of this extraordinary usage are fully treated in the larger *History of India*. It will suffice to state here that Rajas, and other members of the military class of Nairs, were not regularly married, but lived such irregular lives that no one knew who was the father of a child. There was, however, a certainty about a blood relationship between a man and the son of a sister; and accordingly the son of the sister inherited the property or throne as the nearest of the blood lineage.

services in the worship of Krishna, Jagganath, and other similar idols, is of the same materialistic character.

A.D. 1623-1625

Difficulties of travellers in Hindu countries.

Della Valle left Ikkeri and proceeded to the Portuguese port of Mangalore. He was anxious to see the Queen of Olaza, a little kingdom bordering on Mangalore. He found that travelling in Hindu countries was difficult on the score of diet. The Hindus would not furnish him with fish or flesh; they would only supply him with rice, butter, milk, and other inanimate things; this they would only do as a great favour. The people lived by cultivating rice, which was done by overflowing the soil with water; but they complained of the large tribute they were obliged to pay to Venk-tapa, which reduced them to great poverty notwithstanding their hard labour.

Meeting with the Queen of Olaza.

Della Valle heard that the Queen of Olaza was staying at a neighbouring town named Manel. He went to Manel, accompanied by a Brahman interpreter. On going to the bazar to procure a lodging in some house, he saw the Queen coming on foot the same way. She was not attended by women, but only by soldiers. Six soldiers walked before her with swords and bucklers, but without any covering save a cloth about their loins, and a kind of scarf over the shoulder. Other soldiers walked behind her in the same fashion, and one of them carried an umbrella of palm-leaves to shade her from the sun.

A princess of Kanara.

The Queen of Olaza was as black as an Ethiopian. She was corpulent and gross, but not heavy, for she walked nimbly enough. She was about forty years of age. She wore a plain piece of cotton cloth from her waist downwards, but nothing at all from her waist upwards, except a cloth about her head, which hung down a little upon her breast and shoulders. She went bare-footed, but that was the custom of all Hindu women, high and low, at home and abroad. Most of the men went unshod in like manner. A few of the graver sort wore sandals, but very few wore shoes. The Queen was more like a kitchen-maid or a washerwoman than a noble princess; but her voice was graceful, and she spoke like a woman of judgment.

The conference.

The Queen spoke a few words to Della Valle through his Brahman interpreter, asking what had brought him to those woods of hers. She was going into the fields about a mile off, to see some trenches which were being dug for conveying

A.D. 1623-1625

water to certain lands; and when she returned from the fields, she was busied in administering justice amongst her people. She said, however, that she would send for Della Valle in the evening. Della Valle procured a house in Manel, belonging to a Moor; and was thus enabled to procure animal food. He waited however in vain for a message from the Queen. She was heard praising the liberality of Della Valle in paying for poultry and other necessaries. She said, "Do we in India toil and moil for a fanam,[1] whilst this stranger spends money in this fashion?" But for some unknown reason she never invited Della Valle to come and see her.

Social life in Kanara.

The early life of the Queen of Olaza reveals something of social life in Kanara. The Raja of Olaza had died leaving neither son nor nephew. Accordingly his wife succeeded to the Raj. The wife died, and was succeeded by her sister, the present Queen. The new female sovereign married the Raja of a neighbouring territory, called Banghel; but the husband and wife only met at intervals. The Raja had other wives, and the Queen was said to have other lovers. After a while they quarrelled, and the Queen returned all the jewels the Raja had given her. The Raja was so offended that he made war upon her, and called in the aid of the Portuguese. The Queen appealed to Venk-tapa Naik to help her. In the end Venk-tapa annexed the Raj of Banghel, defeated the Portuguese, and compelled the Queen of Olaza to cede a considerable territory. The Portuguese embassy was sent to Venk-tapa Naik at Ikkeri to protest against the annexation of Banghel, on the ground that the Raja was an ally of the King of Portugal.

King of the Yógis.

Before leaving Mangalore, Della Valle paid a visit to a holy man dwelling in a neighbouring hermitage. He was known as the King of the Yógis; a sect of wandering mendicants, who were supposed to abstract themselves from all the cares of the world.[2] The so-called King was lord of a little circle of land, comprising a hermitage, a temple, and

[1] A fanam was a very small silver coin, worth about twopence-halfpenny.

[2] The Yógis are dying out of India. They were common enough in ancient times, but are disappearing before the advancing tide of European civilization. They were supposed to abstract themselves from the world, and to lead a life of religious contemplation, in order to secure the deliverance of the soul from the otherwise endless chain of transmigrations. See *ante*, page 67.

certain habitations for Yógis, together with a few country-houses and villages. The territory had been given to the Yógis by a former Raja of Banghel; and as the Yógis had no wives, the dominion of the hermitage and adjacent lands went by elective succession. The Yógis were not subject to their King in the way of obedience, but only paid him reverence and honour. They went where they listed, and were dispersed amongst different temples; but at certain solemn times they assembled at the hermitage in great numbers, and were supplied with victuals by their King. Many servants and labourers of the King lived at the hermitage, and cultivated the land for his maintenance. It yielded a yearly revenue of about five or six thousand pagodas, or nearly three thousand pounds sterling. Most of the money was spent on feasts; the remainder was devoted to the service of the temple and idols.

A.D. 1623-1625

His appearance.

Della Valle found the King of the Yógis employed in business of a mean sort, like a peasant or villager. He was an old man with a long white beard, but strong and lusty. He had a golden bead hanging from his ear as big as a musket-bullet; and had a little red cap like those worn by Italian galley-slaves. He seemed a man of judgment, but was without learning. He told Della Valle that formerly he had horses, elephants, and a great equipage; but Venktapa Naik had taken all away, so that he had very little left.[1]

Portuguese embassy to the Zamorin of Calicut.

About this time the Portuguese were sending a fleet from Mangalore to the Zamorin of Calicut. There was a question of peace between the Portuguese and the Zamorin. The Zamorin had sued for peace; but the Viceroy would not come to terms unless the Raja of Cochin was included in the treaty. Accordingly a fleet was sent to Calicut with the Viceroy's ultimatum.

People of Malabar.

The better sort of the people of Malabar were Hindus, especially those inland. They mostly belonged to the caste of Nairs, or hereditary soldiers. The sea-coasts were inhabited by Malabar Muhammadans, who lived among the Hindus, and spoke their language, although they differed in religion. The Malabar Muhammadans were corsairs, who had infested the coast, and had been

[1] A representative of the King of the Yógis is living in Mysore to this day, and is still complaining of his loss of wealth and power.

A.D. 1623-1625

the terror of merchant vessels since the days of Pliny, and probably for ages before.[1]

Malabar pirates.

Della Valle went on board the Portuguese fleet with the view of seeing Calicut. During the voyage the Portuguese had two encounters with Malabar corsairs. On each occasion the light vessels of the corsairs escaped to the creeks and mouths of rivers which were scattered along that coast. The Portuguese would not attack them by land, as it belonged to the Zamorin; and they were anxious to respect his territories whilst the peace was in agitation.

Message to the Zamorin.

On arriving at Calicut, messengers were sent to the Zamorin at early morning with the ultimatum of the Viceroy. If he wanted to make peace with the Portuguese, he must immediately send an ambassador on board the fleet, pledged to conclude a treaty with the Viceroy at Goa, in which the Cochin Raja would be a party.

Troubles of the Zamorin.

The proposal was a bitter pill for the Zamorin. His feud with the Raja of Cochin had been handed down for many generations; and he could not bring himself to come to terms with his hereditary enemy. But he was forced to take some action. He had ships with rich cargoes coming from the Red Sea; and unless he made peace with the Viceroy, the Portuguese would capture the ships. Accordingly he sent messengers to the admiral of the fleet. He proposed to make a treaty with the Viceroy first, and then to make a treaty with the Raja of Cochin. Under any circumstances he requested that the fleet would stop at Calicut until he had sufficient time to deliberate with his ministers respecting the proposed treaty. In reply he was told that the fleet would return to Goa at nightfall, whether the ambassador came on board or no.

City and bazar of Calicut.

Meanwhile Della Valle, with the captain of the ship he was in, and some others, went ashore to see the town of Calicut. The streets were long and narrow. The houses were mere cottages built of mud and palm-leaves. The bazar was filled with provisions and other necessaries, but there was not much cloth. Indeed there could have been

[1] Of course the pirates could not have been Muhammadans in the days of Pliny, as their prophet was not born until A.D. 570. Probably during the sixteenth century the pirates had been recruited by the Moors, who had lost their trade with the Red Sea and Persian Gulf after the arrival of the Portuguese.

little demand for clothes; for men and women wore nothing but a piece of cotton or silk, hanging from their girdles to their knees. Della Valle and his party also saw much of the plunder of the Malabar pirates in the bazar; such as Portuguese swords, arms, books, and clothes, which had been taken from Portuguese vessels. No Christian could buy such articles under pain of excommunication. A.D. 1623-1625

When Della Valle and his companions were tired of wandering about the bazar, they walked towards the palace. To their great surprise some persons of quality came up and invited them to enter and see the Zamorin. They accepted the invitation, and entered a large court where they found a number of courtiers. Invitation to the palace.

After a while Della Valle and his party were conducted into a smaller court, and told to sit down on a raised pavement. Suddenly two girls, about twelve years of age, entered the court. They wore no covering of any kind except a blue cloth about their loins; but their arms, ears, and necks, were covered with ornaments of gold and precious stones. Their complexion was swarthy but clear enough; their shape was well proportioned and comely; and their aspect was handsome and well favoured. They were both daughters of the Queen; that is, not of the Zamorin, but of his sister, who was styled the Queen, and was so in effect. These two girls were in fact Infantas of the kingdom of Calicut. Upon their entrance all the courtiers paid them great reverence; and Della Valle and his companions rose from their seats, and saluted them, and then stood before them bareheaded. The girls talked together respecting the strangers; and one of them approached Della Valle, and touched the sleeve of his coat with her hand, and expressed wonder at his attire. Indeed they were as surprised at the dress of the strangers, as the strangers were at the strange appearance of the girls. Malabar princesses.

Presently the Zamorin came in accompanied by more courtiers. He was a young man of thirty years of age, of large bulk of body, and a handsome presence. He had a long beard, and wore nothing except the cloth hanging from his girdle.[1] He had bracelets on his arms, pendants at his Appearance of the Zamorin.

[1] This was not a state occasion like that on which a Zamorin had received Vasco de Gama, more than a hundred and twenty years [prev]iously. The absence of the vestment shows that it was only [ord]inary reception. See *ante*, page 102, note.

A.D. 1623-1625

ears, and other ornaments with jewels and rubies of value. In his hand he carried a stick like a shepherd's staff. He received the salutations of the strangers with smiles and courtesy, standing all the while and leaning on the staff. Many courtiers came in and saluted the Zamorin with joined hands. There were higher cloisters round the court filled with women, who had come to behold the strangers. The Queen sister stood apart in the most prominent place, with no more clothing than her daughters, but abundantly adorned with jewels.

The conference.

The secret now transpired; the Zamorin wanted to sound the party as to the intentions of the admiral of the fleet. The captain declared that he was only a private soldier, and knew nothing of the admiral or his business; whilst all the others were absolutely ignorant of the state of affairs. Finally, after a long interview, the Zamorin requested the captain to persuade the admiral to stop at Calicut until the deliberations were over; and then he dismissed the party. The fleet remained at Calicut all night, and sailed away next morning without any ambassador.

Rajas sacred in battle.

In Malabar the persons of Rajas were sacred in battle. The Nairs fought on either side, but no one fought a Raja, or even struck the royal umbrella. To shed the blood of a Raja was regarded as a heinous sin, and would be followed by a terrible revenge. The Zamorin was of a lower caste than the Raja of Cochin.[1] If the Zamorin was killed, his subjects devoted three days to revenge; they ran "amok," as it was called, killing all they met until they were killed themselves. If the Raja of Cochin was killed, his subjects ran "amok" for the rest of their lives.[2]

[1] The question of caste between the Zamorin of Calicut and the Raja of Cochin was the cause of the feud. According to a religious myth the land of Malabar had been given to the Brahmans by the god Parasu Rama. The Brahmans called in the Nairs for their protection. The Rajas then ruled Malabar as deputies of the Brahmans. The Zamorin affected a superiority over the Brahmans, and ruled as a deputy of the gods. In revenge the Brahmans affected to regard the Zamorin as a Súdra, inferior in caste to the Raja of Cochin. Such a quarrel could not possibly be settled by a treaty with the Portuguese. For more than a century there must have been constant deliberations between the Zamorin and his ministers upon this difficult and delicate question.

[2] This was the origin of the English phrase "running a muck." It prevails amongst Rajpúts, Malays, and other cognate races.

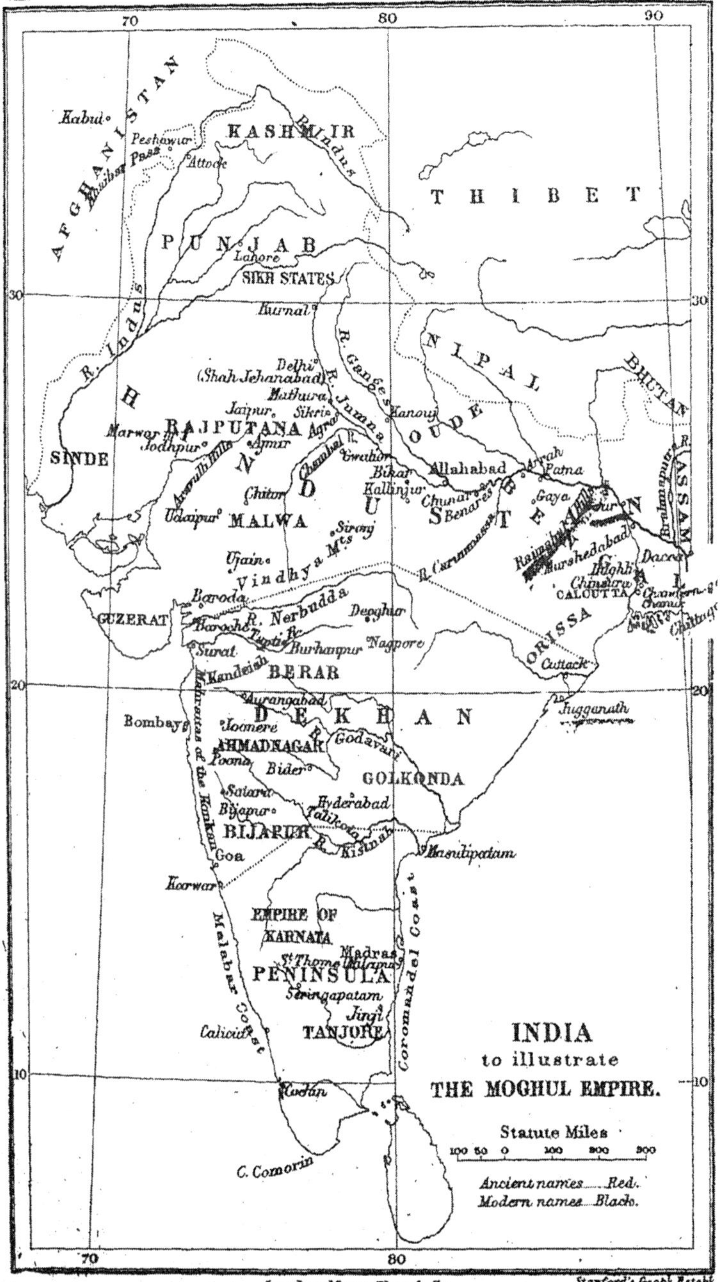
INDIA
to illustrate
THE MOGHUL EMPIRE.
Statute Miles
100 50 0 100 200 300
Ancient names...... Red.
Modern names.... Black.
AFGHANISTAN
Kabul
Peshawur
Khaibar Pass
Attock
KASHMIR
R. Indus
THIBET
PUNJAB
Lahore
SIKH STATES
Kurnal
NIPAL
BHUTAN
Delhi
(Shah Jehanabad)
Mathura
Jaipur
Sikri
Agra
Kanouj
OUDE
RAJPUTANA
Marwar
Jodhpur
Ajmir
SINDE
Gwalior
Allahabad
Arrah
Patna
ASSAM
Chitor
Bikar
Kallinjur
Chunar
Benares
Gaya
Udaipur
MALWA
Seronj
Murshedabad
Ujain
Vindhya Mts
Dacca
Hughli
Chinsura
CALCUTTA
Baroda
GUZERAT
R. Nerbudda
Deoghur
ORISSA
Barochè
Surat
Burhanpur
Nagpore
Cuttack
Kandeish
BERAR
Juggernath
Aurangabad
DEKHAN
Bombay
Joonere
AHMADNAGAR
Godavari
Poona
Bider
GOLKONDA
Satara
Hyderabad
Bijapur
Talikota
BIJAPUR
R. Kistnah
Goa
Masulipatam
Karwar
EMPIRE OF
KARNATA
Malabar Coast
Madras
St Thome
PENINSULA
Seringapatam
Coromandel Coast
Jingi
Calicut
TANJORE
Cochin
C. Comorin
70
80
90
30
20
10

CHAPTER IV.

MOGHUL EMPIRE: BÁBER, HUMÁYUN, AKBAR.

A.D. 1525 TO 1605.

A.D. 1525-1530

Afghans and Moghuls.

During the sixteenth century, whilst the Portuguese were establishing their maritime empire in the eastern seas, two races were contending for the empire of Hindustan, namely, the Afghans and the Moghuls. Both races were associated with a remote past; both have played important parts in the modern history of India.

Jewish origin of the Afghans.

To all appearance the Afghans are of Jewish origin; not Jews of the orthodox type, the outcome of Jerusalem and the temple worship; but Jews of the old turbulent stiff-necked type, who revolted at Shechem against Rehoboam, and set up golden calves at Bethel and Dan. The Afghans claim to be descendants of Saul the son of Kish.[1] They are divided into tribes, clans, and families. They distribute conquered lands by lot; perform the ceremony of the scapegoat, and build shrines on high places. Their features are unmistakably Jewish; but their language is not Hebrew, nor anything akin to Hebrew. It is conjectured that they are the descendants of the Ten Tribes, whom the king of Assyria carried away to the city of the Medes; but the loss of all traces of the Hebrew language militates against the theory, and it is impossible to verify the identity.[2] In

[1] This tradition helps to identify the Afghans with the children of the men who fought against the house of David.

[2] The Jewish features of the Afghans outweighs, to the author's mind, the evidence of language. The face of Shere Ali Khan, the late Amír of Afghanistan, revealed not only the Jewish features but the melancholy mania that belongs to the character of Saul.

A.D. 1525-1530

modern times they are Muhammadans of the Sunní religion, and traditional foes of the Persians or Shíahs.

Early Afghan conquests in India, 1200-1290.

The early conquests of the Afghans in India are obscure. In the thirteenth century a dynasty of Afghan Sultans was reigning at Delhi under the name of Patans; and this name is said to have been derived from an earlier Afghan dominion at Patna.[1] Towards the end of the century the Afghan dynasty was ousted by a Turkish dynasty; and for a century and a half the Afghans fade away from history.

Invasion of Timúr the Tartar, 1398-99.

In 1398-99 Hindustan was invaded by Timúr the Tartar. After his departure the affairs of Hindustan are veiled in darkness. He left officers at Delhi to rule in his name, or rather to collect tribute in his name; and accordingly four princes reigned in succession at Delhi in his name, but nothing is known of them of any moment. The last was swept away by the tide of Afghan invasion.

Afghan Sultans of Delhi, 1450-1525.

In 1450 the Afghans were overrunning the Punjab and Hindustan. They established a dynasty at Delhi, known as the Lodi dynasty. They were bitter persecutors of the Hindus and their religion. They broke down temples and built mosques in their room, as in the days of Mahmúd of Ghazní. A Brahman was put to death by a Sultan of this dynasty for maintaining that the religions of Hindus and Muhammadans were equally acceptable in the eyes of God.

Lawlessness of Afghan rule.

Afghan dominion is always divided and unsettled, excepting at rare intervals, when a man of energy and genius is at the head of affairs. The Afghan Sultans of Delhi had no firm hold on their empire. Lawless Afghans had spread over Hindustan, and some of their leaders had established themselves as independent princes. They occupied fortresses, exercised local dominion, and levied tribute and blackmail, especially in the outlying provinces of Bihár and Bengal. They were often in revolt against the Sultans of Delhi, and often at war amongst themselves. They bore a strong family likeness to their reputed forefathers, who rebelled against the house of David; and they bore an equally strong likeness to their descendants, who have so often rebelled and fought in Herát and Kandahar.

[1] The old capital of Bengal at Gour seems to have been named after the ancient Afghan stronghold of Ghor between Ghazní and Herát.

A.D. 1525-1530

Afghan revenge.

The Afghans have left a bad name in India. Their passion for revenge has become a proverb. No man is said to be safe from the revenge of an elephant, a cobra, or an Afghan.

Tartar origin of the Moghuls.

The Moghuls are men of a different stamp. In history they are associated with the great Tartar invasions under Chenghiz Khan and Timúr. Their so-called annals are bewildering stories of evanescent dynasties. Sometimes they founded a dominion as vast as the empires of Darius and Ahasuerus; and then, after a few generations, it crumbled into fragments, and provinces were transmuted into independent kingdoms.

Moghuls, a ruling tribe.

Father Rubruquis, who travelled through the greater part of Asia shortly after the death of Chenghiz Khan, says that the Moghuls were the ruling tribe amongst the Tartars. This statement is a clue to their history. The Tartars are barbarous nomades, who have wandered over the vast steppes of Asia, from pasture to pasture, from an unknown antiquity. They have no settled habitations, and dwell in huts which they carry about on carts. They probably represent the ancient Scythians; and if so, the Moghuls may represent the Royal Scythians.[1]

Religious toleration.

The Moghuls were proud and arrogant; but they were inquisitive and tolerant, especially in matters of religion. Indeed it was one of the laws of Chenghiz Khan that every priest was to be reverenced who taught the belief in one God. Many became Muhammadans, but they were very lax observers of the Koran, and had none of the bigotry which characterised the Afghans. Marco Polo the Venetian, who was entertained at the court of the great Khan, is loud in praising the Moghuls. Father Rubruquis, who excited their suspicions, complains bitterly of their deceitful ways and coarse mode of life.

Moghuls of the sixteenth century.

In the sixteenth century the Moghuls had lost many of their Tartar features and much of their Tartar manners. The yellow complexions, high cheek bones, and ugly mouths

[1] The Royal Scythians are an interesting but obscure tribe described by Herodotus. Their religion, like that of the Scythians generally, was undoubtedly Vaidik, and Sir Henry Rawlinson has proved that their language was Aryan. Philologists may deny that there is any identity between the terms Σκύθαι and Kshatriya, but there are other similarities which may help to solve the problem as regards the origin of the Vaidik Aryans.

A.D. 1525-1530 — approximate to Persians.

had disappeared; and the Moghuls who conquered Hindustan bore a general resemblance to Persians. These changes have led to confusion. The people of India often include Persians under the general name of Moghuls; but they always mark the distinction between Moghul and Afghan.

Early life of Báber, 1482-1525.

The founder of the Moghul empire in India was a chieftain named Báber. The career of Báber is a romance. He was born in 1482; and claims descent from Timúr and Chenghiz Khan. At the age of twelve he inherited the kingdom of Khokand on the Jaxartes. Whilst still a youth he conquered the whole of Bokhara from the Jaxartes to the Oxus. Subsequently, after years of fighting, he was driven out of Bokhara by the Uzbegs, and founded a kingdom in Afghanistan.

Character of Báber.

The character of Báber is revealed in his memoirs, which are said to have been written by himself. Sometimes he was storming a city or defending a stronghold; at other times he was an exile in the desert broken down by wounds and privations; but on all occasions he had an easy temper, and an affectionate regard for the playmates of his boyhood, his mother and female relatives, and for all old friends. He was fond of a drinking bout with gay companions. He freely describes the temptations which led to these excesses,—the shady wood, the hill with a fine prospect, or the idleness of a boat floating down a river. He also tells the amusements which accompanied them,—extempore verses, recitations in Turki and Persian, sometimes a song, and often a contest of repartee.[1]

Conquers the Afghans of Delhi, 1525.

For years Báber had contemplated the conquest of Hindustan. In 1525 he was encouraged to make the attempt. The reigning Sultan of Delhi was weak and fickle. The whole Afghan empire was disaffected. The Afghan governor of the Punjab invited Báber to invade the country. At the same time the suzerain of the Rajpút princes, the Rana of Chitór, sent messengers to Báber promising to attack Agra if the Moghuls would attack Delhi. Báber obeyed the call. In the winter of 1525-26 he crossed the Indus at the head of ten thousand men. The Afghan Sultan marched against him with an immense army, but was defeated and slain.

Báber occupied Delhi and then marched to Agra. As

[1] Erskine's translation of *Báber's Memoirs*.

he advanced the Hindus fled from the villages, and he fell short of supplies. To crown all, he found the whole army of the Rajpút league arrayed against him, not as a friend and ally, but as an enemy resolved to drive him out of Hindustan.

A.D. 1525-1530

Advance to Agra.

The proceedings of the Rana of Chitór were treacherous but intelligible. He expected Báber to invade Hindustan as Timúr had done; that is, to sack Delhi and then go away, leaving him, the Rana, to re-establish the ancient empire of the Rajpúts over Hindustan and the Punjab. When Báber defeated the Afghan Sultan, the Rana made no advance to Agra but waited for events. When Báber captured Delhi and marched to Agra, the Rana felt aggrieved and went out to fight the invaders.

Hostility of the Rana of Chitór.

The battle between the Moghuls and the Rajpúts was desperate but decisive. Báber aroused the enthusiasm of his Muhammadan troops against the idolaters. He broke up his drinking vessels on the field, and swore that henceforth he would never taste wine. The battle was fought at Sikri, a few miles from Agra. Báber gained the victory, and the Rajpúts fled back to their hills. From that day to this the Rajpúts have never attempted to re-conquer Hindustan.

Victory of the Moghuls.

Báber reigned four years afterwards, but was chiefly occupied in rooting the Afghans out of their strongholds. He died in 1530, and was succeeded by his son Humáyun.

Death of Báber, 1530.

Báber was a bad Muhammadan, inasmuch as he drank wine and allied with the idolatrous Rana of Chitór against Afghan believers. His son Humáyun was a worse Muhammadan, for he relapsed into the old nature worship of the Moghuls. He divided his household affairs according to the four elements of fire, air, water, and earth. He built a pavilion with seven apartments of different colours to represent the sun, moon, and planets; and he sat each day in a different apartment, and transacted business or took his pleasure according to the reigning luminary.

Báber and Humáyun, bad Muhammadans.

Humáyun was engaged like his father in rooting Afghans out of their strongholds; but he lacked his father's energy and decision. An Afghan, named Sher Khan, was in possession of Chunar, an important fortress on the south bank of the Ganges, which commanded the line of communication between Hindustan and Bengal. Humáyun

Humáyun gulled by Sher Khan.

A.D. 1530-1555

demanded the surrender of the fortress, and might easily have dislodged the Afghan; but Sher Khan affected entire submission, sent his son with a troop of horse to fight in the army of the Moghul, and begged to be allowed to hold the fortress in the name of Humáyun. In a word Humáyun was cajoled into leaving Sher Khan in possession of Chunar.

Rajpút affairs.

About this time Humáyun interfered in Rájpút affairs. A Sultan of Guzerat, the very man who invited the Sultan of Turkey to drive out the Portuguese, had invaded the territory of the Rana of Chitór. The city was invested by the Muhammadans, as it had been in the reign of Alá-ud-dín. The women performed another Johur; amongst them was the widow of the Rana who fought against Báber. Before the princess joined the sacrifice, she provided for the escape of her infant son, and sent her bracelet to Humáyun.

Gift of the bracelet.

The gift of the bracelet is a relic of the days of Rajpút chivalry. Whenever a Rajpút lady is in peril, be she wife or maiden, she may select a protector by sending him her bracelet. She thus adopts him as her brother. He may never see her, but he is flattered by the mystery and honour. Humáyun accepted the bracelet and obeyed the summons. Muhammadan historians say that Humáyun was a follower of the Prophet; but his conduct is at variance with the statement. He went to war against a brother Muhammadan on account of a Rajpút princess, and drove the Sultan of Guzerat out of Chitór.

Defeat and flight of Humáyun.

When Humáyun returned to Agra, he found that Sher Khan the Afghan had taken possession of Bengal. He now had reason to curse his folly in leaving the fortress of Chunar in the hands of Sher Khan. He was obliged to capture the fortress before he could enter Bengal; and six months were wasted before the walls before it was starved into surrendering. Next he was blocked up by the Afghans in the narrow defile between the Ganges and the Rajmahal Hills, which is the only opening into Bengal. Finally he entered Bengal at the beginning of the rains, and lost a large portion of his army by fever and dysentery. When the rains were over he tried to return to Agra, but was attacked and routed by Sher Khan. His affairs were so desperate that he had no alternative but to fly to Persia;

and there he remained in exile for a period of fifteen years. A.D. 1530-1535

Afghan rule in Hindustan, 1540-1555.

The Afghan rule of Sher Khan and his successors is a break in the history. It is a strange fact that the Afghans, the bigoted enemies of the Hindus and their religion, should have maintained an empire over the Punjab and Hindustan for fifteen years. Stranger still, the last Sultan of this Afghan dynasty favoured the Hindus and lost his throne in consequence. He appointed a Hindu, named Hemu, to be his minister, and advanced Hindus to rank and power. Accordingly his own nobles rebelled against him, and thus opened a way for the return of Humáyun.

Return of Humáyun to Delhi, 1555.

The adventures of Humáyun during this interval have little bearing on the history. During his flight to Persia, his favourite wife gave birth to the celebrated Akbar. During his residence in Persia he is said to have cast aside the Sunní religion and become a Shíah out of deference to the Shah. In 1555 he raised a force and returned to Hindustan and recovered possession of Delhi and Agra.

Death of Humáyun.

A final struggle was pending between Moghul and Afghan, when Humáyun was killed by an accident. He was ascending the stone steps outside the palace in order to say his evening prayers on the roof, when his foot slipped and he fell lifeless on the pavement below.

Obsolete claims of the Afghans.

The Afghan conquest of Hindustan between 1540 and 1555 has never been forgotten by the Afghan people. In their eyes it gives them a traditional claim to the possession of Hindustan. Báber claimed Hindustan by virtue of the conquest of Timúr; and in after years the Afghans affected to claim Hindustan by virtue of the conquest of Sher Khan. Such assumptions are mere phantoms of oriental imaginations, but nevertheless they often have a bearing upon the current of oriental history.

Akbar, the founder of the Moghul empire.

Akbar, the son and successor of Humáyun, was the real founder of the Moghul empire in India. By wise policy and consummate craft he put an end to the conflict between Afghan and Moghul, and brought about a reconciliation between Muhammadan and Hindu. The annals of his reign open up a new era in the history of India.

Reign of Akbar, 1556-1605.

Akbar, the contemporary of Queen Elizabeth, succeeded his father in 1556. He was only a boy of fourteen; and when Humáyun was dying at Delhi, the young prince was

A.D. 1530-1605

away in the Punjab fighting the Afghans. His guardian was an experienced general named Bairam Khan, and when the boy became Padishah the guardian became regent.[1]

Empire in peril.

The Moghul empire was in sore peril. A host of Afghans had advanced up the valley of the Jumna under the leadership of Hemu, and recovered the cities of Agra and Delhi, and was now marching on to the Punjab.[2] The Moghul officers were in such a panic of fear that they counselled a retreat to Kábul.

Defeat of the Afghans.

Akbar and his guardian resolved on battle. A bloody action was fought, and the Moghuls gained the victory. Hemu was wounded in the eye and taken prisoner. Bairam Khan exhorted Akbar to kill the Hindu and win the title of Ghazi-ud-dín, or "champion of the faith." Akbar refused to slaughter a helpless warrior, and Bairam Khan beheaded the Hindu with his own sword.

Akbar discards his guardian: death of Bairam Khan.

During the four years that followed there were constant wars between Moghuls and Afghans. Meanwhile Akbar reached his eighteenth year, and resolved to throw off the control of his guardian. He left the camp under the plea of a visit to his mother. He next proclaimed that he had assumed the sovereign authority of Padishah, and that no orders were to be obeyed but his own. Bairam Khan saw that he had lost his power. He tried to cajole Akbar into appointing him minister, but the young Padishah was resolved to be his own master. Akbar offered his old guardian any post he pleased excepting that of minister. But Bairam Khan would be minister or nothing, and prepared to go on a pilgrimage to Mecca. He was about to depart when he was assassinated by an Afghan. It was the old story of Afghan revenge. Bairam Khan had killed the father of the assassin in some battle, and was stabbed to death by the son.

Wars of Akbar.

The wars of Akbar are of small interest. He had to restore order in Hindustan after two centuries of anarchy

[1] The term Padishah was the Moghul equivalent for Emperor. The second syllable is the well-known Persian "Shah," signifying origin or lord. "Pad" signified stability and possession. See Abul Fazl's preface to the *Ain-i-Akbari*, translated by Mr. Blochmann.

[2] The history of this crisis is a mystery. Possibly the facts have been misrepresented by Muhammadan historians; but in the absence of other contemporary authorities it is impossible to test their statements. The march of an Afghan army under a Hindu general is opposed to all Asiatic experiences.

A.D. 1556-1605

and misrule. To effect this object it was necessary to capture fortresses in the hands of Afghans, and to stamp out disaffection and revolt amongst his own turbulent chieftains. It was also necessary to subdue and dethrone dynasties of independent Sultans who had built up kingdoms in Guzerat, Malwa, and Bengal, out of the ruins of the old Delhi empire of the Tughlaks. In all these wars he displayed the energy and skill of a practised commander, and the bodily strength of a warrior familiar from his boyhood with the toils of war and the sports of the field.

Energy of Akbar.

But though the wars are of small interest, some traditions have been preserved which serve to bring out the character of Akbar, and illustrate the lawlessness against which he had to contend. An officer named Adham Khan was sent to reduce a Sultan of Malwa. The Sultan fled at his approach and left his treasures behind. Adham Khan took possession of Malwa, but kept back the Padishah's share of the spoil, and only sent a few elephants to Agra. Suddenly he learnt that Akbar was at hand with a strong force and hastened to make submission and reparation. Akbar feigned to be satisfied and returned to Agra. Adham Khan was soon recalled to Agra and another governor sent in his room. Adham Khan found that no command was given to him, and thought that the minister was his enemy; he went to the palace and stabbed the minister to death in the hall of audience. Akbar heard the uproar and rushed to the place. The murderer begged for mercy, but was thrown over the parapet by Akbar's orders, and perished on the spot.

Bravery of Akbar.

Another officer in Bihár kept back the Padishah's share in like manner, and soon found that Akbar was upon him. He, too, made submission and reparation, but then fled from Bihár and joined some rebels in Oude. At that moment Akbar was called away to the Punjab by an invasion of Afghans. Meanwhile the whole region to the north of the Ganges broke out in open revolt. Akbar disposed of the Afghans and then marched back to Allahabad in the middle of the rainy season. He reached the Ganges with his body-guard whilst the rebel army was encamped in perfect security on the opposite shore. At night he swam the river with his body-guard, and fell upon the enemy at daybreak. The thunder of the imperial kettle-drums sufficed to scare away

A.D. 1556-1605 — the rebels. The flight was a stampede. Some of the ringleaders were slain in the pursuit; the greater number were taken prisoners and trampled to death by elephants, after the barbarous custom of Moghul times.

Decay of Muhammadan dominion. The rebellion was crushed out in Oude, but it was soon followed by others. The truth seems to be that the Muhammadan religion had lost its force. The brotherhood of Islam could not bind Moghul, Turk, and Afghan into one united mass as it had united the Arab tribes in the old wars of the Khalifat. The dismemberment of the Muhammadan empire in India had begun two centuries before, at the fall of the Tughlak dynasty and revolt of the Dekhan. Under such circumstances Akbar called in the aid of a new power to restore peace in Hindustan and consolidate a new empire; and the policy which he pursued forms the most important and interesting event in the history of his reign.

Policy of equality of race and religion. Akbar was not a man of culture like the Muhammadan Sultans of olden time. If he had gone with his father to Persia he might have received a schooling; but he stayed with an uncle in Kábul and learnt nothing but war. He could not read or write,[1] but he had listened to histories, and seems to have formed ideas. He was not a zealous Muhammadan, and he certainly did not share in the Muhammadan hatred of idolaters. On the contrary, he was imbued with the religious toleration of Chenghiz Khan, and inclined to regard all religions as equal. He resolved to amalgamate Hindus and Muhammadans into an imperial system, in which the one should be a check on the other. In a word, he foreshadowed that policy of equality of race and religion, which maintained the integrity of the Moghul empire for more than a century, and since then has been the mainstay of the British empire in India.

The first step in the work of amalgamation was the conquest and pacification of the princes of Rajpútana. The Rajpút league, under the suzerainty of the Rana of Chitór, was bound together by a system of intermarriages. Hindus marry but one wife, but polygamy has always been the practice of Rajas. The Rana of Chitór was supposed to be the descendant of Ráma and the old Rajas of Ayodhyá, the noblest

[1] Akbar made up for some of his deficiencies in after years. His Spelling-book was preserved as a curiosity down to modern times.

A.D. 1556-1605

of the children of the sun.[1] Every Raja considered it a high honour to receive a daughter of the Rana in marriage. In like manner every Raja deemed it an honour to give a daughter in marriage to the Rana.

Relic of the Swayamvara.

By this time the old ceremony of the Swayamvara had died out of India. A Rajpút princess no longer appeared in her father's hall, to signify her choice of a husband by the gift of a garland. But the fiction of "self-choice" had been preserved, and continues to this day. A gilded cocoa-nut is still formally sent to a Raja in the name of a princess as symbolical of choice. It is but an empty compliment, for the girl has no voice in the matter; but the cocoa-nut is a relic of a civilization which has passed away.

Rajpút marriages.

The policy of Akbar was to put the Padishah in the room of the Rana; to become himself the suzerain of the Rajpút league, and the commander of all the Rajpút armies. To carry out this object it was necessary that he should take the daughters of the Rajas to be his wives, and give them daughters in return. The idea was repulsive alike to Rajpút and Muhammadan; it was contrary to caste laws; it was contrary to the religion of the Koran unless the bride became a convert to Islam. In a word, the policy could only be carried out by a barbarian and a despot; and such a man was Akbar.

Submission of Rajpút princes.

The wars of Akbar in Rajpútana may be forgotten.[2] It will suffice to say that after bitter struggles Jaipur and Jodhpur yielded to their fate, and each gave a daughter in marriage to Akbar, and paid him homage as their suzerain. In return he added to their territories, raised them to high rank in his court, loaded them with honours, and took their armies into his pay. Other Rajas followed the example and were rewarded in like manner. Akbar thus brought a new political element into existence; and the support which he derived from the princes of Rajpútana enabled him to establish and consolidate an empire.

[1] Of course there are rival families, but the superior claims of the Rana are pretty generally acknowledged.

[2] It is important to bear in mind the relative positions of Rajpútana and Malwa, between the Jumna and the Nerbudda rivers. Rajpútana lies to the west of the river Chambal, and extends to the neighbourhood of the Indus. Malwa lies to the east of the Chambal, and extends in a southerly direction to the Nerbudda river.

A.D. 1556-1605

Resistance of the Rana and destruction of Chitór.

The Rana of Chitór however held out against all threats and temptations. He preferred death to dishonour. In 1567 the city of Chitór was environed by the army of Akbar. The Rajpúts saw that there was no hope of deliverance, and performed the awful rite of Johur. The women threw themselves on burning piles, whilst the men put on saffron garments and perished sword in hand. Chitor was reduced to a ruin. Sir Thomas Roe saw it fifty years afterwards. It contained a hundred temples and innumerable houses, but not a human inhabitant was there.

Foundation of Udaipur: the Rana' vow.

The very name of Chitór was blotted out of the after history of Rajpútana. The Rana was named Udai Singh. He sought a refuge in the Aravulli hills, where he founded the city of Udaipur. Henceforth he was known as the Rana of Udaipur, or Oodeypore. But Chitór was never forgotten. So long as Chitór was a widowed city, the Rana bound himself and his successors never to twist their beards, or eat from gold or silver, or sleep upon anything but straw. To this day the memory of the interdict is preserved in the palace at Udaipur. The Rana never twists his beard. He eats from gold and silver, but there are leaves beneath the dishes. He sleeps upon a bed, but there is a scattering of straw below.

Rajpút element in the Moghul empire.

Meanwhile the Rajpút princes, who had been hated as idolaters since the days of Mahmúd, were treated by Akbar as honoured and valued friends. The marriages of the Padishah with their daughters converted them into kinsmen of the Moghul. Akbar especially employed the Rajpúts to maintain his ascendency over the Afghans, the bigoted and inveterate foes of the Hindus. The history is obscure; and to all appearance has been purposely obscured. But it is certain that one Rajpút kinsman was appointed Viceroy of the Punjab; another commanded the Rajpút army against the Afghans of Kábul; whilst one Rajpút Raja of renown was appointed Viceroy of Bihár and Bengal, which had been at the mercy of Afghan chieftains from a remote antiquity. The historian of Akbar tells us that these Rajas proved able rulers; but in truth nothing is known of the working of Akbar's policy, beyond the bare fact that he employed the Rajpúts to overawe the Afghans.

Two aristocracies and two armies.

Henceforth there were two aristocracies in the Moghul empire, and two armies. Each was distinct from the other, and acted as a balance against the other. The one was Moghul and Muhammadan; the other was Rajpút and Hindu.

Moghul grandees, or official nobles.

The Moghul aristocracy was one of white-complexioned foreigners, chiefly Persians, who went by the common name of Moghuls. The Moghuls had no hereditary nobility outside the royal family. The Padishah was the sole fountain of honour, and the fountain of all honour. He gave rank at will, and all rank was military rank. He gave titles at will, and every title was associated with the idea of loyalty. The emoluments took the form of military pay. Every grandee was appointed to command a certain number of horse; but he rarely maintained more than a third of the number, and received payment for the whole. Rank and title might be given in a moment, and in a moment they might be swept away.

Dependence on the Padishah.

Every Moghul noble and officer was entirely dependent on the Padishah. Their lives and property were at his disposal, He was the heir to the wealth of every one of his grandees. and wives and families of men of the highest rank were sometimes reduced to beggary. Hereditary nobility was thus unknown to the Moghuls. In one generation an Amír, or grandee of the first order, might hold a high command, and enjoy a princely income. His grandsons might be brown-complexioned men serving in the ranks as common soldiers.

Amírs, Mansubdars and Ahadis.

The Amírs were the highest class of nobles, the grandees of the empire.[1] They might be made governors, viceroys, or ministers. A second class was known as Mansubdars, and a third class as Ahadis; but these were military officers. One and all were little better than slaves [illegible] the Padishah.

Rajpút Rajas, hereditary nobles.

The Rajpúts formed a hereditary [illegible]cy on a feudal basis. They held their lands in return [illegible] military service, and all commands were hereditary. The vassal served his lord, the lord his Raja, and the Raja his suzerain. When Akbar became suzerain in the room of the Rana, he raised the Rajas to the rank of Amírs, and sometimes conferred the title of Raja on his grandees.[2]

1 In old books of travel the Amírs are called Umrahs and Omrahs.

2 It is not quite certain that the title of Raja was conferred by Akbar; it was certainly conferred by his successors.

A.D. 1556-1605

Political advantage of religious antagonism.

The religious antagonism between Muhammadan and Hindu was a positive gain to Akbar. Muhammadans could not always be trusted in a war against Muhammadan rebels; and any scruples about fighting fellow-Muhammadans were a hindrance to Akbar in the suppression of a revolt. But no such scruples existed between Muhammadans and Hindus. Muhammadans were always ready to fight idolatrous Rajas. The Rajpúts, on the other hand, were always ready to fight Muhammadan rebels; and they gloried especially in fighting their hereditary enemies, the bigoted Afghans, who had driven their forefathers from their ancient thrones on the Ganges and Jumna.

Personal characteristics of Akbar.

Akbar has often been described by contemporaries. He was proud and arrogant like all Moghuls, but clement and affable. He was tall and handsome, broad in the chest and long in the arms. His complexion was ruddy and nut-brown. He had a good appetite and digestion, but was sparing as regards wine and flesh meat. He was remarkable for strength and courage. He would spring on the backs of elephants who had killed their keepers, and compel them to do his bidding. He delighted in every kind of sport; in fights between buffaloes, cocks, harts, rams and elephants; in the performances of wrestlers, fencers, dancers, and actors of comedies, as well as in those of trained elephants. He often despatched serious business in the midst of these spectacles. He was very fond of hunting. He had no hunting dogs, but kept tame antelopes with nets fastened to their horns to entangle wild ones; also tame panthers to take other wild beasts. He surrounded a whole wood with hunters, and then sent beaters into the jungle to drive out the game.

Akbar, a Muhammadan: his Hindu wives.

All this whi[illegible]r was outwardly a Muhammadan. Thus he made [illegible]w that on the birth of a son he would walk on foot to the shrine of a Muhammadan saint at Ajmír. In 1570 a son was born, who was named Selim, but afterwards succeeded to the throne under the title of Jehangír. Akbar accordingly walked on pilgrimage to the shrine, and paid his devotions to the saint, and built a mosque at Ajmír. Even his Rajpút brides were required to say the formula of Islam as they entered the zenana,—"There is no God but Allah, and Muhammad is the prophet of Allah." But having thus made a show of being converted, the Hindu princesses did as they pleased. They introduced idols and Brahmans into the zenana, and offered sacrifices to their idols; and at last Akbar joined in the idol worship of his wives, like Solomon of old.

A.D. 1556-1605

Ulamá, a collective body of Muhammadan doctors.

In process of time Akbar came in collision with orthodox Muhammadan doctors. In Muhammadan states, the laws are supposed to be based on the Koran. Thus law and religion are blended together, and eminent lawyers are often eminent divines. This class is always numerous at the capital; for judges, magistrates, and law officers in general are chosen from amongst these learned doctors. The whole body is known by the collective name of Ulama; and occasionally they assemble and discuss points of law. The opinions of the Ulamá have great weight in a Muhammadan court, and will often influence the decisions of the Sultan.

Rise of the minister, Abul Fazl.

About 1675 an ambitious young scholar, named Abul Fazl, was introduced to Akbar, and soon found favour in the eyes of the Padishah. He was a born courtier, and by steadily administering to the vanity of Akbar, he became his minister and confidant. He was anxious to master all religions. To use his own language, he longed to study the great religions of the world at their fountain heads; to sit at the feet of the Christian padres of Goa, the Buddhist monks of Thibet, and the Parsí priests who were learned in the Zendavesta. He imbued the mind of Akbar with a like curiosity. At the same time he had good reasons for hating the Ulamá; they had persecuted his father and driven him into exile; they would have persecuted himself in like manner, had they not been afraid of Akbar. They were ignorant, bigoted, and puffed up with pride and orthodoxy.

Religious controversies.

Akbar, like other oriental sovereigns, was fond of listening to religious controversies. He held assemblies on Thursday evenings especially to hear different members of the Ulamá dispute in his presence. At first the proceedings were conducted with the utmost decorum. After a while the disputants became accustomed to the Padishah, and spoke with more freedom and greater warmth. At last one evening there was an uproar, and learned men reviled one another in the very presence of their sovereign.

Degradation of the Ulamá.

Abul Fazl was at the bottom of all the mischief. He was anxious to degrade the Ulamá in the eyes of Akbar; and no mode was so effective as that of involving them in

A.D. 1556-1605

religious controversy. He introduced subjects which he knew could only end in wrangling. He introduced others, like Akbar's marriages, which placed the learned doctors on the horns of a dilemma. If they sought to please the Padishah they sinned against the Koran; and if they stuck to the Koran they offended the Padishah. One orthodox magistrate spoke out conscientiously against the marriages, and was removed from his post. In this way the Ulamá were ruined in the eyes of Akbar; they drifted into disgrace and ruin; they had cursed one another in their speech, and probably in their hearts they were all agreed in cursing Abul Fazl.

Akbar, the arbiter.

Meanwhile Akbar was led by Abul Fazl to believe that he was a far better judge in religious matters, and especially in religious controversies, than the bigoted body of doctors that made up the Ulamá. Akbar eagerly caught at the idea. He was anxious to throw off the influence of the Ulamá, who would have persuaded him to persecute heretics and Hindus. He was resolved, like Henry the Eighth, to become himself the supreme authority in all religious matters.

Akbar's apostasy.

The result of all these experiences was that Akbar became hostile to the Muhammadan religion. He broke up the power of the Ulamá, and banished all refractory professors to the remote regions of Central Asia. He conversed with teachers of other religions,—Brahmans, Buddhists, and Parsís. He sent a letter to the Portuguese viceroy at Goa, requesting that Christian fathers might be sent to Agra to teach him the tenets of Christianity. The religious world at Goa was thrown into a ferment at the idea of converting the Great Moghul. Three fathers duly arrived at Agra, and were permitted to build a church and perform Christian rites without molestation; privileges which would have been accorded, perhaps, in no other Muhammadan city. Both Akbar and his minister Abul Fazl professed the utmost respect for Christianity; Akbar even entered the church and prostrated before the image of the Saviour; but neither the Padishah nor his minister were sufficiently impressed with the truths of Christianity to become baptized.

Expectations of a Muhammadan millennium.

Akbar indulged in religious experiences until he believed himself to be a representative of deity. The sixteenth century was a period of great excitement throughout the Muhammadan world. It was currently believed that at the end of a

A.D. 1556-1605

thousand years from the Hijra, or flight of Muhammad, a new prophet would appear to convert the world and usher in a new millennium. The "Lord of the period," as he was called, was expected to appear in 1591-92; and many pious Muhammadans prepared for his coming by fasting and prayer.[1]

Religion of Akbar.

In the first instance Akbar was induced by Abul Fazl to believe that he himself was the "Lord of the period." Subsequently, when his faith in Islam had died out, the idea took another form. He founded a new religion known as the Divine Faith. He permitted himself to be worshipped as a type of royalty emanating from God; or, to use the symbolical language of Abul Fazl, to be adored as a ray of the divine sun, the supreme soul, that animated the universe. Every morning he worshipped the sun in public. At the same time he was himself worshipped by the ignorant multitude, who were induced to believe that he could work miracles and cure diseases.

Ordinances of Akbar.

All this while, however, Akbar sought to better his subjects by measures of toleration, as well as by improved social laws. He permitted the use of wine, but punished intoxication. He gratified his Hindu subjects by prohibiting the slaughter of cows. He forbade the marriage of boys before they were sixteen, and of girls before they were fourteen. He permitted the marriage of Hindu widows, and did his best to put a stop to widow burning. In after life he tried to check the practice of polygamy amongst the Muhammadans.

Cruelty of Akbar.

But the character of Akbar had a dark side. He was sometimes harsh and cruel. He was jealous of his authority; suspicious of plots and rebellions; and resorted to strong measures which are revolting to civilization. His persecution of Muhammadan doctors was unpardonable. He is, moreover, charged with keeping a poisoner and getting rid of his enemies in this manner without remorse. Such practices are known to have been common to his successors; and there are strong grounds for believing that they were equally common during the reign of Akbar.

Daily life of Akbar.

The daily life of Akbar and his court may be gathered from three institutions of Moghul origin. They were known as the Jharokha, the Durbar, and the Ghusal-khana; in

[1] For a further account of this remarkable movement, the reader is referred to the larger *History of India*, vol. iv. chap iv.

A.D. 1556-1605

English parlance they would be known as the window, the audience hall, and the dressing-room.[1] Details of these institutions will appear in the after history; for the present it will suffice to describe their general character.

Public window.

The Jharokha was a window at the back of the palace, which overlooked a plain below. Every morning Akbar appeared at this window and worshipped the sun, whilst the multitude thronged the plain below and worshipped Akbar. Later in the morning, generally about noon, Akbar appeared at the window, and was entertained with the combats of animals in the plain below.[2] Sometimes he inspected troops, horses, elephants, and camels, from this window.

Hall of audience.

The Durbar was the hall of audience, situated in a large court at the entrance to the palace. Every afternoon Akbar sat upon his throne at the back of the Durbar hall, and gave audience to all comers. Here he disposed of petitions, administered justice, and received Rajas, Amírs, and ambassadors. All the grandees at court were bound to attend the Padishah at the Jharokha and Durbar.

Evening assemblies.

The Ghusal-khana was a private assembly held in the evening in a pavilion behind the Durbar court. None were admitted excepting the ministers and such grandees as received special invitations. Sometimes the gathering resembled a privy council; at other times it was an assembly of grandees and learned men. The assembly of the Ulamá on Thursday evenings would, probably, have been held in this pavilion, but it was not large enough. Consequently another pavilion was prepared expressly for their reception.

Division of lands; Khalisa and Jaghír.

Akbar is famous for having introduced a land settlement into his dominions. It should be explained that under Moghul rule all lands were treated as the property of the Padishah. They were divided into two classes, Khalisa and Jaghír. The Khalisa lands were those held by the Padishah as his own demesnes, and paid a yearly rent to him. The Jaghírs were estates given in lieu of salaries. In this way

[1] The Ghusal-khana was literally the bath-room, and contained a large bath decorated with jewels. The idea of entertaining visitors in a bath-room is apparently peculiar to Moghuls.

[2] It is the custom in India among the wealthier classes to perform their devotions at early morning, and then to take a breakfast and a siesta. This will account for the late hours kept at the evening assemblies.

Jaghírs were given to governors, ministers and grandees; they were also given to queens and princesses in the imperial harem. Every Jaghír paid a fixed yearly rent to the Padishah; and all that could be collected above this amount belonged to the Jaghírdar, or holder of the Jaghír.[1]

Revenue settlement of Todar Mal.

Akbar employed a Hindu, named Todar Mal, to make a revenue settlement; in other words to fix the yearly payments to be made by holders of the land. All lands were measured, whether cultivated or uncultivated. Every piece of land yielding a yearly income of twenty-five thousand rupees, was placed under the charge of an officer known as a Krori; the object being to bring uncultivated lands into cultivation. The Krories are charged with every kind of rapacity and oppression; but the settlement of Todar Mal is lauded to this day. It was the one thing to which landholders and cultivators could appeal against the rapacity of revenue collectors.

Conquest of Kábul and Kashmír.

Towards the end of his reign Akbar conquered Kábul and Kashmír. Kábul, however, was a dangerous acquisition from the lawlessness of the people; and on one occasion Akbar lost an army there, but the details are imperfectly known. Kashmír proved a more acceptable conquest; and Akbar and his successors occasionally resorted to a retreat amongst the mountains of Kashmír, as a pleasant change from the heats of Hindustan.

Embassy to the Sultans of the Dekhan.

Akbar was always anxious to establish his sovereignty over the Muhammadan Sultans of the Dekhan. The battle of Talikota, in which the Sultans defeated the Maháraja of Vijayanagar, was fought in 1565, being the ninth year of the reign of Akbar. Some years afterwards the Padishah sent ambassadors to the Sultans of the Dekhan, inviting them to accept him as their suzerain, and promising to uphold them on their thrones and prevent all internecine wars. One and all, however, refused to pay allegiance to the Moghul.

[1] Land tenures in the Moghul empire involve contradictions not easily explained. The husbandman often possessed a few fields, and had the power of selling and bequeathing them, at the same time that the district in which those fields were included was annually let out by the government to a renter, who paid a certain sum of money to the lord of the country, and received from the cultivator a certain part of his harvests. To seize such lands was regarded as the height of injustice. The Moghul was only anxious to keep down the Amírs, not to deprive the smaller landowners of their hereditary rights.

A.D. 1556-1605

Conquest of Ahmadnagar and Berar.

During the latter part of his reign Akbar conquered the northern half of the Dekhan, including Ahmadnagar and Berar, and would probably have conquered the remaining kingdoms of Bíjápur and Golkonda, when he was called away by the rebellion of his eldest son.

Rebellion of Jehangír: death of Akbar, 1605.

The rebellion of Prince Selim, better known in after years by the name of Jehangír, was apparently a Muhammadan insurrection against the apostasy of Akbar. It was marked by the assassination of Abul Fazl. The rebellion was suppressed, and Akbar became outwardly reconciled to his son; but he was apparently a changed man. He abandoned scepticism and heresy, and returned to the Muhammadan faith. He died in October 1605, aged sixty-four; but there are strong grounds for believing that he was poisoned at the instigation of Jehangír.[1]

[1] For proof of this poisoning, see the larger *History of India*, vol. iv. chap. iv.

CHAPTER V.

MOGHUL EMPIRE: JEHANGÍR AND SHAH JEHAN.

A.D. 1605 TO 1658.

JEHANGÍR succeeded Akbar at the age of thirty-five. He inherited his father's vices, but had none of his virtues. He was not only harsh and cruel, but took pleasure in the sufferings of his victims. He drank wine like a Scythian, and was especially fond of drinking bouts at his evening assemblies. Above all, he was the slave of a crafty intriguing woman, named Núr Mahal. 1605-1627. Jehangír.

Jehangír had not been the favourite of his father. He seems to have joined the Muhammadan party against his father. Akbar's favourite was his grandson Khuzru, the eldest son of Jehangír, and he had intended that Khuzru should succeed him on the throne. Khuzru was a young prince of Akbar's way of thinking, inclined to Christianity, and a great friend of the Rajpúts. Jehangír had always been jealous of Khuzru; and it was this jealousy of Khuzru that led him to rebel during the lifetime of Akbar. Breach between father and son.

From the day that Jehangír ascended the throne, Khuzru was in mortal fear. He expected to be strangled, or poisoned, or at any rate to be deprived of sight, so as to be cut off from all hopes of the throne. At last he fled in a panic from the palace at Agra, and hurried to Lahore. On the way he was joined by large numbers of Rajpúts, but was hotly pursued by Jehangír. He tried to escape into Persia, as Humáyun had done; but he was cruelly betrayed and sent in fetters to his father. Revolt of Khuzru, son of Jehangír.

The revenge of Jehangír upon the rebels was horrible and sickening. It resembled those cruel scenes of slaughter

A.D. 1605-1627 — Revenge of Jehangír on the rebels.

which are to be seen on Assyrian monuments. Hundreds were flayed alive after Moghul fashion. Hundreds were impaled on sharp stakes, and left to die in lingering torture. The wretched Khuzru was conducted through the lines of victims, and forced to hear the shrieks of his followers, and witness their dying agonies. His life was spared, but he was doomed to years of captivity and suffering.

Story of Núr Mahal.

Meanwhile Jehangír became the slave of Núr Mahal. Various stories are told of the early adventures of this celebrated princess. According to general rumour, she was a Persian girl of low birth, and Jehangír fell in love with her during the lifetime of his father. Akbar objected to such connections; and the girl was given in marriage to a Persian, and went with her husband into Bengal. When Jehangír came to the throne he sent for the girl; but her husband raised some natural objections, and was murdered in a fray. The widow was conducted to Agra, and for a long time refused to listen to Jehangír. At last she consented to become his queen; and her brother Asof Khan was appointed minister. She herself is best known by the title of Núr Mahal, or the "light of the harem."

Appearance of the English at Surat.

During the early years of the reign of Jehangír, the English began to appear in the Indian seas. The East India Company had been formed in 1599, in the lifetime of Akbar. It obtained its first charter from Queen Elizabeth in 1600, under which the Company were to monopolise all the English trade in the Indian seas. English ships sailed round the Cape as the Portuguese had done; but they could do nothing in Malabar, for the ports were in the hands of the Portuguese. They sailed northward to Surat within the Moghul's territory. Surat was situated near the mouth of the river Taptí, about a hundred and eighty miles to the north of Bombay.

Portuguese hostility.

The English, however, could do but little business at Surat. The Portuguese thwarted them in every way; bribed the Moghul governor of Surat to prevent the English from buying cargoes; jeered at James I. as a king of fishermen, and scoffed at Great Britain as a contemptible island. In fact the Portuguese treated the English at Surat much in the same way as they themselves had been treated a century before by the Moors of Malabar. The result was that for years the English and Portuguese were natural enemies, and fought one another to the death whenever their ships met on the high seas.

Mission of Captain Hawkins to Agra, 1608-11.

A sea captain, named Hawkins, managed to make his way from Surat to Agra on a sort of mission to the Padishah. Jehangír took a fancy to the Englishman; promoted him to the rank of commander of four hundred horse; and drank wine with him every night in the Ghusalkhana, and asked him a thousand questions about Europe and its princes. In the first instance the head of Hawkins was turned by the favour shown to him by the Great Moghul; but his very success created numerous enemies. The Portuguese had friends in the Moghul court, and managed to excite the suspicions of Jehangír against the Englishman. The Moghul governor of Surat raised an outcry against Hawkins; he had bought many things of Hawkins and had refused to pay for them. One Amír portentously declared in the Durbar hall, that if once the English got a footing in India they would soon become masters. Hawkins found that he could get no redress and no favours, and soon made his escape from Agra.

Early quarrels with the Moghuls.

The English were anxious to buy goods, and willing to pay for them; but the Moghul merchants were afraid to sell lest the Portuguese should seize their ships on the high seas; and for a long time they refused to deal with the English traders. At last the English were provoked to take the law into their own hands. They did not plunder Muhammadan ships and scuttle them, as the Portuguese had done a century before; but they attacked Moghul ships in the Red Sea, seized the cargoes, and paid for them at the market rates which prevailed at Surat. In fact, there was lawless fighting on all sides; and to make matters worse, other English ships appeared in the eastern seas in defiance of the Company's charter; and these interlopers committed acts of piracy on Moghul ships, which gave the English a bad name in the court of Jehangír.

Embassy of Sir Thomas Roe, 1615-18.

Two or three years afterwards an English ambassador, named Sir Thomas Roe, was sent to the Great Moghul by James the First. Roe was a far greater man than Hawkins; he was a lord ambassador, and had [illegible]secretary, a chaplain, and a retinue. He landed at Su[illegible] 1615, attended by a guard of honour made up of capta[illegible]s, merchants, and sailors. The English ships in the river were decked with flags and

A.D. 1605-1627

streamers, and welcomed the lord ambassador with a salute of forty-eight guns. Sir Thomas Roe was to make a treaty with Jehangír, to explain the difference between the ships of the East India Company and those of interlopers, and to establish the Company's trade on a sound footing.

Annoyances at Surat.

Sir Thomas Roe experienced some rudeness at landing from the Moghul officials at the Custom-house. They had little respect for his character as ambassador, and persisted in searching all his servants and opening all his boxes, including those which contained the presents for Jehangír. At length, after a month's delay at Surat, Roe procured carriage and escort as far as Burhanpur, about two hundred and twenty miles due east of Surat. Burhanpur was the head-quarters of the Moghul army of the Dekhan; and here Roe expected to secure fresh carriage and escort to enable him to go as far as the imperial camp, which had been recently removed from Agra to Ajmír.

Desolate country.

Roe was disgusted with what he saw during his journey from Surat to Burhanpur. The country was desolate; the towns and villages were built of mud; and there was not a house fit to lodge in. At one place he was guarded with thirty horsemen and twenty musketeers because of highwaymen. In fact he was travelling through Kandeish, a province partly in Hindustan and partly in the Dekhan, which has been infested by Bhíls and brigands down to modern times.

War in the Dekhan.

At this period the Great Moghul was carrying on a war in the Dekhan. A black Abyssinian, named Malik Amber, had risen to power in Ahmadnagar. Abyssinians, in spite of their colour, were respected on account of their strength and bravery, and often played important parts in political revolutions in India. Malik Amber set up a prince of the fallen house of Ahmadnagar, secured help from Bíjápur and Golkonda, and compelled the Moghul army to retreat northwards to Burhanpur.

Prince Parwíz and the Khan Khanán.

The Moghul army of the Dekhan was under the command of Parwíz, the second son of Jehangír. Parwíz was a drunken prince, and left the army in the hands of an officer known as the Khan Khanán, or Khan of Khans. Meanwhile the Khan Khanán took bribes from the different Sultans of the Dekhan, an[illegible] nothing. At times he tried to deceive Jehangír by feigning to attack Ahmadnagar; but his treachery was already suspected by the Padishah.

A.D. 1605-1627

Roe's visit to Parwíz.

At Burhanpur Sir Thomas Roe was received with some show by the head of the police, known as the Kotwal. He paid a visit of ceremony to Parwíz, who was haughty and arrogant as regards ceremony, but otherwise good-natured. Roe found him sitting in a gallery under a canopy, with a platform below him, railed in for his grandees.

Public audience

Roe ascended the platform and saw the grandees standing below the prince with joined hands, like so many slaves or suppliants. He made a bow, and Parwíz bowed in return. He would have ascended the gallery to speak to the prince, but was stopped by a secretary. Parwíz, however, was ready to grant every request as fast as Roe could make it. He allowed the English to establish a factory at Burhanpur, and promised to supply carriage and escort to enable Roe to get on to Agra. He received Roe's presents very graciously, especially a case of strong liquors. He left the gallery, and said he would send for Roe presently, and speak to him in a private chamber. Roe waited for a while, and was then told that he might leave the palace. He learnt afterwards that Parwíz had opened the liquor bottles, and had rapidly become too drunk to speak to anybody.

Journey to Ajmír: Tom Coryat.

The road from Burhanpur to Ajmír runs through the heart of Rajpútana; yet Roe had few adventures on the way beyond a sharp attack of fever. He paid a visit to the ruins of Chitór; and he met a crack-brained Englishman, named Tom Coryat, who had undertaken a walking tour through Asia. Coryat was one of the most wonderful travellers of his time. He had gone on foot from Jerusalem, through Asiatic Turkey, Persia, and Afghanistan, to the cities of Delhi and Agra, at a cost of about a penny a day; and being regarded as a madman, no one interfered with him. When he met Roe he was going to Surat, where he subsequently died from drinking too much sack, and was buried in the outskirts of the city.

Imperial Durbar hall at Ajmír.

In January 1616 Sir Thomas Roe had his first audience with Jehangír. He describes the Durbar hall as resembling a London theatre. The Padishah was sitting on his throne at one end. The grandees were standing on a platform before him like actors on a stage; they were railed off in three rows according to their respective grades. The common people formed the audience or groundlings, who looked on from behind the third rail.

A.D. 1605-1627

Gracious reception of Roe by Jehangír.

There was at first a question of prostration, but Roe refused to do anything of the kind, and the point was waived. He passed the three rails, making a profound bow at each; and was admitted amongst the grandees of the first grade. Jehangír received the English ambassador with princely condescension. He accepted the presents, consisting of virginals, knives, an embroidered scarf, a rich sword and an English coach. He wanted some one to play the virginals, and one of Roe's retinue complied with his wish. The coach was too large to be brought into the Durbar hall, but Jehangír sent persons to look at it. The Padishah then spoke very graciously to the ambassador, hoped he had got rid of his fever, and offered to send him his own physicians. Altogether Roe went away charmed with his reception.

Childish demonstrations of Jehangír.

When the Durbar was over Jehangír showed himself to be an inquisitive Moghul. He went out and examined the coach, and even got into it and ordered his servants to draw it. He made Roe's English servant array him in the scarf and sword, English fashion; and then strutted about and drew his sword and brandished it. But he complained to the bystanders that the presents were very poor, and said that the King of England ought to have sent him jewels.

Failure of Roe's mission.

Roe's negotiations proved a failure throughout. He wanted too much from the Padishah. Jehangír was willing to issue firmáns or orders to all local officers to grant certain privileges to the English; and a few bribes to the local officers would have ensured attention to these privileges, until by long custom they had hardened into rights. But Roe was smitten with an Englishman's passion for treaties. He wanted a treaty signed and sealed, which would bind the Padishah and his successors for ever, whilst he had nothing to give in return but a few paltry presents. As it was he wasted two years in negotiations, and never got anything beyond firmáns.

Jehangír's suspicions of the Khan Khanán.

The history of the Moghul rule at this period is very suggestive. Jehangír was growing more and more suspicious of the Khan Khanán. Twice he tried to poison him, but failed. He recalled Parwíz from the Dekhan, and sent him to command in Bengal. He then appointed his third son, Prince Shah Jehan, to command the army of the Dekhan. He hesitated to recall the Khan Khanán, lest the

A.D. 1605 1627

latter should break out into rebellion with the army of the Dekhan at his heels.

Story of poisonings.

A kinswoman of the Khan Khanán was in the imperial zenana, and Jehangír consulted her on the subject. He proposed sending a dress of honour to the Khan Khanán as a token of forgiveness. She replied that Khan Khanán would suspect the dress to have been poisoned; that the Khan Khanán was already aware that Jehangír had on two several occasions tried to poison him. Jehangír made no attempt to deny the charge; he only suggested that he should wear the dress for an hour, and that the kinswoman should inform the Khan Khanán accordingly. She replied that the Khan Khanán would trust neither of them. Accordingly Jehangír determined to go in person to the Dekhan.[1]

Moghul festivals.

Sir Thomas Roe saw much of the Moghul court during his stay at Ajmír. He was present at the Nau-roz, or feast of the new year, when the Padishah sat upon his throne in the Durbar, and received presents of great value from all his grandees. He was present at the celebration of Jehangír's birthday on the 2nd of September, 1616. In the morning the Padishah was weighed six times against gold and silver, silks and stuffs, grain and butter; and all the things that were weighed against him were given to the poor. In the afternoon there was a grand procession of elephants before the Durbar.

Drinking bout on the Padishah's birthday.

On the evening of the birthday there was a drinking bout in the Ghusal-khana. Roe was sent for at ten o'clock at night after he had gone to bed. He found Jehangír sitting cross-legged on a little throne, arrayed in his jewels. There was a large company of grandees, and numerous gold and silver flagons, and all present were ordered to drink. Every one got drunk excepting Prince Shah Jehan, the minister Asof Khan, and the English ambassador. Jehangír scattered rupees to the multitude below. He threw about gold and silver almonds for which the nobles scrambled like schoolboys. At last he dropped off to sleep, on which all the lights were put out, and the company were left to grope their way out of the Ghusal-khana in the best way they could.

[1] All that Roe tells about the court of Jehangír may be accepted as truth, as nearly everything that goes on in the zenana of a Moghul sovereign is soon known outside. Nothing is concealed but thoughts or emotions, and even they are often betrayed.

A.D. 1605-1627

Wholesale executions.

On one occasion a hundred thieves were brought before Jehangír in the Durbar hall, and condemned to death without further trial. They were butchered and exposed in the different streets of Ajmír; the head thief being torn to pieces by dogs in front of Roe's house.

Wine drinkers flogged in the Durbar.

At another time there was a terrible scene in the Durbar court. Whenever the Padishah commanded his nobles to drink wine, they were bound to obey; and such had been the case on the evening of the birthday. If, however, Jehangír heard that a grandee had been drinking on any other occasion without his order, the offender was scourged in his presence. One night Jehangír gave a feast to the Persian ambassador, and ordered all present to drink wine. Accordingly, every man drank to the health of the Padishah, and his name was entered in a register according to custom. But Jehangír was so drunk that he forgot all that had passed. Next day there was an allusion to the drinking, and Jehangír asked who had given the order. He was told that the paymaster had given it; an answer that was always returned when the Padishah thought proper to forget his own orders. Jehangír at once called for the register, and began to punish the offenders. They were flogged so unmercifully that some were left for dead; and there was not a man at court, not even a father or a son, that dared to speak a word in behalf of the sufferers.

Roe's warnings to the Company.

About this time Roe reported to London that Shah Jehan was plotting the death of his elder brother Khuzru. He mentioned the fact as a warning to the East India Company not to push their trade too far into the interior. The struggle between the two princes might throw all Hindustan into a ferment. If Khuzru prevailed the English would be gainers, because he loved and honoured Christianity. If Shah Jehan prevailed the English would be losers, because he hated Christianity, and was proud, subtle, false, and tyrannical.

Jehangír's progress towards the Dekhan.

In November 1616 Jehangír left Ajmír and began the journey towards the south. The departure was a grand procession of elephants and palanquins, radiant with jewels and cloths of gold and silver. At setting out there was a notable incident. Jehangír stopped at the door where his eldest son was imprisoned, and called for him to come out. Khuzru appeared and made his reverence. He had a sword and buckler in his hand, and his beard hung down to his waist as a mark of disfavour. He accompanied the imperial camp during its progress through Rajpútana, and hopes were expressed that he might yet succeed to the throne of his father.

A.D. 1605-1627

Camp of the Great Moghul.

The camp of the Great Moghul was like a moving city. The imperial pavilions formed a vast palace of scarlet canvas, surrounded by scarlet screens or walls of arras. The pavilions of the grandees were canvas mansions of white, green, and mixed colours; all were encompassed by screens, and were as orderly as houses. There were also long streets of shops, like the bazar of a metropolis. There was no confusion of any kind, for all the tents and pavilions were laid out and set up in the same order day by day. This regularity, however, disappeared as the camp moved through Rajpútana; for the country was only half conquered, and was infested by robbers, whilst the road sometimes lay through forests and over mountains.

Triumphant policy

As the imperial camp advanced further south some alarm was expressed. It had been expected that the Sultans of the Dekhan would have sent in their submission directly they heard that Jehangír was approaching the frontier. But the Sultans did nothing of the kind, and Núr Mahal proposed that the Padishah should return to Agra under pretence of hunting. But Jehangír declared that his honour was at stake. He continued to advance, but sent on reinforcements to Shah Jehan, who had gone before to take command of the Moghul army of the Dekhan. Suddenly the news arrived of a great triumph of policy. The Sultans of Bíjápur and Golkonda had been detached from the cause of Malik Amber; the Abyssinian had been defeated, and Ahmadnagar was restored to the Moghul.

Jehangír's memoirs.

Sir Thomas Roe left India in 1618. Jehangír went to Guzerat; subsequently he visited Agra and Delhi. In his memoirs written by himself, Jehangír offers certain observations on the country and people, which may be summed up in a few words, and serve as a reflex of his character.

Massacres of brigands and rebels.

"Guzerat," says Jehangír, "is infested with thieves and vagabonds. I have occasionally executed two or three hundred in one day, but I could not suppress the brigandage. From Guzerat I went to Agra, where I became reconciled to my eldest son Khuzru. I next went to Delhi, where I heard of a rebellion in Kanouj, and sent a force to

A.D. 1605-1627

put it down. Thirty thousand rebels were slain; ten thousand heads were sent to Delhi; ten thousand bodies were hung on trees with their heads downwards along the several highways. Notwithstanding repeated massacres there are frequent rebellions in Hindustan. There is not a province in the empire in which half a million of people have not been slaughtered during my own reign and that of my father. Ever and anon some accursed miscreant springs up to unfurl the standard of rebellion. In Hindustan there has never existed a period of complete repose."

Head quarters at Lahore.

Subsequently Jehangír proceeded to the Punjab. He made Lahore his capital, but spent the hot months of every year amongst the cool mountains of Kashmír. Meanwhile Núr Mahal engaged in various intrigues respecting the succession to the throne, which led to tragical consequences.

Four sons of Jehangír: prospects of Shah Jehan.

Jehangír had four sons,—Khuzru, Parwíz, Shah Jehan, and Shahryár. Shah Jehan, the victor in the Dekhan, stood the fairest chance of the throne. For a long time he enjoyed the favour of Núr Mahal; and he had married her niece, a daughter of her brother Asof Khan. Subsequently he excited her wrath by another marriage, and she resolved to work his destruction.

Intrigues of Núr Mahal.

Núr Mahal had a daughter by her previous husband, and she was ambitious for this daughter. She resolved to give her in marriage to Khuzru. This prince was already reconciled to his father Jehangír, and she purposed securing his succession to the throne. But Khuzru was not a Muhammadan, and was averse to polygamy. He was already married to one wife, and he refused to marry a second. Núr Mahal was bitterly angry with Khuzru, and betrothed her daughter to his youngest brother Shahryár. Henceforth she laboured hard to secure the succession for Shahryár.

Intrigues of Shah Jehan.

About this time fresh disturbances broke out in the Dekhan. Shah Jehan was again ordered to take the command of the army of the Dekhan; but he was fearful that Jehangír might die in his absence, and that Khuzru might obtain the throne. He refused to go to the Dekhan unless Khuzru was placed in his charge. Núr Mahal raised no objection; Khuzru would probably be murdered by his unscrupulous brother, but such a catastrophe would forward her own schemes as regards Shahryár. Jehangír was getting old and stupid, and was induced to make over his eldest son to the charge of Shah Jehan.

Assassination of Khuzru: promotion of his son Buláki.

Months passed away. Shah Jehan was again at Burhanpur in charge of his brother Khuzru. Suddenly news arrived at Buranpur that Jehangír was dying. One night Khuzru was strangled to death in his chamber. No one doubted that the murder was instigated by Shah Jehan. Shortly afterwards Jehangír recovered his health. He was so angry at the murder of Khuzru, that he sent for his grandson Buláki, the son of Khuzru, and raised him to the rank of ten thousand horse, the highest rank in the empire. He then declared Buláki to be his successor to the throne of Hindustan.

Desperation of Shah Jehan.

Shah Jehan was driven to desperation by this turn of affairs. The murder of Khuzru, which was to have placed him on the throne, had elevated his nephew Buláki. To crown all, he was deprived of the bulk of his army. An army was despatched from Lahore against Persia under the command of Shahryár; and Shah Jehan was ordered to send a large force to join it; whilst his officers received direct orders from the Padishah to quit the Dekhan and join the army of Shahryár.

Plot of Shah Jehan.

At this crisis a secret plot was hatched between Shah Jehan and his father-in-law Asof Khan. The idea was to seize the imperial treasures at Agra. The court had removed from Agra to Lahore, and Asof Khan persuaded Jehangír to remove the treasure in like manner. Asof Khan proceeded to Agra to conduct the removal; and Shah Jehan was to march his forces with the utmost secresy from the Dekhan and surround the convoy. The plan had nearly succeeded. The treasurer at Agra, much against his will, had loaded the camels with the precious store, when he heard that Shah Jehan was coming up from the Dekhan by forced marches. He saw through the plot in a moment. He unloaded the camels, and lodged the treasure once again in the fortress, and reported the coming of Shah Jehan to the Padishah.

Sack of Agra: flight of Shah Jehan.

Shah Jehan arrived at Agra, but the treasure was beyond his reach. During three weeks he made repeated attacks on the fortress, but failed to capture it. He wreaked his vengeance on the city, plundering and torturing the citizens, and committing cruel outrages on their wives and

A.D. 1605-1627

daughters. Meanwhile Jehangír was marching from Lahore with a large army. Shah Jehan left Agra to encounter his father. A battle was fought at Delhi between father and son; and Shah Jehan was defeated, and compelled to fly to the mountains.

Ravages in Bengal: flight to the south.

The further movements of Shah Jehan are startling from their audacity. His marches resemble the flying raids of 'Alá-ud-dín and Malik Kafur. He resolved to plunder Bengal; and he took the city of Dacca by surprise, and ravaged the country, until the robberies and outrages of his followers were a terror to the Bengalis. At last he was again attacked and defeated by the imperial army. He now fled to the Dekhan, and found an asylum in the courts of Bíjápur and Golkonda, like an exiled prince of the olden time.

Rajpúts and Muhammadans.

All this while there were antagonisms between the Rajpút and Muhammadan armies in the service of the Moghul. Núr Mahal was bitter against the Rajpúts, especially against a Rajpút general who had been converted to Islam, and was known by the name of Mahábat Khan. This general had commanded a Rajpút army in the Dekhan, but was recalled at the instance of Núr Mahal. Subsequently through her instrumentality Mahábat Khan was insulted and degraded; and at last in a fit of desperation he carried off Jehangír, and kept him as a state prisoner under his immediate charge.

Capture of Jehangír by the Rajpúts.

For a brief interval Núr Mahal was baffled; her power was gone, for Jehangír, in spite of his detention, was still permitted to exercise the authority of Padishah. Mahábat Khan treated his sovereign with every mark of respect; and for some time Jehangír expressed thankfulness for his deliverance from the toils of Núr Mahal; but after a while he fled back to his beloved Núr Mahal. Mahábat Khan and his Rajpúts were now in extreme peril. Mahábat Khan would have joined Parwíz with his Rajpút army, but Parwíz was dead. At last he fled to the Dekhan and espoused the cause of Shah Jehan.

Death of Jehangír, 1627.

Jehangír died suddenly, in October, 1627. Before he died he again nominated his grandson Buláki, the son of Khuzru, to succeed him as Padishah.

Short reign of Buláki.

Asof Khan, the minister, installed Buláki on the throne at Delhi. His object was to checkmate his sister Núr

Mahal, and to gain time for furthering the designs of his son-in-law, Shah Jehan. Shahryár was taken prisoner and deprived of sight. The only remaining claimants to the throne were Shah Jehan, the third son of Jehangír, and his nephew Buláki, son of Khuzru.

A.D. 1627-1658

Sham death and burial: Shah Jehan proclaimed Padishah.

The critical state of affairs was brought to a close by one of those strange farces which are peculiar to oriental history. It was given out that Shah Jehan was dangerously ill, and then that he was dead. Permission was readily obtained from Buláki for burying the remains of his uncle and rival in the tomb of Akbar. Mahábat Khan and his Rajpúts conducted an empty bier in sad procession to Agra. Buláki was persuaded to go out with a small escort to conduct his uncle's remains to the tomb of Akbar. He saw a vast procession of Rajpúts, and then suspected a plot and stole away to Lahore. At that moment the trumpets were sounded, and Shah Jehan was proclaimed Padishah, and entered the fortress of Agra amidst universal acclamations.

Massacre of princes: fate of Buláki.

What followed is one of the mysteries of Moghul history. There certainly was a massacre of princes at Lahore; and their bodies were buried in a garden, whilst their heads were sent to Shah Jehan. But the fate of Buláki is uncertain. It was said that he was strangled; but the Duke of Holstein's ambassadors saw the prince in Persia ten years afterwards. Whether he was an impostor will never be known. Shah Jehan sent ambassadors to Persia to demand the surrender of the pseudo-Padishah, but the Shah of Persia refused to deliver up the exile; and henceforth the latter personage lived on a pension which he received from the court of Persia.

Shah Jehan, 1627-58.

The reign of Shah Jehan is obscure. Whilst alive his inordinate love of flattery led to fulsome praises of his administration, which find expression in history; whilst the misfortunes of his later years excited the sympathy of European residents in India, and blinded them to the scandals which stain his life and reign.[1]

Spite against the Portuguese.

Shortly after the accession of Shah Jehan he manifested his hatred against the Portuguese. Goa was beyond his reach, but the Portuguese had been permitted by Akbar to establish a settlement at Húghli, in Bengal, about twenty

[1] For details, see larger *History of India*, vol. iv. chap. vi.

A.D. 1627-1658

miles from the present site of Calcutta. Shah Jehan had a special spite against the Portuguese of Húghli. They had refused to help him in the rebellion against his father Jehangír; and they had joined the imperial army with men and guns, and taken a part in the battle against the rebel son.

Doom of the Portuguese of Húghli.

The fate of the Portuguese of Húghli is one of the saddest stories in the history of India; it has been likened to the Babylonian captivity of the Jews. The settlement was captured in 1632. The Portuguese were carried away captive to Agra, and threatened and tortured to become Muhammadans. Many held out and suffered martyrdom. The flower of the women and children were sent to the imperial zenana; the remainder were distributed amongst the Amírs of the Moghul court; and the veil of oblivion may well be thrown over the unhappy doom of all.

Dangerous antagonism between Rajpúts and Muhammadans.

The antagonisms between Rajpúts and Muhammadans had risen to a dangerous height during the reign of Jehangír, but during the reign of Shah Jehan they became still more alarming. The race hostility between Moghul and Afghan was disappearing, and they were making common cause against the Hindu. A Rajpút army under a Rajpút general had been found necessary in acting against the Muhammadan Sultans of the Dekhan. When, however, Mahábat Khan was recalled from the Dekhan, an Afghan army was sent under an Afghan general named Khan Jehan. The Afghans were Sunnís; so was Malik Amber the Abyssinian. Intrigues naturally followed between the Afghan and the Abyssinian; and Khan Jehan discovered in time that his life was in danger from Shah Jehan, and broke out into rebellion. Then it was found that the Muhammadan army in the service of the Padishah would not fight against the rebel Khan Jehan and his Afghans. The Rajpút army was brought into play, and soon defeated and slew the rebel, and carried off his head to Shah Jehan.

Disaffected Rajpúts.

But whilst the Rajpúts fought bravely against the Afghans, they were disaffected towards the Padishah. They had helped Shah Jehan to obtain the throne, out of hatred to Núr Mahal; but they had no respect for the new sovereign; and an incident occurred at this time, which reveals some of the dangers which were beginning to threaten the imperial throne.

A prince of Marwar (Jodhpur) named Umra Singh, had

entered the Moghul's service with all his retainers. It was the custom for the Rajpút generals to mount guard in turns before the palace, whilst the Muhammadan Amírs mounted guard inside the palace. Umra Singh had a strong aversion to the guard duty. On one occasion he was away for a fortnight without leave, and when he returned he excused himself by saying that he had been hunting. He was fined, but refused to pay the fine. He was summoned to the Durbar hall, and made his appearance whilst Shah Jehan was sitting on his throne. He pressed towards the front as if to speak to the Padishah, and then suddenly drew a dagger from his sleeve and stabbed the minister to the heart. Having thus committed himself to the work of murder, he struck out at those around him; in a word, he ran "amok" until he was overpowered and slain.

Outbreak of Umra Singh.

The turmoil filled the Durbar hall with consternation. Shah Jehan was in such a fright that he left the throne and ran into the zenana. The retainers of Umra Singh heard that their master was dead, and ran "amok" in the old Rajpút fashion. They put on saffron clothes and rushed to the palace, killing all they met. They threatened to plunder Agra unless the dead body of their prince was given to them. Shah Jehan was forced to comply. The dead body was made over to the Rajpúts; the funeral pile was prepared, and thirteen women perished in the flames.

General alarm: running amok.

The Rajpút princes outside the Moghul's service were still more refractory. They were called tributary Rajas, but rarely paid tribute unless they were forced. They were protected by forests and mountains. They often desolated the dominions of the Moghul, harassed his subjects, hindered trade, and plundered caravans. Fortunately they were at constant feud with each other; whereas, could they have united in one national uprising, they might possibly have contended successfully against a sovereign like Shah Jehan.

Tributary Rajas.

Shah Jehan carried out two great works which have served to perpetuate his name. He built the famous Taj Mahal at Agra. He also founded the present city of Delhi, which to this day is known to Muhammadans by the name of Shah Jehanabad, or "the city of Shah Jehan."

Taj Mahal and Shah Jehanabad.

The Taj Mahal is a mausoleum of white marble; a lofty dome supported by four arches. Seen from the outside, the structure is of plain but dazzling whiteness. Inside the

Description of the Taj.

A.D. 1627-1658 walls are inlaid with precious stones of various colours, representing birds and flowers. The marble gates are exquisitely perforated so as to resemble lace. The structure is built in the midst of gardens and terraces, whilst round about are lofty pavilions with galleries and arched ways. The whole must have cost millions sterling. Twenty thousand men are said to have laboured at it for twenty years.

Feminine architecture. This mausoleum was built in honour of Shah Jehan's first and favourite wife Mumtaz Mahal, the daughter of Asof Khan, and niece of Núr Mahal. The spirit of the place is feminine. There is nothing stately or masculine in the buildings; nothing to recall the architecture of Greece or Rome. It is lovely beyond description, but the loveliness is feminine. It is not the tomb of a wife, but the shrine of a mistress. It awakens ideas of fair-complexioned beauty; the soul is dead, but the form, the charm, the grace of beauty are lingering there. The walls are like muslin dresses, radiant with flowers and jewels. The perforated marble gates are like the lace veils of a bride.

The peacock throne. Shah Jehan never lived at Delhi; he made Agra his capital, but sometimes spent the hot months in the cool climate of Kashmír. The new city and palace of Delhi are therefore chiefly associated with the reigns of his successors. But he constructed a peacock of gold and jewels over the imperial throne at Delhi, that has been accounted one of the wonders of the world. Some have attempted to estimate its value. But the historical importance of the peacock lies in the fact that it proves Shah Jehan to have been at heart a Moghul and an idolater, and anything but a Muhammadan. The peacock was an emblem of the sun; and Chenghiz Khan and the Rana of Udaipur claimed alike to be the children of the sun. The image of a peacock was opposed to the direct injunctions of the Koran; but the peacock was the ensign of the old Mahárajas of Vijayanagar, and to this day it is the ensign of the Moghul kings of Burma.

Obsolete wars. Shah Jehan carried on several wars on the frontier, but they are of small importance. On the north-west, Kábul was a bone of contention with the Uzbegs. Further south, Kandahar was a bone of contention with Persia.

Zenana influences. The history of the reign of Shah Jehan is little better than a narrative of zenana influences and intrigues. Every governor of a province was expected to send, not only a fixed yearly sum as the Padishah's share of the revenue, but costly presents to Shah Jehan and the favourite queens. No governor could expect to keep his province except by presents, which were nothing but bribes; and such bribes, if liberally bestowed, would often cover or excuse tyranny and oppression, and secure promotion and titles of honour for the lavish donor.

Four sons of Shah Jehan.

The crowning event of the reign was the fratricidal war between the four sons of Shah Jehan for the succession to the throne. Each of these four sons had a distinctive character; their names were Dara, Shuja, Aurangzeb, and Murád. Dara, the eldest, resided with the court at Agra; Shuja was Viceroy of Bengal, Aurangzeb was Viceroy of the Moghul Dekhan, and Murád was Viceroy of Guzerat. Dara was attached to Europeans, and inclined to Christianity, but he treated the Rajpút princes with arrogance and scorn. Shuja was a Shíah, and friendly towards the Rajpút princes. Aurangzeb was a strict Sunní, and Murád professed to be a Sunní like Aurangzeb.

Sunnís and Shíahs.

The old antagonism between Sunní and Shíah was about to break out in India. The original quarrel between the two hostile camps lies in a nutshell. The Sunnís say that the four Khalifs, who reigned in succession after the death of Muhammad, are the rightful successors of the prophet by virtue of their being elected by the congregation at Medina. The Shíahs declare that the three first Khalifs—Abubakr, Omar, and Othman—are usurpers; that Ali, the fourth Khalif, is the only rightful successor of Muhammad by virtue of his kinship with the prophet; Ali being the husband of Fatima, the prophet's daughter, and the father of Hasan and Husain, the prophet's grandsons. To this day the disputants are cursing and reviling each other, and often resort to fisticuffs, cudgels, and swords, in the vague hope of settling the controversy by force of arms.

Conflicting forms of thought.

But there is something more in the controversy than meets the eye. The Sunní is a puritan of a democratic type, who hates idolaters and unbelievers of every kind, and allows but little speculation in matters of religion. The Shíah, on the other hand, believes in a kind of apostolic succession, and speculates as to how far Muhammad and his son-in-law, Ali, and his grand-sons Hasan and Husain, are emanations of the godhead; and he is certainly neither as puritanical nor as intolerant as the strict Sunní.

A.D. 1627-1658

Aurangzeb, the Sunní fanatic.

The early Padishahs were lusty men, sensual and jovial. Aurangzeb was a lean spare fanatic, abstaining from wine and flesh meat, and living only on fruit and vegetables. His face was pale and livid; his eyes were bright and piercing, but sunk in his head. At one time he is said to have lived as a fakír in the company of fakírs. He always carried a Koran under his arm, prayed often in public, and expressed a great zeal for Muhammad and the law.

Viceroy of the Moghul Dekhan.

Aurangzeb, as already said, was Viceroy of the Moghul Dekhan. He had resided many years in the province, and founded the city of Aurangabad, which was called after his name. He hated the Shíah Sultans of Bíjápur and Golkonda, and was anxious to annex their kingdoms to the empire of the Moghul. He formed a close alliance with Amír Jumla, a rebel minister of Golkonda, and projected the conquest of the two kingdoms; but his projects were thwarted by Dara, and were suddenly brought to a close by reports that Shah Jehan was dying, followed up by rumours that he was dead.

Reported death of Shah Jehan: empire in a ferment.

The whole empire was in a ferment. It was known on all sides that the four brothers would engage in a bloody contest for the throne; and every Amír and Raja was weighing the character and prospects of each of the four. Dara was the eldest son, and was on the spot to assert his rights; but he had alienated the Rajpúts by his insolence; he was disliked by the Muhammadans as a heretic; and he was especially hated by the Sunnís as an infidel and unbeliever. Shuja, as a Shíah, could rely on the support of the Rajpúts, and on the help of all those nominal Muhammadans, who were followers of the Koran from family associations, but detested the puritanism and fanaticism of the Sunnís. Aurangzeb, on the other hand, was a strict Sunní, and relied on the support of all sincere Muhammadans, who mourned over the decay of religion and morals, and yearned after a thorough reformation. His main difficulty was to reconcile his ambitious schemes with his religious views. But craft and fanaticism removed every difficulty, and enabled him to perpetrate the most atrocious crimes out of professed zeal for the prophet and his law.

Revolt of Shuja: its defeat.

Shuja, Viceroy of Bengal, was the first to take the field and march an army towards Agra. An imperial force was sent against him, consisting of a Muhammadan army under

Sulaiman, the eldest son of Dara, and a Rajpút army under the command of Jai Singh, Raja of Jaipur.[1] Jai Singh had no desire to act against Shuja. He hated Dara, who had grievously insulted him by calling him a musician.[2] He assured Shuja that Shah Jehan was still alive, and tried to persuade him to return to Bengal. But Shuja was self-willed, and a battle was the result; but though Shuja was defeated, Jai Singh hung back from a pursuit. Shuja retired with the wreck of his army into Bengal; and the imperial forces saved appearances by following slowly behind. A.D. 1627-1658

Meanwhile Aurangzeb was playing an artful game. He knew that his younger brother Murád had begun to march an army from Guzerat towards Agra. He wrote to Murád proposing that they should make common cause against Dara. All that he wanted, he said, was to prevent an infidel like Dara, or a heretic like Shuja, from succeeding to the throne of Hindustan. He was satisfied that Murád was an orthodox Sunní, and he would gladly help Murád to win the throne; and then he himself would retire from the cares and business of the world, and devote his remaining years to penitence and prayer at the prophet's tomb. Aurangzeb's bait for Murád.

Murád was overjoyed at the proposal. The two armies were soon united, and marching through Rajpútana towards Agra. Aurangzeb continued to observe a studied subservience to his younger brother. He treated Murád as the Padishah, took his orders as regards the movements of the army, and even prostrated himself before him. Murád was completely gulled. He was anything but a fervent Muhammadan, and certainly had none of the fanaticism of Aurangzeb. He professed himself a Sunní for political purposes; and he rejoiced at the blind zeal which had driven Aurangzeb to help him to the throne. Plot thickens.

Dara was a doomed man from the beginning of the war. He sent an imperial force against the two brothers. The Rajpút army was commanded by Jaswant Singh of Marwar; and this Raja was staunch to the imperial cause, for he had married a daughter of Shah Jehan by a Rajpút wife. The Muhammadan army was commanded by a general, who had Victory of Aurangzeb at Ujain.

[1] Jai Singh, Raja of Jaipur (Jeypore), is famous in the after history. So also is Jaswant Singh, Raja of Marwar (Jodhpur).

[2] To call a man a musician is a grave offence in oriental ears. To call a woman a dancing-girl is an equally opprobrious epithet.

A.D. 1627-1658

been insulted by Dara, and was burning for revenge. A battle was fought near Ujain (Oojein), but the Muhammadans would not fire a gun, partly through the treachery of their general, and possibly out of respect for the vaunted piety of Aurangzeb. The whole brunt of the battle fell upon the Rajpúts, and they were cut to pieces. The Raja of Marwar fled with a handful of followers to the city of Jodhpur, only to encounter the fury of his Rani. The princess, though a daughter of Shah Jehan, had Rajpút blood in her veins. She cried out, with the spirit of a Spartan, that the Raja ought to have conquered Aurangzeb or perished on the field of battle. She threatened to burn herself on the funeral pile, since her husband was dead to shame; and she only relented on his making a solemn vow to be revenged on Aurangzeb.

Crushing defeat of Dara on the Chambal river.

Dara was frantic at the defeat. He sent expresses calling up Sulaiman from Bengal, but Jai Singh persuaded Sulaiman to remain where he was. He raised an immense army of raw levies; and refusing to wait any longer, he led it against his two brothers. The Rajpúts in Dara's army were staunch, but the commander of the Muhammadans was burning to be revenged on Shah Jehan; for like other grandees, his wife had been dishonoured by the Padishah. A battle was fought on the banks of the Chambal river. The Rajpút leader was slain, and his men fled in a panic. The Muhammadan troops were persuaded by the wrathful husband that Dara was also slain, and they fled in like manner. Dara saw that all was lost, and galloped off to Agra with a handful of followers; but he dared not remain there, and made his way to the Punjab. He hoped to escape to Persia, as Humáyun had done more than a century before.

Captivity of Shah Jehan.

The victorious army of Aurangzeb and Murád marched on to Agra, and shut up Shah Jehan in his own palace. There was not an Amír or a Raja to strike a blow in defence of the old Padishah, or interfere in his behalf. All were thunderstruck at the revolution, and paralysed with fear. Shah Jehan tried to inveigle Aurangzeb into a private interview; but the latter was warned that he would be murdered by the Tartar women who formed the body-guard to the Padishah, and was thus able to avoid the snare.[1]

[1] An imperial body-guard of Tartar women is an ancient institution in India. Megasthenes tells us that Sandrokottos had such a body-

A.D. 1627-1658

Ruin of Murád.

Aurangzeb next feigned to prepare for the coronation of Murád. Suddenly it was noised abroad that Murád had been found by his brother in a state of intoxication, had been declared unfit to reign, and had been sent as a state prisoner for life to the fortress of Gwalior. Meanwhile Aurangzeb was proclaimed Padishah amidst the acclamations of his soldiers. The whole affair is a Moghul mystery. It is said that Murád was tempted to excess by Aurangzeb himself, and the circumstances confirm the suspicion. Murád was not likely to have indulged in wine, much less to have fallen into a state of intoxication, in the company of his strict brother, without some peculiar temptation. Again, though a zealous Muhammadan might maintain that a drunkard was unfit to reign, yet the fact that Aurangzeb made his brother's drunkenness a plea for seizing the throne, will excite suspicions until the end of time.

Triumph of Aurangzeb, 1658.

The conclusion of the fratricidal war may be briefly told. The fortunes of the contending brothers really depended upon the two Rajpút Rajas, Jai Singh and Jaswant Singh; and both were won over for the time by the cajoleries of Aurangzeb, who forgot his religious scruples whilst seeking the support of Hindu idolaters. In the end Shuja was defeated by Amír Jumla, the staunch ally of Aurangzeb; and was forced to fly with his family and treasures to Arakan, where he is supposed to have perished miserably. Dara was encouraged by Jaswant Singh to hazard another battle, but was abandoned by the Raja, and ruined by the disaffection of his own officers, who were all in collusion with Aurangzeb. Again he fled towards Persia, but was betrayed by an Afghan, and sent in fetters to Delhi; and there he was murdered by hired assassins in the pay of Aurangzeb. His son Sulaiman escaped to Kashmír, but was betrayed by the Raja of Kashmír, and spent the remainder of his days as a state prisoner in the fortress of Gwalior. Shah Jehan was imprisoned for life in his own palace at Agra. Aurangzeb, who had made religion a stepping-stone to the throne, had overcome his brethren mainly by the support of two heathen Rajas. He was installed as Padishah in the city of Delhi, and was accepted as sovereign by the people of Hindustan.

guard; and Raja Dashyanta appears with the same kind of body-guard in the drama of Sakuntalá.

CHAPTER VI.

MOGHUL EMPIRE: AURANGZEB.

A.D. 1658 TO 1707.

A.D. 1658-1707

Fears and anxieties.

AURANGZEB had gained the empire of Hindustan, but he was oppressed by fears and worn by anxieties. He may have felt but little remorse at the fate of his brethren; but he was in constant alarm lest his father Shah Jehan should escape from Agra, or his brother Shuja should turn up in Hindustan. The Sherif of Mecca refused to receive his envoys, although they brought him money presents; he told the pilgrims at Mecca that he knew of no sovereign of Hindustan excepting Shah Jehan.

Religious trimming.

Meanwhile Aurangzeb was obliged to dissemble his religious views; to trim between Muhammadans and Hindus. He tried to conciliate strict Muhammadans by enforcing the law against wine, by prohibiting music and singing, and by banishing dancing-girls. He is said to have conciliated the Rajas by magnificent feasts, at which he offered up prayers in the presence of a burning brazier,[1] as if he were performing sacrifices. But he could not, or would not, conciliate Shíahs. He issued an edict compelling them to cut the long mustachios which they wore in memory of the prophet Ali; and he deprived many Persian Shíahs of the lands which had been specially granted to their families by the tolerant Akbar.

[1] Hindus say their prayers, and read the sacred books, in the presence of a lamp or fire as a representative of deity. Sir William Jones was much censured in bygone days because he yielded to the prejudice of his Brahman pundits, and burnt a lamp whilst studying the laws of Manu.

A.D. 1658-1707

Spite of Auarngzeb.

Aurangzeb was not an amiable man. On the contrary, he was sour, reserved, and resentful, and seemed to delight in wounding the feelings of others. Although he was more than forty years of age, he cherished a grudge against his old tutor, and was mean enough to resent it by stopping his pension. The tutor thought there must be some mistake, and went to Delhi and secured a public audience with the Padishah in the Durbar hall. He expected to be treated with some show of warmth; but to his utter surprise Aurangzeb delivered a long tirade on the poorness of his education. "This tutor," said the Padishah, "taught me the Koran, and wearied me with the rules of Arabic grammar; but he told me nothing at all of foreign countries. I learnt nothing of the Ottoman empire in Africa, nor of the Tartar empire in China. I was made to believe that Holland was a great empire, and that England was larger than France. Meanwhile I was taught nothing of the arts of government and war, and but very little of the towns and provinces of Hindustan."

Maligned tutor.

The set speech of Aurangzeb was promulgated throughout the empire, and lauded to the skies by all the parasites and courtiers; but wiser men saw the malignity which dictated it. The tutor had probably taught Aurangzeb all he knew, and certainly could not have been expected to teach him the arts of government and war. What became of the tutor is unknown.

Description of Delhi.

For some years Aurangzeb made Delhi his capital. This city stood about a hundred miles to the north of Agra, where Shah Jehan was kept prisoner. It presented an imposing appearance in those days, but in reality was little better than a camp. When the court was at Delhi the city was crowded with people; but when the court removed to Kashmír or elsewhere, the city was nearly empty. Only a few houses in all Delhi were built of stone or brick; many were built of clay and whitened with lime; but the greater number were mere hovels of mud and straw; and when the court and army went into camp these huts were left to crumble to pieces beneath the sun and rain.

Streets and lanes.

The city, properly so called, consisted of one broad street, lined with shops and arcades, which was known as the Chandní Chouk. There was also another broad street, without shops, where the grandees dwelt in their several

A.D. 1658-1707 mansions. These streets were intersected by long narrow lanes, peopled with the miscellaneous multitude of soldiers, servants, followers, artisans, bazar dealers, coolies, and all the strange varieties of human beings that make up an Indian capital.

The great square. The city of Delhi was separated from the palace by a great square; and when the Padishah was at Delhi this square was a vast bazar, the centre of city life, its gossip, and its news. Here the Rajpúts mounted guard before the entrance gate of the palace. Here horses and elephants of the Padishah were paraded and mustered. Here the unfortunate Dara was conducted with every mark of contumely before he was doomed to death, in order that the people of Delhi might know that he was captured, and might not be seduced afterwards by any impostor who assumed his name. Here wares of every kind were exposed for sale; mountebanks and jugglers performed before idle multitudes; and astrologers calculated fortunate and unfortunate days and hours.

Delhi astrologers. Astrologers were an institution at Delhi, as indeed they are in most oriental cities. Every grandee kept an astrologer, and treated him with the respect due to an eminent doctor. But there was always a number of poor impostors sitting in the bazar ready to tell the fortune of any man or woman for a penny. They sat cross-legged on pieces of carpet, and handled mathematical instruments, turned over the leaves of a large book which showed the signs of the zodiac, and then feigned to calculate a fortunate time for beginning any business or journey. Women, especially, covered themselves from head to foot in white calico, and flocked to the astrologers, whispering the secrets of their lives with the frankness of penitents at confession. Bernier describes one ridiculous pretender, a Portuguese half-caste, whose only instrument was a mariner's compass, and whose astrological lore consisted of two old Catholic prayer-books, with pictures of the Apostles which he passed off for European zodiacal signs.

Imperial palace: shops and arsenals. The palace at Delhi was on the same plan as all the Moghul palaces. In front, within the entrance gate, were streets of shops and public offices. There also were quarters for the Amírs, who mounted guard in turns within the palace;[1]

[1] Muhammadan Amírs mounted guard within the palace gates; Rajpút Rajas mounted guard in the public square outside. The reason

the arsenals for arms and accoutrements; and the workshops for all the artisans employed by the ladies of the zenana,—embroiderers, goldsmiths, painters, tailors, shoemakers, and dressmakers. A.D. 1658-1707

At the inner end of the palace streets was the Durbar court, which was surrounded by arcades, and enclosed the hall of audience, and other pavilions. Beyond the Durbar court was the zenana and gardens. At the extremity of the gardens was the Jharokha window, looking out on an open plain which stretched to the river Jumna. This was the plain where the multitude assembled every morning to salam the Padishah; whilst later in the day, animal fights and other performances were carried on beneath the window for the amusement of the Padishah and his ladies. Durbar court and Jharokha window.

Shortly after the accession of Aurangzeb, his attention was drawn to the state of affairs in the Dekhan. The northern Dekhan was Moghul territory; further south were the two Muhammadan kingdoms of Bíjápur and Golkonda. The western région near the sea, known as the mountains of the Konkan, had never been conquered by the Muhammadans, and was still held by the Hindus in a state of rude independence. The consequence was that the territories of the Moghul and those of the Sultan of Bíjápur were alike harassed by a lawless chief of the Konkan, known as Sivaji the Mahratta. This man appeared in the twofold character of a rebel against the Sultan of Bíjápur, and a freebooting Esau whose hand was against every man. Affairs of the Dekhan.

The mountains of the Konkan, the cradle of Sivaji, form the northern section of the Western Gháts.[1] They stretch southwards from Surat, past Bombay towards the neighbourhood of Goa. The political geography of the Konkan thus bore a close resemblance to that of Wales; and the chiefs or Rajas of the Konkan maintained a rude independence in these mountains, like that which was maintained by the Welsh princes against the early English kings. Mahrattas of the Konkan.

The father of Sivaji was a vassal of the Sultan of Bíjápur; as such he held the two fortresses of Joonere and Poona, Joonere and Poona.

for this was that the Rajpút Rajas were always suspicious of treachery, and would not enter gates or walls unless accompanied by the whole of their retainers.

[1] The western coast of India, as already stated, was divided into three sections:—Konkan, Kanara, and Malabar.

A.D. 1658-1707

about seventy miles to the eastward of Bombay. The region encloses fertile valleys, but otherwise might be described as a land of precipices and jungles. For an unknown period it had been the home of chieftains, who were sometimes vassals of the Sultan of Bíjápur, and sometimes rebels against his suzerainty.

Sivaji, the Mahratta.

Sivaji was born at Joonere in 1627, and bred in the mountains between Joonere and Poona. Whilst yet a child, his father had gone away south into the Mysore country; nominally to conquer territory for the Sultan, but practically to carve out a Raj for himself amongst the dismembered provinces of the Vijayanagar empire. Meanwhile Sivaji grew up to be a rebel and a freebooter. He was a short tawny mountaineer, with long arms, quick eyes, and a lithe and active frame. He was a rude uncultivated Hindu, cunning and crafty beyond his fellows, and fertile in artful devices and disguises. He boasted of a Rajpút origin; was a constant worshipper of Siva and Bhowaní;[1] and was especially imbued with a superstitious reverence for Brahmans. But in one way the tinge of Rajpút blood showed itself. Sivaji always treated women with respect, and never insulted the religion of his Muhammadan enemies.

Genius of Sivaji.

Sivaji was born with a genius for sovereignty. He was endowed with that mysterious instinct which enables some ignorant barbarian to convert shepherds or cultivators into soldiers, and drill them into submission and obedience. He succeeded in forming the mountaineers of the Konkan into loose but organised armies of horsemen; levying plunder and blackmail on a regular system; devastating the plains during the dry season, but returning at the beginning of the rains to their natural fortresses in the hills.

Exploit with the "tiger's claws."

Long before Aurangzeb obtained the throne, and when he was simply Viceroy of the Moghul Dekhan, he heard of the exploits of Sivaji. Indeed the Mahratta performed a feat at this period, a deed of treachery and audacity, which rendered him notorious far and wide. The Sultan of Bíjápur sent a general against Sivaji at the head of a large army. Sivaji feigned to be in great trepidation, and tendered the most humble offers of service. He inveigled the Muhammadan general into a private meeting, without

[1] Bhowaní was a form of the goddess Dúrgá, also known as Parvatí and Kálí, who was supposed to be the wife of Siva.

A.D. 1658-1707

followers on either side, at which he was to do homage as a faithful feudatory of Bíjápur, and take the commands of the Sultan.[1] Sivaji went to the appointed spot with a secret weapon concealed in his hand; a treacherous and murderous contrivance which reveals the savage instincts of the Mahratta. It consisted of steel blades curled at the points to resemble claws; and the whole was fastened to the fingers with rings, and known as tiger's claws.

Assassination of a Muhammadan general.

The Muhammadan general approached the Hindu with dignified satisfaction. Before he left Bíjápur he had boasted that he would bring the Mahratta rebel from his lair, and cast him in chains at the foot of the throne. Sivaji fell at his feet like an abject suppliant. The Muhammadan told him to rise, and he obeyed with every show of humiliation and submission. At this moment, when the Muhammadan was off his guard, the Mahratta rushed at him like a tiger, tore him down with the horrible claws, and killed him on the spot.

Flight of the Bíjápur army.

It is difficult to describe the turmoil which followed. The surrounding jungle seems to have been alive with Mahrattas. The Bíjápur army discovered that their general was dead, and fled in all directions, whilst the Mahrattas plundered the camp and slaughtered the flying soldiery.

Aurangzeb's attentions to Sivaji.

This exploit seems to have been after Aurangzeb's own heart. It reached his ears at a time when he was planning the conquest of Bíjápur, and brooding over the approaching struggle with his brothers for the throne of Hindustan. He saw that Sivaji might prove a useful ally in the coming wars, and that in the event of defeat or disaster the mountains of the Konkan might offer a secure asylum. Accordingly, he is said to have forgiven all the aggressions of Sivaji on Moghul territory; to have ceded him a certain border territory; and to have come to some sort of treaty or understanding with him. But the Mahratta alliance came to nothing. The fratricidal wars were brought to a close without any appeal to Sivaji. Aurangzeb ascended the throne of Hindustan, and for some years Sivaji was forgotten.

Meanwhile Sivaji was engaged in aggressions on Bíjápur. The government of Bíjápur was weakened by domestic

[1] According to some stories both Sivaji and the Muhammadan general were each accompanied by a few followers.

A.D. 1658-1707

Peace with Bíjápur

troubles, and anxious to make peace with the refractory Mahratta. At last there appears to have been some kind of understanding or compromise. Sivaji was to abstain from all further depredations on Bíjápur, and in return was to be left in possession of certain territories and fortresses.

Aggressions on the Moghuls.

But it was impossible for a restless spirit like Sivaji to settle down to a quiet life. Having come to terms with Bíjápur he began to harass the territories of the Moghul. He worked so much mischief as to attract the attention of Aurangzeb, and at last the Padishah took effectual measures for stopping all further depredations.

Moghuls capture Poona.

Aurangzeb appointed his uncle, Shaista Khan, to be Viceroy of the Moghul Dekhan. He sent his uncle with a large force to capture the fortresses of Sivaji and break up the power of the Mahratta. Shaista Khan was accompanied by a Rajpút army under Jaswant Singh, of Marwar. Aurangzeb had reason to be very suspicious of the Raja of Marwar. Jaswant Singh had married a daughter of Shah Jehan, and might form some plan for the liberation of his captive father-in-law. At any rate it was considered more politic to employ Jaswant Singh in the Dekhan, than to permit him to remain in Hindustan, where he might carry on secret plots and intrigues for the restoration of Shah Jehan to the throne.

Night attack on Shaista Khan.

In 1662 Shaista Khan captured the town and fortress of Poona, and made it his head-quarters during the rains. One night Sivaji penetrated the Moghul camp and suddenly attacked the quarters of the Moghul general. Shaista Khan escaped with the loss of a finger; his eldest son was slaughtered on the spot. A Mahratta army suddenly fell upon the Moghul camp, and all was uproar and confusion. In the end Sivaji stole away with considerable booty.

Disaffection of the Raja of Marwar.

Shaista Khan strongly suspected Jaswant Singh of being concerned in this disaster; and there is every reason to believe that there was a secret alliance between the Rajpút and the Mahratta. If so, it was the first sign of that Hindu movement against Aurangzeb which forms a distinguished feature of the reign.

Sivaji captures Surat, 1664.

Sivaji was soon revenged on the Moghul for the invasion of Shaista Khan. The Moghul port of Surat was separated from Sivaji's territories in the Konkan by a tract of hill and

A.D. 1658-1707

jungle inhabited by Bhíls, and other wild tribes, under the rule of some obscure Raja. Sivaji made an alliance with this Raja and marched a Mahratta army through the Bhíl country. The town of Surat was taken by surprise. Most of the inhabitants fled into the country out of sheer terror of the Mahrattas. The Moghul governor of Surat made no resistance, but threw himself into the fortress, and sent out messengers for succour.

Plunder and atrocity.

Meanwhile the Mahrattas plundered and burnt the houses of Surat at their leisure. They attacked the English and Dutch factories, but both were fortified with cannon; and the European merchants in both houses succeeded in beating off the brigands. The Mahrattas arrested all the inhabitants they could find in the streets or houses, and carried them off as prisoners to Sivaji, who remained in his tent outside the town. One Englishman, named Smith, was also taken prisoner. He saw Sivaji in his tent ordering heads and hands to be chopped off, whenever he suspected that the trembling wretches had hidden away their money or jewels in some secret hoard.

Surat, the treasury of Sivaji.

For years afterwards the name of Sivaji was a terror to Surat. He often threatened to repeat the pillage, and forced large contributions from the inhabitants as the price of his forbearance. He called Surat his treasury. He annexed the intervening Bhíl country on the plea that he could not trust the Bhíl Raja with the key of his treasury.

Aurangzeb in Kashmír: fails to form a navy.

About 1665, Shah Jehan died in the palace at Agra, not without suspicions of foul play.[1] Aurangzeb had been suffering from serious sickness, but after his father's death he was sufficiently recovered to proceed to Kashmír, where he recruited his health in the cool air of the mountains. At Kashmír he attempted to form a fleet which should rival the navies of European countries. Two ships were built by the help of an Italian, and were launched on the lake of Kashmír; but Aurangzeb found that it would be difficult to man them efficiently. No amount of teaching would impart the necessary quickness, nerve, and energy to his own subjects; and if he engaged the services of Europeans, they

[1] The question of whether Aurangzeb was implicated in the death of his father Shah Jehan is treated in the larger *History of India*, vol. iv. chap. vii.

A.D. 1658-1707

might sail away with his ships, and he might never see them again.

Threatened by Persia.

About the same time, Aurangzeb was threatened by the Shah of Persia. Shah Abbas the Second was a warlike prince, and was suspicious of Aurangzeb's journey to Kashmír. He thought it portended some design upon Kandahar, which at this time was Persian territory. Aurangzeb sent an ambassador to the Shah, but the envoy was badly received, and publicly insulted. The Shah hated Aurangzeb for being a Sunní, and severely condemned him for his treatment of his father and brethren. He scoffed at the title which Aurangzeb had assumed of "Conqueror of the World"; and he threatened to march an army to Delhi. Aurangzeb was in the utmost alarm, when the news suddenly arrived that Shah Abbas had died of a quinsy brought on by excessive drinking.

Designs against Sivaji, 1666.

Meantime Aurangzeb returned to Delhi. In 1666 he resolved to be avenged on Sivaji for the plunder of Surat, and he planned a scheme for entrapping the "mountain rat." He professed to be an admirer of Sivaji, and publicly praised his exploits. He declared that if the Mahratta would enter his service, he should be appointed Viceroy of the Moghul Dekhan. Jai Singh of Jaipur was induced to believe that Aurangzeb was sincere, and was empowered to make the offer to Sivaji; but he was required to leave his son at Delhi as a hostage for his good faith in dealing with the Mahratta.

Plot and counterplot.

Vanity is a weakness with Orientals. The pride of Sivaji was flattered with the offer of the Great Moghul. In the reign of Akbar, Rajpút princes had been appointed Viceroys in Kábul and Bengal; and Sivaji may have asked himself—Why should not a Mahratta prince be appointed Viceroy of the Moghul Dekhan? It never crossed the mind of Sivaji that possibly he had been deceived; and he undertook the journey to Delhi in the utmost confidence that he would be appointed Viceroy of the Dekhan. But the suspicions of Jai Singh were awakened; he began to fear that Aurangzeb meditated some treachery; and, as he had pledged his faith to Sivaji, he wrote to his son at Delhi to look after the safety of the Mahratta.

When Sivaji reached Delhi, he soon discovered that he had been deluded. Instead of being praised and petted,

A. D. 1658-1707

he found himself neglected; and a long time elapsed before he was admitted to an audience. At last a day was fixed, and every one about the palace saw that unusual preparations were being made to astonish and overawe the Mahratta. Aurangzeb usually appeared in Durbar in white attire, decorated with a single jewel; and on such occasions he took his seat upon an ordinary throne.[1] But on the day that Sivaji was to be introduced to his notice, the Padishah entered the hall in a blaze of jewels, and took his seat on the peacock throne of Shah Jehan.

Sivaji at Delhi: the Durbar hall.

The Amírs and Rajas were railed off as usual in three compartments on three platforms, according to grades. The highest was of gold, the second of silver, and the third of marble.[2] Sivaji was admitted within the golden rail, but directed to take the lowest place on the platform. He saw that he was refused the rank of a Viceroy of the Dekhan, and could not contain his wrath and indignation. In spite of the pomp and ceremonial of the Durbar hall, and the barbaric pearls and gold of the Great Moghul, he loudly charged the Padishah with breach of faith, called the grandees above him cowards and women, and then left the platform and stalked out of the palace.

Wrath of Sivaji.

Every looker-on was expecting that Sivaji would be arrested and beheaded on the spot; but Aurangzeb listened to his tirade with perfect tranquillity; and nothing was to be seen upon his countenance except a malignant smile that played upon his lips when the Mahratta charged the grandees with cowardice. He sent one of his ministers to tell the wrathful prince that new comers were never placed in the front row; that he had not as yet been invested with the insignia of Viceroy of the Dekhan; and that the investiture would follow in due course, after which he would take the rank of his appointment.

Composure of Aurangzeb.

Sivaji feigned to be satisfied, but his eyes were opened to a new peril: he found himself a prisoner; a guard was

Flight of Sivaji.

[1] It is reasonable to suppose that Aurangzeb had religious scruples as to sitting on the peacock throne, seeing that such a figure savoured of idolatry, and was a violation of the injunctions of the Koran.

[2] It is doubtful whether the platforms were of gold, silver, and marble, or only the rails. In Jehangír's time the distinction turned on the colour of the rails, the highest grade in the empire being enclosed by a red rail.

A.D. 1658-1707

placed over his tent under pretence of protecting him against the offended grandees. At this very time it happened that the son of Jai Singh was mounting guard before the palace, and he discovered enough to warn the Mahratta that there was a plot to murder him. Sivaji had ample grounds for believing that it would be dangerous to remain longer at Delhi. What followed is involved in some mystery. According to the current story, Sivaji was carried outside the city walls in an empty fruit basket, and then made his way to Benares, disguised as a religious mendicant. All that is known for certain is, that after many months he reached the Konkan in safety. In September, 1666, the English merchants in India wrote home to the Directors of the East India Company, that if Sivaji had really escaped, Aurangzeb would soon know it to his sorrow.

Reasons for Aurangzeb's craft

It has always been a matter of surprise why Aurangzeb did not put Sivaji to death, without all this plotting and scheming. In plain truth he was afraid of an insurrection of the Rajas. Other Hindu princes, besides Jai Singh, had become sureties for the performance of Aurangzeb's promises. It was on this account that Aurangzeb assumed an unruffled demeanour in the Durbar hall, and plotted in secret for the assassination of Sivaji without exciting the suspicions of the Rajas. Fortunately his designs were discovered by the son of Jai Singh, and Sivaji escaped the trap which had been prepared at Delhi.

War against Sivaji.

Aurangzeb afterwards sent an imperial force of Muhammadans and Rajpúts against Sivaji. The Muhammadan army was under the command of his eldest son, Shah Alam. This prince was destined to play a part in history. His mother was a Rajpút princess, whom Aurangzeb had married when very young. The Rajpút army was commanded by Jai Singh of Jaipur.

Sham rebellion.

Aurangzeb gave his son Shah Alam secret instructions to feign a rebellion. The object was to discover what officers in the imperial army were disaffected towards the Padishah, and to induce Sivaji to join the pretended rebels, when he would be captured and beheaded. The result showed that all the officers, excepting one, were disaffected towards Aurangzeb, and ready to support the rebellion of Shah Alam. Jai Singh and the Rajpúts were especially enthusiastic in favour of Shah Alam, for they all hated Aurangzeb as a bigoted Sunní, and were anxious to place the son of a Rájpút mother on the throne of Hindustan. A.D. 1658-1707

Wariness of Sivaji.

Sivaji, however, was not to be ensnared a second time. His adventures at Delhi had taught him to be preternaturally suspicious of Aurangzeb. He professed to throw himself heart and soul into the cause of Shah Alam, but nothing would induce him to join the rebels. He told Shah Alam to go on and win the throne of Hindustan; he himself would remain behind and maintain the prince's cause in the Dekhan; and in the event of a failure he would keep an asylum open in the Konkan to the prince and his followers.

Explosion of the plot.

When Shah Alam saw that nothing would move the Mahratta from his purpose, he brought the sham rebellion to a close. Another imperial army appeared upon the scene to protect Shah Alam against the wrath of the officers whom he had deceived. The rebels saw that they had been deluded by Shah Alam; they saw moreover that they had been separated from each other, and that there was no way of escape. All the disaffected soldiers were drafted off to different provinces to serve under other generals. All the rebel generals were put to death or sent into exile. For some years the Rajas of Jaipur and Marwar disappear from history; but the Rana of Udaipur still maintained his independence in his secluded territories as in days of old.

Future rebellion rendered impossible.

But Aurangzeb had effected another object, which reveals the political craft of the Moghul. From the reign of Akbar downwards, the empire had been exposed to rebellion on the part of the eldest son of the Padishah. But the cunning of Aurangzeb had rendered such a rebellion impossible for the future. Henceforth Shah Alam found it impossible to revolt; neither Muhammadan nor Rajpút would trust him after his consummate treachery. Indeed, such was the general fear and universal distrust, that the chances of a successful rebellion were less during the remainder of the reign of Aurangzeb than at any former period in the history of Moghul India.

History prohibited, 1668.

In 1668 an edict was issued forbidding any one to write the history of the reign of Aurangzeb. The reason for this extraordinary prohibition has never been explained. Almost every Moghul sovereign has been anxious that his memoirs should be written and preserved to posterity; and Timúr, Báber, and Jehangír have left

A.D. 1658-1707

memoirs of their lives, ostensibly written by themselves. Possibly Aurangzeb was afraid lest current suspicions of his being implicated in the death of his father would be recorded in the popular histories of his reign. The consequence has been that the reign of Aurangzeb has hitherto been little known to history. The present narrative is based on the contemporary memoirs of Manouchi the Venetian, and a history written from memory many years afterwards by a Muhammadan named Khafi Khan.[1]

Turbulence in Kábul: massacre in the Khaibar Pass.

For some years the attention of Aurangzeb was drawn away from the Dekhan by the troubled state of the north-west frontier. The outlying province of Kábul was included in the Moghul empire, but was only nominally under Moghul rule. The Viceroy lived at Peshawar, and rarely, if ever, attempted to go further. About 1666 a Moghul army was collected on the frontier to oppose the Persian invasion; and when all danger was removed by the death of Shah Abbas, the Viceroy of Kábul led the army through the Khaibar Pass and entered the Kábul plain. No enemy was encountered, and want of supplies soon compelled the Moghul governor to retire towards Peshawar by the way he came. On re-entering the Khaibar Pass, the whole force was surrounded by Afghans, and literally cut to pieces. The Moghul governor escaped to Peshawar in the guise of an Afghan, but with the loss of all his troops and treasure.

Outbreak of Shuja: prince or impostor?

In 1672 there was a mysterious outbreak in Kábul. Shuja, the second brother of Aurangzeb, was supposed to have perished in Arakan some twelve years before. This year, however, a man appeared in Kábul, and declared himself to be the missing Shuja; and the Afghans accepted him as their Padishah. To this day it is impossible to say whether the man was, or was not, Shuja. It is certain, however, that the Viceroy at Peshawar believed him to be the real Shuja, and refused to interfere between Aurangzeb and his brother.

Aurangzeb takes the field.

The revolt in Kábul created the utmost alarm at Delhi. Aurangzeb took the field in person, and for the space of two years carried on operations against the Afghans, but effected nothing decisive. The Moghul army was still harassed by

[1] For particulars respecting these authorities, see the larger *History of India*, vol. iv. part ii.

the Afghans, and Shuja was still secure in the recesses of the mountains.

Treachery and massacre.

At last treachery was tried. Aurangzeb returned to Delhi, and a new Viceroy was sent to Peshawar. A policy of conciliation was adopted. The new Viceroy began to ingratiate himself with the Afghan chiefs, treated them as his friends, abolished imposts, and attended Afghan feasts without armed followers. At last he gave a grand entertainment at Peshawar to celebrate the circumcision of his eldest son. All the Afghan chiefs were invited, and a large number attended without fear or suspicion. There were horse-races, animal combats, wrestlings, and exhibitions of all kinds. The whole wound up with a banquet in a tented pavilion set up in the public square. In the midst of the banquet the Viceroy left the pavilion under pretence of having cut his hand. Immediately afterwards volleys of musketry were poured into the pavilion from the surrounding houses. The air was filled with cries of treachery and murder. There was no way of escape for the frightened guests, for all the avenues were guarded with armed men. How many were slaughtered, how many escaped, can never be told. The massacre spread weeping and wailing throughout Kábul. The Afghan nation was paralysed with terror and sorrow. The man calling himself Shuja fled away from the scene and was heard of no more.

Sivaji collects the Mahratta chout.

Meanwhile Sivaji the Mahratta was renewing his depredations in the Dekhan. All treaties or agreements were violated or ignored. He ravaged alike the territories of the Sultan of Bíjápur and those of the Moghul. He organised a regular system of blackmail, known for more than a century afterwards as the Mahratta chout. It amounted to a fourth part of the revenue of the land. So long as the chout was paid, the Mahrattas abstained from all robberies and devastations; but if the chout was withheld, the Mahrattas pillaged the country as before.

Installed as Maháraja, 1674.

The career of Sivaji at this period reveals the continued decay of the Muhammadan powers in India. The Sultan of Bíjápur was compelled to recognise Sivaji as the independent sovereign of the Konkan; and in 1674 Sivaji was installed as Maháraja with great pomp and ceremony, which have been duly described by English ambassadors from Bombay who were present on the occasion.

A.D. 1658-1707

Conquests in the Lower Carnatic.

In 1677 Sivaji conducted an army of Mahratta horse in a south-easterly direction through the kingdom of Golkonda, and invaded the eastern Peninsula. On this occasion he passed the neighbourhood of Madras, and was duly propitiated with cordials and medicines by the English merchants of Fort St. George. Ultimately he conquered a kingdom of an unknown extent in the country known as the Lower Carnatic, in the eastern Peninsula. This Mahratta empire in the Carnatic was represented down to modern times by the Raj of Tanjore.[1]

Death of Sivaji, 1680.

Sivaji died about 1680, having maintained his independence till his death. During the last two or three years of his life, the Moghul army of the Dekhan operated against him under the command of Shah Alam, but nothing was done worthy of note. Sivaji occasionally made extensive raids with his Mahratta horse, and carried off convoys of treasures and supplies, and escaped back safely to his hill fortresses. The Moghul generals did not care to climb the Western Ghâts, nor to penetrate the dangerous defiles; nor indeed did they want to bring the wars of the Dekhan to a close. So long as the wars lasted the Moghul commanders made large emoluments by keeping small forces in the field whilst drawing the pay for large numbers. At the same time they found no difficulty in squeezing presents and supplies out of the Sultans of Bîjâpur and Golkonda, who were especially anxious to save their kingdoms from invasion by propitiating the officers of the Great Moghul.

Projected conversion of the Hindus to Islam.

About this period, and probably ever since the massacre of the Afghans at Peshawar, Aurangzeb had been bent upon realising the great dream of his life—the destruction of idolatry throughout India, and the establishment of the religion of the Koran from the Indus to the Ganges, and from the Indian Ocean to the Bay of Bengal.

[1] The old empire of Karnata corresponded more or less to the Mysore country, the territory occupied by the Kanarese-speaking people. The area of the empire has often changed, whilst that of the language has remained the same. In the seventeenth century the empire had dwindled into a petty Raj, and then disappeared from history. The name, however, has been preserved to our own times. The whole of the Peninsula, or India south of the Kistna, has been divided between what is known in modern orthography as the Upper and Lower Carnatics; the Upper Carnatic comprising the western table-land, whilst the Lower Carnatic comprises the eastern plain.

A.D. 1658-1707

Policy of Aurangzeb.

The policy of Aurangzeb was directly opposed to that of Akbar. Instead of raising the Rajput princes to rank and influence, he sought to degrade them. Instead of permitting the followers of other religions to worship God their own way, he sought to force them into becoming Muhammadans.

Destruction of idolatry in Moghul India.

In the first instance Aurangzeb confined his operations to his own dominions. He began by destroying idols and pagodas within his own territories, and building up mosques in their room. He burnt down a great pagoda near Delhi. He converted a magnificent temple at Mathura into a mosque. He drove religious mendicants of every idolatrous sect out of Hindustan. He ordered the Viceroys of provinces to carry on the same work throughout the empire, in Bengal and the Dekhan as well as in Hindustan. At the same time he prohibited the celebration of Hindu festivals. He required all Hindu servants of the Moghul government to become Muhammadans under pain of losing their appointments. He imposed the Jezya, or poll-tax on infidels on all of his subjects who refused to become Muhammadans. Even English and Dutch residents in India were subjected to the same obnoxious impost; but they seem to have escaped payment by tendering presents to the Viceroy of the province in which they had established their respective factories.

Hindus dragooned into payment of Jezya.

It is difficult to ascertain the nature and extent of the resistance which the Hindus offered to these innovations. It is certain that bands of fanatics more than once rose in rebellion. On one occasion there was a dangerous rising near Delhi, which threatened the destruction of Aurangzeb as the enemy of gods and Brahmans. But Hindu fanatics, however numerous, could not withstand the Moghuls. Mobs of Hindus crowded the streets of Delhi between the palace and the mosque, and clamoured to Aurangzeb to abolish the Jezya; but they were trampled down and scattered by the elephants of the Padishah, and fled in terror and dismay. At last the Hindus seem to have submitted to their fate in sullen resignation. If the gods themselves could not prevent the destruction of idols and pagodas, why should their worshippers sacrifice their wives and families by refusing to pay Jezya?

Operations in Rajpútana.

Aurangzeb next attempted to introduce the same persecuting measures into Rajpútana; and for a while he seemed to carry his point. Jai Singh of Jaipur was dead; he is said

A.D. 1658-1707

Submission of Jaipur.

to have been poisoned after the sham rebellion of Shah Alam. There was no one to succeed him, for his eldest son was still kept as a hostage at Delhi. Accordingly Jaipur was compelled to submit, and the officers of the Moghul collected Jezya in Jaipur territory.

Compromise with Marwar.

Marwar (Jodhpore) was at first prepared for resistance. Jaswant Singh was dead, but his widow, a daughter of Shah Jehan, refused to permit the collection of Jezya. The Moghuls threatened to invade Marwar, and the heart of the princess failed her; and she compounded with Aurangzeb by ceding a frontier district in lieu of Jezya.

Demands on the Rana of Udaipur rejected.

The Rana of Udaipur had been left alone for a number of years, and seems to have recovered strength. The demands of Aurangzeb fell upon him like a thunderbolt; indeed they were so arrogant that it was impossible he could comply. He was to allow cows to be slaughtered in his territories; pagodas to be demolished; justice to be administered according to the Koran; and the collection of Jezya from all his subjects who refused to become Muhammadans. Possibly the first three demands were only made in order to bully the Rana into permitting the collection of Jezya; as it was, all four were refused.

Protracted wars.

The military operations which followed are very suggestive. It was the old story of Moghuls against Greeks; the hordes of High Asia against the Hellas of India. The Rana and his subjects abandoned the plains and took refuge in the Aravulli mountains. Three armies of the Moghul encamped at three different points under the command of three sons of Aurangzeb,—Shah Alam, Azam Shah, and Akbar. Not one, however, would venture to enter the dangerous defiles. Aurangzeb stayed at Ajmír with a small force awaiting the surrender of the Rana. In this manner the Moghul armies wasted their strength, energies, and resources before these natural fastnesses; and months and years passed away, whilst the submission of the Rana was as far off as ever.

Rebellion of Akbar supported by Rajpúts.

At this juncture Aurangzeb was aroused by the tidings that his third son Akbar had broken out in rebellion, and was already on the march to Ajmír. The dowager Ráni of Marwar was at the bottom of the mischief; she had repented of her compromise with the Moghul, and sent fifty thousand Rajpúts to enable Akbar to rebel against his father. At first Aurangzeb could not believe the story;

A.D. 1658-1707

but the same news reached him from other quarters, and he was at his wits' end. At last he sent a forged letter addressed to Akbar; but the messenger was to allow himself to be taken prisoner, and the letter was to fall into the hands of the general of the Rajpúts in the rebel army.

Forged letter: flight of Akbar.

The artifice was successful. The forged letter was captured and read by the Rajpút general. It told him that Aurangzeb and Akbar were in collusion, and that their only object was to destroy the fifty thousand Rajpúts. The Rajpút general remembered the sham rebellion of Shah Alam, and naturally thought that Akbar was playing the same game. At night he deserted Akbar with the whole of the Rajpút army, and hurried back with all haste to the city of Jodhpore. In the morning Akbar saw that all was lost, and fled for his life. After a variety of adventures he found a refuge in the Mahratta country.[1]

Moghul retreat from Rajpútana.

Aurangzeb was thus compelled to abandon his religious wars in Rajpútana, and to pursue Akbar into the Mahratta country, until by force or craft, he could secure the person of his rebel son, and place him in safe custody. The humiliation of Aurangzeb must have been extreme, but there was no remedy. The shame of the retreat from Rajpútana was partly veiled by a report that the Rana had sued for terms; but there was no disguising the fact that the Rana had successfully held out against the Moghul; and that Aurangzeb was compelled to leave the Rajpúts to worship their gods in peace, and to engage in other wars against the Mahrattas of the Konkan.

Splendour of the imperial army.

Aurangzeb concealed his disgrace from the public eye by a show of pomp and magnificence, which was remembered for generations afterwards. The progress of the Moghul army from Hindustan to the Dekhan resembled that of the Persian army under Xerxes. The cavalcade moved in three divisions, and the order of march may be gathered from the following outline.

Order of march.

A body of pioneers walked in front with spades and hods to clear the way. Then followed a vanguard of cannon, elephants loaded with treasures, carts laden with records and account books, camels carrying drinking water from the Ganges, provisions in abundance, cooks by hundreds,

[1] The details of the Rajpút war and Akbar's rebellion and flight are told at length in the larger *History of India*, vol. iv. part ii.

A.D. 1658-1707 wardrobes of dresses and decorations, and large masses of horsemen.

The Padishah. The approach of the Padishah was heralded by the appearance of smoking cauldrons of incense, which were carried on the backs of camels. Aurangzeb was next seen on an elephant, or on horseback, or in a rich palanquin. On either side were the imperial guards on horseback. After him came the ladies of the zenana on elephants with veiled howdahs. They were followed by flocks of other women and eunuchs on horseback, and numerous cannon drawn on wooden rafts.

Camp followers. The division in the rear comprised a motley host of infantry, camp-followers, sutlers, and servants, with spare horses, tents and baggage.

Aurangzeb in camp, 1682-1707. Aurangzeb continued in camp for the remainder of his reign. From the day of his retreat from Rajpútana, about 1682, until the day of his death in 1707, a period of twenty-five years, he never returned to Delhi. He was warned by the fate of Shah Jehan never to leave his army and live in a city. He was warned by the rebellion of his son Akbar never to trust any of his sons with a force superior to his own. Henceforth he spent his days in camp, wandering to and fro like his Tartar ancestors in the steppes of Asia.

Desultory wars: escape of Akbar. The details of the protracted wars of Aurangzeb would be distasteful to general readers. They furnish studies of character, but tell little of history, and still less of policy. Aurangzeb had a genius for treachery and intrigue; at the same time he had been zealous to root out all idolatry and establish the Koran as the religion of India. It is hard to reconcile such contradictions. Meanwhile none who knew him would trust his word. He tried to cajole Akbar by vows and promises; but the son refused to believe his father's oaths. The prince knew that if he surrendered himself to Aurangzeb he would be a prisoner for life, and perhaps might be blinded or poisoned.[1] In the end he escaped to Persia, where he died and was forgotten.

Aurangzeb made no head against the Mahrattas. He was baffled by an enemy, whose light horse scoured the

[1] This had been the unhappy fate of an elder brother, who had been induced to go over to Shah Shuja at the beginning of the reign, and then had surrendered to Aurangzeb. He perished miserably in the fortress of Gwalior.

open country for plunder, and then escaped to defiles and fastnesses where no one dared to follow them. Sivaji had been succeeded on the throne of the Konkan by a son named Sambhaji. After some years Sambhaji was betrayed to Aurangzeb, and put to a barbarous death. But peace was as far off as ever. The Moghuls could not conquer the Mahrattas, and would not comply with their demands for chout; and thus the Moghul army continued to carry on desultory wars throughout the remainder of the reign.

A.D. 1658-1707

Bootless operations against the Mahrattas.

Between 1686 and 1689 Aurangzeb conquered the Sultans of Bíjápur and Golkonda, and thereby converted their kingdoms into a Muhammadan province. The early Viceroys were called Nawabs and Subahdars, but later on were known as the Nizams of the Dekhan, having their capital at Hyderabad. The conquest is memorable, because it brought the Moghals into the Peninsula, and into close relations with the English at Madras. Otherwise the acquisition effected no change in the Moghul empire.[1]

Conquest of Bíjápur and Golkonda.

Aurangzeb was a very old man when he died in 1707, but there is some doubt as to his actual age. His life closed in weakness and disaster. His intolerance in matters of religion had brought the Moghul empire to the verge of ruin. Had he followed the policy of his ancestor Akbar, he might have extended his sovereignty over all the Hindu kingdoms of the Peninsula. But he had evoked a national spirit of resistance which he could not subdue; and when his years were ended, the Moghul suzerainty had lost its hold on Rajpút and Mahratta.

Revival of Hindu nationality.

From a Muhammadan and Sunni point of view, Aurangzeb was a great and good sovereign. He was zealous for the religion of the prophet, and a devoted follower of the Koran. He had no political sympathies for the Hindus; on the contrary, he was violently hostile towards them; and after he was firmly established on the throne he was consistent in the pursuit of this policy. There is reason to believe that, before he engaged in the unhappy war in Rajpútana, his administration was far superior to that of any of his predecessors, excepting possibly Akbar. He reserved to himself the sole right of passing capital

Able administration of Aurangzeb.

[1] Notices of the local history, so far as it affected the English at Madras, will be found set forth in the next chapter.

A.D. 1658-1707

sentences, and he took care that his orders were implicitly obeyed. Every day he received and studied the reports which he received from the Wakiahnawis, or court writers, as to what was going on in different parts of his dominions; and by these means he often acquired information which enabled him to check the corruption or oppression of the Viceroys of provinces.

Punishment of heinous criminals.

One instance will suffice. Amongst other abuses a strange practice had grown up in preceding reigns of permitting Hindus to acquire religious merit by ransoming condemned criminals. On one occasion some Banians had offered large sums to the Nawab of Surat for the release of certain professed stranglers, known as Thugs. But the arrest of the Thugs had reached the ears of Aurangzeb, and his orders were paramount. The Thugs were condemned to be hung in the jungle. The Banians accompanied them to the place of execution, and gave them tobacco and sweetmeats on the way. The hardened wretches knew their fate, but walked along as gaily as if going to a wedding. They were hung up by the left hand, their legs were cut off, and they were left to bleed to death in lingering agony.

CHAPTER VII.

MOGHUL EMPIRE: CIVILIZATION.

A.D. 1600 TO 1720.

A.D. 1600-1720

Condition of the masses ignored in Moghul history.

THE history of the reigns of Moghul sovereigns throws but little light upon the condition of the people. It brings out the individuality of successive monarchs; it familiarises the reader with court life in cities and camps; and it tells the story of intrigues, plots and treacheries. But it reveals little or nothing of the state of civilization which prevailed in India during the palmy days of Moghul rule.

Happiness of a people under bad rulers.

This lack of information is calculated to convey false ideas as regards the happiness or otherwise of the people. The character of the administration is confounded with that of the reigning sovereign; and if the Padishah is self-willed, self-indulgent, and vicious, like Jehangír or Shah Jehan, the conclusion is drawn that the administration is equally selfish and tyrannical, and regardless of the welfare of the masses. But this inference would be fallacious. The Padishah was certainly a despot; his will was law; and his influence was great for good or evil. The local Viceroys, especially during the reigns of Jehangír and Shah Jehan, may have been corrupt and grasping to the last degree. But the Moghul administration was not the handiwork of individuals or generations; it was the growth of centuries, kneaded into shape by the experience of ages, hedged around by checks which are not always visible to the historian, and controlled by the latent force of custom, habit, and public opinion, to which the most despotic princes and governors are occasionally compelled to bow.

The first element of civilization is free and easy com-

A.D. 1600-1720

Superior roads in the Moghul empire.

munication; and during the greater part of the seventeenth century this was by no means wanting in India. The roads and postal arrangements which prevailed throughout the Moghul empire during the reigns of Shah Jehan and Aurangzeb, were quite as advanced, if not more so, than those of France during the reign of Lewis the Fourteenth, or those of England under Oliver Cromwell and Charles the Second. Whether they were Moghul institutions of Tartar origin, or whether they were inherited from the great Hindu sovereigns of antiquity, such as Asoka or Síláditya, may be open to question; but the fact of the superiority of the means of communication throughout the Moghul empire in the seventeenth century remains the same.

Imperial road between Lahore and Agra, *viâ* Delhi.

The most famous road in India was that running from Lahore through Delhi to Agra, thus uniting the three great capitals of the Moghul empire. It was shaded with trees on either side, which are said to have been planted by every famous sovereign in turn—Moghul, Afghan, and Hindu. It was a continuation of the land route from Ispahan to Lahore, *viâ* Kandahar, Kábul, and Atok, which was open to merchants of all countries in the middle of the seventeenth century. Since then it has been closed against travellers generally, or at any rate against European travellers.

Roads from Agra to Bengal and the Dekhan.

Agra was thus the centre of the road system in India. On the north-west it was connected with Delhi, Lahore, Kábul, and Ispahan. On the south-east it ran through Allahabad, Benares, Patna and Dacca, and thus brought Agra into easy communication with Bihar and Bengal. On the south it was connected with the Dekhan by a road which ran to Golkonda, near the modern Hyderabad, *viâ* Burhanpur and Deoghur.

Roads between Surat and Agra.

Surat, the Moghul port at the mouth of Tapti, was an emporium of trade, and another centre of the road system. It was connected with Agra by two lines of road; one running near the coast, *viâ* Baroche, Baroda, and western Rajpútana; the other running more into the interior, *viâ* Burhanpur, Sironj and Gwalior.

Rough pathways.

These lines of route were not metalled roads like those of modern times. They were little better than rough pathways, often running through jungles, or over rivers and mountains. They were often so uneven that waggons were only kept from overturning by two ropes thrown across each waggon, and held tight by two men walking on either side. A.D. 1600-1720

Coaches drawn by oxen.

Natives generally travelled in a light coach with two seats, which was drawn by two oxen. Tavernier travelled in this way through the greater part of India. He carried his cloak, bag, mattress, and quilt on the spare seat; and a short supply of provisions and small vessel of wine in a box under the coach. Some travellers rode on oxen; but in that case it was necessary to see that their horns were not more than a foot long; for if the beast was stung by flies, he was apt to toss his horns back and gore the stomach of the rider.

Caravan-serais and serais.

But if the roads of Moghul India were as good as those of France and England, hotel accommodation was infinitely inferior. The excellence of English inns in the seventeenth century is duly extolled by Lord Macaulay. But in Moghul India there were no hotels properly so called; nothing but caravanserais and serais. Caravanserais were large commodious buildings constructed out of charity or ostentation, or for the protection of caravans against refractory Rajas. Here travellers found accommodation and shelter, but were obliged to procure all necessaries from the neighbouring bazar. Serais were mere enclosures, in which some fifty or sixty huts of mud and straw were surrounded by a fence or wall. There were men and women at these places, who sold flour, rice, butter, and herbs; and they also made it their business to bake bread, and boil rice. If there happened to be a Muhammadan at a serai, he would go to a neighbouring town and buy a piece of mutton or a fowl for a European traveller; but no flesh meat of any kind was procurable from the Hindus. The people who sold bread and boiled rice always cleansed a hut for the traveller to sleep in; and put in a little bedstead or charpoy, on which the traveller laid his mattress and quilt.

Inconveniences and dangers.

But travelling always had its inconveniences and dangers. In the hot weather the caravanserais were like ovens; in the winter nights they were often bitterly cold; whilst the smell of beasts and their drivers and the biting of ants and musquitoes were often intolerable. Sometimes the traveller met a caravan of several thousands of oxen, carrying grain or salt; and if the way was narrow he might be detained two

A.D. 1600-1720

or three days until the whole caravan had passed. Sometimes there was scarcity of water or provisions. Sometimes it was necessary to travel during the night, and rest in the day time, on account of the heat. If the traveller halted in a fortified town, he had to be careful to leave it before sunset, or he might find the gates shut for the night, and be detained anoth r day. The best way was to leave the city in the afternoon with the requisite supply of provisions, and rest under a tree, or some other shady spot, until it was cool enough to begin the journey. Again, there was always danger from wild beasts, such as tigers and panthers; and there was danger, especially in travelling through Rajpútana or Central India, of being attacked by brigands and highwaymen of various degrees.

Guards of horsemen.

Every European traveller found it necessary to hire from twenty to thirty horsemen, who carried bows and arrows, or else swords and bucklers. But robberies in general were compounded for by the payment of blackmail or transit duty, at so much a head, or at so much a waggon. Sometimes there was a wrangle ending in bloodshed; but if the traveller kept his temper the difficulty could generally be arranged. The brigands were not as a rule professed thieves, but Rajpút outlaws or rebels, so called Rajas, who were content to mulct a traveller or a caravan, and then would escort the party in safety through their respective territories. Sometimes Aurangzeb attacked one or other of these petty Rajas, and slaughtered him and his subjects. At one place was to be seen a tower full of windows, and a bleeding head in every window, as trophies of one of these massacres.

Thugs or stranglers, male and female.

There were, however, professional thieves, afterwards known as Thugs, who infested Guzerat, and especially haunted the Imperial high road between Agra and Delhi. They went about disguised as peaceful travellers, and made acquaintance with those they found on the way, and beguiled the time with pleasant conversation, until they all rested under a shady tree. Suddenly, at a signal from the chief, every Thug threw his noose round the neck of his allotted victim, and strangled him, rifled him and buried him, with a rapidity which defied detection. Sometimes a handsome damsel, with dishevelled hair, appeared sitting at the wayside, weeping and moaning over her misfortunes. Compassion and admiration might tempt a traveller to speak

A.D. 1600-1720

to her, but if so he was doomed. She soon had the noose round his throat, and either strangled him on the spot, or stunned him until her comrades came up and finished the work of murder.

Native grandees and dervishes.

Native grandees travelled in rich palanquins, lined with silk or velvet, and covered with scarlet or cloth-of-gold Sometimes they were accompanied by their wives and families, and attended by a large retinue of soldiers and servants, with led horses, elephants, and banners. Sometimes a Muhammadan dervish travelled in great state in like manner, surrounded by a crowd of disciples and followers.

Hindu saints: idols on pilgrimage.

Further south, outside the Moghul frontiers, a traveller might meet a famous Hindu saint or Guru, mounted on an elephant, or carried in a palanquin, surrounded by a host of religious mendicants. Sometimes a traveller met a pair of idols, male and female, going in grand procession on a pilgrimage to Ramisseram, or some other holy place, accompanied by Brahmans and dancing-girls, music and banners, and a nondescript gathering of worshippers of both sexes and all ages.

Absence of roads in Hindu kingdoms.

Travelling amongst the Hindu kingdoms of the Peninsula was more difficult than in Moghul India. In the Peninsula there were no roads at all, and all travelling was performed in palanquins, not only in the seventeenth century, but throughout the eighteenth, and during many years of the nineteenth. The palanquin-bearers of the Peninsula were generally strong men from the Telinga country, and they went at a faster rate than in any other part of India.

Manaris, or hereditary oxen-drivers.

The carrying trade of India was monopolised by a hereditary caste of oxen-drivers, known as Manaris and Brinjarries. Their caravans are described by Tavernier as consisting sometimes of oxen, and sometimes of waggons. They were to be found in all parts of India, from Comorin to Surat and Agra. They were a nomad race, dwelling in tents with their wives and families, and going about with their oxen and cattle, whom they loved like their own children.

Four tribes with caste marks.

The Manaris were divided into four tribes, each comprising about a hundred thousand souls, and each distinguished from the other three by a particular caste mark on their foreheads. Each tribe was devoted to the carriage of one or other of the four chief commodities of India,

A.D. 1600-1720

namely, corn, rice, millet, and salt: it carried its own particular commodity to the place where it was most wanted, but never dealt with the other three articles, nor followed any other avocation whatever. A caravan of oxen consisted of several thousand of those animals loaded on the back with the same commodity. A caravan of waggons consisted of one or two hundred large carts, each drawn by ten or twelve oxen, and attended by four soldiers, as already stated, to prevent it from being overturned.

Head man of the caravan.

Every caravan had its own chief, who affected as much state as a Raja, and wore a necklace of pearls. If the caravan of corn met the caravan of salt, there were fierce quarrels as to who should give way, which often ended in tumult and bloodshed. Aurangzeb is said to have attempted a reconciliation between the two, but it does not appear whether it was successful.

Women tattooed with flowers.

The women of the Manaris wore calico petticoats folded several times from their waists downwards; and they tattooed the upper parts of their bodies with flowers. They painted these punctures in various colours made from the juice of grapes, so that their skin appeared to be made of flowers.

Worship of the serpent.

Every caravan had its priests and idol. Every morning, whilst the men were loading their oxen, and the women were folding the tents, the priests set up a serpent in wreaths on a perch six or seven feet high in the most convenient part of the camp. Then all the people proceeded in files to worship this serpent, and the women walked three times round it. After the ceremony the priests took charge of the idol, and placed it on an ox which was set apart for the purpose; and the caravan set out on its daily journey to some new camping-ground.

Foot-posts in India.

The foot-post in India was another peculiar institution. Old travellers in India, from Roe downwards, make frequent mention of this foot-post. The several news-writers, or Wakiahnawis, sent their reports to the Padishah from the several cities of the empire by these runners. On every road, at an interval of six miles there was a kind of hut or post-office. Every runner that came up threw his letters on the floor of this hut, as it was a bad omen to give them into a man's hand. The runner appointed to go to the next stage picked up the letters, and set off at full speed. At night he was guided by the trees on either side of the road;

A.D. 1600-1720

and where there were no trees, heaps of stones were set up at every five hundred paces, and kept whitewashed by the inhabitants of the nearest village. The result was that the foot-post was swifter than a horseman; for at night the horseman was obliged to go slowly with a man carrying a torch on either side, whilst the foot-post ran on undeterred by darkness or storm.

Administration of justice: Nawab, Kází, and Muftí.

The administration of justice was much the same throughout the Moghul empire. It had been rather loose during the reigns of Jehangír and Shah Jehan, but had been kept under strict supervision by Aurangzeb. Every town had a Nawab or governor, who administered all civil justice, but left criminal cases to the Kotwal.[1] The Nawab was assisted by a Kází, who was supposed to be learned in Muhammadan law; and there was always a Mullah or Muftí, who superintended all matters pertaining to the Muhammadan religion.

Civil administration by the Nawab.

The Nawab generally rendered speedy justice. If a man sued another for a debt, he had either to show an obligation, or produce two witnesses, or take an oath. If he was a Christian he swore on the Gospels; if a Muhammadan he swore on the Koran; and if a Hindu he swore on the Cow. Many Hindus, however, preferred to lose their cause rather than swear, as they had a strong aversion to such a ceremony.

Kotwals of towns: criminal jurisdiction.

The Nawab left all criminal affairs to the Kotwal. This was the most important official next to the Nawab. The Kotwal discharged the functions of magistrate and judge, and was also head of the police and superintendent of the prison. He ordered criminals to be whipped or cudgelled in his presence, either in his own house or at the place where the crime had been committed. He went abroad on horseback, attended by several officers on foot; some carrying batons and great whips; others carrying lances, swords, targets, and iron maces; but every man had a dagger at his side. At night he paraded the streets, and set guards at different places; and any man found abroad

[1] There is some confusion in the use of Moghul titles. The Viceroy of a province was commonly known as a Subahdar. The Governor of a town or district was properly a Nawab; and such a Nawab was in general subordinate to the Subahdar of the province. Sometimes the Foujdar assumed the title of Nawab, and the Nawab assumed the title of Subahdar.

A.D. 1600-1720

in the streets was committed to prison, and rarely released without being whipped or bastinadoed.

Foujdars of districts.

Whilst the Kotwal maintained peace and order in the town, an officer known as the Foujdar carried out the same duties in the surrounding country. The Foujdar exercised the same authority in the district that the Kotwal exercised in the town.

Travels of Fryer, 1673-1681.

Dr. Fryer, a surgeon in the service of the East India Company, travelled in India between 1673 and 1681, and has left some graphic descriptions of India at a time when Sivaji was harassing the Dekhan, and Aurangzeb was preparing for his persecuting wars in Rajpútana.

Masulipatam on the coast of Coromandel.

Dr. Fryer went in the first instance to Masulipatam, a port on the coast of Coromandel, near the mouth of the river Kistna. It was an emporium of trade on the coast of Coromandel, just as Surat was an emporium on the coast of Malabar. But Surat belonged to the Great Moghul, while Masulipatam belonged to the Sultan of Golkonda, who had not as yet been conquered by Aurangzeb.

Streets and houses.

Masulipatam was a favourable type of a Muhammadan city in India. The principal streets were broad, and the buildings good. The better sort of houses were built of wood and plaster, having balconies with latticed windows, and a stately gateway below leading into a square court with a tank in the middle, and a terrace walk all round it. The poorer sort of houses were mere huts, like thatched beehives, walled round with mud.

Muhammadan supremacy.

The Muhammadans at Masulipatam kept a strict hold on the Hindus, entrusting them with no place of importance, but treating them as mechanics and serving-men. The richer sort lived in great splendour, priding themselves upon having a numerous retinue and handsome followers. They were grave and haughty, taking great delight in sitting cross-legged on chairs at their doors, and smoking their hookahs with much pomp and circumstance. They cloistered up their women from the eyes of all men. Sometimes a woman went abroad in a palanquin, but she was always closely veiled, and it would have been death for any man to attempt to see her face.

Hindu women.

The Hindus had no such strictness. The Hindu women went abroad in the open air, adorned with chains and earrings, jewels in their noses, and golden rings on their toes.

A.D. 1600-1720

Festivals.

The people celebrated their festivals, and especially their weddings, with much show and splendour. They were commonly performed at night with the noise of drums, trumpets, and fifes. The poorest Hindu, except amongst artificers and low-caste men, had a week's jollity at his marriage; going about in a palanquin, attended by guards carrying swords, targets, and javelins, whilst others bore ensigns denoting the honour of their caste. But if any low-caste man attempted the like, he was dragged back to his quarters by the hair of his head.

Barbarous executions

The administration of justice at Masulipatam was barbarous in comparison with that in the Moghul's territories. Capital sentences were carried out immediately after conviction, and the offender was either dismembered or impaled. In cases of murder the nearest kinsman of the murdered person was required to prosecute the offender and to execute him. He began to cut the murderer to pieces, and then the rabble rushed in and finished him.

Madras: White town and Black town.

Dr. Fryer sailed from Masulipatam to Madras, about three hundred miles to the south. In 1639 the English had bought a strip of coast territory from one of the Hindu Rajas of the Peninsula. It was only six miles long and one mile inland, but it is famous as being the first territorial possession which the English acquired in India. Here they built a factory, and raised a wall round it mounted with cannon, and gave it the name of Fort St. George. In a few years two towns had grown up in the neighbourhood outside the wall. The one was occupied by Armenians and other foreign merchants, who were glad to live under the protection of the English. The other was a larger village or town of weavers and other artisans who were mostly in the employ of the English merchants. None but Europeans lived in the fort, which was known as White town; whilst the Armenian and native quarters went by the general name of Black town. The whole settlement was known as Madras, but the origin of this name is unknown.

Yearly rent to the Sultan of Golkonda.

Some years afterwards the Sultan of Golkonda pushed his conquests southward into the Peninsula. The Hindu Raja, who sold the land to the English, fled away to the westward and disappears from history. The generals of the Sultan tried to capture Madras, but were baffled by the guns of Fort St. George. The English, however, agreed to pay

A.D. 1600-1720

the Sultan the same rent which they had previously paid the Raja, namely, twelve hundred pagodas per annum, or about five hundred pounds sterling.

Portuguese and French.

The generals of the Sultan captured the neighbouring Portuguese settlement at St. Thomé, and carried off the guns from the fortifications. The Portuguese fled to Fort St. George, and were welcomed by the English, as adding to the strength and security of their settlement. About this time a French fleet appeared off the coast and took possession of St. Thomé. These little wars are forgotten now, but created no little excitement when Fryer visited the place.

Crossing the surf.

Fryer was paddled over the surf at Madras by one of the same kind of native boats that are still in use. It was not fastened by nails, which would have been wrenched out by the surf; but the timbers were sewn or tied together with strings. These strings yielded to the surf, and passengers were carried in safety, but the boats were apt to take in a good deal of water.

Fort St. George: streets and houses.

Fryer landed in wet clothes, but the beach was so scorching hot that he hurried on to the town. Fort St. George presented an imposing front to the sea. It was oblong, about four hundred yards in length from north to south, and one hundred yards in depth from east to west. At each corner of the walls was a bastion mounted with guns, and the banner of St. George waved bravely over the whole. The streets inside were neat and clean. There were about fifty houses, not very lofty, because it was a garrison-town; but every house had an Italian portico, battlements on the roof, and a terrace walk, and there was a row of trees before the doors. There were no public structures, except the Governor's house in the centre, and a small chapel where the Portuguese celebrated mass.

Sir William Langhorn, Governor.

Sir William Langhorn was Governor of Madras, and superintended all the English factories on the coast of Coromandel, as well as those on the Húghli and Ganges as far as Patna.

Population.

The English population of White town scarcely numbered three hundred souls. The Portuguese numbered three thousand. The native population of Black town and adjoining villages, included thirty thousand Hindus in the service of the Company; but there were hardly forty

Muhammadans in the whole settlement. The country round about was sandy, but provisions were plentiful. A.D. 1600-1720

Bombay: magnificent harbour.

Fryer next sailed from Madras to Bombay. He passed by the coast of Malabar, and noted that the Dutch were already ousting the Portuguese from their ports at Cochin and elsewhere; and that Sivaji, a rebel against the Sultan of Bijápur, had conquered the country round about Goa. At last he entered the harbour of Bombay. It was a magnificent bay, capable of holding a thousand of the finest ships of European build.

Gardens and terraces turned into ramparts.

Bombay had been made over to the English some ten or twelve years before, as part of the dowry of Catherine of Portugal, on her marriage with Charles the Second. The English found a government house, having a pleasant garden with terrace walks and bowers; but the place was so poorly fortified, that the Malabar pirates often plundered the native villages, and carried off the inhabitants as slaves. The English soon altered this state of things. They loaded the terraces with cannon, and built ramparts over the bowers. When Fryer landed, Bombay castle was mounted with a hundred and twenty pieces of ordnance, whilst sixty field-pieces were kept in readiness. Only a few months before his arrival, the Dutch had tried to capture Bombay, but were forced to retire. The place, however, was very unhealthy. The site was unwholesome, and the air was bad; and these evils were aggravated by the intemperance of the English settlers.

Surat in the reign of Aurangzeb.

From Bombay Fryer went to Surat. The place was much changed since Della Valle's visit. It swarmed with fakírs, and there were marks on all sides of the intolerant rule of Aurangzeb. No Christian could appear in the streets of Surat in good clothes, or mounted on a proper horse, without being assailed by Muhammadan beggars. The Muhammadans lived in good houses as at Masulipatam. The Banians, or Hindu brokers, lived in wretched sheds, with three or four families crowded into one hovel, together with goats, cows, and calves. But they had good reason for what they did, for if any one was suspected of being rich, he was squeezed by the Nawab of all his effects, unless he had secured the protection of some powerful grandee.

The poorer inhabitants were entirely at the mercy of

A.D. 1600-1720.

Artisans oppressed.

the Nawab and his soldiers. They were often taken from their occupations and forced to work for the Nawab. Sometimes these seizures led to broils, and artisans were driven to desperation, and murdered their families and then ran "amok."

Flight of Hindus.

Aurangzeb had already begun to collect the Jezya at Surat. The Hindus were pressed to become Muhammadans. The neighbouring Rajas were in rebellion. Many Hindus fled from Surat to Bombay, or to one of the Portuguese settlements. This was all the more remarkable to Fryer, because, as he writes, if the Hindus united against the Muhammadans, they would be as a thousand to one.

Visit to Joonere, 1675.

In 1675 Fryer left Surat and returned to Bombay. About this time the Nawab of the town of Joonere required a European doctor to attend on one of his wives. The Moghuls had captured the fort and town of Joonere from the Mahrattas, and the place was a bone of contention between the two. Fryer readily undertook the journey to the town of Joonere, although it was one of some danger. The country was desolate; the people were wretched to the last degree, being plundered alike by Moghuls and Mahrattas, and reduced to utter poverty and starvation. Even the coolies from Bombay that carried Fryer's luggage pitied the misery of the inhabitants, and contrasted it with their own prosperous lives under British rule.

Medical attendance in a zenana.

Fryer met with some adventures at Joonere. He was not allowed to see the sick lady until the astrologers had fixed on a fortunate day for his visit. At last he was shown into a room where there was a bed surrounded with a curtain, and the hand of the patient was placed outside the curtain to enable him to feel her pulse. To his great surprise, the pulse was that of a perfectly healthy woman; and he did not fail to say so. No one, however, was disconcerted; in fact, a healthy maidservant had been placed in the bed to test the skill of the English doctor. After due explanation, Fryer was permitted to feel the pulse of the sick lady, and he subsequently effected a cure by bleeding. The consequence was, that other ladies demanded to be bled likewise, but it was doubtful whether they had any other object in view beyond satisfying their curiosity as regards the English doctor.

Meanwhile Fryer had many discourses with the Nawab

A.D. 1600-1720

of the town of Joonere. He discovered that the Moghul generals had no desire to conquer Sivaji, or to put an end to the wars in the Dekhan. So long as the war lasted, they made much money by keeping small bodies of troops in the field whilst drawing the pay of large numbers.

Discourses with the Nawab.

The Nawab of the fortress of Joonere also desired to see the English doctor. In all Moghul cities the Nawab of the fortress had a separate command from the Nawab of the town. The visit was of little moment beyond revealing the inside of a Moghul fortress. The place was of some historical importance, as Sivaji had been born within the walls, and was anxious to recover possession of the stronghold. There were enough provisions stored within the fortress to support a thousand families during a seven years' siege, but there was no ammunition except stones, and two misshapen brass pieces of Hindu mould.

A Moghul fortress.

The Nawab was a Brahman who had been converted to the Muhammadan religion. He secretly agreed to surrender the fortress to Sivaji, and received an enormous bribe as a reward; but when the day arrived and seven thousand Mahrattas ascended the hill, they found themselves cut off by an ambuscade, and were all slaughtered. Such treacheries were by no means uncommon in olden times.

Nawab a converted Brahman.

Fryer next visited the town of Karwar, to the south of Goa, where the English had a factory. The town had been recently conquered by Sivaji; but the factory was safe, for the English kept off all assailants by means of the guns which they had planted on their factory walls.

English factory in Sivaji's territory.

Sivaji's government at Karwar resembled that of the Moghuls. He appointed one governor to the town, and another to the fortress; whilst a general with a flying army superintended the whole. Sivaji appointed none but Brahmans to places of trust or authority. These men professed to be mightily jealous for their master's dues; but they always managed in a corner to get more for themselves than for their master. Trade was impossible in Sivaji's country, unless goods could be carried a long way round as at Karwar. The people bitterly complained of exactions and torture; but that was the same all over India; and even Brahmans were subjected to the same pains and indignities whenever it was supposed that they had buried their wealth, or concealed it in some other secret fashion.

Sivaji's government.

A.D. 1600-1720

Troubles in Madras: 1690-1700.

Fryer left India in 1681. Nine years afterwards, in 1689-90, Aurangzeb conquered Bijápur and Golkonda, and sent his armies into the Peninsula. The English of Madras at once offered to pay the Moghul the same yearly rent of twelve hundred pagodas, which they had paid the Sultan of Golkonda; but the Moghuls threatened to dismantle Fort St. George of all its cannon. The whole country was in a troubled state, and the English at Madras were often disturbed by alarming rumours. At last it appeared that the Nawab of the conquered territories would be satisfied with a money bribe; and a present of ten thousand pagodas, equivalent to about four thousand pounds sterling, was sent to the Nawab Zulfikar Khan. The present was graciously received, and the Nawab was further mollified by timely supplies of provisions and ammunition.

Wars between Moghuls and Mahrattas in the Lower Carnatic.

All this while desultory wars were being carried on in the Lower Carnatic between the Moghuls under Nawab Zulfikar Khan and the Mahrattas under Ram Raja, a younger son of Sivaji.[1] The once celebrated hill fortress of Jinjí, about eighty miles to the south-west of Madras, was the bone of contention between Zulfikar Khan and Ram Raja. But the story of the struggle is tedious and bewildering. There were intrigues and treacheries on both sides, and also secret understandings between the two, which excited the suspicion and rage of Aurangzeb, when he was too old and helpless to interfere.

Siege of Madras by the Moghuls, 1701-2.

In 1701-2 another Nawab, named Dáúd Khan, succeeded Zulfikar Khan. He, too, demanded a present of ten thousand pagodas from the English merchants at Madras. Mr. Thomas Pitt, grandfather of the great Earl of Chatham, was Governor of Madras, and he resolutely refused to pay the money. Dáúd Khan surrounded Fort St. George with a large force, cut off all supplies of provisions, and stopped all trade. Mr. Pitt held out for three months, and then deemed it expedient to pay up the amount. He consoled himself with the idea that the Nawab had expended a great deal more than ten thousand pagodas during the siege of the place, and was never likely to repeat the demand.

After this remarkable siege matters quieted down at

[1] Ram Raja had taken possession of the Mahratta dominion in the Peninsula, when his eldest brother Sambhaji had succeeded to the kingdom of the Konkan.

Madras. The yearly rent was regularly paid to the Nawab, and presents were occasionally sent to the Nawab and his grandees. The result was that for a period of thirty years after the death of Aurangzeb, the English at Madras bought and sold, and pursued the even tenor of their way, without interference or hindrance from Mahratta or Moghul.

A.D. 1600-1720

Peace at Madras, 1707-46.

Meanwhile the English settlements in Bengal, after a hard struggle with the Moghul's officers, had become the most important and profitable in India. As far back as 1640 in the reign of Shah Jehan, the English had been allowed to establish a factory at Hughli, about a hundred miles from the mouth of the Ganges, where they hoped to succeed to the trade which had been erewhile carried on by the Portuguese. They founded branch factories at Patna, Dacca, and other half-forgotten localities. From Patna they procured saltpetre, opium, raw silk, and cotton piece-goods. From Dacca they obtained those fine muslins which were long the wonder and admiration of the civilized world. The result was that the English settlements in Bengal were withdrawn from the control of the Governor of Madras, and placed under a separate governor, a Mr. Job Charnock, who soon became one of the most distinguished Englishmen in India.

English settlements in Bengal: Hughli, Patna, Dacca.

But the English traders in Bengal were unable to protect themselves with fortifications and guns as they had done at Madras and Bombay. In Madras they had built Fort St. George and mounted their cannon before the Muhammadans had entered the Peninsula; and consequently they were enabled to set the Moghul generals at defiance. Again, their cannon on Bombay castle sufficed to keep off the Mahrattas. But Bengal had been in the possession of the Moghuls ever since the reign of Akbar, and they had suffered too much from the fortifications and cannon of the Portuguese at Hughli to permit of any such formidable settlements for the future. The English, Dutch, and French, all had factories in the neighbourhood of Hughli; but neither were allowed to build any walls or semblance of fortifications of any sort or kind. Neither were they allowed to carry on any hostilities against each other within the territories of the Moghul; and thus whilst wars might be raging between English and Dutch, or English and French, in other parts of the world, the conflicting nationalities were compelled to keep the peace in Bengal.

Fortifications and cannon prohibited in Bengal.

A.D. 1600-1720

Moghul oppressions.

During the bigoted reign of Aurangzeb, the English in Bengal were subjected to oppressions and exactions, which had been unknown in the tolerant days of Jehangír and Shah Jehan. An attempt was made to collect Jezya from the English, but that was warded off by timely presents to the Nawab. In other ways the English were exposed to insults which were beyond all endurance; and at last, as a crowning indignity, Mr. Job Charnock, the Governor of all the English settlements in Bengal, was arrested and scourged by order of the Nawab.

English declare war against the Moghul, 1685.

Under these circumstances the English declared war against the Moghul. In 1685 two squadrons were sent out by James the Second; the one to cut off all Moghul ships trading with Surat, and the other to operate against the Nawab of Bengal. The factory at Surat was removed out of Moghul territory to the new settlement at Bombay. The English in Bengal collected all their goods from their several factories, and prepared to carry them to Chittagong, the frontier port towards Arakan.

Successful operations off Surat: peace concluded, 1687.

The operations of the squadron off Surat were most successful. Cargoes belonging to the subjects of the Moghul were captured to the value of a million sterling. The merchants of Surat would no longer venture on voyages at sea; whilst native manufactures were at a stand-still, and mechanics were thrown out of employment and complaining loudly of famine. Aurangzeb sent officers to listen to the grievances of the English, and mitigate the oppressions to which they had been exposed. A treaty was concluded in 1687, under which the English were permitted to return to their factories, and guaranteed certain rights and privileges which they had hitherto been denied.

Ill-judged operations in Bengal: flight to Madras, 1689.

The operations in Bengal had been ill-judged and not altogether successful, but still they had sufficed to alarm the Nawab. The war was brought to a close for a while, but Charnock had no faith in the treaty and hesitated to return to Hughli. Meanwhile the commander of the English squadron, a hot-headed captain named Heath, was provoked by the delays and evasions of the Nawab. He opened up a communication with the king of Arakan, and sailed to Chittagong with the view of capturing the port for the king. Finding the fortifications stronger than he expected, he returned to Bengal, and offered to undertake an expedition against Arakan in behalf of the Nawab. Suddenly, however, he took disgust at the proceedings of the Nawab, and sailed away to Madras with all the Company's merchants and goods, declaring that he had been told nothing but lies on all sides.

A.D. 1600-1720

Alarm of the Nawab.

This conduct, crazy and irregular as it was, brought the Moghul government to reason. It was imagined that the contempt displayed by Heath arose from the determination of the English to abandon the trade of Bengal. A new Nawab was appointed to Bengal, and he sent pressing overtures to Madras for the return of the English to Hughli.

Return of the English: Calcutta founded, 1690.

The result was that Charnock and the English went back to Bengal, but they did not return to their factory at Hughli. Ultimately they were allowed to rent three villages about twenty miles nearer the mouth of the river; and all duties and customs of every kind were commuted by the yearly payment of three thousand rupees to the treasury at Hughli. The newly-acquired territory was scarcely half the size of the English territory at Madras. It only extended three miles along the eastern bank of the river Hughli, and one mile inland, and paid a yearly rent of 1195 rupees. But the three villages have become historical. Their names were Chutanutti, Govindpore, and Kalighát. They were the nucleus of the city of Calcutta, which after the lapse of two centuries is now the capital of the British Empire in India and the greatest European city in the eastern world.

Memories of Job Charnock.

Mr. Job Charnock is still regarded as the patriarch of Bengal. His name still survives in the station of Barrackpore, which is called "Chanuk" by the natives to this day. Many stories have been told of his eccentricities, which were household words in a bygone generation. He saved a young Hindu widow from burning herself with her deceased husband, and subsequently married her; but instead of converting her to Christianity, he relapsed into a kind of paganism. She died before him, and ever afterwards he celebrated the anniversary of her death by sacrificing a cock to the goddess Durgá over her tomb.

Rebellion of Hindus in Bengal.

Towards the end of the seventeenth century the persecutions of Aurangzeb, the destruction of pagodas, and subversion of Hindu worship, drove many of the people of Bengal into rebellion. The Europeans complained to the Nawab

A.D. 1600-1720

Fortification of Calcutta, Chandernagore, and Chinsura.

of the unprotected state of their factories. He told them to defend themselves, and they took him at his word. They ran up walls and bastions round their respective factories, and planted them with cannon; and this was the origin of the three European forts or towns, namely, the English at Calcutta, the French at Chandernagore, and the Dutch at Chinsura. Both Chandernagore and Chinsura were in the neighbourhood of Hughli, and consequently about twenty miles from Calcutta.

Houses and people of Calcutta, about 1720.

A few years after the death of Aurangzeb, a Captain Hamilton visited Calcutta, and has left a description of the houses and English inhabitants. He says that the town was built without order, every one selecting a spot best fitted for a garden; consequently most houses had a garden in front. The English built their houses near the river side; but the natives dwelt more inland. Most gentlemen and ladies in Bengal lived splendidly and pleasantly. They dedicated the forenoon to business; they then took their dinners and retired to rest during the afternoon. In the evening they found recreation in chaises and palanquins in the fields or gardens; or went upon the river in budgerows, and diverted themselves with fishing or fowling. Before night they made friendly visits to one another, when pride and contention did not spoil society; but the Captain adds, that much social rivalry often existed amongst the ladies, just as discord and faction prevailed among the men.

Garrison at Fort William.

The garrison at Fort William generally consisted of two or three hundred soldiers, but they were not so much employed for the defence of the settlement, as to guard the fleet coming from Patna with the Company's saltpetre, piece-goods, raw silk, and opium. Captain Hamilton remarks, that the English Company held their colony direct from the Moghul, and consequently had no reason to be afraid of any enemies coming to dispossess them. At the same time he predicted that if they again declared war against the Moghul, the Padishah would soon end the quarrel by prohibiting his subjects from trading with them.

Refractory Rajas.

But Bengal was only half conquered by the Moghul. There were, says Hamilton, some impertinent and troublesome Rajas on the banks of the Ganges, between the Nawab's capital at Murshedabad and the city of Patna, who pretended to tax all goods passing through their territories, and often raised forces to compel payment. But a detachment of European troops from Fort William generally cleared the passage up the river, although some of the English soldiers were occasionally killed in the skirmishes. A.D 1600-1720

From the death of Aurangzeb in 1707, to the year 1756, Calcutta was occasionally threatened by the Mahrattas or mulcted by the Nawab; but otherwise it enjoyed a profound peace, and was, to all appearance, as secure against foreign aggression as any seaport town in the United Kingdom. The English settlement was like an oasis of European civilization in a desert of Hinduism and Islam. The English factory, with its depôts, workshops, offices, and outlying "garden-houses," covered about a hundred acres on the bank of the Hughli. The outward life of the English at Calcutta was altogether of a business type. They bought, sold, kept accounts, wrote letters, and regulated establishments and expenditure. Large ships from Europe brought woollen goods, cutlery, iron, copper, and quicksilver. The same ships carried away cotton piece-goods, fine muslins, silks, indigo, saltpetre, spices, and Indian rarities. A rise or fall in the price of saltpetre in Europe was of more interest to the English merchants at Calcutta than the war between the Moghul and the Mahrattas; and a failure of the silk crop in the up-country stations in Bengal and Behar was of more moment to the Court of Directors in London than the death of a Padishah, or the bloody struggles between his sons for the succession to the Moghul throne. Peace: 1707-56.

CHAPTER VIII.

MOGHUL EMPIRE: DECLINE AND FALL.

A.D. 1707 TO 1748.

A.D. 1707-1712 — Excitement at the death of Aurangzeb.

THE death of Aurangzeb awakened the Moghul empire from its torpor; it sent a thrill through the provinces which might be likened to galvanic life. For years all hopes and aspirations of princes and grandees had been in abeyance under the declining but monotonous rule of the aged Padishah. His sons were waiting for his last breath to begin that fratricidal struggle for the throne which had broken out at the death, or before the death, of every Moghul sovereign of Hindustan from Akbar downwards. The Moghul generals were apparently eager to throw off the religious strictness and bigotry, which had so long oppressed the empire; and were looking forward to the death of the old Padishah as a necessary preliminary to the beginning of a new *régime.*

Fears of the dying Padishah.

The last years of Aurangzeb were saddened by fears of the catastrophe which would accompany or follow his death. Indeed throughout the latter half of his reign he had been subject to constant alarms lest he should share the fate of his father, Shah Jehan; lest his sons should consign him to hopeless captivity, and begin to fight for the throne before death had carried him from the scene. He is said to have formed a plan for averting a fratricidal war by dismembering the empire and dividing it amongst his three sons. But if so the attempt at pacification must have proved a failure. Scarcely was it known that the old sovereign had expired, than all the armies of the empire were on the move, and his three sons were each, in turn, prepared to seize the throne by force of arms, or perish upon the fatal field.

A.D. 1707-1712

Fratricidal war: reign of Bahadur Shah, 1707-12.

A war between brethren may excite the passions of contemporaries, but cannot enlist the sympathies of posterity. The struggle between the sons of Shah Jehan had been more or less associated with religion, but the struggle between the sons of Aurangzeb was only a quarrel for an inheritance. The main struggle was between Shah Alam, the eldest son of Aurangzeb, and Azam Shah, the second son; and the war itself is said to have turned on the ill-timed insolence of Azam Shah, and the consequent disaffection or treachery of his affronted generals. A desperate battle was fought near the river Chambal. It closed in a horrible carnage, in which Azam and his two sons were slain. Shah Alam ascended the throne under the title of Bahadur Shah. There was a third son, the rebel Akbar, who had fled to Persia; but he was dead, or at any rate out of the fray. There was a fourth son named Kam Bakhsh, whose fortunes demand separate consideration.

Destruction of a Christian Sultan.

Kam Bakhsh, whom the Greeks would have called Cambyses, had been nominated by Aurangzeb to rule as an independent Sultan over the newly-conquered kingdoms of Bijápur and Golkonda. Bahadur Shah was an old man, and would probably have consented to the arrangement; but his sons were ambitious to preserve the integrity of the empire. The mother of Kam Bakhsh was a Christian; her son was supposed to be a Christian likewise. The Mullahs were stirred up to protest against the rule of a Christian Sultan; and Bahadur Shah was driven to work the destruction of his youngest brother.

Relations between Delhi and Madras.

The course of events had a remote bearing upon the fortunes of the English at Madras. Bahadur Shah ordered letters to be written to Mr. Thomas Pitt, the Governor of Madras, to prevent the young prince from escaping by sea into Persia. At the same time Bahadur Shah confirmed all the rights and privileges which had been granted to the English by his father Aurangzeb. But these precautions proved unnecessary, for Kam Bakhsh was defeated and slain on the field of battle by Nawab Zulfikar Khan.

Bahadur Shah reigned from 1707 to 1712, but has left no mark in history. He had, in the first instance, to face a rebellion of the Rajpúts in Jaipur and Marwar. The

A.D. 1707-1712

Revolts in Rajpútana and the Punjab.

persecuted Hindus had taken advantage of the death of Aurangzeb to drive out all the Muhammadan officers who had been appointed to collect Jezya, and convert the people to the religion of the Koran. The movement was a revolt of Hinduism against the proselytizing policy of Aurangzeb, and Bahadur Shah was anxious to suppress it; but at this moment alarming news arrived from the north-west. The Sikhs had broken out in revolt in the Punjab, and committed a series of murderous excesses; and Bahadur Shah was compelled to "forgive" the Rajpúts, and march with all haste to Lahore.

Formation of the Sikh brotherhood by Nanuk Guru, about 1500.

The Sikhs originally were not a nationality. They were a mixed community of Rajpúts, Játs, and other races, who had been formed into a religious brotherhood about the end of the fifteenth century by a famous prophet named Nanuk Guru. Their religious faith was a combination of the tenets of advanced Shíahs with those of advanced Hindus; it turned upon the worship of the Supreme Spirit, as the deity alike of Muhammadans and Hindus. At the same time the Sikhs reverenced Krishna and Ráma as incarnations of Vishnu; they recognised the sacred character of Brahmans; and they strictly prohibited the slaughter of cows. Above all, they implicitly obeyed their Guru and his successors, as the representatives of God upon earth; and they regarded the teachings of each in turn as the inspirations of the Supreme Being.

Persecutions of Aurangzeb: execution of Guru Govind.

Such a religion was naturally regarded as a detestable heresy by a strict Sunní like Aurangzeb. The Sikhs were persecuted until they betook themselves to the northern mountains, and formed military clans distinguished by a blue dress and peculiar manners. The fires of persecution raged more fiercely than ever. Guru Govind, the tenth in descent from Nanuk,[1] saw his strongholds taken, his mother and children massacred, and his followers slain, mutilated, or driven into painful exile. At last Guru Govind was taken prisoner by the Moghuls, and executed at Gwalior by the command of Aurangzeb.[2]

[1] The secular name of this Guru Govind was Tugh Bahadur. Further particulars of the Sikhs will be furnished hereafter in dealing with the British wars against the Sikhs and final conquest of the Punjab.

[2] Another story says that Guru Govind was assassinated by an Afghan.

A.D. 1707-1712

Vengeance of the Sikhs under Bandu Guru.

Such severities exalted the fanaticism of the Sikhs to the highest pitch of desperation. A new spiritual leader, known as Bandu Guru, inspired them with a spirit of vengeance against their persecutors. They broke out in revolt, destroyed mosques, butchered Mullahs, and massacred the population of whole towns without regard to sex or age. In a word, they fought to the death for God and their Guru; but they also made their religion a cloak for plunder and outrage of every kind.

Operations of Bahadur Shah: his death, 1712.

Bahadur Shah found it necessary to make Lahore his capital, and to carry on a series of desultory wars against the Sikhs. The details are of no moment; it was impossible to dragoon the Sikhs into submission, and they continued to give trouble down to the death of Bahadur Shah in 1712, and indeed for many years afterwards.

Sahu, Maharaja of the Mahrattas, a vassal of the Moghul, 1707-48.

Meanwhile the greater part of the Moghul empire had been left in the hands of the Viceroys of provinces. Little or nothing is known of the history, beyond the fact that some kind of understanding seems to have been concluded by the Viceroys of Guzerat and the Dekhan with the Mahrattas of the Konkan. When Sambhaji, son and successor of Sivaji, was arrested and put to death by Aurangzeb, his little son Sahu, or Shao, was carried away prisoner by the conqueror, and brought up in the zenana of the Moghul. After the death of Aurangzeb, this boy was placed on the throne of the Konkan, in the city of Satara, and was supposed to reign over the Mahratta kingdom as a vassal of the Great Moghul.

Mahratta claims to chout.

But this arrangement could not possibly satisfy the Mahratta claims to chout or black mail, which extended indefinitely over a great part of the Dekhan, as well as over a large extent of Guzerat and Malwa to the northward. These claims were of a most vexatious character, and were pressed with a pertinacity which was deaf to all arguments. To admit them involved the loss of one-fourth of the land revenue, whilst it abandoned large cultivated tracts to the rude collections of Mahratta soldiery. To resist them was as hopeless as an attempt to resist the depredations of locusts. The loose bands of Mahratta horse were here, there, and everywhere. If driven off by the advance of regular troops, they might disappear like a flock of crows; but they soon reappeared elsewhere, ravaging the country

A.D. 1707-1712

with fire and sword to enforce the Mahratta claims to chout over the whole extent of territory.

Brahman element in the Mahratta constitution.

The constitution of the Mahratta government was such that Maharaja Sahu had little or no voice in the matter. It had been the policy of Sivaji to keep all offices of state, and all collections of revenue, exclusively in the hands of Brahmans; and as all these posts became hereditary according to Hindu custom, Maharaja Sahu found himself surrounded by a Brahmanical hierarchy, ostentatious in its professions of submission and obedience to the grandson of the great Sivaji, whilst practically retaining all the power of the state in its own hands.

Effeminate training of Maharaja Sahu.

Moreover, the personal character of Maharaja Sahu was favourable to the Brahman ascendancy. He had neither capacity nor energy for breaking through so powerful an aristocracy. His grandfather Sivaji was bred like a mountain eagle amidst the rude independence of hills and jungles. But Maharaja Sahu was a tame bird, brought up in the gilded cage of the imperial zenana. He was given to pleasure, with some taste for field sports; somewhat touchy as regards his personal dignity; proud of his vassalage to the Great Moghul, although occasionally indulging his fancy with schemes of conquest and empire. The Brahman ministers and officials well knew how to deal with these weaknesses. They invariably treated him with every possible respect, and took care that every measure of state should appear to emanate from himself, and be carried out solely in his name as the supreme sovereign of the Mahrattas; but at the same time they moulded him to suit their own purposes, and thus prepared the way for that revolution at his death which transferred the Mahratta sovereignty from the grandson of Sivaji to the family of the Brahman minister.

Rise of the Peishwas: secret agreement with Moghul Viceroys.

The chief Brahman minister was known as the Peishwa; and during the reign of Maharaja Sahu, the Peishwa for the time being was to all intents and purposes the ruling power. It was the Peishwa who issued commissions to the different Mahratta leaders to collect chout in Guzerat, Malwa, and the Dekhan, in the name of Maharaja Sahu. It was the Peishwa who concluded secret arrangements with the Moghul Viceroys, under which certain yearly payments were made to the Mahrattas on the condition that they made no attempt to collect chout for themselves, and

A.D. 1712-1713

duly kept within a certain line of frontier. The precise terms of this agreement were necessarily kept in the dark; for at this period the Moghul court would have refused to sanction any arrangement which implied the payment of tribute to the Mahrattas.

Fratricidal war of 1712.

The death of Bahadur Shah in 1712 was followed by another fratricidal war; but the Moghul princes were men without force of character, and indeed were little better than puppets in the hands of ambitious generals. After the usual round of treachery and carnage, a debauched young prince, named Jehandar Shah, was placed upon the throne at Delhi; but all real power was exercised by Zulfikar Khan, the Moghul general, who had been Viceroy of the Dekhan in the reign of Aurangzeb, and who had defeated and slain the youngest son of Aurangzeb at the accession of Bahadur Shah.

Reign of Jehandar Shah, 1712-13: a low drunkard.

Jehandar Shah was a drunkard, who chose his favourites from the dregs of society. Zulfikar Khan was a respectable grandee, who sought to wield the destinies of the empire under the name of prime minister. There naturally followed a struggle for power between the besotted Padishah and the ambitious minister. But the reign was too scandalous to last. The vices of Jehandar Shah were not confined to the recesses of the zenana, but were paraded before the lower orders, and became the common talk of the bazars. Suddenly his headlong career was arrested by the news of a dangerous rebellion in Bengal.

Rebellion of Farrukh Siyar and the two Saiyids.

A young prince, named Farrukh Siyar, a grandson of Bahadur Shah, had been left in Bengal during the fratricidal war which followed the death of Aurangzeb. By strange good fortune Farrukh Siyar had escaped the massacre of princes which accompanied the rise of Jehandar Shah; but still he was in constant peril of his life, and was thus prepared for any desperate measure. When the reign of Jehandar Shah became a scandal to the empire, the minds of men began to turn towards Farrukh Siyar. Two Moghul brothers, known as the two Saiyids, or descendants of the prophet, resolved to head a righteous rebellion in the name of Farrukh Siyar; to depose the debauched sovereign who disgraced the empire, and to place Farrukh Siyar on the throne of Delhi, and govern the empire in his name.

The two Saiyids were men of some standing. One was

the governor of Patna, and the other was governor of Allahabad. By their help, a force was collected, and the two Saiyids began to march to Delhi accompanied by Farrukh Siyar. Numbers joined them on the way. Zulfikar Khan took the field and advanced towards Agra, accompanied by Jehandar Shah; but the young Padishah was an arrant coward, and fled back to Delhi, leaving the imperial forces to be defeated in the neighbourhood of Agra. The cause of Farrukh Siyar triumphed; and the two Saiyids conducted him to Delhi amidst the acclamations of the multitude.

Flight of Jehandar Shah: triumph of Farrukh Siyar, 1713.

Assassination and massacre.

Zulfikar Khan tendered his submission to the two Saiyids, and was received with every mark of favour, but was treacherously assassinated on leaving the tent. Jehandar Shah was put to death, as well as many others who were likely to interfere with the accession of Farrukh Siyar. The new Padishah then ascended the throne of Delhi amidst the firing of cannon and thunder of kettledrums, and was at once accepted by all parties as sovereign of the Moghul empire.

Reign of Farrukh Siyar, 1713-19: intrigues against the two Saiyids.

Farrukh Siyar reigned from 1713 to 1719. From the first he engaged in a series of intrigues for throwing off the yoke of the two Saiyids, and ruling the empire as irresponsible sovereign without check or hindrance. The elder Saiyid, Abdulla Khan, filled the post of minister at Delhi. The younger Saiyid, Husain Ali Khan, was sent to restore the Moghul supremacy in Rajpútana, which had been in a disaffected state ever since the death of Aurangzeb. At the same time it was hoped that by separating the two brothers, by keeping the one at Delhi and sending the other to Rajpútana, it might be possible to effect their destruction.

Shameless treachery of the Moghul court.

The Moghul court had always been pre-eminent for craft and treachery; but during the struggles between Farrukh Siyar and the two Saiyids, there was an utter absence of scruple or shame. Rajpútana had been virtually independent ever since the death of Aurangzeb. Even the border territory of Jaipur, which intervened between the Moghul's territories and the more remote kingdoms of Udaipur and Marwar, had thrown off the Muhammadan yoke, and repudiated all connection with the Moghul court at Delhi. A Rajpút prince, a kinsman of the old royal house, ascended the throne as Raja of Jaipur, and was prepared to set the Moghul suzerainty at defiance so long as the Moghul armies refrained from invading his territories. A.D. 1713-1719

Plots against Husain Ali Khan.

In the first instance Husain Ali Khan was sent to reduce the Raja of Jaipur to obedience. Meanwhile secret letters were sent by the Padishah to the Raja, encouraging him to hold out against the Moghul troops, and instigating him to do his utmost to effect the destruction of Husain Ali Khan. The Jaipur Raja was bewildered by these contradictory proceedings, but was at last reduced to submission, and induced to give his daughter in marriage to Farrukh Siyar.

Intrigues respecting the Vice-royalty of the Dekhan.

Husain Ali Khan discovered the treachery which had been practised upon him as regards the Jaipur Raja, but deemed it expedient to become reconciled to Farrukh Siyar. It is said that this reconciliation was brought about by the mother of Farrukh Siyar; but it would be sheer waste of time to inquire too closely into the intrigues which were at work in the Moghul court. Soon afterwards Husain Ali Khan encountered still more flagrant treachery. In order to keep him at a distance from his elder brother, he was appointed Viceroy of the Dekhan, and ordered to proceed to his new government. At this time Dáúd Khan, the same man who besieged Governor Pitt at Madras, was Viceroy of Guzerat. Dáúd Khan was openly instructed, by letters from the minister Abdulla Khan, to meet Husain Ali Khan on his way to the Dekhan, and pay implicit obedience to his orders. At the same time Dáúd Khan was secretly told, by private letters from Farrukh Siyar, that if he could effect the destruction of Husain Ali Khan, he would receive the viceroyalty of the Dekhan as his reward. The result was that Dáúd Khan strengthened his army by enlisting a force of Mahrattas. When Husain Ali Khan came up, instead of a friendly greeting there was an obstinate battle. The Mahrattas did nothing, but scoured about the plain on horseback, and kept aloof from the fighting until the action was over. Meanwhile Dáúd Khan would have gained the victory, but in the moment of triumph he was shot dead by a musket-ball. His Mahrattas at once went over to the army of Husain Ali Khan, tendered their submission, and then began to plunder the camp of Dáúd Khan.

A few glimpses of Delhi at this period are to be derived from the correspondence of an English mission which was sent from Calcutta to Delhi in 1715, and remained more

A.D. 1713-1719

English mission from Calcutta to Delhi, 1715-17.

than two years at the Moghul capital. The mission was undertaken to secure certain trading privileges from the Great Moghul, and is chiefly remarkable for the delays and evasions of ministers and courtiers. The presents sent by the English merchants at Calcutta were received with great favour by the Padishah and the leading grandees; and the English ambassadors received so many promises of goodwill and patronage, that they wrote cheerful letters to Calcutta, saying that they were sanguine of obtaining all they wanted. When, however, they began to ask for firmáns setting forth the privileges to be granted, so many difficulties were raised on all sides that they began to despair of obtaining any firmáns at all.

Story of Dr. Hamilton.

Meanwhile, an English surgeon named Hamilton, who accompanied the mission to Delhi, had been fortunate enough to heal Farrukh Siyar of a troublesome disease; and the Padishah was willing to show his gratitude by granting a firmán of privileges. But Farrukh Siyar refused to part with the doctor; and the doctor was thrown into a painful fright; for he had a wife and family in England, and was horrified at the idea of spending the rest of his days in gilded exile at Delhi.

Sudden close of the mission.

Suddenly, after a delay of two years, all difficulties were removed. The English had found it convenient to remove their old factory at Surat to their more important settlement at Bombay. This trifling event spread a terror through the Moghul court. The older grandees remembered that the factory at Surat had been removed to Bombay just before the disastrous war of 1686; and they were in mortal fear lest the repetition of the measure should be followed by the reappearance of English men-of-war in the eastern seas. The requests of the English ambassadors were granted with surprising promptitude; even the English doctor was permitted to depart after pledging himself to return with a supply of medicines at an early date;[1] and the mission returned to Calcutta with firmáns of new rights and privileges duly signed and sealed.

Troubled state of Delhi.

The English mission were impressed with the pomp and power of the Great Moghul, but they saw many signs of disturbance at Delhi. The marriage of Farrukh Siyar with the Jaipur princess was celebrated with illuminations and

[1] Dr. Hamilton died shortly after his return to Calcutta. His tombstone is still to be seen inscribed with a record of his services.

fireworks: but the plots for securing the destruction of Husain Ali Khan were widely known. About the same time a Tartar army broke out in mutiny, and the troops were clamouring for their arrears of pay in the streets of Delhi.

A.D. 1713-1719

Wholesale executions of Sikh rebels: a martyred Guru.

Meanwhile the Sikhs were signally defeated in the Punjab, and Bandu Guru was taken prisoner and conducted to Delhi amidst a horrible procession of eight hundred Sikh prisoners doomed to death, and two thousand bleeding heads borne on poles. The executions that followed were ghastly and sickening. The Sikh prisoners were beheaded at the rate of a hundred a day. The captive Guru was clothed in mock robes of state, and exhibited with an infant son in an iron cage. The child was butchered before his eyes, and he himself was tortured to death with hot pincers. But Bandu Guru perished in the glory of martyrdom, exulting in the dream that he had been raised up by God to scourge the sins and oppressions of the age.

Doom of Farrukh Siyar, 1719: massacre of Mahrattas.

In 1719, about a year after the English mission left Delhi, the reign of Farrukh Siyar was brought to a tragical close. Abdulla Khan, the minister, found that his life was in danger, and summoned his brother from the Dekhan. Husain Ali Khan marched to Delhi with an army of Mahrattas, and excited a universal terror. Then followed a night of horror. The army of Abdulla Khan surrounded the palace, whilst the Mahrattas were supposed to keep order in the city. The most alarming reports spread through Delhi. It was said that Abdulla Khan had been murdered in the palace by the Raja of Jaipur. Next it was rumoured that the Mahrattas were plundering the city; and the mob of Delhi rose against the Mahrattas, and slaughtered large numbers, and found so much gold in their saddle-bags as to increase the general alarm.

Assassination and revolution.

Next morning the uproar was over. The trembling Padishah had been dragged from the zenana amidst the screams of women, and thrown into a dungeon and deprived of eyesight; and it was soon known that he had been strangled to death by the bowstring. Meanwhile, an infant prince was taken out of the state prison of Selimghur, which adjoined the palace, and placed upon the throne of the Moghuls. The firing of cannon, and thundering of the imperial kettle-drums at the gate of the palace, announced that Farrukh Siyar had ceased to reign, and that another Padishah was sovereign of the Moghul empire.

A.D. 1719-1738

Infant Padishahs.

It soon transpired that the two Saiyids had assumed the supreme direction of affairs in the name of an infant sovereign. Three months afterwards the infant died, and another young boy was taken out of the state prison and set upon the throne. But the reign of the new puppet was shorter than that of his ill-starred predecessor. In a few weeks he too was hurried to the grave by some insidious disease.

Reign of Muhammad Shah, 1719-48.

A healthier youth was now taken out of the prison, and enthroned under the name of Muhammad Shah. He was destined to reign for a period of nearly thirty years; to witness the mortal blow from Persia which shook the Moghul empire to its foundations; and to leave his successors to be the alternate prey of Afghans and Mahrattas.

Plots against the two Saiyids.

Muhammad Shah ascended the throne as the puppet of the two Saiyids; but by this time a strong party had been formed against the brothers. The succession of three pageant Padishahs within a few brief months had opened the eyes of the leading grandees to the dangerous ambition of the Saiyids, and raised up a host of enemies who were resolved on their downfall.

Fall of the Saiyids.

The two brothers were aware of the secret combinations formed against them, and laboured hard to defeat their designs. Abdulla Khan remained at Delhi to carry on the duties of prime minister. Husain Ali Khan returned to his viceroyalty in the Dekhan, and carried the young Padishah with him as a precautionary measure. But there was treachery in the camp, and a savage Kalmuk agreed to strike the fatal blow. He presented a petition to Husain Ali Khan, and whilst the latter was reading it, the Kalmuk stabbed the Viceroy to the heart. The dead body rolled out of the opposite side of the palanquin. The Kalmuk was cut to pieces by the Viceroy's guards. But Muhammad Shah placed himself at the head of his friends, and his appearance put an end to the confusion and restored order. The army returned to Agra, and thence began the march to Delhi. Abdulla Khan marched out an army to revenge the death of his brother, but found it useless to contend against the revolution. His forces were utterly defeated; his life was spared; but the power of the Saiyids was gone for ever.

Triumphant return of Muhammad Shah to Delhi.

Muhammad Shah entered Delhi with all the triumph of a conqueror. He was received by his mother and ladies of the zenana with all the pomp and ceremonial that accom-

A.D. 1719-1738

panied the installation of Moghul sovereigns. He took his seat upon the great throne; the imperial insignia were displayed on either side; basins of gold coins and jewels were waved around him; and to all outward appearance he began to reign with all the magnificence of a Jehangír or Shah Jehan. But the energies of the imperial rule were already in rapid decay; the life-blood of the empire was ebbing away; and the blaze of splendour which heralded the elevation of Muhammad Shah to the sovereignty was but an empty show to veil the decline of the empire.

Decay of the Moghul empire.

The signs of dissolution must have been already evident to those who could see beneath the surface of things. The Moghul court was torn by factions which could no longer be suppressed by the frown of the Padishah, and which not unfrequently broke out in open broils. The removal of Viceroys from one province to another, which had been so frequent under the despotic rule of Jehangír, Shah Jehan, and Aurangzeb, had become of rare occurrence; for an order for removal, under a weak sovereign like Farrukh Siyar or Muhammad Shah, might have been met by a formidable rebellion which would have engulfed the empire.

Cessation of the imperial progresses.

One sign of weakness was more significant than all the others. The imperial camp was no longer to be seen moving from Hindustan to the Punjab, or from Hindustan to the Dekhan, keeping Sikhs and Rajpúts in awe, and carrying the prestige of the Great Moghul to every part of his dominions. During the reigns of Farrukh Siyar and Muhammad Shah, the Padishah was little better than a pageant confined to the palace; and his progresses in camp were little more than hunting expeditions in the immediate neighbourhood of Delhi.

Latent force of court routine.

Yet still the administration moved on in the well-worn grooves of long-established routine, although much of the vitality of power had passed away. No Viceroy or Subahdar of a province was legally in possession of his post until he had received letters and insignia of investiture from the Moghul court at Delhi; and this simple procedure preserved the prestige of Moghul suzerainty for generations after the authority of the Padishah had dwindled into an empty name.

During the reign of Muhammad Shah a Subahdar might die, and his son might succeed to the post by an assumption

A.D. 1719-1738

Successions to local governments.

of hereditary right, which would have been ruthlessly denied by Aurangzeb or his predecessors; but even during the last years of the empire the succession had no validity or weight in the eyes of the masses until the letters and insignia had been received from Delhi. The same might be said of the subordinate Nawabs of outlying territories. A Nawab might be appointed by a Subahdar, and be succeeded on death by his eldest son; and it will be seen hereafter that this was the case with the Nawab of the Carnatic, under the Nizam or Subahdar of the Dekhan; but neither the original appointment, nor the succession of the son, could be considered legal and secure until letters and insignia had arrived from Delhi with the seals of the empire. The consequence was that a Viceroy never failed to send presents and promises to the Padishah and grandees, to secure the recognised succession of a son or near kinsman; and whenever a Viceroy died every candidate for the government was equally profuse in presents and promises in the hope of securing his own recognition to the exclusion of all others.

Padishah, the sole fountain of honour, rank, and title.

All this while the Padishah was still the sole fountain of all honour, rank, and titles throughout the empire. These rewards were so largely coveted that grandees were often ready to sacrifice the greater part of their wealth in order to obtain them. They were never hereditary, but they elevated the grandee for the time being above his fellows in the eyes of the whole court, and were thus always received with the utmost pride and gladness of heart. Many a Subahdar or Nawab, driven to the verge of rebellion by insult or neglect, has been brought once again within the pale of loyalty and devotion by the receipt of an empty title and a dress of honour from the Great Moghul.

Provincial Dewans, or Accountants-General.

A curious anomaly of the Moghul constitution was the appointment of a Dewan, or financial accountant-general, to every province of the empire. It was the duty of this officer to receive all collections of revenue, to pay all salaries, including that of the Subahdar or Nawab, and to devote his whole attention to the remission of the largest possible yearly balance to the imperial treasury at Delhi. In the reign of Aurangzeb the Dewan had been regarded as the most important officer in the province. The duties of the Subahdar or Nawab had been confined to the maintenance of the public peace and the administration of justice; and all revenue questions had been left to the Dewan. At the same time the Dewan received his appointment direct from the Padishah, and was altogether independent of the Subahdar or Nawab; and by his zeal in the collection of revenue, and remission of the largest possible amount as the Padishah's share, he might hope for promotion or reward.

A.D. 1719-1738

General corruption at court and in the provinces.

During the decline of the Moghul empire, the greediness for rank and titles led to a general corruption in the court and provinces. The grandees grew rich whilst the imperial revenues dwindled year by year. Presents to the ministers, courtiers, and chief ladies of the zenana became of more importance than the remittance of the yearly revenue to the imperial treasury. There were collusions between the Subahdar and the Dewan, and by dint of bribes and presents the two appointments were sometimes given to two different members of the same family, and sometimes were doubled up in the same officer. The result was a growing independence amongst the Subahdars and Nawabs of provinces; a growing tendency on the part of those officers to retain their several governments as the hereditary right of their respective families; a growing disregard to the orders received from the court at Delhi, and a determination to govern their respective provinces according to their own irresponsible will.

Ostentatious reverence to the orders of the Padishah.

Strange to say, whilst there was a general loosening of the tie which bound the Viceroys of provinces to the Moghul court, the tie itself was on all occasions ostentatiously displayed before the multitude. Every Viceroy of a province acted as though he believed that his authority derived its sole lustre and security from its subordination to that of the Great Moghul. Whenever the imperial firmáns, orders, or letters of any description arrived from Delhi, the Subahdar or Nawab went out with all his officers in grand array to receive the documents with every demonstration of respect and honour; to place the imperial commands upon his forehead in token of his profound submission to the will of the Padishah; and to announce the coming of the imperial messengers with a salute of artillery, and every mark of devotion and loyalty.

The richest province of the empire, or that which sent

A.D. 1719-1738

Bengal provinces: isolation of the Nawab.

the largest yearly revenue to the Padishah, was the one which included the outlying territories of Bengal, Behar, and Orissa. But the Nawabs of the Bengal provinces played no part in the history of the empire. They lived to the eastward of the river Carumnasa, and had little or no concern with the Moghul court, beyond remitting the yearly revenue to Delhi.

Two great men of the empire.

The two most important officers in the empire were Saádut Ali Khan, who was Subahdar of Oude; and Chín Kulich Khan, better known by his title of Nizam-ul-mulk, who was Subahdar or Nizam of the Dekhan.[1] The history of these two men is typical of the condition of the Moghul empire during the reign of Muhammad Shah, and thus demands separate consideration.

Saádut Ali Khan, Subahdar of Oude, a Persian Shíah.

The province of Oude in those times included not only modern Oude, but the vast area of fertile territory extending from Benares to Agra, which is comprised in the present day under the general term of North-west Provinces. Saádut Ali Khan was a Persian and a Shíah. He was of low extraction, having been originally a cotton merchant of Khorasan; but by a strange destiny he had become Viceroy and practically sovereign over the greater part of Hindustan, and was the ancestor of the later kings of Oude, who like him professed the religion of the Shíahs.

Nizam-ul-mulk, Subahdar of the Dekhan, a Turk and Sunní.

Nizam-ul-mulk was a rival in race and religion, a Turk and a Sunní. He belonged to what was called a Turanian family, as distinguished from the Iranian, or Persian stock. His early history is obscure, but he and his father before him are said to have held important commands in the reign of Aurangzeb.

Peril in the reign of Jehandar Shah.

During the scandalous reign of Jehandar Shah, the proud spirit of Nizam-ul-mulk had nearly worked his own downfall. Whilst proceeding through the streets of Delhi, his way was impeded by one of the worthless parasites of the hour; a woman who had formerly sold fruit and garden stuff in the vegetable market, but had become the sworn friend of a

[1] Chín Kulich Khan subsequently received the honorary title of Asof Jah, which, according to Muhammadan tradition, was the name of the minister of Solomon. But though he is often called Asof Jah he is best known by the title of Nizam-ul-mulk, or "regulator of the state," given to him on the accession of Farrukh Siyar; and as his successors, the Nizams of Hyderabad, are named after this title, it will be preserved throughout the present volume.

A.D. 1719-1738

dancing-girl who was the ruling favourite of Jehandar Shah. This woman was proceeding to the palace on an elephant, accompanied by a numerous retinue; and as she passed she poured out a torrent of abuse on Nizam-ul-mulk. It is said that the proud Turk gave a signal to his retainers; but whether he did or no, the men dragged the woman from her elephant and maltreated her in the presence of the mob. The woman threw ashes on her head, and hurried off to the palace to demand vengeance from the favourite dancing-girl. Meanwhile Nizam-ul-mulk went to the house of the prime minister Zulfikar Khan, and told him the whole story. The two men were not friends, but Zulfikar Khan saw the necessity for supporting his fellow-grandee against the insolence of the favourite. Accordingly he wrote on a slip of paper "I throw in my lot with that of Nizam-ul-mulk;" and sent the writing to Jehandar Shah. The paper proved to be a sufficient warning for the young Padishah; he saw that revenge was out of the question, and nothing more was heard of the matter.

Jealousy of the Saiyids.

At the accession of Farrukh Siyar, the two Saiyids made much of Nizam-ul-mulk, gave him the title and appointed him Subahdar of the Dekhan. Subsequently they grew jealous of him and transferred him to the government of Malwa between the Chambal and Nerbudda, whilst Husain Ali Khan was appointed Subahdar of the Dekhan between the Nerbudda and Kistna.

The Nizam secures the Dekhan.

After the assassination of Husain Ali Khan, Nizam-ul-mulk crossed the Nerbudda with an army, and took possession of the government of the Dekhan, defeating every commander who was secretly sent to overthrow him, whilst still retaining a paramount influence in Malwa and Guzerat.

Growing power of the Mahrattas: policy of the Brahman Peishwas.

All this while the Mahrattas were the pest of the empire, the horror of the Moghul court, the terror of the Moghul Viceroys of provinces, and the especial enemies of Nizam-ul-mulk. The first Peishwa, Balaji Visvanath, died in 1720, and was succeeded in the post of minister by his son Baji Rao, who is always described as the ablest Mahratta Brahman of the time.[1] The policy of both father and son was to secure the continued recognition of Maharaja Sahu as the vassal of the Great Moghul; to enforce the Mahratta claims

[1] Compare *ante*, p. 206.

A.D. 1719-1738 to chout throughout the Dekhan, Malwa and Guzerat; and to keep the loose bands of Mahratta horsemen, which might prove dangerous to the Brahman government at Satara, continually employed at a distance from the capital. These ends both Peishwas in turn had sought to attain by issuing commissions to different Mahratta leaders to collect chout in all directions in the name of Maháraja Sahu.

Designs against the Moghul empire.

The policy of the Peishwas throws much light upon the political genius of the Mahratta Brahmans. They did not care to create a Mahratta empire with well-defined frontiers. They preferred exercising the right of interference over a large and undefined part of the Moghul empire, and collecting chout under the plea of affording protection and security in return.

Ascendancy over Mahratta military leaders.

The Peishwa parcelled out the right of collecting chout amongst different military leaders in every district, in such a way, that whilst each leader had an interest in increasing the contributions to the general stock, no one had a compact property to render him independent of the Brahman court at Satara. Moreover, by dividing the revenue into innumerable fractions, it threw the military leaders into the hands of Brahman accountants; and thus strengthened the power of the Peishwa by increasing the influence of the caste of Mahratta Brahmans to which he belonged.

Importance of Mahratta history.

Mahratta history has thus an importance which has never been recognised by historians. It illustrates the struggle for political power between the caste of priests and that of soldiers which is the life and soul of ancient history. Glimpses of this struggle are furnished by the annals of Hebrews and Egyptians, but they are obscure and blurred. Mahratta history reveals every secret working in the battle between intellect and brute force, which ended in the triumph of the Brahman. In like manner the after history will tell of the revolt of the military leaders against the Brahman ascendancy, until the power of the Peishwas was reduced to a pageant by Lord Wellesley.

Rise of the Gaekwar, Sindia, Holkar, and the Bhonsla.

It was during this early period of the Brahman ascendancy, that the Mahratta commanders, mostly men of low caste, began to rise to the rank of predatory powers. The family of the Gaekwar of Baroda came to the front in Guzerat; the families of Sindia and Holkar established a hold in Malwa; and the Bhonsla family, the same clan to which

Sivaji belonged, established a dominion in Berar in the Dekhan to the northward of the dominions of the Nizam.

A.D. 1719-1738

Dependence on the Peishwa.

But during the supremacy of the Brahman Peishwas these leaders were little more than military puppets in the hands of the central power at Satara; they were in fact officers of the Peishwa, commanding divisions of his troops, and acting under his commission. It was not until many years afterwards, when the power of the Peishwa was on the wane, that these military leaders ventured to exercise political influence and authority as semi-independent princes of the Mahratta empire.

Dealings of the Peishwa with the Nizam and Padishah.

The dealings of an astute Mahratta Brahman, like Baji Rao, with Nizam-ul-mulk and Muhammad Shah, are too obscure and complicated to be dealt with except in the most general terms. Baji Rao was ever ready to take advantage of the jealousies and rivalries in the Moghul empire to further his own political schemes for power and aggrandisement. He saw the jealous antagonism between the Padishah and Nizam-ul-mulk, and laboured hard to profit by it. He helped the imperial forces to drive the power and influence of Nizam-ul-mulk out of Guzerat and Malwa; and in return he obtained from the Moghul court a grant of chout for the whole of the Dekhan. He carried on a series of desultory wars against Nizam-ul-mulk, until he forced him into a kind of recognition of the Mahratta claims. At the same time there was some sort of compromise between the two. Nizam-ul-mulk obtained better terms from Baji Rao by engaging not to interfere in the Mahratta collections in Guzerat and Malwa. All this while Baji Rao was seeking to obtain from the Moghul court a formal grant of the chout for Guzerat and Malwa.

Resistance of the Moghul court to Mahratta pretensions.

The Moghul court vainly attempted to resist these demands. Their unwieldy masses of regular troops could make no impression on loose bands of Mahratta horsemen, whose home was in the saddle, and who disappeared from the scene one day only to reappear in an unexpected quarter on the morrow. Muhammad Shah made certain concessions to the Peishwa, but only with the view of embroiling him with other powers. He ceded to the Peishwa the right of collecting chout from the Rajpúts; a measure which certainly led to endless predatory wars between Rajpúts and Mahrattas when both ought to have been united in a

A.D. 1719-1738

strong national confederacy of Hindus against the Moghuls. Muhammad Shah also made some additions to the Mahratta claims on the territories of Nizam-ul-mulk. This last measure recalled the Nizam to a sense of his dependence on the Padishah. Henceforth he seems to have resolved on supporting the Padishah against the Mahrattas. At the same time Baji Rao resolved on marching a Mahratta army towards Delhi, and driving Muhammad Shah into making a formal grant of chout for Guzerat and Malwa.

Advance of the Peishwa on Agra and Delhi, 1736.

Such was the general progress of affairs from the beginning of the reign of Muhammad Shah in 1719 down to the year 1736. In the latter year Baji Rao advanced a Mahratta army towards Agra; whilst his light troops, under the command of Mulhar Rao Holkar, began to ravage the surrounding country beyond the Jumna. Suddenly Holkar was attacked and driven back by a force under Saádut Ali Khan, Subahdar of Oude. This check was magnified into a great victory; but Baji Rao retrieved his disgrace by appearing with a Mahratta army at the very gates of Delhi.

Retreat of the Mahrattas, 1737.

This movement of Baji Rao took place in the beginning of 1737, and threw the Moghul capital into the utmost consternation. But the object of Baji Rao was not to provoke, but to intimidate the Padishah. He made no attempt to enter Delhi, and he tried to prevent his troops from devastating the suburbs. Meanwhile Saádut Ali Khan joined his forces to the imperial army; and Baji Rao deemed it expedient to return to the Dekhan. During this retreat of the Mahrattas, Nizam-ul-mulk marched an army to Delhi, and was received at the capital with every mark of favour.

Secret relations between the Mahrattas and the Moghul court.

These movements of rival armies become intelligible by bearing in mind the secret relations between the Moghul court and the Peishwa. The Moghul court was playing off the Mahrattas as a check upon the growing and dangerous power of Saádut Ali Khan and Nizam-ul-mulk. At the same time the Moghul court was in mortal fear of the Mahrattas. It shrunk from the ignominy of making a formal grant of the chout for Malwa and Guzerat; but according to current reports it secretly paid chout for all its own territories round about Delhi, with the view of keeping the Mahrattas at a distance from the Moghul capital. Thus Baji Rao advanced to Agra and Delhi with the view of securing the formal grant of chout for Malwa and Guzerat; but he kept his Mahratta army from plundering the surrounding country lest he should thereby forfeit his claim to chout from the Delhi territories. A.D. 1719-1738

Baji Rao's triumph over the Nizam: the revolution from without.

In 1738 the Nizam was returning from Delhi to the Dekhan, when he came into collision with Baji Rao on the banks of the Nerbudda. There was no actual battle, but the Mahrattas surrounded the Nizam, cut off his supplies, and reduced him to sore distress. In this extremity Nizam-ul-mulk engaged to procure from the Padishah a cession of the chout for Malwa and Guzerat to the Peishwa. The Nizam then returned to Delhi, and Baji Rao took possession of Malwa. At this crisis political affairs were brought to a standstill by a sudden and unexpected blow from the side of Persia, which shook the Moghul empire to its foundations.

The Súfí empire in Persia, 1500-1722.

The modern history of Persia begins with the year 1500, when it was formed into an independent kingdom by a dynasty of Shíah fanatics, known as the Súfí Shahs. The rise of the Súfí empire preceded that of the Moghul empire of Hindustan by a quarter of a century, and its downfall preceded that of the Moghul empire about the same period.

Characteristics of Persian rule.

The rule of the Shahs of Persia differed little from that of the Moghul sovereigns of Hindustan. There were no fratricidal wars at the death of a Shah, but the princes were treated with greater cruelty during the lifetime of their father, often kept in state prisons, and blinded or strangled to prevent rebellion. On the death of a Shah a son or a grandson was taken out of a prison and placed upon the throne; and all his brothers, and all other possible rivals, were butchered wholesale. Each Shah in succession seemed to be more weak, more cruel, and more depraved than his predecessor; and it is difficult to understand how the empire could have been kept together, threatened as it was by the Turks on the west, the Russians on the north, and Afghans and Uzbegs to the eastward.

Afghan rule in Persia, 1722-30.

The dynasty was at last overthrown by an invasion of Afghans. About 1710 the Afghans of Kandahar and Herát threw off the Persian yoke, and established their independence under a chieftain of their own race. In 1722 the Afghans marched to Ispahan, and besieged the city until it was starved into unconditional surrender. Shah Husain,

A.D. 1719-1738

the last of the Súfí dynasty, abdicated his throne in favour of Mahmud, the Afghan conqueror; and for a period of eight years, from 1722 to 1730, the people of Persia were subjected to the indescribable atrocities and outrages of Afghan rule.

Rise of Nadir Kuli Khan, 1730.

Meanwhile Shah Tahmasp, a son of Shah Husain, made feeble efforts to recover his father's kingdom. In 1727 he was joined by a freebooting chieftain named Nadir Kuli, or Nadir the slave. This man was a born general, endowed with an instinct for creating armies and founding empires. He waged such successful wars against the Afghans that, by the year 1730, he had driven them out of Persia and placed Shah Tahmasp on the throne of Ispahan.

Usurps the throne, 1736.

But Nadir Kuli Khan, as he was now called, was only making a stepping-stone of Shah Tahmasp. He went off to Khorasan to complete the subjugation of the Afghans. Meanwhile Shah Tahmasp engaged in war against the Turks, met with some disasters, and concluded a peace by yielding up his right to Armenia, Erivan, and Georgia, which had long been in the possession of Persia. Nadir Kuli Khan affected the utmost indignation at this ignominious peace. He returned to Ispahan, threw Shah Tahmasp into confinement, and placed the Shah's infant son upon the throne. He then carried on a war with Turkey until she was compelled to restore the disputed provinces; and Russia was also induced to restore certain territories bordering on the Caspian which had been seized by Peter the Great. Nadir Kuli Khan was thus all-powerful in Persia. In 1736 the infant sovereign died, and Nadir the slave assumed the full sovereignty under the title of Nadir Shah, or Nadir the king.

Embassies to the Moghul treated with contempt.

In 1737 Nadir Shah was engaged in besieging Kandahar, when he sent two successive embassies to the Great Moghul at Delhi. The Moghul court took no notice of these embassies; it did not even dismiss them and permit them to return to their master. Probably the haughty Moghul was prepared to dispute the title of Nadir Shah to the throne of Persia, and to treat him as an upstart and usurper. The result was that Nadir Shah captured Kandahar and Kábul, and then prepared to march an army to Delhi *viâ* Peshawar and Lahore.

The Moghul court at this crisis was feeble to the last

degree. It had been recently threatened by the Mahrattas, and it was torn to pieces by the dissensions and jealousies of the leading grandees. There was hot rivalry between Saádut Ali Khan and Nizam-ul-mulk, and one or both were at daggers drawn with Khan-dauran, the minister. Indeed it was currently reported that both Saádut Ali Khan and Nizam-ul-mulk had been for some time in secret correspondence with Nadir Shah, and had invited him to invade Hindustan.

Dissensions and treacheries at Delhi.

Nadir Shah's intrigues.

Nadir Shah was certainly familiar with the progress of affairs in India. He charged Muhammad Shah with having failed to collect the Jezya from the unbelieving Hindus, and with having paid a fourth of his revenue to the idolatrous Mahrattas.

March from Kábul through the Punjab, 1738.

Nadir Shah reached Peshawar without difficulty. The Moghul court had been accustomed to pay a yearly subsidy to the hill tribes for the defence of the frontier passes; but for some years previously the money had been appropriated by the corrupt and unscrupulous minister. Consequently the garrisons had been withdrawn, and the disbanded troops not only left the passes open to Nadir Shah, but eagerly joined his army in the hope of sharing in the spoils of Hindustan. The Persian invader met with little or no resistance on his way through the Punjab. The Moghul Viceroy of the province was in communication with Nizam-ul-mulk; and he deemed it more to his interest to permit Nadir Shah to continue his march, than to sacrifice his troops and himself in vain efforts to repel the invasion.

Moghul army advanced to Kurnal.

At last the Moghul court was awakened from its lethargy. A large army marched from Delhi to Kurnal, about sixty-five miles to the northward, under the joint command of Nizam-ul-mulk and Khan-dauran, and accompanied by Muhammad Shah. Shortly afterwards the army of Nadir Shah approached Kurnal, and encamped in the neighbourhood.

Disaster at Kurnal, 1739.

At this crisis Saádut Ali Khan arrived at Delhi with reinforcements, and proposed giving the enemy battle. But the old rivalries were still at work. Saádut Ali Khan and Khan-dauran went out to engage the enemy, but Nizam-ul-mulk stood aloof and refused to join in the fighting. The Moghul army was utterly defeated; Saádut Ali Khan was taken prisoner, and Khan-dauran received a mortal wound.

A. D. 1738-1739

Negotiations with Nadir Shah.

Muhammad Shah was now at the mercy of Nadir Shah. Nizam-ul-mulk was sent to offer terms to the conqueror; he is said to have agreed to pay two crores of rupees, or two millions sterling, provided Nadir Shah returned to Persia without advancing on Delhi. The terms were accepted, and Nizam-ul-mulk returned to the camp of the Padishah with the joyful news, and was rewarded with the coveted rank of Amír of Amírs, or chief of all the Amírs.

Treachery of Saádut Ali Khan.

Saádut Ali Khan was stung with jealousy at the honour conferred on his rival. He told Nadir Shah that two crores were only a flea-bite in comparison with the treasures of Delhi; and he persuaded the invader to pursue his march to the Moghul capital, by promising to collect a subsidy of twenty crores. The offer was accepted, and Saádut Ali Khan hastened back to Delhi.

Nadir Shah's march to Delhi.

Nadir Shah set out on his march to Delhi with the expectation of receiving a subsidy of twenty millions sterling. He ordered Muhammad Shah to go on before him and prepare the city and palace for his reception. He received a visit from Saádut Ali Khan in the suburbs, but treated him with harshness, and asked why he had not begun to collect the subsidy. Saádut saw that his ruin was at hand. He left the presence of Nadir Shah in abject terror, swallowed a dose of poison, and passed away from the scene.

Gloomy entry into Delhi.

Next day Nadir Shah entered the city of Delhi with twenty thousand men. All houses and shops were closed; not a soul appeared in the streets. Amidst this portentous gloom, Nadir Shah posted his troops in various quarters of the city, and proceeded to the palace, where he was duly entertained by Muhammad Shah.

Moghul outbreak: slaughter of Nadir Shah's soldiers.

The soldiers of Nadir Shah were known as the Persian army, but they chiefly consisted of Tartars, Afghans, and Uzbegs; and were naturally regarded with disgust and hatred by the proud Moghuls. Nadir Shah promulgated stringent orders that none of the inhabitants of Delhi should be injured; indeed all that he wanted was to collect the subsidy as thoroughly and rapidly as possible, and this could be best achieved by abstaining from all alarms. But the people of Delhi were driven by terror and shame into acts of madness. On the day after the entry of Nadir Shah, being the 10th of March, 1739, a turmoil arose in the city. Many of the strangers were cut down and

A.D. 1739-1748

slaughtered. A rumour spread through the streets and bazars that Nadir Shah had been slain within the palace. The mob arose in overwhelming force and began to massacre the foreign soldiery, in the same way that they had massacred the Mahrattas some twenty years before. The approach of night increased the uproar. The troops of Nadir Shah retreated to their quarters in the caravanserais and houses of the grandees, and stood under arms throughout the night, whilst all stragglers were butchered by the infuriated multitude.

Nadir Shah's revenge.

At early morning Nadir Shah left the palace with a strong force, and began riding through the streets of Delhi. The sight of the dead bodies of his troops aroused his terrible wrath. At the same moment he was assailed with stones, arrows, and firearms, from the houses, and one of his chiefs was slain by his side. He determined on a deed of vengeance, which has no parallel in modern history. He ordered an indiscriminate massacre of the inhabitants without regard to age or sex. No city taken by storm could have presented greater horrors. The Persian army, maddened by the sight of their bleeding comrades, spread over the city like demons, breaking open shops, houses, and palaces, slaughtering, plundering, burning, destroying, and committing every kind of outrage with an unbridled fury which knew not how to pity nor how to spare.

Seven hours' sack and carnage.

The sack and carnage of Delhi lasted from eight o'clock in the morning until three o'clock in the afternoon. The streets were filled with the shouts of the brutal soldiery and the shrieks of their helpless victims. The atmosphere was reeking with the blood and butchery of thousands of human beings. Houses were set on fire, and numbers perished in the flames. Husbands killed their wives and then murdered themselves. Women threw themselves into wells. Children were slaughtered without mercy, and infants were cut to pieces at their mothers' breasts.

Nadir Shah in the mosque.

All this while Nadir Shah sat in a little mosque in the principal street, which is still pointed out to modern travellers. His presence in his milder moods was sufficient to strike beholders with awe. Six feet high, with swarthy countenance, large eyes, and a voice of thunder, his commanding aspect compelled all men to bend before him. But now as he sat in the mosque, his features were lighted up by a stern ferocity, as if he exulted in the great-

A.D. 1739-1748

ness of his revenge. Nizam-ul-mulk, stung by remorse, threw himself at the feet of the conqueror, and prayed for mercy towards the innocent inhabitants; but he was received with torrents of abuse that must have added to his terrors. Muhammad Shah followed his example, and begged that his subjects might be spared from further slaughter. At last the bloodthirsty warrior began to relent; he sent out orders that the butchery should end, and he was promptly and implicitly obeyed. But the sun set upon a scene of horror and devastation which has rarely been equalled in the annals of Tartar revenge.

Burial and cremation of the dead.

Next morning the survivors were ordered under terrible penalties to dispose of the dead. The corpses of Hindus and Muhammadans were thrown promiscuously together. Many were buried in vast pits; many were cast on piles of timber taken from the falling houses, and burnt in huge holocausts. The number of slain can never be known. According to one wild estimate, more than a hundred thousand souls perished in the massacre; but if the number is reduced to one-fifth or one-tenth, it is sufficient to strike men with terror until the end of time.

Collection of the subsidy.

When the slaughter was over and the murdered heaps had been cleared away, the work of plunder and exaction was carried out with relentless barbarity. The peacock throne and all the jewels of the imperial palace became the spoil of the conqueror; so did the best of the cannon and warlike stores, and the choicest of the elephants, horses, and camels. Contributions were levied from every grandee, and from every dwelling-house in the capital; and any show of reluctance or attempt at concealment was met by threats and tortures. Many who were unable to meet the demand committed suicide rather than fall into the hands of their tormentors. A body of Persian horse was sent to Oude, and confiscated the treasures of Saádut Ali Khan to the value of one or two millions sterling. A like sum was demanded of Nizam-ul-mulk, and a large amount seems to have been obtained; but the treasury of the Dekhan was out of the reach of Nadir Shah; and any force despatched in that direction might have been cut off in the passes of the Vindhya mountains, or exposed to the assaults of the Mahrattas. An attempt was made to secure a subsidy from Bengal; but the treasury of Murshedabad was too remote

A.D. 1739-1748

from Delhi; and not even the avarice of Nadir Shah would induce him to send an army into the defiles of Bihar.

Value of the spoil.

The total value of the gold, silver, jewels, weapons, stuffs, stores, and money carried off by Nadir Shah has been variously estimated from eight to eighty millions; but all such conjectures are the sport of the imagination. Nothing is known beyond the fact that the invader carried off vast and untold treasures; that he gave three months' pay to every soldier in his army, and remitted a year's taxation throughout the whole Persian empire.

Inter-marriage and ceded territory.

Nadir Shah demanded the niece of Muhammad Shah in marriage for his second son. He also demanded the cession to Persia of all territories to the westward of the Indus which had previously belonged to the Moghul. Indeed he he might have made any demand he thought proper, for Muhammad Shah was far too prostrate to attempt any refusal. The marriage of his son to the Moghul princess was solemnised with some show of rejoicing; and the cession of territory was embodied in a formal grant, which was couched in terms of abject submission to the will of the conqueror.

Departure of Nadir Shah.

Nadir Shah reinstated the fallen Moghul in the possession of his throne and empire. He exhorted every vassal and feudatory to be loyal in their devotion to Muhammad Shah; and he threatened to wreak his vengeance on any that should attempt to rebel. He then returned to Persia after a stay of two months in Hindustan.

Nadir Shah assassinated, 1747.

Nadir Shah never reappeared in India. He lived nine years longer, during which he was engaged in wars with the Turks, or in putting down rebellions in his own territories. Unfortunately for him, he interfered with the national religion of Persia. He sought to put an end to the antagonism between Shíahs and Sunnís by declaring the Sunní faith to be the one state religion of the empire. He thus raised a storm of fanaticism against his rule, which no force could allay. In 1747, at the age of sixty, he was cut off by assassins, after a troubled reign of eleven years.

Paralysis of the Moghul empire.

The invasion of Nadir Shah inflicted a mortal blow on the Moghul empire. Muhammad Shah was re-seated on the throne of his fathers, but his sovereignty was little better than a name. The Viceroys of the provinces had become independent princes. The death of a Subahdar or

A.D. 1739-1748

Inundations of the Mahrattas.

Nawab was followed by fratricidal wars like those which attended the demise of a Padishah; and not unfrequently by the elevation of a usurper with no other authority than that derived from the sword. The Mahrattas were no longer to be quieted by payments from the imperial treasury, for the treasury had been emptied by Nadir Shah; and the Mahratta leaders led their hosts of horsemen to the remotest quarters of India, plundering and devastating the two Carnatics in the southern Peninsula, and at the same time spreading like destroying locusts over the fertile plains of Bengal.

Mahratta affairs, 1740-48.

Baji Rao died in 1740, and was succeeded in the post of Peishwa by his son Balaji Rao. Maharaja Sahu died in 1748, the year after the assassination of Nadir Shah, and was succeeded on the throne of Satara by a nominal sovereign named Raja Ram. At the same time a noiseless revolution was carried out, under which the real sovereignty was transferred from the Maharaja to the Peishwa. Raja Ram reigned as a state pageant in the fortress or prison at Satara; whilst Balaji Rao removed the Mahratta court to Poona, and reigned at the old capital of Sivaji as the independent sovereign of the Mahratta empire, but under the old name of Peishwa or minister.

Death of Muhammad Shah, 1748: Afghan invasion.

Muhammad Shah died in 1748, the same year that saw the death of Maharaja Sahu. At this moment a new enemy appeared in Hindustan to contest with the Mahrattas for supremacy. The assassination of Nadir Shah in the previous year had delivered the Afghans from the Persian yoke. Another Asiatic conqueror rose to the front under the name of Ahmad Shah Abdali. He extended the independent empire of the Afghans over the greater part of Central Asia, including the Punjab and Kashmír. He invaded Hindustan for the purpose of re-establishing the old Afghan supremacy in India. The consequence was that the successors of Muhammad Shah were mere pageants in the hands of rival ministers, who in their turn were alternately under the influence of Mahrattas and Afghans.

Revolution in the destinies of India.

At this turning-point in the downward career of the once Great Moghul, the history of India underwent an entire revolution. The Moghul empire was broken up never to be restored. The foundations of a new empire were laid by English settlers, which was destined to extend its para-

mount influence over the whole of India from sea to sea. A.D.
The centre of political interest is thus transferred from the 1739-1748
old Moghul capital of Delhi to the English settlements of Madras and Calcutta. The Hindu nationalities of India, after centuries of repression, were to be educated by British administrators in a knowledge of that civilisation, which has regenerated the western world and established the reign of order and of law. In this manner the people of India are being trained and disciplined by British rule for a new career of national life, which can only be revealed in the unknown world of the future.

PART III.

BRITISH INDIA.

CHAPTER I.

ENGLISH AT MADRAS.

A.D. 1700 TO 1756.

A.D. 1700-1732

Growing importance of Madras.

DURING the early half of the eighteenth century, the English town of Madras grew into an important settlement. It was enlarged by the addition of out villages, which still give their names to different quarters of the modern city.[1] It carried on a profitable trade with Burma and Siam, Sumatra and China. It employed more weavers and manufactured more cotton piece goods than at any previous period; and no settlement in the eastern seas was regarded by the English Company with more pride and complacency than Madras and Fort St. George.

Commercial establishment.

The government of Madras was the natural outcome of a trading agency. The establishment of every English factory in India originally consisted of a certain number of European servants, graded as writers, factors and merchants, who were paid small salaries, but were lodged and boarded at the Company's expense. In the seventeenth century a writer only drew ten pounds per annum, a factor only twenty pounds, and a merchant only forty pounds; whilst the yearly salary of the president or governor was only three or four

[1] In the seventeenth century, Nunkumbaukum, Vepery, Egmore, Royapoorum, and other localities familiar to modern residents in Madras, were native villages outside the Company's grounds.

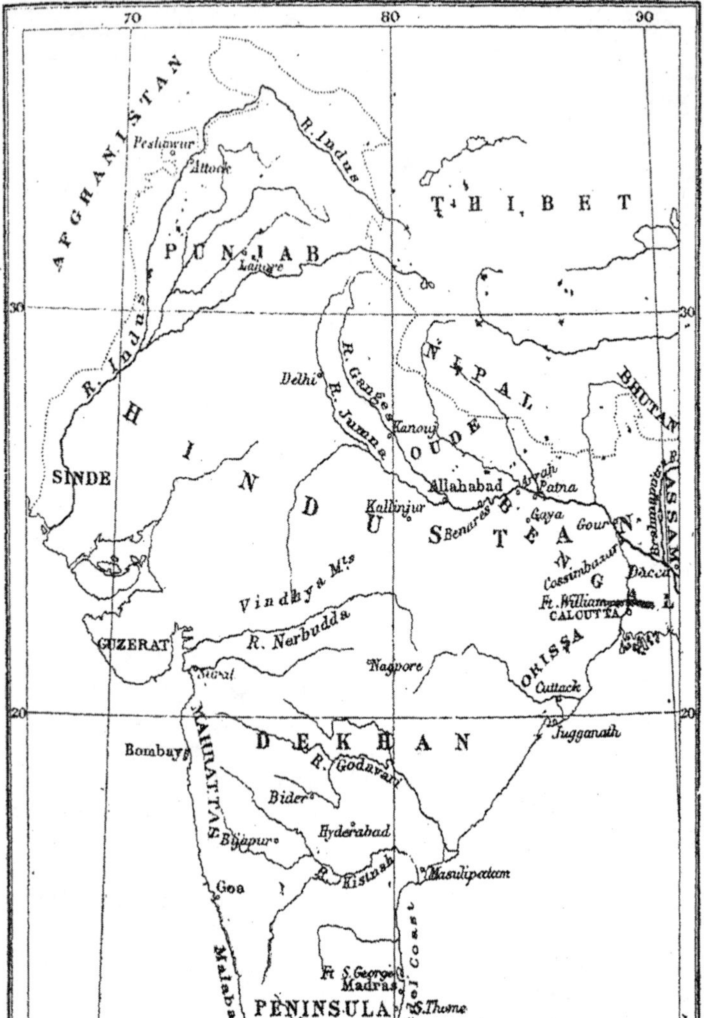
INDIA
to illustrate
EARLY ENGLISH SETTLEMENTS
BEFORE 1750.
Statute Miles
100 50 0 100 200 300
70
80
90
30
20
10
AFGHANISTAN
Peshawur
Attock
R. Indus
PUNJAB
Lahore
THIBET
NIPAL
BHUTAN
ASSAM
R. Indus
SINDE
HINDUSTAN
Delhi
R. Ganges
R. Jumna
Kanouj
OUDE
Allahabad
Arrah
Patna
Kallinjur
Benares
Gaya
Gour
BENGAL
Cossimbazar
Dacca
Ft. William
CALCUTTA
Vindhya Mts
R. Nerbudda
GUZERAT
Surat
Nagpore
ORISSA
Cuttack
Jugganath
DEKHAN
Bombay
MAHRATTAS
R. Godavari
Bider
Hyderabad
Bijapur
R. Kistnah
Masulipatam
Goa
Malabar Coast
Coromandel Coast
Ft. S. George
Madras
S. Thome
PENINSULA
Seringapatam
Ft. S. David
Devicottah
Calicut
C. Comorin

hundred pounds. In the eighteenth century salaries were considerably raised, but were still absurdly small to modern eyes. Every servant of the Company, however, was allowed the privilege of engaging in private trade, so long as he confined it to the ports in the eastern seas, and did not meddle in the Company's monopoly of trade with Europe. A.D. 1700-1732

Governor in Council and Mayor's Court.

The governor of Madras exercised supreme control over the White town, but was helped by a council of selected merchants; and so indeed were the governors of Bombay and Calcutta. Such was the simple origin of the governors in council for Madras and Bombay, and the Viceroy in council for the whole of India. The governor and council at Madras, during the seventeenth and nearly half of the eighteenth centuries, were chiefly engaged in superintending the Company's trade; in selling English manufactures and commodities in Indian markets, and providing Indian products and manufactures for the home markets. They also regulated all matters connected with revenue and expenditure; and investigated and punished all offences committed by Europeans. Besides the governor and council, a court, consisting of a mayor and aldermen, was established by royal charter for the trial of all civil cases in which Europeans were concerned; but there always seems to have been an appeal to the governor and council.

Justices of the peace and Pedda Naik.

The administration of justice amongst the natives in Black town was more simple and oriental. English justices of the peace sat in certain courts or choultries, and promptly disposed of all cases, civil and criminal, by fine, imprisonment, or whipping; and appeals to the governor and council were very rare, except in capital cases, or where there was some doubt about jurisdiction. The duties of the police were carried out by a Hindu official, known as the Pedda Naik, who was bound to make good all stolen property. He was remunerated, Hindu fashion, by a grant of hereditary lands, and small *octroi* duties levied on certain classes of commodities admitted into the town.

Dutch at Pulicat and Sadras.

The English at Madras had always been jealous of the Dutch, but only as rivals in the Indian trade. The Dutch had a fort and town at Pulicat, about twenty-four miles to the northward of Madras; and occasionally civilities and hospitalities were exchanged between the authorities of Pulicat and those of Fort St. George. The Dutch also had a fort

A.D. 1700-1732 — and town at Sadras, about forty miles to the southward of Madras; and the ruins of well-ordered towers and ramparts, prim gardens, neat water channels, and secluded bowers will still meet the eye of the pilgrim, who seeks to recall the old days of Dutch rule in India.

French at Pondicherry. But the English of the eighteenth century hated the French as their natural enemies; and this hatred was intensified in India by the fact that the natural enemies were commercial rivals. The French had built a town and fort at Pondicherry, about a hundred miles to the south of Madras; and whenever a difference arose between the two governments, it was accompanied by a warm correspondence which plainly revealed the hostile feeling which was burning on either side.

Second English settlement at Fort St. David. Besides Madras, the English had founded a settlement at Fort St. David, near the mouth of the southern Pennar river. It was only twelve miles to the south of Pondicherry; and seems to have been a rival establishment to Pondicherry. Fort St. David plays an important part in the after history; for the English at that settlement hated the French with as much warmth as their brethren at Fort St. George.

Interlopers. The English at Madras and Fort St. David were also troubled by so-called interlopers; a name applied to all English adventurers, who were not in the service of the Company, and who were not licensed to dwell as free merchants within the Company's bounds. These interlopers were generally roving captains, who persisted in carrying on an illicit trade in the eastern seas, in defiance of the monopoly granted to the Company by the charter; and who often combined the pursuits of trade with those of slave-dealing and piracy.

Nawab of the Carnatic, subordinate to the Nizam. The political outlook at Madras was confined to the Carnatic.[1] Since the death of Aurangzeb this province had been an appanage of the Nizam of the Dekhan; in other words it was governed by a Nawab, who was appointed by the Nizam, subject to confirmation and investiture by the Great Moghul.

The Moghul province of the Carnatic was supposed to

[1] Properly speaking this Carnatic should be termed "Lower Carnatic," or Carnatic below the Eastern Ghâts, to distinguish it from Mysore and other Hindu countries to the westward, which are sometimes included under the name of "Upper Carnatic," or Carnatic above the Ghâts. The term Carnatic is so often applied to the Lower Carnatic only, that it may be used for the future in its latter application.

A.D. 1700-1732

extend north and south from the neighbourhood of the river Kistna to Cape Comorin, and east and west from the coast of Coromandel to the Eastern Gháts which cut it off from Mysore and Malabar.[1] Politically, however, it was divided into a northern and a southern region by the river Koleroon; and this distinction is the key to the after history.

Division of the Carnatic.

The region to the north of the Koleroon might be termed the Moghul Carnatic. It had been conquered by the Moghuls, and brought under Moghul rule; and all the towns, districts and more important fortresses were under the command of Moghul officers.

Moghul Carnatic.

The region to the south of the Koleroon might be termed the Hindu Carnatic. It was for the most part under the dominion of the Hindu Rajas of Trichinopoly and Tanjore. Both these Rajas had been conquered by the Moghul, so far as to pay a subsidy or tribute; but nevertheless they maintained an independent rule in their respective kingdoms; and no Nawab had ever annexed their territories to his own province. These Rajas had been Naiks, or governors of provinces, under the old Hindu empire of Vijayanagar; and they might be described as the relics of the empire, half conquered by the Moghul, but rarely paying tribute unless compelled by force of arms.

Hindu Carnatic.

Besides the two Rajas there was a class of minor chiefs, known as Poligars. They were to be found both north and south of the Koleroon. They had been feudal barons under the old Hindu rule of Vijayanagar, holding their lands by military tenure; but like the old chiefs of Highland clans, they refused to accept the Moghul *régime*, and indeed were often disaffected towards the Hindu Rajas. Sometimes they were forced to pay tribute or allegiance; but often they maintained a rude independence in some remote stronghold.

Poligars.

The Moghul conquest was hurtful to the people of the northern region. The revenue was mostly derived from the land, and the Moghul Nawabs were harder task-masters than Hindu Rajas. The Hindu kingdoms descended from father to son, and were regarded as family property; and

Moghul and Hindu rule.

[1] The real boundary of the Carnatic province on the north was the little river Gundlacama, half way between the Kistna and the northern Pennar. The tract between the Gundlacama and the Kistna was at one time of some importance in a quarrel about the Northern Circars.

A.D. 1700-1732

self-interest led successive Rajas to encourage cultivators, and keep tanks and irrigation works in repair.[1] But the earlier Nawabs were removed at will by the Nizam or the Great Moghul. They cared only to make money, and paid no heed to the future. They doubled the land assessments, and let the tanks and irrigation works go to rack and ruin; and for some years many lands fell out of cultivation, and grain rose to famine prices.

Decline of trade in the interior.

Meanwhile the inland trade of the English had fallen off. The ravages of the Mahrattas in the Upper Carnatic prevented the Canarese merchants of Mysore and elsewhere from bringing their cotton-yarn to Madras. The removal of the imperial camp from the Dekhan to Delhi after the death of Aurangzeb, had ruined the trade in scarlet and green broad-cloths. The outbreaks of Poligars and free-booters, as well as threatened invasions of Mahrattas, created general alarm; and wealthy natives hoarded their treasures in strongholds, or sent them to Madras or Pondicherry for security.

Flourishing trade in cotton piece goods.

But the prosperity of Madras was increasing. The demand from Europe for cotton piece goods was greater than ever. The English founded two new towns for the exclusive accommodation of spinners, weavers, dyers, washers, and other Hindus engaged in the manufacture. They also planted trees for the accommodation of this class of people, who were accustomed to work in the open air. Hindus of other castes were not allowed to dwell in these towns, always excepting betel sellers, dancing-girls, and Brahmans.[2]

Isolation of the English.

The English at Madras and Fort St. David were mere traders, and cared but little about the country powers. They were industrious and respectable, but curious only as regards products and manufactures. The Moghuls on their part had grown jealous of Europeans, and were anxious to keep them ignorant of all that was going on. The Nawab

[1] The comparative merits of Hindu and Moghul rule are open to question. The Catholic missionaries in Southern India during the seventeenth century are loud in their denunciations of the cruelties and oppressions of the Hindu Rajas.

[2] These two towns are well known to residents in Madras. Collet's petta was founded in 1720; Chindadree petta in 1734. Betel sellers, dancing-girls, and Brahmans are necessities of Hindu life, and no Hindu village is complete without them.

A.D. 1732-1736

kept his court at Arcot, which was only seventy miles from Madras; but the English knew as little of Arcot as they did of Delhi. They paid their yearly rent to the Nawab, and sent him complimentary letters and presents, and that was all.[1]

Accession of a new Nawab: breach between the Nawab and Nizam, 1732.

In 1732 a Nawab died at Arcot. He had been appointed by a Nizam of the Dekhan as far back as 1712, but on his death in 1732, he was succeeded by an adopted son, named Dost Ali, without any reference to the Nizam. This assumption of hereditary right by the Nawab of the Carnatic was very gravelling to Nizam-ul-mulk. To make matters worse, Dost Ali withheld the revenue or tribute which previous Nawabs had paid to the Nizam.[2] But Nizam-ul-mulk was obliged to pocket the affront. He was too much harassed by the Mahrattas, and worried by Delhi intrigues, to interfere with Arcot affairs. Accordingly he nursed his wrath and bided his time.

Trichinopoly and Tanjore.

In 1736 there was a revolution in the Hindu Carnatic. The two kingdoms of Trichinopoly and Tanjore were situated, as already described, immediately to the south of the Koleroon; and they stretched over an unknown tract of country towards Comorin. Trichinopoly was an inland territory, and included the three important towns of Trichinopoly, Dindigul, and Madura. Tanjore lay to the eastward, and stretched to the coast of Coromandel. It was the more fertile territory of the two, for it included the rich delta of the Koleroon and Káveri; and to this day Tanjore is regarded as the granary of southern India. But Tanjore was at the mercy of Trichinopoly. The rivers Koleroon and Káveri were only kept asunder by an embankment; and by breaking down that embankment the Káveri rushed into the Koleroon and Tanjore was robbed of her water supply.

Civil war in Trichinopoly.

In 1736 the Raja of Trichinopoly died, leaving no children. Consequently there was a war for the succession

[1] This ignorance of the surrounding country was peculiar to the English at Madras. It will be seen hereafter that the English at Calcutta were far better acquainted with Bengal.

[2] By this time the office of Dewan, or accountant-general in behalf of the Great Moghul, had become a farce. Dost Ali appointed one Chunder Sahib, to be Dewan, and gave him a daughter in marriage. Subsequently this Chunder Sahib became an important personage.

A.D. 1736-1740

between the brothers of the Raja and the brothers of the Rání; whilst the Rání herself claimed to be regent until the son of her eldest brother should attain his majority.

The Nawab interferes.

The possession of Trichinopoly had long been coveted by the Nawabs of the Carnatic; it was in fact the key the Peninsula. Accordingly the Nawab Dost Ali interfe. in the affairs of Trichinopoly as the pretended friend of the Rání. He sent an army to Trichinopoly under his son Subder Ali and his son-in-law Chunder Sahib.[1]

Chunder gulls the Rání.

The son-in-law was a much sharper man than the son. Chunder Sahib gulled the Rání; pretended to be in love with her; swore on the Koran to be faithful to her cause and finally deluded her into admitting him and his troops into the walls of Trichinopoly. The Rání soon found that she was betrayed; she was thrown into prison, and is said to have taken poison.

Seizes the city and Raj.

Chunder Sahib soon took possession of the city and the Raj. He sent one of his kinsmen to command at Dindigul, and another to command at Madura. The people of Trichinopoly bent as usual to their fate: it was the will of the gods. Subder Ali was enraged at finding that Chunder Sahib was holding Trichinopoly and could not be ousted. Accordingly he nursed his vengeance and returned to Arcot. In like manner the Rajas of Tanjore and Mysore were bitterly incensed against Chunder Sahib for putting an end to the Hindu dynasty of Trichinopoly, and bringing the country under Muhammadan rule. But like Subder Ali, they did nothing and patiently abided their time.

Mahratta invasion, 1740.

In 1740 the Mahrattas invaded the Carnatic, plundering and destroying according to their wont. Some said that the Nizam had invited them in order to punish the Nawab. Others said that the Rajas of Tanjore and Mysore had invited them to punish Chunder Sahib. Others, again, said that the Great Moghul was unable to pay the chout after the invasion of Nadir Shah, and therefore told them to collect it in the Carnatic and Bengal. Such conflicting rumours are always noised abroad in India on like occasions, and it is often impossible to say whether any of them are false or true.

[1] Chunder Sahib was the man who married a daughter of the Nawab, and was appointed Dewan.

A.D. 1740-1743

Defeat and death of the Nawab Dost Ali.

Nawab Dost Ali had tried to keep out the Mahrattas by marching an army to the Eastern Ghâts, and blocking up the passes which led from Mysore into the Carnatic, until he could assemble the whole of his forces from different parts of the province. But there was treachery in his camp. One of his own officers admitted the Mahrattas by a secret pass. The Mahrattas took him by surprise, and assailed his army with the utmost fury. He was slain in the midst of the action; and his troops, seeing that their Nawab was dead, fled in confusion after the manner of oriental armies.

Alarm at the Mahrattas.

The Mahratta invasion spread universal terror. Subder Ali, the son of the deceased Nawab, fled to the strong fort of Vellore, about twelve miles from Arcot. Chunder Sahib sent his wife and treasures to Pondicherry, and collected vast stores of grain within the city of Trichinopoly in order to stand a lengthy siege. The English at Madras began to look after their defences, and shared in the general alarm.

Mahratta agreement with Subder Ali.

The Mahrattas were disappointed of the spoil. All the gold and jewels in the country had been hoarded up in strongholds. The Mahrattas had no guns or battering train of any kind; and it was impossible for loose bands of horsemen to capture fortresses, except by bribery, stratagem, or starvation. Accordingly they accepted an offer of rupees to the value of a million sterling from Subder Ali, to be paid by instalments; they then left the Carnatic, giving out that they were going to plunder some other part of India.

Surprise of Trichinopoly: imprisonment of Chunder Sahib

The departure of the Mahrattas was a *ruse*. Subder Ali had secretly engaged to let them take possession of Trichinopoly, provided they carried off his ambitious brother-in-law, Chunder Sahib, and kept him prisoner at Satara. Their object in leaving the Carnatic was to blind Chunder Sahib, and in this they fully succeeded. Chunder Sahib thought that the Mahrattas would never return, and foolishly sold off all the grain he had stored in Trichinopoly. Suddenly, to his surprise and mortification, the Mahrattas returned to Trichinopoly, and closely besieged the city. Chunder Sahib was helpless; and was soon compelled by sheer starvation to surrender the city. He was then carried off to Satara, and languished in a Mahratta prison for

A.D. 1740-1743

more than six years. Meanwhile the Mahrattas held possession of Trichinopoly. The bulk of the Mahratta army returned to the Konkan; but a general, named Morari Rao, remained in command of Trichinopoly, and kept a watchful eye on the progress of affairs in the Carnatic.

Subder Ali proclaimed Nawab.

For a brief interval Subder Ali was at ease. He had purchased the imprisonment of his dangerous brother-in-law, Chunder Sahib, by permitting the Mahrattas to occupy Trichinopoly. He was still pledged to pay the Mahrattas a subsidy of a million sterling; and this was a matter that required prompt attention. Meanwhile he proceeded to Arcot and was proclaimed Nawab of the Carnatic in succession to his father, who had been slain in the passes.

Wrath of Nizam-ul-mulk.

At this juncture Subder Ali was threatened by a new danger from Hyderabad. Nizam-ul-mulk had been for a long time exasperated at the unauthorised succession of Dost Ali to the Nawabship of the Carnatic, and the non-payment of tribute. Since then the occupation of Trichinopoly by Chunder Sahib had added fuel to his anger; for in spite of domestic dissensions, the acquisition of Trichinopoly had added to the material resources of the Nawab's family, and would doubtless encourage the Nawab himself to persist in disregarding the superior authority of the Nizam. The invasion of Nadir Shah had compelled Nizam-ul-mulk to bottle up his wrath; but the progress of affairs during the interval had not improved his temper. The Mahrattas had secured a dangerous footing in the Carnatic by the occupation of Trichinopoly. Worse than all, Subder Ali had followed the contumacious example set by his deceased father, by assuming the Nawabship of the Carnatic without any reference to Hyderabad or Delhi.

Demand of the Nizam: perplexities of Subder Ali.

Under these circumstances Nizam-ul-mulk demanded the immediate payment of all arrears of tribute from the new Nawab. Subder Ali was at his wits' ends. He was firmly resolved not to pay the demand. Meanwhile he sent his family and treasures to Madras. He shut himself up in the strong fortress of Vellore, which was commanded by another brother-in-law, named Mortiz Ali.[1] He vowed that the Mahrattas had emptied his treasury of his last rupee. He

[1] Chunder Sahib and Mortiz Ali had each married daughters of Dost Ali, and were consequently brothers-in law of the reigning Nawab. Both men played important parts in the after history.

feigned a pious intention of abdicating his throne, and going on pilgrimage to Mecca. He even made one or two journeys to Madras to induce the Nizam to believe that he was going to embark there for Mecca. A.D. 1740-1743

Contributions for the Mahrattas.

All this while Subder Ali knew that he must pay the Mahrattas. The Nizam might be deceived for a while by protestations of poverty, or threats of going to Mecca; but the Mahrattas were the most pertinacious people in all India, and were deaf to all vows and prayers that were not backed up by rupees. Any attempt on the part of Subder Ali to delay payment would be followed by another Mahratta invasion of the Carnatic, and the probable release of Chunder Sahib. Accordingly Subder Ali levied contributions from all commanders of towns and forts throughout the province, in order to pay the subsidy promised to the Mahrattas. Mortiz Ali refused payment of his quota. The Nawab was excessively angry, for Mortiz Ali was the richest man in the province, and unless he was made to pay, other commanders would refuse to pay in like manner.

Demands on Mortiz Ali.

Accordingly the Nawab peremptorily demanded the money. The story of what followed was told with horror at Madras for generations afterwards. The Nawab was quartered in the fortress of Vellore where his brother-in-law Mortiz Ali was commandant; but there was no suspicion of danger; for although the money quarrel was bitter, there was no lack of outward courtesy and politeness on either side.

Subder Ali assassinated.

The great festival of the Muharram approached, when all Sunní Muhammadans devote themselves to feasting and rejoicing, whilst the Shiahs lament and beat their breasts over the martyrdom of Ali and his two sons, Hasan and Husain. The Nawab permitted his officers to leave the fortress in order to keep the festival with their wives and families. At midnight an Afghan broke into his chamber, followed by black Abyssinian slaves. The unfortunate Nawab raised a cry of alarm, and rushed to the window; but was soon cut down and stabbed to death by the poniards of the assassins.

Mortiz Ali proclaimed Nawab.

Next morning the Nawab's army, which was encamped outside the fortress, raised a tumult. They cried out that the Nawab had been assassinated by Mortiz Ali; and they prepared to storm the fortress sword in hand, and avenge

A.D. 1740-1743

the murder But the soldiery were quieted after oriental fashion. Large arrears of pay were due from the dead Nawab; and the men were promised early payment of the whole by instalments, if they would only accept Mortiz Ali as his successor. Accordingly, Mortiz Ali was proclaimed Nawab, and then marched in triumph from Vellore to Arcot, and took up his quarters at the palace.

Revolt of the army.

But the leading men in the Carnatic detested the crime of Mortiz Ali. They applied to Morari Rao at Trichinopoly, who foresaw a new complication, and openly declared against Mortiz Ali. They sent messengers to the English at Madras, begging that the governor would protect the family and treasures of the murdered Nawab. Lastly, they stirred up the army against Mortiz Ali; and the question of the succession seemed to turn upon a matter of pay. The soldiery demanded the immediate payment of all the arrears in full, which they had previously agreed to receive by instalments. Had Mortiz Ali produced the money at once, he might possibly have secured himself in the post of Nawab; but he was seized with a panic, and would not stand the storm. He put on a woman's dress, and entered a covered palanquin, and fled at night time from Arcot to Vellore, accompanied by several female attendants. The result was that the young son of Subder Ali, who had been under the protection of the English at Madras, was proclaimed Nawab of the Carnatic in the room of his father.

Nizam-ul-mulk at Arcot, 1743.

By this time Nizam-ul-mulk resolved to march to Arcot, and settle the affairs of the Carnatic. He had arranged matters at Delhi, where his eldest son had been appointed minister; and he had made his peace with the Mahrattas. Accordingly he left Hyderabad in the beginning of 1743, and in March the same year he encamped at Arcot with an overwhelming army.

Settlement of the Nawabship.

At Arcot the Nizam found the Carnatic at his feet. Every grandee was anxious to pay submission and homage to the great Nizam-ul-mulk, the pillar of the Moghul empire. But he himself was struck with the anarchy which prevailed throughout the Carnatic. Every petty commandant of a fort or district assumed the title of Nawab; and no less than eighteen of these little Nawabs were introduced to the Nizam in one day. The old grandee of the court of Aurangzeb lost his temper at this enormity. He declared

A.D. 1743-1744

that there was but one Nawab of the Carnatic; and he threatened to scourge the first person who should venture for the future to usurp such a title. He appointed a new Nawab of the Carnatic, named Anwar-ud dín; but he gave out that Anwar-ud-dín would be the guardian of the son of Subder Ali; and that when the boy prince became of age, he would be made Nawab of the Carnatic.

English mission to Nizam ul-mulk, 1743.

The Nizam next proceeded to Trichinopoly, and recovered the city from the Mahrattas. The governor of Madras sent a deputation to Trichinopoly to wait on the great man with a letter and presents. The Nizam received the English gentlemen with much state, but with singular courtesy. He praised the presents sent to him, and promised to forward some to the Great Moghul at Delhi, and to say that they came from the English governor of Madras. He said he wanted guns, powder, mortars, and shells, and above all the services of an experienced gunner; but he added that he would take nothing unless he was permitted to pay for it.

Murder of the boy Nawab, 1744.

In March 1744 the Nizam left the Carnatic and returned to Hyderabad. In June the same year the boy Nawab was murdered at a wedding-feast. The details were most tragical. On the morning of the ceremony some Afghans had clamoured for arrears of pay, but apologised for their insolence and retired. Their captain especially appeared to be very repentant. At night whilst the guests were sitting in the hall, the coming of Anwar-ud-dín was announced, and the boy Nawab went out to the vestibule at the head of the stairs to receive his guardian. The Afghan captain ascended the steps with a respectful air as if to repeat his regrets, when he suddenly drew his dagger and stabbed the prince to the heart. In a moment he was cut to pieces, and his Afghans below met with the same fate.

General excitement: Anwar-ud-dín appointed Nawab.

The assassination of the young prince sent a thrill through the Carnatic. He was representative of a family who had ruled the Carnatic for thirty years. No member of the family was eligible to succeed except Chunder Sahib and Mortiz Ali. But Chunder Sahib was in a Mahratta prison, whilst Mortiz Ali was more hated than ever. Meanwhile it was everywhere believed that the murder was instigated by Anwar-ud-dín and Mortiz Ali. But the general opinion had no effect upon Nizam-ul-mulk,

A.D. 1744-1745

and he confirmed Anwar-ud-dín in his post of Nawab of the Carnatic.

War with France, 1745: arrival of an English squadron.

The English at Madras were horrified at the assassinations of two Nawabs in succession; but their attention was soon distracted by more important affairs. War was declared between Great Britain and France. In 1745 an English squadron appeared off the coast of Coromandel, for the purpose of destroying the French settlements in the eastern seas.

Hostilities forbidden by the Nawab.

M. Dupleix, the governor of Pondicherry, was in great alarm. He sent large presents to the new Nawab, and begged for protection. Anwar-ud-dín replied by prohibiting the English from engaging in hostilities within any part of his dominions; but at the same time he assured the English that if the French appeared in superior force, he would prohibit them in like manner.

Capture of Madras by the French, 1746.

In 1746 the English fleet left the Coromandel coast, and a French squadron, under the command of Labourdonnais, entered the Bay of Bengal, and threatened Madras. The defences of Fort St. George were sufficient to strike the natives with awe and wonder, but they were ill fitted to stand a bombardment from European ships. The governor and council of Madras requested the Nawab to fulfil his promise of restraining the French; but they neglected to send a present. Accordingly the Nawab seems to have done nothing. Madras was compelled to surrender to Labourdonnais, under a pledge that it should be restored on payment of ransom. Dupleix, however, refused to recognise the pledge; he rejected all offers of ransom. He was a fervid Frenchman, bent on the ruin of the English in India as the enemies of the French nation. He ordered that all the Company's effects, and all private property except clothes and jewels, should be confiscated as prize. Madras thus became a French settlement, and its inhabitants were sent to Pondicherry as prisoners of war.[1]

Wrath of the Nawab.

The Nawab was very wroth at seeing the French in possession of Madras. Dupleix tried to quiet him by promising to give him the town; but the Nawab soon saw that

[1] Labourdonnais afterwards returned to France, and was thrown into the Bastile. He had rendered great service to France, but was charged by his enemies with collusion with the English at Madras. After three years he was liberated, but died shortly afterwards.

A.D. 1746-1748

the Frenchman was deceiving him with false promises in order to divert him from protecting the English. Accordingly he resolved to deprive the French of their new conquest, and sent an army of ten thousand men and numerous cannon to capture Madras.

Ignominious defeat of the Nawab's army.

To the utter surprise and mortification of the Nawab, the Moghul army was routed by a French force of four hundred men and two guns, and compelled to fly back to Arcot. The disaster was most humiliating to the Moghul grandees. Up to this time they had proudly imagined that it was their own superior military prowess which induced Europeans to treat them with so much respect and deference. The spell was broken by the French at Madras, who defeated a Moghul army with half a battalion.

War in the Carnatic, 1746-48: English at Fort St. David.

The war between the English and French in the Carnatic lasted from 1746 to 1748. It has lost much of its interest since the two nations have become friends, but it was an oft-told story in the last century. The English removed their seat of government from Madras to Fort St. David, near the mouth of the southern Pennar; it was only twelve miles to the south of Pondicherry, and consequently there was much smart fighting between the two settlements; and the Nawab alternately helped the English and the French, according as either appeared to be getting the upper hand.

Failure of an English attack on Pondicherry.

In 1748 Major Stringer Lawrence arrived from England, and took the command of all the Company's forces in India. Another fleet arrived from England under the command of Admiral Boscowen. A grand attack was made on Pondicherry by land and sea; but after a siege of two months, and the loss of more than a thousand Europeans, the English were compelled to retire. A few weeks afterwards peace was proclaimed between Great Britain and France, and Madras was ultimately restored to the English East India Company by the treaty of Aix-la-Chapelle.

Epoch of 1748.

The year 1748 is an epoch in Indian history,—Muhammadan, Hindu, and English. The Afghans, delivered by the death of Nadir Shah from the Persian yoke, were beginning to invade the Punjab and Hindustan. Muhammad Shah, the last of the Moghuls of any note, died at Delhi. The aged Nizam-ul-mulk died at Hyderabad, and left his sons to fight for the possession of his throne. Maháraja Sahu died at Satara, and the sovereignty of the Peishwas

A.D. 1748-1749

began at Poona. Robert Clive gained his first laurels in the defence of the advanced trench before the walls of Pondicherry. Finally, the war between Great Britain and France was brought to a close by the peace of Aix-la-Chapelle.

Career of Clive.

The name of Robert Clive first appeared in the story of the unsuccessful siege of Pondicherry; but in the course of a few years more it was a household word throughout the British Empire. Robert Clive was born in 1725. He grew up a bold and wayward boy, impatient of control, neglecting his studies, but firm and dauntless in all his ways, and especially cool and self-possessed in the face of danger. In 1744, at the age of nineteen, he landed at Madras as a writer in the mercantile service of the Company. When the war broke out with France, he entered the military service of the Company, and obtained a commission as ensign. Subsequently he received the praises of the Court of Directors for his gallantry at Pondicherry.

Aggressions on Tanjore, 1749.

In the beginning of 1749 the English interfered in the affairs of Tanjore, in the delta of the Koleroon and Káveri. They had long wanted to establish a settlement at Devicotta, about twenty miles to the south of Fort St. David, near the mouth of the Koleroon. At last an opportunity presented itself. An exiled member of the reigning family of Tanjore applied to the English for help. He persuaded the governor and council at Fort St. David that he was the rightful Raja, and that the people of Tanjore would join him the moment he appeared at the head of a small force. He also promised to cede Devicotta, and pay all the expenses of the war.

Alarm of the Raja: cession of Devicotta.

The English sent an expedition against Tanjore, but it was a blunder from the beginning. They had no possible excuse for interfering in the Tanjore succession; and would not have made the attempt, had they not wanted Devicotta, and had not the unexpected peace with France placed a small military force at their disposal. To make matters worse, the people of Tanjore would not receive back the pretender, and boldly resisted the English. All at once the Raja agreed to cede Devicotta; to give a pension to the pretender, and to pay all the cost of the English expedition. It turned out that the Raja was anxious for an alliance with the English. Chunder Sahib, the enemy of Hindu Rajas, had been liberated from his Mahratta prison, and

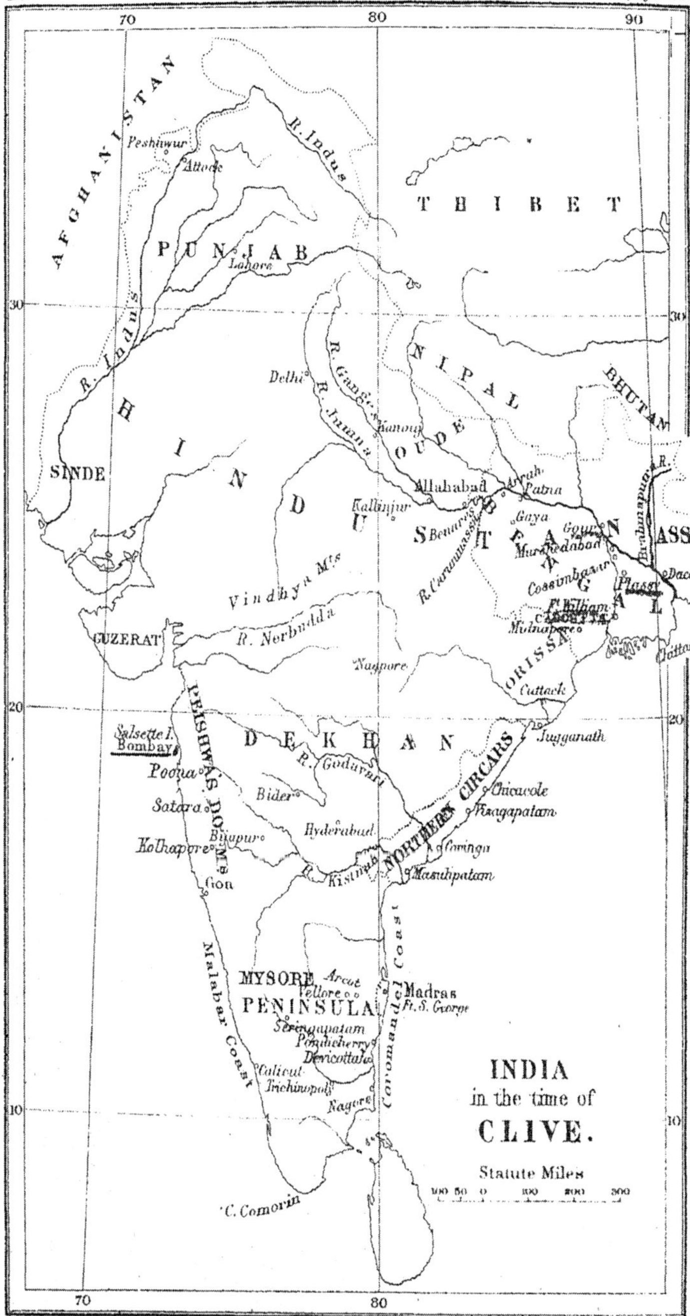

London; Macmillan & Co. Stanford's Geog! Estab!

proclaimed Nawab at Arcot; and the Raja of Tanjore saw that no one but the English could protect him in the coming struggle. A.D. 1748-1749

Designs of Dupleix. Dupleix, the French governor of Pondicherry, was at the bottom of this revolution. Whilst the English were at war for a trading settlement, Dupleix was scheming for an empire. The Frenchman had grown disgusted with trade; the profits of the Indian trade had so diminished as to be, in his opinion, unworthy of the French nation. He turned his attention to the politics of India. He saw that the grandees of the Carnatic were hostile to the Nawab appointed by Nizam-ul-mulk, and hankering after the old hereditary family. He procured the liberation of Chunder Sahib by guaranteeing the payment of a large ransom to the Mahrattas. He was alive to the vast superiority of Europeans over the Moghuls, and he sent a French force to help Chunder Sahib to attack Anwar-ud-dín. He hoped to make Chunder Sahib Nawab of the Carnatic; to establish the French nation as the dominant power in the Peninsula; and to drive the English out of India in the name of the new Nawab.

Death of Nizam-ul-mulk: results in the Carnatic. All this machinery had been set in motion by the death of Nizam-ul-mulk in 1748. Anwar-ud-dín, the Nawab of the Carnatic, had thereby lost his patron and supporter; and was left to contend as he best could against the disaffected officers of the Carnatic who were yearning for the restoration of the old dynasty of Nawabs. At the same time Chunder Sahib was no longer in fear of the interference of the Nizam, and had everything to hope from the enemies of Anwar-ud-dín.

Results in the Dekhan. Meanwhile the death of Nizam-ul-mulk was opening out new fields of ambition to Dupleix. The struggle between two rival Nawabs for the throne of the Carnatic was soon overshadowed by a far grander struggle between two rival Nizams for the throne of the Dekhan; and the attention of Dupleix, which had originally centred at Arcot, began to alternate like a pendulum between Arcot and Hyderabad, until the greater part of India to the south of the Nerbudda river was brought within the sphere of his ambitious designs.

The death of Nizam-ul-mulk had been followed by distractions in his family. His eldest son was at Delhi, but his second son, Nasir Jung, seized the treasures, and pacified

A.D. 1749-1750

Nasir Jung succeeds his father as Nizam.

the army by a timely distribution of money. This prince had rebelled during the lifetime of his father. The crafty Nizam feigned to be in mortal sickness; he wished, he said, to forgive and embrace his son before he died. Nasir Jung was thus lured to his father's camp, and was then put into chains. After the Nizam's death Nasir Jung proved as unscrupulous as his father. He threw his three younger brothers into confinement, and carried them with him wherever he moved his army.

Claims of Muzaffir Jung, the grandson.

Oriental princes love their sons whilst they are children, but grow jealous of them as they approach manhood. Subsequently they often have an affection for grandsons. Nizam-ul-mulk had a favourite grandson known as Muzaffir Jung. After his death this young prince produced a will by which the Nizam bequeathed his treasures and dominions to his favourite grandson. The will was probably a forgery; at any rate Nizam-ul-mulk could not bequeath territories which nominally belonged to the Great Moghul. To add to the absurdity, both the son and grandson affected to receive delegates from the Great Moghul, with insignia and letters of investiture for the government of the Dekhan. Both could not have been real; probably in both cases the delegates were hired and the letters were forged. Such mock ceremonials were soon common in India, and imposed on no one but the credulous mob.

Junction of Chunder Sahib and Muzaffir Jung: brilliant successes.

At this crisis the grandson, Muzaffir Jung, received a proposal from Chunder Sahib that they should unite their forces, conquer the Carnatic, and then conquer the Dekhan. The scheme recommended itself to all parties, to Dupleix as well as to Muzaffir Jung. The would-be Nizam joined his forces to those of the would-be Nawab, and the two allies began career of brilliant successes which took the Carnatic by surprise. They marched through the passes of the Eastern Ghâts, defeated Anwar-ud-dín at Amboor, and left him dead upon the field. They next proceeded to Arcot and proclaimed Chunder Sahib as Nawab of the Carnatic. Finally they went to Pondicherry, and were received with open arms by Dupleix.

Crisis at Trichinopoly.

Meanwhile a son of the slain Nawab, named Muhammad Ali, had fled to Trichinopoly. It was the last stronghold remaining to the family of Anwar-ud-dín, and Muhammad Ali was the last representative of the family. It was obvious to Dupleix that the capture of Trichinopoly, and surrender of Muhammad Ali, would bring the war in the Carnatic to a triumphant close, and enable the allies to bring all their forces to bear against Nasir Jung. Accordingly he urged Chunder Sahib and Muzaffir Jung to march with all speed to Trichinopoly, and waste no time in the reduction of the place; as it would not only establish Chunder Sahib on the throne of the Carnatic without a rival, but prepare the way for ousting Nasir Jung from Hyderabad, and enthroning Muzaffir Jung as Nizam of the Dekhan in the room of his uncle.

A.D 1749-1750

Delays at Tanjore.

But Dupleix had to deal with Asiatic princes, on whom it is dangerous to rely. Both Chunder Sahib and Muzaffir Jung were in pressing want of money, but both were too proud to mention their poverty to Dupleix, lest it should lower them in the eyes of their French ally. They left Pondicherry with music and banners but without funds; and they halted at Tanjore to demand a subsidy from the Raja, as arrears of tribute due to the Nawab of the Carnatic.

Vacillations of the Tanjore Raja.

The Tanjore Raja had been in mortal fear of Chunder Sahib ever since the treacherous capture of Trichinopoly in 1736. He had rejoiced when his Mahratta brethren carried off Chunder Sahib as a prisoner to Satara; and he had hastened to form an alliance with the English the moment he heard of the escape and successes of Chunder Sahib. He knew that he was powerless to contend against a demand for a subsidy which was backed up by the French. He shut himself up in his capital and prepared to stand a siege; but then lost heart and offered to pay a ransom. His sole object was to gain time; and he resorted to all those evasions, procrastinations, hesitations, and vexatious alternations of resistance and submission, by which native potentates often prolong a settlement long after they are convinced of the hopelessness of war. Days and weeks were then frittered away in fixing the gross amount of the subsidy, and the instalments by which it was to be paid. All this while Chunder Sahib and Muzaffir Jung were most anxious to advance to Trichinopoly, but could not move without money; whilst letters from Dupleix were constantly reaching the camp, urging the allies to raise the siege of Tanjore and hasten to the reduction of Trichinopoly.

At last the amount of subsidy was fixed; also the amount

A.D. 1749-1750

Wranglings over money.

of the first instalment, which was to be paid down on the spot. Then the Tanjore Raja had recourse to other artifices. He feigned the utmost anxiety to pay the money, but he had no rupees. One day he sent a package of gold and silver plate; and his officers wrangled like pedlers over the valuation. Another day he sent a lot of old and obsolete coins, which entailed more wrangling. Lastly, he sent jewels and precious stones of dubious or fluctuating value, which led to endless altercations.

Nasir Jung at Arcot, 1750: Muhammad Ali appointed Nawab.

Suddenly the uproar ceased and the Raja was relieved. During the quarrels about the subsidy, Nasir Jung had left Hyderabad with an overwhelming army, and begun to invade the Carnatic. The allies were thrown into a panic. Muzaffir Jung was induced to surrender himself to his uncle by promises of pardon and promotion, and was then chained and imprisoned, as his uncle had been before him. Chunder Sahib fled to Pondicherry. Nasir Jung entered Arcot, and found, like Nizam-ul-mulk, that the Carnatic was at his feet. He appointed Muhammad Ali to be Nawab of the Carnatic, and thus seemed to have brought the ambitious schemes of Dupleix to a final ending.

Victories of Dupleix.

Dupleix, however, was not a man to be cast down by reverses. He was not a soldier like Clive. "Battles," he said, "confused his genius." But he knew how to plan campaigns, and he was anxious to intimidate the English and frighten Nasir Jung. One detachment of the French army surprised the fort of Masulipatam at the mouth of the Kistna. Another French army routed the army of Muhammad Ali at Trivadi, only sixteen miles from Fort St. David. But the crowning exploit was carried out by M. Bussy, a Frenchman destined to win a name in India. Bussy captured the fortress of Jinjí, the strongest in the Carnatic. It was only thirty-five miles from Pondicherry, and was supposed to command the whole country. In the previous century it had been the great bone of contention between the Moghul and the Mahratta.[1]

[1] The fortress of Jingí, formerly spelt Ginjee, was a natural stronghold improved by art; it had been famous for centuries as the citadel of the Carnatic. It consisted of three precipitous rocks or mountains, from 400 to 600 feet in height, forming very nearly an equilateral triangle. They were covered with redoubts, one above each other,

A.D. 1750-1751

Alarm of Nizam Ali.

All this while Nasir Jung was wasting his time in a round of pleasures at Arcot. He was unmoved by the capture of Masulipatam, or the defeat of his Nawab, Muhammad Ali; but the capture of Jinjí opened his eyes to the dangerous prowess of the French. He offered to treat with the French, but the demands of Dupleix were preposterous. Muzaffir Jung was to be liberated; Chunder Sahib was to be Nawab of the Carnatic; Masulipatam was to be formally ceded to the French East India Company; and Jinjí was to be left in the hands of the French. Nasir Jung was so enraged at these demands, that he marched his army towards Jinjí, with the view of overwhelming the French, and recovering the ancient citadel of the Carnatic which had slipped out of his hands.

Influence of Madame Dupleix, *i.e.* Jan Begum.

Dupleix was playing a deep game, which requires some explanation. He was naturally a man of energy and resources but he now displayed a mixture of audacity and craft, which was more oriental than European. These Asiatic proclivities were due to the influence of his wife; a lady of mixed parentage, who was born and bred in India, and whom he had married in Bengal. Madame Dupleix was familiar with the native languages, and well versed in native ways. She carried on a large correspondence with personages at different courts; and was widely known in India as Jan Begum.[1]

There was disaffection and treachery in the army of Nasir

and were connected by lines of works. They thus enclosed a plain in which the town was situated. The night attack of Bussy and his Frenchmen was one of the most brilliant operations in the war. They blew up a gate with a petard, and climbed up all three mountains at once, carrying each redoubt sword in hand, and storming the fortifications on the summits, which were the strongest of all. The modern traveller, who gazes on this rock fortress, may well wonder at the success of the French; but probably no one was more astonished than the French themselves.

[1] Jeanne was the Christian name of Madame Dupleix, but she signed herself Jan Begum. As a specimen of her intrigues it may suffice to mention that Jan Begum carried on a secret correspondence with the native interpreter of the Madras governor; and that this interpreter not only reported to her all that occurred at Fort St. David, but induced the native commanders of the Sepoys in the British service to pledge themselves to desert to the French in the next general action. The plot was discovered in time; the native interpreter was hanged, the native commanders were banished for life to St. Helena, but Jan Begum continued to be as busy as ever at Pondicherry.

A.D. 1750-1751

Treacherous murder of Nasir Jung.

Jung; and Dupleix and his half native wife were corresponding with the rebel commanders. A small French force was sent out from Pondicherry, nominally to fight the overwhelming army of Nasir, but really to co-operate with the traitors. Some of the disaffected officers of the Nizam's army were ordered to charge the French, but refused to stir. Nasir Jung rode up to the rebels, and called them a set of cowards, who were afraid to withstand a mad attempt of a few drunken Europeans. At that moment he was shot dead by a carbine. His death was followed by a complete revolution of affairs. Muzaffir Jung was taken out of his prison, and hailed by the whole army as Nizam of the Dekhan in the room of his dead uncle.

Rejoicings at Pondicherry.

The news was received at Pondicherry with the wildest joy. Chunder Sahib and Dupleix embraced each other like friends escaped from shipwreck. Salutes were fired, and a "Te Deum" was sung in the cathedral. Muzaffir Jung proceeded from Jinjí to Pondicherry, and was solemnly installed in the French settlement as ruler of the Dekhan. Dupleix appeared at the ceremony in the dress of a Muhammadan grandee, and was the first to pay homage to Muzaffir Jung.

Triumphant elevation of Dupleix.

Meanwhile the gratitude of Muzaffir Jung was unbounded. He appointed Dupleix to be governor for the Great Moghul of all the countries to the south of the Kistna. He appointed Chunder Sahib to be Nawab of the Carnatic, but under the authority of Dupleix. He ceded enough territories to the French East India Company to yield a yearly revenue to the value of nearly forty thousand pounds sterling. He distributed money to the value of fifty thousand pounds amongst the French officers and troops, and presented Dupleix with a sum equal to two hundred thousand pounds.

Death of Muzaffir Jung.

Another revolution was impending. The new Nizam returned to the Dekhan with a French force under Bussy. The rebel commanders were dissatisfied with the rewards they had received for the part they had played in the conspiracy against Nasir Jung. Again they broke out in tumult. It was suppressed by the fire of the French artillery, but Muzaffir Jung pursued the fugitives, and received a mortal stroke from a javelin.

The sudden death of the new Nizam threw the whole camp into horrible confusion. The army was greatly in arrears of pay. The grandees were afraid that the troops would break out in mutiny and plunder. The French would have fared worse than all, for the jealousy of their influence was universal. But the coolness of Bussy averted the crisis. The three younger brothers of Nasir Jung were still in confinement. Bussy released the eldest and proclaimed him ruler of the Dekhan under the name of Salábut Jung, amidst the general acclamations of the whole army.

A.D. 1750-1751

Salábut Jung, Nizam, 1751.

Such was the state of affairs in the early part of 1751. Dupleix had realized his wildest dreams of French supremacy in India. The Nizam and the Nawab owed their thrones to Dupleix and his Frenchmen. Not a single rival remained to the French candidates except Muhammad Ali, who had been appointed Nawab of the Carnatic by Nasir Jung; and Muhammad Ali was closely besieged by Chunder Sahib and the French at Trichinopoly, and was already offering terms.

Ascendancy of the French in India, 1751.

Meanwhile the English at Madras and Fort St. David had been utterly bewildered by revolutions, which were contrary to the precedents and institutions of the Moghul empire. Muhammad Ali had been appointed Nawab of the Carnatic by the Nizam; and the English had recognised and supported him as the legitimate Nawab, and sent small detachments from time to time to Trichinopoly. But they were afraid of being drawn into hostilities with the French, in violation of the treaty of Aix-la-Chapelle. They had even allowed Admiral Boscowen and Major Lawrence to return to England on the ground that the war with France was over. In a word, they seemed resigned to a fate which they could not avert, and anxiously awaited fresh instructions from the Directors in England.

Bewilderment of the English.

The news that Muhammad Ali was capitulating with Dupleix aroused the English from their torpor. The instinct of self-preservation drove them to action. If Muhammad Ali submitted to the French, the ruin of Madras and Fort St. David was assured; for Dupleix could issue his own orders for their destruction through his creature, Chunder Sahib. Accordingly, the English sent larger detachments to Trichinopoly, and appointed Captain Cope, and afterwards Captain De Gingen, to take the command.

English driven to action by the instinct of self-preservation.

The military operations at Trichinopoly are forgotten now. Fighting the French is no longer a master passion with the English nation; and the exploits of Cope, De

A.D. 1751-1752

Captain Clive realizes the situation.

Gingen, and Dalton, with absurdly small parties of English soldiers, have died out of the national memory. But Clive, who was now a captain, performed a feat which thrilled through the British empire. He had gone to Trichinopoly, and studied the whole situation. The succession of the Nizams of the Dekhan was practically settled in favour of the French. Nasir Jung and Muzaffir Jung had both been slain; and Salábut Jung had been placed by Bussy on the throne at Hyderabad. The question as regards the succession of a Nawab of the Carnatic turned upon the fate of Trichinopoly. If Chunder Sahib, the French Nawab, captured Trichinopoly, the English would be driven out of the Carnatic. If Muhammad Ali, the English Nawab, held out at Trichinopoly, he might yet be restored to the throne of his father Anwar-ud-dín, and the English settlements would be saved from destruction.

Critical position at Trichinopoly.

The English were terribly outnumbered at Trichinopoly. The Hindu Rajas, especially Mysore and Tanjore, were holding aloof from the contest; they hated Chunder Sahib, but they would not commit themselves by sending forces to help Muhammad Ali. In a word, they were trembling in the balance between the English and French; waiting to see who would get the upper hand in order that they might join the winning side.

Plans of Clive.

The relief of Trichinopoly was of the first importance to the English; it was almost a question of life or death. The problem was solved by Captain Clive. In July, 1751, Captain Clive returned from Trichinopoly to Madras. The road runs due north to Arcot, a distance of some hundred and eighty miles from Trichinopoly; it then runs eastward from Arcot to Madras, a distance of scarcely seventy miles. During the march, Captain Clive saw that the garrisons in the Carnatic, and especially the force at Arcot, had been drawn away to the siege of Trichinopoly; that Arcot was consequently open to attack; and that the capture of Arcot might prove the salvation of Trichinopoly. On reaching Madras he proposed sending an expedition against Arcot. He urged that the capture of the capital of the Carnatic in the name of Muhammad Ali would revive the spirits of the Hindu Rajas, and induce them to rally round his standard at Trichinopoly. At the same time it would weaken the besieging force at Trichinopoly, by compelling Chunder

Sahib and the French to send a large detachment far away to the northward for the recovery of Arcot.

A.D. 1751-1752

Expedition to Arcot.

The proposition was approved, and the expedition from Madras to Arcot proved to be the turning-point in the war. The detachment consisted of only two hundred Europeans and three hundred Sepoys. Captain Clive took the command, and had eight European officers under him; but of these only two had been in action, whilst four of the remainder were commercial clerks who had been fired by his example to draw the sword.

March from Madras.

With this handful of men, and three field-pieces for artillery, Clive marched from Madras. On the way he heard that the fort of Arcot was garrisoned by eleven hundred men, or more than double his force; and he wrote back to Madras for two eighteen-pounders. Spies from Arcot soon announced his approach to the garrison. They reported that the English had marched through a storm of thunder, lightning, and rain without the slightest concern. The garrison at Arcot was so frightened at this astounding audacity, that they fled from the fort and encamped at a distance, leaving fort and town open to the invaders.

Occupation of Arcot.

The English force entered the city, and took possession of the fort, whilst a hundred thousand spectators looked helplessly on. Clive found lead, gunpowder, and eight pieces of cannon. He stored the fort with provisions sufficient to stand a siege. Meanwhile the fugitive garrison from Arcot was reinforced by large numbers, and threatened to storm the fort; but were dispersed by the sallies of Clive.

Fifty days siege.

The forecast of Clive was fulfilled to the letter. Chunder Sahib and the French were taken aback by the English occupation of Arcot; and were compelled to divide their besieging force at Trichinopoly by sending an overwhelming native army, accompanied by a hundred and fifty Europeans, for the recovery of Arcot. For the space of fifty days Clive not only repulsed all attacks, but filled the enemy with constant alarm. Bribes were offered him in vain. His exploits created such an impression on the Hindus, that a body of Mahrattas joined him from Mysore. Other reinforcements were approaching from Madras, when the enemy threw all its force into one final attack. The assault was made at early morning on the festival of the Muharram. The Muhammadan army was drunk with enthusiasm and

A.D. 1751-1752

bhang, and rushed on to the trenches with their ladders in their hands. But Clive had been prepared for the attack and repulsed it at all points, until the energy of the storming parties was exhausted and the fire of musketry and cannon died away. At night the enemy raised the siege and fled in confusion.

Clive's career of conquest.

Captain Clive then took the field, and not only routed and dispersed the retreating enemy, but captured several strongholds in the Carnatic in behalf of Muhammad Ali. In January 1752 the enemy tried to create a diversion by invading the Company's territory of Poonamallee, and plundering the country-houses of the English in the neighbourhood of Madras. Clive again attacked and defeated them, but was suddenly recalled to Fort St. David. His career of individual conquest had been brought to a close. In March 1752 Major Lawrence returned from England, and resumed the command of all the Company's forces.

Major Lawrence at Trichinopoly: obstructions of native allies.

All this while Muhammad Ali and the English still held out at Trichinopoly against Chunder Sahib and the French. Accordingly Major Lawrence marched to Trichinopoly with reinforcements for the besieged, whilst Clive served under him as the second in command. The tide of fortune had turned in favour of Muhammad Ali, and there was consequently no lack of native allies. One force had already come from Tanjore to assist in the defence of Trichinopoly. A still larger army was brought by the regent of Mysore, who had also hired a body of Mahrattas under Morari Rao.[1] Other bands of barbarians were brought up from the southern jungles by a chief known as Tondiman Poligar. But Major Lawrence was worried by his native allies. Splendid opportunities were lost because the stars were not favourable; and he often found that he must either act alone, or be tied down by feasts or fasts, or by lucky or unlucky days.

Murder of Chunder Sahib:

Still the operations of the English under Lawrence and Clive were crowned with success. In May, 1752, Chunder Sahib surrendered himself a prisoner to the Tanjore

[1] The Raja of Mysore was at this time an infant, and the country was governed by his uncle Nunjiraj as regent during his minority. It was at this period that Hyder Naik, the founder of the Muhammadan kingdom of Mysore, was rising to power as an officer in the service of Nunjiraj.

general, by whom he was barbarously murdered. At the same time the French force at Trichinopoly capitulated. The officers gave their parole not to serve against Muhammad Ali or his allies; whilst the private soldiers, to the number of four hundred, were sent to Fort St. David as prisoners.

A.D. 1751-1752

French surrender, 1752.

The year 1752 thus saw the English triumphant at Trichinopoly. French interests seemed to be ruined. Major Lawrence prepared to leave Trichinopoly with his native allies; to recover the fortresses in the Carnatic which had not been surrendered; and to conduct Muhammad Ali to Arcot, and install him as Nawab.

English triumphant.

At this crisis a dangerous quarrel, which must have been secretly brewing for weeks, suddenly broke out between the native allies. Major Lawrence discovered, to his utter surprise and discomfiture, that Muhammad Ali had bought the help of Mysore by promising to make over Trinchinopoly to the regent; and the Mysore regent refused to stir from Trichinopoly, or to take any part in the restoration of Muhammad Ali to the throne of the Carnatic, until the city of Trichinopoly was placed in his possession.

Quarrel between the native allies.

The dispute about Trichinopoly has long been obsolete, but in 1752 it involved serious consequences. It was the key to the Hindu Carnatic, and as such had long been coveted by successive Nawabs; and its occupation by Mysore, or the Mahrattas, or by any other Hindu power, would have been justly regarded as a perpetual menace to the Nawab.

Trichinopoly, the key to the Hindu Carnatic.

Major Lawrence tried to effect a compromise, but soon found that it was impossible. Muhammad Ali was full of excuses and evasions. He confessed that he had pledged himself to make over Trichinopoly; but he urged that the promise had been extorted from him by his extreme distress, and that the Mysore regent was fully aware that he could not fulfil it. Trichinopoly, he said, belonged to the Great Moghul; and if it was given to a Hindu Raja, the Great Moghul would make war, not only upon him, but upon his English allies. He privately proposed to Major Lawrence to amuse the regent by promising to deliver up Trichinopoly at the end of two months. Meanwhile, he added, he hoped to collect enough arrears of revenue to defray the expenses of the regent, and prevent the necessity of parting with Trichinopoly.

Duplicity of Muhammad Ali.

A.D. 1751-1752

Native intrigues.

Major Lawrence thus found himself involved in a web of deceit and intrigue which rendered action impracticable. The Mysore regent professed himself willing to accept payment of his expenses in lieu of Trichinopoly, if the money was paid at once; but he demanded such an enormous sum that money was out of the question. It was thought that Morari Rao could mediate between the two parties, but he made matters worse. Publicly he decided that the Nawab was to make over Trichinopoly at the end of two months. Privately he counselled the Nawab not to surrender Trichinopoly at all. Privately also he counselled the Mysore regent to insist on the immediate surrender of the city under pain of making war on the Nawab, or deserting to the French. By so doing the wily Mahratta secretly made friends with both sides, and obtained large presents from both the Nawab and the regent, who were each anxious for his support. At the same time Morari Rao fomented the rupture between the two, and tried to cajole the Nawab into allowing the Mahratta troops to hold Trichinopoly during the interval, on the treacherous understanding that at the end of the two months he was not to make it over to the Mysore regent, but to give it back to Muhammad 'Ali. Had Morari Rao succeeded in getting inside Trichinopoly he would undoubtedly have kept possession of the place, just as Chunder Sahib had done some fifteen years before.

General defection of the Hindu allies.

This wretched quarrel robbed the English of all the pleasure of their triumph. Moreover, it was followed by plots and intrigues for the seizure of Trichinopoly, which volumes would fail to describe. Meanwhile the fortunes of the French were becoming brilliant in the Dekhan. Dupleix and his wife took advantage of these successes to send letters and presents to all parties at Trichinopoly, representing that the English were a plodding mercantile people, unacquainted with war, and unable to oppose the French, and who owed all their victories to the valour and activity of the Mahratta cavalry. The consequence was that the Mysore regent went over to the French together with the Mahrattas; whilst the contingents of the Tanjore Raja and Tondiman Poligar returned to their own homes, incensed alike against the Nawab and the Mysore regent, and resolved to do nothing more until they could find whether the English or French were likely to win the day.

A.D. 1752-1753

French acquire the Northern Circars.

All this while Dupleix had never despaired. The death of Chunder Sahib, and surrender of the French force at Trichinopoly, had excited consternation at Pondicherry. But Bussy's successes in the Dekhan more than counterbalanced the disasters in the Carnatic. Salábut Jung owed his throne to the French; and would have been deprived of it at any moment by one rival or another, but for the support of Bussy and the French army. Accordingly he ceded a large and valuable territory on the Coromandel coast for the permanent maintenance of the French forces. The French thus acquired a larger territory in India than had ever before been possessed by any European power, not excepting the Portuguese. It stretched along six hundred miles of seaboard, from the Carnatic frontier at the river Gundlacama, northward to the pagoda of Jagganath. It yielded a yearly revenue of more than half a million sterling; and possessed commercial advantages which were vastly improved by the possession of the port of Masulipatam. This territory was afterwards known as the Northern Circars.

Claims of Dupleix to be Nawab of the Carnatic.

At the same time Dupleix professed to have been confirmed by Salábut Jung in the post of ruler of all India to the south of the Kistna. He even feigned to have received insignia and letters of investiture from the Great Moghul. By virtue of this authority he arrogated to himself all the powers of a Nawab.

Peace prevented by Dupleix, 1753.

In 1753 the English were anxious for a peace. They were worn out by the expense of a war which was in reality a national affair, and ought not to have fallen on the East India Company. Captain Clive had returned to England on the score of ill-health; and the operations of Lawrence were indecisive. The English were willing to leave the French in possession of the Northern Circars, and to acknowledge Salábut Jung as Nizam of the Dekhan; but they required the French to acknowledge Muhammad Ali as Nawab of the Carnatic. But Dupleix was impracticable, and rejected the offer with disdain. He claimed to be Nawab of the Carnatic, and unless his authority as Nawab was recognised by the English he would make no terms whatever.

Reference to Europe.

In this dilemma the Court of Directors in London called on the British ministry to put an end to the war in the Carnatic, or to carry it on at the charge of the British nation.

S

A.D. 1753-1756

The question had become of vital importance. Great Britain and France were at peace in Europe, and had been at peace ever since the treaty of Aix-la-Chapelle in 1748. The war between the two nations in the Carnatic was thus not only an anomaly, but a complication which few in Europe could comprehend. London and Paris were confused by dynastic stories of rival Nawabs and rival Nizams setting the Great Moghul at defiance, and fighting for the mastery with the English Company on one side and the French Company on the other. Meanwhile the Directors of both Companies found themselves drawn into hopeless contests, which exhausted their treasuries and obstructed their trade.

Dupleix sacrificed.

Under such circumstances all parties began to throw the blame upon Dupleix. The English charged him with beginning the war by the liberation of Chunder Sahib from his Mahratta prison at Satara. The French denounced his ambitious schemes for his own aggrandisement, which devoured the profits of the French East India Company without adding to the glory of the French nation. Dupleix was sacrificed to the necessities of both nations, to prevent a war between Great Britain and France, and to enable the English and French Companies to escape from political responsibilities which were destructive to the interests of trade.

Peace between the English and French Companies, 1755.

The finale is soon told. A French commissary was sent to Pondicherry with full powers to conclude a peace with the English authorities at Madras. Both sides pledged themselves for the future to renounce all native government and dignity, and to abandon all interference with native powers. The French also agreed to relinquish all territories they had acquired in excess of those acquired by the English. But these conditions were never carried out. Dupleix, however, was removed from the government of Pondicherry, and returned to France a ruined and broken-hearted man.[1]

Armed truce.

The treaty was signed at Pondicherry in Jan. 1755. It was only provisional, and awaited the confirmation of the English and French governments in Europe; and within eighteen months it was cast to the winds. The English excited the jealousy of the French by helping Muhammad Ali to establish his authority in the Carnatic over rebellious Poligars.

[1] Dupleix lived for nine years longer. He died at Paris in the utmost poverty, on the 10th of November, 1764.

At the same time the French occupation of the Northern Circars, and the continued presence of Bussy and his forces in the Dekhan, excited the bitterest animosity of the English. A.D. 1753-1756

Return of Clive to India.

Meanwhile Clive, who had embarked for England in 1753 on the score of ill-health, had returned to Bombay with the commission of a lieutenant-colonel in the service of the Crown. He was to have led a European force from Bombay towards Hyderabad, with the view of co-operating with the Peishwa of the Mahrattas against the Nizam, and compelling Salábut Jung to dismiss Bussy and his Frenchmen. But the expedition was stopped by the treaty of Pondicherry. Accordingly he joined the fleet of Admiral Watson in an expedition against a noted pirate named Angria.

Rise of the Angrias, or pirate chiefs of Gheria.

About the beginning of the eighteenth century, when the Moghul power was beginning to decline, a rebel of the name of Angria founded a piratical empire on the Malabar coast between Bombay and Goa. During the fifty years which followed, the name of Angria had been as great a terror on the sea as that of Sivaji had been on land. A succession of Angrias had pushed their aggressions along the Mahratta coast, until they possessed a seaboard of a hundred and twenty miles in length, with a fort at every creek. Their fleets consisted of fast-sailing vessels of small burden, and rowing-boats of forty or fifty oars, armed with guns and crowded with men. No vessel could pass this coast without paying chout for a pass from Angria, or running the chance of capture. The East India Company alone expended fifty thousand pounds yearly on the maintenance of an armed convoy for the protection of their merchant ships against these dangerous corsairs.

Destruction of Gheria by Clive and Watson, February, 1756.

The capital of Angria was at Gheria, which was supposed to be another Gibraltar, but Clive and Watson made short work of capturing it. The place was bombarded and stormed in February, 1756, and its fortifications and shipping were destroyed. Angria's people were so alarmed that they surrendered all their other forts to the Mahrattas without resistance, and abandoned most of their territory.

Rupture between the Nizam and the French.

Clivé and Watson next proceeded to Madras. Meanwhile there had been a rupture between Salábut Jung and Bussy, brought about by a powerful Muhammadan party at the court of Hyderabad. In July, 1756, Bussy marched his force to

A.D. 1753-1756

Hyderabad, and took up a strong position; whilst Salábut Jung sent urgent messages to Madras imploring the help of the English against the French.

Bad news from Bengal, July, 1756.

Nothing could have been more acceptable to the English authorities. All mention of the Dekhan and the Nizam had been intentionally excluded from the treaty of Pondicherry. At the same time Europe was on the eve of the "Seven Years' War," and a declaration of hostilities between Great Britain and France was expected to arrive in India by every ship. Accordingly, an English force was prepared to take the field for the support of Salábut Jung against the French; but suddenly the march was countermanded. In August terrible news arrived from Bengal. Calcutta had been captured by the Nawab of Bengal, Behar,[1] and Orissa, and a hundred and twenty-three English prisoners had been stifled to death in the Black Hole.

[1] In the previous chapters Behar has been spelt "Bihár" in conformity with the spelling ordered by the British government. But in dealing with the history of British India, it is not worth while to change the spelling of a geographical term which has been in general use for more than a century.

CHAPTER II.

ENGLISH IN BENGAL.

A.D. 1700 TO 1761.

A.D. 1700-1725

Position of the English at Calcutta.

THE position of the English in Calcutta during the early half of the eighteenth century bore a general resemblance to that of the English at Madras. They had a governor and council, and a mayor's court. They had an English officer, who collected revenue and administered justice amongst their native subjects under the name of Zemindar. They had a head policeman, who kept the peace by day and night, under the name of Kotwal. They had Dutch and French neighbours, whose factories were situated some twenty miles off at Chinsura and Chandernagore. They paid rent and customs to the Moghul officer, who commanded the surrounding district under the name of Foujdar, and made Hughli his head quarters.[1]

Court of the Nawab at Murshedabad.

The Nawab of Bengal, Behar, and Orissa, was a grandee of the first water, who kept his court at Murshedabad, about a hundred and twenty miles to the north of Calcutta. The English had few transactions with the great man; they generally carried on all their political negotiations through the Moghul commander at Hughli.

The English at Calcutta knew more of the interior than the English at Madras. There was no water way at Madras to open up the country; and no great roads in the Peninsula like those which traversed Hindustan and

[1] The Dutch factory at Chinsura, the French factory at Chandernagore, and the Moghul town of Hughli, are some three or four miles distant from each other.

A.D. 1700-1725

Inland factories at Cossimbazar, Dacca, and Patna.

the Dekhan. Before the war, Arcot was as remote as Delhi, whilst Madura was a mystery like Pekin or Timbuctoo. But the position of the English at Calcutta was altogether different, for they had established factories at a considerable distance inland. On the north they had a factory at Cossimbazar, the trading suburb of Murshedabad. On the east they had a factory at Dacca, near the Brahmaputra river, whence they procured Dacca muslins. On the west they had the great water-way of the Ganges, and had established a factory at Patna, four hundred miles from Calcutta, for the purchase of saltpetre, raw silk, and opium.

Nawab Murshed Kuli Khan 1700-25: founder of Murshedabad.

The old Nawabs of Bengal were thus better known to the English than the Nawabs of the Carnatic. The founder of the first hereditary dynasty was Murshed Kuli Khan, a man who flourished between 1700 and 1725, and was a type of the rulers formed in the school of Aurangzeb. He rose from some minor post to be Nawab of the three provinces of Bengal, Behar, and Orissa; a territory extending north and south from the mountains of Nipal to the jungles of Gondwana, and east and west from the river Brahmaputra and Bay of Bengal to the little river Carumnassa.[1] He moved his capital from Dacca to Murshedabad, which was so called after his own name.[2]

Oppressive administration.

The secret of the rise of Murshed Kuli Khan lay in his sending a large yearly tribute to the imperial treasury at Delhi, together with large presents for ministers, favourites, and influential grandees. In return he was allowed to fill the two posts of Nawab and Dewan; in other words, to command the three provinces whilst acting as accountant-general for the Great Moghul. He was thus necessarily a strict financier, and many stories are told by native writers of his cruelty and oppression. He imprisoned the leading landholders, known as Zemindars and Rajas, and appointed Bengali Hindus of his own selection to collect the rents from the farmers. He placed other Zemindars on sub-

[1] The Carumnassa is an insignificant stream, flowing into the Jumna near Buxar, which is not always shown in the map. Its importance as a frontier between Behar and the territory of Benares continued until the administration of Warren Hastings, when Benares was annexed to British territory.

[2] Murshed Kuli Khan is known in some histories by the name of Jafir Khan, and must be distinguished from the Nawab Mír Jafir, who appears in the later history.

sistence allowances, whilst his Bengali officers, known as Aumils, collected the rents in like manner. He re-measured estates, and brought fallow and waste lands under cultivation by making advances to the lower class of husbandmen. In a word, he dispossessed most of the Zemindars from their holdings, except a few whom he ventured to trust, and a few powerful Rajas, such as Birbhúm and Kishenghur, who were able to resent or defy any interference with their hereditary estates or territories.

A.D. 1700-1725

Harsh treatment of Hindus.

Murshed Kuli Khan, like all the Moghul officers of the school of Aurangzeb, was very harsh towards Hindus. He allowed no Hindus, not even Zemindars or Rajas, to sit or speak to each other in his presence. He prohibited even the wealthiest Hindus from riding in a palanquin, and required them to use inferior conveyances. He preferred Bengali Hindus to collect the revenue because they were more amenable to threats and punishments, and were too timid to rebel or plot against him. It was a common saying that the Muhammadans squandered their ill-gotten gains on pomp and pleasure, and left no wealth to be confiscated; whilst the Hindus hoarded their gains, and then, like sponges, could be squeezed of all their riches. If a district collector was in arrears the Hindu defaulter was tormented, bastinadoed, hung up by the feet, placed in the hot sun, or subjected to some other exquisite torture. But if there was any fraud, or any failure to make good a deficiency, the Hindu culprit was compelled to turn Muhammadan, together with his wife and family.[1]

Profligate son-in-law.

Murshed Kuli Khan had no son. He had given a daughter in marriage to an officer named Shuja Khan, who was deputy-governor of Orissa. But Shuja Khan was so utterly bad and profligate that his wife left him in Orissa and went back to her father at Murshedabad, accompanied by a son named Sarfaráz Khan.

Favourite grandson.

The old Nawab hated his son-in-law but took a great liking to his grandson. He set aside Shuja Khan and used all his influence at Delhi to secure the appointment of his grandson, Sarfaráz, as his heir and successor to the Nawabship of the three provinces of Bengal, Behar, and Orissa. But he died in 1725, before his intentions were carried into

[1] The original authorities for these statements will be found translated in Stewart's *History of Bengal*.

A.D. 1725-1742

effect, and thus left the throne at Murshedabad to be a bone of contention between a father and a son.

Coup d'état of Shuja Khan.

Meantime Shuja Khan, by means of lavish presents at Delhi, had procured the insignia and letters of investiture from Delhi for his own appointment as Nawab of the three provinces; and shortly after the death of his father-in-law he suddenly produced them at the city of Murshedabad, and was at once proclaimed successor to the throne. His son, Sarfaráz Khan, was totally ignorant of his father's design. He was sitting at a country house near the city, hourly expecting the arrival of his own credentials from Delhi, when he suddenly heard the fire of salutes and roll of kettle-drums at the palace. He had been outwitted by his father, but there was no redress. He submitted to his fate, and set off to offer the customary present and congratulations to the new Nawab.

Easy reign of Shuja Khan, 1725-39: rise of Alivardi Khan.

Shuja Khan was a good-natured man who cared for nothing but pleasure. He released all the imprisoned Zemindars and Rajas, and thereby made himself popular. But he had two favourites, named Hájí Ahmad and Alivardi Khan. The former, by secret services of a questionable character, obtained the post of minister and remained at Murshedabad. His brother, Alivardi Khan, a man of bravery and audacity, was appointed deputy-governor of Behar, and left Murshedabad and took up his quarters at Patna.

Treachery of Alivardi Khan.

In Behar, Alivardi Khan devoted himself to the reduction of all the Hindu Rajas under his government. This he accomplished by the most consummate treachery and craft; ensnaring them by vows and promises, and then putting them to death. These Rajas were often little better than freebooters, and their suppression was indispensable to the tranquillity of the province; but the wholesale destruction carried out by Alivardi Khan was characterised by barbarities which were most revolting.

English voyage from Calcutta to Patna, 1735.

The English had some experience of the atrocities committed by Alivardi Khan. In those days the English boats carried goods and treasure between Calcutta and Patna under the guard of European soldiers. In 1735 a convoy went as usual in charge of an English civilian named Holwell and a Captain Holcombe. Near Monghyr the two gentlemen saw a boat going by with baskets, which they took to contain fish. They hailed the boat, and on its coming alongside they opened the baskets, and found thirty heads of men who had just been murdered.

A.D. 1725-1742

Story of the baskets of human heads.

The story was not a pleasant one. There was an old Hindu Raja near Monghyr, who had sturdily held out against the Moghul. Captain Holcombe knew him well; for the Raja, like others of his stamp, claimed a right to levy duties on all goods coming up or down the Ganges; a point which was generally settled by the sword. This aged warrior died in 1730, and was succeeded by a son, who submitted to Alivardi Khan, and agreed to pay a yearly tribute. To prevent treachery, the young Raja brought his tribute every year to a certain spot accompanied by only thirty followers. In like manner Alivardi Khan was pledged to send an officer with only thirty followers to receive the money. This year the payment had been made the very morning that Holwell and Holcombe hailed the boat. Alivardi Khan had ordered an ambush and a massacre; and the three baskets contained the heads of the Raja and his followers. One man escaped and told the tidings to the young Raja's wife, who thereupon set the palace on fire, and perished in the flames with an infant son and all her female attendants. That same night the Raja's city was attacked, plundered, and burnt by the forces of Alivardi Khan; and the two Englishmen saw the fire and smoke from the place where they lay at anchor.

Sarfaráz Khan, Nawab, 1739-42.

Nawab Shuja Khan died in 1739, the same year that Nadir Shah attacked Delhi. His son Sarfaráz Khan succeeded to the throne, and turned out a worse profligate than his father.[1] He was insolent and tyrannical, and at last gave mortal offence to a Hindu family of great wealth, who had long exercised a commanding influence at Murshedabad.

Hindu family insulted.

Jagat Seth, the patriarch of the family, was the wealthiest banker in the Moghul empire, the Rothschild of Hindustan. The wildest stories are told of the riches of his house. The Mahrattas carried off two millions sterling from his family, and the loss was no more felt than that of two trusses of straw. He knew all that was going on under every court in India; was security for most of the renters

[1] The old Nawabs of Bengal were so abominably wicked that there is not much to choose between them. Their vices were indescribable.

A.D. 1742-1750

in the Bengal provinces; and always had vast sums at his command. His grandson, a mere boy, was married to a girl of tender years. Out of mere caprice the Nawab insisted on seeing the girl without a veil. This matter, so trifling in European eyes, was regarded by Bengalis as an insult and disgrace which abrogated the marriage tie, and for which nothing but death could atone.

Destruction of Sarfaráz Khan, 1741-42.

The result was that a plot was formed by Hindus and Moghuls for the destruction of Sarfaráz Khan. The conspirators invited Alivardi Khan to undertake the task, and engaged to make him Nawab of the three provinces in the room of the doomed prince. It would be tedious to rake up the story of deceit, treachery, and bribery. Sarfaráz Khan was lulled in security, whilst Alivardi Khan was hurrying an army through the narrow pass which leads from Behar into Bengal. At last Sarfaráz Khan was suddenly aroused by the news that a rebel force was at his gates. He marched out with a large army and a train of artillery; but his officers were disaffected, and the guns were loaded with powder only, without ball. The battle was a sham; but Sarfaráz Khan was slain, and Alivardi Khan was proclaimed Nawab in his room.

Alivardi Khan, the usurper, 1742-56.

Alivardi Khan has been styled a usurper. He subsequently displayed the insignia and letters of investiture; but whether they were forged, or were bought from the Delhi Vizier, is a question of no moment. The day was fast approaching when no rights existed in India save those of the sword.

Mahratta invasions of Bengal, 1742-50.

Scarcely had Alivardi Khan secured himself as Nawab, when the three provinces were invaded by Mahrattas. It was said that the Great Moghul was so disgusted at receiving little or no tribute from the Nawab that he told the Mahrattas to collect chout in Bengal. For eight years in succession, from 1742 to 1750, these merciless hordes of miscreants devastated the country to the southward of the Ganges, from October till June, and never retired until the approach of the rainy season. All this was done under pretence of collecting chout; for by this time the Mahrattas began to consider that they possessed an inherent right to collect chout from the whole of India.

In the first instance, Alivardi Khan tried to get rid of the Mahrattas by treachery and massacre. The commanders on either side were to meet in a tent and arrange the terms of chout. The bait was swallowed. A tent was prepared, and the Nawab posted an ambush between a double lining. The meeting took place; the signal was given; the men in ambush rushed out with drawn swords, and the Mahratta general and most of his chief officers were slaughtered on the spot.

A.D. 1742-1750

Treachery and assassination.

The Mahratta army was paralysed for a moment at this horrible murder of their leaders, and then wreaked their vengeance upon the unoffending inhabitants. They ravaged the country with fire and sword, cutting off ears, noses, and hands, and committing countless barbarities in the search of spoil. The wretched Bengalis fled in shoals across the Ganges, to take refuge, or perchance to perish, in the hills and jungles to the northward of the river. It was at this juncture that the native inhabitants of Calcutta began to dig the once famous Mahratta ditch, to keep the enemy's horsemen out of the Company's bounds.[1]

Mahratta revenge: agony of Bengal.

Alivardi Khan found himself powerless to act against the loose bands of Mahrattas. They evaded a general action, and if dispersed from one place, they soon reappeared elsewhere. At the same time there was treachery in his own camp. He relied much on a force of Afghan mercenaries commanded by an officer named Mustafa Khan; but his brother, Hájí Ahmad, grew jealous of Mustafa Khan, and charged the Afghan with being in secret communication with the Mahrattas. Mustafa Khan suddenly fled with his Afghans towards Patna, but was pursued and slain; and Hájí Ahmad cut off his head, and carried it in derision three times through the streets of Patna.

Afghan treachery in Alivardi Khan's army.

The atrocity was soon avenged. Hájí Ahmad fell into the hands of the Afghans, and was put to a cruel death. He was scourged, insulted, and exposed to the derision of the mob, and then tied to the leg of an elephant, and dragged through the streets until death put an end to his agonies.

Afghan revenge.

Such details are revolting to all; but it is necessary at times to lift the curtain from a few of the horrors of anarchy

[1] Every vestige of this once famous ditch has disappeared from Calcutta. It is supposed to have run along the site at present known as the Circular Road.

A.D. 1750-1756

Peace with the Mahrattas: payment of chout, 1750.

and misrule. It will suffice to add that in 1750 Alivardi Khan came to terms with the Mahrattas. The whole province of Orissa was ceded to the Bhonsla Raja of Berar or Nagpore; and the Nawab agreed to pay a yearly sum of twelve lakhs of rupees, or a hundred and twenty thousand pounds sterling, as chout for Bengal and Behar.

Character of Alivardi Khan.

Alivardi Khan was now an old man, but the remainder of his days were spent in comparative peace. There were horrible scandals in his household at Murshedabad, as well as revolts and plots on the part of members of his family; but with all his crimes, he himself was free from vices. It is said that he was never a drunkard nor a profligate; and that in this respect his private life differed from that of most Muhammadan princes in India. A few details of his daily occupations have been preserved by a native writer who enjoyed his patronage.[1] The picture may be somewhat overdrawn, but it serves to illustrate the domestic life of an aged and respectable Muhammadan grandee:—

Domestic life of Alivardi Khan, 1750-56.

"The Nawab Alivardi Khan always rose two hours before daylight, said his prayers at daybreak, and then drank coffee with his chosen friends. From seven o'clock till nine he sat in the hall of audience, where he listened to the representations of those of his officers and grandees who had anything to say. At nine o'clock he retired and amused himself with the company of particular friends, in listening to verses of poetry or pleasant stories, or in superintending the preparation of different dishes, which were cooked in his presence and under his directions. At ten o'clock he partook of the chief meal of the day, but always in company; and when it was over his guests washed their hands and withdrew, and he retired to his couch and was lulled to sleep by the story-tellers. At one o'clock he awoke and drank a cup of water cooled with ice or saltpetre, and performed his mid-day prayers. He next read a chapter of the Koran with a loud voice, according to the rule, and performed his afternoon prayers. Pious and learned men were then introduced, and regaled with coffee and hookahs; and the Nawab drank

[1] *Siyar-ul-Mutaqherin*, by Gholam Husain Ali. Calcutta, 1786. Large use has been made of this valuable work in dealing with the rise of the British empire in India; but the author was a bigoted Shíah, and has strong likings and bitter dislikings, which must always be taken into consideration.

coffee with them but never smoked.[1] A Koran was set up, and conferences, readings and explanations would occupy two hours. Next the chiefs of offices were in attendance, and amongst others the wealthy Jagat Seth made his appearance; and these men read or told him the news from all parts of India. Wits and buffoons followed, with whom he cracked jokes for another two hours. By this time it would be dusk, and the Nawab said his evening prayers. Then the audience hall was cleared of men, and the ladies of the family came to see him. A supper was served of fresh and dried fruits and sweetmeats, and the Nawab generally distributed them amongst the ladies with his own hands. After supper the ladies retired to rest, and the hall was opened to officers of the guard, bed-watchers, and story-tellers; and the Nawab again retired to his couch, and was lulled to sleep by stories. He generally awoke three or four times in the course of the night, but was always awake about two hours before dawn.

A.D. 1750-1756

"The Nawab was troubled by the progress of affairs in the Dekhan; by the assassination of Nasir Jung during his march against the French at Pondicherry, and by the accession of Muzaffir Jung, who was supported by the French. He was troubled still more when Muzaffir Jung was slain, and Salábut Jung was made Nizam of the Dekhan, and supported on the throne by the French foreigners. At the same time he received a pompous letter from Bussy, recommending the French at Chandernagore to his care and protection. He sent no reply to the letter, but he was amazed and perplexed. 'Those hat-men,' he exclaimed, 'will soon possess all the seaboard of India.'"

Alivardi's alarm at the French.

Alivardi Chan had nominated a grandson to succeed him, named Suraj-ud-daula. This young man was insolent and vindictive, as well as cruel and profligate. He was very bitter against the English at Calcutta, and complained to his grandfather of their hostile designs; but the old Nawab was on his dying bed, and was deaf to all such representations. Meanwhile news arrived at Murshedabad that the

Suraj-ud-daula, grandson of Alivardi Khan: his bitterness against the English.

[1] It is a curious fact that Alivardi Khan never smoked. Originally he is said to have been "hookah bearer" to Shuja Khán. His brother Hájí Ahmad is said to have been originally a khitmutgar, or table-servant.

A.D. 1750-1756

English had captured the great fortress of Gheria, the stronghold of Angria. About the same time, it was reported that the English at Calcutta were strengthening their fortifications in order to fight the French at Chandernagore.

Suraj-ud-daula, Nawab, 1756: marches an army against Calcutta.

The old Nawab died in April, 1756. Suraj-ud-daula succeeded to the throne at Murshedabad, in spite of hostile intrigues and plots in favour of other claimants.[1] He was told that one of his enemies had found refuge in Calcutta, and demanded his immediate surrender; but his messenger was regarded with suspicion at Calcutta, and no reply was sent. Next he ordered Mr. Drake, the governor of Calcutta, to demolish his new fortifications. Mr. Drake replied that no new fortifications had been constructed; that nothing had been done beyond repairing a line of guns to prevent the French from capturing Calcutta in the same way that they had captured Madras ten years before. The young Nawab was furious at the idea of the English fighting the French within his dominions. He sent a body of horsemen to surround the factory of Cossimbazar, in the suburbs of his capital, and to bring away the English there as his prisoners. He then assembled an army of fifty thousand men, and a train of artillery, and marched to Calcutta with such haste in the month of June, that many of his troops died of fatigue and sunstroke on the way.

Alarm of the English: inefficient defences.

The English at Calcutta were bewildered by these tidings. They expected some demand for money, but were taken aback by the capture of Cossimbazar. The Mahrattas had caused an occasional scare at Calcutta, but many years had passed away since the English had the slightest grounds for expecting an attack from the Nawab. The defences had been neglected; warehouses had been built adjoining the fort; whilst the fort itself was overlooked by numerous buildings. The English at Calcutta were a mere handful. There were not five hundred men in all Calcutta, including Englishmen and mixed races. There were only a hundred and seventy European soldiers, and of these scarcely ten had seen any service beyond parade. Still, had Clive been there, he would have defied the Nawab and all his rabble host. All

[1] One of these claimants had actually secured letters of investiture from Delhi for the three provinces of Bengal, Behar, and Orissa, by promising to send a yearly tribute to the Moghul treasury of one million sterling.

tall houses would have been demolished; all inconvenient walls would have been thrown down; and any enemy encamped in the neighbourhood would have been kept in constant alarm, by shells during the day, and by sallies at night, until the besiegers thought proper to disappear from the scene. A.D. 1750-1756

Military operations.

But instead of standing a siege in Fort William, as Clive had done in the citadel at Arcot, the English madly attempted to defend the town of Calcutta by isolated outposts at a distance from the fort. The fighting began on Wednesday, the 16th of June. During Thursday and Friday the outposts were driven in by sheer force of numbers; and after much desperate fighting in the streets and avenues the English fell back on the fort. On Saturday, the 19th of June, the enemy opened a cannonade. The women were carried to the ships, and Mr. Drake and some others escaped with them; and then, to the utter disgust of those left in the fort, the ships moved down the river.

Calcutta surrendered on Sunday, 20th June, 1756.

Next morning was Sunday the 20th of June. The enemy tried to escalade the walls, but the rabble soldiery were easily driven back, and there was a lull in the fighting. By this time, heat and fatigue had told on the English garrison. The European soldiers broke into the arrack stores and got drunk. There was a flag of truce and a parley. Meanwhile the native soldiers climbed over the walls, and broke in at different openings, and there was a general surrender.

Tragedy of the Black Hole.

The Nawab entered Fort William in great pomp, but found only fifty thousand rupees in the treasury. He sent for Mr. Holwell, who represented the governor in the absence of Mr. Drake. He swore that no harm should befall the prisoners, but he was very angry at the small amount in the treasury. Mr. Holwell was soon dismissed, and returned to his fellow-prisoners, who were assembled under a strong guard in a low veranda in front of a line of barracks. For some time the Nawab's officers could find no place fitted for the confinement of the prisoners. At last, at the end of the chambers, they found the strong-room of the garrison, known as the Black Hole. It was not twenty feet square. There was no air except what came through the veranda and two little gratings in the door. Into this close dungeon, on one of the hottest nights in a Calcutta June, a

A.D. 1756-1757

hundred and forty-six prisoners were thrust by swords and clubs. The door was then shut, and the shrieking captives were left to die. Next morning, twenty-three fainting wretches were dragged out alive; the remaining hundred and twenty-three were dead corpses.

Strange indifference of Asiatics.

The question of who was to blame for this catastrophe has often been argued, but has long ceased to be of any moment. Suraj-ud-daula may have been free of blame. He left the custody of the prisoners to his officers, and then retired to rest, and no one dared to wake him. But next morning he was utterly callous to all that had happened, and only anxious to know where the English had secreted their vast treasures. The native inhabitants of Bengal were equally callous. The tale of horror thrilled through the British empire; and would have excited the same indignation had it occurred in the remotest village in England or Ireland. But in India it excited no horror at all; it fell on the listless ears of Asiatics and was forgotten, if indeed it was ever known. Muhammadan historians tell the story of the capture of Calcutta, but they say nothing of the Black Hole.[1]

Hostile preparations at Madras.

The terrible tidings of the capture of Calcutta and catastrophe of the Black Hole reached Madras in August. It created a stir in the settlement which is perhaps without a parallel in Madras history. Bussy and the French were forgotten; and it was speedily resolved that the force intended for the Dekhan should be despatched with all speed to Bengal.

Recapture of Calcutta by Watson and Clive, January, 1757.

The fleet left Madras in October, 1756, under the command of Admiral Watson; the land forces were commanded by Colonel Clive. The expedition reached Calcutta on the 1st of January, 1757. There was very little fighting. The Moghul commander at Hughli had been appointed governor of Calcutta, and he fled in a panic on the arrival of the English. On the 2nd of January the English flag was hoisted on Fort William. On the 10th the English advanced

[1] This utter want of political ties among the masses of natives of India is the cause of their depression. Individually they are the kindest and most compassionate people in the world, but outside their own little circle of family or caste they are utterly heedless of what is going on. Within the last few years there has been a change for the better; the famines have enlarged their sympathies, and the political future of the Hindu people is more hopeful now than at any former period of their history.

to the native town of Hughli, and speedily took possession of the place.[1]

A.D. 1757-1761

Alarm of the Nawab Suraj-ud-daula.

All this while the Nawab had been puffed up by the capture of the European fortress at Calcutta. He threatened to punish the French and Dutch in like manner; but they professed implicit obedience, and sent him large sums of money. He released his English prisoners, and thought that hostilities were at an end. It never crossed his mind that the English would return in force and demand compensation and revenge. But the recovery of Calcutta and

[1] Some of the details of the fighting are valuable as illustrations of Asiatic warfare. The approach to Calcutta was guarded by the fort of Budge-budge, now spelt Baj-baj. Colonel Clive, over-confident and contemptuous of the natives, expected to capture the place without much resistance; and laid an ambuscade to cut off the retreat of the Muhammadan garrison. The enemy however attacked the ambuscade by surprise; and nothing but the cool intrepidity of Clive saved it from destruction. Meanwhile the artillery in the fort played upon the English squadron, and was only silenced by a heavy fire from the shipping.

Under these circumstances Clive prepared to storm the place on the following morning. At night, whilst the storming party was resting on the ground, and all on board the shipping were retiring to rest, a roar of acclamation was heard from the shore, and news was brought to Admiral Watson that Baj-baj had been captured. It appeared that a drunken sailor, named Strahan, having a cutlass in one hand and a pistol in the other, had scaled a breach single-handed, fired his pistol, and rushed on the Muhammadan sentinels with wild huzzas. Two or three other sailors heard the uproar, and followed their comrade with shouts and yells. The garrison fled in a panic. The storming party of soldiers burst in pellmell, without order or discipline, and found themselves in possession of the fort, with eighteen cannon and forty barrels of powder.

Admiral Watson thought it necessary for the sake of discipline to be very angry with Strahan; but the fellow said that he meant no harm, and promised never to take a fort again without orders. Subsequently the Admiral would have made the man a boatswain, but his habits were against him. It was afterwards discovered that Strahan's ambition was to be appointed cook on board one of the ships, but whether his ambition was gratified is unknown to history.

Another absurd occurrence took place after the capture of Hughli. Three English sailors were missing, and were supposed to have been killed or seriously wounded. At night the officers on board the ships saw that several villages were in flames. Next morning the three sailors appeared floating on a raft. They had found themselves deserted by their companions, and had set the villages on fire to make the inhabitants believe that the English forces were still on shore. Subsequently they had found the raft, and escaped in safety before the natives had recovered from their panic.

A.D. 1757-1761 —— capture of Hughli filled him with alarm. He marched a large army towards Calcutta, but professed a desire for peace and friendship, and promised to compensate the English for all their losses.

Clive's anxiety for peace. At the same time Clive himself was anxious for peace. All his thoughts were occupied by the coming war with France. He would have abandoned all ideas of punishment or revenge, provided that the Nawab compensated the English for their losses, and permitted him to capture the French settlement at Chandernagore.

Vacillations of the Nawab: English capture Chandernagore. The Nawab agreed to everything that Clive proposed, but he was resolved in his own heart to do nothing. A treaty was concluded without the slightest difficulty; but Clive soon found that the Nawab had only made peace in order to gain time and procure help from the French. The Nawab promised to compensate the English for their losses at the capture of Calcutta, but he evaded every demand for a settlement. He sent letters and presents to Bussy, requesting him to march up from the Dekhan and drive the English out of Bengal. He forbade the English to attack the French; but news arrived that the Afghans had captured Delhi, and intended conquering Bengal. In his terror he implored Clive to help him against the Afghans. Under the influence of this terror he permitted the English to attack Chandernagore, but then withdrew his permission. Both Clive and Watson considered the withdrawal as an indignity, and sailed against Chandernagore and captured it. The Nawab then sent letters of congratulation to Clive and Watson; and actually offered to make over the territory of Chandernagore to the English on the same terms that it had been held by the French.

Hostility of the Nawab. Meanwhile the dissimulation of the Nawab reached a climax. He harboured the French refugees from Chandernagore; and then supplied them with funds, and sent them up country. He posted a force at Plassy, on the way to Calcutta, under the command of an officer named Mír Jafir; and when Clive remonstrated with him on this hostile demonstration, he joined Mír Jafir at Plassy with the whole of his army.

Conspiracy against the Nawab At this juncture there was a widely spread disaffection against the Nawab. Mír Jafir at Plassy and Jagat Seth, the Hindu banker at Murshedabad, were deeply implicated, and they invited Clive to join in the general conspiracy. It was agreed that Clive should march an army to Plassy, and that Mír Jafir should desert the Nawab and join the English army with all his forces; and a treaty was concluded under which Suraj-ud-daula was to be dethroned, and Mír Jafir was to be proclaimed Nawab in his room.

A.D. 1757-1761

Mír Jafir joined by Clive.

Unfortunately the communication between the head conspirators and Clive was carried on through a Hindu named Omichund. This man threatened to divulge the whole plot to Suraj-ud-daula unless an article was inserted in the treaty pledging Mír Jafir to pay him three hundred thousand pounds sterling as the price of his silence. There is no doubt that Omichund was a consummate rascal without honour or shame; but the mode adopted for keeping him quiet was a slur upon the English character. Omichund was duped with a sham treaty containing the desired clause, which was omitted from the real treaty. Clive and others signed the sham treaty, but Watson refused to sign any treaty but the real one. Clive added the name of Watson to the sham treaty with the full knowledge of the admiral; and he invariably urged to the day of his death that he was fully justified in all he had done.[1]

Treachery of Omichund.

Clive advanced from Calcutta to Plassy with a small force of three thousand men and nine pieces of artillery. The army of the Nawab consisted of fifty thousand foot, eighteen thousand horse, and fifty pieces of artillery.[2] The famous battle was fought on the 23rd of June, 1757. It was little better than a cannonade. Mír Jafir did nothing, and the whole brunt of the fighting fell upon the English. At last the English advanced to storm the camp of the Nawab, and Suraj-ud-daula was seized with a panic and fled from the field.

Decisive battle of Plassy, 23rd June, 1757.

[1] This sham treaty is the one blot on Clive's public character. He did not personally derive any advantage from it; he thought himself justified in taking such a step for defeating the perfidy of a villain like Omichund. He would not have been condemned by the public opinion of orientals, who regard all such fabrications as justifiable against an enemy. But it has been universally condemned by the public opinion of Europe, and will stain the memory of Clive until the end of time.

[2] No reliance whatever can be placed upon the estimated numbers of any native army. It is mere guess work. Clive himself reckoned the army of the Nawab to consist of thirty-five thousand foot, fifteen thousand horse, and forty pieces of cannon.

A.D. 1757-1761

Mír Jafir installed as Nawab: presents and promises.

Clive next went to Murshedabad and placed Mír Jafir on the throne. The new Nawab was profuse with his presents and promises, but his resources are supposed to have been greatly exaggerated. The treasures of Suraj-ud-daula had been estimated at forty millions sterling, but only a million and a half was realised. Mír Jafir engaged to pay a million to the East India Company; three-quarters of a million to the inhabitants of Calcutta, natives as well as Europeans; and vast presents to Clive and other members of government. As a first instalment, a hundred boat-loads of silver, to the value of eight hundred thousand pounds, were sent down the river to Calcutta, and the whole population of the English settlement was wild with joy.

Territory rented to the Company.

Besides money the new Nawab ceded a large tract on the river Hughli, which had long been coveted by the East India Company. It was given as a jaghír according to Moghul fashion; the Company collected the yearly revenue, valued at a hundred thousand pounds sterling, but was required to pay a quit-rent of thirty thousand pounds, nominally to the Great Moghul.

Clive's jaghír.

Clive was a great stickler for Moghul forms. It will be seen hereafter that the recognition of the effete sovereignty of the Great Moghul was the keystone of his policy. Mír Jafir was virtually created a Nawab by Clive; for all practical purposes he was an independent sovereign; yet he deemed it necessary to procure letters of investiture from the Moghul court for the three provinces of Bengal, Behar, and Orissa. At the same time Clive was created an Amír of the Moghul empire, with the honorary rank or command of six thousand foot and five thousand horse. Of course the force only existed on paper, but Clive asked for the jaghír supposed to be given for its maintenance. Mír Jafir was perplexed at the demand, but finally made over the quit-rent of the jaghír previously granted to the Company. Thus Clive came into possession of thirty thousand a year payable by the East India Company, who were supposed to be his honourable masters.

Responsibilities of the English.

The revolution effected by the battle of Plassy involved the English in endless difficulties which no one had foreseen. The process of dethroning Suraj-ud-daula and setting up Mír Jafir in his room was a simple affair; but Mír Jafir had no hold upon the grandees, and was soon regarded

A.D. 1757-1761

with jealousy and hatred, especially when they saw the boats loaded with silver going down to Calcutta. It was soon evident that as the English alone had placed Mír Jafir on the throne of Bengal and Behar, so the English alone would be able to keep him there.

Incapacity of Mír Jafir: atrocities of his son Miran.

To make matters worse, it was discovered that Mír Jafir was unfit for the dignity. He had served with credit as a commander in the field, but he had no administrative ability, civil or military. He idled away most of his time under the influence of bhang, or in the company of singing and dancing girls. He complained of an empty treasury, and his army was mutinous for want of pay; but he always appeared loaded with costly jewels, with five or six bracelets of different gems on his arms, and three or four chaplets of pearls hanging from his neck.[1] His son Miran rendered himself detestable by murders and assassinations. Ten days after the battle of Plassy, Suraj-ud-daula was taken prisoner and cruelly murdered in the palace at Murshedabad. Other members or partisans of the family, male and female, were put to death in like manner. Mír Jafir threw all the blame upon his son Miran.

Colonel Clive's Jackass.

The English were anxious to maintain the dignity of the new Nawab by showing him every kind of deference; but his dependence on the "hat wallahs," and his morbid terror of Clive, rendered him the laughing-stock of his courtiers. Within a few months of his accession he was nicknamed

[1] There is reason to believe that the English were duped as regards the treasures of Murshedabad, and that enormous wealth to the value of many millions sterling was concealed in the recesses of the Nawab's palace, and shared by Mír Jafir and some others. The author of the *Siyár-ul-Mutaqherín* says that the English only knew of the outer treasury. "Those renowned English," says Gholam Husain Khan, "who looked down with contempt on the intellects and abilities of the Bengalis, and yet are perpetually baffled and duped by them, did not know anything of the inner treasury, said to contain money and jewels to the value of eight millions sterling, and which, pursuant to a custom well known in India, was kept in the *Zenana*, or women's apartments. This inner treasury was shared by Mír Jafir and three natives." The author adds that two of the natives were writers in the service of Clive, whose respective salaries were only sixty rupees a month, or about four shillings per diem; yet ten years afterwards one of these men died worth a million and a quarter sterling, whilst the other spent ninety thousand pounds on his mother's funeral alone.—*Siyár-ul-Mutaqherín* vol. i., page 773.

A.D. 1757-1761

"Colonel Clive's Jackass," and he retained the title till his death. The story is told of a fray between the followers of a Moghul grandee and the servants of Clive. The Nawab warned the grandee against any rupture. The grandee replied with a sneer: "My lord Nawab, I am not likely to quarrel with the Colonel. I never rise in the morning without making three salams to his Jackass, and am the last man to fall out with the rider." Such stories tell more of the current feeling at Murshedabad than pages of description.[1]

Revolution of political ideas.

In truth the change of Nawabs had revolutionised the political ideas of all the great men at court. Before the capture of Calcutta, the English had only appeared at Murshedabad as supplicants for trading privileges. After the battle of Plassy they were lords and masters, to be propitiated as the representatives of a new and paramount power. Under such circumstances it was only natural that they should be feared and hated; and those Moghuls who were loudest in their praises of the English would gladly have seen them at the bottom of the sea.

Disaffection of Hindu grandees.

Another circumstance was calculated to exasperate Mír Jafir and the Moghuls against the English. Alivardi Khan had filled all the higher offices and commands with Hindus, who were raised to the rank of Rajas, and thus served as checks upon the Zemindars, who were mostly Muhammadans. His prime minister was a Hindu, and a so-called Raja; so were the governors of most of the towns and districts. Such nominal Rajas were more amenable to orders, and less likely to rebel, than turbulent Muhammadans. Mír Jafir wanted to remove them from their posts, and replace them by his own kinsmen and dependants. The result was that plots and intrigues were seething in all directions. Some of the Hindu Rajas were in fear of their lives, and implored the protection of the English. Clive guaranteed the lives of some of these Hindus, but he could not keep them in their posts; and thus disaffection was spreading over the province, whilst the English were more feared and hated than ever.

English blamed for

But this fear and hate were only felt by the grandees. The general complaint of the natives was that the

[1] Mill tells the story in his *History of India*, and Macaulay copies it in his Essay on Clive; but both missed the point from ignorance of Mír Jafir's nickname. See Stewart's *History of Bengal*. Also Scott's *Dekhan*, vol. ii., page 376.

A.D. 1757-1761

English did not interfere to protect the people. A native contemporary observes that the presence of mind, firmness of temper, and undaunted bravery of the English were beyond all question; but they took no heed of the husbandmen, and were apathetic and indifferent to the suffering masses.

non-interference.

Mahrattas demand chout

Suddenly Mír Jafir was threatened with new dangers. The Mahrattas demanded arrears of chout for Bengal and Behar, and it was difficult to evade the claim.[1] They had compelled Alivardi Khan to pay chout; and they consequently claimed it as their right from his successors. They did not enforce the payment by the actual invasion of Bengal; but it is evident that they were only restrained by a wholesome fear of Clive.

Claim of the Shahzada to Bengal, Behar, and Orissa.

In 1758 the eldest son of the Great Moghul, known as the Shahzada, appeared in force near the Behar frontier at the river Carumnassa, proclaiming that he had been appointed to the government of Bengal, Behar, and Orissa by the Great Moghul. His cause was supported by Shuja-ud-daula, the Nawab of Oude; and also by a body of Frenchmen under M. Law, the ex-governor of Chandernagore. At the same time the Hindu deputy-governor of Behar, who had been threatened by Mír Jafir, was naturally intriguing with the Shahzada, and inclined to open the way to the invaders.

Progress of affairs at Delhi, 1748-58.

The appearance of the Shahzada brings the Great Moghul upon the stage, and necessitates a glance at the progress of affairs at Delhi. Ever since the death of Muhammad Shah in 1748, the Moghul capital had been torn by distractions. Muhammad Shah had been succeeded by his son Ahmad Shah. The new Padishah found himself threatened by the Afghans on one side, and the Mahrattas on the other. At the same time the post of Vizier was a bone of contention between the Sunnís and the Shíahs: the Sunnís as represented by a grandson of Nizam-ul-mulk, named Ghazi-ud-dín; and the Shíahs as represented by the Nawab of Oude.[2] In the end the Sunnis triumphed, and Ghazi-ud-dín became Vizier.

[1] The chout for Behar and Bengal was claimed by the Bhonsla Raja of Berar or Nagpore. At this time Janoji Bhonsla was the reigning Raja. The history of the Mahratta empire and its feudatories will be given hereafter in Chapter V.

[2] The Nawab of Oude at this time was Sufdar Jung. He had married a daughter of Saádut Ali Khan, and succeeded to the govern-

A.D. 1757-1761

Usurpation of the Vizier: change of Padishahs.

Ghazi-ud-dín aspired to exercise the sovereign power under the name of Vizier, just as the Saiyids had done in a previous generation. He found Ahmad Shah restive and dangerous, and consequently dethroned him, blinded him, and consigned him to the state prison of Salimghur. He next placed an imbecile old prince on the throne of Delhi, under the name of Alamghir. He then treated the Padishah as a pageant, and usurped the sovereign authority, selling titles and letters of investiture to Nawabs in remote provinces, and raising money in every possible way.

Interference of Ahmad Shah Abdali, ruler of Afghanistan.

In 1757, the year of the battle of Plassy, matters were brought to a terrible stand-still. Ahmad Shah Abdali, the founder of the Afghan empire, appeared at Delhi with a large army, and levied contributions from the inhabitants, with all the merciless ferocity of an old officer of Nadir Shah. He next marched down the valley of the Jumna to the sacred city of Mathura, plundering and destroying after the manner of Mahmud of Ghazní. He seems however to have had some respect for the sovereignty of the Great Moghul. He allied himself with the family of the Moghul by marrying a daughter of the deceased Muhammad Shah. He appointed an Afghan, named Najib-ud-daula to be Amír of Amírs, and to act as guardian for Alamghir in the room of Ghazi-ud-dín, the Vizier, who had fled into exile. Having thus arranged matters to his satisfaction, Ahmad Shah Abdali left Delhi and returned with the bulk of his army to Kandahar.

Rising power of the Afghans in the Punjab and Rohilkund.

The Afghans at this period were threatening to become a formidable power in India. They already occupied the Punjab, and neither Sikhs, Moghuls, nor Mahrattas could drive them out. They had long founded a powerful principality in Hindustan to the north-east of Delhi, in a region known as the Rohilla country; it has disappeared from modern maps, but the principality is represented to this day by the little

ment of Oude on the death of his father in 1739. (See *ante*, page 224.) He obtained the post of Vizier during the reign of Ahmad Shah, son of Muhammad Shah; but was subsequently forced to leave Delhi through the intrigues of Ghazi-ud-dín. In 1753 Sufdar Jung collected a large force, and besieged Delhi; and ultimately compelled the Moghul court to give him a formal grant of the provinces of Oude and Allahabad for himself and his heirs. He died shortly afterwards, and was succeeded by his son, the celebrated Shuja-ud-daula. His tomb is one of the sights at Delhi.

state of Rampore. Najib-ud-daula, the new guardian of the Moghul sovereign, was an Afghan of the Rohilla country. In a word the Afghans were in a fair way of supplanting the Moghuls, and once again becoming the dominant power in Hindustan. A.D. 1757-1761

Return of the Vizier to Delhi, supported by the Mahrattas.

No sooner, however, had Ahmad Shah Abdali gone off to Kandahar, than Ghazi-ud-dín, the ex-Vizier, subverted the Afghan power at Delhi. He raised a vast body of Mahratta mercenaries; drove out Najib-ud-daula; murdered or imprisoned all the grandees who had opposed him; reduced Alamghir to the condition of a puppet, and sought to murder the Shahzada, or eldest son and heir of Alamghir.

Flight of the Shahzada.

Thus it was that the Shahzada fled from Delhi in terror of his life. For a year the imperial exile fished in troubled waters, seeking in turns the protection of the Rohilla Afghans and the Mahrattas. At last he took refuge with Shuja-ud-daula, Nawab of Oude, the hereditary Shíah and mortal enemy of Ghazi-ud-dín.[1] But the Nawab of Oude was in no hurry to commit himself. He cared nothing for the Shahzada, but was very anxious to get the Bengal provinces into his own hands. He sent a force to accompany the Shahzada to the Behar frontier, and then waited for events.

Clive's relations with the Moghul court at Delhi.

Meanwhile Clive and Mír Jafir were drawn into an extraordinary correspondence with the Shahzada, and also with the Moghul court at Delhi. Clive received friendly letters from the Shahzada, who was anxious to win the support of the ever-victorious English general. Mír Jafir, however, received orders from the Vizier, and also from the Great Moghul, to arrest the Shahzada, and send him prisoner to Delhi. So Clive wrote back to the Shahza a that he had been created an Amír of the empire, and was consequently bound to support Mír Jafir, who had been invested by the Great Moghul with the government of Bengal, Behar, and Orissa.

The military operations that followed are of no interest.

[1] Ghazi-ud-dín was, as already said, the grandson of Nizam-ul-mulk, and consequently the hereditary Turk and Sunní. The race difference between Moghul and Turk, and the religious antagonism between Shíah and Sunní, will clear up much of the confusion that has prevailed in the history of Muhammadan India.

A.D. 1757-1761

Defeat and flight of the Shahzada, 1758.

Mír Jafir was in a helpless state of terror, and wanted to bribe the Shahzada to go away. Clive vehemently remonstrated against this ruinous proceeding, and marched an English force to Patna, and soon disposed of the Shahzada. The helpless prince fled into obscurity, but was reduced to such distress that Clive sent him a present of five hundred gold mohurs, or about eight hundred pounds sterling, which was gladly accepted.

Helpless condition of the French in Hindustan.

M. Law and his Frenchmen, who had accompanied the Shahzada through all his troubles, were again thrown upon their own resources. Law remarked to an intelligent native that he had travelled over the whole country from Bengal to Delhi, and witnessed nothing but oppression. The grandees of Hindustan thought only of their own aggrandisement, and let the world go to ruin. He had proposed to both the Vizier at Delhi and the Nawab of Oude to restore order to the Moghul empire, as the re-establishment of the authority of the Moghul throughout Hindustan would render it easy to drive the English out of Bengal; but no one paid the slightest heed to his representations. Law failed to perceive that the order which he proposed to restore would have been destructive alike to the Delhi Vizier and the Nawab of Oude.

Dekhan affairs: Bussy's wars against the Hindu Poligars.

Meanwhile the successes of the French in the Dekhan and Peninsula were forced upon the attention of Clive. In 1756 the collision between the English and French in the Dekhan had been averted for a while by the disaster at Calcutta, which called away the English force from Madras on the eve of its march to Hyderabad. In 1757 Bussy made his peace with Salábut Jung, and returned to the Northern Circars, where he came into collision with Hindu Poligars of the old Rajpút type. Amidst all the vicissitudes of Moghul rule these Poligars had maintained a secure independence in hills and jungles; they were nominally pledged to pay tribute to the Nizam, but they withheld payment whenever they had an opportunity. Had they been united they might have resisted the demands of the French; but they were at deadly feud with each other; and one of them, known as the Raja of Vizianagram, managed to turn the wrath of Bussy against his neighbour of Bobili, who for generations had been his mortal enemy.

A.D. 1757-1761

Feud between the Rajas of Bobili and Vizianagram.

The Raja of Bobili claimed to be a Rajpút of high descent, whose ancestors had fought under the ancient Maharajas of Jagganath in the old mythical wars against the south. He affected to scorn his Vizianagram neighbour as a low-born chieftain of a new creation; and his retainers wreaked their spite, by turning off the rivulets which ran into Vizianagram territory. Bussy was induced to take a part in the rivalry; and ultimately to revenge some unexplained outrage by driving the Bobili Raja out of his hereditary territories.

Horrible self-sacrifice of the Bobili Rajpúts.

The catastrophe that followed is a terrible story of Rajpút desperation and revenge. The Bobili Raja retired to a remote stronghold in a deep jungle. Bussy broke down the battlements with his cannon, but for a long time failed to capture the place. The Rajpút garrison was exposed to a withering fire, but resisted the escalading parties with the ferocity of wild beasts defending their dens and families. At last resistance was in vain. The garrison gathered all the women and children into the habitations in the centre of the fort, and set the whole on fire, stabbing or cutting down any one who attempted to escape. They then returned, like frantic demons, to die upon the walls. Quarter was refused, and the Raja perished with all his retainers, sword in hand. The French entered the fort in triumph, but there was no joy in the victory, and the sight of the horrible slaughter moved them to tears. Presently an old man appeared with a little boy; he had saved the son of the Raja contrary to the will of the father.

Rajpút revenge.

The death of the Bobili Raja was followed by speedy retribution. Four retainers had seen him fall, and had escaped to the jungle, and sworn to be revenged. One night two of them crept to the quarters of the Raja of Vizianagram, and stabbed him to death; they were cut to pieces by the guards, but died exulting in their crime. Had they failed, the other two remaining in the jungle were bound by the same oath to avenge the death of their Raja or perish in the attempt.[1]

Submission of the Poligars.

The other Poligars in the Northern Circars were so terrified by the fate of Bobili that they hastened to settle

[1] Rajpút revenge is the same in all ages. The revenge of the men of Bobili is paralleled by the revenge of Aswatthâma and his comrades on the sons of the Pándavas, after the war of the Mahá Bhárata.

A.D. 1757-1761

all arrears of tribute. The Poligar of Gúmsur alone held out, but was compelled in the end to submit in like manner.

Bussy's successes against the English.

During this expedition Bussy received letters from Suraj-ud-daula, inviting him to Bengal; and he would have marched to the relief of the Nawab, but was stopped by the news of the fall of Chandernagore. In revenge for that capture he drove the English out of Vizagapatam, and took possession of three other factories which they had established further south on the coast of the delta of the Godavari.

Contrast between Bussy and Clive.

A native contemporary writer contrasts the personal appearance of Bussy with that of Clive, and treats each in turn as a type of the French and English nations. Bussy wore embroidered clothes or brocade. He and his officers rode on elephants, preceded by "chopdars," or mace-bearers with silver sticks, whilst musicians and eulogists were singing his praises. He received state visits while sitting on a throne embroidered with the arms of the King of France. His table was served with plate, and with three or four services. Clive always wore his regimentals in the field, and never wore silk except in town. He always rode on horseback. He kept a plentiful table, but in no way delicate, and never with more than two services.[1]

French force under Lally reaches Pondicherry, 1758.

In 1758 the fortunes of the French in India underwent an entire change. In April a French fleet arrived at Pondicherry. It brought a large force under the command of Count de Lally, who had been appointed Governor-General of the French possessions in India. Lally was imbued with a bitter hatred against the English, and a profound distrust in the honesty or patriotism of his own countrymen in India. No sooner had he landed at Pondicherry than he organised an expedition against Fort St. David; but he found that no preparations had been made by the French authorities. There was a want alike of coolies, draught cattle, provisions, and ready money. But the energy of Lally overcame all obstacles. The French authorities at

[1] Gholam Husain Ali in the *Siyár-ul-Mutaqherín*. He adds that Warren Hastings, who plays a part in the after history, always wore a plain coat of English broad-cloth, and never anything like lace or embroidery. His throne was a plain chair of mahogany. He was sparing in his diet, and his table was sometimes neglected. His address showed little of pride and still less of familiarity.

A.D. 1757-1761

Pondicherry accused him of pressing natives and cattle; but Lally retorted by declaring that the oppressions and rapacity of the French government, and the extortions of its native servants, had alone prevented his obtaining all that he required.

Lally captures Fort St. David, and recalls Bussy.

In June, 1758, Lally captured Fort St. David. He then prepared to capture Madras as a preliminary to an advance on Bengal. He recalled Bussy from the Dekhan to help him with his Indian experiences; and he sent the Marquis de Conflans to succeed Bussy in the command of the Northern Circars.

Reluctance of Bussy: Lally's suspicions.

Bussy left the Dekhan with the utmost reluctance. He had secured a paramount influence in the Northern Circars, and was anxious to remain and protect Salábut Jung against the designs of his younger brother Nizam Ali. Lally however was deaf to all remonstrances. He believed that Bussy was either deluded by others or desirous of deceiving him; and he was confirmed in this belief when he found that Bussy, notwithstanding his alleged conquests and commanding position, had no funds at his disposal, and was unable to raise any money for the prosecution of the war against the English.

Successes of English in the Northern Circars, 1758.

The departure of Bussy from the Northern Circars was disastrous to the French. The Raja of Vizianagram revolted against the French and sent to Calcutta for help. Clive despatched an English force to the Northern Circars, under the command of Colonel Forde; and in December, 1758, Colonel Forde defeated the French under Conflans, and prepared to recover all the English factories on the coast which had been captured by Bussy.

Desperate condition of the French.

Meanwhile Count de Lally was actively engaged at Pondicherry in preparations for the siege of Madras. He hoped to capture Madras, and complete the destruction of the English in the Carnatic; and then to march northward, capture Calcutta, and expel the English from Bengal. But he was without resources; there was no money to be had in Pondicherry. At last he raised a small sum, chiefly out of his own funds, and began the march to Madras; his officers preferring to risk death before the walls of Madras to certain starvation within the walls of Pondicherry.

Lally reached Madras on the 12th of December, 1758, and at once took possession of Black Town. He then

A.D. 1757-1761

Unsuccessful siege of Madras, 1758-59.

began the siege of Fort St. George with a vigour and activity which commanded the respect of his enemies. His difficulties were enormous. For six weeks his officers and soldiers were on half pay; for another six weeks they received no pay at all. During the last fifteen days they had no provisions except rice and butter. Even the gunpowder was nearly exhausted. At last on the 16th of February, 1759, an English fleet arrived at Madras under Admiral Pocock, and Lally was compelled to raise the siege. Such was the state of party feeling amongst the French in India, that the retreat of Lally from Madras was received at Pondicherry with every demonstration of joy.

French disasters in the Dekhan.

The career of Lally in India lasted for two years longer, namely from February, 1759, to February, 1761; it is a series of hopeless struggles and wearying misfortunes. In the Dekhan, Salábut Jung had been thrown into the utmost alarm by the departure of Bussy and defeat of Conflans. He was exposed to the intrigues and plots of his younger brother Nizam Ali, and he despaired of obtaining further help from the French. Accordingly he opened up negotiations with Colonel Forde and the English. Forde on his part recovered all the captured factories, and drove the French out of the Northern Circars. He could not however interfere in the domestic affairs of the Dekhan, by helping Salábut Jung against Nizam Ali. In 1761 Salábut Jung was dethroned and placed in confinement; and Nizam Ali ascended the throne at Hyderabad as ruler of the Dekhan.[1]

Disasters in the Carnatic.

In the Carnatic the French were in despair. In January, 1760, Lally was defeated by Colonel Coote at Wandiwash, between Madras and Pondicherry. Lally opened up negotiations with Hyder Ali, who was rising to power in Mysore; but Hyder Ali as yet could do little or nothing.

Fall of Pondicherry, 1761.

At the end of 1760 Colonel Coote began the siege of Pondicherry. Lally still held out at Pondicherry, but he

[1] Two years afterwards Salábut Jung was murdered. By the treaty of Paris, concluded between Great Britain and France in 1763, both nations agreed to recognise Salábut Jung as the rightful ruler of Hyderabad territory, although at that moment Salábut Jung was confined in a fortress, and Nizam Ali occupied the throne of Hyderabad. Nizam Ali however removed all diplomatic difficulties by putting his brother to death. Nizam Ali lived on till 1803. Next to his father, Nizam-ul-mulk, Nizam Ali is the best known ruler of the dynasty.

was ill in health, and worn out with vexation and fatigue. The settlement was torn by dissensions. In January, 1761, the garrison was starved into a capitulation, and the town and fortifications were levelled with the ground. A few weeks afterwards the French were compelled to surrender the strong hill-fortress of Jingí, and their military power in the Carnatic was brought to a close. A.D. 1757-1761

Melancholy end of Count de Lally.

The fate of Lally is more to be pitied than that of Dupleix. He had not sought his own aggrandisement, but the honour and glory of the French nation; and he had been thwarted by the apathy of selfish traders who cared only for themselves. On his return to France he was sacrificed to save the reputation of the French ministers. France was furious at the loss of her possessions in India, and the enemies of Lally combined to make him the victim. The unfortunate Count, after an honourable service of forty-five years, was thrown into the Bastille; and a number of vague or frivolous charges were trumped up against him. He was tried by the parliament of Paris, but backbiting and detraction had poisoned the mind of the nation against him, and Lally was a ruined man. In May, 1766, he was condemned not only to death, but to immediate execution. The suddenness of the doom drove him frantic. He took a pair of compasses with which he had been sketching a map of the coast of Coromandel, and tried to drive them to his heart. His hand was stayed, his mouth was gagged, and he was dragged with ignominy to execution. Thus fell the last of the three martyrs of the French East India Company,—Labourdonnais, Dupleix, and Lally.

Clive's departure to England, 1760.

Meanwhile there had been great changes in Bengal. In June, 1758, Clive had been appointed Governor of all the Company's settlements in Bengal. In 1759 Lally had been compelled to raise the siege of Madras, and Forde had pursued his career of victory in the Northern Circars. There was nothing further to fear from the French in India; and in February, 1760, Clive resigned his post in Bengal and returned to England. He was succeeded for a few months by Mr. Holwell, and afterwards by Mr. Vansittart; but the times were out of joint. No one but Clive seemed to comprehend the revolutionary character of the crisis; and the Company's government in Bengal drifted on, it knew not where, like a ship labouring through a troubled sea.

A.D. 1757-1761

Necessity for a permanent European force in Bengal.

Before Clive left India he was convinced that so long as Mír Jafir was allowed to reign as Nawab, the Company's settlements in Bengal would be exposed to sore peril. Hindustan was swarming with adventurers at the head of warlike bands, Mahratta and Afghan; and Mír Jafir and his rabble army would have been powerless of themselves to contend against such hardy warriors. A permanent force of two thousand European soldiers, and a corresponding army of drilled sepoys, could maintain Bengal and Behar against all comers; but who was to pay the cost? The entire revenue of the provinces was swallowed up by the Nawab; and it was out of the question that the Company should maintain such a force out of the profits of their trade, even supposing that they could bear the strain.

Clive's scheme for the acquisition of Bengal by the British nation.

Under these circumstances Clive made a proposal to Mr. William Pitt, the great war minister of England; and coming, as it did, from a servant of the Company, it must have somewhat staggered that illustrious statesman. He proposed that the British nation, and not the Company, should take possession of Bengal, Behar, and Orissa in full sovereignty. He explained that the Great Moghul would readily grant the three provinces to any one who would guarantee the regular yearly payment of some half million sterling to the imperial treasury. He further explained that the Vizier had already offered him the post of Dewan, or collector of the revenue for the three provinces, on these conditions. He summed up the advantages to the British nation as follows. The total revenue was certainly two if not three millions. Thus after deducting half a million as tribute to the Great Moghul, and another half a million for the maintenance of a military force, there would remain a handsome surplus for the payment of the national debt. or any other national undertaking.[1]

[1] Clive's letter to Pitt was dated 7th of January, 1759. (See Malcolm's *Life of Clive*, vol. ii.) Strange to say, a similar proposal had been drawn up by a Colonel James Mill as far back as 1746. Colonel Mill planned the conquest of Bengal, Behar, and Orissa, under the flag of Germany, and in behalf of the Great Moghul. The original paper may be found in the Appendix to Bolt's *Affairs in Bengal*. The following remarks throw a curious light on the contemporary condition of the Moghul empire:—

"The Moghul empire," says Colonel Mill, "is overflowing with gold and silver. She has always been feeble and defenceless. It is a miracle

Pitt was not inclined to accept Clive's proposal. He feared that the acquisition of Bengal would render the British Crown too powerful, and might endanger the liberties of the English people. Thus the grand scheme for acquiring possession of Bengal for the British nation, rather than for the East India Company, was allowed to drop into oblivion.

A.D. 1757-1761

Objections of Pitt.

About this time there was another revolution at Delhi. The Vizier discovered that his imperial master, Alamghir, was corresponding with Ahmad Shah Abdali, and inviting the Afghan ruler to return to Delhi. Accordingly he treacherously assassinated the aged Padishah, and tried to set up another puppet to represent the Great Moghul. But his career of ambition and atrocity was drawing to a close. The avenging army of Afghans once more advanced to Delhi under their dreaded ruler; and the Vizier fled away from Delhi to begin a new set of intrigues;—to stir up the Mahrattas against the Afghans, and to oppose the return of the Shahzada to Delhi.

Revolution at Delhi: murder of Alamghir, 1759.

The Mahrattas soon began to dispute with the Afghans for the possession of the Moghul empire. The war lasted some months, but was brought to a close in January, 1761, by the

Struggle between Afghans and Mahrattas:

that no European prince with a maritime power has ever attempted the conquest of Bengal. By a single stroke infinite wealth might be acquired, which would counterbalance the mines of Brazil and Peru.

"The policy of the Moghuls is bad; their army is worse; they are without a navy. The empire is exposed to perpetual revolts. Their ports and rivers are open to foreigners. The country might be conquered, or laid under contribution, as easily as the Spaniards overwhelmed the naked Indians of America.

"A rebel subject, named Alivardi Khan, has torn away the three provinces of Bengal, Behar, and Orissa, from the Moghul empire. He has treasure to the value of thirty millions sterling. His yearly revenue must be at least two millions. The provinces are open to the sea. Three ships with fifteen hundred or two thousand regulars would suffice for the conquest of the three provinces, which might be carried out in the name of the Great Moghul, for the destruction of a rebel against his lawful suzerainty."

The proposals of Colonel Mill have been overlooked by Indian historians; but they are valuable as the outcome of his twenty years experience of India during the second quarter of the eighteenth century. The so-called Moghul empire had reached a crisis and its conquest was inevitable; and as no Asiatic power was able to effect it, and no European power would accept the responsibility, the conquest was forced on a company of English traders, a contingency which alone saved the people of India from becoming alternately the prey of Mahrattas and Afghans.

A.D. 1757-1761

Decisive battle of Paniput, January, 1761.

terrible battle of Paniput in the neighbourhood of Delhi.[1] This battle was one of the bloodiest in the annals of the world. On the 7th of January the Mahrattas were defeated with horrible slaughter. A mob of fugitives escaped to the village of Paniput, with a multitude of women and children. The Afghans surrounded the village throughout the night to cut off all chance of escape. Next morning the male prisoners were brought out in files and beheaded in cold blood. The women and children were carried away into hopeless slavery. Generations passed away before the bloody field of Paniput was forgotten by the Mahrattas. It was said that two hundred thousand Mahrattas had fallen in that murderous campaign.

Ahmad Shah Abdali at Delhi.

Ahmad Shah Abdali was once more the arbiter of the fate of the Moghul empire. He would have placed the Shahzada on the throne at Delhi, but the heir of the murdered Alamghir was a fugitive and an exile. Accordingly he placed a son of the Shahzada, named Jewan Bakht, upon the throne, to reign as the deputy of his father. He also appointed Najib-ud-daula, the Rohilla Afghan, to act as guardian of the young prince under the title of Amír of Amírs, in the same way that he had previously appointed him to be guardian of the murdered Alamghir.

[1] The details of Mahratta history, before and after the battle of Paniput, will be told hereafter in Chapter V.

CHAPTER III.

REVOLUTIONARY THROES.

A.D. 1761 TO 1765.

A.D. 1761.

Eventful character of the year 1761: Shah Alam the new Padishah.

THE year 1761, like 1748, is an epoch in Indian history. It saw the fall of Pondicherry, the overthrow of the Mahrattas, and the ascendancy of the Afghans. The revolution at Delhi brought the Shahzada once more to the front, and the Moghul prince began to play a part in the history. He was proclaimed Padishah under the title of Shah Alam; and he assumed the dignity of Great Moghul by taking his seat upon a throne surmounted with the umbrella of sovereignty. Finally he appointed Shuja-ud-daula, Nawab of Oude, to the honorary but nominal post of Vizier of the Moghul empire.

Views of the Nawab Vizier of Oude.

Shuja-ud-daula gladly accepted the empty title, and hoped to obtain solid advantages. The Mahrattas were prostrate; the Afghan conqueror was favourable to Shah Alam; and Clive had gone to England. Accordingly the Nawab Vizier contemplated wresting Behar and Bengal from the feeble hands of Mír Jafir in the name and under the authority of the Great Moghul.

Incapacity of Mír Jafir, Nawab of Bengal.

Shah Alam and the Nawab Vizier once more appeared with a large army on the Behar frontier and threatened Patna. The incapacity of Mír Jafir at this crisis was insufferable. He was worse than useless, whilst his army was a rabble in a chronic state of mutiny for want of pay. Mr. Vansittart was Governor at Calcutta, and thought to meet the difficulty by appointing a grandee of capacity to act as a deputy-Nawab, who would do all the work, whilst Mír Jafir retained the name and dignity.

A.D. 1761.

Vacillations of Governor Vansittart.

Mír Jafir had a son-in-law, named Mír Kasim, or Cossim, who seemed a likely man for the post. Accordingly Governor Vansittart proceeded to Murshedabad, and proposed the measure to the Nawab and his son-in-law, but found them both to be impracticable. Indeed both men were disgusted with the proposal. Mír Kasim had been scheming to become Nawab, and was angry at being offered the post of deputy. Mír Jafir saw that he was to be shelved, and was furious at the threatened loss of power. Accordingly, after some vacillation, Governor Vansittart determined to dethrone Mír Jafir and set up Mír Kasim.

Treaty with Mír Kasim.

Of course there was a preliminary treaty with Mír Kasim, and the Nawab expectant naturally yielded to every demand. He pledged himself to respect every privilege that had been granted to the English by Mír Jafir. He also agreed to pay up all arrears due to the English from Mír Jafir; to contribute fifty thousand pounds sterling towards the expenses of the war against the French in the Carnatic; and to cede the three districts of Burdwan, Midnapore, and Chittagong, which yielded a yearly revenue of half a million sterling. By this last measure Mír Kasim hoped to guard against the money disputes which had embittered the relations between the English and Mír Jafir; as it provided for the military defence of the provinces on the scale recommended by Clive, without the necessity of paying hard cash out of the Nawab's treasury.

Vansittart refuses a bribe.

In oriental countries little can be done without presents. Mír Jafir had been profuse in his presents to Clive and other English officers and members of council; and Mír Kasim was prepared in like manner to purchase the favour and goodwill of the English gentlemen at Calcutta. Accordingly Mír Kasim offered twenty lakhs of rupees, or two hundred thousand pounds sterling, to Governor Vansittart to be shared by himself and members of the council. Vansittart, however, refused to take the money. Mr. Mill, the historian of India, declares on the evidence of a native, that the money was accepted;[1] but recent researches in the government records at Calcutta prove beyond all question

[1] For many years this groundless charge, originating with Mr. Mill, has clung to the memory of Governor Vansittart. The evidence contradicting it may be found in Chapter IX. of *Early Records of British India*, published by the author of the present volume.

A.D. 1761.

that the money was refused, and that Mr. Vansittart was an upright and honourable man.

Peaceful change of Nawabs.

The change of Nawabs was carried into effect without any opposition. The people of Bengal were indifferent to the revolution. Mír Jafir yielded to his fate, and gave up the title as well as the dignity. But he was conscious that his life was no longer safe at Murshedabad; and that he would be murdered without scruple by the new Nawab to prevent further complications. Accordingly, in spite of his anger at the English for dethroning him, he hastened to Calcutta and placed his family and treasures under their protection.

Defeat and flight of the Nawab Vizier of Oude.

The new Nawab soon paid off the arrears due to the English government at Calcutta, and also satisfied the claims of his own army. He then took the field against Shah Alam, accompanied by an English force under Major Carnac. The army of Shah Alam was utterly routed, and the Nawab Vizier fled back to Oude.

Negotiations with Shah Alam.

But there was a political difficulty as regards Shah Alam. He was generally recognised as the rightful Padishah and Great Moghul; and though the assumed sovereignty was but the shadow of a name, it was thought necessary to come to terms with him. Accordingly Major Carnac paid a complimentary visit to Shah Alam, and conducted the pageant Padishah to Patna, the capital of Mír Kasim's province of Behar.

Installation of the Great Moghul at Patna.

At Patna the English factory was converted into a palace for the installation of the Great Moghul. The centre room was hung with stuffs and formed a hall of audience. The dining-tables were covered with carpets and turned into an imperial throne. Shah Alam was carried in grand procession to the factory and enthroned on the dining-tables. Mír Kasim entered the hall and paid his homage to the Padishah, and presented a honorary gift of a thousand and one gold mohurs.

Letters of investiture.

The English were dazzled with the ancient glory of the Great Moghul; and Shah Alam profited accordingly. Letters of investiture were procured from the Padishah conferring the Nawabship of Bengal, Behar, and Orissa, on Mír Kasim; but in return Mír Kasim was obliged to pledge himself to pay a yearly tribute of a quarter of a million sterling to Shah Alam. Mír Kasim could have made better terms, since he

A.D. 1761-1762

had Shah Alam in his power, and might have compelled him by threats or torture to do his bidding; but the English interfered to protect the Great Moghul, and Mír Kasim was foiled. But the English were foiled in their turn. They asked Shah Alam to grant them letters of investiture for the three districts of Burdwan, Midnapore, and Chittagong, which had been ceded by Mír Kasim. Also, as a legal safeguard against any future contingency, they asked for letters of investiture in behalf of Muhammad Ali, the Nawab they had set up in the Carnatic. The English seemed to expect that these letters would be granted for nothing as a matter of course; or at any rate as a mark of gratitude on the part of Shah Alam towards his foreign protectors. But Shah Alam refused to give any letters of investiture unless a corresponding yearly tribute was paid into the imperial treasury. Accordingly Governor Vansittart was told that if the English would pay tribute for the three districts, and if the Nawab would also pay tribute for the Carnatic, letters of investiture would be granted, but not otherwise.

Proposed advance of the English to Delhi.

At this time however Shah Alam would have granted almost any request, provided only that the English would conduct him to Delhi. Strange to say, the English were prepared to carry out this extravagant scheme, and were only prevented by sheer force of circumstances. Mír Kasim refused to join in a mad-cap expedition to Delhi. Then again the services of European soldiers were absolutely necessary; and at this juncture a European regiment was detained in the Carnatic to carry on the war against the French. Accordingly Vansittart was induced to negative a proposal which would have withdrawn a British force to a distance of a thousand miles from Calcutta, and left it to struggle as it best could against the successive attacks of Mahrattas and Afghans.

Secret negotiations.

Shah Alam made Governor Vansittart the same offer of the post of Dewan of Bengal, Behar, and Orissa, which had been made to Clive. But Vansittart was afraid to embroil himself with Mír Kasim, and declined the offer. Accordingly, Shah Alam returned to Oude, still harping upon going to Delhi, and hoping that the Nawab Vizier would conduct him there.

Mír Kasim had some inkling of these negotiations between Shah Alam and the English; especially of the offer made

A.D. 1762.

Suspicions of Mír Kasim: secret preparations for war.

to Vansittart of the post of Dewan for the three Bengal provinces; and he must have been perfectly aware that they foreboded no good to the permanence of his own authority. Indeed, from this time Mír Kasim appears to have made preparations for coming to a collision with the English. He reduced his expenditure; forced the Zemindars to pay up arrears; and squeezed Hindu officials and grandees of their hoarded wealth. He discharged a large portion of his rabble soldiery, and formed an army of picked men. He cut off all close relations with the English by removing his capital from Murshedabad, which was little more than a hundred miles from Calcutta, to Monghyr, which was more than three hundred miles. At Monghyr he drilled his army in English fashion, cast guns, manufactured muskets, and prepared for war.

Quarrel about private trade, 1762.

In 1762 disputes arose between the English and Mír Kasim about the payment of transit duties. Bengal was traversed by water ways, and at every important turning a toll-house was set up for collecting duties on all goods going and coming. In former times the English had obtained firmáns from the Moghul court at Delhi, granting them the privilege of carrying goods, duty free, to any part of the three provinces. Every boat claiming the privilege was obliged to carry the English flag, and the Company's "permit" or dustuck, bearing the Company's seal. In return for this privilege the Company paid yearly a block sum of three thousand rupees into the Nawab's treasury at Hughli.

Freedom from duties.

Before the battle of Plassy this right of dustuck was restricted by the Nawab to goods imported or exported by sea. Moreover, it was confined to the goods belonging to the Company, and was never extended to private goods belonging to the Company's servants. Indeed, before the battle of Plassy none of the Company's servants had attempted to trade with the people of Bengal on their private account. But after the battle of Plassy there was an entire change. The English were masters, and Mír Jafir pledged himself to permit all goods of every kind and sort to be carried, duty free, under the Company's dustuck, without any reservation as to whom they belonged.

The consequence was that the Company's servants, whose incomes depended infinitely more upon their private trade than upon their official salaries, began to trade in the

A.D. 1762.

Trade in country commodities and sale of dustucks.

products of the country, such as salt, tobacco, betel, dried fish, oil, ghee, rice, straw, ginger, sugar, and opium. Freedom from duties enabled them to undersell all native dealers, and they began to absorb the whole commerce of the country, to the detriment of the Nawab's revenue, and the ruin of native dealers. To crown all, every servant of the Company claimed the privilege of using the Company's seal and selling dustucks; and young writers, whose official salaries were only fifteen or twenty pounds a year, were to be seen at Calcutta spending fifteen hundred or two thousand.

Outrageous proceedings of native agents.

The conduct of the native agents of the English gentlemen was still more outrageous. Bengalis of no character or position, who had been seen in Calcutta walking in rags, were sent up country as agents or gomastas of the English. They assumed the dress of English sepoys, displayed the English flag and Company's dustuck, set the Nawab's servants at defiance, and gave themselves all the airs of men in office and authority. They compelled the natives to sell their goods at half their market value, and to pay double for all they required. They thus bullied sellers and buyers, insulted the Nawab's officers, and probably cheated their English masters. Mír Kasim bitterly complained that the English gentlemen were crippling his revenues by withholding payment of duties, whilst their gomastas were bringing his government into contempt in the eyes of the people of the country.

Violent debates at Calcutta.

Governor Vansittart was fully alive to these evils. So was Mr. Warren Hastings, who at this time was a rising man of thirty, and the youngest member of the Calcutta council. Both Vansittart and Hastings contended that trade in the country commodities ought not to be carried on by the Company's servants to the prejudice of the Nawab's government. But they spoke to men whose daily gains were at stake, and who were blind to all other considerations. Moreover, at this very time complaints arrived at Calcutta that the Nawab's officers had stopped the boats belonging to the Company's servants and demanded payment of duties. The passions of the council were aroused. The majority demanded the fulfilment of the privilege granted by Mír Jafir and confirmed by Mír Kasim; and no amount of pleading from Vansittart or Hastings could lull the storm.

A.D. 1762-1763

Failure of Vansittart as an arbitrator.

Governor Vansittart tried to bring about a compromise by paying a visit to the Nawab at Monghyr; but he lacked judgment and firmness of temper, and vacillated between the Nawab and his own council. In fact no one, but a strong-minded man like Clive, could have arbitrated between a Nawab, indignant at the loss of revenue, and a body of Englishmen, infuriated at the threatened loss of income. The question of right or wrong was cast to the winds. The Nawab considered himself to be an independent prince, confirmed in his sovereignty by the letters of the Great Moghul. The majority of the English considered that the Nawab was a creature of their own, whom they had raised to the throne, and might dethrone at will.

Factious opposition of Amyatt.

To make matters worse, the council at Calcutta was torn by faction. Hitherto the Company's servants had been generally promoted by seniority; but Mr. Vansittart had been brought up from Madras, and appointed Governor of the English settlements in Bengal, through the personal influence of Clive. Vansittart had thus superseded a Bengal civilian named Amyatt; and Amyatt opposed every measure proposed by Vansittart, and was warmly supported by a majority of the Calcutta council.

General abolition of all duties, 1763.

In 1763 Mír Kasim brought matters to a crisis. He abolished the payment of all duties; and thus granted the same privileges to his own subjects which had been monopolised by the English gentlemen. This measure put the question on a totally new footing. It stopped the sale of dustucks. It silenced all wrangling as to the right of the servants of the Company to deal in country commodities. It narrowed down all controversy to the single point of whether the Nawab had or had not a right to grant a remission of duties to his own subjects.

New controversy.

The majority of the council at Calcutta decided that the Nawab had no such right. The decision was unjust and absurd; but still the majority had a show of reason on their side. They contended that the spirit and intention of the treaty arrangements with Mír Jafir and Mír Kasim were to grant exclusive privileges to the English servants of the Company; and they argued, that the general exemption of all his subjects from the payment of duties destroyed the value of those exclusive privileges, and was thus a violation of the spirit and intention of the treaties. They failed to see that

A.D. 1763. the monopoly had been broken by the force of circumstances, and could not be restored without a violation of public law. Warren Hastings saw the point clearly. "The Nawab," he said, "has granted a boon to his subjects; and there are no grounds for demanding that a sovereign prince should withdraw such a boon, or for threatening him with war in the event of refusal." In reply Hastings was told that such language became an agent of the Nawab rather than a member of the Calcutta council. Then followed a retort, a blow, and a duel: and though Warren Hastings obtained an apology from the offender, the resolution of the council remained the same.

Violent conduct of the English at the up-country factories. Meanwhile the isolated Englishmen at remote factories were as violent as the council at Calcutta. If the Nawab's officers stopped English boats, they were liable to be beaten by English sepoys; and in some instances the Nawab's people were sent down to Calcutta for trial by the English for having obeyed the orders of their master. Mr. Ellis, the chief of the factory at Patna, rendered himself particularly obnoxious to the Nawab; yet his position was one of real peril, for he was posted with a mere handful of European troops more than four hundred miles from Calcutta; and was moreover cut off from Calcutta by the Nawab's capital and army at Monghyr.

Deputation of Amyatt and Hay to Monghyr. In April, 1763, the Calcutta council sent two of their number, Messrs. Amyatt and Hay, to present an ultimatum to the Nawab. Before the deputies left Calcutta the Nawab had refused to receive them; "he had abolished all duties," he said, "and consequently there was nothing to settle." On reaching Monghyr, however, they met with a hospitable reception; for the Nawab performed all the duties of an oriental host towards his European visitors. He *fêted* them, gave them presents, and entertained them with music and dancing-girls. But all this while he kept them under strict surveillance. He remembered the secret plots that led to the destruction of Suraj-ud-daula, and he was constantly suspecting his grandees of a design to betray him to the English. He ordered the two grandsons of Jagat Seth to be arrested at Murshedabad and sent to Monghyr. He sent to Shah Alam and the Nawab Vizier of Oude for help against the English. He was for ever lying in wait for signs of some understanding between his grandees and the English.

In May a boat arrived at Monghyr laden with goods for the factory at Patna, and laden also with five hundred fire-locks for the English garrison. The sight of the arms filled the Nawab with fresh suspicions and alarms. He stopped the boat and refused to allow the firelocks to go on to Patna. He permitted Amyatt to return to Calcutta, but kept Hay as a hostage at Monghyr for the safety of certain officers of his own who had been arrested by the English.

A.D. 1763.

Stoppage of arms at Monghyr.

The story that follows is a mournful page in Indian history. Mr. Ellis, at Patna, was in correspondence with Amyatt, and he foresaw that the moment Amyatt reached Calcutta the council would declare war against the Nawab. The factory in the suburbs of Patna would then be in extreme peril. It was untenable, and might be easily surrounded and captured by the Nawab's troops. Accordingly Mr. Ellis resolved to attack and occupy the town and fort of Patna as a better place of defence in the event of a war.

Peril of Mr. Ellis at the Patna factory.

At early morning on the 25th of June, 1763, the English took the town of Patna by surprise; the native commandant fled in a panic with most of his troops. The English next attacked the fort but were repulsed. They then began to disperse over the streets and bazars. The sepoys were plundering shops and houses, and European soldiers were getting drunk and incapable. There was no idea of danger, and consequently no measures were taken for the defence of the town against any return of the fugitive garrison.

Capture of Patna by the English, June, 1763.

Suddenly, at hot noon, the flying garrison recovered heart and re-entered the town of Patna. They had been joined by a reinforcement coming from Monghyr, and had, moreover, been told that the fort at Patna was still holding out against the English. They met with little resistance, and were soon in possession of the town. The English were bewildered and overpowered, but they managed to spike their guns and retreat to the factory.

Recovery of Patna by the Nawab's troops.

The English in the factory were utterly cast down by the disaster. They saw that they were being surrounded by the Nawab's troops; and they hurried off to their boats with the vain hope of escaping up the river Ganges into the territory of the Nawab Vizier of Oude. But they found every outlet closed against them, and, instead of cutting

Flight and surrender of the English.

A.D. 1763. their way through the Nawab's troops, they committed the fatal error of surrendering to Asiatics. They were all sent as prisoners to Monghyr, and found that they were not alone in their misfortunes. The factory of Cossimbazar, in the suburb of Murshedabad, had been captured and plundered by the Nawab's troops; and all the English at Cossimbazar had been sent to Monghyr as prisoners of war.

Elation of Mír Kasim. All this while Mír Kasim had been waiting at Monghyr in an agony of suspense. News arrived of the loss of Patna, and filled him with despair. At dead of night other tidings arrived; the town had been recovered, and the English were at his mercy. The Nawab was intoxicated with joy and exultation. He ordered the kettledrums to announce the glorious victory to the sleeping city. Next morning every grandee in Monghyr hurried to the palace with presents and congratulations; and Mír Kasim sent out circulars ordering his officers throughout Behar and Bengal to attack the English wherever they were to be found, and to slaughter them on the spot or bring them away as prisoners to Monghyr.

Murder of Amyatt. The capture of the English factory at Cossimbazar was the first result of this cruel order, but Mr. Amyatt was the first victim. The unfortunate gentleman was proceeding down the river towards Calcutta, when his boat was hailed by a detachment of the Nawab's troops, and he was invited by the native commander to an entertainment on shore. The dancing-girls were there, but Amyatt had his misgivings, and sent his excuses. Next he was peremptorily ordered to come on shore, but refused to go. Shots were fired; the Nawab's troops boarded the boat. Amyatt went ashore and mounted the bank with a pistol in each hand; but he was overwhelmed by numbers, and hacked to pieces, and his head was carried off in trumph to the Nawab at Monghyr.

Cries for war and revenge. The news of the barbarous murder of Mr. Amyatt filled the Calcutta council with horror; and the majority clamoured for prompt vengeance on the Nawab. Vansittart begged them to remember that Mr. Ellis, and a multitude of Englishmen from Patna and Cossimbazar, were at the mercy of Mír Kasim; and that it would be better to make terms, and secure the lives of their fellow-countrymen, before they talked of war and revenge. But his

A.D. 1763.

warning was unheeded; scarcely a soul in the council would listen to his words. They loudly declared,—and they wrote out their declaration on paper and affixed their signatures,—that they would not come to terms with Mír Kasim, nor defer their revenge, although every prisoner in his hands was slaughtered to a man.

Mír Jafir proclaimed Nawab.

The council then left the chamber, and proceeded to the house of Mír Jafir within the precincts of Calcutta, and proclaimed him Nawab of Bengal, Behar, and Orissa. The ex-Nawab was overjoyed at his unexpected restoration to a throne, and readily agreed to everything that the council wanted. He pledged himself to compensate the Company and its servants for all losses; to pay the expenses of the war against Mír Kasim; and to reverse the measures of Mír Kasim, by collecting the duties from his own subjects, and permitting the English servants of the Company to trade in the commodities of the country duty free.

English advance to Monghyr.

In July the avenging army of the English was on its way to Plassy and Patna accompanied by Mír Jafir. The English captured Murshedabad and defeated the flower of the Nawab's army; but they found the enemy stronger than they had anticipated. The Nawab's troops had been drilled and disciplined in English fashion, and fought better than any native army had ever fought before under a native commander. But the steadiness of the European forces overcame every obstacle; and after a series of victories, they began to advance towards Monghyr.

Flight of Mír Kasim to Patna.

Meanwhile Mír Kasim was inflamed by his reverses to commit fresh acts of cruelty. He ordered several Hindu prisoners to execution, including the two grandsons of Jagat Seth. He collected his scattered forces at Monghyr, and finally proceeded to Patna, carrying with him all his English prisoners, to the number of a hundred and fifty souls.

Fall of Monghyr: frenzy of Mír Kasim.

Terrible news followed him to Patna. The English had captured his new capital at Monghyr. Then followed one of the most awful massacres of Europeans which is recorded in the history of British India. In a paroxysm of rage at the loss of Monghyr, Mír Kasim ordered the English prisoners to be put to death in cold blood The native commanders shrank from the slaughter of unarmed men; but a European deserter of the worst character agreed to perform the hateful

A.D. 1763.

service, which has handed down his name to everlasting infamy.

Sombre, *alias* Sumru.

A morose Franco-German, named Walter Reinhardt, had deserted more than once from the English to the French and back again. He had re-enlisted in an English regiment under the name of Somers; but his comrades nicknamed him Sombre on account of his evil expression. Finally he had deserted to the service of Mír Kasim, and obtained the command of a brigade under the Hinduised name of Sumru.

Massacre of a hundred and fifty Englishmen.

The English prisoners were lodged in a house or palace which had belonged to Hají Ahmad, the ill-fated brother of Alivardi Khan. It was a large range of buildings with a square court in the centre, like a college quadrangle. On the fourth of October 1763, the prisoners were deprived of their knives and forks by Sumru's orders, under pretence of a feast on the morrow. The morrow came. The house was surrounded with sepoys. Messrs. Ellis, Hay, and Lushington were called upon to come out, and were slaughtered outside. The sepoys climbed to the roof of the buildings, and fired upon the prisoners in the square, but were attacked with brickbats, bottles, and articles of furniture. They were struck with admiration at the courage of the English. They cried out that they would not fire upon men without arms. "They were sepoys," they said, "and not executioners!" But Sumru was furious at the hesitation. He struck down the foremost with his own hands, and compelled them to fire until every prisoner was slain.

Storming of Patna: flight of Mír Kasim into Oude.

The massacre at Patna sent a thrill of horror through the British empire. The errors of the victims were forgotten in their sufferings, and the cry for vengeance was universal. The Nawab was still hoping that the English would come to terms; possibly he thought that they would be frightened into an accommodation; but he soon found that the bloody deed had sealed his doom. In November Patna was taken by storm, and Mír Kasim fled away into Oude with his family and treasures, accompanied by the infamous Sumru.

Schemes of the Nawab Vizier: mutiny in the English army.

The Nawab Vizier had bound himself by an oath on the Koran to support Mír Kásim against the English; but his only object was to secure the Bengal provinces for himself. The moment was most favourable for an advance of the Nawab Vizier against the English. The victorious army, which had fought its way from Plassy to Patna, was in a state of mutiny. Soldiers and sepoys had expected extraordinary rewards for their extraordinary successes, but had received nothing beyond their pay and were starving for want of provisions; and they had talked themselves into such a state of disaffection that many were prepared to desert their colours and go over to the enemy.

A.D. 1763-1764

Repulse of the Nawab Vizier at Patna, April, 1764.

Weeks and months passed away. In April 1764 the Nawab Vizier, accompanied by Shah Alam, invaded Behar with what appeared to be an overwhelming army. The English force was encamped on the frontier, but was disheartened at the numbers of the enemy, and retreated slowly towards Patna. But the invading army is described by a native eyewitness as a mob of highwaymen.[1] The lawless soldiery of the Nawab Vizier fought, murdered and plundered each other in the middle of the camp; or went out killing and marauding in the surrounding country. A battle was fought in the neighbourhood of Patna, and the Nawab Vizier was repulsed. He then threw over Mír Kasim, and tried to make separate terms with Mír Jafir; but he insisted on the cession of Behar. At the same time the English insisted on the surrender of Mír Kasim and Sumru; and the Nawab Vizier, unscrupulous as he was, shrunk from the infamy of surrendering fugitives. Accordingly nothing was done, and as the rainy season was approaching, the Nawab Vizier returned to Oude.

Hector Munro stops the mutiny: blowing from the guns.

Subsequently Major Hector Munro arrived at Patna with reinforcements. He found the English troops threatening to desert to the enemy and carry off their officers. Shortly after his arrival, an entire battalion of sepoys went off to join the Nawab Vizier with their arms and accoutrements. Munro pursued them in the night, found them asleep, and brought them back as his prisoners. He ordered the native officers to select twenty-four ringleaders, and to try them by court-martial. The whole were found guilty of mutiny and desertion; and Munro ordered eight to be blown from guns on the spot, and sent the rest to other cantonments to be executed in like manner. He then told the remainder that if they were not satisfied with their present pay, they might lay down their arms and be dismissed the service, for they

[1] Gholam Husain Ali, in the *Siyár-ul-Mutaqherín*.

A.D. 1764.

would get no better terms. The delinquents expressed their penitence, and promised to serve the Company very faithfully for the future.[1]

Decisive battle of Buxar, October, 1764.

In September the rainy season was over, and Major Munro took the field. On the 23rd of October he defeated the Nawab Vizier in the decisive battle of Buxar; and the English army then advanced to Lucknow. The Nawab Vizier fled away to the Rohilla country; whilst Shah Alam joined the English, complaining that he had been set up as the Great Moghul, and then kept as a state prisoner by his own Vizier.

Importance of the victory.

Next to Plassy, the battle of Buxar is the most famous in the history of British conquest in India. It broke up the strength and prestige of Shuja-ud-daula, the last and greatest of the Moghul Viceroys of provinces, excepting perhaps the Nizam. It threw the whole of the territories of Oude into the hands of the English; placed the Moghul Padishah under British protection; and established the British nation as the foremost power in India.

Negotiations.

The Nawab Vizier was seeking the help of the Rohilla Afghans and the Mahrattas, whilst his minister was trying in the name of his master to make peace with the English. The demand for the surrender of Mír Kasim and the infamous Sumru was the main difficulty. But Mír Kasim had been despoiled by the Nawab Vizier of the bulk of his treasures, and fled away to the north-west, where he subsequently perished in obscurity. As regards Sumru it was proposed on the part of the Nawab Vizier to invite the miscreant to an entertainment, and put him to death in the presence of any English gentleman who might be deputed to witness the assassination.[2]

[1] Mr. Mill tells the story somewhat differently, but here as elsewhere the original authorities have been consulted. The narrative in the text is based on Major Munro's own account of the transaction in a letter to Governor Vansittart, dated 16th September, 1769.

[2] The after career of Sumru or Sombre is a strange episode in Indian history. He deserted the Nawab Vizier with a battalion of sepoys and a body of European outcasts, the scum of different nations. He entered the service of the Raja of the Játs, the ancestor of the present Raja of Bhurtpore. Lastly he entered the service of the so-called imperial army of Moghuls under Najib-ud-daula the Rohilla. Subsequently he married a dancing-girl, who afterwards became known as the Begum Sombre.

The villain who murdered the English at Patna afterwards became a

A.D. 1764-1765.

Rise of Raja Shitab Rai.

About this time a Hindu grandee, named Raja Shitab Rai, came to the front. He was a shrewd, keen-witted native, who had started in life as a small office clerk at Delhi, and risen to posts of power and wealth in Bengal and Behar. He was a fair type of the Hindus of capacity, who made themselves useful, and were ultimately rewarded with the title of Raja. He was demonstrative in his friendship for the English, and busied himself in all that was going on. He was an agent for the English in the negotiations with the Nawab Vizier. He brought over the Raja of Benares, Bulwunt Singh, from the cause of the Nawab Vizier to that of the English. He had been mixed up in some secret intrigues for inducing the commanders of fortresses in Oude territory to surrender to the English. In a word, he lost no opportunity of ingratiating himself with the English in the hope of profiting by their ascendancy.

English occupy Oude.

Meanwhile the English refused to listen to the proposals for the assassination of Sumru. They took possession of the territories of the Nawab Vizier; appointed officers to the command of the several districts; and intrusted the settlement of the revenue and judicial administration to Shitab Rai and Bulwunt Singh.

Final defeat of the Nawab Vizier.

The Nawab Vizier was still reluctant to come to terms. He sought the help of Rohilla Afghans and Mahrattas. The Rohilla chiefs engaged to join him, but did nothing. The Mahrattas under Mulhar Rao Holkar were eager for the plunder of Oude, and readily marched to his support. But Holkar was not accustomed to English artillery. He and his Mahratta horsemen advanced against the English army, but were received with such a terrible fire that they galloped off in consternation.

Nawab Vizier surrenders to the English.

The Nawab Vizier saw that his cause was ruined. He complained bitterly of the Rohilla chiefs, but they plied him with excuses. He had no alternative but to proceed to the English camp, and throw himself upon the mercy of the conquerors. Raja Shitab Rai was again busy as a negotiator; and the Nawab Vizier was led to believe that the

prince, and acquired great wealth, after the manner of Hindu and Muhammadan adventurers of the eighteenth century. The territory of Sirdhána was granted him in jaghír by the Moghul court for the maintenance of his sepoys and Europeans. He died in 1778, leaving his wealth and principality to the Begum Sombre.

A.D. 1764-1765

payment of fifty lakhs, or half a million sterling, would enable him to recover his lost territories.

Change of Governors at Calcutta.

About this time there was a change of Governors at Calcutta. Vansittart returned to England, and was succeeded by a Mr. Spencer; whilst a scheme was brewing for making over Oude to Najib-ud-daula, the Delhi minister, and conducting Shah Alam to Delhi. The scheme came to nothing, but it probably accounts for the reluctance of the Rohilla chiefs to join the Nawab Vizier.[1]

Death of Mír Jafir, January, 1765. Scheme of Spencer

Mír Jafir died in January, 1765; and the appointment of a successor to the Nawabship of Bengal and Behar was a question of grave importance. Spencer was only a temporary Governor. He knew that Clive, now an Irish Peer, was coming to Bengal with the powers of a dictator; and he would have acted wisely if he had awaited the arrival of Lord Clive; but he resolved to forestal Lord Clive in the disposal of the vacant throne at Murshedabad. There were two claimants to the succession, namely, an illegitimate son of Mír Jafir, aged twenty, and a legitimate grandson, aged six, a son of the deceased Miran; and the question was, which of the two was likely to prove the most subservient to the interests of the Company. No doubt the boy would have been most amenable to the will of the English; but Spencer chose the elder claimant, in spite of his illegitimacy, as the most amenable to the pecuniary rapacity of himself and his colleagues.

Sale of Bengal and Behar

Four members of the Calcutta council proceeded as a deputation to Murshedabad, and made a hurried bargain with a clever Mussulman grandee, named Muhammad

[1] The scheme of Governor Spencer was more extravagant than that of Governor Vansittart. The proposal to conduct Shah Alam to Delhi was wild but possible; and had an English officer, endowed with the genius of an Alexander or a Napoleon, been appointed to the command, he might have established a British empire over Hindustan. But the proposed cession of all the territories of the Nawab Vizier of Oude to his rival, the Afghan guardian at Delhi, would have been ruinous to the English There was only one way by which Najib-ud-daula could have occupied Oude, namely, by parcelling out the whole country as military jaghirs, or fiefs, amongst the Rohilla chiefs. This occupation would have amounted to the re-establishment of an Afghan empire down the valleys of the Jumna and Ganges as far as the Carumnassa, which would have proved a perpetual menace to Behar and Bengal.

A.D. 1764-1765

Reza Khan. It was agreed that the illegitimate son, aged twenty, should be proclaimed Nawab; that Muhammad Reza Khan should exercise all real power, under the name of Naib, or deputy Nawab; and that twenty lakhs of rupees, or about two hundred thousand pounds sterling, should be distributed to the Governor and certain select members of the council at Calcutta.

The Nemesis of history.

The bargaining at Murshedabad, and virtual sale of Bengal and Behar to Muhammad Reza Khan, was the last public act of the counting-house administrators of Calcutta. The Company's servants at this period were no better and no worse than the Prætorian guards, who sold the throne of the Cæsars to the highest bidder; but they were followed by men of the stamp of Robert Clive and Warren Hastings, who knew something of courts and armies, and were anxious to maintain a character in the eyes of their countrymen. The transaction however was strictly mercantile; and had it been concluded in the name of the East India Company, and not as an underhand stroke of private trade, it might have been regarded by the merchants of Leadenhall Street as a financial success. Indeed commercial statesmen might still be found, who would sell India back to native princes as the readiest means of getting rid of the supposed incubus of an Indian empire. But crimes against history are avenged by history. The men who sold Bengal and Behar to fill their own pockets are remembered only to be despised. But the soldiers and administrators that came after them, who delivered the native populations from the bondage of oriental despotism, and laboured to raise them to the level of Englishmen, have left a mark upon the people of India which will remain for all time.

CHAPTER IV.

DOUBLE GOVERNMENT: CLIVE, ETC.

A.D. 1765 TO 1771.

A.D. 1765-1767

Startling tidings.

LORD CLIVE, who at this time was on his way to India, was forty years of age. He had been named by nearly all parties in England as the only man who could save the Company's affairs in India. He reached Madras in April, 1765, and was greeted with startling tidings. Nizam Ali, who had murdered his brother Salábut Jung in 1763, had invaded the Carnatic with unusual ferocity; but had been compelled to retire to Hyderabad before the united forces of the English and Muhammad Ali. This matter was allowed to stand over; Lord Clive had already made up his mind how to deal with the Nizam. But another event struck him nearer home. He was told that Mír Jafir had died in the previous January.

Contemplated policy of Lord Clive.

Lord Clive was delighted at the news, for it enabled him to carry out a part of the grand scheme that he had unfolded to Pitt more than seven years before; namely, to take over the sovereignty of Bengal and Behar in the name of the East India Company, but to veil this sovereignty from the public eye by the forms of Moghul imperialism. He wanted a Nawab, who should be only a cypher; and the legitimate grandson of Mír Jafir, aged six, was ready to his hand. Lord Clive proposed to leave the native administration under the puppet Nawab and native ministers, who should be wholly dependent on the English; but to take over the entire revenue of the provinces. He calculated that after paying for the defence of the country, and the maintenance of the state pageant, there would remain a yearly surplus of one or two millions sterling for the use of the Company.

A.D. 1765-1767.

Clive at Calcutta, May, 1765: his wrath at Spencer.

Lord Clive reached Calcutta in May, and soon discovered the corrupt transactions of Governor Spencer. Of course he was furious with rage. Governor Spencer and his council had forestalled him only to fill their own pockets. They had placed a grown-up Nawab on the throne only to facilitate their corrupt bargaining with Muhammad Reza Khan. Clive declared in his wrath that the whites had united with the blacks to empty the public treasury. In vain he was told that the Governor and council had only followed the example which he had himself set at Murshedabad after the battle of Plassy. He retorted that he had rendered great public services by his victory at Plassy, whilst Spencer and the others had rendered no services whatever; that after Plassy, presents had been permitted, but that at the death of Mír Jafir they had been strictly forbidden by the Court of Directors. But Lord Clive was powerless to compel the offenders to refund, or to punish them in any way whatever; and most of them resigned the service and returned to England to fight the question with the Directors in the courts of law.

Arrangements of Clive at Murshedabad and Patna.

Lord Clive made the best arrangement he could under the circumstances. He accepted the Nawab who had been set up by Governor Spencer. He left Muhammad Reza Khan to act as deputy Nawab at Murshedabad, and he appointed Raja Shitab Rai to act in the same capacity at Patna. Both men wielded enormous powers. They were at the head of law and justice; they superintended the collections of revenue; and they were supposed to make over the whole of the proceeds to the English. But the story of their doings or misdoings will be told hereafter.

English sovereignty veiled by Moghul forms.

Lord Clive felt that whilst the English exercised sovereign powers in Bengal and Behar, it was necessary to conceal that sovereignty from the eyes of the world; as it would only excite the murmurs of the English parliament, and provoke the jealousies of French and Dutch rivals.[1] Accordingly Lord Clive planned that the English were to act solely in the name of the cypher Nawab, and under the affectation of

[1] The Seven Years' War between Great Britain and France was brought to a close by the Treaty of Paris in 1763, under which Chandernagore and Pondicherry were restored to the French.

A.D. 1765-1767

being the officers of the Great Moghul. In other words, the English were to accept from Shah Alam the post of Dewan, or manager of the revenues of the Bengal provinces; to pay the salaries of the Nawab and his officials; to set aside a fixed yearly sum as tribute to the Great Moghul as represented by Shah Alam; to provide for the defence of the provinces against all external and internal enemies;[1] and to transfer the surplus revenue to the coffers of the Company.

Policy as regards the Great Moghul.

Lord Clive's idea was to resuscitate the Moghul empire under Moghul forms, whilst keeping Shah Alam as a puppet or pageant in his own hands. He utterly scouted Spencer's scheme of policy. To have ceded Oude to the Rohilla Afghans would have drawn the Afghans to the frontier of Behar. To have conducted Shah Alam to Delhi would have carried the English army hundreds of miles from the frontier, and have embroiled the British authorities with Afghans or Mahrattas. Lord Clive was anxious to keep Shah Alam in the Bengal provinces,—at Patna, if not at Calcutta; and to set him up as a symbol of the Great Moghul. In other words, Shah Alam was to have been an imperial idol; and the English were to have issued their orders and commands as the oracles of the idol.

Restoration of Oude to the Nawab Vizier.

At the same time Lord Clive determined to restore Oude to the Nawab Vizier. It was too remote from Calcutta for the English to hold it as a conquered territory. Its defence would have drawn the European troops far away to the north-west, and left Behar and Bengal exposed to the demands or assaults of Mahrattas or Afghans. Its administration would have been out of the reach of all control from Calcutta. But the restoration of Oude to the Nawab Vizier would relieve the Company of all further expense and responsibility, and convert the government of Oude into a natural barrier for Behar and Bengal against the Afghans and Mahrattas of Hindustan.

Settlement at Allahabad.

Full of these grand schemes, Lord Clive left Calcutta, and hastened up the Ganges to meet Shah Alam and the Nawab Vizier at Allahabad. There, to use the language

[1] The military defence of a province under Moghul rule was not the duty of the Dewan, but of the Nawab Nazim. The exigencies of the time compelled Lord Clive to overlook the niceties of Moghul forms as regards the relative functions of Dewan and Nawab Nazim.

A.D. 1765-1767

of a native contemporary, he disposed of provinces with as much ease as if he had been selling cattle.[1] Without any of the endless negotiations, cavillings, and delays, which are the pride and glory of native diplomatists, he settled all questions by his own authority as the supreme arbiter of the destinies of Hindustan. The Nawab Vizier eagerly agreed to receive back his lost territories; to pay a sum of half a million sterling towards the expenses of the late war; and to cede by way of tribute to Shah Alam the revenues of Korah and Allahabad. On the other hand, Shah Alam was equally ready to accept the provinces of Allahabad and Korah in lieu of a tribute which for many years had never been paid. But Shah Alam refused to remove to Patna, or to any other place in Behar or Bengal. He was much chagrined at the refusal of Lord Clive to conduct him to Delhi; and he was still bent on going there at the first opportunity. Accordingly he decided on living at Allahabad in the empty state of a Great Moghul without a kingdom, but in the immediate neighbourhood of Shuja-ud-daula as his Vizier. A British force was posted at Allahabad for his protection; and it may be remarked that at this period, and for years afterwards, the forces of the Company were formed into three brigades, one of which was posted at Monghyr, a second at Patna, and a third at Allahabad.

Office of Dewan of Bengal, Behar, and Orissa.

The affairs of the Bengal provinces were settled with the same ease as those of Oude. Shah Alam gave letters patent to Lord Clive investing the English Company with the office of Dewan; and in return Lord Clive agreed that the English should pay him as Padishah a yearly tribute of something like a quarter of a million sterling, or about the same amount that Mír Kasim had agreed to give Shah Alam under the settlement of 1761.

Distinction between the Nawab Nazim and the Dewan.

It has already been explained that under the constitution of the later Moghul empire every province was administered by two officers, a Nawab and a Dewan. The Nawab, or Nawab Nazim, held the military command, and in that capacity superintended the administration of law, justice, and police. The Dewan was the accountant-general or finance minister, and looked solely after the revenue and expenditure.

Under Lord Clive's scheme the Company became nomi-

[1] *Siyár-ul-Mutaqherín*, by Gholam Husain Ali. Calcutta translation.

A.D. 1765-1767

Double powers of the Company.

nally Dewan, and practically Nawab Nazim; for the English compelled the young Nawab Nazim to disband his rabble army, and took upon themselves the military defence of the country, as well as the disposal of the revenue. The duties of the Nawab Nazim were thus limited to the nominal superintendence of law, justice, and police; and it will be seen hereafter that the English were soon forced by the general anarchy to take these branches of the administration into their own hands. Thus within a few years the Nawab Nazim dwindled into a pageant, having no duties to perform beyond the superintendence of his own household.[1]

Political results.

The political result of this arrangement was that the English remained in military charge of Bengal and Behar, with a claim on Orissa whenever they could procure it from the Mahrattas. Shuja-ud-daula was converted into a friendly ally; and it was hoped that he would succeed in guarding the English frontier at the Carumnassa river from Mahrattas and Afghans.

Financial results.

The financial results were still more satisfactory. The yearly revenue of Bengal and Behar was roughly estimated at three or four millions sterling, but hopes were expressed that it might reach five millions. Out of this gross sum the English were to pay half a million to the Nawab, and a quarter of a million to Shah Alam; and were then at liberty to appropriate the remainder.

Golden prospects of the East India Company.

The political system of Lord Clive must have appeared on paper to be the perfection of wisdom. So far as the Company believed in his golden dreams of the future, it held out most brilliant prospects. The civil administration in all matters of law, justice, and police was left in the hands of the natives, so that there were no responsibilities on that score. At the same time it was fondly expected that the surplus revenues of Bengal would meet

[1] The yearly allowances of the Nawab Nazim were fixed in the first instance by Lord Clive at fifty-three lakhs of rupees, or more than half a million sterling. The first puppet Nawab died within a year of his accession from sheer self-indulgence; his successors were equally useless and equally worthless, and, within seven years, the yearly allowance was reduced to 160,000*l*. Strange to say, this latter rate has been maintained down to our own time; and thus, for more than a century, a yearly expenditure, which would have supported a university, has been wasted on a useless pageant without duties and without claims.

A.D. 1765-1767

all charges against the Company in India; including all the expenses of the Company's settlements, all the civil and military salaries, and even all investments in India and China goods. Could these visions have been realised, the East India Company would have enjoyed the grandest monopoly the world ever saw. The Company already carried on a trade with India and China, from which all other Englishmen were excluded; and the further convenience of making the people of Bengal and Behar pay for all they bought in the east, would have enabled them to pocket the gross receipts of all they sold in England. Meanwhile, and for many years, so much secrecy was observed, and so much confusion was created by the use of oriental terms, that few outside the Company's service could possibly understand or realise the actual state of affairs.

External policy of non-intervention.

The external policy of Lord Clive was more clear and intelligible to men of business. In theory it was a strict adherence to the principles of non-intervention, amounting to political isolation. The English in Bengal were to leave all the native states outside the frontier to their own devices. They had formed an alliance with Shah Alam and his Nawab Vizier, but they were to abstain from making any other alliances whatever. Afghans and Mahrattas might fight each other, and kill each other like Kilkenny cats; the English were not to interfere, especially as the territories of the Nawab Vizier were supposed to form a political barrier against both the antagonistic races.

Misgivings about the Mahrattas.

Lord Clive had some misgivings about the Mahrattas of Berar. The Bhonsla Raja of Berar, or Nagpore, was pressing for the payment of chout for Bengal and Behar with arrears; and Clive was inclined to keep him quiet by paying the chout, on the condition that the Raja ceded the province of Orissa, which he had held ever since the agreement with Alivardi Khan in 1750. Again the Mahrattas were recovering from their defeat at Paniput, and beginning to re-assert their ascendancy in the Dekhan and Hindustan. Accordingly, Lord Clive threw out some hints of an alliance with the Nizam of the Dekhan which should maintain the balance of power against the Mahrattas.

Non-intervention.

The Directors in London took the alarm. They saw no necessity for paying chout; they did not want Orissa; and

A.D. 1765-1767 — enforced by the Directors.

they protested vigorously against any alliance with the Nizam, or any other native power. "The Carumnassa," they repeated, "is your boundary; go not beyond the Carumnassa! Leave the Mahrattas to fight the Afghans, and the Nizam to fight the Mahrattas, and devote all your attention to revenue and trade!"

Breach with Nizam Ali.

But Lord Clive had already dealt with Nizam Ali according to his peculiar scheme of imperial policy. On arriving in India in 1765, he had been told that Nizam Ali had been ravaging the Carnatic; and he saw that strong measures must be taken to repress such a troublesome and refractory neighbour. The quarrel was about the Northern Circars; namely, the five maritime districts on the coast of Coromandel, extending northward from the frontier of the Carnatic to the pagoda of Jagganath.[1] Salábut Jung had ceded this territory to Bussy and the French, and afterwards to Colonel Forde and the English; but his younger brother, Nizam Ali, who usurped the throne at Hyderabad in 1761, and murdered Salábut Jung in 1763, refused to submit to the loss of territory.

Firmán of a puppet Padishah.

Lord Clive tried to settle the question by putting forward Shah Alam as the rightful sovereign of India. Shah Alam, as the Great Moghul, was encouraged to maintain a little court at Allahabad; but he was otherwise treated as the tool and creature of the English; and a story is told that the English officer in command at Allahabad refused to allow the pageant prince to sound the imperial kettle-drums, because they made too much noise. However, Lord Clive obtained a firmán from Shah Alam, granting the Northern Circars to the English in full sovereignty, in defiance of the hereditary claims of Nizam Ali.

Assumption of Moghul sovereignty.

The assumption was enormous. It amounted to an assertion, on the part of Shah Alam, of a sovereign right to dispose at will of all the territories of the old Moghul empire, although the provinces had been practically converted into hereditary kingdoms ever since the invasion of Nadir Shah. If Shah Alam possessed the right to cede a portion of a province, like the Northern Circars, it would have been impossible to deny his right to cede whole provinces like Oude, Hyderabad, or the Carnatic.

[1] See *ante*, pages 255, 285, and 286.

A.D. 1765-1767

Clive, a Moghul Peishwa.

Had Lord Clive been an Asiatic conqueror, remaining for the rest of his life in India, he might possibly have ruled over the whole empire of Aurangzeb in the name of the Great Moghul. Shah Alam would have been the half-deified symbol of sovereignty. Lord Clive would have been prime minister or Peishwa; and as such might have compelled all rebellious Viceroys and refractory Rajas to do his bidding. He was already the virtual sovereign of Behar and Bengal. He had disposed of Oude at will; and had he remained in India he would have held the Northern Circars under the authority of the firmán. His genius was cast in the iron mould of military despotism; and the prestige of his name was sufficient to render the decrees of Shah Alam as irresistible as those of Aurangzeb.

Thwarted by Madras.

But Lord Clive was thwarted by the Madras authorities. In 1766 he sent an expedition under General Calliaud to take possession of the Northern Circars. But the English at Madras were alarmed at reports that Nizam Ali was making prodigious preparations for the invasion of the Carnatic; and they ordered General Calliaud to proceed to Hyderabad, and conclude a peace on almost any terms with Nizam Ali.

Treaty of 1766 with Nizam Ali.

At the end of 1766 General Calliaud negotiated a treaty with Nizam Ali. The firmán of Shah Alam was ignored. The English agreed to pay Nizam Ali a yearly tribute of seventy thousand pounds for the Northern Circars.[1] At the same time the English and Nizam Ali agreed to assist each other against any enemy; and in the first instance resolved on a joint expedition against Hyder Ali of Mysore, who had already threatened the dominions of Nizam Ali, and aroused the jealousy of the English by his leanings towards the French.

Clive succeeded by Verelst, 1767.

In January, 1767, Lord Clive left India never to return.[2] He was succeeded by Mr. Verelst as Governor of Bengal. Meanwhile the joint expedition of Nizam Ali and the

[1] There was some special arrangement as regards the Guntoor Circar, between the Gundlacama and Kistna rivers, which had been assigned as a jaghír to Basalut Jung, the eldest brother of Nizam Ali. The Circar of Guntoor was not to be made over to the East India Company until after the death of Basalut Jung.

[2] Lord Clive was only forty-two when his career in India was brought to a close. He died in England in 1774, at the age of forty-nine.

A.D. 1767-1771

English against Hyder Ali of Mysore was opening out a new phase in Indian history.

Mysore: rise of Hyder Ali.

The rise of Hyder Ali is a sign of the times. This adventurer was a Muhammadan of obscure origin. He is said to have served as a soldier in the French army.[1] Subsequently he left the French army and raised a body of troops on the basis of plunder, giving his men the half of all they stole, and taking care that nothing was stolen without his knowledge. Hyder's men seized every description of property, great and small; they would carry off sheep, cattle, or grain, or they would strip the villagers of their clothes and ear-rings.

Tricks and treacheries.

Hyder Ali next appeared as a commander in the service of the Hindu Raja of Mysore during the operations against Trichinopoly. He received a money allowance for every man under his command, and a donation for every one who was wounded; and he naturally cheated the Hindu government by false musters, and by bandaging men without a scratch, in order to pass them off as wounded. Meanwhile the Mysore government was distracted by a rivalry between a young Raja, who was a minor, and an uncle, named Nunjeraj, who acted as regent, and Hyder Ali did not fail to take advantage of the occasion. Gradually, by tricks and treacheries as bewildering as the feats of a conjuror, Hyder Ali destroyed the influence of the regent and used the Raja as a pageant, until at last he assumed the sovereign power in his own name.

Founds a Mysore empire.

Hyder Ali was not a mere freebooter. He subjugated several small states to the north and west of Mysore, including Kanara and Malabar. In this fashion he converted the Hindu Raj of Mysore into the seat of a new Muhammadan empire. He formed no political alliances. He committed raids on the territories of all his neighbours; on the Mahrattas of Poona, the Nizam of Hyderabad, and the Nawab of the Carnatic. At the same time he excited the jealous alarm of the English by secret dealings with the French of Pondicherry.

1 The author of the *Siyár-ul-Mutaqherín* states that Hyder Ali was originally a French sepoy. The story is extremely probable, although it would be suppressed or denied by the court annalists at Mysore or Seringapatam. It would explain Hyder Ali's subsequent leanings towards the French, which are otherwise inexplicable.

Nizam Ali joins Hyder Ali: invasion of the Carnatic.

The English were soon disgusted with their alliance with Nizam Ali. The united armies invaded Mysore and captured Bangalore. Meantime Nizam Ali was secretly intriguing with the Mysore court. He tried to win over the regent Nunjeraj; but Hyder Ali discovered the plot, and nothing more was heard of Nunjeraj. Nizam Ali next tried to win over Hyder Ali. This plot succeeded. Nizam Ali deserted the English, and joined his forces with those of Hyder Ali; and the new confederates began to attack the English and invade the Carnatic.

Humiliation of Nizam Ali: treaty of 1768.

The English army was taken aback at this sudden treachery, and retired towards Madras; but reinforcements came up, and they succeeded in inflicting two decisive defeats on the Muhammadan confederates. Nizam Ali was much alarmed at these disasters. He had expected to crush the English and recover the Carnatic from Muhammad Ali; but he began to fear that his own dominions were in danger. Accordingly he repented of his treachery, deserted Hyder Ali, fled towards Hyderabad, and sued the English for peace. In 1768 another treaty was concluded between the English and Nizam Ali, and relations were restored to their former footing.

Second firmán of a puppet Padishah.

Nizam Ali had grounds for his alarm. Whilst he was uniting his forces with Hyder Ali against the English, the puppet Padishah at Allahabad was once more brought into play. Mr. Verelst, the successor of Lord Clive, thought to checkmate Nizam Ali, and put an effectual stop to his intrigues with Hyder Ali, by procuring a blank firmán, with the seals of the Great Moghul, granting the whole of the Nizam's dominions to any one whom the English might choose. The firmán was actually sent to Madras, leaving the English there to fill in the name of any candidate that pleased them. The Directors loudly condemned this transaction and ordered it to be cancelled.[1]

[1] The cool attempt of Mr. Verelst to deprive Nizam Ali of his dominions by a simple firmán from Shah Alam excited great wrath and astonishment at the time. Nevertheless Verelst continued to regret that the design was not carried out. At a subsequent period, when Shah Alam had fled from Allahabad to Delhi, it was discovered that Hyder Ali of Mysore had been equally clever. Hyder Ali had actually purchased letters of investiture from the pageant Padishah at Delhi, under which he himself was appointed to the government of all the dominions of the Nizam.

A.D. 1767-1771

Successes of Hyder Ali, 1768-1769.

Strange to say, Hyder Ali was relieved by the defection of Nizam Ali. He retired to Mysore; but after collecting his resources, he fought the English with varying success, and then engaged in a series of rapid marches, which resembled the movements and surprises of Sivaji. He exacted a contribution from the Raja of Tanjore; re-opened communications with the reviving French settlement at Pondicherry; and threatened to join the Mahrattas of Poona against the English, unless the English joined him against the Mahrattas. Finally he appeared at St. Thomé, near Madras, with an army of six thousand chosen horsemen.

Offensive and defensive treaty at Madras, 1769.

The English at Madras were filled with consternation. Their resources were exhausted; they were alarmed for the safety of their garden houses in the suburbs of Madras; and they hastened to make peace, because, as they said, they had no money to carry on the war. In April, 1769, they concluded an offensive and defensive treaty with Hyder Ali. Each party agreed to restore all conquests, and to help the other in the event of an invasion from the Mahrattas or any other power.

Crisis in Bengal, 1770-71.

All this while the affairs of the Company in Bengal were drifting into financial anarchy. There was no war, nor rumours of war, beyond an occasional demand from the Bhonsla Raja of Berar for the payment of chout; but there was an alarming decline in the public revenue; money was disappearing from Bengal, and many of the native population were sinking into helpless penury. In 1770 Mr. Verelst returned to England, and was succeeded by Mr. Cartier as Governor of Bengal. But there was no prospect of improvement. In 1770-71 a terrible famine in Bengal added to the general desolation. At last in 1771 Lord Clive's political sham of a Moghul empire suddenly collapsed. Shah Alam threw himself into the hands of the Mahrattas, and went off to Delhi; and the destinies of the native powers of India entered upon a new phase, which is closely associated with the Mahratta empire, and will demand separate consideration in the following chapter.

Rapid fall in land revenue, 1767-71.

The system of government introduced by Lord Clive had turned out a total failure. This was obvious before Lord Clive left Calcutta; but for three or four years the system was lauded to the skies as the grand discovery of the age. At last the rapid diminution of the revenues of Bengal and

A.D. 1767-1771

Behar opened the eyes of the Directors, and induced them to break up the political sham, and to intrust the collection of the land rents and the administration of justice to their European servants.

Double government, not party government.

The system introduced by Lord Clive was a double government, under which the English took over the revenue and garrisoned the country, and left the administration in the hands of native officials without prestige or authority. This double government must not be confounded with party government. There never has been a party government in India with the natives on one side and the English on the other. In the double government of Lord Clive the English cared for nothing but the money, and left the native officials to prey upon the people and ruin the country without check or hindrance, so long as they collected the land rents and paid over a satisfactory block sum into the English treasury.

Protection of native administration.

This anomaly was not the fault of Lord Clive. It was forced upon him, partly, as already seen, from motives of policy as regards the French and Dutch, and partly also by the force of public opinion in England. Strong indignation had been felt in England at the interference of the servants of the Company in the administration of Mír Kasim; and strong opinions had been expressed that native officials should be left alone. Accordingly Lord Clive had been induced to recognise Muhammad Reza Khan as deputy Nawab at Murshedabad, and to appoint Raja Shitab Rai as deputy Nawab at Patna, in order that these two officials might conduct the native administration. He also appointed a British Resident at both places for the twofold purpose of taking over the revenue from the deputy Nawabs, and of protecting the native administration from any encroachments of the English. He overlooked the fact that the power which takes over the revenue is responsible for the well-being of the people. The result was that all the vices of oriental rule were left to fester in the native administration; whilst the restrictions imposed upon the British Residents prevented the possibility of any reform.

Zemindars and Ryots.

In Bengal and Behar the bulk of the revenue was derived from the land, which was assumed to be the property of the state. The Ryots cultivated the land, paying rent to the

A.D. 1767-1771

Zemindar of the district. The Zemindar collected the rents of his district in the mixed character of landholder and revenue-collector, and made monthly payments into the treasury at Murshedabad or Patna. The income of the Zemindar was thus derived, not from his rental, but from profit. It comprised the difference between the gross rents he received from the Ryots and the net proceeds which he paid into the treasury at headquarters.

Oppressive treatment of the Ryots.

The Ryots were mostly Hindus,—servile, timid, and helpless. The Zemindars were mostly Muhammadans from Persia, bred amidst the tyranny and corruption which prevailed in Persia, and devoid of all sympathy for the Hindu population.[1] They collected not only rents but irregular cesses; and whenever there was a marriage in the house of a Zemindar, or a son was born, or a fine was levied on the Zemindar on account of some delay or defalcation, the Ryots were compelled to contribute according to their means. There was no way of escape, except by bribing the servants of the Zemindar, reaping the crops at night and hiding the grain, or throwing up the holding and flying the country.

Judicial powers of the Zemindars.

All this while the Zemindar was magistrate of the district. He could fine, imprison, torture, and even execute heinous offenders, and there was no one to control him. There were Muhammadan Kázís and Brahman Pundits to decide civil cases, and there were higher courts of appeal; but no one could obtain redress without a large expenditure in presents or bribes, or the interference of some powerful grandee.

Deputy Nawabs.

In addition to the Zemindars, there always had been governors or deputy Nawabs of the same type as Muhammad Reza Khan and Raja Shitab Rai. They governed large towns or circles; received the collections from the Zemindars; and kept the peace throughout their respective jurisdictions. Originally their posts had been filled by Muhammadan officers; but later Nawabs preferred promoting Hindu officials, and giving them the honorary title of "Raja."[2]

[1] See Verelst's *Bengal*. Also *Early Records of British India*.

[2] Muhammadan governors were often turbulent and refractory; and they squandered all their ill-gotten gains on pomp and pleasure. Hindus were more amenable to authority, and delighted in hoarding up gold and jewels; so that as occasion served they could be squeezed

A.D. 1767-1771

Check on the Zemindars.

The only check on Zemindars and deputy Nawabs was the right of petition to the Nawab; and this check in olden time had exercised a restraining influence on oppression. Former Nawabs would often sit in state, and spend a great part of their days in hearing petitions and passing judgments with the assistance of law officers. Sometimes the iniquitous oppressions and exactions of a Zemindar were forced on the attention of a Nawab, and were punished by the confiscation of his goods and removal from his Zemindary. Sometimes, justly or unjustly, a Hindu Raja was recalled from his post, deprived of all his goods and chattels, and put to an ignominious death as a punishment for his misdeeds, or in order to replenish the coffers of a grasping Nawab.

Aggravation of evi under the double government.

But under the double government created by Lord Clive, embezzlement, corruption, and oppression flourished as in a hotbed. Not only was there no check, but there was every temptation to guilty collusion. No Zemindars could have been anxious to swell the collections of revenue for the benefit of the East India Company; nor were the deputy Nawabs eager to detect defalcations and abuses, when they might be bribed to silence by a share in the spoil. The new puppet Nawab Nazim had no inducement to hear petitions, and no power to enforce judgment. The deputy Nawabs, Muhammad Reza Khan at Murshedabad and Raja Shitab Rai at Patna, were supposed to hear petitions; but they had a thousand interests to consult, of Englishmen as well as Zemindars, and it is impossible to know whether they performed their duties well or ill. Meanwhile the English servants of the East Indian Company were merchants, educated for the counting-house, skilled in bargaining and commerce, and impressed with the conviction that the one aim and object of life in India was to make a fortune and return to England at the earliest possible opportunity.

The outward working of the Nizamut may be gathered from a solemn farce which was played every year at Mur-

of all the riches they had absorbed. Mir Jafir removed some of the Hindu Rajas, and appointed Muhammadan kinsmen of his own to the vacant posts. Muhammad Reza Khan was a fair sample of a Muhammadan grandee; whilst Shitab Rai was a favourable specimen of a Hindu Raja.

A.D. 1767-1771

Mock pageantry at Murshedabad.

shedabad. The annual revenue settlements were arranged at a yearly festival known as the Poona. The Zemindars assembled at the capital to make their agreements as regards the monthly payments of revenue for the ensuing year. The Nawab Nazim took his seat on the throne in empty dignity; whilst the English Governor of Bengal and Behar stood on his right hand as representing the Honourable Company in the quality of Dewan.

Bengal drained of silver.

One result of the new system of government was the rapid disappearance of rupees. Silver was no longer imported from Europe for the purchase of commodities or payment of salaries; whilst large quantities were exported to Madras and China, or carried to Europe by the Company's servants, who retired with large fortunes. The old Nawabs of Murshedabad had squandered enormous sums on pomps and pleasures, which, however useless in themselves, had kept the money in the country. Under the English *régime* these expenses had been largely curtailed; the army was disbanded, the vast menageries of animals and birds were broken up, and there were large reductions in the household and zenana. But the money thus saved was sent out of Bengal; and a host of native soldiery and parasites were reduced to beggary. A native contemporary remarked, in the language of oriental hyperbole, that grain had become exceedingly cheap because there was no money to buy it; that a native horseman was becoming as rare as a phœnix; and that but for the money spent by the English in the purchase of raw silk, opium, and white piece goods, a silver rupee, or a gold mohur, would have been as rare as a philosopher's stone.[1]

Verelst's experiences of native administration.

The stoppage of the exports of silver from Bengal to China, and increased public expenditure in Bengal, lessened the evils arising from the outflow of silver; but nothing would check the rapid decline of the revenue. Mr. Verelst, who succeeded Lord Clive as Governor of Bengal, seems to have understood the causes of the decrease. For years he had overlooked the revenue administration in Burdwan, Midnapore and Chittagong, and had seen the roguery which pervaded all classes of native officials, and the unblushing rascality of their servants and dependants. But Verelst

[1] *Siyâr-ul-Mutaqherin*, by Gholam Husain Ali.

A.D. 1767-1771

was hampered by Clive's political system of non-interference, and was compelled to use the utmost caution in introducing European supervision.

English supravisors and committees.

In the first instance Verelst appointed English supravisors into the different districts, with instructions to report all that was going on, but not to interfere in the native administration. Subsequently the English Residents at Murshedabad and Patna were encouraged to inquire into the conduct of affairs; and ultimately committees of Englishmen were appointed in association with Muhammad Reza Khan and Shitab Rai.

Closer relations between English and natives.

At this crisis the natives were taken aback by a social revolution. Hitherto the English had kept aloof from native gentlemen, and taken no pleasure in their society; but now they began to form intimacies with Muhammadan and Hindu grandees, and to converse with them on political affairs. It was remarked by the native writer already quoted, that the English eagerly inquired into the laws, usages, and modes of transacting public business, and wrote down all they heard in books for the information of other Englishmen. Meanwhile the native grandees were envious and jealous of each other; and every one was ready to report the misdoings of the others, in order to win the favour of the English gentlemen, or to conceal his own backslidings and short comings.

Native administration of justice.

The English gentlemen, it was said, also attended courts of justice, and sometimes expressed surprise at what they saw or heard. When an offender was convicted and fined, his accuser also was required to pay a fine by way of thanksgiving. The English could not understand this, and asked why a man should be fined who had committed no offence? They were told it was the custom of the country. Again, when a Zemindar or Kází tried a civil case, he took a fourth-part of the amount in dispute as his fee. This again the English could not understand, as they had no such custom in their country.

An English gentleman at Patna.

Under such circumstances the native grandees would be most polite and obliging, whilst an Englishman would be sometimes gulled. A Mr. George Vansittart[1] was sent to Patna, where Raja Shitab Rai was acting as deputy Nawab;

[1] This was a brother of Governor Vansittart, who perished at sea during a return voyage to India.

Company's servants returned to England loaded with wealth, which they were supposed to have wrung out of native princes, or acquired by oppressing the native population. A.D. 1767-1771

It is needless to dwell on obsolete scandals. No doubt presents were received from native contractors, and "dustoori," or commission, from native dealers and manufacturers. No one was better acquainted with the Company's trade at the factories up country than Warren Hastings; and he bitterly complained that the Directors were rigid about salaries, whilst they were indifferent about perquisites, though the former were but pittances, whilst the latter amounted to lakhs.[1] Corruption was equally rampant at Calcutta. Contracts were given to Europeans for every kind of public expenditure, whilst the work was entrusted to natives; and whoever obtained a contract seemed to make a fortune. The Directors saw that large sums were entered in the public accounts, which they were unable to audit, and which only confirmed their worst suspicions. General corruption in Bengal.

All this while the people of the country were bitterly complaining of being abandoned to the oppression and extortion of native officials. The author of the *Siyár-ul-Mutaqherín* testifies to the superiority of the English, but denounces their selfish neglect of the masses. "When," he says, "the Shahzada invaded Behar, the people prayed that he might be victorious and prosperous, for they remembered the good government and favours they had enjoyed under his ancestors. But when they found themselves harassed and plundered by his disorderly soldiery, and saw that the English never touched a blade of grass, nor injured the weakest individual, they changed their minds; and when the Shahzada was proclaimed Padishah, and invaded Behar under the name of Shah Alam, they loaded him with reproaches, and prayed for victory and prosperity for the English army. But they soon ceased to pray for the English; for the new rulers paid no attention to the concerns of the people of Hindustan, and suffered them to be mercilessly plundered, oppressed and tormented, by officers of their own appointing." Native opinion turned against the English.

In 1771 matters were brought to a climax by a horrible famine in Bengal. It is needless to dwell upon the details of death and desolation. Indian famines have been Bengal famine of 1770-71.

[1] Gleig's *Memoirs of Warren Hastings*, vol. i. chap. viii.

A.D. 1767-1771

English gentleman; for it was currently believed by every native of standing and experience that all Englishmen, especially officials, were gratified with the language of flattery and adulation. The Raja was also ever ready with his explanations, having probably learnt them by heart before Mr. Vansittart's arrival; being well aware that nothing exasperates an Englishman so much as boggling or prevarication, and that almost any lie may be swallowed so long as it is prompt and plausible. Meanwhile, the number and value of the Raja's presents could scarcely fail to make a gratifying impression on Mr. Vansittart, and have thoroughly satisfied that gentleman of his faithfulness and capacity. The public conduct of the Raja towards petitioners was modelled after that of the most polished oriental statesmen, as being the best calculated for confirming friends and disarming enemies. Unfortunately Shitab Rai found that he must keep on good terms with English gentlemen at any price; and consequently he was driven to commit those acts of embezzlement and oppression, which his best friends must have deplored, and for which the Englishmen of those days were more or less responsible.

Wrath of the Directors at their English servants.

Meanwhile, the Directors in England threw all the blame of the declining revenues on the crafty practices of the native officials, and the corrupt collusion between their own English servants and the deputy Nawabs at Murshedabad and Patna—Muhammad Reza Khan and Raja Shitab Rai. How far they were justified in these conclusions may be gathered from the admissions of Gholam Husain Ali, who evidently entertained a high opinion of Shitab Rai. Gholam Husain Ali was infinitely more bitter against Muhammad Reza Khan, charging him with pride and insolence, corruption and crime; but as the writer was notoriously an enemy to Muhammad Reza Khan, it would be invidious to repeat the accusations.

Losses in the Company's trade.

The Directors in England were exasperated beyond measure by their losses in trade. The Indian commodities, and manufactures had risen in price and deteriorated in value, chiefly, it was believed, through the culpable heedlessness, or still more guilty connivance, of their servants in the different factories. At the same time, the public expenditure in Bengal had risen to such a pitch that the Company was brought to the verge of ruin. Yet year after year the

A.D. 1767-1771

or impatient at the extravagance of their demands; and he never used a harsh word, or the language of abuse or reprimand. He was generous and hospitable, after the manner of a middle-class Moghul Amír of Hindustan. Whenever a person of distinction came to Patna the Raja always sent him a number of trays of sweetmeats, delicacies, and dressed victuals according to his rank and station.

Failings of the Raja.

"But Rajah Shitab Rai was not wholly free from blame. He was too fond of obliging and gratifying his friends and acquaintances. He religiously abstained from appropriating the public money, but his salary and private means fell very short of his expenses, and he was obliged moreover to bestow sums of money on Europeans. In order, therefore, to adjust his means to his expenses, he adopted two methods, which were both iniquitous. When a man was indebted to the public treasury it was customary to send one or two constables to compel payment, and to charge their diet money to the debtor. But Shitab Rai sent dozens of constables, and entered but a very small part of the diet money in the book of receipts, and kept the remainder to expend on his liberalities. Again, Shitab Rai called upon all jaghírdars and other landholders to produce their title-deeds on the pretence that some English gentlemen wanted to examine them; and he refused to return the documents until the incumbent had contributed a sum of money in proportion to his means. All these contributions he bestowed on Englishmen that had been recommended to him; and seemed to be wholly occupied in keeping the gentlemen of that nation in good humour."[1]

Results of the collision between Europeans and Hindus.

The observations and admissions of Gholam Husain Ali sufficiently reveal the early results of the collision between the European and Hindu mind during the rise of British power in Bengal. Raja Shitab Rai was a type of the native grandees and officials of the eighteenth century, and a prototype of a considerable number of the nineteenth. By readiness and business habits, and a constant study of the temper of his employers, he had gradually risen from one post to another, until he had gained the favour of Lord Clive, and was appointed deputy Nawab at Patna. Of course the Raja was most attentive and profoundly respectful to the

[1] *Siyár-ul-Mutaqherín*, Calcutta translation.

A.D. 1767-1771

and Gholam Husain Ali describes the circumstances of their meeting, and the ultimate results, with much apparent truthfulness and simplicity:—

Fears of Raja Shitab Rai.

"When it was known that Mr. Vansittart was coming to Patna, all the enemies of Shitab Rai conceived mighty hopes from the change. The capacity and politeness of the Raja were such that few could have found fault with his administration; but many were envious of his greatness, and prepared to light up a mighty flame, so that he himself was fearful of the consequences. The hem of his robe was pretty free from dirt, and the blemishes in it were few in comparison with his many services; yet he was so alive to the inconveniences that might arise from the difference of nation and language, and his ignorance of Mr. Vansittart's character and genius, that he was very doubtful of his fate.

The Raja and the Englishman.

"When Mr. Vansittart approached Patna, the Raja went out to meet him, took him on his elephant, and brought him into the city. This was very mortifying to the enemies of the Raja, who were hastening to wait on Mr. Vansittart in order to set up a shop of chicanery and malice. They were all struck dumb by his artful behaviour. As a great statesman and accountant, he had ready every kind of paper that could be called for. He was firm and steady in his behaviour and answers; never boggled or prevaricated; never hesitated to furnish any information that was required; and answered with so much propriety as to leave no opening for an imputation on his character. Accordingly Mr. Vansittart was so convinced of his fidelity, wisdom, and knowledge, that he opened the gates of friendship and union. Nor was the Raja wanting to himself in such an overture. By respectful behaviour, and a number of curious presents, he gained so much on the mind of Mr. Vansittart, that the latter gentleman was thoroughly satisfied.

Politeness and generosity of the Raja.

"Raja Shitab Rai behaved to men of virtue and distinction with a modesty and humility that disarmed envy. He was quick at understanding the intent of every man's petition. If he granted a request it was with the utmost condescension; if he refused a petition it was with handsome excuses and in condoling language. He was engaged in business, and in conferences with different people, from daybreak till noon, and from evening till three o'clock in the morning. He never seemed fatigued with the number of applicants,

A.D. 1767-1771

familiarised to readers of the present generation, but were intensified in the eighteenth century by the inadequacy of the measures taken to meet the evil. Many English gentlemen, as well as Shitab Rai, and perhaps other grandees, laboured hard to alleviate the general suffering by feeding thousands at their own expense, and bringing down stores of grain from cheaper markets. But alarming news had reached England that certain Englishmen had confederated with Muhammad Reza Khan to profit by the national disaster by hoarding up large stocks of grain and selling it out at famine prices.

Warren Hastings Governor of Bengal, 1772-85.

The result of all these complicated suspicions and charges was that the Directors determined on a radical reform; and to entrust this important work to Mr. Warren Hastings by appointing him to be Governor of Bengal. Hastings was a man of large Indian experience and clear-headed capacity; and up to this period was regarded as a man of probity. Accordingly the Directors expected Hastings to bring back their European servants to a sense of duty, moderation, and loyalty to the Company; and to remodel the administration by transferring the collection of the revenue from natives to Europeans.

Contemporary history of Bombay and the Mahrattas.

The advent of Warren Hastings is the beginning of a new era. He introduced British administration into Bengal and Behar; and he was drawn by the Bombay government into hostilities on a large scale against the Mahrattas. Accordingly, before entering on the history of his government, it will be as well to review the progress of affairs in Bombay and the neighbouring empire of the Mahrattas.

CHAPTER V.

BOMBAY: MAHRATTA EMPIRE.

A.D. 1748 TO 1772.

A.D. 1748-1772

The three Presidencies.

DURING the eighteenth century Madras, Calcutta, and Bombay had each a political life of its own. This individuality is disappearing in an age of railways and telegraphs; but it has left lasting marks on the traditions of the past; and before proceeding further with the history, it may be as well to sum up the distinctive characteristics in the annals of each of the three Presidencies.

Madras on the Coromandel coast.

Madras is seated in an open roadstead on the sandy and surf-bound coast of Coromandel. On the sea side it looks over the large expanse of the Bay of Bengal towards Burma, Siam, Sumatra, the Eastern Archipelago, and the more remote territories of China and Japan. On the land side it was associated with the establishment of the Nawabs of the Carnatic and Nizams of Hyderabad as independent princes; with old wars between England and France; with the capture of Madras by Labourdonnais, the ambitious dreams of Dupleix, the siege of Trichinopoly by Chunda Sahib and the French, the defence of Arcot by Clive, the victory of Eyre Coote at Wandiwash, and the temporary destruction of Pondicherry in 1761; and finally with the rise of Hyder Ali in the western table-land of Mysore.

Calcutta, a hundred miles up the river Hughli.

Calcutta is situated a hundred miles up the river Hughli, amidst green rice-fields and overgrown jungles. It is remote from the sea and busied with shipping in the river. Before the age of railways a water communication united Calcutta with Patna and Benares, and opened up the heart

A.D. 1748-1772

of Hindustan. The English settlement was associated with memories of the Black Hole, the recovery of Calcutta from the Nawab, the expulsion of the French from Chandernagore, the triumph at Plassy, the setting up of Nawabs at Murshedabad, the acquisition of Bengal and Behar in 1765, the subsequent introduction of British administration into Bengal and Behar by Warren Hastings, and the rise of a British empire which was to overshadow Hindustan and establish a dominion from the Brahmaputra to the Indus.

Bombay, facing Persia and the Red Sea: land-locked by Mahrattas.

Bombay is a small island on the Malabar coast, commanding the finest harbour on the eastern seas, and looking over the Indian Ocean towards Muscat and Madagascar, the Persian Gulf and the Red Sea. It was the dowry of Catherine, the Portuguese wife of Charles the Second. On the land side it was hemmed round with Mahrattas, who exercised dominion, or collected chout, from Bombay to Bengal, from Guzerat to Orissa, and from Malwa to Mysore.

Maritime neighbours: Seedees and Angrias.

The other neighbours of the English settlement at Bombay were maritime powers. On the north and south were the Abyssinians of Surat and Jinjeera, whose hereditary chiefs, known as the Seedees, or Sidis,[1] were the nominal lord high admirals of the Moghul; the protectors of Moghul traders and Mecca pilgrims against the pirates of Malabar. Further to the south were the Mahratta pirates of Malabar; the hereditary Angrias of Gheriah; the representatives of the Malabar corsairs, who had been the terror of the Indian Ocean since the days of Pliny and the Cæsars.

Mahratta empire and feudatories.

The frontiers of the great Mahratta empire were ever changing like those of the Parthians. In fact, the Mahrattas were the Parthians of India, and their dominion extended as far as the Mahratta horsemen could harry and destroy. But a distinction must be drawn between Maharashtra proper, the homes of the Mahratta-speaking people, and the outlying military dominion of Mahratta feudatories. Maharashtra proper was the hereditary kingdom of the Maharajas of the house of Sivaji. The military lieutenants outside the Mahratta pale, were freebooting chiefs, who originally held

[1] The term Seedee, when assumed by the Africans, is a term of dignity corresponding to the Arabic term Saiyid, or lord. In India however it was sometimes used as a term of reproach, rather than of distinction.—*Grant Duff.*

commissions from the reigning Maharaja, but who gradually grew into vassal princes; whilst the outlying territories which they plundered, hardened into semi-independent provinces of a loose Mahratta empire. A.D. 1748.

The seats of the home government of the Mahratta country are indicated by three important fortresses, running from north to south, and known as Poona, Satara, and Kolhapore. Poona was situated about seventy miles to the south-east of Bombay; it was originally the stronghold of Sivaji, the founder of the Mahratta empire, but was subsequently surrendered to the generals of Aurangzeb. Satara was the capital of Sahu, the grandson of Sivaji, and last of the Bhonsla dynasty. Kolhapore was the capital of an independent principality founded by a rival branch of the same Bhonsla family.[1] Mahratta country: Poona, Satara, Kolhapore.

The four leading Mahratta feudatories have already been mentioned; namely, the Gaekwar in Guzerat; Holkar and Sindia in Malwa, between the Nerbudda and the Chambal rivers; and the Raja of Berar and Nagpore to the north of the Nizam of Hyderabad.[2] The three former were of low caste; but the Berar Raja belonged to the tribe of Bhonslas, of which Sivaji was a member. The Bhonsla Raja of Berar was also the most powerful of the four; for he had conquered large territories from the Nizam of the Dekhan, and occupied the Orissa country to the south of Behar and Bengal. Outlying feudatories: Gaekwar, Holkar, Sindia, Bhonsla Raja of Berar.

The early history of the Mahratta feudatories is a confused narrative of family quarrels, assassinations, and predatory exploits, varied by frequent disputes with the Maharaja's government as to the amount of revenue or chout to be paid into the Maharaja's treasury. About the middle of the eighteenth century the four great feudatories were beginning to found dynasties, namely, Damaji Gaekwar, Mulhar Rao Holkar, Ranuji Sindia, and Rughuji Bhonsla. Early annals.

Maharaja Sahu, grandson of Sivaji, died at Satara in 1748. For some years before his death he had been nearly imbecile.

[1] The Raj of Kolhapore was held by a younger brother of Sahu, known as Sambhaji the Second, to distinguish him from his father, the first Sambhaji, who was executed by Aurangzeb. See *ante*, page 181. Further south, near Goa, was the Bhonsla chief of Sawant Waree, but he has played little or no part in history.

[2] See *ante*, pages 218, 219.

A.D. 1748.

Death of Sahu, 1748: his imbecility

A favourite dog had saved his life while hunting a tiger. He conferred a jaghír on the dog, and provided it with a palanquin and bearers. He dressed the dog in brocade and jewels, placed his own turban on its head, and in this fashion received Mahratta chiefs in full durbar. He was conscious of his dependence on his Brahman prime minister, or Peishwa, and boasted that he had conquered India from the Muhammadans and given it to the Brahmans.

Plots for the succession: Tara Bai and Raja Ram.

Sahu died childless; consequently before his death there had been plots in the zenana as regards the succession. An old princess of the family, named Tara Bai, produced a boy, named Raja Ram, whom she declared was her own grandson. Nothing was known of the boy, but she persuaded the dying Sahu that he was the legitimate descendant of Sivaji, and consequently the rightful heir to the throne at Satara. Her object was to secure the throne for the boy, and then to rule the Mahratta empire as regent during the minority of her reputed grandson.[1]

Sukwar Bai: her vow.

Sukwar Bai, the chief wife of Sahu, was hotly opposed to the scheme of Tara Bai. She had no notion of seeing Tara Bai occupy the post of regent. She declared that Raja Ram was an impostor. She intrigued in behalf of a claimant of the house of Kolhapore, who was also a descendant of Sivaji. She secretly won over several partisans, but sought to conceal her plans by publicly declaring that on the death of Sahu she would burn herself alive on his funeral pile.

Schemes of Balaji Rao, third Peishwa.

All this while Balaji Rao, the third Peishwa, was bent on usurping the sovereignty of the Mahratta empire.[2] Like his predecessors, he was a type of those secular Brahmans who

[1] Tara Bai was a widow of Raja Ram, the youngest son of Sivaji. When Sambhaji the First, the elder son of Sivaji, was executed by Aurangzeb in 1689, Raja Ram succeeded to the sovereignty of the Mahrattas. Raja Ram died in 1700, and Tara Bai became regent during the minority of a son who was an idiot. In 1708 Tara Bai was deposed and imprisoned. Forty years afterwards, she was, as stated in the text, once more intriguing for the regency. Pertinacity is a national characteristic of the Mahrattas, male and female.

[2] There were three Peishwas, who successively exercised supreme power at Satara as the hereditary prime ministers of Maharaja Sahu. Balaji Vishvanath, the grandfather, died in 1720. Baji Rao, the son, died in 1740. Balaji Rao, the grandson, and third Peishwa, succeeded to the post in 1740, and usurped the sovereignty in 1748. See *ante*, pages 217—223, 238.

ignore the religious duties of their caste in order to pursue their ambitious designs. He kept a watchful eye on the two princesses, who were plotting for the sovereign power, which he was resolved to secure for himself and his son after him. For a long time he was anxious and hesitating as to whose cause he should espouse. At last he professed to believe in the legitimacy of Raja Ram; intending in the end to set aside the regency of Tara Bai, and treat the boy Maharaja as a puppet of his own.

A.D. 1748-1751

Cruel treatment of Sukwar Bai.

On the death of Sahu, Balaji Rao occupied Satara with troops, and threw the partisans of Sukwar Bai into prison. He then got rid of Sukwar Bai by insidiously begging her not to burn herself, whilst persuading her kinsfolk that the family would be dishonoured by the violation of her vow. Maddened with wrath against the Peishwa, the distracted widow was forced to perish in the flames which consumed the body of her deceased husband.

Tara Bai befooled: caste ordeal of Raja Ram.

Balaji Rao behaved very differently to Tara Bai. For a while he treated her with the utmost respect and deference. Indeed her influence was necessary to secure the allegiance of the great feudatories of the Mahratta empire; the Gaekwar in Guzerat, Sindia and Holkar in Malwa, and the Bhonsla Raja of Berar. The Bhonsla Raja of Berar was especially dreaded by the Peishwa; for he not only belonged to the same tribe as Sivaji, but he had always nursed a secret design on the throne of Satara by virtue of his kinship to Sivaji. The Bhonsla on his part was very jealous of the ascendancy of the Brahmans; very suspicious of Balaji Rao; and very sceptical as regards the legitimacy of Raja Ram. Tara Bai, however, clenched the matter by eating with Raja Ram in the presence of the Bhonsla tribe, and swearing on the food that he was her legitimate grandson. The Bhonsla of Berar was thus compelled to acquiesce in the succession of Raja Ram; and none of the other feudatories were prepared to resist the authority of the hereditary Peishwa.

Balaji Rao removes the capital to Poona.

Balaji Rao next proceeded to Poona, the old stronghold of Sivaji, leaving Tara Bai and Raja Ram at Satara. He produced a deed, purporting to be under the hand of the deceased Sahu, granting to himself, as Peishwa, the guardianship of the Mahratta empire, so long as he maintained a descendant of the famous Sivaji on the throne of Satara.

A.D. 1748-1751

He removed all the officials and records to Poona; and henceforth Poona, and not Satara, was regarded as the capital of the Mahratta empire.

Eight Purdhans, or ministers.

At Poona Balaji Rao retained the forms of the old Mahratta constitution. Sivaji had appointed eight Purdhans or ministers, beginning with the Peishwa or premier, and including a treasurer, public record keeper, private record keeper, war minister, foreign minister, chief justice, and head Shastri.[1] Balaji Rao retained these ministers in nominal employ; but he kept all real power in his own hands.

Mahratta invasions of the Dekhan and Carnatic.

Balaji Rao was soon prepared to take advantage of the troubled politics of the times. The year 1748, as already stated, was an epoch in India.[2] The war between the English and French in Southern India had been brought to a close by the treaty of Aix-la-Chapelle; but rival Nizams were fighting for the throne of Hyderabad, and rival Nawabs were fighting in the Carnatic for the throne of Arcot; and in spite of the peace between Great Britain and France, the English and French were soon fighting against each other under pretence of taking opposite sides in the native wars for the succession. Under such circumstances, Balaji Rao, like a true Mahratta, was soon invading both the Dekhan and Carnatic; not to take any part in the dissensions, unless he was paid for it, but chiefly to collect chout and annex districts, whilst the regular forces, which might have checked his inroads, were fighting elsewhere.

Tara Bai plots at Satara.

Suddenly Balaji Rao was recalled to Satara. Tara Bai had resolved to throw off his yoke. She tried to stir up the boy Raja Ram to assert his sovereignty; and she called on Damaji Gaekwar to deliver the lad from the thraldom of the Brahman. Raja Ram was too stupid or feeble for her purpose; but Damaji Gaekwar obeyed her summons. Meanwhile she struck at the root of the Peishwa's authority by confessing that Raja Ram was no descendant of Sivaji,

[1] The head Shastri was an important member of the Mahratta government. He was the expounder of Hindu law and scriptures, and general referee in all matters of religion, criminal law and judicial astrology. At a later period the office was held by a celebrated Brahman, named Ram Shastri, who played an important part in the history.

[2] See *ante*, page 243.

A.D. 1751-1755

but a low-caste boy who had been changed for her grandson. Accordingly she threw Raja Ram into a dungeon, and vowed to atone for her perjury by rites and sacrifices on the bank of the holy Kistna.

Counter plotting of Balaji Rao.

Balaji Rao was equal to the emergency. He feigned to make terms with the Gaekwar, and then treacherously surrounded him and carried him off prisoner to Poona. But Tara Bai set the Peishwa at defiance; refused to surrender Raja Ram; and prepared to stand a siege at Satara. Balaji Rao left her alone for a while; he saw that the Mahratta people still regarded her as their rightful regent; and meanwhile she was ruining her claim to the regency by shutting up the boy Maharaja in the fortress, and declaring him to be an impostor.

Mahratta aggressions and ravages, 1751-55.

For some years Balaji Rao carried on a variety of operations in the Dekhan and Carnatic. Villages were ruthlessly plundered, and village officials were put to the torture; and if a fortress ventured to hold out, and was reduced by force of arms, the whole garrison was put to the sword.

Intrigues with Delhi.

All this while Balaji Rao was carrying on some obscure intrigues with Delhi. Muhammad Shah, the last of the Moghul Padishahs worthy of the name, had died in 1748, the same year as Sahu. Since then the Moghul court at Delhi had presented a troubled scene of anarchy and bloodshed. The successors of Muhammad Shah were mere pageants, who were set up, deposed, or murdered by the Vizier; whilst the grandees plotted against each other, or intrigued with Afghans or Mahrattas, in order to obtain the post of Vizier, or that of Amír of Amírs. Ghazi-ud-dín, the grandson of Nizam-ul-mulk, carried on a secret correspondence with the Mahrattas, and ultimately obtained the post of Vizier. Nothing however is known of these intrigues beyond the characteristic fact that Balaji Rao found it convenient to procure from the Vizier imperial firmáns for all the territories which he had acquired on the side of Hyderabad during the wars for the succession. In return Balaji Rao gave help or countenance to Ghazi-ud-dín.

Obstinacy of Tara Bai.

Damaji Gaekwar was still a prisoner at Poona, whilst Tara Bai was fretting and fuming at Satara. Balaji Rao did his best to conciliate the old lady; but she insisted that he should come to Satara and acknowledge her authority as regent. He sent a force to invest Satara; and her

A.D. 1751-1755

commandant, thinking that her cause was hopeless, formed a plan for carrying Raja Ram out of the fort, and making him over to the besiegers. But Tara Bai discovered the plot, and ordered the traitor to be beheaded; and the garrison was persuaded to put their own commandant to death, together with other officers who had been implicated in the conspiracy.

General reconciliation.

The protracted imprisonment of Damaji Gaekwar was inconvenient to the Peishwa. So long as the Gaekwar was shut up in Poona, no revenue or tribute was forthcoming from Guzerat. Accordingly the Peishwa and Gaekwar were forced to come to terms; and the latter was released and returned to Guzerat. At the same time Tara Bai was persuaded to come to Poona. She still hated Balaji Rao and the Brahmans, but submitted to her destiny. Balaji Rao was still anxious that Raja Ram should remain shut up in Satara; and he effected his object by entreating the old lady to release the boy. Tara Bai was deaf to the feigned entreaties of the Peishwa, and persisted in keeping Raja Ram a close prisoner until her death.

Relations of the Peishwa with Bombay.

The English at Bombay were on friendly terms with Balaji Rao. They would have joined him in an expedition to drive the French out of the Dekhan, but for the treaty of Pondicherry in 1755, which put an end to the war.

Joint expedition against Gheriah pirates.

Subsequently the English and Mahrattas concerted a joint attack on the piratical forts of Angria. Colonel Clive and Admiral Watson stormed the strongholds at Gheriah, but the Mahratta generals held off, and carried on some treacherous negotiations with Angria. Ultimately the forts and territory were made over to the Peishwa according to a previous arrangement; but Balaji Rao was very angry because the English kept the treasure and stores as prize for the forces engaged.[1] He wrote wrathful letters to the Governor of Madras and King George the Second on the subject. Subsequently he heard that the Nawab of Bengal had captured Calcutta, and that Great Britain was at war with France, and he began to bluster. The victory at Plassy, however, brought him to his senses, and nothing more was heard of the Gheriah prize-money.

[1] The treasure in the forts at Gheriah fell very far short of what was expected. But Angria escaped from the place before the engagement began, and there is no doubt that he bribed the Mahratta generals.

A.D. 1754-1759

Administration of Balaji Rao.

Balaji Rao himself was neither a soldier nor an administrator. He was an intriguing Brahman,—restless, tortuous, and crafty, but otherwise indolent and sensual. He gave the command of his army in Hindustan to his brother, Rughonath Rao, who was associated with Mulhar Rao Holkar and Jyapa Sindia.[1] He entrusted the civil administration at Poona to his cousin, Sivadás Rao Bhao;[2] but often employed him to command his expeditions in the Dekhan and Carnatic.

Mahratta wars from the Punjab to Mysore.

Mahratta affairs at this period resembled a stormy sea. The tides of war and plunder were ever and anon bursting on remote quarters:—on Mysore and the Carnatic in the Peninsula; on Hyderabad and Orissa in the eastern Dekhan; on Guzerat, Malwa, and Bundelkund in Hindustan; and as far northward as Lahore and the Rohilla country. To trace these impetuous currents of bloodshed and desolation would be tedious and bewildering. It will suffice to say that wherever there was weakness or war, black swarms of Mahratta horsemen flew like vultures to the prey; whilst their presence excited as great a panic at Delhi and Lahore as at Arcot or Seringapatam.

Mahrattas at Delhi and Lahore.

Meanwhile the reign of terror in Delhi was followed by a revolution. In 1754 the Vizier, Ghazi-ud-dín, deposed and blinded Ahmad Shah, the son and successor of Muhammad Shah. He next set up an old Moghul prince, named Alamghir, as a pageant. In these violent proceedings he was supported by the Mahratta army under Rughonath Rao, the brother of the Peishwa, who was encamped in the neighbourhood of Delhi. From Delhi, Rughonath Rao advanced to Lahore, and for a brief period the Mahrattas were masters of the Punjab in the room of the Afghans.

Delhi tragedies.

All this time the new Padishah, Alamghir, was in fear of his life, and began to open up secret negotiations with Ahmad Shah Abdali the Afghan. His eldest son, known as the Shahzada, shared his terrors, and fled from Delhi towards Bengal, where he fell into the hands of Clive. In

[1] Jyapa, eldest son of Ranuji Sindia, succeeded to the command or principality of his father about 1754. Jyapa Sindia was assassinated at Jodhpur in 1759, and was succeeded by a younger brother, named Mahadaji Sindia, who played an important part in the later history.

[2] This Mahratta officer is known to readers of Grant Duff's Mahratta history by the name of Sewdasheo Bhow.

A.D. 1759-1761

1759 the Vizier put Alamghir to death on suspicion of intriguing with the Afghans; and he then placed another puppet on the throne at Delhi; whilst the Shahzada, as the eldest son of the murdered Moghul, was proclaimed Padishah in Oude and Behar, under the name of Shah Alam.

Afghan supremacy at Delhi.

At this crisis the avenging Nemesis appeared upon the scene in the person of Ahmad Shah Abdali, the Afghan conqueror, who had been building up an Afghan empire ever since the death of Nadir Shah. Ahmad Shah Abdali was furious at the audacity of the Mahrattas in entering his province of the Punjab. He drove out Rughonath Rao and advanced to Delhi, and became for a while the arbiter of the destinies of the Moghul throne. Ghazi-ud-dín fled from his wrath into perpetual exile. Jewan Bakht, a son of Shah Alam, was placed upon the throne of Delhi as the deputy of his father; and Najib-ud-daula, the Rohilla Afghan, was appointed regent, or guardian of the Moghul throne, under the title of Amír of Amírs.

Repulse of the Mahrattas.

The tide of Mahratta conquest was thrown back by the Afghan invasion. Rughonath Rao returned to Poona, and was reproached for the heavy losses he had incurred in the Punjab. He had left Holkar and Sindia to maintain their hold on upper Hindustan; but news soon reached the Dekhan that both had been routed by the Afghans and were flying from the Jumna to the Chambal.

Surging up of Hindus against Afghans.

The pride of Balaji Rao was deeply wounded by these repulses. He had been puffed up by his conquests, and was burning to wipe away the disgrace which had fallen upon his armies. At the same time a national spirit seemed to kindle the Hindoo people against the Afghan invaders. The Mahratta army of the Dekhan was pushed to the northward over the Nerbudda to the Chambal under the command of Sivadás Rao Bhao. Beyond the Chambal the Mahratta army was joined by Holkar, Sindia, and the Gaekwar. Many Rajpút princes also hastened to support the national cause; whilst Játs, Pindharies, and other irregular forces, flocked to the increasing host, to reap a harvest of plunder, if not to share in the glory of driving the Afghans out of Hindustan.

Crushing disaster at

In January, 1761, the Mahrattas received a crushing defeat at Paniput. The details of that horrible slaughter have been told in a previous chapter.[1] The tidings of the massacre spread weeping and wailing throughout the Mahratta empire. Balaji Rao died broken-hearted at the disaster. His death was followed by that of Tara Bai at the advanced age of eighty-six, exulting in the thought that she had lived to see the end of her hated and successful rival.[2]

A.D. 1761-1762

Paniput, 1761: death of Balaji Rao.

Balaji Rao was succeeded on the throne at Poona by his young son, Mahdu Rao. The boy Peishwa, the fourth of the name and second of the dynasty, was a minor of seventeen; and his uncle Rughonath Rao, who planted the Mahratta flag at Lahore and then retreated to Poona, became regent during the minority.

Mahdu Rao, fourth Peishwa, 1761-62.

The reign of Mahdu Rao began with the solemn farce which is the main feature of Mahratta history. The young Peishwa, accompanied by his uncle, the regent, proceeded from Poona to Satara to receive his investiture as Peishwa, or minister, from the puppet descendant of Sivaji, who was reigning in a state prison at Satara as Maharaja of the Mahratta empire. Mahdu Rao however was an amiable youth, and his sympathies were enlisted in behalf of his imprisoned sovereign. Accordingly, Ram Raja was released from the fortress, and permitted to live henceforth as a prisoner at large in the town of Satara.

Farce of investiture at Satara.

At this juncture, the war for the succession to the throne of Hyderabad was brought to a close. Salábut Jung was a prisoner whilst his younger brother Nizam Ali reigned in his room. Nizam Ali took advantage of the disaster of the Mahrattas at Paniput to advance an army towards Poona, in the hope of recovering the territories which Balaji Rao had wrested from the Hyderabad dominion. The threatened invasion was stopped by a compromise, and Nizam Ali was pacified with the cession of a part of the debateable territory.

Aggressions of the Nizam.

At this period Mahdu Rao was hemmed round with enemies. He was anxious to take a part in the government, but was thwarted by his uncle the regent. The Mahratta

[1] See *ante*, page 290.

[2] The life of Tara Bai would make a Mahratta romance. She was born in 1675, when Sivaji was reigning at Poona and Charles the Second was reigning at Whitehall. She died in 1761, the first year of the reign of George the Third.

A.D. 1761-1762

Enemies of Mahdu Rao: Rughonath Rao, Janoji Bhonsla, and Nizam Ali.

feudatories were growing disaffected, especially the Bhonsla Raja of Berar. Rughuji Bhonsla died in 1754; but his son and successor, Janoji Bhonsla, had inherited the family jealousy of the Brahmans, and the latent desire to seize the Mahratta suzerainty. All this while Nizam Ali of Hyderabad was watching the progress of affairs at Poona; ready to take advantage of the quarrels between Mahdu Rao and his uncle, or of the secret designs of Janoji Bhonsla, or of any other turn in affairs, which might enable him to recover territory and revenue from the Peishwa, or cripple the Mahratta power.

Quarrels between the Peishwa and his uncle: movements of Nizam Ali and the Berar Raja.

The disputes between Mahdu Rao and his uncle ended in the flight of Rughonath Rao from Poona; but the fugitive regent bought the support of Nizam Ali by promising to cede more territory. At the same time Janoji Bhonsla of Berar advanced an army towards Poona, without any avowed purpose, but, like Nizam Ali, with the intention of profiting by any change that turned up. These complications were brought to a close by the young Peishwa, who suddenly submitted himself to his uncle, Rughonath Rao, and was promptly imprisoned. Nizam Ali then demanded the cession of territory which had been promised him; but as the regent had got the better of his nephew, and was strong enough to defy the Nizam, he refused to fulfil his promise. Nazim Ali saw that fortune was in favour of the regent, and feigned great pleasure at the submission of the nephew to the uncle, and withdrew for a while from the scene.

Violence of Rughonath Rao: Brahman intrigues.

Rughonath Rao, finding himself uncontrolled regent at Poona, proceeded, after oriental fashion, to revenge himself on his domestic enemies by removing them from office, and confiscating their property. This led to plots against him; and the leaders made overtures to the Brahman minister of Nizam Ali.[1] The Brahman suggested to his Muhammadan master that the best way of overturning the regency of

[1] Both Nizam Ali of Hyderabad and Hyder Ali of Mysore were Muhammadan princes, and as such were natural enemies of Hindu idolaters like the Mahrattas; but both entertained Brahman ministers, and consequently, in spite of any open wars that were being carried on, there were constant undercurrents of intrigue between the Brahman rulers of Poona and the Brahman ministers at Hyderabad and Mysore.

Rughonath Rao was to declare that the Bhonsla Raja of Berar was the rightful regent of the Mahratta empire.[1] A.D. 1761-1763

Duplicity of Nizam Ali.

Accordingly, Nizam Ali authorised his minister to complete the negotiations with the Berar Raja, and Janoji Bhonsla entered very warmly into the scheme for his own aggrandisement. Meanwhile Nizam Ali, with his characteristic duplicity, opened up a secret correspondence with another member of the Bhonsla clan, known as the Raja of Kohlapore, in order to have a competitor in reserve in the event of Janoji Bhonsla proving troublesome.

Plunder of Berar.

Rughonath Rao soon had an inkling of the coming danger. His nephew, Mahdu Rao, although still kept in confinement, supported him with influence and counsel. Moreover he was joined by Damaji Gaekwar of Baroda and Mulhar Rao Holkar; and the three Mahratta armies formed a junction in order to give battle to Nizam Ali and the recreant Bhonsla of Berar. Suddenly however the three armies avoided an action, and rushed off in Mahratta fashion to plunder Berar territory by way of punishing the perfidious disloyalty of Janoji Bhonsla.

Plunder of Poona.

Nizam Ali and the Bhonsla tried to overtake the enemy, but found it impossible, and accordingly followed their example, and marched with all haste to the plunder of Poona. The inhabitants of Poona were thrown into a panic at the report of their approach, and most of them fled for refuge to the neighbouring mountains. The united armies ransacked the city, and burnt and destroyed every house that the inmates were unable to ransom.

Plunder of Hyderabad: duplicity of the Berar Raja.

Meanwhile Rughonath Rao had gone on to Hyderabad, and raised a contribution from the Nizam's capital. He also opened up a secret correspondence with Janoji Bhonsla, who began to think that he had been deceived by the Brahman minister of Nizam Ali; and the Bhonsla was bought over, by a promised cession of territory, to desert Nizam Ali at a fitting opportunity, and join his forces to those of Rughonath Rao.

The hour soon arrived for carrying out the scheme. Rughonath Rao became reconciled to his nephew, the young

[1] This incident is remarkable, as showing the absence of caste sympathy between the Brahman minister at Hyderabad and the Brahman regent at Poona. The former was proposing to set up a Bhonsla as regent in the room of a Brahman.

A.D. 1764-1765

Treacherous slaughter of half the Nizam's army.

Peishwa, and moved towards the camp of Nizam Ali on the bank of the river Godavari. One half of the Nizam's army crossed the river, leaving the remaining troops under the command of his Brahman minister to guard the spot until the baggage and stores had been sent over. Janoji Bhonsla lay encamped with the Brahman, but feigned to be offended at the non-payment of some money, and retreated to a distance. The movement was a signal to Rughonath Rao, who fell upon the forces of the Brahman minister and inflicted a crushing defeat. The battle raged for two days; the losses of the Mahrattas are unknown; but ten thousand of the enemy were reported to have fallen on the field, and the Brahman minister was amongst the slain.

Reconciliation of Nizam Ali and Rughonath Rao.

During the battle Nizam Ali tried to open a cannonade from the opposite bank, but without effect; and he was compelled to witness the slaughter of his soldiery, and then to beat a retreat into his own territories. Rughonath Rao followed with his Mahratta army, but a reconciliation was effected. The matter is inexplicable. It is only known that Nizam Ali visited Rughonath Rao, expressed contrition, laid the blame of all that occurred on the dead Brahman minister, and so worked on the weakness or good-nature of the Mahratta regent, that the latter forgave all that had happened, and actually presented Nizam Ali with territory yielding a yearly revenue of about a hundred thousand pounds sterling.

Berar Raja rebuked by the Peishwa.

Rughonath Rao paid the Berar Raja the price of his treachery; but the young Peishwa publicly reproached Janoji Bhonsla for his duplicity towards both parties, and especially for having joined the Muhammadan, Nizam Ali, in trying to subvert the house of the Peishwas, to whom the Mahratta princes owed all their power.

Mahratta successes against Hyder Ali of Mysore, 1764-5.

About 1764, the rise of Hyder Ali in Mysore excited the alarm of the Mahrattas. Rughonath Rao had become reconciled to his nephew, and Mahdu Rao marched a large army to the south for the subjugation of Hyder Ali. The campaign was successful, and Mahdu Rao tried to keep on good terms with his uncle, by inviting Rughonath Rao to join the Mahratta camp, bring the war to a close, and conclude a treaty of peace.

Subsequently fresh quarrels broke out between Mahdu Rao and his uncle, and were inflamed by two Mahratta

A.D. 1766-1772

princesses, namely, the mother of the Peishwa and the wife of Rughonath Rao. Mahdu Rao was urged by his mother to imprison his uncle, but he put off doing so. He was afraid that his uncle would gain the support of Nizam Ali, or of Janoji Bhonsla, or of both combined. Mahdu Rao next joined Nizam Ali in an invasion of Berar; and Janoji Bhonsla was compelled to cede back nearly all the territories he had acquired by his double treachery.

Fresh quarrels between Mahdu Rao and his uncle.

Subsequently Rughonath Rao engaged in some secret intrigue with Mulhar Rao Holkar, for the purpose of dividing the Mahratta suzerainty; but Holkar died in 1767 and the design was abandoned. Rughonath Rao next proposed to retire from the world, and devote the remainder of his life to religious contemplation at Benares. In 1768 he broke out in open rebellion, and was ultimately overpowered and imprisoned in a fortress, where he remained until the close of the reign.

Imprisonment of Rughonath Rao, 1768-72.

The death of Mulhar Rao Holkar in 1767 is an important event in the history of the Holkar dynasty. Mulhar Rao had obtained commissions for collecting chout in Malwa as far back as the reign of Maharaja Sahu. He left no heir. His son was dead, but his son's widow carried on the civil administration, and appointed an officer, named Tukaji Holkar, to be commander-in-chief. This daughter-in-law of Mulhar Rao Holkar is celebrated in Mahratta history under the name of Ailah Bai. She was very superstitious and extremely lavish to the Brahmans. Accordingly she is much praised in Brahmanical traditions as the incarnation of every virtue, masculine and feminine. Otherwise there is no reason to believe that she was anything more than a clever Mahratta queen of the ordinary type, who conciliated the Brahmans by her largesses, and appointed a favourite to be commander-in-chief.

Death of Mulhar Rao Holkar: accession of Ailah Bai and Tukaji Holkar, 1767.

A characteristic anecdote is told of Mahdu Rao. At one time he sought to fulfil his religious obligations as a Brahman by engaging in divine contemplations for the deliverance of his soul from the vortex of transmigrations. At this period the head Shastri in the Poona cabinet was an eminent Brahman, named Ram Shastri. One day Ram Shastri visited the Peishwa on business, and found Mahdu Rao absorbed in pious abstraction from the world, with every faculty of mind and body engaged in meditations on the

Religious vagaries of Mahdu Rao.

A.D. 1765-1772

Supreme Spirit. Ram Shastri hastily left the room, but next day begged permission to retire from court and go to Benares. Mahdu Rao saw he had given offence, and apologised for his apparent neglect on the previous day, but defended it on the score of piety. Ram Shastri, however, rebuked him, saying that if he wished to fulfil his duties as a Brahman he should abdicate the throne and devote the remainder of his days to contemplating the Supreme Spirit at Benares; but that if he chose to reign as Peishwa he should give all his time and energies to the welfare of his people, as the only way by which the Brahman Peishwas could justify their assumption of sovereignty. Mahdu Rao received the rebuke in a becoming spirit, and abstained ever afterwards from all religious practices which interfered with his duties as a sovereign.

Ram Shastri, the upright Brahman.

Ram Shastri is celebrated in Mahratta annals as a pure and upright judge. He was born at a village near Satara, but left his home at an early age to study at Benares. Later on he was selected, without any solicitation on his part, for the post of head Shastri at Poona; and when Mahdu Rao began to take a part in the government, it was Ram Shastri who instructed him in the conduct of the administration. The greatest evil-doers at Poona are said to have stood in awe of Ram Shastri; and although persons of rank and riches occasionally tried to corrupt him, yet no one dared to repeat the experiment, or to impeach his integrity.

Mahratta demands on the English in Bengal.

Throughout the whole reign of Mahdu Rao, the English in Bengal were struggling through a sea of difficulties. Janoji Bhonsla, Raja of Berar, was incessantly demanding chout for Bengal and Behar, first from Mír Jafir, then from Mír Kasim, and finally from Lord Clive; and Clive was prepared to pay the chout provided the Mahrattas ceded Orissa, but the Directors in England utterly scouted the idea. Fortunately, as already seen, the Bhonsla was too busy with the intrigues at Hyderabad and Poona, and too much alarmed at the artillery and battalions of the English Company, to attempt to collect the chout by force of arms.

Relations between Bombay and Poona.

All this while the English at Bombay were making friendly advances to Mahdu Rao, the Peishwa. They were anxious to possess the island of Salsette and peninsula of Bassein, in the immediate neighbourhood of Bombay, for the protection of their harbour; but the Mahrattas had conquered those places from the Portuguese, and were so proud of their success against Europeans that they would not part with either on any terms. In 1767, and again in 1772, an English Resident was sent to the court of Poona. He was instructed to cultivate friendly relations with the Peishwa and his ministers, and to leave no stone unturned that would induce the Poona government to part with Salsette and Bassein by sale, or by any other way.

A.D. 1761-1763

Dilemma of the English at Madras.

These relations between Bombay and the Peishwa led to an awkward diplomatic difficulty in the relations between Madras and Hyder Ali of Mysore. In 1769 a defensive treaty had been concluded with Hyder Ali. Subsequently Hyder Ali engaged in a fresh war with the Peishwa, and called upon the English at Madras to help him in accordance with this treaty. The English at Madras were thus placed in a dilemma. It would have been the height of folly for Madras to have helped in a war against the Peishwa, whilst Bombay was trying to coax the Peishwa into parting with Salsette and Bassein. Again the English at Madras could not possibly secure the Carnatic from invasion. If they helped Hyder Ali the Mahrattas would invade the Carnatic, and if they did not help him the Mysore army would invade the Carnatic. Under such circumstances the Madras government could do nothing but lament the unfortunate treaty which had drawn them into such a muddle.

Delhi affairs: regency of Najib-ud-daula the Rohilla, 1761-70.

Meantime the court at Delhi was attracting the attention of the Mahrattas. Najib-ud-daula, the guardian of the Moghul throne, must have been a man of capacity. He had risen from the command of a small body of horse to the supreme authority at Delhi; and from the battle of Paniput in 1761, until his death in 1770, he retained the sovereign power in his own hands, in spite of the enemies that threatened him on every side.

Ját principality at Bhurtpore.

In 1763 Delhi was threatened by the Játs. This mysterious race are supposed to have been akin to the ancient Getæ. They may be described as Hinduised Scythians, who had entered the Punjab at some remote period and established outposts in Hindustan. Many of the Játs who settled in the Punjab became Sikhs. Those in Hindustan founded a principality between Ulwar and Agra on the basis of freebooting and plunder; and this predatory power

A.D. 1764-1765

has since been converted into a peaceful state, and is represented in the present day by the Raj of Bhurtpore.

Suraj Mal, the Ját hero: his fortresses.

The hero of the Játs in the eighteenth century was a rude warrior named Suraj Mal. The exploits of this semi-barbarous chieftain resemble those of Sivaji. Like Sivaji his strength lay in his fortresses. He built, or perhaps only repaired, four vast fortresses of mud baked in the sun, of which Bhurtpore and Deeg are existing types. They were impervious to cannon, and were regarded as impregnable down to comparatively modern times.

Slain near Delhi.

In 1764 Suraj Mal was joined by the infamous Sumru, the Patna miscreant who had fled from the Nawab Vizier of Oude, and was glad to enter the service of the Ját Raja. Suraj Mal was puffed up by this addition to his forces, and began to threaten Delhi; and Najib-ud-daula sent an envoy with a present of flowered chintz to conciliate him. Suraj Mal was delighted with the chintz, and ordered it to be made into a suit of clothes; but he refused to talk of anything else, and the envoy retired in disgust. Suraj Mal advanced with an army to Delhi, but instead of besieging the city, he went out to hunt, by way of bravado, in the imperial park of the Great Moghul. He and his retinue were surrounded by a flying squadron of Moghul horse, and were slaughtered to a man. The dead body of the Raja was found arrayed in the chintz. The head was cut off, and carried on a lance; and the Játs were so terrified at the sight that they fled back to their own country.

Ranjít Singh, the Ját.

The Ját principality then became a scene of horrible turmoil. The sons of Suraj Mal were all fighting or murdering one another. At last a surviving son named Ranjít Singh secured the chiefship. His territory bristled with forts, and was reckoned to yield a yearly revenue of two millions sterling, and to maintain an army of sixty thousand men.[1] Ranjít Singh was one of the predatory powers of Hindustan who had learnt to trim between Afghans and Mahrattas.

In 1764—65 Najib-ud-daula was intriguing with the

[1] A native army in the last century was a mere mob of followers, without discipline or organisation. The reports as regards the number of troops in such an army are altogether unreliable, and there is no possible means of checking the native estimate.

A.D. 1765-1771

English at Calcutta. He was expecting Governor Spencer to cede the territory of Oude, and to send Shah Alam to Delhi. Had these measures been carried out, Najib-ud-daula would have been exalted to the real sovereignty of Hindustan; whilst the ascendancy of the Rohilla Afghans would have been extended from the upper Jumna to the Carumnassa. But Lord Clive, as already seen, broke up the whole scheme; and Oude, instead of being a menace to Behar and Bengal, was converted into a barrier against Afghans and Mahrattas.

Relations between Delhi and Calcutta, 1764-65.

In 1767, the same year that Lord Clive left India for ever, Ahmad Shah Abdali advanced an Afghan army for the last time against Delhi, in the hope of once more enriching his coffers with the plunder of Hindustan. Najib-ud-daula feigned to join the invaders, but created delays and thwarted operations, until Ahmad Shah was at his wit's end. The Afghan troops were harassed by the Sikhs, oppressed by the hot weather, and threatened with the approach of the rainy season. At the same time they were breaking out in mutiny from want of pay or plunder. At last Ahmad Shah was obliged to rest content with a small supply of money from Najib-ud-daula, and to return baffled and disheartened to Kábul and Kandahar.

Last invasion of Ahmad Shah Abdali, 1767.

By this time the Mahrattas had recovered their losses at Paniput. In 1769 the army of the Peishwa crossed the Chambal to the number of fifty thousand horse. They levied arrears of tribute from the Rajpút princes to the value of a hundred thousand pounds sterling. They next entered the territory of the Játs, under pretence of helping one of the sons of Suraj Mal, and exacted a contribution of more than six hundred thousand pounds. Najib-ud-daula was thrown into alarm, and made overtures to the Mahrattas for an accommodation; but he died in 1770, and was succeeded in the post of Amír of Amírs by his son, Zabita Khan.

Mahratta aggressions in Hindustan, 1769-70.

Meanwhile Mahadaji Sindia appeared upon the scene.[1] This ambitious warrior, like the other feudatories of the Mahratta empire, was of low origin. In a previous generation, his father, Ranuji Sindia, had been trusted with the menial duty of carrying the Peishwa's slippers, but had subsequently

Rise of Mahadaji Sindia.

[1] See *ante*, page 337, *note*.

A.D. 1765-1772

risen to high military commands, and secured a territorial estate for his family. Mahadaji Sindia was an illegitimate son; but he was a man of undoubted capacity, and had won his laurels in the Dekhan wars of 1751. Subsequently the question of succession to the territorial estate was referred to the Peishwa as suzerain; and Rughonath Rao opposed the claims of Mahadaji, whilst Mahdu Rao supported them.

Ambitious designs on Shah Alam.

In 1771 Mahadaji Sindia was the hero of an achievement which startled all Hindustan. He drew the Padishah, Shah Alam, out of his protected retreat at Allahabad, and conveyed him to the Moghul capital. Shah Alam was restored to the throne of his fathers; Zabita Khan fled to the Rohilla country; and the Mahrattas recovered their supremacy at Hindustan.

Death of Mahdu Rao, 1772.

In 1772 Mahdu Rao Peishwa died of consumption, and was succeeded by his younger brother, Narain Rao. Mahratta history entered on a new phrase. The plots and intrigues at Poona drew the Bombay settlement into a vortex which culminated in the first Mahratta war. The story of this war belongs to the administration of Warren Hastings, and will be told in the following chapter.

Importance of Mahratta history.

Mahratta history, as told in the foregoing pages, will appear bewildering to European readers; but it is nevertheless of value as a reflex of Hindu politics and ruling ideas. It brings out the characteristics of Hindu princes and priests in the eighteenth century; and it also furnishes a key to Hindu history from a remote antiquity. Indeed the Mahratta empire may be accepted as a type of all Hindu empires. It was founded by warriors who were little better than freebooters, and governed by Brahman ministers, who often, as in the case of the Peishwas, succeeded in usurping the sovereign power.

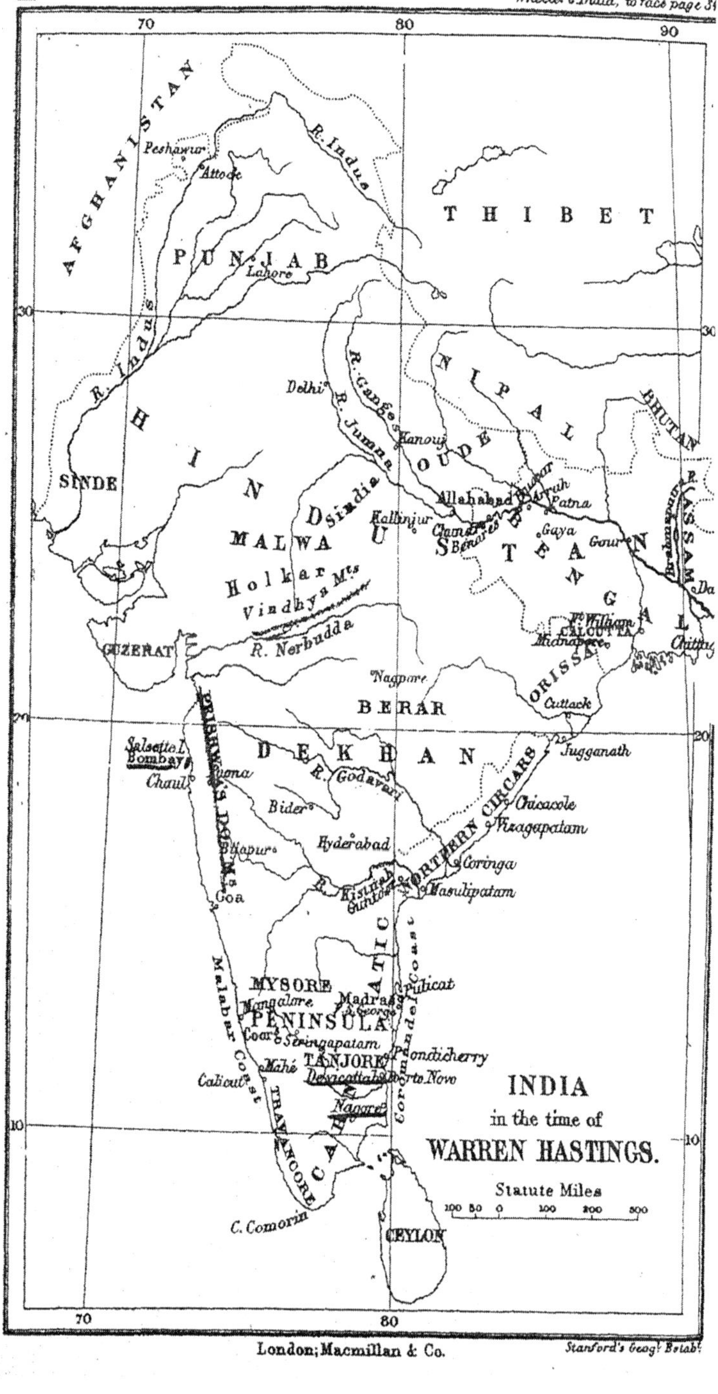

London; Macmillan & Co.

Stanford's Geog! Estab!

CHAPTER VI.

ENGLISH RULE: WARREN HASTINGS.

A.D. 1772 TO 1785.

A.D. 1772-1774

Confused history.

THE government of Warren Hastings is perhaps the most important in the history of British India. It was, however, so blackened by his enemies and belauded by his friends, that few of his contemporaries understood its real character; and the records of the period are a mass of controversy and confusion.

Previous career of Hastings.

The previous career of Hastings is creditable as far as it is known. In 1750, at the age of eighteen, he landed at Calcutta for the first time. For seven years longer the Company was a mere firm of merchants. Hastings was employed to sort silks and muslins, and to invoice opium and saltpetre; but he managed to learn Hindustani and pick up some knowledge of Persian. After the victory at Plassy he entered into political life as Resident at Murshedabad. Next he played an important part in the council of Governor Vansittart at Calcutta. In 1764 he returned to England and became poor. In 1769 he came back to India as member of council at Madras. Three years afterwards he was selected for the most important post in the Company's service, namely, that of Governor of Bengal.

Reforms in the revenue administration.

Governor Hastings was forty years of age, and had evidently read much and thought much. Within a few months after his arrival in Calcutta he placed the whole of the administration, revenue and judicial, on a reformed footing. He turned the European supervisors into collectors of revenue; abolished the more obnoxious cesses; and reduced the number of inland custom-houses. He went on a tour

A.D. 1772-1774

through the districts, accompanied by four members of council, and leased out the lands for five years at fixed rates. Whenever a Zemindar came to terms he was retained in the possession of his district. Whenever a Zemindar held out he was granted a subsistence allowance and the land was leased to the highest bidder. So far Hastings acted much after the fashion of Nawab Murshed Kuli Khan, in the old days of Moghul rule.

Reforms in the administration of justice.

Governor Hastings transferred all judicial powers from the Zemindars to the European collectors. He established a civil and a criminal court in each district, in which the European collector sat as President, and was assisted by Muhammadan and Hindu officials. He abolished the judge's fee of one quarter of the amount in dispute, which under native rule had always been levied in civil cases. He drew up a simple code of regulations for the new courts, which abolished all the glaring evils which had existed under the native system. The details are of no interest in the present day, excepting so far as they redound to the credit of Warren Hastings, who was unquestionably the ablest and most successful administrator that ever governed Bengal.

Charges against Muhammad Reza Khan and Shitab Rai.

Meanwhile Muhammad Reza Khan and Raja Shitab Rai were brought down to Calcutta; and the conduct of their respective administrations was brought under judicial investigation. Nothing, however, could be judicially proved. No charges were substantiated, except by accusers acting from interested motives, or by men of a notoriously bad character. No native of standing and respectability, who had learnt to know and fear the deputy Nawabs, was likely to bring charges against men who might be eventually restored to authority and power. Moreover there must have been many Englishmen anxious to screen the accused. In the end both were acquitted. Raja Shitab Rai was restored to his post and died shortly afterwards; but Hastings utterly refused to restore Muhammad Reza Khan.[1]

[1] Judicial inquiries are always unsatisfactory in India. The law will often acquit a known criminal from the contradictory character of the evidence. Mr. James Mill had emphatically a judicial mind, and it has led him into grave historical errors. He convicted Governor Vansittart of receiving a bribe on native evidence alone; and that evidence has been proved by government records to be absolutely false. Again, Mr. Mill accepted the acquittal of both Muhammad Reza Khan and

A.D. 1772-1774

Transfer of the capital to Calcutta.

But native administration had received its death-blow; the authority of the deputy Nawab Nazims was gone for ever. The central offices of revenue were removed to Calcutta, and placed under the supervision of English officials, under the name of a Board of Revenue. Two new courts of appeal were established at Calcutta, in which the Governor or a member of council sat as President, assisted by learned Munshís and Pundits. Henceforth Calcutta was the capital of Bengal and Behar; and Murshedabad dwindled into insignificance as the residence of a Nawab Nazim without authority or power.

Delhi affairs: severance of the English from the Great Moghul.

Meanwhile the flight of Shah Alam from Allahabad to Delhi in 1771 had broken the political ties which bound the English to the Great Moghul. Henceforth the English held possession of Bengal and Behar, not by a sham association with a puppet Nawab Nazim, nor by the affectation of acting as Dewan to a puppet Padishah, but by the right of the sword, and the sword alone.

Shah Alam and the Mahrattas.

Shah Alam had deserted the English for the Mahrattas, in the wild hope of reigning over Hindustan, like another Aurangzeb or Akbar. The Mahrattas, under Mahadaji Sindia drove out the Rohilla guardian of the Moghul empire, and restored Shah Alam to the throne at Delhi.[1] But the new Padishah suffered very considerably by the change. He had been a mere pageant under the protection of the English; and he was still a mere pageant in the hands of Mahadaji Sindia; but he had thrown away the tribute from Bengal and Oude, which had been given to him under Lord Clive's settlement of 1765, and which not only relieved him from his previous penury, but sufficed for the maintenance of his sham suzerainty at Allahabad.[2]

These losses were a painful surprise to Mahadaji Sindia

Raja Shitab Rai, when it was impossible that they should have been innocent. Nevertheless the treatment of both men was harsh and oppressive. It was what might have been expected from oriental potentates, but was unworthy of the British government.

[1] Najib-ud-daula, the guardian of the Moghul empire, died at Delhi in 1770, and was succeeded in the post by his son, Zabita Khan. On the approach of Shah Alam and the Mahrattas to the city of Delhi, Zabita Khan fled to the Rohilla country. Thus for a brief period the ascendancy of the Rohilla Afghans at Delhi was superseded by that of the Mahrattas.

[2] See *ante*, pages 311, 314.

A.D. 1772-1774

Demand for tribute from Bengal and Oude.

as well as to Shah Alam. Mahadaji Sindia had restored Shah Alam to his throne for the sole purpose of ruling over Hindustan in the name of the Great Moghul; and he had fondly expected to receive the yearly tribute of a quarter of a million sterling for the Bengal provinces, as well as the revenues of Allahabad and Korah, which had been assigned to Shah Alam in lieu of tribute from Oude. Accordingly Mahadaji Sindia demanded the payments in the name of Shah Alam, very shortly after his arrival at Delhi, but met with an unqualified refusal.

Refused by the English.

The English in Bengal decided that as Shah Alam had broken off his relations with the East India Company by his flight to Delhi, he had in like manner forfeited his claim to the imperial tribute which he had drawn under their guarantee. At the same time the English knew that the money, if granted, would only go into the pockets of the Mahrattas;—the predatory power which had been the terror of India for more than a century.

Question of equity.

The equity of this refusal of the English Company to continue the payment of the imperial tribute was much debated at the time, but to no practical purpose. The Moghul empire was politically dead when Lord Clive tried to re-habilitate Shah Alam as a spectre of the past; and the flight of Shah Alam back to Delhi was like the return of the spectre to its cemetery. So long as the Padishah remained under the protection of the English, they had been willing to maintain him as a pageant to be fluttered in the eyes of the French and Dutch as a show of Moghul sovereignty. But when he threw himself on the protection of the Mahrattas, there was nothing to be gained by paying the tribute; and the refusal to pay was equivalent to a declaration of war and assertion of independent sovereignty, which Moghul or Mahratta could only set aside by force of arms.

Mahrattas threaten Oude.

But although the Mahrattas were not prepared to wage war against the English, they were pertinacious in urging their claims. Accordingly they began to threaten the Nawab Vizier of Oude; and they invaded and plundered the Rohilla country on his north-western frontier. But they were willing to forego further plunder in the Rohilla country, provided that Hafiz Khan, the Rohilla ruler, would permit them to march unmolested through his territory for the invasion and plunder of Oude.

A.D. 1772-1774

Claims of the Nawab Vizier against the Rohillas.

The Nawab Vizier had fenced off the evil day by making a treaty with Hafiz Khan. He engaged to drive the Mahrattas out of the Rohilla country; but in return for this service he had exacted a pledge from Hafiz Khan to pay him forty lakhs of rupees, or four hundred thousand pounds sterling. Subsequently the Mahrattas were drawn away from Hindustan by domestic troubles. Mahdu Rao Peishwa had died at Poona, and disputes had arisen as regards the succession; and Mahadaji Sindia and Tukaji Holkar deemed it expedient to return to the Dekhan. Consequently the Mahratta scare passed away from the Rohilla country; whilst the Nawab Vizier of Oude was relieved from all danger of Mahratta invasions. Under such circumstances the Nawab Vizier recovered sufficient heart to form plans for his own aggrandisement. He turned a covetous eye on the Rohilla country, and began to show his teeth by demanding payment of the forty lakhs from Hafiz Khan. The claim was disavowed by Hafiz Khan, and possibly on good grounds; but at this distance of time it would be useless to inquire into the rights of a money dispute between the Nawab Vizier and the Rohilla ruler.

Nawab Vizier applies for an English brigade.

The Nawab Vizier, doubtless, had his own quarrel with the Rohilla Afghans. He was a Shíah and they were Sunnís; and as he could not rely on their friendship, he was anxious to extirpate their power, and take possession of their country. But he wanted the services of one of the Company's brigades; and he offered to pay Governor Hastings the expenses of the brigade so long as it remained in his country, and to make over the forty lakhs into the bargain. Accordingly in 1773 Governor Hastings agreed to meet the Nawab Vizier at Benares.

Dangerous position of the Rohilla Afghans.

The Rohillas were doubtless a troublesome people; and, like Afghans in general, they were often at war amongst themselves. They had established a dominion over the Hindu population between the eastern bank of the Ganges and the north-western frontier of Oude. They were a thorn in the side of the Nawab Vizier. They might possibly have proved a barrier to Oude against the Mahrattas; but possibly they might come to terms with the Mahrattas, and not only permit the Mahratta marauders to march through their country, but take a part in the invasion and plunder of Oude.

A.D. 1772-1774

Political reasons for English neutrality.

Warren Hastings had also to consider the Rohilla question from an English point of view. The Rohilla Afghans were a long way off; not only beyond the British frontier, but beyond the Oude frontier; and the Directors had repeatedly ordered its servants in Bengal to keep within the river Carumnassa. Moreover the English had no quarrel with the Rohillas; and they knew nothing of the rights or wrongs of the rupture between the Nawab Vizier and the Rohillas beyond what the Nawab Vizier might choose to tell them.

Financial reasons for English interference.

But the Bengal treasury was empty, and the Directors were pressing Governor Hastings for funds; moreover the promised supply would not only fill the treasury, but relieve the Company of nearly one-third of its military expenditure in Bengal. Accordingly, Governor Hastings came to terms with the Nawab Vizier at Benares; and moreover made over Allahabad and Korah to the Nawab Vizier for another sum of fifty lakhs, or half a million sterling.

Suspicious action of Warren Hastings.

The only question was whether the Nawab Vizier did not remove the scruples of Governor Hastings by a private present of a few lakhs for himself. The character of Hastings up to this date would contradict such a suspicion; but in England he had felt the pressure of want; he had seen his fellows coming home with large fortunes; and the temptation must have been strong to a man schooled in dealings with natives. Innocent or guilty, he laid himself open to suspicion. He conducted the negotiations at Benares with the utmost privacy; and the English commander-in-chief of the Bengal army was especially angry at being shut out from all share in the dealings with the Nawab Vizier. Hastings could have had no object in maintaining so much secresy in his money dealings with the Nawab Vizier, otherwise than that of securing a money present for himself; and the commander-in-chief of the Bengal army could have had no ground for exasperation at being shut out from the interview, had he not in like manner reckoned on receiving a handsome douceur. However, the bargain was concluded, and nothing further could be said; but it is easy to believe that the enemies of Hastings had formed their own opinion of what at best was a dubious transaction.[1]

[1] It is a current article of faith amongst Orientals that wherever there is secresy there is either treachery or corruption. Accordingly a native

A.D. 1774.

Rohilla war: cowardice and cruelty of the Nawab Vizier.

In January, 1774, the English brigade was marched through Oude into the Rohilla country, accompanied by the Nawab Vizier and a large army. The Rohillas were defeated by the English, and by the English alone. The Rohillas fled in all directions, leaving Hafiz Khan amongst the slain. The Nawab Vizier was equally cowardly and cruel. He kept his troops at a distance during the battle, but when it was over he let them loose on the unhappy country to murder, plunder, and commit every atrocity of which Asiatics are capable. The English commander of the brigade was utterly disgusted with the cowardice and cruelty displayed on all sides. "The English," he declared, "have had all the fighting, whilst these bandits have had all the plunder."

Hastings not to blame.

It was unfortunate for the honour of the nation that the English should have appeared to sanction such barbarities; but this was the curse of native alliances in the eighteenth century, and it is difficult to blame Hastings for the atrocities committed by the Nawab Vizier. In other respects the war was brought to a satisfactory conclusion. The Nawab Vizier concluded a treaty with a surviving son of Hafiz Khan, named Faiz-ullah Khan, under which Faiz-ullah Khan became his vassal. Henceforth Faiz-ullah Khan and his descendants were known as the Nawabs of Rampore.

Middleton appointed Resident in Oude: revolution at Calcutta.

Meanwhile Governor Hastings had appointed an English servant of the Company, named Middleton, to reside at Lucknow as the medium of all his correspondence with the Nawab Vizier. The amounts due to the Company were being paid by instalments, and matters seem to have been progressing smoothly. Suddenly there was a revolution in the English government at Calcutta, which nearly drove Warren Hastings from his post and threatened to undermine the Company's power in India.

New government of India, 1774.

The disordered state of the Company's affairs had induced the British ministry to reorganise the Bengal government. In 1774 Warren Hastings was appointed Governor-General of all the British settlements in India, as well as Governor

envoy will often refuse an interview unless his leading followers are present, or unless he actually contemplates treachery or corruption. The enemies of Hastings not only complained of his mysterious secresy, but whispered that he was in pressing need of money to provide for Imhoff, the portrait painter, and to defray the expenses of the divorce of Mrs. Imhoff, who afterwards became his wife.

A.D. 1774.

of Bengal. The council at Calcutta had hitherto consisted of ten or twelve members who were servants of the Company. This was abolished, and a council of five was nominated in its room. Mr. Hastings took his seat as president by virtue of his office, with a single vote as member of council, and a casting vote when parties were equally divided. Mr. Barwell, a servant of the Company in India, was also appointed member of the council. The three additional members were sent out from England, namely, General Clavering, Colonel Monson, and Mr. Philip Francis.

Supreme Court at Calcutta.

At the same time a Supreme Court of judicature was created at Calcutta, consisting of a chief justice and three puisne judges, who were sent out from England by the direct appointment of the Crown.[1]

Majority in council.

The three new members of council from England were strongly prejudiced against the Company's government. They soon formed a united opposition to Hastings; but the life and soul of the opposition was Philip Francis.

Philip Francis: author of *Letters of Junius.*

This extraordinary man was born in 1740, and was consequently only thirty-four years of age on his arrival in India; but he had spent some years in the War Office in London, and was known to the initiated as a man of large capacity. Of late years it has been discovered that Francis was the author of the *Letters of Junius.* The *Letters* had created a great sensation in London by their lofty assumption of patriotism, and their bitter invectives against men in power; and it is shrewdly suspected that the secret of the authorship was known to the British ministers, and that Philip Francis was sent to India on a salary of ten thousand a year to get him out of the way. Macaulay describes Francis as capable of patriotism and magnanimity, and free from vices of a sordid kind; but otherwise vindictive, arrogant, and insolent; confounding his antipathies with his duties, and mistaking his malevolence for public virtue.[2]

[1] A distinction must be drawn between the Supreme Court at Calcutta, with judges appointed by the Crown, and the two Courts of Appeal established by Warren Hastings, which were known down to 1861 as the Sudder or Company's Courts. (See *ante,* page 351.) Subsequently similar courts were created at Madras and Bombay. In 1861 the Sudder and Supreme Courts were amalgamated at each of the three Presidencies into what is at present known as the High Court.

[2] This opinion is worth bearing in mind, as it is confirmed by Mr. Herman Merivale, editor of the Correspondence and Journals of Francis.

A.D. 1774-1775

Condemnation of the Rohilla war: suspicions of Francis.

The new triumvirate landed at Calcutta in October 1774; their first action was to condemn the Rohilla war, and to call for the correspondence between Hastings and Middleton. Had Hastings produced those papers he would have silenced all suspicion; but he refused, on the ground that much of the correspondence referred to private matters, and he would only agree to produce extracts. From that hour Philip Francis seems to have believed that Hastings had been bribed by the Nawab Vizier.

Middleton superseded by Bristow at Lucknow.

Philip Francis next moved that Middleton should be recalled to Calcutta, and that a Mr. Bristow should be sent as Resident to Lucknow. This measure was carried out in the teeth of Hastings and Barwell by a majority of three votes against two. Hastings saw that his authority was set aside; and for many months Philip Francis was supreme in the Calcutta council, being supported by the votes of General Clavering and Colonel Monson.

Ability of Philip Francis.

The ability of Philip Francis is beyond all question. He had scarcely been four months in the country when he sent to England a scheme for the government of Bengal, which corresponded very much to what has been since carried out in India. The King of Great Britain was to be the only sovereign in Bengal. The jurisdiction of the Supreme Court was to extend over all the natives in the Bengal provinces. The English language was to be used in all affairs of government. The lands were to be granted to the Zemindars, and in many cases to the Ryots, in perpetuity or for life, with fixed rents, and fixed fines on the renewal of leases.

Factious opposition.

But Philip Francis had a fixed purpose which destroyed all his usefulness; namely, to ruin Hastings and succeed him as Governor-General. Right or wrong, he opposed Hastings in everything.

Death of Nawab Vizier of Oude, 1775: interference of Francis.

In 1775 the Nawab Vizier died,—the once famous Shuja-ud-daula; he was succeeded on the throne of Oude by his son, Asof-ud-daula. This event opened up new troubles for Hastings. He proposed that the treaty relations which had been formed with the father should continue to be binding on the son. Francis opposed this view, and was anxious to make better terms. He insisted that the new Nawab Vizier should cede the suzerainty of Benares to the Company, and pay a larger monthly allowance for the services of the Company's brigade, which had been

A.D. 1775.

maintained by the Nawab Vizier within his own dominions ever since the Rohilla war.

Acquisition of Benares.

The cession of the suzerainty of Benares is of some importance. It was the only territory acquired by the Bengal government during the administration of Warren Hastings; and the acquisition was not the act of Warren Hastings, but of Philip Francis. Lord Clive had laid down the Carumnassa as the boundary of British territory, and that boundary would have been maintained down to the time of Lord Wellesley but for the interference of Philip Francis.

State treasures of Oude.

The next dispute related to the treasures of the deceased Nawab Vizier. Under oriental rule there is often no distinction between the revenues of the state, and the private property of the ruler. Shuja-ud-daula had left accumulated hoards of surplus revenue amounting to two or three millions sterling. His son and successor, Asof-ud-daula, declared that the money was state property. But the mother and grandmother of the new Nawab Vizier, who were popularly known as the two Begums, claimed the whole of this large sum on the ground that it had been made over to them as his private property.

laim of e two egums.

The claim of the Begums was preposterous. The deceased Nawab Vizier could never have been justified in making over two millions sterling of state revenue to a couple of old ladies shut up in a zenana, whilst leaving his son and successor with an empty treasury, to defray the large debts due to the East India Company.

npolitic ter- rence f the esident.

The money question, however, between the new Nawab Vizier and the two Begums, was one in which the English government ought not to have interfered. Such was the opinion of Warren Hastings, but such was not the opinion of Philip Francis. Mr. Bristow, the new Resident who had been sent to Lucknow at the instance of Philip Francis, interfered in behalf of the two Begums; and the two ladies paid some quarter of a million sterling to the Resident, on account of the debt due by the Oude government to the East India Company, and were then confirmed in the possession of the remainder. Hastings condemned the interference of the Resident, but Francis and his colleagues sanctioned all that had been done.

By this time it was widely known amongst the natives that Hastings had lost his authority; that Francis was the rising

A.D. 1775.

Charges brought against Hastings by Nund-komar.

man; and that he and his two colleagues, Clavering and Monson, were giving ready ear to all charges brought against the Governor-General. A host of informers soon appeared with accusations of bribery and corruption, which were greedily swallowed by the triumvirate. It is impossible to say that the whole were either true or untrue. But two distinct charges were brought against Hastings by a man named Nund-komar, which deserve consideration. Hastings had appointed a widow of Mír Jafir, named Muni Begum, to manage the household of the Nawab Nazim. He had also appointed a son of this very Nund-komar to act conjointly with Muni Begum. Hastings was accused by Nund-komar of receiving a bribe of thirty-five thousand pounds sterling in return for these appointments. He was also accused by the same man of having received a hundred thousand pounds to connive at the embezzlements of Muhammad Reza Khan.

Hastings declines to meet the charges.

The character of Nund-komar was utterly bad. He was a high-caste Brahman, but he was known to have forged seals and signatures, and to have carried on a treasonous correspondence with Shah Alam and the French governor of Pondicherry. But the two charges of bribery involved an aggregate of a hundred and thirty-five thousand pounds sterling, and might have been disproved by the production of accounts. Hastings, however, preferred to stand on his dignity. He refused to answer charges brought by such a miscreant, or to be tried like a criminal by his own council. Francis persisted in giving his full belief to Nund-komar, and he voted that the charges were proved.

Trial and execution of Nund-komar.

Hastings, in self-defence, brought an action against Nund-komar, in the Supreme Court of judicature at Calcutta, for conspiracy. The judges admitted the charge, but suffered Nund-komar to go out on bail. Six weeks afterwards Nund-komar was arrested for forgery, tried by the new chief justice, Sir Elijah Impey, convicted by a jury of Englishmen, condemned to be hanged, and finally executed at Calcutta in the presence of a large multitude.

Judicial murder.

There is no doubt that Nund-komar committed forgery; but it is questionable whether he would have been arrested on the charge if he had not brought accusations against Hastings. Again, there is no doubt that Nund-komar had committed offences worthy of death; but it is questionable

A.D. 1772-1773

whether he ought to have been hanged for forgery. Such a punishment for such an offence was unknown to the people of Bengal. The execution of Nund-komar has therefore been regarded by many as a judicial murder, and the guilt has been equally distributed between Warren Hastings and Elijah Impey.

Charges against Hastings stopped.

The execution of Nund-komar filled Calcutta with terror. From that time forth not a single native dared to whisper a charge against Hastings. Even Francis was paralysed. Possibly he discovered, when it was too late, that he had been more or less the dupe of Nund-komar. Subsequently, when a petition in the name of the dead man passed through the council, it was Francis who moved that it should be burnt by the common hangman.

Mahratta affairs: relations between Bombay and Poona.

Meanwhile the relations between the English settlement at Bombay and the Peishwa of the Mahrattas at Poona were beginning to alarm the Governor-General and council at Calcutta. In order, however, to take in clearly the current of events it will be necessary to review the progress of Mahratta affairs.

Narain Rao, fifth Peishwa, 1772.

Mahdu Rao, fourth Peishwa, died in November, 1772, aged twenty-eight. He left no son, and his widow perished on his funeral pile. His younger brother, Narain Rao, succeeded to the throne at Poona as fifth Peishwa; and went to Satara to receive the dress of investiture from the puppet Maharaja. The uncle, Rughonath Rao, was released from prison, and re-appointed guardian.

Jarring elements.

All the jarring elements which had been at work during the reign of Mahdu Rao, broke out afresh under his successor. The natural jealousy between the uncle and the nephew was inflamed to fever heat by the wife of the one and the mother of the other. The discord was aggravated by a secret rivalry between two Brahman ministers. The elder, Sakaram Bapu, supported the pretensions of the uncle guardian, Rughonath Rao; whilst the younger Brahman, destined to become famous under the name of Nana Farnavese, was plotting his own advancement by courting the favour of the young Peishwa.

Murder of Narain Rao, 1773.

In April, 1773, the uncle guardian was arrested and imprisoned in the palace of Poona, where the young Peishwa was residing. In the following August Narain Rao was murdered. To this day the story is a mystery.

During the morning of the 30th of August, the Peishwa's troops were clamouring at the palace for arrears of pay. The young Peishwa ordered the palace to be secured, and retired to his afternoon siesta. His orders were neglected; the clamour increased; the troops, led on by two conspirators, broke into the palace. The young Peishwa started from his slumbers, and ran to his uncle's apartments and prayed for protection. Rughonath Rao interfered, but the conspirators declared they had gone too far, and slaughtered Narain Rao on the spot. By this time the palace was surrounded by troops; armed men thronged the streets; the shops were shut throughout the city; and the inhabitants of Poona ran to and fro in consternation. At last the news transpired that Narain Rao was murdered, but nothing was known of the murderers.[1]

A.D. 1772-1773

Rughonath Rao, sixth Peishwa.

Rughonath Rao was unquestionably implicated. Ram Shastri investigated the case, and charged him with having set on two conspirators to assassinate his nephew. Rughonath Rao admitted having authorised the arrest of his nephew, but denied having ordered the murder. Ram Shastri recovered the original document, and discovered that the word signifying "to seize" had been changed into the word signifying "to kill." Henceforth it was the general belief that the alteration was made by Ananda Bai, the unscrupulous wife of Rughonath Rao. The result was that Rughonath Rao ascended the throne of Poona as the successor to his murdered nephew, and began to reign as sixth Peishwa; but Ram Shastri retired from Poona refusing all employment under the new regime.[2]

The distractions at Poona encouraged Nizam Ali to take the field from Hyderabad. But the Bhonsla of Berar came to the help of the new Peishwa;[3] and Nizam Ali was

[1] Here, as elsewhere in dealing with the Mahrattas, the details are given on the authority of Grant Duff's Mahratta history.

[2] Rughonath Rao, sixth Peishwa, plays an important part in the after relations of the English with the Mahrattas. He is frequently mentioned in the records of the eighteenth century under the name of Ragoba, but Rughonath Rao is his correct name. He was the father of Baji Rao, the eighth Peishwa and last of the dynasty, who was dethroned in 1818, and died in 1851, leaving the infamous Nana Sahib as his adopted son.

[3] Janoji Bhonsla died in 1773, leaving no natural kin. He had a brother named Mudaji Bhonsla; and he left the Raj of Berar to the

A.D. 1774-1775

Befooled by Nizam Ali.

defeated, and compelled to cede territory yielding a yearly revenue of about two hundred thousand pounds. But Nizam Ali once again worked on the weakness of Rughonath Rao; paid him a visit, praised his wisdom, and made over his seal of state, telling him to take as much territory as he wanted. Rughonath Rao was cajoled and befooled. Not to be outdone in generosity, he actually gave back the ceded territory to Nizam Ali; a senseless act of generosity which proved fatal to his authority; for had he distributed the territory judiciously, amongst the Mahratta chiefs, he would have bound them closely to his cause.

Revolution at Poona, 1774.

Rughonath Rao was indeed born to be outwitted. He marched an army towards the south to attack Hyder Ali; and was suddenly astonished by the news of a revolution at Poona. During his absence from the capital the widow of Narain Rao gave birth to a son. The infant was placed upon the throne, and a council of regency was formed at Poona; and Rughonath Rao was shut out from the capital. Accordingly the baffled Peishwa proceeded northward into Malwa and Guzerat to raise forces for the destruction of the council of regency, and the recovery of the throne of Poona, by force of arms.[1]

Rughonath Rao applies to Bombay for help, 1775.

At this crisis Rughonath Rao applied to Bombay for succour. He engaged to cede Salsette and Bassein to the English government, and to assign the territory and revenue of Baroche towards the expenses of the war. At this time there was no evidence that Rughonath Rao was a murderer; indeed it was generally believed that the infant son of the deceased Narain Rao was a supposititious child.

Treaty of Surat:

Accordingly, in 1775, the Bombay government concluded a treaty with Rughonath Rao at Surat, and then took

son of Mudaji Bhonsla, named Rughuji Bhonsla. The nephew however was placed under the guardianship of his own father. The result was that Mudaji Bhonsla, the father, became the real ruler of Berar. Mudaji Bhonsla helped Rughonath Rao in order to obtain the confirmation of the Peishwa to his authority.

[1] It would be tedious and needless to trace the movements of the greater Mahratta feudatories during the struggle between Rughonath Rao and the council of regency. Each feudatory was guided solely by considerations of his own individual interest, and wavered between the two, or deserted the one for the other, without scruple or shame. Indeed the policy of Mahratta chiefs in general has been to trim between conflicting parties until the struggle is drawing to a close, and then to declare for the winning side.

possession of Salsette and Bassein, and began operations for restoring Rughonath Rao to the throne at Poona. The army of the Mahratta regency was utterly defeated by the new allies, and there was every prospect of brilliant success, when the war was suddenly brought to a close by orders from Calcutta.

A.D. 1775-1775

Bombay begins the war.

It will be remembered that Warren Hastings had been appointed Governor-General, and that his government had been invested with authority over Madras and Bombay. Both he and his council condemned the Mahratta war as impolitic, dangerous, unauthorised, and unjust. As, however, war had begun, Hastings wished to push it to a speedy conclusion; but Francis and his supporters would not listen to any such compromise. The Bombay government was ordered to withdraw its forces and cease from all further hostilities; and Colonel Upton was sent from Calcutta to Poona as an agent of the supreme government of Bengal to conclude a treaty with the Mahratta council of regency, but to insist on the cession of Salsette and Bassein and the territory of Baroche to the Company.

War condemned by the Bengal government.

The Mahratta council of regency at Poona had been much cast down by the loss of Salsette and Bassein; and they had been still more disheartened by the successes of the Bombay army. Accordingly they were delighted at the clashing between Bengal and Bombay. They extolled the great governor of Calcutta, who had ordered Bombay to put an end to the war; but they refused to cede either Salsette and Bassein, or the territory of Baroche. They urged, and with a show of reason, that as the Bengal government had justly condemned the war, the English could not intend to profit by its aggression. At last they took alarm at some preparations for a renewal of the war, and agreed to cede Salsette, but no more. In 1776 a treaty was concluded at Purundhur on this basis, to the mortification of Warren Hastings and the Bombay government.

Difficult diplomacy: treaty of Purundhur, 1776.

Subsequently despatches were received from the Directors approving the treaty of Surat but condemning the treaty of Purundhur. By this time Hastings was no longer in a minority. Colonel Monson died soon after the treaty of Purundhur, and Hastings was enabled to carry his measures by a casting vote.

Interference of the Directors.

Peace with the Mahrattas was impossible. England and

A.D. 1776-1779

French intrigues at Poona.

France were on the eve of a war on account of the help furnished by the French to the American colonies. A French adventurer, named St. Lubin, arrived at Poona with presents from the King of France, and asserted that a French force was following him to drive the English out of India. The leading member of the council of regency, named Nana Farnavese, showed great attention to St. Lubin, granted him the port of Chaul, near Bombay, and was evidently disposed to hostilities with the English.

Bombay invited to restore Rughonath Rao.

Meanwhile there were more plottings and intrigues in the council of regency. Sakaram Bapu, the elder Brahman, was anxious for the return of Rughonath Rao, and jealous of Nana Farnavese. Sindia and Holkar were beginning that baleful interference in the affairs of Poona which ultimately brought about the destruction of the Peishwa.[1] Mahadaji Sindia was absent from Poona, pursuing his ambitious designs in Hindustan. He owed a grudge against Rughonath Rao, on account of the opposition to his succession to the family Jaghír; but he sought to trim between the contending factions until he could appear in person at Poona. Tukaji Holkar joined the party of Sakaram Bapu, and plotted against Mahadaji Sindia. Nana Farnavese was obliged to succumb to his rivals. A party was formed at Poona for the restoration of Rughonath Rao; and letters were sent to Bombay, signed by Sakaram Bapu, Tukaji Holkar, and others of the party, inviting the English to conduct Rughonath Rao to Poona, and place him once more on the throne of the Peishwa.[2]

Warren Hastings resolved on war, nominally for the

[1] Sindia and Holkar divided between them the greater part of Malwa between the Nerbudda and Chambal rivers; but their territories were so intermixed and confused that it was impossible in former times to draw a line of boundary between the two. They are best distinguished by their later capitals, namely, Gwalior the capital of Sindia, and Indore the capital of Holkar.

[2] Nana Farnavese was the paramour of the widow of Narain Rao Peishwa, who was murdered by Rughonath Rao. He was thus personally interested in maintaining the infant Mahdu Narain Rao on the throne of Poona, under the regency of the Rání mother. Subsequently the Rání mother died, and Nana Farnavese lost his influence, whilst his rivals in the regency intrigued for the restoration of Rughonath Rao to the throne at Poona.

restoration of Rughonath Rao, but in reality for the purpose of defeating the designs of the French. A force under Colonel Goddard was sent from Bengal overland through Bundelkund and Malwa to the Mahratta country. At the same time a force was sent from Bombay to Poona to conduct Rughonath Rao to the Mahratta capital.

A.D. 1776-1779

Hastings sends Goddard.

Bombay expedition to Poona, 1778.

The Bombay expedition marched towards Poona in 1778, but none of the Mahratta chiefs came out to join Rughonath Rao. There had been another revolution in the Mahratta court. Mahadaji Sindia had arrived at Poona, and violently interfered in behalf of Nana Farnavese. Sakaram Bapu fell into the clutches of his rival, and ultimately perished miserably. Tukaji Holkar fled from Poona to Indore. All the other men who had invited Rughonath Rao were thrown into prison. The movement at Poona in behalf of Rughonath Rao died out with the fall of his supporters; and the ruling party were prepared to resist any attempt which might be made to restore Rughonath Rao to the throne of the Peishwa.

Convention of Wurgaum, January, 1779.

The Bombay forces advanced within eighteen miles of Poona, and then were so alarmed at the rumours which reached them on all sides, that they turned back towards Bombay. They were attacked in their retreat by a large Mahratta army under Mahadaji Sindia. The enemy was repulsed by Captain Hartley, a gallant officer who was famous in his day; but the troops lost heart, and Hartley's superior officer was bewildered, and wanted to come to terms with the Mahrattas. Captain Hartley warmly opposed the measure, and pointed out a safe way of retreat, but was overruled. Terms were offered; Nana Farnavese was in the Mahratta camp, and insisted on the surrender of Rughonath Rao. Mahadaji Sindia was more amenable to reason. The result was that Rughonath Rao threw himself on the protection of Sindia, whilst the English agreed to restore Salsette and to countermand the march of Colonel Goddard. This unhappy business is known in history as the convention of Wurgaum.

Movements of Colonel Goddard.

Colonel Goddard had reached Burhanpore on the Nerbudda river, when he was stopped by the convention of Wurgaum, and marched northward to Surat. By this time, however, the governments of Bengal and Bombay had repudiated the convention; and as war annihilates treaties,

A.D. 1779-1782

preparations were being made for war. Indeed, war against France had already been declared, and war against the Mahrattas was found to be inevitable.

First Mahratta war, 1779-82.

The hostilities which followed are known as the first Mahratta war; they lasted from 1779 to 1782. From first to last the operations were directed by Warren Hastings, who might have been called the Chatham of India, if like Chatham he had been free from suspicions of corruption. The march of Goddard from Bengal to Burhanpore was condemned at the time as a frantic exploit; but the marches of Ala-ud-dín and Sivaji were equally frantic, and so was the defence of Arcot and battle of Plassy.

Territory acquired in Guzerat: capture of Gwalior, 1780.

The operations of the first Mahratta war were extended from Bombay into Guzerat, and from Bengal into the heart of Hindustan. Colonel Goddard entered Guzerat, and took possession of a large territory belonging to the Peishwa. Subsequently he was more or less surrounded by dense clouds of Mahratta horse, under Mahadaji Sindia and Tukaji Holkar; and he could neither leave Guzerat nor bring the enemy to a decisive action. At this crisis Warren Hastings made a splendid diversion from the side of Bengal. He sent Captain Popham at the head of two thousand four hundred sepoys, and a small detachment of artillery, to make his way through Hindustan towards Malwa. With this little army Captain Popham scattered a Mahratta force that was levying contributions, and after some other successes, electrified half India by the capture of Gwalior, one of the strongest fortresses in Hindustan.

Mahadaji Sindia becomes neutral.

The loss of Gwalior compelled Mahadaji Sindia to return to Malwa for the defence of his own territories. He still however avoided a general action, and after some delay made overtures of peace, which ended in his engaging to remain neutral on condition that certain conquered districts on the Jumna were restored to him. It will be seen hereafter that this neutrality on the part of Mahadaji Sindia added greatly to his influence during the later negotiations for a general peace with all the Mahratta powers.

British administration in conquered provinces.

Whilst the Mahratta war was raging, the territory acquired in Guzerat was placed under the charge of Mr. Forbes, a civilian of Bombay. The inhabitants, who had been hitherto accustomed to the exactions of the Moghuls, and still more grinding cruelty and rapacity of the Mahrattas, hailed the change in the administration as the greatest of earthly blessings. Forbes was a mild and amiable man, to whom cruelty was impossible, and corruption as revolting as crime. His jurisdiction extended over five large towns, and a hundred and fifty villages. He gratified Brahmans and other Hindus by prohibiting his European soldiers from molesting monkeys, pelicans, cranes, and water-fowl; and above all by forbidding the slaughter of cows, except in a private manner. He administered justice with the help of four Brahmans and four Muhammadans, besides native merchants and heads of castes. Each case was tried by a punchayet, or jury of five natives; two being chosen by the plaintiff, two by the defendant, and one by himself as judge. In some cases, but with great reluctance, he allowed of trials by ordeal. Such a man seems to have approached the Hindu ideal of a perfect ruler.

Crisis at Calcutta.

Meanwhile, events of importance were transpiring at Calcutta. Hastings had expressed through a friend in England some intention of resigning the government; and the Directors had taken him at his word, and appointed General Clavering to succeed him as Governor-General. When orders reached Calcutta, Hastings had regained his ascendancy in council, and withdrew his resignation. A quarrel ensued which caused the utmost excitement. Clavering took his seat as Governor-General in one room with Francis, whilst Hastings took his seat in another room with Barwell. Clavering sent for the keys of Fort William, but Hastings had already brought the military authorities to obey no orders but his own. In this extremity the dispute was referred to the Supreme Court of judicature at Calcutta, and decided in favour of Hastings. Clavering died shortly afterwards, and a Mr. Wheler came out to India as member of council and supported Francis. But Hastings was still supported by Barwell, and secured a majority by means of his casting vote.

Failure of the land settlement in Bengal.

About this time it was discovered that the five years' leases of lands in Bengal and Behar had proved a failure. Many Zemindars and others had taken lands beyond their value, and were unable to pay the rent. Francis urged his plan of a permanent settlement, and it was sent to England for the consideration of the Court of Directors. Pending the receipt of orders from England, the lands were let on yearly leases.

A.D. 1779-1782

Duel between Hastings and Francis: return of Francis to Europe.

In 1780 the quarrel between Hastings and Francis reached a climax. Mr. Barwell, the supporter of Hastings, was anxious to proceed to England, but would not leave Hastings to contend alone against Francis and Wheler. Overtures were made to Francis, and a compromise was effected; Hastings making some concessions to Francis, and Francis engaging not to oppose Hastings in the conduct of the Mahratta war. Barwell embarked for Europe; and then Francis opposed the war as bitterly as ever. Hastings declared that he had been betrayed. Francis explained that he was only pledged to support the war so long as it was confined to the Malabar coast; but that when Hastings extended it to the heart of Hindustan, the obligation ceased. The result was a duel in which Francis was wounded; and the discomfited statesman left India for ever, burning with disappointed ambition, and breathing the direst vengeance against Hastings.

Troubles at Madras.

Whilst Hastings was carrying on the Mahratta war from Bengal, the settlement of Madras was in sore danger. Muhammad Ali, Nawab of the Carnatic, had proved as useless an ally to the English at Madras, as old Mír Jafir had been to the English in Bengal. Muhammad Ali had ceded a territory to the English, which was known as the Company's Jaghír; but the revenues of the Jaghír were insufficient to pay for the defence of the Carnatic, threatened as it was from time to time by one or other of the three great powers of India,—Nizam Ali, Hyder Ali, and the Mahrattas.

Debts and difficulties of the Nawab of the Carnatic.

All this while Muhammad Ali was hopelessly in debt. He had ostensibly borrowed large sums from English servants of the Company, most of which were presents under the name of loans, and yet were charged with high interest. Englishmen in the service of the Madras government, whose means were notoriously small, and who could never have sent a rupee to Arcot, were nevertheless put down as creditors to the Nawab, and were thus bribed with both principal and interest. In a word, the Nawab had been lavish of money, or of acknowledgments of the receipt of money, in the hope of securing friends and supporters in both India and England; whilst his revenues, which ought to have been available for the defence of the Carnatic against all invaders, were pawned away to the servants of the Company, in return for loans, which were mostly nominal.

A.D. 1772-1776

Aggressions on Tanjore, 1773.

In this extremity the Nawab had often turned a wistful eye to the Hindu territory of the Raja of Tanjore, which included the delta of the Kávari and Koleroon, and was regarded as the granary of Southern India. He invaded and ravaged the territory of Tanjore, and called upon the English to help him to crush the Raja. The Madras authorities were blind to all considerations excepting their own immediate gains; and were consequently eager to put the Nawab in possession of territories, which would enable him to liquidate their supposititious claims. In 1773 they deposed the Raja and made over his kingdom to the Nawab.

Tanjore restored to the Raja by Lord Pigot, 1776.

The Court of Directors was furious at this proceeding. Mr. Wynch, the Governor of Madras, was turned out of the service. Lord Pigot was sent out as Governor in his room, with orders to restore the Raja to his kingdom. The Nawab is said to have offered a large bribe to Lord Pigot to delay taking action; but the money was refused. In 1776 Lord Pigot proceeded to Tanjore and restored the Raja to his throne and territories.

Claims of Mr. Paul Benfield.

A Mr. Paul Benfield then appeared upon the scene. This man had been a servant of the Company on a salary of three hundred rupees a month, but had subsequently entered the service of the Nawab. Benfield put forward claims on the Nawab for nearly a quarter of a million sterling, for which the Nawab had given him an assignment on the revenues and standing crops of Tanjore. Benfield produced no vouchers, but urged that the Nawab would acknowledge the debt. It was obvious that the whole affair was a sham, got up with the connivance of the Nawab for diverting the revenues of the Tanjore Raja to the payment of the Nawab's creditors.

Vacillations of the Madras government.

The members of Lord Pigot's council were swayed by conflicting motives. The demand of Benfield was so preposterous that in the first instance they could not avoid rejecting it. But they subsequently discovered that by rejecting his claims they were imperilling their own. Accordingly they rescinded their vote, and declared that the assignments to Benfield of the revenue and crops of Tanjore were valid.

Lord Pigot in his wrath suspended two members of council

A.D. 1776-1780

Death of Lord Pigot, 1777.

on his own authority, and arrested the commander-in-chief of the Madras army. In return he was himself suddenly arrested by the opposition members of the Madras council, and placed in confinement. He died in May 1777, eight months after his arrest, and one month before the orders for his release were received from the Court of Directors.

Rumbold, Governor of Madras, 1778-80.

In 1778, the same year that wars were beginning against France and the Mahrattas, a Bengal civilian, named Sir Thomas Rumbold, was appointed Governor of Madras. He was a shrewd man of business, and possibly an able administrator; but either he knew nothing of the dangers which threatened Madras, or else he wilfully shut his eyes to the actual state of affairs.

Formidable power of Hyder Ali, 1778.

By this time Hyder Ali had become the most formidable power in the Peninsula. He had strengthened his army by absorbing all the floating European elements which were abroad in Southern India;—deserters from the Company's army; runaways from the Company's ships; scamps and tramps from the desk or warehouse, who preferred oriental licence to duty and routine; discharged Frenchmen and others from the service of the Nawab or the Nizam; bodies of native infantry or cavalry, which had been raised, trained and disciplined, by English officers to meet sudden emergencies, and then had been broken up, or had broken themselves up, from sheer want of pay. With these nondescript forces Hyder Ali had conquered all the Rajas and Poligars of Mysore and Malabar, and compelled them all to pay tribute, excepting the remote Rajas of Coorg and Travancore. He was still sore at the failure of the English at Madras to help him in his wars against the Mahrattas; but he saw with satisfaction that Bengal and Bombay were engaged in hostilities against the Peishwa at Poona; and he was prepared to take advantage of the distractions in the Mahratta empire, whilst planning secret designs against his brother Muhammadan at Hyderabad. On the whole he was willing to be at peace with the English at Madras, provided that the English would leave him alone.

Wrath of Hyder Ali.

In 1778 the English at Madras began the war against France by the capture of Pondicherry. They next threatened to capture the French settlement at Mahé on the coast of Malabar, within the dominions of Hyder Ali. Mahé was very serviceable to Hyder Ali; he obtained European

A.D. 1778-1780

recruits and stores through Mahé. He declared that if the English attacked Mahé, he would desolate the Carnatic. But the English at Madras were bent on rooting the French out of the Peninsula. An expedition was sent from Madras against Mahé, partly by sea round Ceylon, and partly by land through Mysore. At this crisis news reached Madras that the Bombay army had been driven back from Poona; but neither the disaster at Wurgaum, nor the expected wrath of Hyder Ali, could induce Rumbold to recall the expedition, and eventually Mahé surrendered to the English without a blow.

Mission of Swartz to Hyder Ali.

Meanwhile Governor Rumbold hoped to pacify Hyder Ali by sending Swartz, the German missionary, with messages of peace to Seringapatam. Swartz was well fitted for the work. He could speak Hindustani, which was a rare accomplishment in those days; and he had already won golden opinions amongst the natives of Southern India by his unassuming life and self-sacrificing toil. He was unwilling to be mixed up with political affairs, but undertook the mission in the hope of averting a war. He was received by Hyder Ali with the respect due to his sacred calling; but unhappily during his stay at Seringapatam, reports arrived that English sepoys were marching through Mysore for the capture of Mahé. Hyder Ali was filled with wrath at this violation of his territories. He dismissed the missionary with kindness and consideration; but Swartz returned from his bootless errand with sad forebodings of coming disaster.

Dealings with Basalut Jung of Guntoor.

About the same time Governor Rumbold managed to exasperate Nizam Ali. There had long been a soreness about the English occupation of the Northern Circars; but, as already stated, the English had settled the quarrel by agreeing to pay Nizam Ali a yearly rent of seventy thousand pounds for the territory in question. The Circar or province of Guntoor had however been assigned for life to Basalut Jung, the eldest brother of Nizam Ali; and the cession of Guntoor was accordingly postponed until the death of Basalut Jung.[1] But the war with France brought on further complications. Basalut Jung had entertained a French force for his protection against Hyder Ali; and the English compelled him to disband it. He then made over Guntoor to the English in return for a yearly rent; and the English

[1] See *ante*, page 315.

A.D. 1778-1780

in their turn transferred Guntoor to Muhammad Ali, the Nawab of the Carnatic, on similar terms.

Jealous suspicions of Nizam Ali.

The wrath of Nizam Ali was kindled at the separate negotiations with Basalut Jung, and especially at the transfer of Guntoor to Muhammad Ali. He suspected that the English were plotting with the Nawab to work his destruction, and set up Basalut Jung on the throne at Hyderabad. In reality Guntoor was transferred at the instance of the Nawab's creditors, who wanted the revenue for the payment of their claims. Nizam Ali manifested his hostility by taking into his service the French troops who had been dismissed by Basalut Jung. To make matters worse, Governor Rumbold chose this particular moment for asking Nizam Ali to remit the rent due for the Northern Circars, on the ground that the war against France had emptied the Madras treasury.

Interference of Bengal: retirement of Rumbold.

These proceedings were most irritating to the government of Warren Hastings. The war against France was already hampered by the war with the Mahrattas; and now Madras had provoked this ill-timed quarrel with Hyder Ali and Nizam Ali. Accordingly the Bengal government, as the supreme authority, ordered the immediate restoration of Guntoor to the Nizam. Rumbold however resented the interference of the Governor-General; refused to restore Guntoor; and embarked for England in April 1780, ignorant or regardless of the coming storm.

Whitehill, Governor of Madras, 1780.

Rumbold was succeeded as Governor by a Madras civilian named Whitehill; but there was no improvement in the conduct of affairs. The air of Madras was reeking with scandals and intrigues, growing out of money transactions between servants of the Company and the Nawab of the Carnatic. Whitehill was as obstinate as his predecessor in refusing to restore Guntoor to Nizam Ali and in neglecting to provide the means of defence against Hyder Ali. Meanwhile corrupt Europeans were appropriating the revenues of the Carnatic to the payment of their fabricated claims, and amusing the Nawab Muhammad Ali with hopes of being relieved from all obligations to the East India Company by the direct interference of the English parliament and Court of St. James's.

Hyder Ali invades the Carnatic, 1780.

In July 1780 the storm burst upon the Carnatic. Hyder Ali, at the head of a hundred thousand men, poured through the passes which separate the table-land of Mysore from the

A.D. 1778-1780

Carnatic plain. The whole country was overrun by the invaders,—eastward to the coast of Coromandel, northward to the river Kistna, and southward to the Káveri and Koleroon.[1] Villages were set on fire, crops were destroyed, cattle were driven off; wives and daughters were shamelessly carried away, and Brahmans were wantonly cut down and slaughtered without scruple or remorse. Fifty years afterwards the atrocities committed were still remembered in remote villages; and persons who are still living have spoken to ancient crones who shuddered as they told of the avenging army of Hyder Ali.

Hostile confederacy of Nizam Ali, Hyder Ali, and the Mahrattas.

Shortly before the invasion of Hyder Ali, Hastings received a mysterious communication from the Bhonsla[2] Raja of Berar. The Raja informed Hastings that the three great powers of India—Hyder Ali, Nizam Ali, and the Mahrattas, —were about to make simultaneous attacks on the three English settlements in Bengal, Bombay, and Madras; and that Nizam Ali was at the bottom of the confederacy. The Berar Raja added that he had received orders from the Peishwa's government at Poona to send a large army for the conquest of Bengal and Behar; that he had been obliged to obey the orders, but had instructed his Mahratta commanders to abstain from hostile operations. In return for this act of friendship he requested payment of arrears of chout from Bengal and Behar, aggregating some three millions sterling.

Disasters in the Carnatic.

The fact of a confederacy was partly proved by news from Madras. Hyder Ali had entered the Carnatic and drawn a circle of flaming villages round Madras and Fort St. George. The English army under Sir Hector Munro, the hero of Buxar, had marched against Hyder Ali; but by

[1] The army of Hyder Ali included 20,000 infantry formed into regular battalions, and mostly commanded by Europeans. His cavalry numbered 30,000, including 2,000 Abyssinian horse who formed a body guard, and 10,000 Carnatic horse well disciplined. Half of the Carnatic horse had belonged to Nawab Muhammad Ali, and after being trained by English officers, had either deserted or been disbanded from want of pay. Hyder Ali also had 100 pieces of cannon managed either by Europeans, or by natives who had been trained by the English for the service of the Nawab. Above all, Hyder Ali had a corps of Frenchmen or other Europeans to the number of 400 men, under the command of a Monsieur Lally, who had left the service of the Nizam for that of the Mysore ruler.

[2] Mudaji Bhonsla. See *ante*, page 361, *note*.

A.D. 1780-1784

some bad generalship had permitted an English detachment to be surrounded by overwhelming numbers. After desperate heroism, the English were induced to surrender on promises of quarter; but no sooner had they laid down their arms, than the savages rushed on them with unbridled fury, and would have butchered every man upon the spot but for the timely interference of the French officers. As it was, two hundred Europeans were carried off prisoners to Mysore, and subjected to cruelties and indignities which were never forgotten by the survivors.

Spirited proceedings of Hastings.

Never did the genius of Warren Hastings burn more brightly than at this epoch in the Mahratta war. He discovered that Hyder Ali had procured a grant of the whole of the Nizam's territories from Shah Alam at Delhi; and he detached Nizam Ali from the confederacy by informing him of the treacherous transaction. He secured the neutrality of the Berar Raja by negotiations and a small present of money. He sent an English force under Colonel Pearse to march overland through the Berar Raja's territories towards Madras. He deposed Whitehill, the Governor of Madras, on his own authority; and further mollified Nizam Ali by the restoration of Guntoor. At the same time Sir Eyre Coote left Bengal and proceeded to Madras by sea, to take the command of the Madras army with full and independent powers.

Successes of Eyre Coote.

Eyre Coote is one of the half-forgotten heroes of the eighteenth century. He defeated Hyder Ali at Porto Novo,[1] and followed up his success by a series of brilliant victories which have won him a lasting name in the annals of British India, although the details have long since died out of the memory of the British nation.

Empty treasury in Bengal.

All this while the Bengal government was sorely pressed for money, and Hastings sought to replenish the public treasury by demanding a subsidy from the Raja of Benares, and calling on the Nawab Vizier of Oude to pay up all arrears due to the Company. The details are interesting from the fact that they formed the basis of the more important charges in the subsequent impeachment of Warren Hastings.

Cheit Singh, Raja of Benares, was a feudatory of the

[1] Porto Novo is situated near the mouth of the Koleroon, immediately to the south of Fort St. David.

A.D. 1780-1784

Political status of Raja of Benares.

British government. His father, Bulwunt Singh, had joined the English after the battle of Buxar, and died in 1770; and the Nawab Vizier of Oude would have confiscated the territory of Benares but for the interference of the English, who upheld the rights of Cheit Singh. On the accession of a new Nawab Vizier in 1775 the sovereignty of Benares was ceded to the British government, whilst the territory still remained in the possession of Cheit Singh.

Hastings demands money from Cheit Singh.

Cheit Singh paid a tribute to the British government of about two hundred thousand pounds per annum; but by the laws and customs of India, Moghul or Mahratta, he was also subject to the extraordinary demands of his suzerain for money or military service. Hastings demanded an extra fifty thousand pounds per annum and the service of two thousand horse. The Raja complied for a while, and then evaded the demand on the plea of poverty. Hastings, knowing that the Raja had large treasures, imposed a fine of half a million sterling.[1]

Submission and rebellion.

About this time Hastings was proceeding to the city of Benares to negotiate a peace with the Mahrattas. As he entered Benares territory he was met by Cheit Singh, who offered to pay something less than half the fine; but Hastings persisted in demanding the half million. Subsequently, after reaching the city, Hastings sent four companies of sepoys to arrest the Raja. The mob of Benares, always the most turbulent in India, rose against the sepoys, who had no ammunition, and were slaughtered on the spot.

Flight and deposition of Cheit Singh.

Cheit Singh fled in terror from Benares. Hastings was in personal danger, but escaped to the fortress of Chunar. Cheit Singh prayed for a reconciliation, but Hastings refused to overlook such open rebellion against the British supremacy. Cheit Singh tried to raise the native princes against the dominant power, but was defeated and deposed, and ultimately found an asylum in Sindia's territories. The nephew of Cheit Singh was then placed upon the feudatory throne of Benares, and the yearly tribute was nearly doubled.

[1] Had the Raja of Benares resisted the demands of a Moghul or Mahratta sovereign he would have been imprisoned and squeezed, until nothing was left of his treasures. In modern times the rights of feudatory princes of India have been defined and respected, if not absolutely created, by the British government, and they are only expected to contribute to imperial necessities in the form of loans.

A.D. 1780-1784

Demands on the Nawab Vizier of Oude: affair of the two Begums.

The proceedings of Hastings as regards the Nawab Vizier of Oude were more dubious. Asof-ud-daula could not or would not pay up the arrears due to the Company, unless he was put into possession of the state treasures which had passed into the hands of the two Begums. Hastings was told that the Begums were implicated in the rebellion of Cheit Singh. Moreover, he acknowledged having received a present of a hundred thousand pounds from the Nawab Vizier, which may possibly have warped his judgment, and which will call for some special remarks hereafter. The result was that he withdrew the guarantee which Bristow had given to the two Begums, and which had been approved and sanctioned by the Bengal government during the supremacy of Philip Francis and his two colleagues in the triumvirate. Above all, he connived at the imprisonment of the servants of the Begums by the Nawab Vizier until the treasures were surrendered.

Criminality of Hastings.

There can be no doubt that Asof-ud-daula ordered the servants of the Begums to be subjected to indignities, privations, and sufferings, common enough in the households of oriental despots, but revolting to civilization. His father, Shuja-ud-daula, is said to have subjected the ladies of Mír Kasim to like cruelties in order to compel the ex-Nawab to surrender his secret hoards. But there is no extenuation for Hastings, and he must share the blame of the whole transaction. Subsequently he reported the receipt of the hundred thousand pounds to the Court of Directors, and requested permission to keep the money. The Directors refused the request, which ought never to have been proffered. Indeed, it would have been better for the reputation of Hastings if he had never accepted the money, or had promptly placed the whole matter on public record. As it stands, the money bears all the stamp of a bribe, intended to remove the scruples of Hastings as regards the abandonment of the Begums and their servants to the tender mercies of the Nawab Vizier.

Close of the first Mahratta war, 1781-82.

In 1781-82 the first Mahratta war was brought to a close. Nana Farnavese was at this time too much afraid of Hyder Ali to ratify a treaty of alliance with the English. But Mahadaji Sindia exercised a predominating influence in the councils of the Peishwa, and was more inclined to the

A.D. 1780-1784

alliance. Negotiations were thus concluded with Mahadaji Sindia but evaded by Nana Farnavese.

Treaty of Salbai.

At the end of 1782 it was known that Hyder Ali was dead; and Nana Farnavese ratified the treaty which had been concluded with Mahadaji Sindia, and was known as the treaty of Salbai. The terms of this treaty are simple and intelligible. The English and the Mahrattas were mutually pledged to withhold all help from the enemies of the other. Rughonath Rao was set aside and pensioned. The infant Peishwa, Mahdu Rao the Second, was recognised as the legitimate head of the Mahratta empire. The council of regency was also recognised as represented by Nana Farnavese. Salsette and some small islands were retained by Bombay, but all other conquests were restored to the Mahrattas. The important districts acquired in Guzerat were made over to Mahadaji Sindia as an acknowledgment of his moderation at Wurgaum; but the grief of the inhabitants at being restored to the grasping oppression of their Mahratta rulers was profound and sincere, and caused many pangs of regret to the amiable Forbes.

Death of Hyder Ali, 1782.

The death of Hyder Ali in 1782 is a landmark in the history. He was cruel and often brutally so; he was also self-indulgent to an extreme after the manner of eastern potentates. Like Akbar he could neither read nor write, yet he was shrewd, sagacious, indifferent in matters of religion, and tolerant towards Hindus.

Hyder Ali at home at Seringapatam.

Swartz the missionary has left a striking description of the government of Hyder Ali. The palace at Seringapatam had an open space in front, with ranges of civil and military offices on either side, so that Hyder Ali could overlook the whole from his balcony. Two hundred men with whips were constantly in attendance to scourge all offenders,—gentlemen, horsekeepers, tax-gatherers, and even his own sons. Not a day passed without a number of officials being flogged. The offenders were not dismissed from his service, but sent back to their offices, with the marks of the stripes on their backs as public warnings.

Evidence of Swartz the missionary.

One evening Swartz went to the palace, and saw a number of men of rank sitting round in great tribulation. He was told that they were revenue collectors of districts, but they looked more like criminals expecting death. One wretched defaulter was scourged in the most horrible manner, whilst

A.D. 1780-1784 — his shrieks rent the air. Yet there was a great struggle for these posts, especially amongst the Brahmans. They outbid one another in order to be appointed collectors, and then practised similar cruelties towards the people in order to add to their gains.

Lord Macartney, Governor of Madras, 1781-86. At this period Lord Macartney was Governor of Madras. He had landed in India in 1781, and distinguished himself by pushing on the war against Hyder Ali; but his administration was chiefly marked by differences with the Bengal government which have long since been forgotten. He was distinguished by a spotless purity in money matters, which has handed down his name to posterity as the first Governor of a new *régime*.[1]

Treaty of peace with Tippu Sultan, 1784. In 1784 Lord Macartney sent envoys to Tippu, the son and successor of Hyder Ali, to negotiate a peace. A treaty was concluded at Mangalore by which both the English and Tippu were mutually bound to withhold all help from the enemies of the other; and a large number of European prisoners, who had passed years of suffering, privation, and and torture in Mysore, were at last restored to life and freedom.

Assumption of the Carnatic. During the war against Hyder Ali, Lord Macartney assumed the management of the revenues of the Carnatic. The Nawab agreed to the measure, reserving a sixth part for the maintenance of his family and dignity. Indeed he was unable to offer any opposition. The Carnatic was virtually occupied by the armies of Hyder Ali; and for a period of eighteen months the Nawab had not contributed a single rupee towards the expenses of the war; whilst the native renters had often endangered the very existence of the forces in the field by keeping back supplies, either for their own profit, or out of treacherous collusion with the enemy. Indeed on one occasion Eyre Coote had placed a native renter in irons for having endeavoured to betray the fortress of Vellore to Hyder Ali. The new arrangement ensured the regularity of supplies; protected the Nawab from the rapacity of his creditors; whilst delivering the

[1] In 1781 the English were at war with the Dutch, and Lord Macartney captured the two Dutch sea-ports of Pulicat and Sadras, in the neighbourhood of Madras, to prevent their falling into the hands of Hyder Ali or the French. The dismantled fortifications are still to be seen within easy communication from Madras, and will well repay a visit, as they form the most interesting relics of Dutch dominion which are to be found in all India.

people from the merciless exactions of the native renters. In a word, Lord Macartney was driven by the instinct of self-preservation to take the revenues of the Carnatic under direct control, as the only possible way of saving the country, the people, the Nawab himself, and the Company's possessions, from utter destruction.

A.D. 1784-1785

Proposals for reducing the Nawab to a pageant pensioner.

When the war was over Lord Macartney resolved on perpetuating an arrangement, which had enabled him to provide for the expenses of the war as well as for the maintenance of the Nawab. Accordingly he refused to restore the revenues to the control of Muhammad Ali and his native renters. Large bribes were offered to him, but he was immovable. For thirty years it had been obvious to all parties concerned—to the Nawab himself, as well as to the Madras government and the Court of Directors—that the East India Company alone could protect the Carnatic from the horrible ravages to which it had been exposed from Hyder Ali, Nizam Ali, or the Mahrattas. It was equally obvious that unless the English held the power of the purse they could not wield the power of the sword. The sixth part of the revenues had been regularly paid to the Nawab, and in reality yielded him more money for his private purposes than he had ever enjoyed before. Lord Macartney was willing to continue the payment, and to investigate and liquidate all the just claims of the Nawab's creditors; but he was determined that henceforth the Nawab should be powerless for evil; and for this purpose it was necessary to depose Muhammad Ali from his sovereign authority, and reduce him to the condition of a pageant pensioner like the Nawab Nazims of Bengal.

Dubious equity.

The equity of the measure was open to question. So long as the English maintained a helpless Nawab on the throne of the Carnatic, so long they were responsible for the sufferings of his wretched subjects. On the other hand, for more than thirty years, the East India Company, for purposes of its own, had treated the Nawab as an independent prince; and his sovereignty had been acknowledged alike by the English parliament and the Crown. In a word, the Nawab of the Carnatic was a political Frankenstein, the creation of the Company, galvanised into artificial life by the Company's own servants; and he could not be deposed from his sovereignty unless it could be proved to the

A.D. 1784-1785

satisfaction of the English parliament that his extinction was essential to the safety of British interests in Southern India.

Mr. Pitt's bill of 1784: the Board of Control.

Meanwhile Indian affairs had been hotly debated in the English parliament. Indian wars and conquests had been denounced, and alliances with native princes had been condemned as the cause of all Indian wars. In 1784 an act was passed, known as Mr. Pitt's bill, under which a Board of Control was nominated by the Crown to exercise supreme authority over the civil and military administration of the Company's servants. It consisted of six members, but all real power was vested in the President of the Board, who played the part of an additional Secretary State, and was directly responsible to parliament and the Crown.[1] It was enacted that for the future no alliances should be formed with any native prince without the consent of parliament. It was also enacted, with the view of preventing future scandals, that no servant of the Company should engage in any monetary transactions with any native prince, without the express sanction of the Governor-General of India.[2]

Zeal of the Nawab's creditors.

All this while the creditors of the Nawab were straining every effort to procure his restoration to the sovereignty of the Carnatic. Indeed unless Muhammad Ali was replaced in the possession of the revenues, his creditors could never hope to realize the enormous fortunes which for years had dazzled their imaginations and perverted their moral sense. Emissaries from the Nawab, including the notorious Mr. Paul Benfield, appeared in London with large means at their disposal for the purchase of seats in parliament, and otherwise bringing corrupt influences to bear upon men in high places.[3]

[1] The Board of Control consisted of six members of the Privy Council, chosen by the Crown, and always including the Chancellor of the Exchequer and one of the Secretaries of State. In the absence of the Chancellor and Secretary of State, the senior member acted as President of the Board, and practically was the sole authority. Mr. Dundas, afterwards Lord Melville, was the first President of the Board of Control. The Board was maintained down to the year 1858, when it was amalgamated with the Court of Directors, and the whole was transformed into a Secretary of State for India in Council.

[2] By a subsequent act, 37 of George III., this prohibition was extended to all European subjects of the British Crown.

[3] The lives of the English adventurers who preyed upon the Nawab of the Carnatic, and other native princes, during the latter half of the

A.D. 1784-1785

It would be tedious to rake up a forgotten controversy in which there was much to be said on both sides. The Board of Control eventually decided that as the war with Hyder Ali had been brought to a close, there was no necessity for lowering the status of the Nawab, and no excuse for retaining the management of the Carnatic. With this view the Board of Control ordered, not only that the Carnatic should be restored to the Nawab, but that all claims against the Nawab should be liquidated out of the revenues of the Carnatic without any further investigation. Lord Macartney retired from the service rather than obey such orders; but many of the Company's servants acquired large fortunes, Mr. Benfield alone realizing about half a million sterling.[1]

Orders of the Board of Control: Carnatic restored.

Warren Hastings returns to Europe, 1785.

Meanwhile the government of Warren Hastings drew towards a close. His proceedings as regards Cheit Singh

eighteenth century, would make an instructive volume. Their intrigues in London would perhaps prove more curious than those at Arcot and Madras. Their parade of wealth and jewels at the Court of St. James's was the marvel and envy of the aristocracy. Mrs. Paul Benfield astonished London by driving through the parks in a chariot of cerulean blue. Mr. Paul Benfield ultimately lost all his fortune, and died at Paris in extreme poverty. Mr., afterwards Sir John, Macpherson, who for a brief period succeeded Warren Hastings as Governor-General, was originally the purser of a ship, who entered the service of the Nawab of the Carnatic, and afterwards went to London and gained the ear of the Duke of Grafton. The magazines and journals of the day would furnish equally suggestive details respecting Mr. Holland and others. All these men were at one time or other in the Company's service. There were also adventurers at Seringapatam, Hyderabad, and Lucknow, who had never been in the service. In the story of "Lame Jervis" Miss Edgeworth describes one of these men who visited the Court of Tippu, and proved a favourable specimen of his class. There were others whose careers would vindicate the proceedings of the Court of Directors in prohibiting the advent of Europeans into the dominions of native princes.

[1] The settlement of the debts of Muhammad Ali was accompanied by ministerial scandals which will never be cleared up, and which belong to the history of England rather than to the history of India. Burke denounced Benfield, Dundas, and all concerned; but his invectives were so coarse and extravagant that they failed to make any lasting impression. It will suffice to say that between 1784 and 1804, five millions sterling were paid away. In 1805 commissioners were appointed to investigate the further claims of private creditors; and between 1805 and 1814 claims to the amount of twenty millions were brought under examination, during which nineteen millions were rejected as bad, whilst little more than a million was treated as true and lawful debt.

A.D. 1784-1785 — and the Begums were severely censured by the Court of Directors, and he lost the support of his colleagues in council. Accordingly he resigned the service, and left India in February, 1785, never to return.

Impeachment and acquittal of Hastings. The subsequent impeachment and acquittal of Warren Hastings are great events in English history, but they made no impression on the people of India. A storm of indignation was raised by Philip Francis, and turned to a hurricane by the hot eloquence of Burke, Fox, and Sheridan; but the people of Bengal only knew Hastings as a deliverer, a protector, and a conqueror, and they were bewildered by the remote thunder in Westminster Hall.

Review of the charges. The three most important charges against Hastings referred to the Rohilla war, and the treatment of Cheit Singh and the Begums; but the animus of the charge was that Hastings had exercised and countenanced cruelty and oppression for the sake of money. Lord Clive had accepted presents, but he was not accused like Hastings of taking bribes. Bribery and corruption, however, are difficult of judicial proof, whether in England or India; and grave suspicion will often ensure a moral conviction when a legal conviction is wanting; but in the case of Warren Hastings the national resentment was neutralised by the obvious vindictiveness of Francis, and the dreary procrastination of a state trial, until it had spent its force and died away. Posterity will possibly decide that the services of Hastings have thrown his failings into the shade; that Hastings deserved approbation and reward at the hands of the East India Company; but that William Pitt was in the right when he refused to recommend Warren Hastings for a peerage, or for honourable employment under the British Crown.[1]

[1] Lord Macaulay acquits Hastings of money corruption on the ground of want of evidence; had he been familiar with the workings of native courts in India, he would have found Hastings guilty. Hastings acknowledged to having taken a hundred thousand pounds from Asof-ud-daula in 1782. The inference follows that in 1773 he received a like sum from Shuja-ud-daula, and silently pocketed the money. Officers of any political experience would be satisfied that Asof-ud-daula would never have offered the hundred thousand pounds to Hastings unless a like sum had been previously offered by his father, Shuja-ud-daula, and accepted by Hastings.

Whilst Warren Hastings was preparing to defend himself against his enemies, he was harassed by the thought that he had left an old bureau behind at Calcutta, containing papers of such secresy that he

A.D. 1784-1785

End of Philip Francis.

Philip Francis may be consigned to oblivion. His talents might have gained him a lasting name in the history of India, but were frittered away in attempts to advance himself at the expense of Hastings. He intrigued for the post of Governor-General until his hopes were shattered by old age. To this day he is only remembered as the writer of the "Letters of Junius," and as the vindictive enemy of Warren Hastings.

could not entrust them to his closest friends. At least seven references to this lost bureau are to be found in his published correspondence (Gleig's *Life of Hastings*, vol. iii. pp. 238, 240, 268, 286, 290, 297, and 327). Nowhere is it said that the bureau was recovered. Had it fallen into the hands of Francis, it might have made short work of the trial at Westminster Hall.

CHAPTER VII.

LORD CORNWALLIS AND SIR JOHN SHORE.

A.D. 1785 TO 1798.

A.D. 1785.

India in 1785.

IN 1785 the British empire in India comprised Bengal and Behar in eastern Hindustan; a very little area round Bombay in the western Dekhan; and a larger area round Madras in the eastern Peninsula. There were also two protected princes, namely, the Nawab Vizier of Oude, and the Nawab of the Carnatic. Outside the area of British supremacy were the three native powers who were the bugbear of English statesmen,—Nizam Ali, Tippu Sultan, and the Mahrattas.

Mahratta empire.

The Mahrattas were regarded as the most formidable power in India. The heart of the Mahratta empire was weak and palpitating; half shattered by domestic commotions and its recent struggles against the English. The Peishwa at Poona was an infant, and the council of regency was in mortal fear of Tippu Sultan. The real head of affairs at Poona was Nana Fatnavese, an able Brahman but no soldier. But the feudatory princes of the Mahratta empire were strong and nominally subordinate to the Peishwa's government. The Gaekwar of Baroda, Sindia and Holkar in Malwa, and the Bhonsla Raja of Berar, although practically independent, admitted, one and all, their obligations to obey the Peishwa as suzerain of the Mahratta empire; and the confirmation of the Peishwa was necessary to the validity of every succession to a feudatory state or throne.

Growing power of Mahadaji Sindia.

Of all these feudatory princes, Mahadaji Sindia was the most powerful and the most ambitious. Whatever prestige he had lost during the Mahratta war he had recovered during

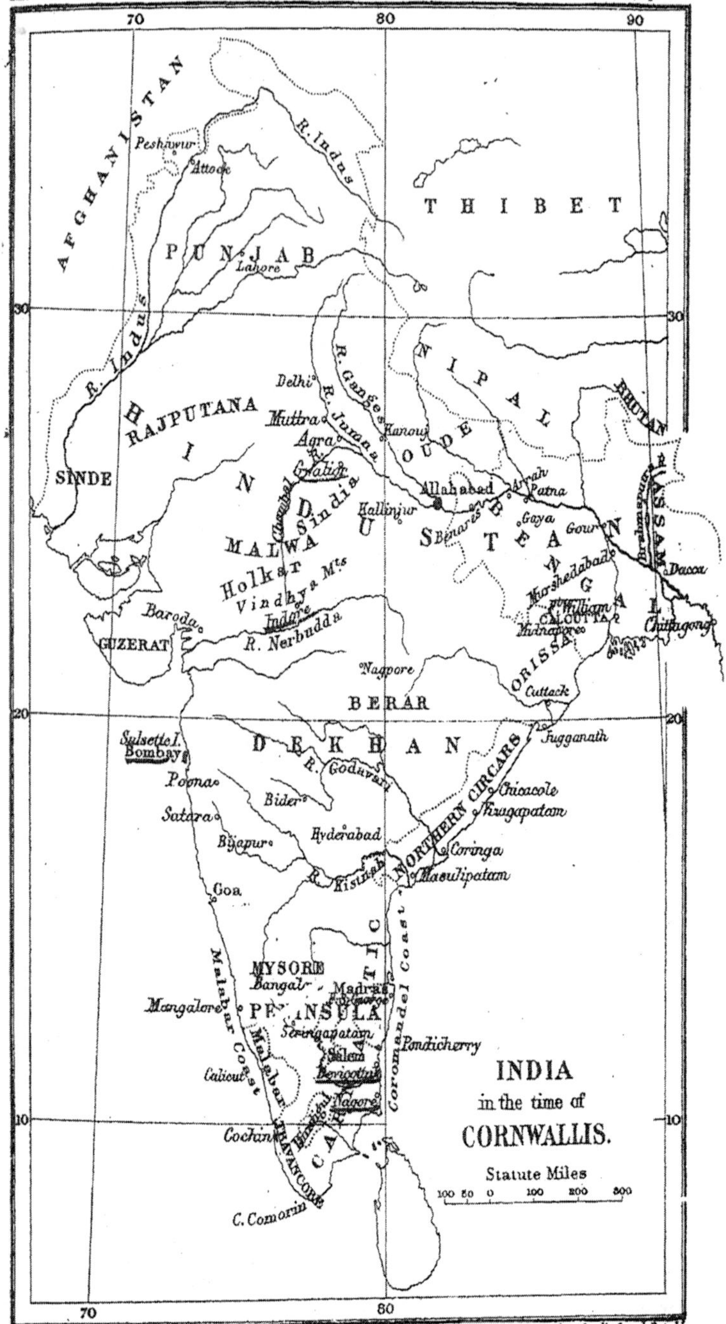

London: Macmillan & Co.

Stanford's Geog. Estab.

A.D. 1785.

the negotiations which ended in the treaty of Salbai. Being a neutral at the conclusion of the treaty, he had acted as the representative of all the Mahratta princes, from the Peishwa downwards; and he was the sole guarantee for the fulfilment of the treaty. To crown all an English Resident, named Anderson, was sent to his camp to transact all business between the English and the Mahrattas.[1]

Designs at Delhi and Poona.

The lot of Mahadaji Sindia was cast in a revolutionary era. His career was marked by restlessness and cunning, and by those sudden changes of fortune which befall the leading actors in oriental revolutions. He was swayed to and fro by conflicting motives. He was afraid of the English but proud of his connection with them. He was anxious to exercise a paramount ascendancy at Delhi as well as at Poona; indeed he could not rivet this ascendancy in either court unless he was master at both. He could not be supreme at Delhi unless he was backed up by the Peishwa's government; and he could not be supreme at Poona unless he was backed up by the authority of the Great Moghul.

Distractions at the Moghul court.

For years the Moghul court at Delhi had been the scene of distractions, intrigues, and assassinations at once tedious and bewildering. Shah Alam was a weak prince, who clung to the name and dignity of sovereignty, but was without authority or power. The government was carried on by a prime minister, or lord protector, who was known as the Amír of Amírs, a title higher than that of Vizier, and implying the guardianship of the Padishah. The Amír of Amírs for the time being collected revenue and tribute by force of arms, and carried on petty wars with Rajpúts, Játs, and other neighbouring chieftains. In 1784 there had been a crisis. The ruling Amír of Amírs had obtained his post by the murder of his predecessor, and was in mortal fear of being murdered in his turn. Accordingly he invited Mahadaji Sindia to Delhi, and Shah Alam joined in the invitation.

Mahadaji Sindia at Delhi.

It is difficult to realise the horrible complications which must have prevailed at Delhi to induce the Muhammadan minister and Muhammadan sovereign to invite the help of a Mahratta chieftain, who was at once a Hindu and an idolater, an alien in race and religion. Mahadaji Sindia, on

[1] Mr. Mostyn, the English Resident at Poona, had died just before the first Mahratta war, and no one had been sent to supply his place.

A.D. 1785.

his part, was only fearful of offending the English; and having duly sounded the English Resident, and ascertained that the English rulers at Calcutta would not interfere in his doings at Delhi, he left Poona and proceeded to the Moghul court. Shortly afterwards it was reported that the Amír of Amírs had been murdered at the instigation of Mahadaji Sindia; and that the Mahratta chieftain had taken Shah Alam under his protection, and assumed the administration of the relics of the Moghul empire.[1]

Deputy of the Peishwa at Delhi.

Mahadaji Sindia would not accept the title of Amír of Amírs; it would have clashed with his position at Poona. He artfully procured the title of "deputy of the Padisbah" for his nominal sovereign the Peishwa; and then procured for himself the title of "deputy of the Peishwa." Thus for the nonce he appeared at Delhi as the deputy of the Peishwa. In this capacity Mahadaji Sindia performed all the duties of an Amír of Amírs, administered the government at Delhi and Agra, commanded the rabble army of the empire, and collected tribute from Rajpúts and Játs in the name of the Great Moghul.

Sindia's kingdom in the North-west.

In reality Mahadaji Sindia was founding a new Mahratta kingdom between the Ganges and Jumna, and extending Mahratta influence over an unknown region to the westward. He was raising battalions of regular sepoys, who were being trained and disciplined by a Frenchman, celebrated in after years as General De Boigne. He became inflated with

[1] The following summary of events may suffice to explain the position of affairs on the arrival of Mahadaji Sindia at Delhi. Before Shah Alam returned to Delhi in 1771, the Rohilla Afghan, Najib-ud-daula, had filled the post of Amír of Amírs; but this man died in 1770, and was succeeded by his son, Zabita Khan, who fled from Delhi at the approach of Shah Alam. A Persian, named Najaf Khan, then came to the front. He had been in the service of Shah Alam at Allahabad, and accompanied him to Delhi in command of his army. Then followed an obscure intrigue in which the Mahrattas expelled Najaf Khan and restored Zabita Khan to the post of Amír of Amírs. Next another intrigue, in which Zabita Khan fled to the Játs, and Najaf Khan took a part in the war against the Rohillas. Najaf Khan formed an alliance with the Nawab Vizier of Oude, and was appointed deputy Vizier. Then followed fresh plots and fresh wars between Najaf Khan and Zabita Khan. Najaf Khan died in 1782. His son, Afrasiab Khan, is the Amír of Amírs mentioned in the text, who murdered his predecessor, and was subsequently murdered by Mahadaji Sindia. The details are told at length in Mr. Keene's *Fall of the Moghul Empire.*

A.D. 1785.

his own greatness, and once again called upon the British government to pay chout for Bengal and Behar. In reply he was told that the demand was a violation of the treaty of Salbai. The rebuff smote him with apprehension; and both Sindia and Shah Alam sent a solemn disavowal of the demand to Calcutta under their respective seals.

English alarm at the French: Resident at Poona.

At this time the dominant feeling of the English was alarm at the French. The war between Great Britain and France had been brought to a close in 1784 by the treaty of Versailles; but there was constant expectation of a renewal of hostilities; and for many years the English were discovering or imagining French intrigues at almost every court in India. A French agent was already residing at Poona. Accordingly an English agent, Mr. Charles Malet, was posted to Poona to look after English interests and frustrate French designs.)

Sindia's offended dignity.

The dignity of Mahadaji Sindia was hurt by this proceeding. He had been guarantee to the treaty of Salbai, and considered himself the sole agent in all transactions between the Mahrattas and the English. He was quieted by the assurance that Mr. Malet would send all correspondence between the Peishwa and the Governor-General through the Resident in attendance at his camp. Moreover, in order to smooth the ruffled feathers of the Mahratta, Mr. Malet was sent to the camp of Sindia in the neighbourhood of Agra, to arrange matters with Mr. Anderson.

Agra in 1785.

Agra in 1785 presented the most melancholy objects of fallen grandeur. Mosques, palaces, gardens, caravanserais, and mausoleums were mingled in one general ruin. In the midst of this chaotic desolation, a splendid building burst upon the view in resplendent beauty and complete repair. It was the famous Taj Mahal, whose white domes and minarets of marble stood out in brilliant relief above groves and gardens. As Mr. Malet approached the spot he found that he was expected to take up his quarters in the Taj Mahal. The tomb of the favourite wife of Shah Jehan had been appropriated by Mahadaji Sindia for the accommodation of the English Resident and his retinue.

Sindia's camp at Muttra.

Sindia himself was encamped some thirty miles off at Muttra, the ancient Mathura. He kept Shah Alam in his camp as a kind of state prisoner, whilst Mr. Anderson as English Resident was in attendance. Mr. Malet was

A.D. 1785-1786

honoured by an interview with Sindia, and afterwards by an audience with Shah Alam.

Fallen state of the Great Moghul.

The Great Moghul, the representative of the famous family of Timúr, was an object of interest. He was about sixty years of age,—placid, benignant and dignified. He received the rich presents of Mr. Malet with calm approval. In return he conferred on the English gentleman a tiara of diamonds and emeralds, a charger, and an elephant; but his gifts were emblematical of his own fallen condition, and had all been provided by Mahadaji Sindia. The diamonds were false; the emeralds were nothing but pieces of green glass; the horse was dying from old age; and the elephant was a mass of disease from the shoulder to the tail.

War between the Peishwa and Tippu.

Mr. Malet was soon obliged to take up his post of Resident at Poona. War had broken out between the Peishwa's government and Tippu Sultan of Mysore. The dread of Tippu was very strong, and the Brahman government of the Peishwa formed an alliance with Nizam Ali against Tippu; and Nizam Ali, notwithstanding his Muhammadan faith, eagerly helped the Mahrattas against the dangerous Sultan of Mysore. It was expected that the British government would furnish help in like manner. But the English were bound by the treaty of Salbai not to help the enemies of the Mahrattas; and they were equally bound by the treaty of Mangalore not to help the enemies of Tippu. The question of the day was, whether Tippu Sultan had not himself broken the treaty of Mangalore by forming an alliance with the French, who were the avowed enemies of the English; and this question was not solved until a later period in the history.

Mr. Macpherson, Governor-General, 1785-6.

When Hastings returned to England in 1785, he left a Mr. Macpherson to act as Governor-General. At this time it was decided that the future Governor-General should not be a servant of the Company, but a nobleman of rank. Lord Macartney was offered the post, but declined it; and in 1786 Lord Cornwallis landed at Calcutta as Governor-General and Macpherson passed away.

The introduction of an English nobleman in the place of a merchant ruler produced beneficial results. Vansittart and Hastings had been powerless to effect reforms which touched the pockets of the servants of the Company. Indeed, Hastings had been often driven to distribute contracts and

Lord Cornwallis, Governor-General, 1786-93: social reforms.

sinecures in order to secure personal support. But Lord Cornwallis was strong enough, by virtue of his rank as an English peer, to abolish all such abuses. He even forced the Court of Directors to replace the system of perquisites by that of large salaries. At the same time his respectability of character elevated the tone of English society at Calcutta. Under Warren Hastings there had been painful scandals in high quarters; whilst gambling had risen to such a pitch that within one month Philip Francis won twenty thousand pounds at whist from Barwell. But under the severe and stately morality of Lord Cornwallis excesses of every description were discountenanced; and the increasing number of ladies from Europe introduced a refinement and decorum which had long been wanting.

Permanent land settlement.

Lord Cornwallis carried out a startling change in the land settlement. He abolished the system of leases, granted the lands in perpetuity to the Zemindars, and fixed a yearly rental for the several estates which was never to be enhanced. The details of this important measure were worked out by Mr. Shore, afterwards known as Sir John Shore and ultimately as Lord Teignmouth. Mr. Shore argued however that a change which was to last for all futurity should not be made irrevocable until further inquiries had been made as to the value of the land, the nature of the different tenures, and the rights of landlords and tenants as represented by Zemindars and Ryots. He proposed that the settlement should be made for ten years, and then declared permanent if it proved satisfactory. Lord Cornwallis's views, however, were referred to the ministers in England, and after some delay the perpetual settlement became the law of the land.

Results, good and evil.

To this day the good and evil effects of the perpetual land settlement are matters of controversy. It raised the condition of Zemindars from that of tax collectors to that of landed proprietors; but it did not raise them to the position of a landed aristocracy, capable of administering patriarchal justice among their tenantry, or of legislating for the welfare of the masses. It proved an immediate relief to the Zemindars, but opened out no prospects of relief to Ryots or farmers. Worst of all, as the rental of land is the backbone of the Indian revenue, it fixed the limit of the receipts of government, without making provision for the future requirements of the country, when military

A.D. 1786-1788 — defences would call for a larger expenditure, and the wants of advancing civilisation would be pressed upon the attention of government. Consequently the permanence of the landed settlement tended to fossilize the people of Bengal, until an English education broke the trammels of ages, and opened out new careers of advancement to the rising generation.

Reforms in the judicial administration. Lord Cornwallis carried out a thorough reform in the administration of justice. He separated the judicial branch from the revenue branch by restricting the English collectors to their fiscal duties, and appointing a separate class of English magistrates and judges. He appointed magistrates to towns and districts to deal with civil and criminal cases. He established courts of appeal in the four cities of Calcutta, Dacca, Murshedabad, and Patna; each court consisting of a judge, a registrar, and qualified assistants. These courts of appeal disposed of all civil cases, with a final appeal to the Sudder court at Calcutta, which was nominally composed of the Governor-General and members of council. The same courts also held a jail delivery twice every year, by going on circuit in their several circles for the trial of criminal cases committed by the district magistrates.

Sindia retreats to Gwalior. 1788 Meanwhile Mahadaji Sindia received a check in Hindustan. Shah Alam suddenly left the camp at Muttra and returned to Delhi. The Muhammadan party at Delhi persuaded the imbecile old prince that his imperial sovereignty had been insulted by the Mahrattas. They stirred up the Rajpút princes to revolt against Sindia. They carried on secret intrigues with the Muhammadan officers in Sindia's army. The result was that when Mahadaji Sindia attempted to suppress the Rajpút revolt, the Muhammadans in his army deserted him in a body, and joined the Rajpút rebels. In a moment he lost all his acquisitions between the Jumna and the Ganges. He was reduced to worse straits than when he had fled from the battle of Paniput more than a quarter of a century before. He had no alternative but to fall back on Gwalior, and implore Nana Farnavese to send him reinforcements from Poona.

But Shah Alam had soon cause to lament the absence of Mahratta protection. Zabita Khan, the Rohilla ex-Amír of Amírs, died in 1785. In 1788 his son, Gholam Kadir,

A.D. 1788-1790.

Horrible outrages in the palace at Delhi, 1788.

entered Delhi with a band of freebooters, and took possession of the city and palace. The atrocities perpetrated by these miscreants in the palace of the Great Moghul reduced the wretched pageant and his family to the lowest depths of misery and despair. Gholam Kadir plundered and insulted the aged Padishah, smoked his hookah on the imperial throne, forced princesses to dance and play before him, and scourged and tortured princes and ladies in the hope of discovering hidden treasures. In one mad fit of passion at the supposed concealment of money or jewels, he threw Shah Alam on the ground, and destroyed his eyes with a dagger. For two months this infamous ruffian and his barbarous followers ran riot in the palace, and there was no one to deliver the helpless family of the Great Moghul from their unbridled excesses.[1]

Schemes of Nana Farnavese for checking Sindia.

Nana Farnavese at Poona was agitated by conflicting passions. He was jealous of the growing power of Mahadaji Sindia, but anxious to maintain the Mahratta ascendancy to the northward. He determined to play Holkar against Sindia. He sent reinforcements to Sindia under the command of Tukaji Holkar, accompanied by a kinsman of the infant Peishwa, named Ali Bahadur;[2] but he insisted that all territories acquired to the northward of the Chambal river should be equally shared by the Peishwa and Holkar, as well as by Sindia.

[1] It is to be hoped that Gholam Kadir and his followers are not fair types of the Rohilla Afghans, who were so much praised by Lord Macaulay. Gholam Kadir was the son of Zabita Khan and grandson of Najib-ud-daula. The outrages which he committed at Delhi were the outcome of the struggle for supremacy at the Moghul court between the families of Najib-ud daula the Rohilla, Najaf Khan the Persian, and Mahadaji Sindia the Mahratta. See *ante*, page 379, *note*.

[2] The kinship between a Muhammadan like Ali Bahadur and a Brahman like the Peishwa is the outcome of the laxity of Mahratta courts. The father of Ali Bahadur was the son of Baji Rao, the second Peishwa, by a Muhammadan woman. According to Hindu law, the offspring of such illicit unions belonged to the same caste as their mother; and in this case caste was equivalent to religion.

Ali Bahadur was associated with a military Guru, or soldier-saint, named Himmut Bahadur, who commanded a large force of Gosains, or religious devotees, in the army of Mahadaji Sindia. Subsequently Ali Bahadur deserted Sindia, and was instigated by Himmut Bahadur to attempt the conquest of Bundelkund. Ultimately Himmut Bahadur, the spiritual teacher and military leader of the army of yellow-robed Gosains, went over to the English during the second Mahratta war.

A.D. 1788-1790

Sindia's return to Delhi.

Thus reinforced Mahadaji Sindia marched to Delhi with the allied army of Mahrattas, and was hailed by the Muhammadan population with the greatest joy. The wretched inmates of the imperial palace were delivered from their misery. Gholam Kadir fled at the approach of the Mahrattas, but was captured and put to death with horrible tortures.

Dangerous power of Tippu of Mysore.

About this time the proceedings of Tippu of Mysore began to excite the serious alarm of the English. This prince, unlike his father Hyder Ali, was a bigoted Muhammadan of the persecuting type. He committed horrible ravages in the Malabar country, and converted thousands of Hindus and Brahmans to the Muhammadan religion by forcibly subjecting them to the rite of circumcision. He asserted a sovereign authority far beyond that of any other native ruler in India. The Nawab Vizier of Oude, and even the Peishwa of the Mahratta empire, continued to acknowledge the Moghul Padishah as the suzerain of Hindustan. But Tippu threw away every pretence of dependence on the Great Moghul, and boldly assumed the independent and sovereign title of Sultan of Mysore.

Enmity against the English.

In 1787 Tippu Sultan took fright at some military reforms of Lord Cornwallis, and hastily made peace with the Mahrattas and Nizam Ali. At the same time he was known to be a bitter enemy of the English, and to be in secret communication with the French at Pondicherry; and he was naturally regarded by the English as a dangerous enemy, who was not to be bound by treaties, and who might at any moment take advantage of a war with France to invade and plunder the Carnatic as his father had done before him.

Attack on Travancore.

By the treaty of Mangalore the Hindu Raja of Travancore, to the south of Malabar, had been placed under British protection. But the Raja was in terror of Tippu Sultan. He purchased two towns from the Dutch on his northern frontier, and built a wall of defence which was known as "the lines of Travancore." Tippu declared that the two towns belonged to the Raja of Cochin, who was his vassal. The Raja of Travancore refused to resign them, and applied to the British government for protection. Lord Cornwallis ordered an inquiry to be made into the merits of the case, and Tippu to be informed that the British government would defend the rights of the Raja; and at the same time he desired the Madras government to make the necessary preparations for war. A.D. 1788-1790

Corruption and inaction of the Madras government.

Unfortunately the Madras government was at this time as corrupt and demoralised as it had been in the days of Hyder Ali. A Company's servant named Holland had been appointed Governor of Madras. Holland was deeply implicated in loans to the Nawab of the Carnatic; and he set the Governor-General at defiance, refused to make preparations for the coming war, and appropriated the revenues of the Carnatic to the payment of the Nawab's debts. Finally he wrote to the Raja of Travancore, offering to help him with a British detachment, on condition of receiving a present for himself of a lakh of pagodas, or some thirty-five thousand pounds sterling.

Lord Cornwallis resolves on war.

Meanwhile Tippu attacked the lines of Travancore, but, to his utter surprise, he was repulsed by the Hindu army of Travancore. Accordingly he ordered a battering train from Seringapatam, and called for reinforcements from every quarter. At this news Lord Cornwallis resolved to take the field. But Holland was incorrigible. He provided no cattle, but proposed to appoint commissioners to settle all differences with Tippu. Lord Cornwallis was much exasperated, and Holland fled from his post and embarked for England.

Native alliances forbidden by Parliament.

Lord Cornwallis now resolved on forming alliances with Nizam Ali and the Mahrattas against Tippu; but the British authorities in India were prohibited by Mr. Pitt's bill of 1784 from making any more alliances with native princes. Lord Cornwallis violated the letter of the act, but respected its spirit by providing that the treaties should cease to have effect after the conclusion of the war.

Nizam Ali accepts the British alliance.

Negotiations with Nizam Ali were comparatively easy. He was anxious for the humiliation of Tippu, and he was still more anxious for British protection against the Mahrattas, who claimed vast sums of money from him, under the head of arrears of chout. He would gladly have secured the permanent protection of the English government against the Mahrattas; but this could not be granted by the English government, without giving mortal offence to the Mahrattas. Accordingly Nizam Ali was obliged to be content with the British guarantee for the protection of his territories until the conclusion of the war; and in

A.D. 1790-1791

return he promised to join the English army with ten thousand horsemen.

Peishwa's government vacillates.

The Peishwa's government professed equal readiness to join the English army against Tippu with another body of ten thousand horsemen. But Nana Farnavese secretly played a double game. He entertained Tippu's envoys at Poona, and delayed the march of the Mahratta contingent for several months, in the hope of inducing Tippu to purchase the neutrality of the Peishwa's government by a large cession of territory.

Sindia withdraws.

Mahadaji Sindia was equally anxious to render the war against Tippu subservient to his own individual interests. He offered to join the confederation against Tippu, provided the British government would guarantee him in possession of the territories he had acquired in Hindustan, and help him to conquer the princes of Rajpútana. Lord Cornwallis was obviously unable to accede to such conditions. Accordingly Mahadaji Sindia refused to take any part in the war against Tippu.

Mysore war: campaign of Medows, 1790.

In 1790 the war began with a campaign under General Medows, who had been appointed Governor of Madras and commander-in-chief of the Madras army. But its operations were futile, and Lord Cornwallis proceeded to Madras and took the command in person. Meanwhile Tippu had desolated the Carnatic, and proceeded towards the south in the hope of procuring a French force from Pondicherry.

Campaign of 1791: inaction of Nizam Ali and the Peishwa.

In 1791 Lord Cornwallis advanced through the Carnatic to the Mysore country, and captured the fortress of Bangalore. Up to this date neither of his native allies had joined him. Nizam Ali would not leave his frontier until he heard that Tippu had gone away to the south; and then, when he entered Mysore, it was not to fight but to plunder. When he heard of the fall of Bangalore, he joined the force of Lord Cornwallis. His cavalry had good horses and showy costumes, but were disorderly, undisciplined, and unfitted for field duties; and they only helped to consume the grain and forage. Meanwhile, for reasons stated, the Mahratta contingent of the Peishwa never appeared at all.

The result of the campaign of 1791 was that Lord Cornwallis advanced towards Seringapatam, and was then compelled to retreat from sheer want of supplies and carriage bullocks. Shortly afterwards he was joined by a

A.D. 1792.

Retreat of Lord Cornwallis: grasping demands of the Mahrattas.

Mahratta force under Hari Pant. Had the Mahrattas come up a week earlier they might have changed the fate of the campaign. They had abundance of supplies, but were imbued with the spirit of hucksters, and refused to part with grain or provisions of any kind to their English allies excepting at exorbitant prices. They had done nothing but rob and ravage the Mysore country from the day they left their frontier; and the bazar in their camp was stored with the plunder of towns,—English broadcloths, Birmingham cutlery, Kashmír shawls and costly jewellery, as well as with oxen, sheep, and poultry. Yet Hari Pant pleaded poverty, and demanded a loan of fourteen lakhs of rupees; and Lord Cornwallis was forced to give him the money, not on account of his services, but to prevent the Mahratta contingent from deserting to Tippu.

Final campaign of 1792.

In 1792 Lord Cornwallis renewed the campaign in Mysore on a scale which had not been seen in India since the days of Aurangzeb. He engaged large numbers of Brinjarries, the hereditary carriers of India, who have already been described under the name of Manaris.[1] His infantry, battering-train, field-pieces, and baggage moved in three parallel columns, followed by a hundred waggons loaded with liquors, and sixty thousand bullocks loaded with provisions. The resources of the English struck the natives of India with awe; and Tippu is said to have exclaimed, "I do not fear what I see, but what I do not see."

Advance on Seringapatam.

Lord Cornwallis was soon joined by the gaudily dressed horsemen of Nizam Ali, and a small force of Hari Pant's Mahrattas; and after a long march at last drew up his artillery on a rising-ground which commanded Seringapatam. Tippu had constructed three lines of earthworks, protected by three hundred pieces of cannon, and covered by a bound hedge of thorny plants. British valour carried the defences by storm, and British cannon were soon playing on the fortifications of Seringapatam.

Submission of Tippu: treachery of Nizam Ali and the Mahrattas.

Tippu was bewildered and confounded. His losses in killed and wounded were severe, and the levies whom he had pressed into his service deserted him in large numbers. He saw that nothing but prompt submission could save his throne. He suddenly accepted the terms which had been offered by Lord Cornwallis, namely, (1) to cede a moiety of

1 See ante, page 187.

A.D. 1792.

his territories, to be equally divided between the English, the Nizam, and the Peishwa; to pay three millions sterling towards the expenses of the war (3) and to deliver up his two sons as hostages for the fulfilment of the terms. In after years it was discovered that the sudden submission of Tippu had defeated the treacherous intentions of the Mahrattas and Nizam Ali. Both were engaged in a clandestine correspondence with Tippu, but both were checkmated by the arrival of his sons as hostages in the camp of the English army.

Changes in British policy.

The Mysore war marks a change in the policy of the British government. Lord Cornwallis had undertaken it to protect the Raja of Travancore from the Mysore Sultan, but his main objects were to cripple the power of Tippu, to sever his connection with the French, and to shut him out of the Carnatic. The policy of political isolation, which had been enjoined by the English parliament, the Board of Control, and the Court of Directors, had proved a failure. Accordingly Lord Cornwallis proposed to go a step further;—to keep the peace in India in the same way that it was supposed to be kept in Europe, namely, by a balance of power. With this view he sought to convert the confederation of the English, the Nizam, and the Peishwa against Tippu into a basis for a balance of power, in which the British government should hold the scales.

Political system of a balance of power.

But there was a fatal obstacle to such a political system. There was not a government in India, excepting that of the British, that cared for the maintenance of the public peace, or hesitated to disturb it at any moment for the promotion of some immediate and individual advantage. Indeed Warren Hastings had reported, ten years before, that the want of faith amongst native states, and the blind selfishness with which they pursued their individual schemes of aggrandisement, regardless of the obligations of treaties or the interests of allies, had rendered such a balance of power as was possible in Europe altogether impossible in India.

Failure of Lord Cornwallis's scheme.

The result of Lord Cornwallis's negotiations was that Nizam Ali was willing to join in any confederation which would protect him from the Mahratta claims; whilst the Mahrattas refused to join in any alliance which would hamper their demands for chout upon Nizam Ali or any one else. But English statesmen at home had been charmed with the scheme for keeping the peace in India by a balance of power. They could not abandon the political idea; and for years it haunted their imaginations, and perverted public opinion as regards the government of India. A.D. 1792.

Antagonism between Sindia and Nana Farnavese.

As if further to show the impossibility of a balance of power, Mahadaji Sindia and Nana Farnavese took opposite views of the British government. Sindia contended that the English had become too powerful in India, and that it would be necessary to support Tippu as a counterpoise. The Nana, on the other hand, was anxious to gain the help of the British government against Mahadaji Sindia; but he insisted on the right of the Peishwa to claim arrears of chout, not only from Nizam Ali but from Tippu Sultan. Lord Cornwallis was thus obliged to abandon his political project in despair.

Commanding position of Mahadaji Sindia, 1792.

In 1792 Mahadaji Sindia had grown to enormous power. He had augmented his French battalions under De Boigne, and raised his standing forces to eighteen thousand regular infantry, six thousand irregulars, two thousand irregular horse, and six hundred Persian cavalry, besides a large train of artillery. This military power was accompanied by territorial aggrandisement, for it was maintained by formal grants of land revenue in the Doab, to the westward of Oude, which Sindia procured from Shah Alam as the Great Moghul.[1] At the same time Agra was becoming a most important fortress in the hands of Mahadaji Sindia; it was a depôt of cannon and arms, and a stronghold which commanded upper Hindustan.

Sindia at Poona: installation of the Peishwa as deputy of the Great Moghul.

In 1792 Mahadaji Sindia marched an army from Delhi to Poona to confer the hereditary title of "deputy of the Great Moghul" upon the young Peishwa. Nana Farnavese tried to prevent the Peishwa from accepting the post; it was opposed, he said, to the constitution of the Mahratta empire. It was indeed a strange anomaly for the Brahman suzerain of the Mahratta confederacy to accept the post of deputy to an effete Muhammadan pageant like Shah Alam. But Sindia insisted, and Nana Farnavese was obliged to give

[1] The Doab, or region between the two rivers, might be called the Mesopotamia of Hindustan. It lies between the Jumna and Ganges, just as Mesopotamia lies between the Tigris and Euphrates. It is impossible to draw a line of strict demarcation at this period between the territories of the Great Moghul and those of the Nawab Vizier of Oude.

A.D. 1792-1794

way. The empty ceremony was accordingly celebrated with the utmost pomp and magnificence at Poona.

Mock humility of Mahadaji Sindia.

Mahadaji Sindia sought to allay all suspicions of his ambitious designs by a mock humility which imposed on no one. His father, Ranuji Sindia, claimed to be the hereditary head man, or Patell, of a village; and he had been originally appointed to carry the slippers of one of the former Peishwas. Accordingly Mahadaji Sindia refused to be called by any other title but that of Patell, and ostentatiously carried the slippers of the young Peishwa at the ceremony of his installation as deputy of the Great Moghul.

Demands of Sindia on the Peishwa.

But the would-be Patell and slipper holder had a keen eye for his own interests. Mahadaji Sindia demanded payment from the Peishwa's government of the expenses he had incurred in extending the Mahratta empire to the northward; and he requested that Tukaji Holkar and Ali Bahadur, who had been sent to his assistance after his retreat to Gwalior, might be recalled from Hindustan to Poona.

Demands of the Peishwa on Sindia.

But Mahadaji Sindia met his match in Nana Farnavese. The Brahman statesman, who had been schooled in diplomacy at Poona, was not to be foiled by the son of a Patell. Nana Farnavese called upon Mahadaji Sindia to produce the revenue accounts of the territories in the Doab and elsewhere, which he had acquired for his sovereign master the Peishwa. Sindia had conquered these territories with the utmost ease, and enjoyed them for a considerable period; and the astute Mahratta minister urged, with some show of reason, that it was high time that the servant should pay the revenue into the treasury of his master.[1]

Death of Mahadaji Sindia, 1794.

While Sindia and the Nana were plotting against each other at Poona, hostilities were breaking out between the armies of Sindia and Holkar in Hindustan. There had been a quarrel over some plunder, and Tukaji Holkar had

[1] The rivalry between Sindia and Nana Farnavese furnishes a strange instance of the instability of native alliances. Sindia had rescued the Nana from the grasp of the conspirators, including Tukaji Holkar and his confederates, who were plotting to restore Rughonath Rao to the throne of the Peishwa. Since then Tukaji Holkar had been appointed, as the faithful ally of Nana Farnavese, to the command of the troops which were at once to support Sindia and to check his growing power. In reality Holkar was sent because of his known rivalry to Sindia; and it will be seen from the text, that this rivalry culminated in a battle between Tukaji Holkar and Sindia's force under De Boigne.

been defeated by De Boigne, the French general in the service of Sindia, and compelled to retire to his capital at Indore. At this crisis the rivalry between Mahadaji Sindia and Nana Farnavese was brought to a close by death. Mahadaji Sindia expired at Poona in February, 1794, and was succeeded by a boy of fourteen, afterwards known as Daulat Rao Sindia. Thus Nana Farnavese was left without a rival in the Mahratta empire.

A.D. 1794-1795

Lord Cornwallis leaves India, 1793.

Meanwhile there was peace and prosperity in Bengal. In 1793 the permanent land settlement was promulgated, and Lord Cornwallis returned to England, leaving Sir John Shore, the servant of the Company, to succeed him in the post of Governor-General. Important events were occurring in Europe; Great Britain had declared war against France and the French revolution; and the British authorities in India took possession of Pondicherry for the third time in Indian history.

Sir John Shore, Governor-General, 1793-98.

Sir John Shore was a model Indian civilian, free from all suspicion of corruption,—honourable, honest, high-minded, and of undoubted industry and capacity. He was the real author of the land settlement, for Lord Cornwallis can only claim the credit of making it perpetual. The British ministry were so impressed with his merits that he was knighted, and appointed to succeed Lord Cornwallis as Governor-General. But he knew little of the history of the world, and was apparently blind to the significance of political events in India.

Alarming breach between the Mahrattas and Nizam Ali.

At this time the progress of affairs at Poona and Hyderabad was exciting universal alarm. The Mahrattas insisted on a final settlement of their claims on Nizam Ali for arrears of chout. They had been put off for years by the war against Tippu, and the evasions and procrastinations of Nizam Ali; and after the conclusion of peace with Tippu they became more pressing in their demands for an immediate settlement. Nizam Ali could neither pay the money, nor hope to repel the Mahratta invasion. In sore distress he implored the help of the English against the Mahrattas, but Sir John Shore declined to interfere. Indeed the British parliament and Court of Directors had strictly enjoined a policy of non-interference. Sir John Shore was fully alive to existing dangers. He saw that without the interference of

A.D. 1794-1795

the British government, Nizam Ali would be crushed by the Mahrattas. He also saw that the destruction of Nizam Ali would remove the last check on the growing power of the Mahrattas, and leave the British government without an ally of any weight to resist Mahratta encroachments. But Sir John Shore was the last man to disobey orders; and he persistently refused to protect Nizam Ali.

Nizam Ali's French battalions.

Nizam Ali, losing all hope of help from the English, had naturally sought it from the French. Forty years before, his elder brother Salábut Jung, owed his throne to the French, and maintained himself against the Mahrattas, as well as against all domestic rivals, solely by the aid of Bussy and the French. Accordingly Nizam Ali entertained a Frenchman, named Raymond, who had originally served in the army of Hyder Ali, and who raised a force of sepoy battalions, trained and disciplined by French officers. In the beginning of 1795 Nizam Ali possessed an army of twenty-three battalions of regulars commanded by Raymond. He was now independent of the English, and ceased to be afraid of the Mahrattas.

Mahratta envoy insulted at Hyderabad.

The Peishwa's government demanded arrears of chout to the amount of nearly three millions sterling. The accounts were swelled by high rates of interest and other exasperating items. They were drawn up with much precision and nicety by Mahratta Brahmans, and were perplexing, if not unintelligible, to every one else. A Mahratta envoy carried the accounts to Hyderabad, and requested payment. The Muhammadan minister of the Nizam treated the Mahratta with haughty insolence. He told the envoy in open durbar that Nana Farnavese must come in person to Hyderabad to explain the items; and that if he refused to come he must be brought. This threat was regarded by both sides as a declaration of war.

Inflated hopes of Nizam Ali.

Nizam Ali was puffed up with hopes of victory. The dancing-girls glorified his triumphs in prophetic songs. The soldiers boasted that they would sack and plunder Poona. The minister at Hyderabad was a Muhammadan like his master; and he bragged that no treaty should be concluded with the Mahrattas until the Brahman Peishwa had been sent on pilgrimage to Benares, to mutter his incantations on the banks of the Ganges, with a cloth about his loins and a pot of water in his hand.

A.D. 1794-1795

The Mahrattas were one and all eager for the war. All the feudatories of the empire,—Sindia and Holkar, the Gaekwar and the Bhonsla,—and even the smaller chieftains of the southern Mahratta country,—were burning to share in a settlement of the Mahratta claims. For the last time in Mahratta history the summons of the Peishwa was obeyed throughout the length and breadth of Mahratta dominion.

Mahratta powers eager for war.

The decisive battle was fought near the small fortress of Kurdla in March 1795. The Nizam's cavalry were routed with rockets and artillery, but the French battalions under Raymond stood their ground. Nizam Ali, however, was seized with a panic from the outset. He fled to the fortress of Kurdla, repeatedly calling on Raymond to follow him. The bulk of his troops dispersed in all directions, plundering the baggage of their own army as they fled from the field. The banditti in the Mahratta army, known as Pindharies, rushed after the fugitives and stripped them of their ill-gotten spoil; whilst the Mahrattas swarmed round the fortress of Kurdla, animated by the thought that the Nizam and all his treasures were within their grasp.

Decisive battle of Kurdla, 1795.

Nizam Ali held out for two days in the fortress of Kurdla; then yielded to every demand. He surrendered his offending minister, ceded nearly half his territory, and pledged himself to liquidate the whole of the Mahratta claims.

Submission of Nizam Ali.

The victory of Kurdla raised Nana Farnavese to the height of prosperity; but within six months he was plunged in a vortex of distractions, which well-nigh worked his ruin.

Reverses of Nana Farnavese.

The Peishwa, Mahdu Rao Narain, had reached his twenty-first year. He had all his life been kept in galling tutelage by Nana Farnavese, and saw no hope of throwing off the yoke and exercising his sovereign rights as Peishwa of the Mahratta empire. In a fit of despair he threw himself from a terrace of the palace, and died two days afterwards.

Suicide of the Peishwa, 1795.

The nearest kinsman was Baji Rao, son of the Rughonath Rao whom the English had supported in the first Mahratta war. Baji Rao was at this time a young man of twenty; but had long been kept in confinement by Nana Farnavese. He was too old and too cunning to be a puppet; and the unscrupulous minister was anxious to override his claims by prevailing on the widow of the dead Peishwa to adopt a son. But Baji Rao, within the walls of his prison, was already engaged in a counter-plot. He tried to play Sindia against

Claims of Baji Rao.

A.D. 1794-1795

Nana Farnavese. He secretly opened a correspondence with the young Daulat Rao Sindia, and promised to cede him a large territory if Sindia would place him on the throne of Poona as the Peishwa of the Mahrattas.

Reconciliation of the Nana and Baji Rao.

Nana Farnavese discovered the plot and forestalled Sindia by releasing Baji Rao and declaring him to be Peishwa. But the minister could not trust the new Peishwa, and the new Peishwa could not trust the minister, until Nana Farnavese had taken the most solemn oaths on the tail of a cow to be faithful to Baji Rao, and Baji Rao had taken oaths equally solemn to keep Nana Farnavese at the head of the administration.

Bewildering plots.

The plots which followed are tortuous and bewildering. Daulat Rao Sindia marched an army to Poona. Nana Farnavese fled to Satara, under pretence of procuring the insignia of investiture from the pageant Maharaja. Baji Rao came to terms with Daulat Rao Sindia by promising to pay him a sum of two millions sterling. All this while, in spite of oaths and promises, and in spite of his being a Hindu and a Brahman, Baji Rao sent messengers to Nizam Ali, the Muhammadan ruler at Hyderabad, imploring his help against both Sindia and the Nana, and promising to restore all the territory ceded after the battle of Kurdla, and to forego the balance due on the Mahratta claims.

Anarchy at Poona.

These plots threw the city of Poona into tumult and anarchy. Nana Farnavese was induced to return to Poona, and to pay a visit to Daulat Rao Sindia; but he was treacherously seized and thrown into prison with all his chief partisans. Parties of Mahratta soldiers were sent off to plunder the houses of the imprisoned chieftains. They found the doors barricaded, and the inmates posted with arms at the windows and on the roof. The firing was incessant and spread universal alarm; and there was nothing but uproar, plunder and bloodshed, throughout the city.

Plunder and treachery.

Sindia next demanded his two millions of Baji Rao, and was told to plunder Poona. Sindia took the hint and plundered the capital of his suzerain without mercy. All the wealthy inhabitants were scourged and tortured until they had given up their hoarded treasures. In the end Baji Rao made an attempt to entrap Sindia, by inviting him to the palace for the purpose of murdering him; but his heart failed him at the last moment, and he hesitated

A.D. 1796-1798

to give the necessary signal to the assassins. Accordingly Sindia left the palace without injury, but not without suspicions; and henceforth he was more distrustful than ever of the good faith of Baji Rao.

Weakness of Sir John Shore.

Sir John Shore was not the man to deal with such distractions. The Mahratta empire was breaking up, and non-intervention would not solve the problem. A statesman of European experience and original genius was required to deal with the crisis; a man of stronger brain and firmer will. At the same time a dangerous disaffection broke out in the English army in Bengal. Sir John Shore was devoid of all military experience, and found that he had not nerve enough to suppress the growing disorders, and he requested the Court of Directors to send out a successor.

Oude affairs, 1797-98.

Before Sir John Shore returned to England, he was forced to give his attention to the state of Oude. The administration was at once weak and oppressive. The money wrung from the Ryots was withheld by the Talukdars,[1] or squandered in wasteful luxury at the capital; whilst nothing but the presence of the British battalions prevented the whole country from being overrun by the Mahrattas. Sir John Shore remonstrated with the Nawab Vizier, but only wasted his words. Asof-ud-daula died in 1797, and Sir John Shore recognised a certain Vizier Ali as his successor. Subsequently it turned out that Vizier Ali was illegitimate, and that Saádut Ali, the brother of the late ruler, was the legitimate and rightful Nawab Vizier. Accordingly Vizier Ali was pensioned off and sent to reside at Benares. Saádut Ali was placed upon the throne and effected a change in the aspect of affairs. He devoted his energies to hoarding up the revenues which his predecessors had been accustomed to squander on their pleasures.

Shore embarks for Europe

In March, 1798, Sir John Shore, now Lord Teignmouth, embarked at Calcutta for Europe. Meanwhile a Governor-General was coming out to India of a very different stamp. At first he was only known as Lord Mornington, but in the history of British India, he is more widely known by his later title of Marquis of Wellesley.

[1] The Talukdars of Oude corresponded generally to the Zemindars in Bengal, but in some cases they were mere collectors of revenue, whilst others corresponded to a feudal nobility. Under the rule of a Nawab Vizier it is impossible to say what they were.

CHAPTER VIII.

MYSORE AND CARNATIC: WELLESLEY.

1798 TO 1801.

A.D. 1798.

Lord Mornington, aged thirty-eight.

LORD MORNINGTON landed at Calcutta in the thirty-eighth year of his age. At the time he left England he had three objects in view, namely, to drive the French out of India; to revive the confederacy with Nizam Ali and the Peishwa against Tippu of Mysore; and to establish the balance of power which Lord Cornwallis had failed to create, and which was still the darling object of the English ministry.

National hatred against the French: Tippu an ally of France.

At this time the hatred of the British nation towards the revolutionary government in France had risen to fever heat. The reign of terror, the horrors of the guillotine, the execution of Louis the Sixteenth and Marie Antoinette, the rise of Napoleon, and the threatened invasion of England, had stirred up depths of antagonism which later generations can scarcely realise. The new Governor-General shared in the national sentiment, but his wrath was mingled with alarm as he heard that one army of French sepoys was in the service of Nizam Ali; that another French army was in the service of Daulat Rao Sindia; and that Tippu Sultan, the hereditary enemy of the British nation, was entertaining French officers, and courting a French alliance which might endanger British power in India.

Balance of power impossible in India.

But Lord Mornington soon discovered that whilst it was possible to revive the old confederation against Tippu, it was utterly impossible to frame a network of alliances which would establish a balance of power, and maintain the peace

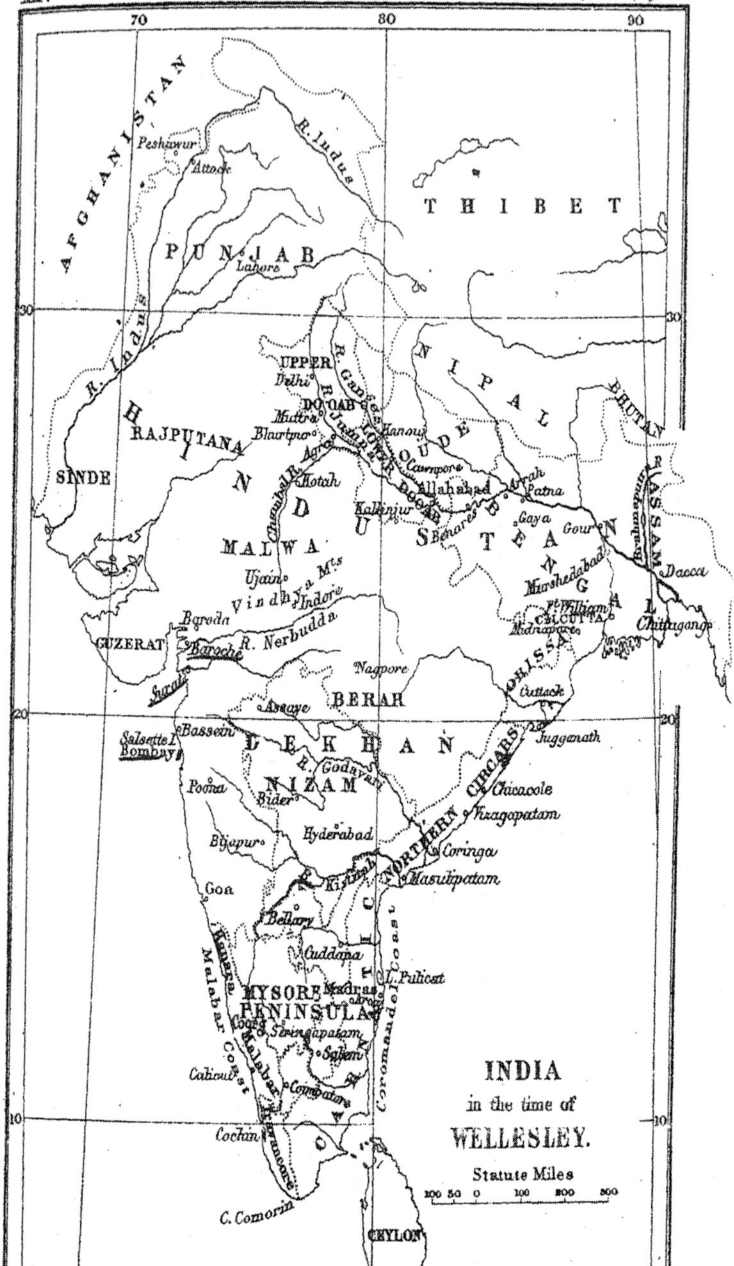
INDIA
in the time of
WELLESLEY.
Statute Miles
100 50 0 100 200 300
AFGHANISTAN
Peshawur
Attock
R. Indus
THIBET
PUNJAB
Lahore
SINDE
RAJPUTANA
HINDUSTAN
UPPER DOOAB
Delhi
Muttra
Bhurtpur
Agra
R. Ganges
R. Jumna
LOWER DOOAB
Hansi
Cawnpore
Allahabad
OUDE
NIPAL
BHUTAN
ASSAM
Arrah
Patna
Benares
Gaya
Gour
BENGAL
Dacca
Kotah
Chambal R.
Kallinjur
MALWA
Ujain
Vindhya Mts
Indore
Murshedabad
Ft William
CALCUTTA
Midnapore
Chittagong
Baroda
GUZERAT
Baroche
R. Nerbudda
Surat
Nagpore
BERAR
ORISSA
Cuttack
Assaye
Juggannath
Salsette I.
Bombay
Bassein
DEKHAN
R. Godavari
NIZAM
Poona
Bider
NORTHERN CIRCARS
Chicacole
Vizagapatam
Hyderabad
Bijapur
Coringa
R. Kistnah
Masulipatam
Goa
Bellary
Cuddapa
L. Pulicat
Madras
Arcot
MYSORE
PENINSULA
Kanara
Malabar Coast
Coromandel Coast
Seringapatam
Salem
Calicut
Malabar
Coimbatore
Cochin
Travancore
CARNATIC
C. Comorin
CEYLON
70
80
90
30
20
10

of India on the basis of international relations. Indeed the progress of events had rendered such a task still more hopeless in 1798 than it had been in 1792. In 1792 the Nizam and the Peishwa were at any rate substantive states, although they could not be formed into trustworthy allies. But in 1798 the power of the Nizam was shattered by his humiliation at Kurdla; whilst the Peishwa's government was distracted by the dissensions between Baji Rao, Daulat Rao Sindia, and Nana Farnavese. Accordingly, the idea of a balance of power was abandoned; and Lord Mornington saw that the work before him was to secure the disbandment of the French battalions, and to revive the confederation against Tippu.

A.D. 1798.

Alliance with Nizam Ali against Tippu.

Lord Mornington began with the Nizam. There was little difficulty, except what arose from the alarms, the prevarications, and the fickle temperament of Nizam Ali himself. In the end, Nizam Ali agreed to disband his French battalions, and to maintain an English force in their room, with the understanding that the British government would mediate in the Mahratta claims, and, if necessary, protect him against the Mahrattas. Nizam Ali further pledged himself to take no Frenchman or other European into his service without the consent of the British government. Finally, he promised to furnish a contingent force to serve in the coming war against Tippu.

Disbandment of the French battalions.

The disbandment of the French battalions at Hyderabad was attended with anxiety, but carried out without bloodshed. An English force was on the ground. The disbandment was proclaimed, and then the French sepoys broke out in mutiny for arrears of pay, and the French officers fled for protection to the English lines. The French sepoys were re-assured by the discharge of their pay and arrears, and submitted to their fate; and within a few hours the French battalions had melted away.

Mahrattas avoid a British alliance.

Lord Mornington also opened negotiations with the Mahrattas, but he found them impracticable. Baji Rao and Nana Farnavese had become reconciled; for both were Brahmans, and both were threatened by Daulat Rao Sindia. But they would not form a close connection with the English; they were jealous of the English alliance with the Nizam; and they were especially jealous of any interference of the English in the Mahratta claims. But whilst evading

A.D. 1798-1799

a treaty they avoided all cause for quarrel. Nana Farnavese promised that in the event of a war against Tippu, the Peishwa's government would send a Mahratta contingent to co-operate with the armies of the English and the Nizam.

Open hostility of Tippu.

Meanwhile the hostility of Tippu was proved beyond a doubt. He sent envoys to the French governor of the Mauritius with despatches for the government at Paris, proposing an offensive and defensive alliance against the English. The matter was blazoned forth in a public proclamation at the Mauritius; and it was republished in the Indian journals, and confirmed by advices from the Cape. Shortly afterwards news arrived in India that a French army under Napoleon had landed in Egypt; and it was also rumoured that a French fleet was on its way down the Red Sea bound for the coast of Malabar. Under such circumstances Lord Mornington resolved on the final extinction of Tippu.

Explanations demanded.

But Lord Mornington did not rush blindly into a war. He demanded an explanation from Tippu, and proposed sending a Major Doveton to come to a thorough understanding with the Sultan. But Tippu sent back lame explanations, charging the French authorities with untruthfulness and malice, and refused to receive Major Doveton.

Last war against Mysore, 1799.

The war began in 1799. An English army under General Harris marched from Madras to the Mysore country, accompanied by Colonel Arthur Wellesley, afterwards famous as the great Duke of Wellington. The expedition was joined by a force from Hyderabad, but the Mahrattas made no appearance. Another English force from Bombay entered the Mysore country from the westward, to form a junction with the Madras army.

Tippu overwhelmed: refuses humiliation.

Tippu made some efforts at resistance, but was routed and compelled to fall back on his famous capital and stronghold at Seringapatam. He seemed bewildered and infatuated as the forces from Madras and Bombay closed around him. He sued for peace, and was required to cede half his remaining territories, and to pay a sum of two millions sterling. The terms were hard, but the hearts of the English were steeled against him. They remembered his cruelties towards his English prisoners, and were enraged at his intrigues with the French. Tippu spurned the proffered conditions. "Better," he said, "to die like a soldier, than to end my days as a pensioned Nawab."

A.D. 1799-1800

Storming of Seringapatam and death of Tippu.

In May, 1799, the fortifications of Seringapatam were taken by storm. Tippu himself was found dead in a gateway; his remains were treated with becoming respect, and buried with funeral honours in the mausoleum of his family.

Relief and pity

Thus fell the dynasty of Hyder Ali after a brief existence of forty years. The downfall of Tippu and capture of Seringapatam thrilled through India like the victory at Plassy. Every Englishman felt a relief; every native prince was alarmed at the rapid success of the conquerors. There were few in India to lament the fate of Tippu, excepting the members of his own family and the Muhammadans of Mysore. He was denounced as a cruel persecutor of Hindus and Christians; as a foe of the English and a friend of the French. He was not a born genius like his father Hyder Ali, but he was more zealous and consistent as a Muhammadan.

Veiling of territorial conquest.

Territorial conquest in India was distasteful to the people of England. Lord Mornington was hailed as the conqueror of Tippu, and rewarded with the title of Marquis of Wellesley; but, like Lord Clive, he deemed it prudent to veil his conquest from European eyes. A part of Mysore was formed into a Hindu kingdom; and an infant representative of the extinct Hindu dynasty was taken from a hovel, and placed upon the throne as Maharaja. The remaining territory was divided into three portions; one to be retained by the English; one to be given to the Nizam, who had joined in the war; and the third, under certain conditions, to be made over to the Peishwa, who had taken no part in the hostilities.

Picturesque glimpses of the Carnatic and Mysore in the year 1800 are furnished by Dr. Buchanan, who was deputed by Lord Wellesley to undertake a journey through the newly opened territories of Mysore and Malabar.

Madras to Malabar, 1800.

Company's Jaghír.

Dr. Buchanan left Madras in April, 1800, and marched towards Arcot. His journey in the first instance lay through the Company's Jaghír; and it is curious to note the changes which the Jaghír had undergone. It had been ceded to the East India Company by Muhammad Ali, Nawab of Arcot, many years previously, in return for the services rendered by the English. It extended along the Coromandel coast, north and south, from Pulicat lake to the river Palar, and

A.D. 1800.

inland from Madras to Conjeveram. It was thus about a hundred miles long and forty broad.

Ravages of Hyder Ali.

The Company's Jaghír was twice ravaged by Hyder Ali with fire and sword. The devastation was so complete that at the end of the war in 1784, there were few signs that the country had been inhabited, beyond the bones of those who had been murdered, and the naked walls of houses, temples, and choultries that had been burnt. The havoc of war was succeeded by a destructive famine, which drove many of the wretched survivors to emigrate from the country.

Mr. Place, the English collector.

In 1794, ten years after the war, the Company's Jaghír was formed into a collectorate under the management of Mr. Place, who was long remembered by the natives. Mr. Place retired in 1798. Two years later Dr. Buchanan was on his way from Madras to Mysore.

Face of the country.

Dr. Buchanan found the weather very hot and dry, as is generally the case in April. After leaving the plain occupied by the white garden houses of the Europeans, Dr. Buchanan entered a level country covered with rice-fields. The roads were good, and many of the mud huts were covered with tiles, and consequently appeared better than those in Bengal.

Resting-places and choultries.

Dr. Buchanan was struck with the resting-places and choultries which had been built for the accommodation of travellers by rich native merchants of Madras. The resting-places were mud walls four feet high, on which porters deposited their loads during intervals of rest, and took them up again without stooping. The choultries were square courts enclosed by low buildings, divided into apartments in which the poorest travellers obtained shelter from sun or rain, and a draught of water or milk without expense. In some choultries provisions were sold; in others they were distributed gratis, at least to Brahmans or other religious mendicants. The village choultry was also the place of assembly for all the head men and elders, when they met together to settle disputes or discuss other public matters.

Collection of land rents.

In collecting rents in the Company's Jaghír, the crops were not kept on the ground until the rent was paid, as was the case in Bengal. On the contrary, the grain was cut, threshed, and stacked, and then sealed with clay bearing a stamp, until the cultivator paid his rent in coin or kind.

A.D. 1800.

Great tank.

The great water-tank of Saymbrumbaukum on the road to Conjeveram was then as now an object of wonder. It was not dug like the tanks in Bengal, but was formed by shutting up, with an artificial bank, an opening between two natural ridges. The sheet of water was seven or eight miles in length and three in width. During the rains it was filled by neighbouring rivers, and during the dry season it was let out in small streams. In the event of the rains failing, it sufficed to water the lands of thirty-two villages for a period of eighteen months.

Measures of Mr. Place.

Mr. Place, the English collector,[1] had repaired this tank, and given great satisfaction to the cultivators whilst augmenting the revenue. Mr. Place had also caused every village to be surrounded by a hedge of bamboos, which served to keep off small parties of horsemen during a hostile invasion, whilst extending the cultivation of bamboos.

Conjeveram: streets and houses.

Buchanan halted at Conjeveram, or Kanchi-puram, about forty miles from Madras. To this day Conjeveram is a type of the Hindu cities in the Peninsula. The streets were tolerably broad and lined with cocoa-nut trees, and crossed one another at right angles. The houses were built of mud in the form of a square, with a small court in the centre. They appeared much more comfortable than the houses in the country towns in Bengal.

Worship of Siva and Vishnu.

There was a large temple at Conjeveram dedicated to Siva and his wife. Three miles off was another temple dedicated to Vishnu. There were a hundred Brahman families and a hundred dancing-girls employed in the service of these temples. Twice a year the images of Vishnu and his family were carried in procession on a visit to Siva; but Siva returned the visit only once a year. On those occasions there were frequent disputes between the worshippers of Siva and those of Vishnu, leading to abusive language and blows, which the English collectors were sometimes obliged to put down with the bayonet.

Three sects.

The Brahmans of Southern India were divided into three leading sects, namely, the Smartal, the Vaishnava, and the Madual.

The Smartal were the most numerous, and comprehended

[1] In Madras the civil officers are termed collectors and deputy-collectors; in Bengal and elsewhere they are termed commissioners and deputy-commissioners.

A.D. 1800.

The Smartal.

half the Brahmans in the Lower Carnatic. Its members were followers of Sankhara Achárya. They were commonly said to be worshippers of Siva, but they considered Brahma, Vishnu, and Siva to be the same god assuming different persons as the creator, preserver, and destroyer of the universe. They believed their own souls to be portions of the divinity, and did not believe in transmigration as a punishment for sin. They were readily distinguished by three horizontal stripes on the forehead made with white ashes.[1]

Type of a Smartal.

Buchanan met with a Smartal Brahman, who was a fair type of his class. He was reckoned a man of learning, but he denied all knowledge of Jains, Buddhists, or other sects, beyond having heard them mentioned. He considered the doctrines of all sects, save his own, to be contemptible and unworthy of notice. He believed in a supreme god, called Náráyana, or Para Brahma, from whom proceeded Siva, Vishnu, or Brahma; but he regarded all of them, individually and collectively, as one and the same god. His sect prayed to Siva and Vishnu, as well as to many of their wives, children and attendants, among whom were the Sakhtis, or destructive powers. Siva however was the principal object of their worship; for they considered him to be a most powerful mediator with Náráyana, who was rather too much elevated to attend to their personal requests. They abhorred bloody sacrifices, but did not blame the Súdras for practising such a form of worship; they said it was the custom of the Súdras, and that it was a matter of very little consequence what such low people did. The Smartals believed that when a good Brahman died, his spirit was united to God; but that the soul of a bad Brahman was punished in purgatory, and then passed through other lives, as an animal or as a person of low caste, until at last he became a Brahman and had another opportunity by the performance of good works to become united to God.

[1] Sankhara Achárya, the apostle of the Smartals, was a Nambúri Brahman of Malabar, who flourished about the eighth century of the Christian era. His disciples taught that he was an incarnation of Siva, who appeared on earth to root out the religion of the Jains and regulate and reform the Brahmans. In 1871 a representative or successor of this apostle was still living. His name was Narsingh Achárya. He was called by his disciples the Jagat Guru, or teacher of the world. See larger *History of India*, vol. iii. chap. 8.

A.D. 1800.

The Vaishnava and A'ayngar.

The followers of Rámánuja Achárya were the most numerous sect of Brahmans, next to the Smartals, and formed about three-tenths of the whole. They were called Vaishnava and A'ayngar, and were readily known by three vertical marks on the forehead, connected by a common line above the nose, and formed of white clay. They abhorred Siva, calling him the chief the Rákshasas, or devils; and they worshipped only Vishnu and the gods of his family. They formed two sects; those who believed in transmigration and those who did not.[1]

The Madual

The Maduals formed the remaining two-tenths of the Brahmans. They wore the vertical marks on the forehead, which were appropriate to the followers of Vishnu, but they also worshipped Siva. They believed in the generation of the gods in a literal sense, thinking Vishnu to be the father of Brahma, and Brahma to be the father of Siva.

Brahmans, spiritual and secular.

The proper duty of a Brahman was meditation on things divine; and the proper mode of procuring a livelihood was by begging. But the common people were not so charitable as in a former age, nor so willing to part with their money. Accordingly most of the Brahmans in the Lower Carnatic followed secular professions. They filled the different offices in the collection of revenue and administration of justice; and were extensively employed as guides and messengers, and as keepers of choultries. They rented lands, but never put their hands to the plough, and cultivated their farms by slaves who belonged to the inferior castes.[2] Hence arose the distinction between the Vaidika and Lókika Brahmans: the Vaidika devoting their days to

[1] Rámánuja Achárya, the apostle of the Vaishnaras and A'ayngars, flourished about the twelfth century. He made Conjeveram his head quarters, but undertook missionary circuits over the whole of the Peninsula. One of his disciples, named Rámánand, founded another celebrated sect at Benares, who worshipped Vishnu through his incarnations of Râma and Krishna, and threw off all ties of caste. See larger *History of India*, vol. iii. chap. 8.

[2] The lower-castes, or rather outcastes, were by far the most hardy and laborious people in the Carnatic, but the greater number were slaves. Hyder Ali was alive to their value, and during his incursions in the Carnatic he sought to carry them away to Mysore, where he settled them down in farms. They are divided into numerous tribes or castes, distinguished by a variety of names, but are best known to Europeans by the general term of Pariahs. Properly speaking the Pariahs or Pareyars form only a single tribe.

A.D. 1800.

study, contemplation, and the education of younger Brahmans; whilst the Lókikas engaged in the government revenue and other worldly concerns. The mercenary Brahmans who officiated in pagodas for a livelihood were despised alike by Vaidikas and Lókikas.

Separate streets for Brahmans and Súdras.

Throughout both Carnatics, except at Madras and some other exceptional towns, the Brahmans appropriated to themselves a particular quarter, generally that which was the best fortified. A Súdra was not permitted to dwell in the same street as a Brahman, and Pariahs and other low-castes were forbidden to dwell in the same quarter as the Súdras. Indeed the Pariahs, and others of the same stamp, generally lived in wretched huts about the suburbs, where a Brahman could not walk without pollution.

Fortified villages and towns.

Buchanan paid a passing visit to Arcot and Vellore. He saw nothing remarkable except the Muhammadan women, who rode about on bullocks, and were entirely wrapt up in white veils. He ascended the Eastern Gháts and entered Mysore. The country was exceedingly bare and the population scanty. All the houses were collected in villages; the smallest villages of five or six houses were fortified with a wall six feet high, and a mud tower on the top to which the only access was by a ladder. If a plundering party approached the village, the people ascended the tower with their families and valuables, and drew up the ladder, and defended themselves with stones, which even the women threw with great force and dexterity. The larger villages had square forts, with round towers at the angles. In towns the defences were still more numerous; the fort served as a citadel, whilst the town or pettah was surrounded by a weaker defence of mud. The inhabitants considered fortifications as necessaries of existence, and incurred the whole expense of building them and the risk of defending them. Indeed for a long series of years the country had been in a constant state of warfare; and the poor inhabitants had suffered so much from all parties that they would not trust in any.

Bangalore.

Buchanan halted at Bangalore, which has since become a favourite resort of the English in India. Bangalore was founded by Hyder Ali, and during his reign was an emporium of trade and manufactures. Hyder built the fort at Bangalore after the best fashion of Muhammadan

A.D. 1800.

military architecture; but Tippu destroyed it after he found that it could not resist English valour. Tippu also ruined the town by prohibiting all trade with the subjects of the Nawab of Arcot and Nizam of Hyderabad, whom he held in detestation.[1] It was plundered during the Mysore war of 1791-92 by the forces of Lord Cornwallis and his native allies, and the inhabitants fled in all directions. Subsequently Tippu induced the refugees to return with the wreck of their fortunes; and then, having got them under his thumb, he fleeced them of all they possessed, down to the most trifling ornaments, on the pretence that they had favoured the English. Since the fall of Tippu in 1799 the inhabitants began once more to flock into Bangalore under the assurance of British protection.

Seringapatam: palace and warehouses of Tippu.

At Seringapatam Buchanan saw the palace of Tippu Sultan. It was a large building surrounded by a wall of stone and mud. Tippu's own rooms formed one side of the square, whilst the three remaining sides were occupied by warehouses. Tippu had been a merchant as well as a prince; and during his reign he filled his warehouses with a vast variety of goods, which the Amildars, or governors of provinces, were expected to sell to the richer inhabitants at prices far in excess of their real value. Much corruption and oppression resulted from this forced system of trade. Those who bribed the Amildar were exempt from making large purchases. Those poor wretches who were unable to bribe, were forced to buy; and as they were equally unable to pay, they were stripped of all they possessed, and written down as debtors to the Sultan for the outstanding balances.

Brahman officials.

Tippu persecuted Hindus, and especially Brahmans, as bitterly as Aurangzeb; but his bigotry rarely stood in the way of his interest. He might be unmerciful towards the temple Brahmans, but he spared the seculars. Indeed, the secular Brahmans were the only men in his dominions who were fitted for civil administration. His Dewan, or financial minister, was a Brahman of singular ability, named Purnea. Tippu was anxious that Purnea should become a Muhammadan; but Purnea was so horrified at the idea that the intention was abandoned.

[1] Tippu sought to punish both the Nawab and Nizam by stopping the trade with Arcot and Hyderabad, much in the same way that the first Napoleon tried to punish England by the Berlin decrees.

A.D. 1800.

Corruption and oppression.

All this while the Brahmans were so avaricious and corrupt, that Tippu would gladly have displaced them could he have found capable men of other castes to fill their posts. He tried to check their malpractices by appointing Muhammadan Asofs, or lord-lieutenants, to superintend the administration in the provinces; but this measure only aggravated the evil. The Asofs were indolent, ignorant, and self-indulgent; and hungered after money bribes to supply their wants. Consequently the Brahmans doubled their exactions in order to satisfy the Asofs. Every native supposed to be rich was exposed to false charges, and there was no escape except by bribery.

Purnea, the Brahman, Dewan of Mysore.

Under the new government introduced by the Marquis of Wellesley, Purnea remained in the post of Dewan, and conducted the administration of Mysore under the supervision of an English Resident. He was a Brahman of the Madual sect, a good linguist, and well versed in the affairs of the country. The revenue establishments were largely reduced, and consequently the Brahmans were the loudest in their complaints against the new government. Those who were retained in the public service were paid liberal salaries to place them above temptation, but the result was not satisfactory. The people of Mysore acknowledged that they were delivered from the licentiousness of Tippu's soldiery, and the arbitrary exactions of his government; but they complained that the Brahman officials took more money than ever.

Distinction between the left and right "hands."

Buchanan explains the remarkable distinction which prevails in the two Carnatics between the left and right "hands." This distinction is confined to the Pariahs, and low-castes generally. The "left hand" comprised nine tribes or castes, including blacksmiths, carpenters, masons, gold and silver-smiths, oil makers, hunters, shoemakers, and some others. The "right hand" comprised eighteen tribes, including Pariahs properly so called, calico-printers, shepherds, potters, washermen, palanquin-bearers, barbers, painters, cowkeepers, and others. The Pariahs proper were the chief tribe of the "right hand."

Quarrels and bloodshed.

The origin of this division of the Hindu low-castes was involved in fable. It was said to have been carried out at Conjeveram by the goddess Kálí. It was also said that the rules to be observed on either side were engraved

A.D. 1800.

on a copper plate, and preserved in the great temple of Siva. The existence of the plate, however, was more than doubtful. The pretensions of both hands were diametrically opposed, yet both appealed to the plate as an authority, and no one produced a copy. The antagonism originated in claims to the exclusive possession of certain honorary distinctions, such as the privilege of using twelve pillars to the temporary building under which the marriage ceremonies were performed; the right of riding on horseback in processions; or the claim to carry a flag painted with the figure of the monkey god Hanuman.[1]

Gurus and Swamis: initiation and confirmation.

Buchanan saw something of the working of Gurus and Swamis in the Brahmanical hierarchy.[2] They were the bishops of their respective sects, exercising a jurisdiction in all things relating to religion or caste. The Gurus and Swamis performed certain ceremonies of initiation and confirmation in their respective sects. They imparted to every disciple a mysterious sentence, known as the Upadása, which was to be uttered orally in their devotions, and was never to be written down or revealed. Sometimes a Guru gave a Upadása and some images to a favourite disciple, and appointed him as a kind of deputy to manage affairs at a distance. In the Vaishnava sect every disciple was branded with the spear of the god Vishnu. This ceremony was known as the Chakrántikam.[3] The spear was made

[1] The division between the left and right "hands" is unknown in Hindustan, but prevails throughout the Peninsula and a great part of the Dekhan. The disputes amongst the low-castes at Masulipatam (*ante*, page 191) were connected with this distinction. The English at Madras and the French at Pondicherry were often troubled in the last century by disputes between the left and right "hands," which sometimes were productive of bloodshed, and necessitated the interference of the military. Abbé Dubois relates a remarkable instance at which he himself was present. A terrible feud had broken out between the Pariahs and Cobblers, which spread through a large district. Many of the timid inhabitants began to remove their effects and leave their villages, as if they had been threatened by a Mahratta invasion. Fortunately matters did nor come to an extremity, as the chief men came forward to mediate between the vulgar castes, and to disband the armed ranks just as they were awaiting the signal for battle. The cause of this dreadful commotion was a trifle. A Cobbler had stuck red flowers in his turban at a public festival, and the Pariahs insisted that none of his caste had a right to wear them.

[2] See *ante*, part i., chap. iv., page 65.

[3] This branding ceremony was not practised by the Smartal sect who worshipped Siva.

A.D. 1800.

hot and applied to the shoulder so as to burn the skin. The Upadása was imparted to the disciple only once during life; but the Chakrántikam or branding was performed several times.[1]

Money demands.

The Gurus were entirely supported by the contributions of their disciples; but these were so burdensome that a Guru seldom continued long in one place. The contributions of a rich town like Madras would not support a Guru or Swami for more than one or two months; and the visits of a Guru were often regarded with dread like the incursions of a Mahratta.[2]

Visitations of the Gurus.

The Gurus travelled in great state, with elephants, horses, palanquins, and an immense train of disciples, the least of whom considered himself as elevated far above ordinary mortals by his superior sanctity. They generally travelled at night in order to avoid their Muhammadan or European conquerors, who would not show them that veneration, or adoration, to which they considered themselves entitled On the approach of a Guru to any place, all the inhabitants of the higher castes went out to meet him; but the lower castes were not admitted to his presence. The Guru was conducted to the principal temple, and bestowed Upadása, or Chakrántikam, on such as had not received those ceremonies, and also distributed holy water. He then inquired into matters of contention, or transgressions against the rules of caste; and having settled or punished all such offences, he heard his disciples and other learned men dispute on theological subjects. This was the grand field for acquiring reputation among the Brahmans.

[1] At the Madras Presidency College many years ago, the author often heard educated Hindus speak of the ceremonies described by Buchanan. He believes that the Upadása imparted to the higher castes corresponded to the Gayatri, or invocation of all the Vaidik deities as represented by the sun. The Upadása imparted to Súdras and others was nothing more than the name of some particular god, which was to be constantly repeated by the worshipper. The ceremony of branding was sometimes a subject of mirth to those who were not required to submit to it.

[2] A hundred pagodas a day, or about thirty-six pounds sterling, were as little as could be offered to a Guru on his tour, and the Raja of Tanjore was said to have given his Guru something like ninety pounds a day whenever the great spiritual teacher honoured him with a visit. There is reason however to believe that the disciples exaggerated the value of past gifts in the hope of exciting the emulation of current worshippers.

A.D. 1800.

Popular forms of ecclesiastical government.

Besides the Gurus however there were popular forms of ecclesiastical government. Throughout every part of India, wherever there was a considerable number of any one caste or tribe, there was usually a head man, and his office was generally hereditary. His powers were various in different sects and places; but he was commonly entrusted with authority to punish all transgressions against the rules of caste. His power was not arbitrary; as he was always assisted by a council of the most respectable members of his tribe. He could inflict fines and stripes, and above all excommunication, or loss of caste, which was the most terrible of all punishments to a Hindu.

Satires against Gurus and Brahmans.

Whilst Gurus, and Brahmans generally, were held in such outward veneration, an undercurrent of antagonism occasionally found expression in the language of revolt. Satirical songs were current, showing up the incapacity of the Gurus; and sarcastic tales were told of the vanity or stupidity of Brahmans. Abbé Dubois has preserved a specimen of these compositions, which sufficiently illustrates the popular sentiments, and may be reproduced in a condensed paraphrase:—

Dubois' story of the four Brahmans.

"Once upon a time four Brahmans were going on a journey, when they met a soldier, who cried out,—'Health to my lord!' All four replied with a benediction, and then quarrelled amongst themselves as to which of the four had been saluted by the soldier. Accordingly they ran back and put the question to the soldier, who replied that his salutation had been intended for the greatest fool of the four.

Question of the greatest fool.

"The four Brahmans next quarrelled as to which of them was the greatest fool. Accordingly they proceeded to the choultry of a neighbouring village, and put the question to the elders who were assembled there; and in order to arbitrate on this knotty point, each Brahman was called upon in turn to prove his claim to the salutation.

The dog's tail.

"The first Brahman said that a rich merchant had given him two of the finest pieces of cloth that had ever been seen in his village. He purified them by washing, and hung them out to dry, when a dog ran under them; and neither he nor his children could tell whether the dog had touched them so as to render them impure. Accordingly he crawled under the cloths on his hands and knees without touching them; but his children decided that the trial was of no

A.D. 1800.

avail, as the dog might have touched them with his turned-up tail, whilst their father had no such appendage. This decision so exasperated the Brahman that he tore the cloths to rags, and was then laughed at as the greatest fool in the village, because he might have washed the cloths a second time, or at any rate have given them to a poor Súdra.

The shaven wife.

"The second Brahman then told his story. His head had been shaved by a barber, but his wife had given the man two annas instead of one, and the barber refused to give back the extra anna. After much wrangling the barber agreed to shave the head of the Brahman's wife for nothing. The husband agreed, but the wife screamed with terror, for shaving her head was equivalent to charging her with infidelity. However the Brahman was determined not to lose his anna, and the wife was shaved by force. The result was that the wife ran away to her parents, whilst the husband was railed at as the greatest fool in the world.

The prattlers and the betel-leaf.

"The third Brahman next put in his claim. One evening he remarked that all women were prattlers. His wife replied that some men were greater prattlers than women. After some disputing it was agreed that the one who spoke first should give a leaf of betel to the other. The night passed away without a word. Morning came, but neither would speak or rise. The village was alarmed, and a multitude of Brahmans, men and women, gathered round the house fearing that the inmates were murdered. At last the carpenter broke down the door. The husband and wife were still lying on the couch, and neither would speak or move. Some of the bystanders declared that the pair were possessed of devils; and a magician was called in, but his incantations had no effect. At last a wise old Brahman brought a bar of red-hot gold in a pair of pincers, and applied it to the feet of the husband; but the man bore the torture without a word. Next the bar was tried on the wife, with a different effect; she rose up with a shriek and gave her husband a leaf of betel. The man took the leaf, saying,—'Was I not right when I said that all women were prattlers?' The multitude looked on with amazement, but when they discovered that the husband had aroused the whole village for the sake of a leaf of betel, they declared that he was the biggest fool they had ever seen.

"At last the fourth Brahman asserted his right to be regarded as the greatest fool of the four. For some years he had been betrothed to a girl, and at last she was old enough to be his wife. His mother would have fetched the damsel from her father's house, but was too sick to go. Accordingly she sent her son, but knowing him to be a brute, she implored him to be careful in his behaviour. The father of the damsel entertained his son-in-law with all hospitality, and then dismissed him with his bride. The day was excessively hot, and the road ran through a desert which scorched their feet. The damsel had been tenderly brought up, and fainted with the heat, and lay down upon the ground and declared that she wished to die. A rich merchant came up, and offered to save her life by carrying her away on one of his bullocks; he also offered twenty pagodas to her husband as the value of her ornaments. Accordingly the bridegroom parted from his bride, and went home with the twenty pagodas. When his mother heard the story she overwhelmed him with curses. Presently the wife's relations came to the village, and would have murdered him had he not fled to the jungle. As it was, the chiefs of the caste fined him two hundred pagodas, and prohibited him from ever marrying again.

A.D. 1800.

The lost bride.

"Meanwhile the elders at the choultry had been convulsed with laughter at the stories of the four Brahmans, and so had all the people who had gathered around to hear what was going on. When the fourth Brahman had finished his tale, the elders delivered their judgment. They decided that each of the four Brahmans might consider himself entitled to the salutation of the soldier; and thereupon all four rushed out of the choultry in great delight, each one declaring that he had won the cause."

Decision of the village elders.

The foregoing tale cannot be regarded as history proper; but it is a specimen of folk lore, and reveals the current of feeling which was running through Peninsular India at the beginning of the present century, and is still flowing. It will now be necessary to resume the thread of the narrative, which has been interrupted ever since the Mysore war was brought to a close by the destruction of Tippu and downfall of Seringapatam.

Resumption of the history of British India.

A.D. 1800-1801

Tanjore and the Carnatic brought under British rule.

The conquest of Mysore was followed by vital changes in Tanjore and the Carnatic, similar to those which Lord Clive had carried out in Bengal and Behar some thirty-five years before, but without the sham of Moghul suzerainty. English administration was introduced into both countries in the place of native rule; and the Raja of Tanjore and Nawab of the Carnatic were reduced to the condition of titular princes like the Nawab Nazim of Murshedabad. How far Lord Wellesley was justified in carrying out such radical reforms may be gathered from the following facts.

Tanjore Raj conquered by Mahrattas.

The Hindu Raj of Tanjore had been favoured by nature beyond all the other principalities in the Peninsula. It has already been described as the delta of the Koleroon and Káveri; a well-watered garden, vieing in fertility with the delta of the Nile, and forming the granary of Southern India. It had been conquered in the seventeenth century by a Mahratta prince of the house of Sivaji; but it was cut off from the homes of the Mahratta-speaking people in the western Dekhan by the intermediate territories of the Carnatic Nawab.[1]

Independent of Satara and Poona.

Tanjore had suffered much from the encroachments of the Moghuls, but was otherwise an independent principality. Isolated from the Mahratta empire, the Mahratta Rajas of Tanjore paid no such allegiance to the Maharajas at Satara, or Peishwas at Poona, as was paid by Sindia or Holkar, the Gaekwar or the Bhonsla of Berar. For many years the frontiers of Tanjore were oscillating, like those of the Mahratta empire; but during the eighteenth century they became fixed, and the Raj of Tanjore is described as a compact territory, seventy miles long from north to south, and sixty miles from east to west. It was bounded on the north by the Koleroon, on the east by the Bay of Bengal, on the south by the Marawar

[1] Tanjore was originally a province of the old Hindu empire of Vijayanagar. After the battle of Talikota, the Hindu viceroy or Naik became an independent Raja. Then followed intermittent wars between Tanjore and Trichinopoly. The Tanjore Raja was overpowered, and called the Mahrattas to his help. In 1680 the Mahrattas helped him with a vengeance. They saved him from destruction and then overran his territory, and took possession of his kingdom in payment for their services. See *ante*, page 176.

country,[1] and on the west by Trichinopoly and the Tondiman's country.[2] A.D. 1800-1801

Mahratta rule described by Swartz.

Swartz, the missionary, was favourably disposed towards the Raja who was reigning in 1775 when Tanjore was restored by Lord Pigot. Indeed the Raja had permitted him to preach and establish schools. But the evidence of Swartz reveals the agony of Tanjore. The people were groaning under oppression and misgovernment. The Raja was a slave in the hands of Brahmans; he lived immured in the recesses of the palace, surrounded by a multiplicity of wives, and left the administration in the hands of a rapacious minister. The cultivators were at the mercy of renters, who took sixty or seventy baskets of rice out

[1] The Marawar country is a relic of Hindu antiquity, and closely associated with the legendary wars of Ráma and Rávana. The people were primitive, and included the caste of Kalars, or hereditary robbers. In modern times the tract fell into the possession of the Rajas of Sivaganga and Ramnad, the former of whom was known as the little Marawar, whilst the latter was known as the great Marawar. The Ramnad estate was granted to the ancestors of the great Marawar, with the title of Sethipati, or "Commander-in-chief," for the defence of the road and protection of pilgrims resorting to the sacred pagoda of Ramisseram.

[2] The Tondiman was originally a Zemindar, who rendered great services to the East India Company during the wars in the Carnatic, and was rewarded by the title and dignity of Raja. One incident in the family history is suggestive of old Hindu life. There was an ancient dispute between the Tondiman and Sivaganga Rajas respecting a small tract of land about ten miles long. Generation after generation fought for this land, so that four-fifths of it became jungle, whilst the remainder was sowed sword in hand, and reaped with bloodshed. Many attempts were made to settle the dispute, but without avail. At last a Major Blackburne, Resident at Tanjore, summoned the representatives on either side to bring all their documents and vouchers. After six weeks' laborious investigation, Major Blackburne discovered beyond all doubt that most of them were forgeries. Both parties, seeing that the fact was patent, admitted that every document of importance had been fabricated for the occasion; but they confidently appealed to the boundary stones, which they swore had been set up from a remote antiquity. On inquiry however Major Blackburne found that four years previously none of the stones had been in existence. Major Blackburne then decided the case on his own authority by dividing the land equally between the Tondiman and Sivaganga Rajas, and setting up new boundary stones under the seal of the British government. By so doing he offended both parties, but he put an end to the interminable wars, and before long the whole jungle was brought under cultivation. This measure, in the eyes of natives, was one of the oppressions of British rule.

A.D. 1800-1801

of every hundred; and sometimes the entire harvest was reaped by the servants of the Raja, whilst the cultivators looked helplessly on. In 1786 it was reported that sixty-five thousand of the inhabitants had fled from Tanjore; and that many of those who remained refused to cultivate the lands unless there was a change in the administration.

Responsibility of the British government.

Unfortunately the English government at Madras was more or less responsible for this tyranny. When Lord Pigot restored Tanjore to the Raja, he engaged that there should be no interference for the future in the administration. The Madras government could consequently only remonstrate with the Raja, and its advice was thrown away. At last a committee of inspection was appointed, and Swartz was nominated a member. The Raja appealed to the pledges given him by Lord Pigot, and promised to amend his administration; but he did little or nothing, and the Madras government left matters to drift on.

Disputed succession: decision of Tanjore Pundits.

The Raja died without issue in 1787. His death was followed by a disputed succession. There was an adult half-brother, named Amar Singh, and an adopted son, aged ten, named Serfoji. The recognition of the Madras government, as the superior authority in the Peninsula, was necessary to settle the case. Accordingly, the Madras government nominated twelve Pundits, who decided against the adoption, on the ground that the boy was disqualified by reason of his age, and by being the only son of his natural father. Under such circumstances Amar Singh, the half-brother, was placed upon the throne of Tanjore by the Madras government.

Wretched rule of Amar Singh: counter-decision of Madras Pundits.

The administration of Amar Singh was as oppressive as that of his predecessor. He placed the boy Serfoji in close confinement, together with the widows of the deceased Raja. After some delay, and repeated complaints, the Madras government insisted on the liberation of the prisoners, and Serfoji and the widows were removed to Madras. Then followed a petition from Serfoji, claiming the throne of Tanjore by the right of adoption. More Pundits were consulted, who decided in favour of the adoption. The Madras government, after long and careful consideration, determined that a mistake had been made, and resolved on dethroning Amar Singh in favour of Serfoji.

A.D. 1800-1801

Orders of Lord Wellesley: a cypher Raja.

Amidst the contradictory interpretations of Sanskrit law, and the conflict of authority on the part of the Pundits, it is impossible to say who was the rightful Raja. Indeed it is impossible to say how far the Pundits on either side may have been swayed by undue influences. Swartz intimates pretty plainly that the Tanjore Pundits were bribed by Amar Singh; while it is equally probable that the Madras Pundits were bribed by Serfoji. Lord Wellesley solved the problem by placing Serfoji on the throne on the condition that the entire administration should be transferred to the Company's officers. Accordingly Serfoji was put in possession of the town and fort of Tanjore and maintained by a yearly grant of thirty-five thousand pounds, together with one-fifth of the revenues of the Raj; whilst a yearly stipend of about nine thousand pounds was awarded to the ex-Raja Amar Singh.

Carnatic affairs: treaty of 1792.

Carnatic affairs had drifted into still greater confusion. The introduction of British administration had become a crying necessity, not only for the deliverance of the people from oppression, but for the security of the East India Company's possessions in the Peninsula. In the war against Tippu in 1791-92 Lord Cornwallis had followed the example set by Lord Macartney during the invasion of Hyder Ali, and assumed the entire management of the Carnatic, as the only safeguard against underhand practices and failure of supplies. After making peace with Tippu in 1792, Lord Cornwallis concluded a treaty with Nawab Muhammad Ali, under which the Company was to assume the management of the Carnatic in all future wars, and the Nawab was pledged to carry on no correspondence whatever with any other state, native or foreign, without the sanction of the British government.

Suspicious action of the Nawab in the Mysore war, 1799.

Muhammad Ali died in 1795, and was succeeded on the throne at Arcot by his eldest son, Umdut-ul-Umra. In 1799 Lord Wellesley prepared for the conquest of Mysore; but as he purposed to make short work with Tippu, he would not hamper his operations by taking over the Carnatic. He soon regretted his forbearance. The Nawab and his officers created such obstructions at critical moments that it was impossible to avoid the suspicion that they were guilty of systematic treachery.

After the capture of Seringapatam the treachery came to

A.D. 1800-1801

Discovery of treachery at Seringapatam.

light. A clandestine correspondence was discovered which had been carried on with Tippu by both Muhammad Ali and his son Umdut-ul-Umra. Some sympathy between a Muhammadan prince at Arcot and another at Seringapatam was perhaps to be expected; although the Carnatic had been ravaged and plundered by Tippu only a few short years before. But the primary duty of Lord Wellesley was to secure the safety of the Company's rule in India; and it was impossible for him to overlook deliberate treachery, which threatened the existence of the Company, and which certainly violated the treaty of 1792, and put an end to all confidence in the future good faith of the Carnatic family.

Disputed succession: a cypher Nawab, 1801.

Umdut-ul-Umra was on his death-bed. Lord Wellesley refused to disturb his last moments; and nothing was done beyond investigating the correspondence until after his death in July, 1801. The family was then told of the treachery which had been discovered, and the resolution of the Company, that henceforth the Carnatic was to be brought under the same system of government as Tanjore and Bengal. The dynasty was not to be subverted. There was to be a titular Nawab of Arcot in the same way that there was a titular Nawab Nazim of Murshedabad; but he was no longer to exercise any civil or military authority, and the entire administration was to be transferred to the servants of the Company. There were two claimants of the throne, a son and a nephew; and the nephew was said to have a better claim to the succession because the son was illegitimate. In the first instance the throne was offered to the son of Umdut-ul-Umra, but he refused the proffered terms. It was then offered to the nephew and accepted. An allowance of about fifty thousand pounds a year was assigned to the new Nawab for his personal expenses; and a yearly grant of one-fifth of the revenues of the Carnatic was set apart for the maintenance of the family.[1]

[1] The Nawab of the town of Surat on the side of Bombay was equally dependent on the British government, equally helpless in defending the place, and equally incompetent to manage its internal affairs. In 1800 the dynasty of Surat shared the fate of that of the Carnatic. Advantage was taken of a disputed succession to assume the government and revenues of Surat, and to reduce a favoured claimant to the position of a titular pensioner.

A.D. 1800-1801

Madras Presidency predominant in the Peninsula.

By these autocratic measures Lord Wellesley put an end to the anarchy and oppression which had prevailed for centuries in Southern India. At the same time he established the British government as the dominant power in the Peninsula. British administration was introduced into the Moghul Carnatic, and into the newly-acquired territories in Mysore, from the Kistna to the Koleroon, and from the Bay of Bengal to the frontier of the Mysore Raj. It was also introduced into the countries to the south of the Koleroon; and not only Tanjore and Trichinopoly, but Tinnevelly and Madura became British territory.[1] Further to the west, on the Malabar side, Malabar proper and Kanara were in like manner brought under British administration; whilst the states of Coorg, Cochin, and Travancore were brought into feudatory relations with the British government, which have continued, with the exception of Coorg, down to our own time.[2] Thus the Madras Presidency, which was originally restricted to a sandy tract on the Coromandel coast of six miles in length and one inland, was extended westward to the coast of Malabar, northward to the Kistna and Godavari, and southward to Cape Comorin.

[1] The English collectorate of Madura includes Dindigul and the two Marawars, Sivaganga and Ramnad.

[2] The general character of these feudatory relations will be sufficiently described in the next chapter. In 1834 the Raja of Coorg declared war against the British government, and was speedily reduced by British arms. His country, at the expressed and unanimous desire of the people, was then brought under the Company's rule. The incident belongs to the administration of Lord William Bentinck, and will be told hereafter.

CHAPTER IX.

MAHRATTA WARS: WELLESLEY.

A.D. 1799 TO 1805.

A.D. 1799-1802 — Abandonment of a balance of power.

THE Mysore war did something more than establish the British government as the dominant power in the Peninsula. It put an end to the phantom of a balance of power in the Dekhan and Hindustan. The Nizam was helpless; his very existence depended on the British government. The Peishwa's government was faithless; it sent no contingent to join the forces of the English and the Nizam, and kept the envoys of Tippu at Poona long after the war began, in order to carry on underhand negotiations with the enemy. Henceforth it was for the British government, and for that government alone, to keep the peace of India by the exercise of a paramount power.

Political system of Lord Wellesley: the paramount power and its feudatories.

The political system contemplated by the Marquis of Wellesley lies in a nutshell. The native states were to surrender their international life to the British government in return for British protection. They were to make no wars, and to carry on no negotiations with any other state whatever, without the knowledge and consent of the British government. They were not to entertain Frenchmen or any other Europeans in their service, without the consent of the British government. The greater principalities were each to maintain a native force commanded by British officers for the preservation of the public peace; and they were each to cede certain territories in full sovereignty to meet the yearly charges of this force. The lesser principalities were to pay tribute to the paramount

A.D. 1799-1802

power. In return the British government was to protect them, one and all, against foreign enemies of every sort or kind. This system had already been carried out as regards the petty Hindu principalities of Travancore and Coorg, which had been left intact in the Peninsula. Its extension was now to be urged on the greater powers of the Dekhan and Hindustan.

The Nizam becomes a feudatory.

The Nizam of Hyderabad was the first to enter into the new political system; the first to become a feudatory of the British government. Nizam Ali agreed to the maintenance of a native force under British officers, known as the Hyderabad Subsidiary Force; and he ceded back to the British government all the territories which had been given him after the Mysore conquests in 1792 and 1799, to meet the charges of the Hyderabad Subsidiary Force. This was the beginning of the new political system of a British empire over native feudatories.[1]

The Peishwa refuses.

Lord Wellesley next tried to bring over the Peishwa's government to the subsidiary system. He offered to make over the remaining share of the Mysore country, provided the Peishwa would agree to the same terms as the Nizam. Baji Rao and Nana Farnavese were anxious for the proffered territory, but would not accept the conditional treaty. They urged that the Peishwa was endowed with the inherent right to collect chout for the whole of the Mysore territory; and they tried to convince Lord Wellesley that it would be politic to make over the proposed share of the Mysore conquest to the Peishwa as an equivalent for the collection of the chout throughout the whole of the Mysore territory. They met all other proposals by diplomatic evasions. The Peishwa would help the English against the French, but would not dismiss the Frenchmen in his service. He would take English battalions into his pay provided he might employ them against his refractory feudatories. But he would not accept the mediation of the English in the claims of the Mahrattas against the Nizam, nor pledge himself as regards wars or negotiations with other states or principalities.

Daulat Rao Sindia was still more refractory. He was

[1] A distinction must be made between the Hyderabad Subsidiary Force and the Hyderabad Contingent. The Contingent was a later creation.

A.D. 1799-1802

Stubbornness of Daulat Rao Sindia.

barely nineteen years of age, but he exercised a preponderating influence in the Mahratta empire, and was puffed up with exaggerated ideas of his own importance and power. Lord Wellesley refrained from exciting his suspicions by any premature disclosure of his larger political views, and only attempted to engage him in a defensive alliance against the Afghans. Lord Wellesley himself was in some alarm about the Afghans. Zeman Shah, the reigning sovereign of Afghanistan, was a grandson of the once famous Ahmad Shah Abdali, and longed to tread in the footsteps of his illustrious progenitor. In 1796 he had advanced into the Punjab as far as Lahore; but was compelled to return to Kábul the following year on account of distractions in his own territories. Later on he sent a letter to Lord Wellesley announcing his intention to invade India, and inviting the British government to help him to drive the Mahrattas out of Hindustan. Lord Wellesley forwarded this letter to Daulat Rao Sindia, and proposed an alliance between the English and Mahrattas against Zeman Shah. But Daulat Rao Sindia was not to be terrified by an Afghan invasion. The slaughter of the Mahrattas at Paniput in 1761 had died out of the memory of the rising generation. Accordingly Daulat Rao Sindia treated the letter of Zeman Shah as the idle vapourings of a distant barbarian; and refused to hamper himself with an English alliance for resisting an invasion which might never be attempted.[1]

Lord Wellesley's alarm at the Afghans.

Lord Wellesley was exasperated at the apathy of Daulat Rao Sindia, for he was seriously afraid of the Afghans. He knew nothing of their domestic wars and endless feuds; he only knew that they had more than once established a dominion in Hindustan, and must be anxious to recover their lost power. He was in great alarm lest the Afghans should invade Oude; for Oude had nothing to protect her but a few English battalions, and a rabble army, in the pay of the Nawab Vizier, that would be worse than useless in the event of an invasion.

[1] In a previous generation, when the Afghan armies of Ahmad Shah Abdali were overrunning the Punjab, and threatening Hindustan, neither the Moghuls nor the Mahrattas ever troubled themselves about the Afghans until the invaders reached Delhi. Since then thirty years had passed away. Ahmad Shah Abdali died in 1773, and his sons were too much occupied in fighting one another for the throne to attempt a renewal of their aggressions on Hindustan.

Under these circumstances Lord Wellesley called on the Nawab Vizier of Oude to disband his own army, and devote the money thus saved to the maintenance of a larger number of the Company's battalions. The Nawab Vizier refused to do anything of the kind. Lord Wellesley was imperious and peremptory; he was not disposed to give in to the Nawab Vizier as he had given in to the Peishwa and Daulat Rao Sindia. He considered that unless Hindustan was in a sufficient state of defence against the Afghans, the British empire in India would be in peril. Accordingly he compelled the Nawab Vizier to cede half his territories and revenues for the protection of the remaining half; and he devoted the additional income thus acquired to the permanent defence of Hindustan.

A.D. 1799-1802

Demands on the Nawab Vizier of Oude.

As a matter of fact the threatened invasion of Zeman Shah turned out a bugbear. In 1800 the would-be conqueror of Hindustan was dethroned and blinded by one of his brothers, and ultimately compelled to seek a refuge in British territory. But Lord Wellesley had no means of knowing what was going on. Kábul in those days was associated with the invasions of Timúr, Nadir Shah, and Ahmad Shah Abdali; and for aught Lord Wellesley knew to the contrary, hosts of Tartars and Afghans might have rushed into Hindustan like a destroying flood. Moreover no help was to be expected from native princes. The Mahrattas would have held aloof and played a waiting game. The Muhammadans expected Zeman Shah to deliver them from the English. The Rajpúts expected him to deliver them from the Mahrattas. Then again there was no knowing what the French might be doing in the background. Under such circumstances Lord Wellesley was driven by the instinct of self-preservation to take extreme measures for the permanent defence of Hindustan against foreign invaders.

Justification of Lord Wellesley.

Meanwhile Lord Wellesley turned an anxious eye towards Persia. During the anarchy which followed the assassination of Nadir Shah in 1747, the old trade between Bombay and Persia had dwindled away. Persia was the theatre of bloody struggles between the Persian and the Turkoman, otherwise known as the Zend and the Kajar. For a brief interval the Zend gained the mastery, but in 1794 was compelled to succumb to the Kajar, amidst massacres and atrocities too horrible for description. A Kajar dynasty was

Persian affairs: triumph of the Kajar over the Zend.

A.D. 1799-1802

founded by Agha Muhammad Khan. For a brief interval it was exposed to Russian aggression.[1] Subsequently there was reason to suspect that it might be made an instrument of French intrigue. Accordingly, having got rid of Tippu as a creature of the French in the southern Peninsula, it was natural that Lord Wellesley should provide against any possible danger that might be brewing to the north-west of Hindustan.

Malcolm's mission to Persia, 1800.

In 1800 Lord Wellesley sent Captain John Malcolm on a mission to Persia, to create a diversion against Zeman Shah on the side of Khorassan, and to counteract any designs that might be entertained by France. The mission has left no mark in history; but Malcolm was a man of his time, and destined to play an important part in the later affairs of India. He distinguished himself in Persia by a lavish distribution of presents amongst the Shah and his courtiers, who were equally poor, vain, and mercenary; and he concluded a treaty, under which the Shah agreed to act, if necessary, against Zeman Shah, and to exclude all Frenchmen from his dominions.[2]

Mahratta affairs: death of Nana Farnavese, 1800.

Meanwhile the progress of Mahratta affairs had engaged the anxious attention of Lord Wellesley. In 1800, Nana Farnavese, the famous Mahratta minister, was gathered to his fathers. He was a Brahman statesman of the old Hindu type. For many years he had grasped the real power, and treated the late Peishwa, Mahdu Narain Rao, as a child; but Baji Rao, the successor af Mahdu Narain, was older, more experienced, and consequently more troublesome, and

[1] The Kajar conqueror, Agha Muhammad Khan, was extending his conquests to the eastward, when he was called away by Russian aggression in Georgia; but he was saved by the death of Catherine the Second in 1796, and the unexpected recall of the Russian army by her son and successor the Emperor Paul. In 1797 Agha Muhammad Khan was assassinated, and after another interval of wars and distractions, was succeeded by his nephew, Futih Ali Shah, the second sovereign of the Kajar dynasty, who died in 1834.

[2] John Malcolm belonged to the old military school of political officers. In 1783 he landed at Madras as a boy ensign of fourteen. In 1784 he took charge of the prisoners surrendered by Tippu after the treaty of Mangalore, and caused some amusement on the occasion by reason of his extreme youth. In 1791 he distinguished himself in the Mysore war under Lord Cornwallis. In 1798 he took an active part in the disbandment of the Nizam's French battalions. He was only thirty-one when he was sent by Lord Wellesley on his mission to Persia.

was for ever intriguing against his authority. The death of Nana Farnavese released Baji Rao from a state of ministerial thraldom, but exposed him more than ever to the galling dictation of Daulat Rao Sindia. Shortly afterwards Sindia was called away to the northward by disorders which had broken out in Holkar's territory; and Baji Rao was left alone at Poona to follow his own devices without any interference whatever.

A.D. 1799-1802

Affairs of Holkar: foundation of Indore.

The dominion founded in Malwa by Mulhar Rao Holkar was at this period passing through a crisis, which tempted the interference of Daulat Rao Sindia. Ailah Bai, the daughter-in-law of Mulhar Rao, had carried on the civil administration of the state ever since his death in 1767.[1] She had transformed the village of Indore into a wealthy capital; and henceforth the name of Indore was applied to the state as well as to the capital. She died in 1795, leaving the state of Indore in the sole possession of her commander-in-chief. Tukaji Holkar.

Troubles in the Holkar family: rise of Jaswant Rao Holkar.

Tukaji Holkar died in 1797, leaving two legitimate sons, one of whom was an imbecile. Daulat Rao Sindia hurried away from Poona to Indore, and played the part of a suzerain. He placed the imbecile son of Tukaji Holkar on the throne, and put the other in prison and eventually murdered him; his object being to render his own influence paramount at Indore. But an illegitimate son of Tukaji appeared upon the scene under the name of Jaswant Rao Holkar. This man had no pretensions to the throne, for they were barred by the baseness of his birth. He had professed to be the partisan of the half-brother whom Sindia had set aside; but when the half-brother was murdered, Jaswant Rao fled to the jungles and turned outlaw and freebooter after Rajpút fashion. He was joined by a host of the predatory rascals who infested Central India at this period,—Bhíls, Pindharies, Afghans, and Mahrattas. In this fashion he became so formidable that Daulat Rao Sindia was compelled to march against him with a large army and attempt to suppress him by main force.

The army of Jaswant Rao Holkar was reckoned at twenty thousand men, all of whom were maintained by plunder. It is needless to dwell upon the details of rapine,

[1] See *ante*, page 343.

A.D. 1799-1802

Defeat of Jaswant Rao Holkar.

desolation and bloodshed which characterised his proceedings, and rendered him the pest of Malwa and Berar. In October, 1801, he was attacked and routed by Sindia and his French battalions; but defeat in those days was of little avail in suppressing a freebooting chief, whose name alone was a tower of strength for outlaws and refugees of every kind, and a rallying point for all the brigands and blackguards in Central India.

Cruelties of Baji Rao at Poona.

Meanwhile Baji Rao was free from all restraint. Nana Farnavese was dead, and Daulat Rao Sindia was busied in establishing his influence over the territory of the Holkar family in Indore. Accordingly, the young Peishwa at Poona pursued a wild career of revenge upon all his enemies, real or supposed. It would be tedious to dwell on his acts of savage ferocity; a single instance will serve as a type. A brother of Jaswant Rao Holkar had given some offence, or committed some crime, and was condemned to die by being dragged through the streets of Poona tied to the foot of an elephant. Baji Rao was not only deaf to the humblest prayers for mercy, but revelled in the sufferings of his victim. He looked on with delight whilst the wretched man was being dragged by the elephant from the palace yard, and filling the air with his shrieks at the prospect of a death of lingering agony.

Jaswant Rao Holkar at Poona.

Baji Rao had soon reason to repent of his cruelty. News arrived at Poona that Jaswant Rao had re-assembled his scattered forces, inflicted some small defeats on Daulat Rao Sindia, and was marching to Poona to be revenged on the Peishwa for the tortures which had been inflicted on his brother.

Defeat of the Peishwa, 1802.

Baji Rao was in great consternation. He was half inclined to agree to the treaty with the English, and accept their protection. Sindia, however, prevented the British alliance for a while by despatching a large force to reassure the Peishwa. In October, 1802, the decisive battle of Poona changed the fate of the Mahratta empire. The united armies of Sindia and the Peishwa were defeated by Jaswant Rao Holkar; and Baji Rao fled for his life to the western coast, and escaped on board an English ship to the port of Bassein, about twenty miles to the northward of Bombay.

Baji Rao was paralysed by the disaster. Another Peishwa

was set up by Jaswant Rao Holkar at Poona, and Baji Rao saw nothing before him but ruin. In this extremity he agreed to sign the obnoxious treaty, provided the English restored him to his throne at Poona. Accordingly the treaty of Bassein was concluded on the last day of December, 1802.

A.D. 1802-1803

Treaty of Bassein, 31st Dec. 1802.

By the treaty of Bassein Baji Rao severed all the ties which bound the Mahratta princes to him as Peishwa, lord paramount, and suzerain. He absolutely abdicated the headship of the Mahratta empire. He pledged himself to hold no communication with any other power, not even with the great feudatories of the empire, such as Sindia and Holkar, the Gaekwar and the Berar Raja, without the consent of the British government. He also ceded territory for the maintenance of a Poona Subsidiary Force. He thus secured his restoration to the throne of Poona; but, as far as treaties were binding, he had ceased to be lord paramount of the Mahratta empire; he had transferred his suzerainty to the East India Company; and henceforth was bound hand and foot as a feudatory of the British government.

The Peishwa becomes a feudatory.

The treaty of Bassein is a turning-point in the history of India. It established the British empire as the paramount power in India, but it rendered a Mahratta war inevitable. It was impossible for a Mahratta prince of Baji Rao's character and surroundings to fulfil the obligations involved in such a treaty; he was certain, sooner or later, to attempt to recover the lost headship of the Mahratta empire. It was equally impossible for Daulat Rao Sindia to respect the terms of a treaty which shut him out from the grand object of his ambition, namely, to rule the Mahratta empire in the name of the Peishwa.

Objections to the treaty of Bassein.

In 1803 Baji Rao was conducted by a British force from Bassein to Poona. The Madras army under Colonel Wellesley, and the new Hyderabad Subsidiary Force under Colonel Stevenson, were moving up from the south in the same direction for his protection. Yet at this very time Baji Rao was secretly imploring Daulat Rao Sindia and the Bhonsla Raja of Berar to march to his assistance, and deliver him from the English supremacy.[1]

Treachery of the restored Peishwa.

[1] Mudaji Bhonsla died in 1788, and was succeeded on the throne of Berar by his eldest son Rughoji Bhonsla, who reigned twenty-eight years, and died in 1816. Baji Rao was imploring the help of Rughoji Bhonsla.

A.D. 1803.

Stupefaction of Sindia and the Bhonsla.

Sindia and the Bhonsla had each taken the field with a large army, and were restlessly moving near the western frontier of the Nizam's dominions. They were closely watched by Wellesley and Stevenson, but they were stupefied by the treaty of Bassein, and knew not what to do. They had no particular regard for Baji Rao; indeed they were opposed in theory to the supremacy of the Brahman Peishwas. Daulat Rao Sindia had long been intriguing to gain the ascendency at Poona, and rule the Mahratta feudatories in the name of the Peishwa; whilst every successive Raja of Berar nursed the design of overthrowing the Brahmanical supremacy, and seizing the throne at Poona as the representative of Sivaji. But both Sindia and the Bhonsla preferred the Brahman sovereignty to the British; and they hesitated to conclude treaties with Lord Wellesley, or to begin a war.

Crafty proceedings of Jaswant Rao Holkar.

Meanwhile both Sindia and the Bhonsla used every effort to induce Jaswant Rao to join them. They were prepared to make any sacrifice; to ignore the legitimate branch of Holkar's family, and to acknowledge Jaswant Rao as Mahá-raja of Indore. But Jaswant Rao was richly endowed with the craft and cunning of his race. He was profuse in promises to join the allies against the English; and by these means he procured from Sindia and the Bhonsla all the recognition and countenance he wanted; and then he went back to Indore, to strengthen his position and await the result of the expected collision with the English. At Indore he received repeated invitations from Sindia and the Bhonsla; but he replied to all with seeming frankness,—"If I join you in the Dekhan, who is to take care of Hindustan?"

Alarm of Lord Wellesley at Sindia's French battalions.

All this while Lord Wellesley was full of alarms at the presence of Sindia's French battalions between the Jumna and the Ganges. De Boigne had returned to Europe, and was succeeded in the command by a violent French republican named Perron, who was known to be hostile to the English. Perron collected the revenues of the Doab for the maintenance of his French battalions; and the imagination of Lord Wellesley was so fired by his fear and hatred of the French, that he pictured Perron as a French sovereign of upper Hindustan, with the Great Moghul under his thumb, and unbounded resources at his command.

A.D. 1803.

Alarm at the designs of Napoleon.

The state of affairs in Europe gave a fresh impetus to these alarms. Napoleon's expedition to Egypt had revealed the vastness of his ambition. The young Corsican was prepared to march in the footsteps of the great Macedonian from Egypt to Persia, and from Persia to Hindustan. The peace of Amiens in 1802 was only an interval of preparation for grand designs. News of a renewal of the war between Great Britain and France was expected by every ship from Europe; and many besides Lord Wellesley imagined that the imperial dreamer at the Tuileries was still longing to outdo Alexander by conquering the oriental world from the Mediterranean to the mouths of the Ganges.

Fears of a French landing at Baroche.

Lord Wellesley brooded over the map of India with a jealous eye. He pondered over every vulnerable spot on the coast of India where a French armament could anchor. He was especially alarmed at the convenient position of Baroche on the western coast to the northward of Surat. Baroche was a port belonging to Sindia, situated at the mouth of the Nerbudda river. Accordingly, the fevered imagination of Lord Wellesley was again at work. He pictured a French armament sailing down the Red Sea, and across the Indian Ocean, to Sindia's port of Baroche; a French flotilla going up the Nerbudda river from Baroche to the neighbourhood of Indore; a French army marching through Malwa, followed by a host of Mahrattas and Rajpúts, joining Perron at Agra and Delhi, and pretending to conquer India in the name of the Great Moghul.[1]

Instructions to General Lake.

At this time, General Lake, commander-in-chief of the Bengal army, was posted at Cawnpore on the frontier of Oude. He was told by Lord Wellesley that a Mahratta war was impending; and that directly the war note was sounded he was to march towards Delhi, break up Sindia's French battalions, and occupy the whole territory between the Jumna and the Ganges.

Meanwhile Colonels Wellesley and Stevenson continued to watch Sindia and the Bhonsla in the Dekhan. Sindia was still waiting to be joined by the recreant Jaswant Rao

[1] Baroche, or Broach, had fallen into the possession of the English, together with other territories in Guzerat, during the first Mahratta war in the days of Warren Hastings, but had been needlessly and heedlessly made over to Mahadaji Sindia at the treaty of Salbai in 1782. See *ante*, page 374.

A.D. 1803.

Hostile tone of Sindia in the Dekhan.

Holkar, but his language as regards the British government and its allies was more hostile. He threw out hints to the British Resident, who accompanied his camp, that he meant to collect chout in the Nizam's territory. He was doubtful, he said, whether there would be peace or war between the Mahrattas and the English; and he could arrive at no decision on this point until he had talked the matter over with the Bhonsla Raja of Berar.

Professions of friendship.

Sindia had a meeting with the Bhonsla, but nothing was decided. The two chiefs professed to be the friends of the British government, but naturally cavilled at the treaty of Bassein. They said they ought to have been consulted before it was concluded, and that many of the articles required more discussion.

Wellesley's test.

In August, 1803, Colonel Wellesley put an end to these vacillations. "If," he said, "Sindia and the Bhonsla are such friends of the British government as they profess to be, let them prove their sincerity by marching back their armies to their respective dominions." Sindia replied that the English ought to set the example; in other words, that the English were to leave Sindia and the Bhonsla with their armies of freebooters to threaten the frontier of the Nizam, whilst Wellesley returned to Madras and Stevenson withdrew to Hyderabad. Sindia forgot that he had threatened to plunder the Nizam's dominions, and had doubted whether there was to be peace or war. Sindia was accordingly told that it was he, and not the British government, who had broken the peace, and that therefore he must take the consequences.

Second Mahratta war, 1803.

Thus began the second Mahratta war. The Resident left Sindia's camp. Sindia and the Bhonsla moved towards the south-east, as if to threaten Hyderabad; but their operations were feeble and undecided. They marched and countermarched more to delay action than to carry out any definite plan.

Victory at Assaye, September, 1803.

At last Wellesley and Stevenson agreed to make a combined attack on the united armies. By some accident Wellesley alone came upon the enemy near the village of Assaye on the Nizam's frontier, and resolved to fight a battle single-handed. His force only numbered four thousand five hundred men, whilst that of the Mahrattas numbered fifty thousand. The battle of Assaye was fought on the 23rd of

September, 1803. The Bhonsla Raja fled at the first shot, and Sindia soon followed his example. The Mahratta artillery, however, worked great execution; and Wellesley only won the battle by cavalry and infantry charges. It was the clashing of a fiery few of Europeans against a host of Mahrattas; and the fiery few won the day.[1] The victory was decisive, but one-third of the European force in the British army lay dead or wounded on the field.

A.D. 1803.

End of the Dekhan campaign, December, 1803.

The victory of Assaye was followed by the capture of fortresses, and another victory at Argaum. It would be tedious to dwell on the details of the military operations, which, however much they redounded to the credit of the youthful Wellesley, were destined to be overshadowed by the glories of the Peninsula and Waterloo. It will suffice to say that by the end of the year 1803 the Dekhan campaign was over, and Sindia and the Bhonsla sued for peace.

Lake's campaign in Hindustan: battles of Alighur and Delhi.

Meanwhile General Lake had carried on another brilliant campaign in Hindustan. He left Cawnpore in August, 1803, defeated Perron's cavalry at Alighur, and captured the Alighur fortress. He next marched on to Delhi, defeated the French infantry, and entered the capital of the Moghuls as a hero and a conqueror. More than forty years previously the last representative of the dynasty of the Great Mogul, the unfortunate Shah Alam, had fled from Delhi to Bengal, and taken refuge with the English. Ten years later he fled back from his protected retreat at Allahabad to the city of his fathers under the wing of the Mahrattas. In 1803 he was pondering over his deliverance from the Mahrattas, and the advent of his English protectors at the capital of Aurangzeb and tomb of Humáyun.

Settlement with Shah Alam.

The imperial family were much excited by the arrival of the English army. Some finery and tinsel were furbished up to enable the blind and aged Shah Alam to give a reception to the English general. The tottering descendant of Aurangzeb then placed himself under British protection; and was left to dwell in the palace, supported by a liberal pension from the British government.

[1] "This is he that far away
Against the myriads of Assaye
Clash'd with a fiery few and won."

TENNYSON'S *Ode on the Death of the Duke of Wellington.*

A.D. 1803-1804

End of the campaign in Hindustan.

General Lake left the city of Delhi in charge of Colonel Ochterlony, and brought the campaign to a close by the capture of Agra and victory at Laswari. The battle of Laswari broke up the French battalions for ever, and put the English in possession of the whole of upper Hindustan.

Perron in private life.

The fate of Perron was somewhat extraordinary. At the very beginning of the campaign he appeared as a suppliant to the English general. He was in bad odour with Sindia; his life was in danger; and he was anxious to retire to British territory with his private fortune. Permission was granted, and Perron ultimately took up his abode in the French settlement at Chandernagore, and then dropped into oblivion.

Sindia and the Bhonsla become feudatories.

Sindia and the Bhonsla had no alternative but to accept the dictation of the British government. Accordingly they concluded treaties on the basis of the treaty of Bassein. Sindia renounced all pretensions to the regions northward of the Jumna and westward of the Chambal; all hold on the Great Moghul; all claims to collect chout or plunder from the Rajpúts, Játs, or other native princes. To all appearance his power for mischief had gone for ever.[1] The Bhonsla

[1] The negotiations with Daulat Rao Sindia were conducted by Major Malcolm and General Wellesley. Sindia's prime minister was a veteran Brahman and born diplomatist, with a sour, supercilious, inflexible countenance, which nothing could disturb. The most startling demand or unexpected concession was received without the movement of a muscle. Malcolm said that he never saw a man with such a face for a game of brag; and henceforth the grey-haired Mahratta went by the name of "Old Brag." Years passed away, and Wellesley returned to Europe and became Duke of Wellington. Malcolm met him and asked him about Talleyrand. Wellington replied that he was very much like "Old Brag," but not so clever.

Negotiations under such circumstances were not easy. Malcolm went to Sindia's camp, and found the young Maháraja almost as grave as his minister. A meeting took place in a large tent amidst a storm of rain. Suddenly a volume of water burst in torrents through the canvas, and fell upon an Irish officer named Pepper. The Maharaja screamed with laughter at the catastrophe, and all present joined in the chorus. All gravity was at an end. The rain was followed by a storm of hail, and the diplomatists and their followers fell to work at collecting the hailstones, which are as refreshing as ices in the hot plains of India.

But nothing could stop the pertinacity of "Old Brag." On a subsequent occasion he demanded that an article should be inserted in the treaty that out of respect for the caste of Brahmans of which the Peishwa was a member, and out of friendship for Maharaja Sindia, and

Raja belonged to a smaller fry. He ceded Cuttack on the east and Berar on the west; and was henceforth known as the Raja of Nagpore. But Lord Wellesley was afraid to vaunt his conquests in the eyes of the people of England, unless he could prove that they were necessary for protection against the French. He kept possession of Cuttack because it was the only vulnerable tract on the Bay of Bengal that was open to invasion from the sea; but he made over the territory of Berar proper as a free gift to the Nizam of Hyderabad.

A.D. 1803-1804

Complection of Lord Wellesley's political system: Holkar excepted, 1804.

In 1804 Lord Wellesley had completed his political scheme for the government of India. The Gaekwar of Baroda accepted the situation, and ceded territory for the maintenance of a Subsidiary Force. The Rajpút princes and theJát Raja of Bhurtpore gladly surrendered their old international life, with all its wars and feuds, for the sake of protection against the Mahrattas. The cession of Cuttack by the Berar Raja removed the only break on the British line of seaboard from Calcutta to Comorin. Only one power of the slightest moment remained outside the pale of the new political system; and that was Jaswant Rao, the Mahratta freebooter who had usurped the throne of Holkar.

Status of Jaswant Rao Holkar: objections to a protective alliance.

In those days the British government had no interest or concern in the rightness or wrongness of Jaswant Rao's pretensions. It was in no way responsible for his usurpation, for that had begun before the subsidiary treaties were concluded with the other Mahratta powers. The British government might have arbitrated, but it could not force the people of Indore, nor the Mahratta princes in general, to accept its arbitration. It could not conclude any subsidiary or protective treaty, which would guarantee Jaswant Rao Holkar in the dominions of the Holkar family; because, according to the common understanding of the Mahratta states, Jaswant Rao Holkar was a rebel against the Peishwa, and an illegitimate son of the late ruler, whilst the legitimate

for the purpose of increasing its own reputation, the British government should prohibit the slaughter of cows throughout Hindustan. Such a wholesale demand was perilous to the well-being of European soldiers, to say nothing of Englishmen in general, who are supposed to owe their superiority to beef. Accordingly the proposition was rejected as inadmissible.

A.D. 1803-1804

heir was still alive. But Lord Wellesley was willing to leave Jaswant Rao alone, provided only that he abstained from all aggressions upon the territories of the British government, or upon those of its allies.

Predatory instincts of Jaswant Rao Holkar.

But Jaswant Rao was a free lance of the old Mahratta type; a man of the stamp of Sivaji with the instinct of a freebooter running in his blood. He did not aspire to be a warrior and hero like the Sindias. He preferred plunder to political power; and consequently took more delight in commanding loose bodies of predatory horsemen, like another Sivaji, than in directing the movements of drilled battalions of infantry, like Mahadaji Sindia or Daulat Rao. It was the boast of Jaswant Rao Holkar that his home was in the saddle, and that his dominions extended over every country that could be reached by his horsemen.

Formidable power in 1804.

In 1803, whilst English and Mahrattas were engaged in wars in the Dekhan and upper Hindustan, Jaswant Rao Holkar collected a golden harvest in Malwa and Rajpútana. Subsequently he was joined by deserters or fugitives from Sindia and the Bhonsla; and but for the presence of the English in Hindustan might have become the most formidable predatory power in Central India.

Ideas of Jaswant Rao.

But Jaswant Rao Holkar was ill at ease. He was an Esau amongst the Mahratta powers, without fear or love for any one of them. He was alarmed at the victories of the English. It was obvious to his mind, moulded by Mahratta culture, that he had an inherent right to collect chout, which the English were bound to respect. As a matter of fact, he could not keep his forces together without plunder or chout. But he feared that the English were unable or unwilling to recognise the sacred rights of the Mahrattas, and were bent on putting a stop to his future expeditions.

Rebuffed by General Lake.

Jaswant Rao proceeded to work upon the English with all the wariness of a Mahratta. He wrote an arrogant letter to General Lake, full of pretensions as regards what he called his rights, but still professing much friendship. He continued the work of collecting chout and plunder from the protected allies in Rajpútana, and at the same time he urged them to throw off their dependence on the British government. He was told by General Lake that the English had no desire to interfere with him, but that it was absolutely necessary that he should withdraw to Indore territory, and abstain from all aggressions on the British government or its allies. A.D. 1803-1804

Jaswant Rao then took a more decided tone. He requested permission to levy chout according to the customs of his ancestors. He offered to conclude a treaty, provided the British government would guarantee him in the possession of Indore territory. But he refused to withdraw from Rajpútana until the English complied with his demands. He wrote letters still more peremptory to General Wellesley in the Dekhan, threatening to burn, sack, and slaughter by hundreds of thousands in the event of refusal. He invited Daulat Rao Sindia to join him in an attack upon British possessions; but Sindia was already disgusted with his duplicity, and not only refused to have anything more to do with such a faithless chieftain, but reported Jaswant Rao's proffered alliance to the British authorities. Arrogant demands and threats.

There was no alternative but to reduce Jaswant Rao to submission. General Lake was ordered to move southward into Rajpútana, whilst General Wellesley moved northward from the Dekhan; and Jaswant Rao would then have been hemmed in between the two armies, and compelled to surrender at discretion. But there was a famine in the Dekhan; the rains had failed, and the country had been ravaged by the armies of Sindia and the Bhonsla. General Wellesley could not move from the Dekhan, but ordered Colonel Murray to march from Guzerat towards Malwa with a sufficient force to co-operate with any force which might be sent by General Lake. Daulat Rao Sindia also offered to co-operate with the English for the reduction of Jaswant Rao, whom he declared had forfeited all claim to consideration from his treacherous refusal to join the allied Mahratta armies before the battle of Assaye. Preparations for war against Jaswant Rao Holkar.

In April, 1804, General Lake moved an army into Rajputana, and sent a detachment in advance under Colonel Monson. Jaswant Rao beat a hasty retreat through Rajpútana towards Indore territory in the south. In May the English force captured Holkar's fortress of Rampoora, known as Tonk-Rampoora. The rains were now approaching, and General Lake left Colonel Monson to keep Jaswant Rao in check, and then returned to cantonments. General Lake in Rajpútana: retreat of Jaswant Rao.

The force under Colonel Monson consisted of five

A.D. 1804.

Monson's advance into Holkar's territory.

battalions of sepoys, a train of artillery, and two bodies of irregular horse, one under a Lieutenant Lucan, and the other under Bapoji Sindia, a kinsman of Daulat Rao. In June Monson crossed the river Chambal and reached Kotah, and was joined by a body of troops in the service of the Rajpút ruler of Kotah, who was anxious for the friendship of the British government. Monson was daily expecting to be joined by Murray with the force from Guzerat, as well as by a force which Daulat Rao Sindia promised to send from Ujain. Accordingly he advanced through the pass of Mokundra into Holkar's territory, and continued his march some fifty miles further to the southward.

Untoward events.

In the beginning of July Colonel Monson was staggered by a succession of untoward events. His supplies were running very low.. Treachery was in his camp of which he was ignorant; Bapoji Sindia was sending secret messages to Jaswant Rao to turn back and advance against the English brigade. Next Monson heard that Colonel Murray had taken fright and was retreating to Guzerat; and that Jaswant Rao had stayed his onward flight and turned back, and was marching against him with overwhelming forces, and a vast train of artillery.

Monson's retreat to the Mokundra pass.

Colonel Monson ordered a retreat to Mokundra pass, leaving the irregular horse to follow. Shortly afterwards Bapoji Sindia came up with a story that Jaswant Rao had routed the irregular horse, and that Lucan was taken prisoner. Monson reached the Mokundra pass; and Bapoji Sindia filled up the measure of his iniquity by deserting the English and going over bodily to Jaswant Rao with all his horsemen. Shortly afterwards Monson was attacked by the whole army of Holkar, but succeeded in repulsing the enemy.

Retreat to Kotah and Agra.

Unfortunately, instead of holding out at the Mokundra pass, Colonel Monson continued his retreat to Kotah. The ruler of Kotah lost heart at seeing the fugitives, and shut his gates against them. The rainy season was at its height. Colonel Monson continued his retreat towards the north, but his supplies were exhausted, and his guns sank hopelessly in the mud. He was obliged to spike his guns and destroy his ammunition to prevent their falling into the hands of the enemy. Sindia's commander came up to join him with the expected detachment from Ujain: but when the Mahratta saw the wretched state of the fugitives, he turned his guns upon the English force and went over to Jaswant Rao. It is needless to dwell on further details of disasters in crossing rivers, and privations and sufferings beneath the pitiless rains. The retreat became a disorderly rout, during which the English sepoys were constantly exposed to the charges and surprises of Jaswant Rao Holkar. About the end of August, 1804, the shattered remains of Monson's brigade managed to reach Agra.

A.D. 1804-1805

Disastrous political results.

Monson's retreat was one of those disasters which will upset the designs of the ablest statesmen. The political system of Lord Wellesley was in imminent danger. For a brief interval British prestige vanished from Hindustan. Jaswant Rao Holkar was exaggerated into a Mahratta hero, and was joined by most of the predatory bands of Central India. Even the Rajpút and Ját princes, the protected allies of the British government, were shaken in their allegiance by the successes of the victorious Mahratta.

Jaswant Rao Holkar at Muttra, Delhi, and Bhurtpore.

Jaswant Rao took possession of Muttra, and then with happy audacity hastened to Delhi, to seize Shah Alam, and plunder Hindustan in the name of the Great Moghul. He was beaten off from Delhi by a small force under Ochterlony; but meanwhile a new ally had sprung up in his rear. The Ját Raja of Bhurtpore threw off his dependence on the British government, and declared in favour of Jaswant Rao Holkar. The fortress of Bhurtpore was the strongest in Hindustan. The huge walls of hardened mud rose round the city like a rampart of mountains. They were a godsend to Jaswant Rao. He sent his guns and infantry within the walls, and began to ravage the Doab with his army of horsemen, like a Tartar Khan of the olden time.

Lake defeats Holkar and besieges Bhurtpore, 1805.

General Lake took the field with his cavalry, and soon routed and dispersed the Mahratta horse. The English captured the fortress of Deeg, which also belonged to the Bhurtpore Raja. But then, instead of completing the destruction of Jaswant Rao, General Lake advanced against Bhurtpore, and endeavoured to capture the impregnable fortress without even a siege-train. For a period of four months, from January 1805 to the following April, he wasted the strength of the English army in trying to storm these enormous earthworks. To make matters worse, Daulat Rao

A.D. 1805.

Sindia threw off his allegiance to the British government, and declared for Jaswant Rao Holkar.

Submission of Bhurtpore and Sindia: arrival of Lord Cornwallis, July, 1805.

The fortunes of the English soon began to brighten. The Raja of Bhurtpore grew frightened, and was restored to the protected alliance on paying a fine of two hundred thousand pounds to the British government. Subsequent defeats inflicted on Jaswant Rao brought Daulat Rao Sindia to his senses. Difficulties were being removed, and tranquillity was about to be restored, when negotiations were upset by the home authorities. At the end of July, 1805, Lord Cornwallis landed at Calcutta, and took up the office of Governor-General, and the policy of the British government underwent an important change. Shortly afterwards Lord Wellesley returned to England.

Genius and policy of Wellesley.

Lord Wellesley was a statesman of the highest order, who brought the political experiences of western culture to bear upon the conditions of Asiatic rule. His genius was untrammelled by the narrow ideas which grew out of a trading monopoly, and which swayed the better judgment of Robert Clive and Warren Hastings. He valued the security and prestige of the British empire in India at a higher rate than the commercial privileges of the East India Company; and consequently he raised up a host of enemies, who could not appreciate his comprehensive foresight. But, in the teeth of all opposition, he established the sovereignty of the British government over the greater part of India, and put an end for ever to the English-born fantasy of a balance of power.

Wellesley and Akbar.

Lord Wellesley has been compared with Akbar. Consciously or unconsciously, he sought to build up a British empire in India on similar foundations to those of the Moghul empire of Akbar. He avoided, however, the spirit of oriental intrigue, which balanced one element of race or religion against another; and he laboured to provide for the peace and security of India by establishing the British government as a paramount power over Moghuls and Mahrattas, and protecting the chieftains of Rajpútana against the predatory incursions of Sindia and Holkar. He formed a school of political officers, whose aspirations were linked with the well-being of the British empire, rather than with the maintenance of the Company's monopoly; and thus he

A.D. 1805.

led to the identification of British interests with those of India, which has been the main work of the nineteenth century. Small in stature and imperious in will, he was known to his admirers as the "glorious little man;" and as long as the Anglo-Indian empire retains a place in history, the name of the Marquis of Wellesley will rank amongst its most illustrious founders.

Errors of Wellesley the outcome of genius.

Lord Wellesley was led into errors, but they were the errors of genius—the outcome of a foresight which credits enemies with the entertainment of designs beyond their power of execution. Wellesley gauged the ambition of the first Napoleon, and foreshadowed the dreams which would have carried a French army from the Mediterranean to the Ganges; but he overrated the resources as well as the prescience of the imperial dreamer, and he underrated the obstructions and difficulties which beset Napoleon in Europe, and checked his advance in the footsteps of Alexander. He provided for the defence of India against plans which had no real existence, excepting in his own imagination, but which nevertheless might have proved substantial dangers had Napoleon been a Wellesley, or Wellesley a Napoleon.

Remodelling of the Indian Civil Service.

Lord Wellesley was the founder of the Indian Civil Service on its existing footing. The old servants of the Company were emphatically merchants; and he rightly considered that mercantile training is of small use to civil administrators in comparison with a knowledge of history, law, political economy, and Indian languages. Moreover, during the old commercial period, money-making too often became a master passion, and certainly exercised an undue influence on the Indian rulers of the eighteenth century. With these views Lord Wellesley founded a College on a grand scale at Calcutta, with a competent staff of professors, for the special education of young civilians fresh from Europe; and although his plans were dwarfed for a while into insignificance by the Court of Directors, yet in the end they led to the establishment of a College at Haileybury, which served as a training-school for Indian civil servants until the introduction of the competitive system in comparatively modern times.

CHAPTER X.

CONCILIATION: LORD CORNWALLIS, SIR GEORGE BARLOW, AND LORD MINTO.

A.D. 1805 TO 1813.

A.D. 1805-1807 — Reaction against Lord Wellesley's imperial policy.

THE second coming of Lord Cornwallis to India was the result of a political reaction. The British nation was alarmed at Lord Wellesley's conquests, and his large assumption of political power. It was always averse to territorial aggrandisement except for colonial purposes, or to humble France; and it was especially averse to conquests in India, which provided no outlet for the superfluous population of England, but only transferred large provinces from the government of native princes to that of the servants of the East India Company. The Directors themselves were equally alarmed at the extension of their dominion and responsibilities; for they had learned by bitter experience that wars and conquests only added to the expenditure, without increasing the profits of the Company, or otherwise promoting the interests of trade. Above all, neither the British nation nor the Company could understand the new political dogma, that India could only be governed in peace by reducing her princes to the condition of feudatories, and setting up the British government as the paramount power. The policy of Lord Wellesley savoured too much of that of Napoleon to be acceptable to the people of England; and it was accordingly attacked on all sides tooth and nail.

The real fact was that the native powers in India were not states after the European model. They were for the most part new and crude principalities, which had grown up

A.D. 1805-1807

Popular errors respecting native powers.

within the previous half century.[1] Rebel Muhammadan Viceroys had thrown off their dependence on the Great Moghul, and converted their provinces into kingdoms. Mahratta freebooters had created an empire over feudatory princes on the basis of plunder; and their dominions had been consolidated by Brahmans, who played the part of ministers, accountants, and collectors of revenue. There were no political constitutions or hereditary aristocracies in either the Moghul or the Mahratta empires; nothing but bodies of officials, organised chiefly for the collection of revenue, bound by no national ties, and only held together by a system of red-tape and routine, which in times of revolution or disaster was either broken up or dwindled into hereditary names and sinecures.

Contrast between European states and native principalities.

The older states of Europe may have been created in a similar fashion; but they have endured for a thousand years, and the traditional experiences of a past history have converted subject populations into nationalities, and rude warrior barons into landed nobilities. The kingdoms of India, with the exception of the Rajpút principalities, were things of yesterday, without national life or organisation. The kingdoms of Europe had undergone a political training under kings and emperors, parliaments, popes, and priests, which had moulded them into substantive states, quickened them with international life, and fitted them for the exercise of political power within their respective circles, and the observance of their obligations and duties in the European states system.

Absence of political training.

The princes and nobles of India required the same training as the old feudal kings and barons of Europe. The Great Moghul, the last symbol of imperialism, had shrivelled into a feeble pageant. The little vitality that remained in the name had died out under a Vizier, or an Amír of Amírs, who might be Moghul or Mahratta, Afghan or Arab, according to the daily game of revolutions and shuffling of factions at the Moghul capital. Lord Wellesley was a generation in advance of his age. He saw, with that true genius which is rarely understood or recognised by contemporaries, that a new paramount power was necessary for the

[1] The only exceptions of importance were the Rajpúts, and they were overrun by Mahrattas, and were as shattered as the Nizam after the battle of Kurdla.

A.D. 1805-1807

salvation of India; and that such a power could be exercised by the British government and by that government alone.

Errors of Lord Wellesley.

But Lord Wellesley made mistakes, like all other statesmen who are dealing with a present which is imperfectly known, and a future that can only be conjectured. He had over-rated the strength of the Mahrattas, and the danger of Sindia's French battalions. Since then he had underrated the powers of mischief which were still left in the hands of the Mahratta princes. He was consequently taken aback at the outbreak of Jaswant Rao Holkar; especially when it was followed up by the defection of Sindia and the protected Rajas of Rajputana.

Return to neutrality and isolation.

The result of the embroglio was that the home authorities resolved to reverse the policy of Lord Wellesley, and revert to that of Sir John Shore; to abandon the system of subsidiary and protective alliances, and return to that of neutrality and isolation; and, above all, to conciliate the Mahratta princes to British ascendency by the restoration of conquered territories, and surrender of captured fortresses.

Mortification of Lord Wellesley.

That Lord Wellesley was bitterly mortified by this decision may well be imagined; but every statesman who is in advance of his generation must be prepared to see his ideas ignored, misunderstood, or held up to derision, until popular errors are corrected by public disasters, and the foregone conclusions of those in power are educated by a larger experience to a right understanding of the evils and their cure.

Extreme views of Lord Cornwallis.

Lord Cornwallis was prepared to go extravagant lengths in the way of conciliation and neutrality. He would have withdrawn the Great Moghul and all his family to Bengal, and made over Delhi to Daulat Rao Sindia, with liberty to recover his lost territories between the Ganges and the Jumna. He would have abandoned the protective treaties with the Rajpút and Ját princes, and left them to the tender mercies of the Mahrattas.

Death of Lord Cornwallis, 1805.

Fortunately for the interests of philanthropy, Lord Cornwallis did not live to carry out these reactionary intentions. He was sixty-seven years of age; he had landed at Calcutta at the end of July to be exposed to the damp heats of a Bengal August, when every breeze from the south was laden with the feverish malaria of the Sunderbunds. In the month of September, the most trying month in the plains, he was travelling towards the north-west; and the fatal result might have been foreseen. The anxious veteran became weak in mind and body, sank into a state of insensibility, and finally, died on the 5th of October, 1805, before he had been ten weeks in the country.

A.D. 1805-1807

Sir George Barlow, Governor-General, 1805-7: his character.

The successor of Lord Cornwallis was a man of a different culture. Sir George Barlow was not an independent nobleman, educated in European politics; but a civil servant of the Company, pliant under superior authority, but self-willed in his own sphere of action. He had been a member of council in the time of Lord Wellesley, and had steadily supported Wellesley's imperial policy. Subsequently, however, he accepted the policy of conciliation and neutrality, which Lord Cornwallis was preparing to carry out in accordance with the will of the home authorities.

Political apostasy unavoidable.

The political apostasy of Barlow has been much condemned, but perhaps without sufficient cause. He adopted the imperial system of Lord Wellesley when that nobleman was in power; but it was impossible for him to resist the reaction in public opinion, which had recalled Lord Wellesley and placed Lord Cornwallis at the head of affairs. Such open rebellion against all the home authorities, including both houses of parliament, would have been an unwarrantable assumption, and have ended in a political suicide from which nothing was to be gained.

Submission of Jaswant Rao Holkar.

By the end of 1805, Lord Lake had pursued Jaswant Rao Holkar into the Punjab, and forced him to come to terms. A half-hearted treaty was concluded by Sir John Malcolm with the Mahratta adventurer, which satisfied no one. There was enough concession to the new policy of concilation to exasperate Lord Lake, and enough spice of Wellesley's policy of imperialism to exasperate Sir George Barlow. All Holkar's territories were restored to Jaswant Rao, except the fortress of Tonk Rampoora; but he was bound over not to commit any aggressions on the British government, or on any of its allies, including the Rajpút Rajas.

Arrogant pretensions.

This unexpected liberality revived the audacity of Jaswant Rao. He claimed the territories in Hindustan and the Dekhan, which he had demanded from Lake and Wellesley before the beginning of the war. He claimed a right to collect contributions from the Raja of Jaipur. Lord Lake was so disgusted with these arrogant demands on the part of

A.D. 1805-1807

a prostrate foe, that he stopped the negotiations; and then, of course, Jaswant Rao Holkar gave in, and withdrew all demands, and accepted the proffered terms.

Mistaken concessions.

But Sir George Barlow was not satisfied with this treaty. He ordered the fortress of Tonk Rampoora to be restored to Jaswant Rao. The recovery of the fortress was most gratifying to the faithless Mahratta, and he naturally thought he could do as he pleased. Accordingly he broke all his pledges, and exacted enormous sums from the Jaipur Raja; whilst Lord Lake, who had returned to head-quarters to save the expense of his field force, was prevented from putting a stop to his depredations.

Annulment of protective treaties with Rajpút states.

Sir George Barlow next annulled the protective treaties which had been concluded with the chiefs of Rajpútana. He declared that the chiefs had forfeited British protection by the countenance they had subsequently given to Jaswant Rao Holkar during the retreat of Colonel Monson. The Rajpút chiefs had certainly deserted the English and helped Holkar when they saw Monson running away. But in like manner they deserted Holkar and helped the English when they saw Jaswant Rao running away. The question in dispute however became a matter of personal quarrel between Lake and Barlow. Lake had promised to restore the Raja of Jaipur to the protective alliance provided he resisted the advance of Holkar. The Raja performed his part, but Barlow annulled the protective treaty with Jaipur, and Lake was naturally indignant that his pledges should be ignored. But Barlow was deaf to all the protests of Lake, and abandoned the Rajpúts to the irregular demands of the Mahrattas, with the exception of the Rajpút state of Ulwar and the Ját state of Bhurtpore, whose claims to protection could not be set aside.

Turn of the tide.

But the violence of the reaction against the policy of Lord Wellesley went too far for even Sir George Barlow. The home authorities proposed to restore all the territories which had been acquired by Lord Wellesley during the Mahratta war. Barlow replied that such a restitution would be most dangerous. Instead of inducing the Mahrattas to keep the peace, it would only tempt them to renewed efforts for the subversion of the British power in India, and a return to the wars and anarchy of the eighteenth century. Meanwhile the Mahratta feudatories heard of the proposal, and were puzzled by the restoration of territory and fortresses to Jaswant Rao Holkar. The Raja of Nagpore especially demanded the restoration of Cuttack and Berar, although Cuttack was essential to the maritime defence of British India, and Berar had been ceded to the Nizam. The Raja of Nagpore, however, was a true Mahratta; and down to his death, in 1816, he never ceased to implore the British government for compensation on account of Cuttack and Berar.

A.D. 1805-1807

Brief interval of peace.

For a brief interval the policy of non-intervention appeared to be a success. The predatory powers confined their depredations to Malwa and Rajpútana, and respected the territories of the British government and its allies. There were frequent rumours of confederacies against the British power, but they were generally discredited. To all outward appearance the Peishwa was politically dormant, or too much engaged in trying to reduce the smaller refractory feudatories within his own dominions, to attempt to carry on secret intrigues with other powers outside his frontier. At the same time Sindia and Holkar were afraid of each other, and chiefly busied themselves with exacting revenue and chout for the maintenance of their overgrown armies.

Disaffection in the Madras army: mutiny at Vellore, 1806.

In 1806 there was a great alarm in the Madras Presidency. There was a sudden rising of the sepoys at Vellore, and the Madras army was said to be disaffected. The fortress of Vellore, which had been the scene of many tragedies in the past history of the Carnatic, had been turned into a residence for the Mysore princes of Tippu's family. It was held by a garrison of about four hundred European soldiers, and fifteen hundred sepoys. The sepoys arose in the night, and attacked the European barracks, firing through the Venetian windows until half the force were killed or wounded. Other parties of sepoys attacked the European houses and shot down thirteen English officers, who had rushed out to learn the cause of the uproar. All this while the Mysore princes and their followers were in active communication with the mutineers, supplied them with provisions, and hoisted the flag of Mysore over the fortress.

Prompt action of Gillespie.

Unfortunately the Europeans had no ammunition, but the survivors made a sally from the barracks, and managed to maintain a position on a gateway under cover of a bastion. Every officer was killed, but a gallant resistance was

A.D. 1805-1807 — maintained by a Sergeant Brodie, who was the hero of the day. Meanwhile news of the outbreak was carried to Arcot, eight miles off, where Colonel Gillespie was in command. Relief was soon at hand. Colonel Gillespie galloped to Vellore with a troop of European dragoons, and two field guns. Gillespie rode far in advance of his men, and reached the gateway, amidst a furious fire, just as Brodie and his small party were burning their last cartridge. A chain of soldiers' belts was let down by Brodie, and Gillespie dragged himself to the top of the gateway, and placed himself at the head of the survivors, who welcomed him as their deliverer. At his word of command the soldiers promptly formed, and drove back the enemy with the bayonet. Presently the dragoons came up with the galloper guns. The gates of the fortress were blown open; the soldiers rushed in; four hundred mutineers were cut down; others were taken prisoners; and a few only escaped by dropping from the walls.

Needless innovations at the bottom of the mutiny.

A searching inquiry was made into the cause of the mutiny. It was ascertained that the military authorities at Madras had issued orders forbidding the sepoys from appearing on parade with ear-rings or caste marks, and requiring them to shave their beards and trim their moustachios. Above all, an obnoxious head-dress had been introduced, which was totally unlike the beloved turban, and bore a closer resemblance to the European hat, which has always been an eyesore to orientals.

Aggravated by taunts and wild rumours.

These innovations had rankled in the hearts of the Madras sepoys, and exposed them to taunts and derision. At Vellore the disaffection was aggravated by the presence of the Mysore princes, and the fact that many of Tippu's old soldiers were serving in the English garrison. Moreover alarming rumours were whispered abroad that the new army regulations were only a preliminary to the forcible conversion of the sepoys to Christianity. The prompt action of Colonel Gillespie put a stop to further troubles; but there were some disturbances at Hyderabad, which showed that the disaffection was widely spread.

Recall of Bentinck from Madras.

The Court of Directors were so alarmed at this sepoy mutiny, that they recalled Lord William Bentinck, the Governor of Madras, as well as Sir John Craddock, the commander-in-chief of the Madras army, for having sanctioned such dangerous innovations. Lord William Bentinck protested against his removal, but the Directors were inexorable. Twenty years afterwards he obtained tardy redress by being appointed Governor-General of India.

A.D. 1807-1813

In 1807 Sir George Barlow was succeeded at Calcutta by Lord Minto. The new Governor-General was strongly impressed with the wisdom of the policy of non-intervention. He was bent on eschewing the errors of Lord Wellesley and walking in the ways of Lord Cornwallis. Moreover Great Britain was engaged in wars against Napoleon, and peace in India was to be maintained at any price.

Lord Minto, Governor-General, 1807-13.

Immediately after Lord Minto's arrival in Bengal, attention was called to the state of affairs in Bundelkund; and he discovered to his surprise and disappointment that the policy of non-intervention was sometimes not only inexpedient but impossible. The territory of Bundelkund stretches to the southward of the Jumna from Behar to Malwa. It was parcelled out amongst a number of turbulent chieftains, who had been partly conquered by Ali Bahádur,[1] but who were supposed to acknowledge the suzerainty of the Peishwa. A large tract of Bundelkund had been ceded by the Peishwa to the British government for the maintenance of the Poona Subsidiary Force; but it was found that the country had never been completely subjected by the Peishwa, and that territory had been ceded which had never acknowledged his suzerainty. Bundelkund was overrun with military freebooters. A hundred and fifty fortresses were held by as many chiefs of banditti, who were permitted on the principles of non-intervention to settle their disputes by the sword.

Turbulence and anarchy in Bundelkund.

Sir George Barlow had sacrificed revenue and prestige rather than violate the new policy; but Lord Minto resolved to take action. Military operations were undertaken with the usual success. The result was that peace and order were established in Bundelkund; and the turbulence and anarchy which had prevailed in these jungle tracts since the days of Aurangzeb, were banished out of the land under the protective influence of British rule.

Departure from the policy of non-intervention.

The Punjab next attracted the attention of Lord Minto. A Sikh chieftain, named Runjeet Singh, had brought the Sikh Sirdars under his authority, and established a sovereignty

Rise of Runjeet Singh, the Lion of Lahore.

[1] See *ante*, page 391.

A.D. 1807-1813

which kept down rebels and bandits by the iron heel of military despotism. The territories of Runjeet Singh included the old battle-grounds where Alexander fought against Porus; and fears were entertained that Napoleon would march in the steps of the great Macedonian and attempt the conquest of Hindustan.[1]

Aggressions on the Cis-Sutlej states, 1807.

In 1807 Runjeet Singh was making aggressions on the Sikh principalities of Sirhind, between the Sutlej and the Jumna. These Cis-Sutlej Sikhs had paid allegiance to the British government ever since the campaign of Lord Lake; and they now applied for British protection against Runjeet Singh. The case was a difficult one, for it was necessary to conciliate Runjeet Singh as regards French invasion, whilst maintaining British supremacy on the banks of the Sutlej.

Mission of Charles Metcalfe, 1808.

In 1808 Lord Minto sent a young civilian, named Charles Metcalfe, to conduct the negotiations with Runjeet Singh; and by firmness on the part of the envoy, and the advance of a military force to the Sutlej, Runjeet Singh was induced to give in, and withdraw his troops to the westward of the river. Mr. Metcalfe established his reputation for tact and discretion by his able conduct of the mission, and lived to play an important part in Indian history.[2]

Rebellion against Holkar: insanity of Jaswant Rao.

Later on the affairs of Jaswant Rao Holkar fell into disorder. His subjects rebelled against him as a usurper, and he sought to retain the throne by murdering his legitimate brother and nephew. Next he took to drinking brandy, until at last he was pronounced to be insane, and placed in confinement; and his wife Tulsí Baí assumed the government of Indore with the help of an Afghan adventurer named Amír Khan.

[1] According to the latest orthography "Runjeet" is spelt "Ranjít," and this spelling has been adopted in dealing with Ranjít Singh, the Ját Raja, who is unknown to European readers. But the name of Runjeet Singh, the "Lion of Lahore," has become classical.

[2] Besides Metcalfe's mission to the Punjab, Lord Minto sent a mission, under Colonel Malcolm, to the court of Persia, and another, under Mr. Mountstuart Elphinstone, to the court of Kábul, to counteract the supposed designs of the Emperor Napoleon. Neither mission was followed by any practical result, and both might be passed over as obsolete. It is, however, curious to note that Elphinstone never reached Kábul, but met Shah Shuja, the nominal sovereign of Afghanistan, at Peshawar. By this time the Afghan empire, founded by Ahmad Shah Abdalí, was broken up; the whole country was distracted by civil wars, and Shah Shuja was driven into exile shortly after Elphinstone left Peshawar.

A.D. 1807-1813

Career of Amír Khan, the Afghan freebooter.

The career of Amír Khan, the founder of the Tonk principality, reveals the wretched condition of Rajpútana and Malwa. Originally Amír Khan was a leader of bandits, and as such he had been an associate of Jaswant Rao Holkar. His banditti grew into an army, maintained by forced contributions and robberies. When Jaswant Rao became insane, Amír Khan interfered in the affairs of Indore; he professed to protect the state of Holkar, whilst exacting large grants of territory and revenue from the weak government of Tulsí Baí.

Aggressions of Amír Khan on Nagpore.

Amír Khan, like all the predatory powers at this period, was constantly in want of means to support his lawless soldiery. Rajpútana and Malwa were exhausted, and he was compelled to look abroad. He revived some dormant claim of Holkar against the Bhonsla Raja of Nagpore, and invaded Nagpore territory with a large army.

Interference of Lord Minto

Lord Minto sent a force to protect Nagpore, and the result was that Amír Khan was forced to retire to his own territories. But Lord Minto felt that this interference was a violation of the policy of non-intervention; and he explained to the Court of Directors that he had interfered in behalf of the Raja of Nagpore as a measure of self-defence, to prevent any alliance between two Muhammadan powers, like Amír Khan and the Nizam. By this time, however, the home authorities were awakening to the fact that war, brigandage, and anarchy were on the increase in Central India; and they not only approved of what Lord Minto had done, but expressed a wish that he had made an end of Amír Khan.

Quarrel between Jodhpur and Jaipur respecting the daughter of the Rana.

One episode will suffice to reveal the horrible state of turmoil which prevailed in the fertile regions of Rajpútana. Every Rajpút chieftain was anxious to marry a daughter of the Rana of Udaipur. The reigning Rana had only one daughter, and she had been betrothed at an early age to the Raja of Jodhpur. The Raja died, and was succeeded by a prince named Mán Singh. Meanwhile the princess had been betrothed to the Raja of Jaipur; but Mán Singh claimed her hand on the ground that she had been betrothed to the throne of Jodhpur, and not to the mere occupant for the time being.

Desolating wars, 1806-10.

From 1806 to 1810, Rajpútana was convulsed by this domestic struggle between Jodhpur and Jaipur. Nearly all

A.D. 1807-1813

the chiefs in Rajpútana took a part in the war, just as their forefathers had fought on either side in the war of the Mahá Bhárata.

Interference of Amír Khan.

Amír Khan went from one side to the other with his army of banditti, as best suited his own interests. Originally he was bought over by Jaipur, and helped to defeat Mán Singh, and shut him up in his fortress of Jodhpur, whilst ravaging the surrounding country. Next he was bought over by Mán Singh, who offered to pay him a yearly tribute of some half a million sterling. Meanwhile Amír Khan was guilty of treacheries and wholesale assassinations, which alone would suffice to brand his character with infamy.

Ravages of Mahrattas and Afghans.

All this time the Rana of Udaipur took no part in the war; but his territories were exposed to the ravages and depredations of Daulat Rao Sindia and Amír Khan. The marches of the Mahratta and Afghan armies were to be traced by blazing villages and ruined harvests; and wherever they encamped they turned the garden of Rajpútana into a desert and desolation.

Rajpút appeals for British interference, 1809.

In this extremity the Rana of Udaipur claimed the protection of the British government as the paramount power. He offered to cede half his territories for the defence of the other half. The rival princes of Jodhpur and Jaipur joined in the solicitation. They declared that there always had been a paramount power in India to protect the weak against the strong; and as the East India Company had become the paramount power it was bound to fulfil its duties.

Results of non-intervention.

The interference of the British government would have put an end to all this frightful anarchy; but it would have been an open and undisguised violation of the policy of non-intervention. The Rana of Udaipur was refused all help. Driven by despair, he bought the protection of Amír Khan by the cession of a quarter of his dominions; and stooped to the ignominy of exchanging turbans with the Afghan freebooter.

Murder of the princess, 1810.

Still the war was raging between Jodhpur and Jaipur. Amír Khan proposed to stop it by taking the life of the innocent cause of the quarrel; and he threatened to carry off the princess, and make her over to Mán Singh of Jodhpur, unless his advice was followed. The miserable Rana gave his consent to the murder of his child; and the Rajpút maiden accepted her doom, and drank the poison which was to put an end to her existence. The terrible tragedy filled western India with shame and horror; and there was not a chieftain in Rajpútana who did not lament the fate of the unhappy princess, and execrate all concerned in the heartless atrocity.

A.D. 1807-1813

Successes of the French in eastern waters.

But other causes were at work, besides the policy of non-intervention, to prevent Lord Minto from interfering in western India. The war between Great Britain and France was being fought in eastern waters. The Mauritius was a depôt for French frigates and privateers, which swept the seas from Madagascar to Java.. The merchants of Calcutta alone estimated their losses at two millions sterling since the beginning of the war, whilst, in one year, the East India Company estimated their losses at half a million.[1]

British occupation of the Mauritius and Java, 1810-11.

In 1810 Lord Minto sent an expedition against the Mauritius and captured the island. In 1811 he sent expeditions against the Dutch settlements in India, which had passed into the hands of Napoleon. The island of Java was captured and occupied by the English down to the end of the war with France; but eventually it was restored to the Dutch, and irretrievably lost to the British nation.

Death of Jaswant Rao Holkar: increasing anarchy.

Lord Minto accompanied the expedition to Java, but returned to Calcutta in 1812. Anarchy still prevailed in Malwa and Rajpútana. Jaswant Rao Holkar died in 1811, and was succeeded by an infant, named Mulhar Rao Holkar, who had been adopted by his widow Tulsí Baí. This, however, was a matter of small moment in comparison with the dark clouds which threatened India in the shape of organised battalions of bandits under Amír Khan, and the loose bands of marauders, who were known by the dreaded name of Pindharies.

Rise of the Pindharies.

The Pindharies were a low class of freebooters, who had been attached to the Mahratta armies during the desolating wars of the eighteenth century. Their origin is lost in obscurity, but one body, as already seen, joined the Mahratta host that fought at Paniput.[2] The Mahratta horsemen of any respectability affected to look down upon the Pindharies; but it was only a difference between regular and irregular

[1] The merchants at Calcutta chiefly confined their trading to the eastern seas, and consequently suffered most severely. The East Indiamen from Europe were armed like men of war.

[2] See *ante*, page 338.

A.D. 1807-1813

banditti; between gentlemen highwaymen who were ready to fight, and pickpockets and pilferers who were ready to run away.

Connection with Sindia and Holkar.

Before the Mahratta wars of 1803 and 1804 the Pindharies had been distributed amongst different Mahratta chieftains. One body was known as Sindia's Pindharies; another body as Holkar's Pindharies; and lands were assigned by Sindia and Holkar to different Pindhari leaders for the maintenance of their respective hordes. When the wars were over the Pindharies still formed separate and independent bodies, but followed the fortunes of any turbulent chieftain or lawless adventurer. They were not divided by differences of race and religion, but were the riff-raff of Hindus and Muhammadans bound together by no tie save that of plunder.

Pindhari leaders, Chetu and Khurím.

Two notorious Pindhari leaders were known by the names of Chetu and Khurím. There was no union between the two; on the contrary they were jealous of each other and often at open enmity; and they were entirely wanting in the military strength and organisation which characterised the army of Amír Khan.

Extended depredations.

At first the Pindharies confined their depredations to Rajpútana and Malwa. Sometimes they made raids on the territories of Sindia and Holkar. On one occasion Daulat Rao Sindia captured the two Pindhari leaders, and kept them in confinement; but was at last induced to liberate them on payment of a ransom of a hundred thousand pounds sterling. Subsequently, they extended their raids into the Dekhan, and invaded the territories of the Peishwa, the Nizam, and the Raja of Nagpore.

Periodical incursions.

In 1809-10, Captain Sydenham, the Resident at Hyderabad, described the proceedings of the Pindharies. Their incursions, he said, were as regular as the periodical monsoons. They seemed to wait with malicious pleasure until the crops were ripe upon the ground, and then robbed the unfortunate husbandmen of the fruit of their labours at the moment they expected to reap them. Every villain who escaped from his creditors, or was expelled for flagrant crimes, or was disgusted with an honest and peaceable life, fled to Central India and enrolled himself amongst the Pindharies.

Foreign invasions.

The Pindharies generally invaded a country in bands varying from one thousand to four thousand men. On

A.D. 1807-1813

reaching the frontier they dispersed in small parties of two or three hundred. They advanced with such rapidity that the story of their depredations was generally the first news of their approach. They were not encumbered with tents or baggage, but carried only their arms, and slept on their saddle-cloths. Both men and horses were accustomed to long marches, and they never halted except to refresh themselves, to collect plunder, or to commit the vilest outrages on the female population. They subsisted on the grain and provisions which they found in the villages; took everything that was valuable; and wantonly destroyed all that they could not carry away.

Departure of Lord Minto, 1813.

Lord Minto left India in 1813, and was succeeded as Governor-General by Lord Moira, afterwards Marquis of Hastings. One of the last acts of Lord Minto's administration was to impress on the Court of Directors the necessity for adopting large measures for the purpose of suppressing the Pindharies; and thus from an early period the attention of Lord Moira was directed to the annual depredations of these organised banditti.

Lord Moira adopts the policy of Wellesley.

Lord Moira landed at Calcutta in the fifty-ninth year of his age. Before he left England he had denounced the ambitious policy of Lord Wellesley in seeking to establish the British government as the paramount power in India. But his attention had already been directed to the yearly expeditions of the Pindharies; and soon after his arrival in Bengal he began to modify his political views. He reported to the Court of Directors that the battalions of Amír Khan and hordes of Pindharies numbered some fifty thousand men; that they subsisted by plunder alone, and extended their ravages over an area as large as England. He emphatically declared that the affairs of the Company would never prosper until the British government was placed at the head of a league which embraced every native state in India, and was enabled to bring the whole strength of the league to bear upon any single power that disturbed the public peace.

This sudden conversion of Lord Moira from the policy of non-intervention to that of a paramount power had no effect upon the home authorities. There was still the same morbid dread of the Mahrattas, which misled the British nation at the beginning of the century. Daulat Rao Sindia was still

A.D. 1807-1813

Opposition of the home authorities: dread of the Mahrattas.

regarded as a dangerous power like Chenghiz Khan or Timúr. In reality he was a prince in sore distress, worried by an army which was in frequent mutiny from want of subsistence, and paralysed by a terror of the English, which never left him after the battle of Assaye. He had been anxious to follow the advice of the British Resident, who still accompanied his camp; but the Resident was a victim to the policy of non-intervention, and refused to advise Sindia. Thus in India and in England every one, save Lord Moira, was a strict adherent to the policy of non-intervention. Accordingly, Lord Moira was told by the Directors that no league was to be formed, or any step taken for the suppression of the Pindharies, that was likely to embroil the British government with the Mahrattas, or to give offence to Daulat Rao Sindia.

Threatened war with Nipal, 1813.

Meanwhile black clouds were gathering over the Himalayas. For years the Ghorka rulers of Nipal had been making systematic encroachments on British territory. The English in Bengal remonstrated in vain. They were anxious for peace at any price short of abject submission; but the Ghorkas were beyond all bearing: appropriating villages and districts without a shadow of a claim, and turning a deaf ear to all representations, or stubbornly insisting that the abstracted territory had always belonged to Nipal. Lord Minto sent an ultimatum to Khatmandu before he left Bengal, and Lord Moira sent another shortly after his arrival. The result was the Ghorka war of 1814 and 1815; but before describing the military operations it will be as well to review the history of the Ghorka conquest of Nipal.

CHAPTER XI.

NIPAL HISTORY: GHORKA CONQUEST.

A.D. 1767 TO 1814.

A.D. 1767.

Nipal, Bhutan, and Thibet.

NORTHWARD of Hindustan, a square mass of territory extends over the Himalayas beyond the British frontier towards the great desert of Gobi or Shamo, the terror of Marco Polo.[1] On the west, this irregular quadrangle is bounded by Kashmír and the upper streams of the Sutlej and Ganges; on the east by China proper and the courses of rivers which are as yet unfamiliar to modern geographers. The southern side of the quadrangle, immediately to the northward of British territory, is occupied by the mountain range of the Himalayas, which includes the valley of Nipal and heights of Bhutan. Northward of the Himalayas the flat table-land of Thibet stretches over little-known tracts towards the great desert. Southern Thibet is watered by the Brahmaputra river, which coils like a huge serpent round the northern slopes of the Himalayas, and finally flows southward through Assam, and helps to form the delta of the Ganges.

Religious empire of Buddhism transplanted from Hindustan.

A veil of religious mystery hangs over the Himalayan mountains and the Thibetan table-land beyond. Buddhism, which once overshadowed Hindustan, was driven northward between the eighth and twelfth centuries of the Christian era by the great Brahmanical revival which was associated with the reformed worship of Vishnu and Siva. The monasteries and the monastic colleges, which once flourished on the banks of the Ganges and Jumna,

[1] It was known to Marco Polo as the desert of Lop, and was said to be haunted by evil spirits or goblins.

A.D. 1767.

reappeared amidst the mountain scenery of the Himalayas and pathless wastes to the northward. But Hindustan was never forgotten. The memories of the holy land of Behar and Gaya, sanctified by the footsteps of Sakya Muni and his disciples, were treasured in the hearts of the inmates of every monastery, from the boy neophyte of twelve or fourteen to the venerable Lama or abbot, who ruled as lord and master. To this day pious legends of Magadha and Benares are still the subjects of religious thought and teaching in those remote regions, which are a *terra incognita* to the European.[1]

Great Lama at Lhassa: Teshu Lama at Digarchi.

Buddhism, like Christendom, has its bishops and its heresies. The city of Lhassa, seated on the southern bank of the Brahmaputra, forty days' journey from Pekin, is the Rome of Thibetan and Chinese Buddhism. At Lhassa a succession of Great Lamas, the supposed incarnations of Sakya Muni, exercise a spiritual dominion resembling that of the Holy See. At Digarchi, ten days' journey to the westward of Lhassa, the Teshu Lama is worshipped and protected by the emperors of China as their spiritual father.[2]

Description of Nipal.

The valley of Nipal is located in the southern slopes of the Himalaya range. It is shut out from Hindustan by the lower shelves and precipices of the Himalayas; whilst the still lower range of mountains, at the base, is guarded by a broad belt of dense forest, from which a low marshy plain stretches out towards the south, the whole being known as the Terai. Nipal has rarely been invaded by Muhammadans or Moghuls, and to this day the Muhammadans form no part of its population.[3]

From a remote period this fertile and secluded valley has

[1] The holy land of Magadha is identical with the modern Behar or Vihar. The word Vihar signifies a Buddhist monastery.

[2] Both the Great Lama of Lhassa and the Teshu Lama of Digarchi are pontiffs of the yellow sect, the orthodox and reformed Buddhism of the court of Pekin. But the followers of the red sect, who retain much of the old devil-worship and incantations in their religious observances, continue to maintain monasteries and Lamas of their own in Thibet and Bhutan.

Thibet is nominally subject to the Chinese emperor, but little is known of the extent of Chinese jurisdiction in that quarter. Lhassa is the capital of what is called Chinese Thibet, and is the abode of a Chinese viceroy as well as of the Great Lama.

[3] Muhammad Tughlak sent an army over the Himalayas in the fourteenth century, but it perished miserably. See *ante*, page 87.

A.D. 1767.

been inhabited by a peaceful and industrious race of Hindu Buddhists, known as Newars. Like India, the whole country was parcelled out into petty Hindu kingdoms each having its own Raja; but in the early half of the eighteenth century the whole were absorbed in three kingdoms, of which Khatmandu was the chief. Indeed, at this period the Newar Raja of Khatmandu was always treated by the East India Company as the ruler of Nipal.

Hindu Buddhists.

In those early times the valley of Nipal might have been likened to the happy valley of Rasselas. The Newars were devoted to agriculture and trade, and pursued the even tenor of their way under the mild influence of Buddhism. The East Indian Company carried on a profitable trade with Nipal; and numerous commodities, including quantities of gold from Thibet, were imported into Behar and Bengal.

Happy valley of the Newars.

About 1767, ten years after Plassy, the Ghorkas of Kashmír, a race of Rajpúts and Brahmans, invaded the happy valley of Nipal. There was no apparent cause of quarrel. The Ghorkas were a military people, hungering after territory and revenue; and the valley of Nipal, with its peaceful population of Buddhist Newars, was open to their inroads. They preserved the usages of caste, and worshipped the same gods as the Rajpúts of Hindustan; and the Ghorka conquest may have been a later wave of the great Brahmanical revival, which convulsed India in mediæval times, and drove Buddhism out of Hindustan.

Ghorka conquest of Nipal, 1767.

The Newars were as helpless to resist the Ghorkas as sheep when attacked by wolves. The Newar Raja of Khatmandu abandoned his territories to the invaders, and shut himself up in his capital, and implored the help of his mercantile friends in Bengal. Strange to say, the English rulers responded to his prayers. Their trade was slack, their revenues were falling away, and specie itself was vanishing from Bengal. Moreover, the spirit of Clive was still abroad, and the Company's servants were burning with military glory as well as commercial enterprise. A small force was sent to the Himalayas under a Captain Kinloch to deliver the Newar Raja from the Ghorkas, and re-open the outlets of gold from Thibet. Unfortunately Kinloch set out at the worst season of the year. He made a desperate effort to march through the Terai in the middle of the rains, but was beaten back by malaria and want of provisions;

British intervention a failure.

A.D. 1767-1771

and the Newars and their Rajas were abandoned to their doom.

Prithi Narain, the Ghorka hero: horrors of the conquest.

Maháraja Prithi Narain was the hero and sovereign of the Ghorkas. He conquered the Nipal valley by the aid of his Bharadars or barons. He made a great slaughter of the Newar Rajas, and massacred every Newar of distinction throughout the country. The horrors of the Ghorka conquest were beyond all telling. A European eye-witness, Father Guiseppe, describes Prithi Narain as a monster of inhumanity—as crafty, treacherous, and bloodthirsty as any Tartar conqueror of the olden time. Atrocities and outrages were committed which must be left to the imagination. At one city, six miles from Khatmandu, the whole of the inhabitants were deprived of their lips and noses in punishment for their long and obstinate resistance to the invaders.

Ghorka constitution: king and barons.

The Ghorka conquest throws valuable light on the ancient constitution of the Rajpúts. The valley of Nipal was parcelled out amongst the Ghorka Bharadars, much in the same way that England was parcelled out amongst the Norman barons under William the Conqueror. The Maháraja reigned at Khatmandu as sovereign and despot; but the Bharadars claimed for themselves and families an exclusive right to all offices and commands, as well as a voice in the national councils. Accordingly the Maháraja selected his ministers exclusively from the Bharadar aristocracy; and in times of national emergency all the Bharadars in the kingdom were summoned to a council of state at Khatmandu.

Three armies maintained at the expense of one.

The strength of the Ghorkas lay in their military organisation. They maintained three armies at the expense of one, each army numbering about twelve thousand men. About the end of every year the existing army returned to civil life, whilst a new army was enrolled, which generally consisted of old soldiers. Thus three trained armies could be brought into the field in cases of emergency, whilst only one army was kept on military duty, and drew military pay.

Yearly Panjani.

The old army was disbanded and the new army was enlisted at a yearly festival known as the Panjani. At every Panjani there was a redistribution of all offices and commands amongst the Bharadars and their families. Indeed, under the old Ghorka constitution, the Panjani was the great institution of the year, when there was a change of ministers as well as officers and generals, and nothing remained permanent excepting the Mahárаja. A.D. 1771-1792

Prithi Narain, the hero founder of the Ghorka dynasty in Nipal, died in 1771, leaving two sons. The elder succeeded to the throne, but died in 1775, leaving an infant son, a babe in arms. Then followed the usual complication. The baby grandson of Prithi Narain was placed upon the throne under the name of Run Bahadur. The uncle of the infant, the younger son of Prithi Narain, became regent and guardian. But the queen-mother also claimed to be regent and guardian; and for some years there was a struggle for supremacy between the queen-mother and the uncle—a struggle which used to be common to every Hindu court in India.[1] In 1786, when the boy Mahárаja was eleven years of age, the queen-mother died, and the uncle became supreme. Henceforth the uncle surrounded the boy with all the young profligates of the court, and permitted him to indulge in every species of vice and cruelty, in the hope of thereby perpetuating his own authority as regent. It will be seen hereafter that he sowed the wind and reaped the whirlwind.

Death of Prithi Narain: Run Bahadur and his uncle, 1775-86.

Meanwhile the Ghorkas were troublesome and aggressive towards all their neighbours—westward towards Kashmir and the Punjab, and eastward towards Sikhim and Bhutan. One Ghorka army invaded Thibet and plundered the temples at Lhassa and Digarchi. The audacity and sacrilege kindled the wrath of the Chinese emperor and court of Pekin; and in 1792 a Chinese army of seventy thousand men advanced against Nipal.

Chinese invasion, 1792.

The Ghorkas were wild with alarm, and began to make advances to the English. Hitherto they had affected to disdain trade and traders, and had displayed a haughty and exclusive spirit in their dealings with the Bengal government. But the victories of the English in the first Mahratta war had inspired them with respect, and they hungered for the help of British arms and soldiers.[2] They hastily

Ghorkas conclude a treaty with the English, 1792.

[1] Such rivalries and jealousies between a minister and a queen-mother have been frequent in all oriental courts from a remote antiquity. Sometimes the quarrel is prevented by a criminal intimacy between the two parties. In India the British government arbitrates as the paramount power, and all quarrels about a succession or a regency are thus nipped in the bud.

[2] The old trade between Bengal and Behar had died out under the military despotism of the Ghorkas, and every effort to recover it had

A.D. 1792-1795 — offered to negotiate a treaty of commerce and friendship with the English Resident at Benares; and a treaty was concluded in 1792, under which certain privileges were granted to traders from British territories, and a fixed duty of two and a half per cent was to be charged by either government on all commodities imported on either side.

Apply for help against China.

The commercial treaty was a blind. The Ghorkas amused the Bengal government with hopes of a revival of trade, and then asked for British help against China. Lord Cornwallis replied that the English had no quarrel with the Chinese emperor, but would willingly mediate between Nipal and China; and for this purpose he sent Colonel Kirkpatrick on a mission to Khatmandu.

Humiliation of Nipal.

Before Kirkpatrick left Patna the Ghorkas were routed by the Chinese and driven back to Nipal through the snows of the Himalayas. The Chinese army advanced to Nayakote, within a day's march of Khatmandu, and dictated their own terms. The Ghorka regency was compelled to restore all the plunder that had been carried from the temples, and to pay tribute for the future to the court of Pekin.

Mission of Kirkpatrick: its failure.

The Ghorkas were now disgusted with their treaty with the English, and only anxious to keep the English out of Nipal. Kirkpatrick was met by messengers, who announced the peace with China, and tried to induce him to go back. But the Bengal government was anxious to establish friendly relations with the Ghorka government, and Kirkpatrick pushed on to Khatmandu. He was received with every show of courtesy and respect, but thwarted in every attempt at negotiation. He soon found that his presence at Khatmandu was useless and dangerous, and returned to Bengal. Henceforth the treaty was a dead letter.

Revolution of 1795: downfall of the regent uncle.

In 1795 there was a revolution at Khatmandu. Mahá-raja Run Bahadur had reached his twentieth year. He had been nurtured in the worst possible school, and the natural ferocity of his temper had been encouraged rather than controlled. At last he cunningly worked the destruction of his uncle. He suddenly announced in open durbar that he had assumed the sovereignty; and the Bharadars hailed

hitherto proved a failure. In 1774 Warren Hastings sent a mission to Thibet under Mr. Bogle; and in 1783 he sent another under Mr. Turner; but there was no practical result.

A.D. 1795-1800

the declaration with a burst of loyalty. The regent uncle was powerless to contend against the voice of the nobles, and compelled to give place to his nephew. For a few months he was treated with decent respect, but was then arrested, loaded with chains, and thrown into a dungeon. Nothing more was heard of him. Some said that he was starved to death; others that he was assassinated by his royal nephew.

Run Bahadur, the Nero of Nipal, 1795-1800

Run Bahadur reigned over Nipal like another Nero. Day by day he took a savage joy in beholding tortures, mutilations, and executions. His marriages and amours were the scandal of Khatmandu. His chief wife was childless. His second wife gave birth to a son, and was then neglected. Run Bahadur, in spite of his Kshatriya caste, was bent on securing a Brahmaní bride. He carried off a young Brahmaní widow from her father's house in the plains, and made her his queen, in violation of the laws against widow marriages and the mixture of castes; and a son was born of the Brahmaní queen, who was destined to change the fortunes of the dynasty.

Death of the Brahmaní queen.

Run Bahadur was deeply enamoured of his Brahmaní bride. She was his prime favourite, the idol of his soul. She was seized with small-pox, and Run Bahadur was frantic with grief and alarm. He spent vast sums on offerings to the gods at the different temples. He summoned the ablest physicians from Benares to attend the sick lady. But prayers and medicines were of no avail, and the Brahmaní queen was soon numbered with the dead.

Madness of Run Bahadur.

Run Bahadur was driven to madness by the loss of his Brahmaní queen. He broke out in fits of ungovernable fury, which spread a wild terror through the court and capital. He flogged the physicians, cut off their noses, and sent them back to Benares. He wreaked his vengeance on the gods of Nipal by firing cannon at the sacred statues in the temple of Pusput Nath, the great national shrine of Siva and Parvatí in the suburbs of Khatmandu. He threw up the sovereignty, and vowed to spend the remainder of his days in religious seclusion at Benares; and he actually placed the little son of his dead queen on the throne of Nipal, and called on the Bharadars to swear allegiance to the infant. He sought to smooth matters by appointing his second wife to be regent, and her young son to be

A.D. 1800-1802 — prime minister. The result was a baby sovereign aged four, a child premier aged six, and a regent stepmother. But Run Bahadur remained at Khatmandu. He had abdicated the throne, but persisted in exercising supreme authority.

Feigned abdication. The abdication of Run Bahadur was a mere caprice of insanity. He wished to honour his dead queen by placing her son upon the throne; but he continued to wreak his ferocity on those around him. Some officers of government were scourged; others were hung up by the heels to branches of trees. In a word, the sovereign was dangerous to his subjects; and neither rank, age, nor caste could protect any one from his blind anger.

Pandey conspiracy; flight of Run Bahadur to Benares, 1800. Meanwhile the Bharadars began to conspire against the headstrong Maháraja; and Damodur Pandey, the head of the once famous Pandey family, was the moving spirit of the conspiracy. The Bharadars urged that their allegiance had been solemnly transferred to the infant son, and they called on Run Bahadur to complete his abdication of the throne by going into exile. Damodur Pandey had already gained over the army; indeed, he was a type of those Hindu ministers who, at different intervals, have dragged their country and its princes at the heels of a military car. A civil war broke out, and Run Bahadur was worsted. He saw that his life was in sore peril, and suddenly left Khatmandu in the night time, and fled to Benares, accompanied by his neglected chief queen and a young Bharadar named Bhím Sein Thapa, who was the head of the Thapa family, and bitter rival of the Pandeys.

Pandeys in power: plots and counterplots. The flight of Run Bahadur placed Damodur Pandey at the head of affairs. He was appointed prime minister to the infant Mahárajа and regent stepmother; and he filled all the ministerial posts with members of the Pandey family. Henceforth there were constant plottings at Benares for the destruction of the Pandeys and restoration of Run Bahadur to the throne of Nipal; and at the same time constant counterplots at Khatmandu for the forcible detention of the royal exile in British territory, and the destruction of Bhím Sein Thapa.

Lord Wellesley's dealings with Run Bahadur. At this period Lord Wellesley was Governor-General of India. The sudden appearance of the ex-Mahárаja of Nipal within British territory stirred up that active nobleman to attempt the recovery of the lost trade. Run

Bahadur was received by the British authorities at Benares with every mark of honour and distinction. Money from the Company's treasury was advanced for his support. A Captain Knox was appointed Political Agent, to carry on all communication with the royal exile, and to open up negotiations in his behalf with the regency at Khatmandu.

A.D. 1802-1803

Mission of Captain Knox. 1802.

The government of the East India Company was conducted on mercantile principles. It was therefore deemed necessary to apply to the Ghorka government for a repayment of the moneys advanced to the ex-Maháraja, and also for a suitable pension for his future maintenance. Accordingly Captain Knox was sent to Khatmandu in 1802 to make the necessary arrangements, and also to establish a cordial friendship with the ruling powers, and open up a trade through Nipal with Thibet and Bhutan. Knox was welcomed at Khatmandu with respect and courtesy, but soon found that he was hedged around with spies, and played upon by mendacious intriguers. There was a great show of business and much pretended negotiation, but nothing was concluded. At heart the Ghorkas were as jealous and exclusive as ever, and evidently imagined that Lord Wellesley was scheming to restore Run Bahadur, overthrow the Ghorka dominion, and take possession of Nipal. After much prevarication and vacillation they agreed to pay certain yearly allowances to the ex-Maháraja, as long as he was detained in British territory. In return, the ex-Maháraja pledged himself to devote the remainder of his life to the worship of the Supreme Spirit at Benares, under the religious title of "Swami." But the money was never sent to Benares, and Run Bahadur only professed to be a Swami until a way was opened for his restoration to the throne at Khatmandu.

Revolution of 1803: the chief queen becomes regent.

Suddenly the chief queen left the ex-Maháraja at Benares, and made her way to Nipal. She was resolved to oust the second queen from the regency, and take the government into her own hands. Her approach threw the court of Khatmandu into confusion. Cannon were drawn up before the city gates; guards were posted in every avenue; ammunition was served out; and hurry, noise, and disorder prevailed in every quarter. Damodur Pandey began to vacillate, and went out to make terms with the chief queen. In his absence the second queen fled from the palace with

A.D. 1803-1804

the infant Maháraja, and took refuge in the temple of Pusput Nath. Meanwhile the chief queen was joined by Damodur Pandey, and entered Khatmandu in triumph, and assumed the post of regent. The infant Maháraja was then brought back from the temple, and placed upon the throne; and the second queen saved her life by timely submission to her older rival.

Failure of Knox's mission.

The new government was profuse in promises to Captain Knox, but only to cajole and thwart him. The new queen regent evaded the terms which had been accepted by her predecessor; and Knox left Khatmandu in disgust as Kirkpatrick had done ten years previously. Accordingly Lord Wellesley formally announced to the new government that the alliance with Nipal was dissolved, and told the ex-Maháraja that he might leave Benares, and go where he pleased.

Run Bahadur returns to Nipal, 1804.

In 1804 Run Bahadur returned to Nipal accompanied by Bhím Sein Thapa. Damodur Pandey came out to meet him at the head of the Ghorka army, prepared to join him or fight him as occasion might arise. But the Ghorka soldiery were still loyal at heart towards the ex-Maháraja. Run Bahadur fearlessly advanced towards the opposing column, and threw his royal bonnet into the air, exclaiming, "Now, my Ghorkas, who is for me, and who is for the Pandeys?"

Downfall of the Pandeys.

At once the whole army received their sovereign with acclamations. Damodur Pandey was arrested on the spot, loaded with chains, and carried off to Khatmandu, and beheaded with many of his adherents. The chief queen resigned the government into the hands of her husband; but Run Bahadur dared not assume the title of Maháraja. The army had sworn fidelity to the son of the Brahmaní queen; and Run Bahadur was obliged to be content with the post of regent, and to carry on the government in the name of his son, with Bhím Sein Thapa for his prime minister.

Counter conspiracy.

The revolution, however, was not yet over. The air of Khatmandu was heavily charged with plots and intrigues. Many Bharadars had supported the Pandeys, and they now dreaded the resentment of the Thapas. A conspiracy was formed under the leadership of the brother of Run Bahadur for the overthrow of the new government, and the destruction of the Thapas; but the scheme exploded before it was ripe for execution.

A.D. 1804-1813.

Murder of Run. Bahadur.

Bhím Sein Thapa discovered the plot, and made his arrangements accordingly. By his advice Run Bahadur ordered his brother to attend the durbar, and then directed him to join the Ghorka army on the western frontier. The brother returned an insolent reply, and was ordered off to immediate execution. The brother drew his sword before he could be arrested, and slaughtered Run Bahadur on the spot, but was then cut to pieces on the floor of the hall.

Massacre at Khatmandu.

The bystanders were horror-stricken at the double murder. Every man was cowed, and thought only of his own safety. Bhím Sein Thapa alone was master of himself and the situation. By his orders every enemy of the Thapa family was put to the sword on the charge of being implicated in the murder of Run Bahadur. Fifty officers of the army are said to have been executed amidst the general massacre. Meanwhile the remains of the dead sovereign were carried off to the place of burning; and his second queen, the deposed regent-mother, was forced to immolate herself on the funeral pile.

Rule of Bhím Sein Thapa and the chief queen.

The deeply laid plot of Bhím Sein Thapa was soon revealed to the people of Khatmandu. It turned out that he was the secret paramour of the chief queen. Accordingly the chief queen resumed her post of regent-mother, and Bhím Sein Thapa continued to hold the post of prime minister, whilst he was virtually the sole ruler of Nipal. For some years there was a lull in the domestic politics of the Ghorkas, but meanwhile the Ghorka rulers were forcing the British government into a war against Nipal.

CHAPTER XII.

NIPAL WAR: LORD MOIRA (HASTINGS.)[1]

1814 TO 1816.

A.D. 1804-14

Aggressions of Nipal on British territory.

IN 1813, eight years after the elevation of Bhím Sein Thapa, Lord Minto resigned the post of Governor-General of India into the hands of Lord Moira. Ever since the dissolution of the alliance by Lord Wellesley in 1804, there had been constant wrangling between the two governments. The Ghorka authorities had been gradually absorbing British territory along the whole line of frontier to the north of Hindustan, from the neighbourhood of Darjeeling to the neighbourhood of Simla. Sir George Barlow had remonstrated, and Lord Minto had remonstrated, but to no purpose. Each Governor-General in turn had overlooked the aggressions in order to avoid a war; until at last it was discovered that within the previous quarter of a century more than two hundred British villages had been added to Nipal territory; and it was obvious that the aggressions were conducted on a regular system, having for its object the extension of Nipal dominion to the banks of the Ganges.

Occupation of British districts by the Nipalese.

At last two large districts were annexed by the Ghorka authorities, respecting which there could not be a shadow of doubt. At this date Lord Minto was still Governor-General, and he invited the Nipal government to send a commissioner to investigate the claim to the two districts, in association with a British commissioner. The investigation lasted over a year. In the end it was ascertained that the districts in question had always belonged to Oude; and

[1] Lord Moira was not created Marquis of Hastings until after the Nipal war, but he is best known to history by the latter title.

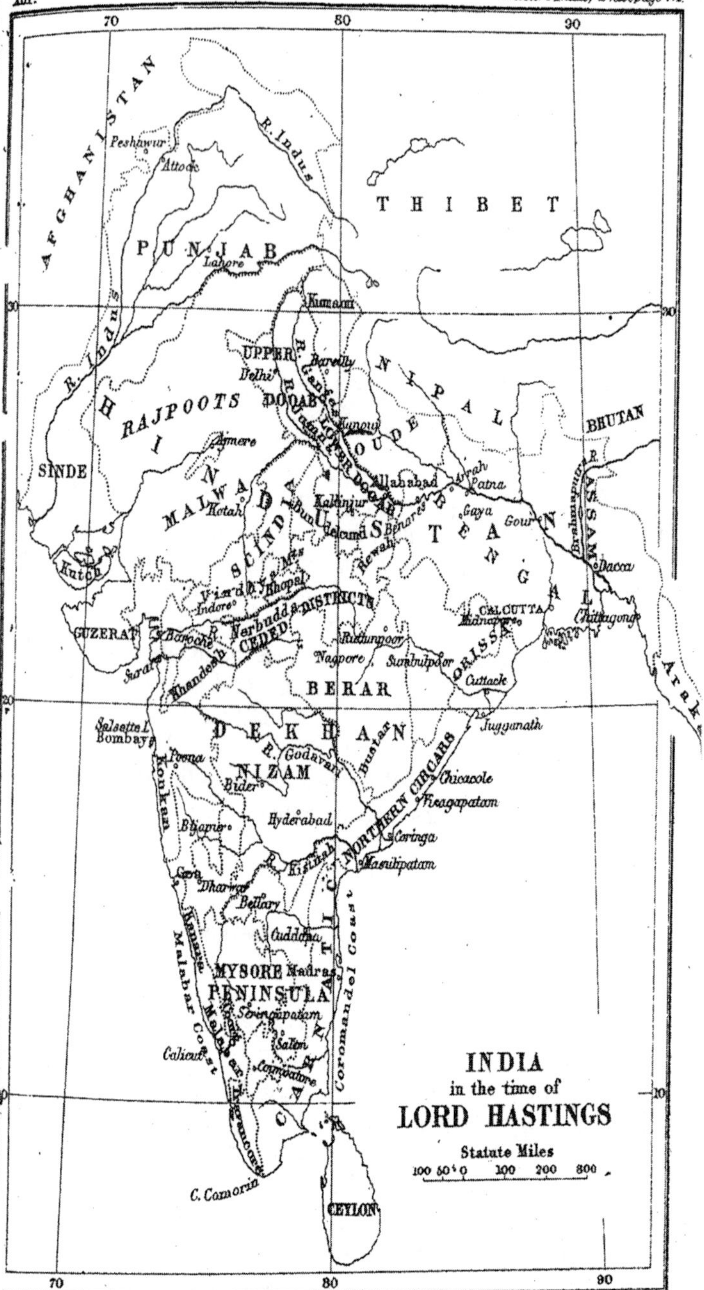
INDIA
in the time of
LORD HASTINGS
Statute Miles
100 50 0 100 200 300
AFGHANISTAN
Peshawur
Attock
R. Indus
THIBET
PUNJAB
Lahore
Kumaon
UPPER
Bareilly
Delhi
DOOAB
R. Ganges
R. Jumna
NIPAL
BHUTAN
RAJPOOTS
HINDUSTAN
Ajmere
SINDE
OUDE
LOWER DOOAB
Allahabad
Arrah
Patna
MALWA
Kotah
Kalinjur
Bundelcund
Benares
Gaya
Gour
BENGAL
R. Brahmaputra
ASSAM
Dacca
Kutch
SCINDIA
Rewah
Vindhya Mts
Bhopal
Indore
CALCUTTA
Midnapore
Chittagong
GUZERAT
Baroche
R. Nerbudda
CEDED DISTRICTS
ORISSA
Surat
Khandesh
Nagpore
Sumbulpoor
Ruttunpoor
Cuttack
Arakan
BERAR
Salsette I.
Bombay
DEKHAN
Juggunath
Poona
R. Godavari
Bustar
NIZAM
Bider
Chicacole
Vizagapatam
NORTHERN CIRCARS
Konkan
Bijapur
Hyderabad
Coringa
R. Kistnah
Masulipatam
Goa
Dharwar
Bellary
Cuddapa
CARNATIC
Coromandel Coast
Malabar Coast
Kanara
MYSORE
Madras
PENINSULA
Seringapatam
Salem
Coimbatore
Calicut
Travancore
C. Comorin
CEYLON
70
80
90
30
20
10

A.D. 1813-1814

that they formed a part of the territory which the Nawab Vizier had ceded to the British government in 1801. The Nipal commissioner was unable to disprove this fact, or to show that his government had any claim whatever to the disputed territory.

The ultimatum.

The Nipal government dealt with the case in characteristic fashion. They recalled their commissioner, and stoutly maintained that the investigation proved their right to the two districts. Lord Minto then brought matters to a crisis. He sent an ultimatum to the effect that unless the districts were restored they would be recovered by force. The answer was not received until after the arrival of Lord Moira; it was to the effect that the districts belonged to Nipal, and would not be surrendered.

Recovery of the districts.

Lord Moira followed up the action of his predecessor by sending another ultimatum, fixing the day on which the districts were to be restored. The Nipal government allowed the time to pass; and a British detachment took possession of the districts without opposition, and set up police-stations for their protection.

Council of Bharadars at Khatmandu.

But although the Ghorka government had treated the ultimatum with apparent contempt, the letter of Lord Moira had nevertheless created a profound sensation, and led to a division of parties in Nipal. Bhím Sein Thapa foresaw that the local dispute about frontier districts was broadening into a question of peace or war. He summoned the Bharadars to a council of state at Khatmandu, and twenty-two Bharadars assembled to discuss the question.

Ghorka debates on peace or war.

Amar Singh, the most renowned general in the Ghorka army, was opposed to the war. He had faced Runjeet Singh, the "lion" of the Punjab; and he knew something of the fighting powers of Englishmen, and the resources of the British government. "Fighting against the Newars," he said, "was like hunting deer; but fighting against Englishmen would be like battling with tigers." Other chiefs joined Amar Singh in deprecating a collision with the British government; but Bhím Sein Thapa held a different opinion. "What power," he asked, "can fight against us in Nipal? Not even the great Alexander of Macedon could carry his rams into our mountains.[1] Our hills and fastnesses are the

[1] Alexander the Great is known to Asiatics by the name of Sekunder. Bhím Sein Thapa alluded to him as Sekunder, but the name would

A.D. 1814-1816

work of God, and are not to be taken by mortals. As for the English, they could not even capture the fortress of Bhurtpore, which is the work of men's hands; how then shall they reduce our strongholds, which were created by the Almighty? There can be no peace between Nipal and the English, until the Company have surrendered all their provinces to the northward of the Ganges, and made the Ganges their boundary against us."

Ghorka slaughter of British police.

The council of Bharadars resolved on war; but a war after oriental fashion. They did not make a declaration of hostilities, and prepare for a solemn appeal to the God of battles; but they sent a large force into the disputed districts which had been recovered by the English, and attacked a police station, and slaughtered eighteen police constables. The Ghorka army then hastened back to Khatmandu, leaving the English to make their way through the swamps and forests of the Terai, and climb the heights of the Himalayas, before they could exact retribution for the cowardly crime.

Lord Moira's plan of a campaign.

Lord Moira soon planned a campaign against Nipal. Four British divisions, aggregating thirty thousand men and sixty guns, proceeded to enter Nipal at four different points: the western column on the Sutlej, the eastern column on Khatmandu, and the other two columns on intermediate positions.

Disastrous operations of 1814.

The operations of 1814 proved very nearly a failure. The Ghorkas exhibited a pluck and bravery which took the English by surprise. General Gillespie, the hero of Vellore, who commanded one of the columns, was shot dead whilst recklessly attempting to storm a mountain fortress without a siege train. Other generals showed a strange incompetency, and one of them on setting out was so alarmed at the density of the forests in the Terai, that he galloped back to Dinapore, leaving his division behind him.

Brilliant successes of Ochterlony, 1814-15.

General David Ochterlony, who commanded the division advancing by the way of the Sutlej and Lúdhiana, was pitted against Amar Singh, the Ghorka general who had deprecated the war. Ochterlony was a Company's officer of the old heroic type. In his younger days he had fought against Hyder Ali in the Carnatic under Sir Eyre Coote. At a later

convey no idea to English readers, and has accordingly been modified in the text.

A.D. 1814-1816.

day he had held Delhi against the Mahratta army under Jaswant Rao Holkar. His advance up the Himalayas was a marvel of caution and audacity. Those who have visited Simla will realise the difficulties of his march along shelves and precipices, dragging up eighteen-pounders, and opening roads by blasting rocks, and battering down obstructions with his field guns. For five months, at the worst season of the year, in the teeth of snowstorms and mountain blasts, he carried one fortress after another, until not a stronghold was left in the hands of the enemy excepting Maloun.

Fall of Maloun.

The fortress of Maloun was situated on a shelf of the Himalayas, with steep declivities of two thousand feet on two of its sides. Amar Singh was shut up in Maloun. After a desperate attack on the British works, he held out till the British batteries were about to open on his stronghold, and then came to terms, and was permitted to march out with the honours of war.

Nipalese sue for terms.

The fall of Maloun shook the faith of Bhím Seín Thapa in his heaven-built fortresses, and he sent commissioners to make terms with the British government. He ceded all the conquests of the Ghorkas to the westward of the Kali river, together with the whole of the Terai; and he also agreed to receive a British Resident at Khatmandu; but nothing was said about a subsidiary force.

Sudden renewal of the war.

The negotiations were closed; Lord Moira had even signed the treaty; when a question arose as to whether the Terai, which had been ceded to the English, included the forest on the lower slopes of the Himalayas, or only the marshy plain at the foot of the mountain. At this moment Amar Singh returned to Khatmandu, and persuaded the Bharadars to defend their mountain territory to the last, and if conquered to retire towards China, rather than yield to the demands of the British government.

Treaty of Segowlie 1816.

Lord Moira, who had been honoured with the title of Marquis of Hastings, at once prepared to renew the war. In the beginning of 1816, General Sir David Ochterlony, who had been made a baronet, advanced towards Khatmandu with an army of twenty thousand men, and defeated the Ghorka army within fifty miles of the capital. The original treaty was then concluded in hot haste by the Thapa regent; the red seal was attached; peace was

A.D. 1814-1816 — concluded at Segowlie, and the British army was withdrawn from Nipal. But the difference about the Terai was renewed in other forms with a tenacity peculiar to the Ghorka character; it ended by the British government tacitly abandoning its rights rather than renew the war. The other mountain territory ceded by the treaty has however proved a valuable acquisition; it has furnished sites for the principal hill stations in India,—for Simla and Mussoorie, Landour and Nynee Tal.

CHAPTER XIII.

PINDHARI WAR, AND FALL OF THE PEISHWA: LORD HASTINGS.

A.D. 1815 TO 1823.

A.D. 1815-1817

Pindhari raids on British territories, 1815-16.

In 1815-16, whilst Sir David Ochterlony was bringing the Nipal war to a close, the Pindharies began to make raids on British territories. One horde of eight thousand horsemen swept the Nizam's territories as far south as the Kistna river. Another and a larger horde of twenty-five thousand Pindharies entered the Madras Presidency, and plundered three hundred villages on the coast of Coromandel. A third band of five hundred horsemen rode through the Peishwa's dominions, and plundered the villages along the coast of Malabar for a distance of two hundred miles, and then returned up the valley of the Taptí river to their homes in Malwa.

Lord Hastings resolves on the extinction of the Pindharies.

Lord Hastings determined, in spite of all orders to the contrary, to take steps for the extermination of these execrable miscreants. Other Pindhari raids were carried out in the cold weather of 1816 and 1817, and confirmed him in this resolution. He tried to form such a league with the Mahratta powers as would at least prevent them from interfering in behalf of the Pindharies. At the same time he secretly and silently made his own preparations for a campaign on such a large scale against the homes of the Pindhari hordes as would ensure their destruction once and for ever.

Indignation in England at Pindharí atrocities.

Meanwhile the horrible details of Pindharí atrocities were told in England, and created a revulsion of public opinion. Even the Mahrattas were forgotten in the stern resolution to punish the Pindharies and put an end to their cruel raids.

A.D. 1815-1817

Stories were related of villages surrounded by swarms of savage banditti; of fire and sword, rapine, murder, torture, and outrage, which spread universal alarm, and were proved by unquestionable testimony. At the approach of the Pindharies, fathers were known to pile fire-wood round their dwellings, and perish with all their families in flames kindled by their own hands; and in some cases the whole female population of a village threw themselves into wells rather than fall into the hands of such merciless marauders. Under such circumstances the home authorities violated their own policy of non-intervention, and hastened to sanction the most vigorous measures for the protection of British subjects. The British cabinet concurred with the Court of Directors in authorising hostilities against Sindia, Holkar, or any other native power, that should venture to protect the Pindharies against the just resentment of the British government.

Intrigues of Baji Rao Peishwa.

At this moment, and indeed for some years previously, the British government was aware that certain secret intrigues were being carried on at Poona by Baji Rao Peishwa, and his minister Trimbukji Dainglia, with Sindia and Holkar's governments, and even with the Pindharí leaders. The main object of these intrigues was to re-establish political relations with Sindia and Holkar contrary to the treaty of Bassein; to restore the Peishwa to the headship of the Mahratta empire; and to form a general confederacy of native powers for the overthrow of the British government.

Underhand breaches of treaty.

The objects which the Peishwa and his minister had in view might possibly be justified as patriotic efforts to throw off a foreign yoke; but the underhand means employed to carry them out were of a nature to provoke the hostility of the British government. The Peishwa had certain money claims against the Nizam of Hyderabad and the Gaekwar of Baroda; and these claims were to have been settled by the arbitration of the British government in accordance with the treaty of Bassein. But the Peishwa evaded all such arbitration, and it was discovered that these claims were used as a cover for carrying on secret negotiations with the Nizam and the Gaekwar, like those which had been carried on with Sindia, Holkar, and the Pindharí leaders.

In 1815 it was proposed that the Gaekwar should send his minister to Poona to settle the claims of the Peishwa

A.D. 1815-1817

against Baroda. This minister was a Brahman of high caste, named Gungadhur Shastri. His sacred character would have ensured his safety in any other court in India; but the unscrupulous treachery of Baji Rao was notorious, and the Shastri would not go to Poona until the British government guaranteed his safety.

Mission of Gungadhur Shastri to Poona.

Gungadhur Shastri was coldly received at Poona. He was suspected of being a friend of the British government, and was treated with so much reserve and covert hostility that he prepared to return to Baroda. His departure, however, would have put an end to all further communications with the Gaekwar. Accordingly the Peishwa and his minister turned round, and won him over by flattery and cajolery. The Shastri was told that the Peishwa had been so much struck by his talents, that he was to be appointed minister at Poona directly the claims against Baroda were settled. Moreover a marriage was arranged between the son of the Shastri and a sister-in-law of the Peishwa.

Strange reception, cold and hot.

The result of this cajolery was that Gungadhur Shastri was brought to agree to a settlement of the claims, which was more favourable to the Peishwa than to the Gaekwar. The proposals were sent to Baroda for ratification, but the Gaekwar was very angry and sent no reply. The Shastri became alarmed; he was afraid that the Gaekwar would think that he had neglected his master's interests in order to form a marriage connection with the Peishwa. Accordingly he broke off the marriage.

Halting between the Gaekwar and the Peishwa.

The Peishwa was mortally offended at this proceeding, but betrayed no sign of anger to the Shastri. On the contrary, the Shastri was treated with more kindness and cordiality than ever. He was invited to accompany the Peishwa and his minister on a pilgrimage to the temple of Punderpore. He was warned of danger, but was too much puffed up with the deference paid to him to take any heed. He went to Punderpore, dined with the Peishwa, proceeded to the temple, performed his devotions, took leave of the Peishwa and minister on the veranda of the temple, and set out to return to Poona. He had scarcely gone three hundred yards from the temple gateway, when he was attacked and cut to pieces by assassins who had been hired by the minister, Trimbukji Dainglia.

Murder of Gungadhur Shastri.

There was no doubt of the guilt of Trimbukji Dainglia.

A.D. 1815-1817

Surrender of the Peishwa's minister.

Mr. Elphinstone, the British Resident at Poona, investigated the case, and found that it was Trimbukji who hired the assassins. The general voice of the country pronounced that Trimbukji was the murderer of the Brahman. There was no moral doubt that the Peishwa was also implicated, but that was allowed to pass. The British government had guaranteed the safety of the Shastri, and the Peishwa was called upon to surrender the murderer. The Peishwa tried to evade the demand, but was at last terrified into compliance; and Trimbukji was placed under confinement in the fortress of Thanna on the island of Salsette, near Bombay.

Romantic escape of Trimbukji Dainglia, 1816.

Trimbukji Dainglia was confined at Thanna from September, 1815, to December, 1816. To prevent the possibility of escape, his guard was composed entirely of Europeans. He felt that his case was hopeless. He admitted to the officers of his guard that he had planned the murder of the Shastri, but declared that he only acted under the orders of the Peishwa. Subsequently Baji Rao managed to communicate with his favourite. A Mahratta horsekeeper in the service of one of the officers of the garrison passed the window of the prisoner every day with his master's horse. He carelessly sung a Mahratta song under the window, which the European guards neither understood nor suspected, but which told the ex-minister how to escape.[1] A number of Mahratta horsemen were lying in wait in the neighbourhood, and one night Trimbukji Dainglia was missing. He had escaped over the wall, joined the party of horsemen, and fled northward to the hills and jungles of Kandeish, where he found refuge amongst the Bhíls. No one doubted that Baji Rao had abetted the escape of his favourite; but nothing could be proved, and the matter was allowed to drop.

[1] Bishop Heber turned the Mahratta ballad into English verse as follows:—

"Behind the bush the bowmen hide
The horse beneath the tree.
Where shall I find the knight will ride
The jungle paths with me?

"There are five-and-fifty coursers there,
And four-and-fifty men;
When the fifty-fifth shall mount his steed,
The Dekhan thrives again."

Heber's Journal.

A.D. 1816-1817

Fresh intrigues of the Peishwa.

All this while, however, the Peishwa was actively but secretly negotiating with Sindia, Holkar, Amír Khan, and the Pindhari leaders, against the British government. He was enlisting troops in all directions, and sending large sums of money to Trimbukji Dainglia to enable him to raise a force in like manner. Subsequently Mr. Elphinstone discovered that Trimbukji had assembled an army within fifty miles of Poona. The Peishwa denied all knowledge of the fact, but continued to aid and abet his exiled favourite, and encouraged him to make war on the British government.

Increasing dangers.

The conduct of Baji Rao Peishwa at this crisis was as provoking to Lord Hastings as the conduct of Jaswant Rao Holkar had been to Lord Wellesley. It threatened to interfere with his plans for the extermination of the Pindharies. Lord Hastings had been most anxious to avoid a breach with Baji Rao, and had consequently ignored the Peishwa's connivance at the murder of the Shastri and escape of the minister. But Baji Rao was enlisting large bodies of troops in spite of the Resident's remonstrances; and he was placing his forts in a state of preparation, and sending his treasures out of Poona. At the same time the number of rebels under Trimbukji was increasing daily. It was obvious that the Peishwa was engaged in a conspiracy against the British government in order to effect the restoration of Trimbukji Dainglia to power, and possibly to carry out designs of a more serious character.

The Peishwa threatened: treaty of Poona, June, 1817.

At last in April, 1817, Mr. Elphinstone told the Peishwa that unless he put a stop to his hostile preparations, active measures would be taken against him by the British government. The Peishwa was now alarmed, and made a show of disbanding troops; but all this while he was raising fresh levies, and re-enlisting the disbanded troops in other quarters. In May the Resident sent an ultimatum; and after endless evasions and delays the Peishwa came to terms, and delivered up three important fortresses as pledges of his future good behaviour. In June, 1817, a treaty was concluded at Poona, under which the Peishwa ceded a considerable territory, and pledged himself to hold no further communication with any power whatever, Mahratta or otherwise, excepting the British government.

Lord Hastings was at this time completing his military

A.D. 1817

Military preparations for exterminating the Pindharies.

preparations; he was assembling the largest army that had ever appeared in India under British colours. Lord Cornwallis brought thirty thousand men to bear against Tippu. Lord Wellesley assembled nearly sixty thousand during the second Mahratta war. Lord Hastings called together the armies of the three Presidencies, which, together with native contingents and irregular troops, numbered nearly a hundred and twenty thousand strong. He was resolved, not only to exterminate the Pindharies, but to take decisive measures with the three predatory powers,—Sindia, Holkar, and Amír Khan.

Pindharies hemmed in.

Lord Hastings planned a campaign for placing the Pindharies between two fires; between the Bengal army from the north under his own command, and the Madras army from the south under Sir Thomas Hislop. On the north four Bengal divisions were to march from the Jumna, and to close round Malwa from the side of Bundelkund, Agra, and Rajpútana. At the same time four Madras divisions were to move from the south, cross the Nerbudda, and drive the Pindharies out of their haunts towards the river Chambal, where a Bengal force was lying in wait to receive them.

Attitude of the three predatory powers—Sindia, Holkar, and Amír Khan.

The three predatory powers were aware of the movements of the Madras army from the southward, but they had no inkling of the decisive operations which Lord Hastings proposed to carry out on the northward from the side of Bengal. They imagined that the greater part of the British forces on the Madras side were to be employed in defending the frontiers of the Nizam, the Raja of Nagpore, and the British possessions. They expected that a British detachment would make a push upon the homes of the Pindharies to the northward of the Nerbudda; but they calculated that the Pindharies would hide themselves for a while, either by enlisting in the predatory armies of the three powers, or by retiring to remote villages. Moreover they chuckled over the idea that when the storm had blown over, and the British troops had returned to cantonments, the Pindharies would revenge the British attack on their homes by still more savage and extensive raids on British territories.

Daulat Rao Sindia was the most decided supporter of the Pindharies. As far back as 1816 he engaged to help in the expulsion of the Pindharies; but he hoped to evade his

A.D. 1817

promise by some delusive action against the Pindharies, which might be managed in concert with their chiefs. He permitted the British to establish posts in his territories for operations against the Pindharies, but made no attempt to co-operate with the British officers for the destruction of his old retainers. On the contrary, his officers maintained cordial relations with the Pindhari leaders, in spite of the remonstrances of Captain Close, the British Resident.

Sindia leans to the Pindharies.

In 1817, at the beginning of the campaign, Daulat Rao Sindia was asked to issue orders for the friendly reception of the Madras army, which was crossing the Nerbudda into his territories in order to dislodge the Pindharies from his dominions. He was thunderstruck at the demand, and said that it required time for consideration. He was told by Captain Close that deliberation was out of the question; that the Madras forces were hastening northward on the faith that he was acting in concert with them for the extirpation of the Pindharies; and that these movements were combined with those of the Bengal army, which was about to cross the Jumna under the command of the Governor-General in person. Sindia saw that he was outwitted, and in imminent danger of being overwhelmed. He was overawed by the threatened approach of the Bengal army under Lord Hastings. Next day he sent to say that he had despatched orders to his officers for the friendly reception of the British troops within his own territories.

Yields to British pressure.

Lord Hastings was fully alive to the fact that the sympathies of the three predatory powers were with the Pindharies; and that the Pindharies looked to them for refuge and protection during the coming storm. Consequently he foresaw that the mere expulsion of the Pindharies from their haunts would not secure the peace of India, or prevent the revival of the predatory system. Accordingly he resolved to disarm the three predatory powers before rooting out the Pindharies.

Necessity for disarming the three predatory powers.

Daulat Rao Sindia soon felt that his powers for mischief were ebbing away. He was told that he had violated existing treaties by carrying on secret negotiations with the Peishwa, as well as with Runjeet Singh, the ruler of the Punjab. Nevertheless Lord Hastings was willing to leave him in possession of his territories, but was determined to deliver the Rajpút states out of the clutches of the predatory

Negotiations with Daulat Rao Sindia.

A.D. 1817

powers by reviving the protective treaties that had been annulled by Sir George Barlow.

Treacherous negotiations with Nipal.

At this crisis Daulat Rao Sindia was singularly unlucky. Whilst solemnly protesting that he had carried on no negotiations contrary to treaty, two of his messengers were arrested on the road to Nipal conveying letters to the Ghorka government at Khatmandu. Other letters were discovered between the leaves of a Sanskrit book, which had been glued together, and concealed amongst the baggage of the messengers. The contents proved that Daulat Rao Sindia was making proposals to the Thapa ministry for a combined attack of Ghorkas and Mahrattas on the British government.

Ignored by Lord Hastings: new treaty with Sindia, 1817.

Lord Hastings, however, was not inclined to press matters too hardly upon the Mahratta. He directed the British Resident to make over the documents to Daulat Rao Sindia in open durbar, briefly stating what they were and what they contained. Sindia was dumb with astonishment and alarm; he could make no defence whatever. He agreed to a new treaty under which the Rajpút states, and all other native states that desired it, were taken under British protection. He also pledged himself to co-operate for the expulsion of the Pindharies, and to prevent the future formation of any predatory gangs in his dominions.

Treaty with Amír Khan.

Negotiations were next opened with Amír Khan, through Mr. Charles Metcalfe, the British Resident at Delhi. The Afghan freebooter was growing old, and could not contend against the British government. He agreed to a treaty which converted a leader of bandits into a prince, and turned a predatory power into a native state under the guarantee of the British government. In return, Amír Khan engaged to abstain from all depredations for the future; to reduce his troops to a specified number; to surrender his artillery to the British government at a certain valuation; to refrain from all foreign conquest and aggrandisement; to exclude Pindharies and plunderers of every kind from his dominions; and to oppose to the utmost of his power the revival of the predatory system. Amír Khan thus appears in history as the founder of a Muhammadan dynasty, which is represented to this day by the Nawab of Tonk in Rajpútana.

The territories of Holkar were in a different condition to

A.D. 1817-1818

Holkar's government at the mercy of the army.

those of Sindia or Amír Khan. The government had been rapidly declining ever since the insanity of Jaswant Rao; and after his death it had fallen into a state of imbecility, and was literally at the mercy of the so-called army of Holkar. The best provinces were usurped by military chiefs, or mutinous bodies of armed men. The regent-mother, Tulsí Baí, and the young prince, Mulhar Rao Holkar, had sought refuge in a remote fortress from the outrages of the turbulent soldiery, who were clamouring for arrears of pay. Under such circumstances the regent-mother was naturally anxious for British protection against the army.

Destruction of the Pindharies, 1817-18.

In October, 1817, Lord Hastings left Cawnpore and began to cross the Jumna; and the different divisions of his army took up the positions assigned them. Meanwhile the Pindharies had been dislodged from their haunts by the Madras army, and fled with their wives and families to the northward; and now found themselves checkmated by the Bengal forces, and barred out of Rajpútana and Bundelkund. They were panic-stricken at the open defection of Sindia, and knew not where to go. All their anxiety was to avoid a conflict with the British troops. One body managed to escape in a southerly direction, with the loss of nearly all its baggage; the rest were forced to abandon their horses and hide themselves in the jungles, where numbers perished miserably. The body that escaped towards the south received a severe defeat, and suffered so much in smaller encounters that in the end it was completely dispersed. Many were slain in these actions and the subsequent flight; and many fell by the hands of the villagers in revenge for their former cruelties.

Extinction of the predatory system.

In this state of misery and despair some of the Pindhari leaders threw themselves upon the mercy of the conquerors. Khurím was provided with a landed estate in British territory, and permitted to reside there with his family. Chetu was killed in the jungles by a tiger. Several of the subordinate chiefs, and some of their followers, were settled in agricultural pursuits in the territories of the Newab of Bhopal, and converted into peaceful and profitable subjects. Others who survived the conflict mingled with the population and melted away, insomuch that after a very few years not a trace of the Pindhari gangs remained.

CHAPTER XIV.

MAHRATTA CONQUEST: LORD HASTINGS.

A.D. 1817 TO 1823.

A.D. 1817-1823

Mahratta affairs: Lord Hastings thwarted.

FROM the very beginning of the Pindhari war the attention of Lord Hastings was distracted by untoward events. He had hoped to suppress the predatory system in India, without disturbing one of the established principalities, or adding a rood of land to the British empire. This politic intention was thwarted by sheer force of circumstances. Whilst he was advancing against the Pindharies, Daulat Rao Sindia and Amír Khan remained true to their engagements, but the Peishwa, the Raja of Nagpore, and the army of Holkar, broke out in open hostilities to the British government, and his hopes of maintaining the existing political system were at an end.

Desperate designs of Baji Rao Peishwa.

Baji Rao Peishwa could no more keep the treaty of Poona than he could keep that of Bassein. It was equally opposed to his nature as a Mahratta, his culture as a Brahman, and his experiences as a Peishwa. It was just as reasonable to suppose that he could remain at Poona content with the loss of his suzerainty, as to suppose that the first Napoleon would have remained at Elba content with the loss of his empire.

Duplicity of the Peishwa.

Meantime Baji Rao Peishwa was playing his old game of duplicity. He had signed the treaty of Poona in June, 1817, and he then tried to throw dust in the eyes of the British Resident by pretending to disband his army. He discharged large bodies of cavalry, but gave the officers seven months' pay in advance, and sent them to their respective villages with orders to return to Poona with their friends and followers directly they received his summons. In July he left Poona, and went on a pilgrimage to the temples of Punderpore, the scene of the murder of Gungadhur Shastri. From Punderpore he went to another sacred place, named Maholi, which was situated near Satara, the later capital of the dynasty of Sivaji.

A.D. 1817

Meeting with Sir John Malcolm at Maholi.

At this crisis Sir John Malcolm was at Poona, busied with political arrangements connected with the approaching Pindhari war. Malcolm knew the Peishwa well, having accompanied him on his restoration to Poona in 1803. Accordingly Malcolm received a pressing invitation from Baji Rao to visit him at Maholi, and readily accepted it in the hope of reconciling the Peishwa to his new situation. Baji Rao welcomed Malcolm most cordially, spoke of his restoration in 1803, declared that John Malcolm and Arthur Wellesley were his best friends, and dilated on his lasting gratitude to the English. But he was evidently smarting under the treaty of Poona. He bitterly complained of his loss of position and territory, and especially harped upon the three fortresses which he had been forced to surrender as pledges of his good faith.

Malcolm outwitted.

An officer of Malcolm's experience ought to have known that Baji Rao was only cajolling him, in the hope of getting back the three fortresses before committing himself to a war. But Malcolm believed in the sincerity of the Peishwa, and tried to soothe him with promises of future reward and consideration. He explained the coming operations against the Pindharies, and exhorted the Peishwa to co-operate heartily with the English during the campaign. He then returned to Poona, so convinced of the good faith of the Peishwa that he actually induced Mr. Elphinstone to restore the three fortresses.

Scepticism of Elphinstone.

Elphinstone however had lost all faith in Baji Rao. He restored the fortresses because he would not throw cold water on Malcolm's hopes; but he was by no means carried away by Malcolm's generous enthusiasm, and events soon proved that Elphinstone was in the right.

Treachery of Baji Rao.

Baji Rao returned to Poona in September, and took enormous numbers of horsemen into his pay, declaring that he was going to make war on the Pindharies. Elphinstone was not deluded, for Baji Rao was enlisting double the number of troops that could possibly be required.

A.D. 1817 Moreover Baji Rao evaded sending any troops to the northward, although their presence was urgently required on the Nerbudda. At the same time he was putting his fortresses into a state of defence, strengthening the garrisons, and storing them with provisions and treasure. It was also discovered that he was trying to seduce the English sepoys from their allegiance by bribes and promises; sending secret emissaries to the Raja of Nagpore, as well as to Sindia, Holkar, and Amír Khan; and planning to assassinate Elphinstone, either by treacherously inviting him to an interview, or by surrounding the Residency with a rebel force under Trimbukji Dainglia.

Preparations of Mr. Elphinstone for defence.

Elphinstone knew pretty well what was going on, but was anxious not to precipitate a rupture, and accordingly proceeded very cautiously with his preparations for defence. The Poona Subsidiary Force under General Smith had gone to the northward to join in the operations against the Pindharies; but a detachment remained at Poona, and Elphinstone obtained the services of a European regiment from Bombay. The whole British force at Poona only numbered two thousand sepoys and eight hundred European soldiers; and it was deemed expedient to remove the troops from Poona to Khirkí, a village about four miles from the British Residency.

Movements of the Peishwa.

The arrival of the European regiment from Bombay was the one thing above all others which disconcerted Baji Rao. For more than sixty years the presence of a European regiment had been regarded with terror by every native prince. Accordingly, on the arrival of the Europeans, Baji Rao feigned to be alarmed at the intentions of the British government. He threatened to withdraw from Poona unless the European regiment was sent back to Bombay. The removal of the British force to Khirkí re-assured him; he ascribed it to fear. On the 5th of November Elphinstone himself left the Residency and joined the force at Khirkí.

Battle of Khirki: repulse of the Peishwa, November, 1817.

Baji Rao was at this time buoyed up by false hopes. He believed that Daulat Rao Sindia and Amír Khan had taken the field against the British government. He knew that the Raja of Nagpore and the army of Holkar were preparing to support him. Accordingly on the afternoon of the day that Elphinstone left the Residency, Baji Rao attacked the British force at Khirkí with an army of eighteen thousand horse, eight thousand foot, and fourteen pieces of artillery. Notwithstanding these overwhelming numbers, he was repulsed with the loss of five hundred killed and wounded. That same night the Residency was plundered and burnt, and Elphinstone lost a magnificent library which no money could restore. A.D. 1817

The Subsidiary Force under General Smith, which had been sent to co-operate against the Pindharies, had already been recalled to Poona. It soon made its appearance, and prepared to attack the Peishwa's army on the morning of the 17th of November. But the heart of Baji Rao had already failed him. He left Poona on the night of the 16th, and thus surrendered his dominions without a blow. The British troops occupied Poona, and General Smith set out in pursuit of Baji Rao. Peishwa flies from Poona.

Meanwhile the Raja of Nagpore secretly made common cause with the Peishwa. Rughoji Bhonsla died in 1816; his son and successor was an idiot, and his nephew Appa Sahib became regent. The idiot was murdered by Appa Sahib, and the regent became Raja without any discovery of his crime. Appa Sahib conciliated the English by concluding a subsidiary treaty. At the same time he secretly maintained an active correspondence with the Peishwa, and played the same game as the Peishwa. He was somewhat sobered by the treaty of Poona, which Baji Rao had been compelled to accept in June; but he soon renewed his secret negotiations with the Peishwa, and began to levy troops on a large scale. When news arrived of the attack on the British Residency at Poona, Appa Sahib talked at great length to Mr. Jenkins, the Resident at Nagpore, on the treachery of Baji Rao, and the impossibility that he should ever be induced to follow so bad an example; yet all this while Appa Sahib was preparing to falsify every protestation by making common cause with the Peishwa against the British government. Nagpore affairs: treachery of Appa Sahib, November 1817.

The story reveals the double-faced duplicity of the Mahratta. In November, 1817, when Baji Rao was already at war with the English, he appointed Appa Sahib to the honourable but nominal post of commander-in-chief of the army of the Peishwa. Such empty dignities had been common enough in the palmy days of the Mahratta empire, and often served to revive the fading loyalty of a disaffected Appa Sahib appointed commander-in-chief by the Peishwa.

A.D. 1817

feudatory, and bind him in closer allegiance to his suzerain. But such an appointment in November, 1817, was a gross violation of the treaties of Bassein and Poona, and was obviously made for the purpose of drawing Appa Sahib into hostilities with the British government.

Warned by Mr. Jenkins.

On the night of the 24th of November Appa Sahib sent word to Mr. Jenkins that he had accepted the post of commander-in-chief of the army of the Peishwa, and was to be invested with the insignia of office on the following morning in the presence of all his troops; and he invited Mr. Jenkins to be present on the occasion, and requested that a salute might be fired by the English in honour of the investiture. Mr. Jenkins declined having anything to do with the ceremony, and warned the Raja that it might lead to dangerous consequences.

Preparations for war.

Next morning Mr. Jenkins discovered that treachery was abroad. All communication between the city of Nagpore and the Residency had been interdicted by the Raja; and the Raja and his ministers were sending their families and valuables out of the city. He foresaw that an attack would be made on the Residency; and he ordered up the British troops from the neighbouring cantonment and posted them on the Sitabuldí hill, between the Residency and the city of Nagpore. On the following evening the Raja brought up all his forces and began the attack on the hill.

Battle of Sitabuldí.

The battle of Sitabuldí is famous in the annals of British India. The English had no European regiment on the spot, as they had at Khirkí; they had scarcely fourteen hundred sepoys fit for duty, including three troops of Bengal cavalry, and only four six-pounders. Appa Sahib had an army of eighteen thousand men, including four thousand Arabs, the best soldiers in the Dekhan; he had also thirty-six guns. The battle lasted from six o'clock in the evening of the 26th of November until noon the next day. For many hours the English were in sore peril; their fate seemed to hang upon a thread. The Arabs were beginning to close round the Residency, when a happy stroke of British daring changed the fortunes of the day.

Fitzgerald's charge.

Captain Fitzgerald, who commanded the Bengal cavalry, was posted in the Residency compound and was anxious to charge the Arabs; but he was forbidden by the commander of the British forces. Again he implored permission, but was

A.D. 1817-1818

told to charge at his peril. "On my peril be it!" cried Fitzgerald, and gave the word to charge. Clearing the enclosures, the Bengal cavalry bore down upon the enemy's horse, captured two guns, and cut up a body of infantry. The British sepoys posted on the hill hailed the exploit with loud huzzas, and seeing the explosion of one of the enemy's tumbrils, they rushed down the hill, driving the Arabs before them like sheep. The victory was won, but the English had lost a quarter of their number in killed and wounded.

Dealings with Appa Sahib.

Foiled in this treacherous attempt, Appa Sahib sent envoys to Mr. Jenkins to express his sorrow, and to deny having authorised the attack. Reinforcements were now pouring in from all directions; but Mr. Jenkins affected to believe the statement of the Raja, and even promised to be reconciled, provided he disbanded his troops. But Appa Sahib was still playing his old game. He continued his correspondence with the Peishwa, and stirred up his own chiefs to rebellious outbreaks, in order to keep his territories in a state of alarm and disorder.

Deposition and flight.

At this juncture it was discovered that Appa Sahib had been guilty of the murder of his predecessor. Under these circumstances he was arrested, and sent as a prisoner to Allahabad; but on the way he managed to bribe his guards and make his escape. Henceforth Appa Sahib was a fugitive; and after a precarious existence for many years in the Vindhya and Sátpúra mountains, he finally found refuge in the territories of the Raja of Jodhpur.[1]

Boy Raja of Nagpore: Mr. Jenkins supreme.

An infant grandson of Rughoji Bhonsla, aged nine, was then placed upon the throne of Nagpore. He was a son of Rughoji's daughter, but was formally adopted by Rughoji's widow in order that he might take the name of Bhonsla. The widow was appointed regent, but her

[1] The Raja of Jodhpur was called upon to surrender Appa Sahib to the British authorities, but pleaded that he would be disgraced in the eyes of his brother chieftains in Rajpútana, if he gave up a fugitive who had found an asylum within his territories. As Appa Sahib had not committed an offence which placed him outside the bar of mercy, and as he was powerless for further mischief, the plea was admitted on the Jodhpur Raja becoming responsible for his good behaviour. In the end a provision was made for the support of the wretched exile, and his latter days were soothed by the medical attendance of the English doctor at the Jodhpur Residency.

A.D. 1817-1818

authority was nominal, as the whole administration was placed in the charge of Mr. Jenkins until the boy Raja attained his majority.

Holkar's government declares for the Peishwa.

Affairs in Holkar's state of Indore ran nearly in the same groove as at Nagpore, but the circumstances were different. The regent-mother, Tulsí Baí, was no longer anxious to place the infant, Mulhar Rao Holkar, under the protection of the British government. The Peishwa had reduced the army of Holkar to obedience by discharging all arrears of pay out of his own treasury. The regent-mother and her ministers recovered their ascendancy over the soldiery, avowed themselves the partisans of the Peishwa, and led the army towards the south to make war upon the British government in support of the Peishwa.

Desperate proceedings of the army of Holkar.

At this moment, the Madras army, under Sir Thomas Hislop, was moving northward in pursuit of the Pindharies. In December, 1817, it met the army of Holkar near Ujain; and Sir John Malcolm, who accompanied the Madras army in a diplomatic capacity, opened up negotiations with the regent-mother and her ministers. The latter seemed inclined to come to an arrangement with the British government; but the military chiefs were bent on war, and suspected that the ministers and regent-mother were making secret terms with the British authorities. Accordingly the army rose against their rulers, put the ministers under confinement, and carried off the regent-mother to a neighbouring river, and cruelly beheaded her on the bank, and threw her remains into the stream.

Battle of Mehidpore, December, 1817.

The barbarous murder of a woman and a princess cut off all hope of pacification. An action was inevitable; indeed, the army of Holkar began operations by plundering the English baggage. The battle was fought at Mehidpore on the 21st of December, 1817. Sir John Malcolm commanded the English troops on that occasion, and gained a complete victory. The army of Holkar was utterly routed, and all their guns and military stores fell into the hands of the English.

Lord Hastings constructs a new imperial system.

The Mahratta powers were thus prostrate, and Lord Hastings prepared to construct the new political system, which has continued without material change down to the present day. The arrangements with Sindia, Amír Khan, and the infant Raja of Nagpore, were already completed, or

A.D. 1817-1818

were in course of completion. It may, however, be added, that Sindia was required to cede the territory of Ajmír in Rajpútana; as it was deemed essential to the security of the public peace in India, to shut out all Mahratta influences from Rajpútana. The only princes remaining to be dealt with were Baji Rao Peishwa and Mulhar Rao Holkar.

Movements of the Peishwa: annexation.

The Peishwa had fled from Poona southward towards Satara. He sought to strengthen his hereditary claims on the allegiance of the Mahratta powers by causing the pageant Raja of Satara to be brought to his camp. His movements, however, were little more than desperate efforts to avoid a collision with the British forces in pursuit; and all hope of recovering his position as suzerain of the Mahratta empire died out of his restless brain, and reduced him to the depths of despair.

Glorious defence of Korygaum, 1st January, 1818.

The glorious defence of Korygaum belongs to this interval; it was regarded as the most brilliant exploit of the war, and is celebrated to this day in Mahratta songs in all parts of the Dekhan. A detachment of Bombay sepoys and irregular horse, not exceeding 800 men, reached the village of Korygaum, on the bank of the river Bhima, under the command of Captain Staunton. There were only ten English officers, and twenty-four European artillerymen with two six-pounders. Suddenly Staunton saw the whole army of the Peishwa drawn up on the opposite bank, to the number of 25,000 horsemen and about 6,000 Arab and Gosain infantry. Staunton at once occupied the village of Korygaum, and prepared for defence. The enemy surrounded the village with horse and foot, whilst three picked bodies of infantry attempted to storm the English position with rockets. Then followed a series of charges and repulses, which lasted till nightfall. Without provisions, and without water—for all access to the river was cut off—the Bombay sepoys and their European officers fought with a pluck and desperation which broke the spirit of the enemy. Staunton lost a third of his sepoys, and eight out of his ten officers; but the Mahrattas left six hundred killed and wounded on the field. Baji Rao witnessed the whole action from a neighbouring hill, and was beside himself with anger and mortification. Next morning his army refused to renew the fight, and rapidly disappeared from the scene.

For six months longer Baji Rao remained at large, but

A.D. 1817-1818

Pursuit of Baji Rao.

his career was run. There was another battle at Ashti, but he cowardly fled at the first shot, leaving his army to be defeated by General Smith, whilst the pageant Raja of Satara fell into the hands of the English. Indeed, from a very early period, the defection of Daulat Rao Sindia, the destruction of the Pindharies, the crushing defeat of the army of Holkar, and the deposition of Appa Sahib at Nagpore, had combined to deprive Baji Rao of all hope of recovering his throne, and to render his capture a mere question of time.

Extinction of the Peishwa.

The Peishwa was doomed to extinction. The treaty of Bassein had failed to break up the Mahratta confederacy; it had failed to prevent the Mahratta states from regarding the Peishwa as their lawful suzerain, and leaguing under his authority against the British government. Nagpore and Holkar had waged war against the British government in obedience to the call of the Peishwa; and Sindia would probably have done the same had he not been taken by surprise, and bound over to keep the peace before committing himself to a suicidal war.

State necessity for the extinction.

It was thus obvious to Lord Hastings that the abdication of Baji Rao would have proved wholly insufficient to secure the peace of India. To have set up another Peishwa in his room would only have led to a revival of the old intrigues against the British government. To have transferred the territories of the Peishwa to a prince bearing another title would have proved equally dangerous and delusive. The other Mahratta powers would still have deemed it their duty to award to the new prince the indefeasible right of the Peishwa to command their armies, in spite of the change of name; and Poona would have continued to be the rallying point for disaffection, not only to every Mahratta feudatory, but possibly to every Hindu prince in India. Accordingly, Lord Hastings determined that henceforth the Mahrattas should be without a Peishwa.

Proposed elevation of the Raja of Satara.

It was a question whether the Raja of Satara might not have been raised from the condition of a pageant to that of sovereign of Poona. But the representative of Sivaji had long been shut up as an idol at Satara, and was now a forgotten idol. The traditions of the once famous Bhonsla family had lost their hold on the Mahrattas. The dynasty of Sivaji had been superseded by the dynasty of Brahmans;

and the descendant of Sivaji could no more have been restored to sovereignty than the descendant of the Great Moghul. Accordingly Lord Hastings resolved to abolish the Peishwa, annex his territories, and reduce Baji Rao to the condition of Napoleon at St. Helena. He delivered the Raja of Satara from the thraldom of generations, and assigned a territory for his support out of the possessions of the Peishwa.

A.D. 1817-1818

Final decision of Lord Hastings.

In June, 1818, Baji Rao was surrounded by British troops under the command of Sir John Malcolm, and had no alternative but to die sword in hand, or throw himself on the mercy of the British government. The terms offered by Malcolm were so liberal as to excite much controversy. Whilst the great Napoleon was condemned to pass his last days on a solitary rock in the southern ocean, with a comparative pittance for his maintenance, the ex-Peishwa was permitted to live in luxury in the neighbourhood of Cawnpore on a yearly stipend of eighty thousand pounds. Trimbukji Dainglia was captured shortly afterwards, and was doomed to spend the remainder of his days in close confinement in the fortress of Chunar.

Final terms with the Peishwa.

Lord Hastings refused to annex Holkar's territories. The hostile action of the army of Holkar had compelled the British government to treat the shattered principality of Indore as an enemy; but Lord Hastings had no desire to annihilate the remains of Holkar's government, or to dethrone the family of Jaswant Rao. Accordingly the Holkar state was required to cede certain territories, and to confirm the grants it had already made to Amír Khan; it was also required to surrender its international life, and become a subsidiary state under the guarantee of the British government. But in all other respects the infant Mulhar Rao Holkar was treated as an independent prince, and the administration was left in the hands of the ministers and durbar, aided by the advice of the British Resident.

Settlement of the Holkar state.

The policy of Lord Hastings did not meet with the full approval of his contemporaries, but its success is proved by the after history. From the extinction of the Peishwas in 1818, and the suppression of the Pindharies, there has been no serious attempt at an armed confederation of native states against the British government. Possibly had Lord Wellesley extinguished the Great Moghul as thoroughly as Lord Hastings extinguished the Mahratta Peishwa, the

Success of Lord Hasting's policy.

A.D. 1817-1823

mutinies of 1857 might never have occurred, Delhi might have been as loyal as Poona, and any outbreak of deluded sepoys would have hurt no one but themselves.

Education of the natives.

In other directions the administration of Lord Hastings marks a new era in the history of India. He was the first Governor-General that countenanced and encouraged the education of the native populations. Previous to his time it had been the popular idea that the ignorance of the natives insured the security of British rule; but Lord Hastings denounced this view as treason against British sentiment, and promoted the establishment of native schools and native journals. In so doing he was in advance of his time, and consequently he was condemned in his generation.

Affairs of the Nizam of Hyderabad.

The dealings of Lord Hastings with the Nizam's government have been much criticised. The Nizam profited by the extinction of the Peishwa more than any other native prince in India, for he was relieved by the British government from the Mahratta claims for arrears of chout, which had hung like a millstone on the necks of the rulers of Hyderabad for the greater part of a century. But the Nizam eschewed all business, and cared only for his pleasures. A Hindu grandee named Chandu Lal was placed at the head of the administration, and found it necessary to keep on good terms with both the Nizam and the British government, much in the same way that Muhammad Reza Khan in a previous generation had tried to secure his hold on the administration of Bengal. The result was that nothing flourished but corruption. Every public office was put up for sale; judicial decrees could only be purchased by bribes; the revenues of the state were farmed out to the highest bidders; and the farmers became all powerful in the districts, and were left to practice every species of oppression and extortion without control. In the end the people were driven by exactions to become rebels and bandits; villages were deserted; lands fell out of cultivation, and provisions rose to famine prices.

British supervision in the Nizam's territories.

In 1820, Mr. Charles Metcalfe was appointed Resident at Hyderabad. Having made a tour of the country, he deemed it expedient to place his political assistants, and British officers of the Nizam's Contingent,[1] in charge of

[1] The Nizam's Contingent was a body altogether different from the Nizam's Subsidiary Force. By the treaty of 1800 the Nizam was

A.D. 1817-1823

different districts, in order to superintend a new revenue settlement, check oppression, and control the police. There is no question that this measure contributed largely to the improvement of the country and well being of the people; but it was naturally unpalatable to the Nizam and Chandu Lal, and in 1829 the supervision of British officers was withdrawn.

Bank of Palmer and Co. at Hyderabad.

Meanwhile as far back as the year 1814, a bank had been established at Hyderabad by a firm known as Palmer and Co. It received loans from deposits bearing twelve per cent. interest, and lent the money to the Nizam at twenty-four per cent. on the security of assignments of land revenue. According to act of parliament all such transactions were prohibited to British subjects without the express sanction of the Governor-General; but this sanction had been obtained from Lord Hastings, who believed that such dealings were better in the hands of European bankers, than in those of native money-lenders. Moreover, one of the partners had married a ward of Lord Hastings; and thus, under a variety of circumstances, the Governor-General was enabled to throw the veil of his authority over the transactions of Palmer and Co.

Condemned by Mr Metcalfe.

Mr. Metcalfe reported that this bank had become a source of corruption. In 1820, Chandu Lal had obtained the sanction of the British government to a new loan of sixty lakhs of rupees, or six hundred thousand pounds sterling, nominally to pay off and reduce public establishments, to make advances to the ryots, and to clear off certain debts due to native bankers. Mr. Metcalfe, however, discovered that the new loan was a sham. Eight lakhs of the money was transferred as a bonus to the partners in Palmer and Co.; whilst the remainder was appropriated to paying off money lent to the Nizam, or said to have been lent to him, without the knowledge of the British government.

bound to furnish a Contingent of fifteen thousand troops in time of war, but those which he supplied during the Mahratta war of 1803 were little better than a rabble. Subsequently the force was reduced in numbers, and its efficiency was increased by the employment of British officers; and it was retained by the Nizam as a permanent force in time of peace for the reduction of refractory zemindars and other domestic purposes.

A.D. 1817-1823

In a word, the new loan of sixty lakhs was a deception, which filled the pockets of interested parties without liquidating the real claims; whilst, in consequence of the sanction inconsiderately given by Lord Hastings, the British government was more or less compromised in the matter. Accordingly it was resolved to pay off all debts due by the Nizam to the bank, and put an end to the relations between the Nizam's government and Palmer and Co. The matter ended in the insolvency of the firm.

Payment of the Nizam's debts.

The money for paying off the Nizam's debts was provided for in a peculiar fashion. Some half a century previously the East India Company had agreed to pay the Nizam a yearly rent of seventy thousand pounds sterling for the Northern Circars; and in spite of political changes this yearly sum had been regularly paid down to the time of Lord Hastings. Accordingly the rent was capitalised, and the money was devoted to the payment of the Nizam's debt to Palmer and Co.

Error of Lord Hastings.

The error of judgment committed by Lord Hastings in sanctioning the money dealings of Palmer and Co., blotted his reputation in the eyes of his contemporaries, and is only worthy of record as containing a useful political lesson for all time.

Leaves India 1st January, 1823.

Lord Hastings left India on the 1st of January, 1823, at the advanced age of sixty-eight. His last years were embittered by the reproaches of the Court of Directors; but he will live in history as the Governor-General who carried the imperial policy of Lord Wellesley to its legitimate conclusion, and established the British government as the paramount power in India.

Lord Amherst, Governor-General, 1823.

Lord Amherst was appointed Governor-General in succession to Lord Hastings, but he did not reach India until August 1823. During the interval Mr. Adam, a civil servant of the Company, acted as Governor-General; but his short administration is only remarkable for his sharp treatment of the public press. An obnoxious editor, named Buckingham, had written unfavourably of government officials in a Calcutta newspaper, and was forthwith deprived of his licence, and sent to England.[1] Nothing further is known of

[1] Before the year 1833 no European was permitted to reside in India unless he was in the service of the late East India Company, or had

Mr. Adam; he perished at sea on his return voyage to England. A.D. 1817-1823

The all-important event in Lord Amherst's administration was the first Burmese war of 1824-25; but before describing the military operations, it may be as well to bring the country and people of Burma under review.

obtained a license from the Court of Directors. These restrictions were removed on the renewal of the charter of the late East India Company in 1833.

CHAPTER XV.

BURMAN HISTORY: AVA AND PEGU.

A.D. 1540 TO 1823.

A.D. 1540-1823 — Geography of Burma.

BURMA is an irregular oblong, lying west and east between Bengal and China, and between the Bay of Bengal and the kingdom of Siam. On the north it touches Assam and Thibet. On the south it runs downwards in a long narrow strip of sea board, like the tail of an animal, and terminates at the Siamese frontier on the river Pak Chan.

Ava and Pegu.

Burma includes the valley of the Irawadi, which is destined at no distant period to play as important a part in the eastern world as the valley of the Ganges. Burma proper, or Ava, comprises only the upper valley. The lower valley, although included in the general term of Burma, is better known as Pegu.[1]

[1] Ava, or Burma proper, is an inland country entirely cut off from the sea by the territory of Pegu. It has no outlet to the sea excepting by the river Irawadi, which runs through Pegu, and forms a Delta towards the Gulf of Martaban. In ancient times, and down to the middle of the last century, Ava and Pegu were separated into different kingdoms, and were often at war with each other. Indeed, there was some obscure antagonism of race, the people of Ava being known as Burmans, and the people of Pegu as Talains. Besides Ava and Pegu there are two long strips of coast territory facing the Bay of Bengal, which are respectively known as Arakan and Tenasserim; but they also formed independent kingdoms, and had no political connection with either Ava or Pegu until a recent period. Arakan runs northward from the Delta of the Irawadi towards the frontier of Bengal on the river Náf. Tenasserim runs southward towards the frontier of Siam, on the river Pah Chan. Tenasserim is the "territorial tail" indicated in the opening paragraph to the present chapter.

A.D. 1540-1823

Description of the Burmese people.

The people of Burma belong to the Indo-Chinese race, having Mongolian features, with tolerably fair complexions, varying from a dusky yellow to a clear whiteness. They are Buddhists in religion; converts from the old Vedic worship of Indra, Brahma, and other gods, which still lingers in the land. They are without caste, without hereditary rank save in the royal family, without nobility save what is official and personal, and without any of the prejudices which prevail in India as regards early marriages and the seclusion of females. They are a joyous race in comparison with the grave and self-constrained Hindus; taking pleasure in dramatic performances, singing, music, dancing, buffoonery, boat-racing, and gambling. They revel in shows and processions on gala days, at which young and old of both sexes mingle freely together. They indulge in much mirth and practical joking at the water festival and other feasts which have been handed down from the old nature worship of Vedic times. They are imbued with military sentiments akin to those of Rajpúts; and leave all menial appointments to slaves and captives.

Life and manners.

Burma is a land of sun and rain. There are no cold blasts from the Himalayas like those which sweep over Hindustan during the winter season; and the south-west monsoon, which begins early in May and lasts till September, empties its torrents on the soil far more abundantly than on the plains of India. The villages are generally on the banks of rivers. They consist of wooden huts built on piles, so as to be raised above the floods during the rainy season. The ordinary villagers seem to saunter through life, caring only for their cattle and harvests, their fields, fisheries, and fruit-trees; knowing nothing of the outer world, and caring for nothing, except as regards famous pagodas or renowned places of pilgrimage. All real business is generally transacted by wives and daughters, who attend to the cares of the household, and often carry on a traffic in the bazar, and are most exemplary in the discharge of their religious duties.

Buddhist monks, monasteries, and schools.

In every village throughout Burma there is at least one Buddhist monastery built of wood or brick, with a separate building for a monastery school. There are no endowments of money or land of any sort or kind. Every morning the monks go their rounds through the village, clad in yellow

A.D. 1540-1823

robes, and carrying bowls to receive the alms of the villagers in cooked food, after the manner of Gótama Buddha and his disciples. The daily alms are never wanting, for every Burmese man and woman is imbued with the faith that by such acts of benevolence and loving-kindness they secure a higher and better life in the next existence in the chain of transmigrations. When the monks return to the monastery, they take their breakfast, which with them is the chief, if not the only meal of the day. The younger monks then engage in teaching reading, writing, and arithmetic to a daily gathering of village boys; whilst the older monks are teaching the sacred language of Pali to more advanced neophytes, or studying Pali scriptures, or pondering over the mysteries of life and transmigrations of the soul.

Buddhist pagodas: worship and worshippers.

In Burma the pagodas of Buddhists are to be seen everywhere, and are sometimes substantial buildings of masonry. Statues of Buddha are to be found in all parts of the building, or in neighbouring chapels. There are figures squatting on the ground, representing Gótama about to become a Buddha; and there are horizontal figures representing Gótama in the act of dying, or entering into the sleep of Nirvána. Sometimes miniature figures are placed in small niches; sometimes there is a colossal statue many feet high. The images are covered with gilding, or are painted red, or are made of white alabaster, with the features tinted in gold and colours. On festival days the pagodas are decked with flags and garlands, and thronged with people of both sexes and all ages, who prostrate themselves before some great statue of Gótama Buddha, and chant his praises in sacred verses. Fathers and mothers go with all their families. Infants are carried about, sometimes in arms, but generally in baskets yoked to the shoulders like milk-pails. Old men and matrons march along with grave countenances, mingled with swaggering young men in gay attire, and demure damsels with graceful forms, radiant in divers colours and bright adornments, with flowers of every hue lighting up their coal-black hair. All go trooping up the aisles of the pagoda, to make their prostration to Buddha; and then they go out into the temple inclosure to hammer at the pagoda bells with antelopes' horns, as part of some mystic rite of which the meaning is forgotten.

There is one institution in Burma which reveals the marked

contrast between Hindus and Burmese. In India marriages are contracted by the parents between boys and girls of a tender age, when the children themselves can have no voice in the matter. In Burma marriages are brought about by mutual liking, which is developed by an innocent custom of pastoral simplicity. The interval between sunset and retiring to rest is known as courting-time. Any young daughter of a house who is desirous of receiving visitors, attires herself in her best, adorns her hair, takes a seat on a mat, and places a lamp in her window as a hint that she is at home. Meantime all the young men of the village array themselves in like manner, and pass the hours of courting-time in a round of visits, at which there is always much talking and laughing. Sometimes the hour may be a little late; sometimes there may be a little quarrelling between jealous rivals; but as a rule the party breaks up at a suitable time without any serious incident to mar the pleasure of the evening. In this way young men and maidens meet and exchange their sentiments in a perfectly innocent and natural manner, until partners are selected for life, marriages are celebrated, and for them the courting time is over.

A.D. 1540-1823

Marriage institutions: courting time in Burma.

This richly favoured country has been exposed from a remote period to cruel oppressions and bloody wars. It was anciently parcelled out, like India, amongst petty kings, who waged frequent wars on each other. There was constant rivalry between the Burmese people of Ava on the upper valley of the Irawadi and the Talains of Pegu on the lower valley.[1] Other kings warred against each other in like manner; whilst ever and anon an invading army from China or Siam swept over the whole country, and deluged the land with blood. Sometimes there were insurrections under a rebel prince or schismatic monk, followed by sack and massacre without a parallel in recorded history, except amongst Tartar nations. To this day the whole region of Pegu and Ava bears the marks of these desolating contests; and vast tracts of culturable lands lie utterly waste from sheer want of population.

Despotic tyranny and devastating wars.

In the sixteenth century many Portuguese adventurers and desperadoes found a career in Burma. They were for the most part the scum of Goa and Malacca;—renegade

Portuguese in Burma, 1500-1600.

[1] See *ante*, page 500, *note*.

A.D. 1540-1823

priests or runaway soldiers, who had thrown off the restraints of church or army to plunge in the wild license of oriental life, and to reappear as pirates, bravos, or princes in the remoter eastern seas. One Portuguese deserter got possession of the island of Sundiva at the entrance to the Sunderbunds, and created a fleet of pirate-galleys, which was the terror of Arakan and eastern Bengal. He was followed by an Augustine monk known as Fra Joan. Another scoundrel got possession of a fort at Syriam, over against Rangoon, and was the terror of the Burmese kings on the Irawadi. Others entered the service of different kings of Burma, and often changed the fortunes of war by their superior physique and fire-arms.

A Burmese hero, 1540: conquest of Pegu.

About 1540 a Burmese warrior, named Byeen-noung, rose to the front, and became a conqueror of renown.[1] Originally he was governor of Toungoo;[2] then he made himself king of the country; and subsequently he marched an army of Burmans towards the south, and conquered the Talain kingdom of Pegu and slew the Talain king.

Siege of Martaban, 1546.

Byeen-noung next resolved on the conquest of Martaban. This kingdom lay to the eastward of Pegu, between Pegu and Tenasserim; it was separated from Pegu by an arm of the sea, known as the Gulf of Martaban. Byeen-noung raised a large army of all nations, in addition to his army of Burmans, by promising them the sack of Martaban, and with these united forces he invested Martaban by land and sea.

Obstinate resistance: wrath of Byeen-noung.

The siege lasted six months. The king of Martaban had married the daughter of the slaughtered king of Pegu; and the queen and all her ladies spurred on the king and his generals to resist Byeen-noung to the uttermost. The people of Martaban were starved out and driven to eat their elephants. The king had taken several hundred Portuguese into his service, but they had all deserted him, and entered

[1] Byeen-noung is so named in Burmese annals. He was known to the Portuguese as Branginoco. See Faria y Sousa's *Portuguese Asia*.

[2] Toungoo, the Portuguese Tangu, lies in the interior of Burma, between Pegu and Ava. In the present day it is the frontier district of British Burma. In the sixteenth and seventeenth centuries it was sometimes a province of Ava, sometimes an independent kingdom, and sometimes the seat of a Burmese empire; indeed, at one time the city of Toungoo is said to have been the capital of Upper Burma or Ava. Such shifting of provinces, kingdoms, empires, and capitals, is one of the conditions of old Burmese history.

the service of Byeen-noung. The king was reduced to such extremities that at last he offered to make over his kingdom to Byeen-noung, provided he might retire from Martaban with his queen and children; but Byeen-noung was furious at the obstinate resistance he had encountered, and burning to be revenged not only on the king, but on the queen and all her ladies, and he demanded an unconditional surrender.

Council of war a failure.

The king of Martaban was in despair. He called his generals to a council of war, and one and all pledged themselves to die like warriors; to slaughter all their women and children, throw their treasures into the sea, set the city on fire, and rush out and perish sword in hand. But when the council broke up, one of the chief commanders turned traitor or coward, and fled away to the camp of Byeen-noung. Then the rest of the generals lost heart, and threatened to open the gates of the city to Byeen-noung, unless the king gave himself up without further parley.

Surrender of the king.

Accordingly the king of Martaban held out a white flag on the city wall. He then sent a venerable Buddhist priest to Byeen-noung to request that he might be allowed to turn monk, and spend the rest of his days in a monastery. Byeen-noung was very reverential towards the priest, and promised to forget the past, and provide an estate for the king of Martaban, but no one could trust his word.

Preparations for receiving the royal captives.

Next morning there was a great parade of soldiers and elephants, music and banners, throughout the camp of Byeen-noung. A street was formed of two lines of foreign soldiers from the tent of Byeen-noung to the gate of the city; and all the Portuguese soldiers were posted outside the gate, with their captain, Joano Cayeyro, in their midst; and many of the Burmese princes and nobles of Byeen-noung went into the city, with a host of Burmese guards, to bring the king of Martaban in a great procession to the feet of his conqueror.

The scene is thus described by an eye-witness:[1]—"At one o'clock in the day a cannon was fired as a signal. After a

[1] Fernam Mendez Pinto. Modern writers have doubted the veracity of Pinto, but his truthfulness was never doubted by his contemporaries, and the author has resided long enough in Burma to vouch from his own personal knowledge for the credibility of Pinto's accounts of that country. In fact, Pinto, like Herodotus and Marco Polo, is trustworthy about what he saw, but he was simple enough to believe any absurd

A.D. 1540-1832

Sad procession.

while the procession from the palace inside Martaban approached the gate of the city. First came a strong guard of Burmese soldiers, armed with harquebuses, halberts, and pikes. Next appeared the Burmese grandees mounted on elephants, with golden chains on their backs, and collars of precious stones round their necks. Then at a distance of nine or ten paces came the Roolim of Mounay, the sovereign pontiff of Burma, who was going to mediate between the king of Martaban and the high and mighty conqueror Byeen-noung. After him the queen of Martaban was carried in a chair on men's shoulders, together with her four children—two boys and two girls—of whom the eldest was scarcely seven. Round about the queen were thirty or forty young ladies of noble birth, who were wonderfully fair, with cast-down looks and tears in their eyes, leaning on other women. After them walked certain priests, like the capuchins in Europe, with bare feet and bare heads, praying as they went, with beads in their hands, and ever and anon comforting the ladies, and throwing water upon them when they fainted, which they did very often. Presently the king appeared, mounted on a little elephant, in token of poverty and contempt of life. He wore a cassock of black velvet; and his head, beard, and eyebrows were all shaven; and there was an old cord round about his neck by which to render himself to Byeen-noung. He was about sixty-two years of age, and tall in stature;, and although his countenance was worn and troubled, he had all the bearing of a generous sovereign.

Lamentations at the city gates.

"A great throng of women and children and old men were gathered round the city gate; and when they beheld their king in his garb of woe, they set up a terrible cry, and struck their faces with stones until the blood ran down. The spectacle was so horrible and mournful that even the Burmese guards were moved to tears, although they were men of war and the enemies of Martaban.

"Meanwhile the queen fainted twice, and her ladies fainted

fable that he was told. His stories of Byeen-noung are confirmed by Burmese annals and Portuguese historians. It should be added that the passages in the text, marked with inverted commas, are not taken from Pinto's original narrative, which is tedious and prolix to the last degree; they are extracted from a reproduction of Pinto's travels and adventures, with notes and commentaries, which is in course of preparation for the press.

around her; and the guards were fain to let the king alight, and go and comfort her. Whereupon, seeing the queen upon the ground in a swoon, with her children in her arms, the king kneeled down upon both his knees, and cried aloud, looking up to heaven, 'O mighty power of God, why is thy divine wrath spent upon these innocent creatures?' This said, he threw water on the queen and brought her round.

A.D. 1540-1823

Fainting ladies: anguish of the king.

"After a while the king was remounted on his elephant, and the procession moved through the gate. Then the king saw the Portuguese deserters dressed in their buff coats, with feathers in their caps, and harquebuses in their hands; whilst their captain, Cayeyro, stood in front apparelled in carnation satin, making room for the procession with a gilt partisan. The king withdrew his face from the Portuguese deserters, and exclaimed against their base ingratitude; and the Burmese guards fell foul of the Portuguese, and drove them away with shame and contumely.

Wrath at the Portuguese.

"After this the king of Martaban went through the street of soldiers until he came to the tent where the conqueror, Byeen-noung, was sitting in great pomp surrounded by his lords. The king threw himself upon the ground, but spake never a word. The Roolim of Mounay stood close by, and said to Byeen-noung, 'Sire, remember that God shows his mercy to those who submit to his will. Do you show mercy likewise, and in the hour of death you will clear off a load of sins.' Byeen-noung then promised to pardon the king; and all present were greatly contented; and Byeen-noung gave the king and queen in charge of two of his lords.

Prostration and mediation

"Now Byeen-noung was a warrior of great craft; and he posted Burmese captains at all the twenty-four gates of the city of Martaban, and bade them let no one in or out on pain of death, as he had promised to give the sacking of the city to his foreign mercenaries. Meanwhile, and for the space of two days, he brought away all the treasures of the king of Martaban, including very many wedges of gold, and strings of precious stones of inestimable value. When he had carried away all that he wanted, he abandoned the city to the soldiery. A cannon was fired as a signal and they all rushed in pell-mell, so that many were stifled to death at the gates; and for three days such horrible murders

Plunder and sack of Martaban.

A.D. 1540-1823

and wickedness were committed that no man can imagine or describe.

Twenty-one gibbets on the hill Beidao.

"Whilst the city of Martaban was being sacked, Byeen-noung left his quarters in the Burmese camp, and pitched his tent on the hill Beidao, which was close by. One morning, when the work of plunder and destruction was nearly over, twenty-one gibbets were set up in stone pillars on the hill, and guarded with a hundred Burmese horsemen. Presently there was a great uproar in the Burmese camp, and troops of horsemen came out with lances in their hands, and formed a street from the camp to the hill, crying aloud, 'Let no man approach with arms, or speak aloud what he thinks in his heart, on pain of death!'

Procession to the hill.

"Then the marshal of the camp came up with a hundred elephants and a host of foot soldiers. Next followed bodies of cavalry and infantry, and in their midst were a hundred and forty ladies bound together four and four, accompanied by many priests, who sought to comfort them. After them marched twelve ushers with maces, followed by horsemen, who carried the queen of Martaban and her four children on their horses.

Terrible vengeance of Byeen-noung.

"The hundred and forty ladies were the wives and daughters of the chief captains of Martaban, on whom the tyrant Byeen-noung was wreaking his spite because they had persuaded their husbands and fathers to hold out against him. They were for the most part between seventeen and twenty-five years of age, and were all very white and fair, with bright auburn hair, but so weak in the body that oftentimes they fell down in a swoon; and certain women on whom they leaned endeavoured to bring them to, presenting them with comfits and other things, but they would take nothing. Indeed, the poor wretches were so feeble and benumbed that they could scarcely hear what the priests said to them, only now and then they lifted up their hands to heaven.

Priests and children.

"Sixty priests followed the queen in two files, praying with their looks fixed on the ground, and their eyes watered with tears; some ever and anon saying one prayer in doleful tones, whilst others answered weeping in like manner. Last of all three or four hundred children walked in procession, with white wax lights in their hands, and cords about their necks, praying aloud with sad and lamentable voices, saying,

A.D. 1540-1823

'We most humbly beseech thee, O Lord, to give ear unto our cries and groans, and show mercy to these thy captives, that with a full rejoicing they may have a part of the graces and blessings of thy rich treasures.' Behind this procession was another guard of foot soldiers, all Burmans, armed with lances and arrows, and some with harquebuses.

Condemnation of the queen and ladies.

"When the poor sufferers had been led in this fashion to the place of execution, six ushers stood forth and proclaimed with loud voices that the ladies were condemned to death by the king of Burma, because they had incited their husbands and fathers to resist him, and had caused the death of twelve thousand Burmans of the city of Toungoo.

Horrible farewells.

"Then at the ringing of a bell all the officers and ministers of justice, pell-mell together with the guards, raised up a dreadful outcry. Whereupon, the cruel hangman being ready to put the sentence of death into execution, these poor women sobbed and embraced each other, and addressed themselves to the queen, who lay at that time almost dead in the lap of an old lady. One of them spoke to the queen in the name of all the others, and begged her to comfort them with her presence whilst they entered the mournful mansions of death, where they would present themselves before the Almighty Judge, and pray for vengeance on their wrongs. To this the queen, more dead than alive, answered with a feeble voice, 'Go not away so soon, my sisters, but help me to sustain these little children.' This said, she leaned down again on the bosom of the old lady, without speaking another word.

Execution of the ladies.

"Then the ministers of the arm of vengeance—for so they term the hangmen—laid hold of those poor women, and hung them all up by the feet with their heads downwards upon twenty gibbets, namely, seven on each gibbet. Now, this death was so painful that it made them give strange and fearful groans and sobs, until at length in less than an hour the blood had stifled them all.

Death of the queen.

"Meantime the queen was conducted by the four women on whom she leaned to the remaining gibbet; and there the Roolim of Mounay made some speeches to her to encourage her the better to suffer death. Then, turning to the hangman, who was going to bind her two little boys, she said, 'Good friend, be not, I pray you, so void of pity as to

A.D. 1540-1823

make me see my children die; wherefore put me first to death, and refuse me not this boon for God's sake.' She then took her children in her arms, and kissing them over and over in giving them her last farewell, she yielded up the ghost in the lady's lap upon whom she leaned, and never stirred afterwards. On this the hangman ran to her, and hanged her as he had done the rest, together with her four little children, two on each side of her, and she in the middle.

Mutiny of the Pegu army.

"At this cruel and pitiful spectacle the whole multitude set up a hideous yell; all the soldiers of the army that belonged to Pegu broke out in mutiny; and Byeen-noung would have been murdered had he not surrounded himself with the Burman soldiers he had brought from Toungoo. Even then the tumult was very great and dangerous throughout the day, but at last night set in and quieted the fury of the men of Pegu.

Drowning of the king of Martaban.

"That same night the king of Martaban was thrown into the river with a great stone tied about his neck, together with sixty of his male captives, whose wives and daughters had been executed a few hours before on the hill Beidao."

Byeen-noung invades Siam.

The remaining adventures of Byeen-noung may be told in a few words. After the desolation of Martaban, he returned to Pegu, and advanced up the river Irawadi and conquered Prome, and attempted the conquest of Ava.[1] Two years later he invaded Siam with a large army, but was suddenly called back by rebellion in Pegu.

Revolt of the royal monk at Pegu.

Here it should be explained that when the king of Pegu was put to death by Byeen-noung, his brother turned monk and became the most famous preacher in all that country. Accordingly, whilst Byeen-noung was gone away to Siam, this royal monk ascended the pulpit in the great pagoda at Pegu, and harangued a vast audience on the sufferings of the Talains, and the crimes committed by the Burmans from Toungoo on the royal house of Pegu. The sermon threw the whole congregation into an uproar. The people seized their arms and rose as one man against the Burmese yoke. They slaughtered every Burman in Pegu, and carried the monk to the palace, and placed him in

[1] Some sickening tragedies were perpetrated at Prome, but enough has been said about such horrors.

possession of all the treasures, and hailed him as their king.

National outbreak of Talains.

Byeen-noung was furious at the tidings. He hurried back his army with all speed to Pegu, and put down the revolt with his Burmese soldiers, and secured possession of the city; whilst the royal monk fled from Pegu to the kingdom of Henzada. But the spirit of insurrection could not be quenched by force of arms. At Pegu Byeen-noung was assassinated, and his foster-brother was deserted by the mercenaries, and compelled to fly back to Toungoo. At Martaban the people rose up against the Burmese garrison, slaughtered them to a man, and declared for the royal monk.[1] Finally the royal monk was joined by many nobles and great men in the kingdom of Henzada, and raised a mighty host, and returned to Pegu in triumph, and was again crowned king.

Recovery of Pegu by the foster-brother of Byeen-noung.

Meanwhile the foster-brother of Byeen-noung enlisted a large army amongst the barbarous hillmen round about Toungoo, and promised to give them the plunder of Pegu if they would help him to recover the city. He marched his army towards the south, as Byeen-noung had done before him, and scattered the army of the monk; and he entered Pegu in triumph, whilst the monk fled for his life to the mountains between Pegu and Arakan. But his successes led to great perplexities. He had promised to give the plunder of Pegu to his mercenary army; but the people of Pegu had submitted to his yoke, and he was horrified at the idea of abandoning them to the tender mercies of the barbarians from the hills. The mercenaries demanded the fulfilment of his pledge, and when he explained why he would not bear the burden of the crime, they broke out into mutiny. He fled from the camp and took refuge in a pagoda, and protected himself for a while with his Burmese soldiers. At last he held a parley with the ringleaders from the walls of the pagoda; and after much debating, it was agreed that he should distribute amongst the mercenaries a large sum from his own treasures as ransom for the city of Pegu.

After a while the fugitive monk was taken prisoner. He

[1] The resuscitation of a town in Burma in the course of a few weeks or days is by no means surprising. The houses are built of wood, and can be set up very quickly.

A.D. 1540-1832

Capture of the monk.

had thrown off his monastic vows, and married the daughter of a mountaineer; but he had discovered his rank to his wife, and her parents betrayed him to the Toungoo king, for the sake of the reward offered for his capture.

Public execution.

The execution of the royal monk was a piteous spectacle. He was taken out of his dungeon; dressed in rags and tatters; crowned with a diadem of straw garnished with mussel-shells, and decorated with a necklace of onions. In this guise he was carried through the streets of Pegu, mounted on a sorry jade, with his executioner sitting behind him. Fifteen horsemen with black ensigns proclaimed his guilt, whilst fifteen others in red garments were ringing bells. He was strongly guarded in front and behind by a long array of horse and foot and elephants. He was led to the scaffold; his sentence was read aloud to the multitude; and his head was severed from his body by a single blow.

Episode of Diego Suarez.

During the revolt at Pegu, one of the Portuguese soldiers, who had been in the service of Byeen-noung, met with a fearful doom. His name was Diego Suarez. When Byeen-noung was alive and at the height of his prosperity and power, he took a great liking to Diego Suarez, and appointed him governor of Pegu. The man thus became puffed up with pride and insolence, and did what he pleased without regard to right or wrong, keeping a body-guard of Turks to protect him in his evil ways. One day there was a marriage procession in the streets of Pegu, and Diego Suarez ordered his Turks to bring away the bride. A great tumult arose, and the bridegroom was slain by the Turks, whilst the bride strangled herself with her girdle to save her honour; but the father escaped with his life, and swore to be revenged upon the wicked foreigner who had brought such woe upon his household.

Terrible revenge.

Years passed away, but the wretched father could do nothing but weep. Diego Suarez rose into still higher favour with Byeen-noung, and was honoured with the title of "brother of the king." At last the people of Pegu broke out in revolt, and the father saw that the time had come for wreaking his vengeance on the wicked man from Portugal. He rushed into a pagoda, carried away the idol, and harangued the multitude, telling aloud the story of his wrongs. The people of Pegu rose up in a wild outbreak of fury. The officers of justice were forced to arrest Diego Suarez, and, in spite of prayers and bribes, to deliver him up to the mob; and he was then stoned to death in the market-place of Pegu, whilst his house was demolished so that not a tile remained.

A.D. 1750-1823

Byeen-noung, a type of Burmese conquerors.

The story of Byeen-noung is typical. It tells of a forgotten conqueror who flourished in the sixteenth century; but it also reveals the general conditions of life in Burma, from a remote antiquity down to our own times. Byeen-noung was but the type of Burmese warriors who have arisen at intervals in that remote peninsula; played the part of heroes; conquered kingdoms and founded dynasties; crushed out rebellions by wholesale massacres; and have been followed in their turn by other kings of smaller genius, but equally cruel and tyrannical.

Rise of Alompra the hunter, 1750.

In the middle of the eighteenth century, more than two hundred years after Byeen-noung, there was a warrior of the same stamp who founded the dynasty of Burmese kings still reigning at Mandalay. During the earlier years of that century the Talain kings of Pegu gained the mastery of the kings of Ava, and the people of upper Burma groaned under Talain domination. But about 1750 a deliverer appeared in the person of a man of low origin, known as Alompra the hunter.[1] He headed a popular insurrection, which at first only numbered a hundred men, but was soon joined by multitudes. Alompra and his newly created army threw off the Talain yoke, and swept down the Irawadi, subverted the Talain dynasty in Pegu, and founded a maritime capital at Rangoon. The English at that time had a factory at Negrais, off the coast; and the merchants were weak enough to court the friendship of Alompra, whilst selling powder and ammunition to the Talains. A French adventurer informed Alompra of their misdeeds, and the result was that nearly every Englishman at Negrais was massacred by the Burmese.

Reign of Bhodau Phra, 1779-1819.

The successors of Alompra followed in his steps. Bhodau Phra, his third son, was the sixth sovereign of the dynasty. He reigned from 1779 to 1819, and is regarded by the Burmese as the hero of the line next to his illustrious father.

[1] Alompra is the most familiar name to English readers: properly it should be Alompara, or Alom Phra.

A.D. 1750-1823 — He conquered Arakan as far as the boundary of Bengal, and Martaban and Tenasserim as far as the frontiers of Siam. His cruelties were boundless, and were the outcome of the same savage ferocity as those of Byeen-noung. He not only put his predecessor to death, but ordered all the women and children of his victim to be burnt alive. On another occasion, on discovering that a plot had been hatched against him in a particular village, he collected together the whole population of the village, including women, children, and Buddhist monks, and burnt them all alive in one vast holocaust. Father Sangermano, a Catholic missionary who was in Burma about the same time, has left authentic details of the horrible cruelties perpetrated by Bhodau Phra.

Phagyi-dau, 1824-25. The successor of Bhodau Phra was Phagyi-dau, who brought on the Burmese war of 1824–25; but the story of his reign belongs to the after history.

Public life of the kings of Burma. The kings of Burma from Alompra downwards were rude despots of the old Moghul type. They generally maintained large harems; and every high official was anxious to place a sister or a daughter in the royal household, to watch over his interests and report all that was going on. Kings and queens dwelt in palaces of brick and stucco painted white and red; with roofs, walls and pinnacles of carved timber covered with gilding and dazzling as picture-frames; with durbars, reception halls, thrones, canopies, and insignia of all kinds, radiant with bits of looking glass and gilding. Sometimes they went on water excursions in large vessels shaped like huge fishes, and covered with gilding; and they were accompanied by long war-boats, each one covered with gilding, and rowed or paddled by fifty or sixty men. Sometimes a king went on a royal progress through his dominions, like the old Moghul sovereigns of Hindustan, carrying his queens, ministers and law courts with him. Each king in turn was constantly exposed to insurrection or revolution, in which he might be murdered, and all his queens and children massacred without regard to age or sex; whilst a new king ascended the throne, and removed the court and capital to some other locality, in order to blot out the memory of his predecessor. Thus during the present century the capital has been removed from Ava to Amarapura and back again;

and at this present moment it is fixed in the comparatively new city of Mandalay. The kings of Burma have always been utterly ignorant of foreign nations; regarding Burma as the centre of the universe, and all people outside the Burman pale as savages and barbarians.

A.D. 1750-1823

Burmese adminis-tration a network of officialism.

The despotic power of the sovereign, however, was kept in check by an old Moghul constitution, which seems to have been a relic of the remote past. The aristocracy of Burma consists only of officials, who have spread a network of officialism over the whole kingdom. There are heads of tens and hundreds; heads of villages, districts, and provinces; and all are appointed, punished, or dismissed at the mere will of the sovereign. But the ministers and officials at court exercise a power in their collective capacity, to which a king is sometimes obliged to bend; for there have been critical moments when a king has been deposed by the ministers, and another sovereign enthroned in his room.

Hlot-dau, or supreme council.

Four chief ministers, with the king or crown prince as president, sit in a great hall of state within the palace inclosure, known as the Hlot-dau. This collective body forms a supreme legislative assembly, a supreme council of the executive, and a supreme court of justice and appeal. There are also four under-ministers, and a host of secretaries and minor officials, who conduct the administration at the capital in the name of the king, but under the orders of the Hlot-dau.

Byadeit, or privy council.

Besides the Hlot-dau, or public council of state, there is a privy council, sitting within the palace itself, and known as the Byadeit. This council is supposed to advise the king privately and personally, and to issue orders in his name, whenever it is deemed inexpedient to discuss the matter in the Hlot-dau.

Faulty working of the councils.

The real working of these councils has always been obscured by oriental intrigues. It is however obvious that they lack the authority of a hereditary assembly, such as the council of Bharadars at Khatmandu; whilst the bare fact that they are exclusively composed of officials, nominated by the king, and depending for their very existence on the king's favour, deprives them of any authority they might otherwise have exercised as popular or representative bodies.

CHAPTER XVI.

BURMESE AND BHURTPORE WARS: LORD AMHERST.

A.D. 1823 TO 1828.

A.D. 1823

Origin of the Burmese war.

THE difficulties of the British government with Burma began about the end of the eighteenth century. Bhodau Phra had conquered Arakan, but the people rebelled against him, and some of the rebels fled into eastern Bengal. The Burmese governor of Arakan demanded the surrender of the fugitives. Sir John Shore was weak enough to comply rather than hazard a collision; but his successor Lord Wellesley refused to deliver up political refugees who had sought an asylum in British territory, and who would probably be tortured and executed in Burmese fashion the moment they were surrendered to their oppressors.

Pride and ignorance of the Burmese court.

Meanwhile every effort was made to come to a friendly understanding with the Burmese government. Colonel Symes was sent on a mission to Ava; and after him a Captain Canning and a Captain Cox. But the Burmese court was impracticable. Bhodau Phra and his ministers were puffed up with pride and bombast. They despised the natives of India, and had been ignorantly led to believe that the English were traders without military capacity, who paid the black sepoys to fight their battles.

Violence and insolence of the officials.

At last the Burmese authorities grew violent as well as insolent. They repeated their demands for the surrender of political refugees, who had escaped into British territory; claimed possession of an island on the English side of the frontier at the Náf river; and threatened to invade Bengal unless their demands were promptly conceded.

A.D. 1823-1824

Hostilities forced on the British government.

The wars of Lord Hastings had secured the peace of India, but had been vehemently denounced in England. Lord Amherst was therefore most reluctant to engage in a war with Burma; he was ready to make any concession, short of acknowledgment of inferiority, to avert the threatened hostilities. But the Burmese refused to listen to reason, and were resolutely bent on a rupture. In 1822 their general Bundúla invaded the countries between Burma and Bengal; conquered the independent principalities of Assam and Munipore, and threatened Cachar. Subsequently Bundúla invaded British territory, and cut off a detachment of British sepoys. Lord Amherst was thus forced into hostilities, and in 1824 an expedition was sent against Rangoon under the command of Sir Archibald Campbell.

British expedition to Rangoon, 1824.

Meanwhile the Burmese were inflated by the successes of Bundúla, and looked forward with confidence to the conquest of Bengal. Bundúla was ordered to bind the Governor-General in golden fetters, and send him as a prisoner to Ava. But the British expedition to Rangoon took the Burmese by surprise. They purposed invading Bengal, and they may have expected to encounter a force on the frontier; but they never reckoned on an invading army coming to Rangoon by sea. At the same time the English invaders were almost as much surprised as the Burmese. They had been led to expect a foe worthy of their steel; but they soon discovered that the Burmese army was the most despicable enemy that the British had ever encountered. It was composed of raw levies, miserably armed, without either discipline or courage. Their chief defence consisted in stockades, which were however constructed with considerable skill and rapidity.

Flight of the Burmese.

In May 1824 the English expedition arrived at Rangoon. The Burmese had constructed some strong stockades, but they were soon demolished by British artillery. The troops were then landed, and found that Rangoon was empty of population and provisions. The Burmese governor had ordered the whole of the inhabitants—men, women, and children—to retire to the jungle with all their flocks and herds and stores of grain. As for the Burmese soldiery, they had fled in terror at the first discharge of British guns. Shortly after the landing the rains began; and the British

A.D. 1824-1825

army was forced to remain at Rangoon, and to depend for its subsistence on the supplies that arrived from Madras and Calcutta.

Repulse of Bundúla.

In December 1824 Bundúla approached Rangoon from the land side with an army of sixty thousand men. Within a few hours the Burmese soldiery had surrounded the British camp with stockades, and then burrowed themselves in the earth behind. But Bundúla was attacked and defeated; his stockades were carried by storm; and he fled in a panic with the remains of his army to Donabew, a place further up the river Irawadi, about forty miles from Rangoon,

Earth-works at Donabew.

Bundúla was resolved to make a stand at Donabew. He constructed field-works and stockades for the space of a mile along the face of the river. He sought to maintain discipline by the severity of his punishments; and one of his commanders was sawn asunder between two planks for disobedience of orders.

Death of Bundúla: Burmese panic-stricken.

Early in 1825 the British force advanced up the river Irawadi towards Ava, leaving a detachment to capture Donabew. The detachment however was repulsed by the Burmese, and the main army returned to Donabew, and began a regular siege. A few shells were discharged to ascertain the range of the British mortars, and next morning the heavy artillery began to play upon the works, but there was no response. It turned out that one of the shells on the preceding evening had killed Bundúla. The brother of Bundúla was offered the command of the army, but was too frightened to accept it; and he then made his way with all speed to Ava, where he was beheaded within half an hour of his arrival. Meanwhile the Burmese army at Donabew had dispersed in all directions.

Advance to Prome. 1825.

The British expedition next proceeded to Prome. All the mad women in Ava, who were supposed to be witches or to have familiar spirits, were collected and sent to Prome to unman the British soldiers by their magic arts. Another Burmese army was sent to attack Prome, but was utterly defeated. The court of Ava was frantic at its losses, but could not realise its position, and showed itself as arrogant as ever. A brother of the king, named Tharawadi, bragged that he would drive the English to the sea, and left Ava for the purpose, but soon returned in the greatest terror.

A.D. 1825-1826

Advance towards Ava.

The British expedition left Prome, and advanced towards Ava; and the court of Ava, and indeed the Burmese generally, were panic-stricken at the invaders. It was noised abroad that the white foreigners were demons, invincible and bloodthirsty; that European soldiers kept on fighting in spite of ghastly wounds; and that European doctors picked up arms and legs after an action, and replaced them on their rightful owners.[1]

Treaty of Yandabo, 1826.

Early in 1826 a treaty of peace was concluded at Yandabo. The whole country from Rangoon to Ava was at the mercy of the British army. Phagyi-dau, king of Ava, engaged to pay a crore of rupees, about a million sterling, towards the expenses of the war; and the territories of Assam, Arakan, and Tenasserim, were ceded to the British government. The king was left in possession of the whole of Pegu and Upper Burma, and was even permitted to retain the maritime city of Rangoon; whilst the British head-quarters were fixed at Moulmein in Tenasserim.

Crawfurd's mission to Ava, 1826

Later on Mr. John Crawfurd was sent to Ava to conclude a commercial treaty with the king. But the Burmese had already forgotten the lessons of the war, and entertained but little respect for an English envoy after the British army had retired from the scene. Accordingly Crawfurd could effect nothing of any substantial importance to either government. He found the Burmese officials ignorant, unprincipled, and childish, and in no instance endowed with the artifice and cleverness of Hindus and other Asiatics. Some of them had risen from the lowest ranks of life by the favour of the king; one had been a buffoon in a company of play-actors, whilst another had got a living by selling fish in the bazar. They did not want any treaty whatever. They evaded every proposition for a reciprocity of trade, and only sought to cajole the envoy into restoring the ceded territories and remitting the balance still due of the money payment. The country was only sparsely cultivated, and there were few if any indications of prosperity. Phagyi-dau was in the hands of his queen, the daughter of a jailer, who was older than her husband, and far from handsome. She was known as the sorceress, as she was

[1] Fytche's *Burma, Past and Present.* General Albert Fytche's work contains many interesting facts in connection with Burmese history.

A.D. 1825-1828

supposed to have rendered the king subservient to her will by the power of magical arts and charms.

Political ferment in India.

The first Burmese war is forgotten now by the princes and chiefs of India; but in 1824 and 1825 the current of events was watched with interest and anxiety by every native court. The different chiefs and princes of India had not quite settled down under the suzerainty of the British government; and many restless spirits amongst the warriors and freebooters of a previous generation would gladly have hailed the defeat of the British troops in Burma, the overthrow of order in India, and the revival of the predatory system of the eighteenth century.

Outbreak at Bhurtpore, 1825.

Suddenly, in the crisis of the campaign in Burma, there was a fiasco in the Ját state of Bhurtpore on the British frontier near Agra, which had been under the protective alliance of the British government ever since the days of Lord Wellesley. The Raja of Bhurtpore died in 1825, leaving a son aged seven, named Bulwant Singh. The British government recognised the succession of Bulwant Singh under the guardianship of his uncle; but a cousin of the infant Raja, named Dúrjan Sál, corrupted the army of Bhurtpore, put the guardian to death, imprisoned the little prince, and took possession of the principality.

Active proceedings of Ochterlony.

Sir David Ochterlony, the British Resident at Delhi, was agent of the Governor-General for Rajpútana and Malwa. He belonged to the once famous school of soldier-statesmen, which began with Robert Clive, and boasted of men like Sir Arthur Wellesley and Sir John Malcolm. His Indian experiences were perhaps larger than those of any living English officer. He had fought against Hyder Ali in the old days of Warren Hastings and Sir Eyre Coote; and ten years previous to the fiasco at Bhurtpore he had gained his crowning laurels in the Nipal war. He saw that a conflagration was beginning in Bhurtpore that might spread over Central India; and he ordered a force to advance on his own authority to maintain the peace of Hindustan, support the rights of the infant Raja, and vindicate the offended suzerainty of the British government.

Countermanded by Lord Amherst.

Lord Amherst considered that the military preparations were premature. He doubted the right of the British government to interfere in the Bhurtpore succession; and

A.D. 1825-1828

he was alarmed at the strength of the great fortress of clay, which had resisted the assaults of Lord Lake, and had long been deemed impregnable by every native court in India. Accordingly he countermanded the movement of the troops.

Death of Ochterlony.

Sir David Ochterlony was much mortified at this rebuff. In the bitterness of his soul he resigned his appointment, and died within two months, feeling that an illustrious career of half a century had been brought to an inglorious close.

Growing danger of the outbreak.

The vacillation of the British government induced the usurper to proclaim that he would hold the fortress of Bhurtpore, and maintain his hold on the Bhurtpore throne, in defiance of the Governor-General. The dangerous character of the revolution was now imminent, for Rajpúts, Mahrattas, Pindharies, and Játs were flocking to Bhurtpore to rally round the venturous usurper.

Capture of Bhurtpore, 1826.

Lord Amherst saw his error and hastened to retrieve it; indeed his council were unanimous for war. An army was assembled under Lord Combermere and began the siege of Bhurtpore. The British artillery failed to make any impression on the heavy mud walls. At last the fortifications were mined with ten thousand pounds of powder. A terrific explosion threw vast masses of hardened clay into the air; and the British troops rushed into the breach, and captured the fortress which had hitherto been deemed impregnable. The usurper was confined as a state prisoner, and the infant Raja was restored to the throne under the guardianship of the British government. The political ferment died away at the fall of Bhurtpore, and all danger of any disturbance of the public peace disappeared from Hindustan.

Lord Amherst leaves India, 1828.

Lord Amherst embarked for England in February, 1828, leaving no mark in history beyond what is remembered of Burma and Bhurtpore. He was the first Governor-General who established a vice-regal sanatarium at Simla.

CHAPTER XVII.

NON-INTERVENTION: LORD WILLIAM BENTINCK.

A.D. 1828 TO 1835.

A.D. 1828-1835

Lord William Bentinck Governor-General, 1828-35.

LORD WILLIAM BENTINCK succeeded to the post of Governor-General, and held the reins of government for seven years, namely, from 1828 to 1835. Twenty-two years had passed away since 1806, when he had been recalled from the government of Madras amidst the panic which followed the mutiny at Vellore. During the interval he had protested in vain against the injustice of his recall; and his nomination to the high office was regarded as an atonement for the wrong he had suffered.[1]

Domestic administration successful.

The government of Lord William Bentinck covers a peaceful era. He remodelled the judicial system; introduced the village revenue settlement into the north-west provinces; reduced the allowances of civil and military officers; and employed natives in the public service far more largely than had been done by his predecessors. He promoted English education amongst the natives, and founded a medical college at Calcutta. He laboured hard to introduce steam navigation between England and India *viâ* the Red Sea. He took active measures for suppressing the gangs of Thugs, who had strangled and plundered unsuspecting travellers in different quarters of India ever since the days of Aurangzeb. Above all he abolished the horrible rite of Satí, or burning widows with the remains of their deceased

[1] Lord Amherst left India in February, 1828. Lord William Bentinck did not arrive until the following July. During the interval Mr. Butterworth Bayley, the senior member of council, was provisional Governor-General.

husbands, which had been the curse of India from the earliest dawn of history. Lord William Bentinck thus established a great reputation for prudence, integrity, and active benevolence, which has endured down to our own times.

A.D. 1828-1835

Political relations with Mahrattas and Rajpúts.

The state of affairs in Malwa and Rajpútana was soon forced on the attention of Lord William Bentinck. Lord Hastings had established closer political relations with the Mahrattas and Rajpúts, and his measures were beginning to bear fruit during the administration of Lord Amherst. British officers were appointed Residents at native courts for the purpose of mediating between conflicting native rulers, and otherwise keeping the peace. They were strictly prohibited from all interference in the internal administration; and each native state was left to deal with faction, rebellion, or disputed succession, after its own manner. Closer acquaintance, however, showed that such extremes of non-intervention were incompatible with the duties of the paramount power; and the subsequent history of India betrays a necessary conflict between the principle and practice, which has continued till the present day.

Degree of non-intervention in Mahratta states.

At first there was little difficulty as regards the Mahratta states. The policy of non-interference was preached by the British government; but the British Residents at Gwalior and Indore were occasionally driven to employ detachments of the Subsidiary Force, or other British troops, to suppress mutiny or rebellion, or to root out some dangerous outlaw. Daulat Rao Sindia was weak and impoverished, and anxious to meet the wishes of the British government. Mulhar Rao Holkar was a minor, and the provisional administration was equally as subservient to the British Resident as that of Sindia. In Nagpore the Resident, Mr. Jenkins, was virtually sovereign; and during the minority of the Raja, Mr. Jenkins conducted the administration through the agency of native officials in a highly successful fashion. Meanwhile the subjects of both Sindia and Holkar regarded the British government as the supreme authority, to whom alone they could look for redress or security against the mal-administration of their rulers; and a Resident often found it necessary to use his own discretion in the way of remonstrance or expostulation, without infringing the non-intervention policy.

A.D. 1828-1835

Shattered condition of Rajpút states.

In Rajpútana circumstances were different. Captain James Tod, one of the earliest political officers in that quarter,[1] has left a picture of the country which recalls the plots, assassinations, treacheries and superstitions revealed in Shakespeare's tragedy of *Macbeth*. There was the same blind belief in witches and wise women; the same single combats, bloody murders, and flights into foreign territory. Every Raj was distracted by feuds; and the princes and chiefs of Rajpútana had been impoverished by Mahrattas or Pindharies just as the old kings of Britain were harassed and plundered by the Danes. The Thakúrs, or feudatory nobles, were as turbulent, lawless, and disaffected as the Thanes of Scotland, and often took the field against their sovereign, like the Thane of Cawdor, with bands of kerns and gallowglasses. Many a kinsman of a Mahárajá has played the part of Macbeth; whilst Lady Macbeths were plentiful in every state in Rajpútana. The hill tribes, including Bhíls, Mínas, and Mhairs, were as troublesome as the Highland clans; they made frequent raids on peaceful villages, plundered and murdered travellers, and found a sure refuge in inaccessible and malarious jungles.

Active interference of Captain Tod.

Captain Tod was endowed with warm sympathies and an active imagination. He was distressed at the sight of depopulated towns, ruined villages, and pauper courts; and he could not resist the appeals for his personal interference which met him on every side. He was charmed with the relics of the feudal system which he found in Rajpútana. To him they recalled a picture of Europe during the middle ages. One usage especially delighted him. Occasionally a princess of Rajpútana sent him her bracelet as a token that she looked to him for protection. In other words she claimed his interference as her chosen knight, on whom she might rely for succour, but whom she was never destined to see.

Wretched condition of Meywar and Marwar.

The condition of the three leading Rajpút principalities at this period proves the necessity for the interference of British authorities. In Meywar (Udaipore), the reigning Rana, the acknowledged suzerain of Rajpútana, was dependent for his subsistence on the bounty of the ruler of

[1] Afterwards Lieut.-Colonel Tod, and author of *Annals and Antiquities of Rajasthan*.

A.D. 1828-1835

Kotah. In Marwar (Jodhpur), the Maháraja had for years been feigning insanity, and had abdicated the throne, out of terror of Amír Khan of Tonk; but on the extension of British protection to the states of Rajpútana, he once more ascended the throne, and resumed the administration of the Raj. Subsequently he quarrelled with his ministers and feudatory nobles; treating them with savage violence, putting many to death, and seeking the help of the British government to support him in these barbarous proceedings. Indeed the endless broils between the rulers of Rajpútana and their refractory Thakúrs, have at different intervals compelled the British government to interfere for the maintenance of the public peace; and it has often been difficult to decide whether to interfere in behalf of a tyrannical Raja or in support of oppressed Thakúrs.

Critical condition of Jaipur: a dissolute Ráni.

In Jaipur, which is much nearer British territory, matters were even worse than in Marwar. The Raja of Jaipur had died in 1818, and was succeeded by a posthumous infant son, under the regency of the mother, assisted by the minister of the deceased Raja. Then followed a series of complications not unfrequent in oriental courts. The regent mother had a Jain banker for her paramour, as well as other worthless favourites. She squandered the revenues of the state on these parasites, and especially on a Guru, who was her religious teacher or adviser. She set the minister at defiance, quarrelled with him on all occasions, and tried to oust him from his office; and on one occasion there was a bloody conflict within the palace, which ended in the slaughter of thirty men. Next she prevailed on the Jaipur army to break out in mutiny and march to the capital; and there she distributed money amongst the rebel soldiery, whilst the minister fled for refuge to his jaghír or estate in the country.

Conflicting councils of Thakúrs, or feudatory nobles.

The British government was compelled to interfere by ordering the Jaipur army to retire from the capital, and sending a British officer to effect a settlement of affairs. A great council of Thakúrs was summoned to court, and after much debate and uproar, decided on deposing the regent mother, and recalling the absent minister to fill the post of regent. Such a measure would have been the best possible solution of the existing difficulty, and would consequently have been most satisfactory to the British

A.D. 1828-1835

government. But such off-hand debates and resolutions, however right in their conclusions, and however much in accordance with the unwritten traditions of Rajpúts, were not in keeping with that passion for order and formality which is a deeply rooted instinct in Englishmen. Accordingly Sir Charles Metcalfe, the Resident at Delhi, proceeded to Jaipur, and convened a second and more formal council, and subjected the votes to a careful scrutiny. Then it appeared that a small majority had been won over to consider the regent mother as the rightful ruler of Jaipur. To make matters worse, the regent mother insisted upon appointing her paramour to be minister of Jaipur, to the scandal of the whole country; and Lord Amherst's government was so pledged to the policy of non-intervention, that he declined to interfere, and thus left a legacy of difficulties to his successor.

Political administration of Lord William Bentinck.

Such was the state of affairs in Malwa and Rajpútana when Lord William Bentinck assumed the post of Governor-General. Like other Anglo-Indian statesmen, before and since, he landed in India with a determination to carry out a large and liberal scheme of imperial government, which was based more on the visionary ideal of home philanthropists, than on a practical acquaintance with the people and princes of India. The result was that his conduct of political relations with native states was the outcome, not of fixed political views, but of a conflict between sentiment and reality, during which his romantic aspirations died out, and he was gradually awakened to a sense of the actual wants and needs of native feudatories. The political administration of Lord William Bentinck was thus a period of probation and enlightenment; and it might be said of him, and perhaps of nearly all his successors, that he was never so well fitted for the post of Governor-General of India as when he was quitting its shores for ever.

Experimental policy.

It should however be borne in mind that at this period the policy of the British government towards native states was purely experimental. Non-interference was strongly advocated by the home authorities, and strictly pursued by the new Governor-General; but at this stage of political development native rulers required counsel and discipline rather than license. Before the British government became the paramount power, native rulers were afraid lest their

A.D. 1828-1835

subjects should rebel; and were thus kept to their duties by the law of self-preservation. After the establishment of British suzerainty, native rulers found themselves deprived of their old occupation of predatory war or foreign intrigue, and sought consolation in unrestrained self-indulgences. They neglected their legitimate duties, and looked to the British government for protection from rebellion. On the death of a native ruler, disorders often reached a climax, especially if there was a disputed succession, or the heir was a minor; for then queens and ministers intrigued against each other for power, and the country was torn by faction and civil war. In the end the British government was compelled to interfere in almost every case to save the state from anarchy and ruin; whereas, if it had only interfered in the first instance, there would have been no disorders at all.

Gwalior affairs: death of Daulat Rao Sindia.

The progress of affairs in Gwalior, the most important of the Mahratta states, is a case in point. Daulat Rao Sindia, the same who had been defeated by Wellesley at Assaye, died in 1827, leaving no son to succeed him. He had been repeatedly advised by the British Resident to adopt a son, but he had persistently refused. Latterly he had been inclined to give way, but nothing was concluded; and when he was dying he sent for the Resident, and told him to settle the future government of the Gwalior principality as he might think proper. After his death, his widow, Baiza Baí, proposed to adopt a son, and carry on the government as queen regent during the minority. But Baiza Baí wanted to adopt a boy out of her own family, instead of out of Sindia's family; and as this would have been odious to the court and camp at Gwalior, and would have probably led to serious commotions, the British government refused to sanction the measure. Accordingly Baiza Baí adopted a son out of Sindia's family, known as Jankoji Rao Sindia.

Civil war stopped by intervention, 1833.

In course of time it appeared that Baiza Baí was bent on becoming queen regent for life, and continuing to govern the state after the young Maháraja had attained his majority. In 1833 Lord William Bentinck proceeded to Gwalior, and both the queen regent and the young Maháraja were prepared to abide by his decision; but he declined to interfere. The result was that a civil war broke out in Gwalior and the army took different sides. The young Maháraja at the

A.D. 1828-1835

head of one body of troops besieged the queen regent in the palace at Gwalior. The queen regent escaped from the palace, placed herself at the head of another body of troops, and marched towards the British Residency. On the way the two armies met, and there would have been a deadly collision, had not the British Resident hastened to the spot and prevented the conflict by his personal influence. Lord William Bentinck was then forced to interfere, and recognise the accession of the young Maháraja to the throne, whilst the queen regent was obliged to retire from the scene. Had the Governor-General ordered this arrangement during his visit at Gwalior all these disorders would have been averted.

Indore affairs: civil war stopped by intervention, 1833.

In 1833 there was another complication at Indore. Mulhar Rao Holkar died, and left no son to succeed him. His widow adopted a son, and proposed, as in the case of Sindia, to carry on the administration as queen regent during the minority; and the British government recognised the arrangement. Another claimant next appeared in the person of a collateral kinsman of mature years, named Hari Rao Holkar, who was supported by the general voice of the country. Lord William Bentinck might have settled the dispute by a word, but again he declined to interfere. A civil war broke out in Indore, and at last Lord William Bentinck was forced to put an end to the anarchy by persuading the queen regent to retire from the contest with her adopted son, and sending a British force to the capital to place Hari Rao on the throne of Holkar.

Outrageous proceedings in Bundelkund.

Matters were even worse in the petty states of Bundelkund, to the eastward of Malwa. A Raja of Sumpthur died, leaving two queens or Ránís; the elder was childless, but the younger had an infant son. The son was placed upon the throne, and the younger Ráni became regent-mother. Then followed a fierce contest as to who should be appointed manager. The minister of the deceased Raja would have been the best man for the post, but other candidates were put forward by the rival queens, and the British government declined to interfere. The ex-minister fled to his estate, but was attacked by a body of troops belonging to the regent-mother. Finding his affairs desperate, he placed his women and children on a funeral pile built over a mine of gunpowder; he then destroyed them all in a terrific explosion, and rushed out and perished with his

A.D. 1828-1835

adherents, sword in hand. Lord William Bentinck decided that the regent-mother was responsible for the catastrophe, and still declined to interfere.

Distractions in Rajpútana.

In Rajpútana the policy of non-intervention brought forth equally bitter fruits. Meywar and Marwar were distracted by broils between the rulers and their feudatory nobles. In 1828 the Rana of Meywar died, and seven queens and a concubine perished on his funeral pile.

Jaipur affairs: Lord William Bentinck declines to interfere.

In Jaipur, where the regent-mother had appointed her paramour to be minister, there was another tragedy.[1] The young Maháraja reached his majority, but the regent-mother, and her paramour Jhota Ram, still remained in power, and the country was in a state of anarchy. In spite of appeals from the natives, Lord William Bentinck refused to interpose the authority of the British government for the prevention of disorders. In 1832 Lord William Bentinck went on a tour to the upper provinces, and had an interview with Jhota Ram at Agra; but he was persuaded by the artful minister that it was the British authorities that were to blame, and not the Jaipur government, and accordingly he still declined to interfere.

Poisoning of the Maháraja.

In 1834 the regent-mother died, after keeping Jaipur in a state of turmoil for sixteen years. Shortly after her death the young Maháraja died under most suspicious circumstances, and all the leading people in Jaipur were convinced that the prince had been poisoned by Jhota Ram. Indeed Jhota Ram found the minds of the Thakúrs so inflamed against him, that he was forced to tender his resignation.

Murder of Mr. Blake: intervention and tranquillity.

At this crisis Major Alves, agent for the Governor-General in Rajpútana, and his assistant, Mr. Blake, proceeded to Jaipur, and were only just in time to prevent a bloody contest between Jhota Ram and the Thakúrs. The ex-minister was ordered to remove to a distance from the capital; and there he concocted a scheme of revenge. In June, 1835, after a morning attendance at the durbar, the two English officers were attacked in the streets of Jaipur by assassins who had been hired by Jhota Ram. Major Alves was severely wounded, and Mr. Blake was barbarously murdered. A judicial inquiry was held, and the offenders were convicted and suitably punished. An

[1] See *ante*, p. 525.

A.D. 1828-1835 — infant son of the deceased Maháraja was placed upon the throne, and a British officer was appointed to conduct the administration; and the country was rapidly brought to a state of peace and prosperity.

Lord William Bentinck threatens the king of Oude.

But whilst Lord William Bentinck was so lenient towards Mahratta and Rajpút states, he felt deeply the serious responsibilities incurred by the British government in perpetuating misrule in Oude. He could not shut his eyes to the growing anarchy of the Talúkdars; the abominable oppressions practised on the Ryots; the lawlessness of the Oude soldiery; and the weakness and debaucheries of successive rulers, who chose to call themselves kings. He felt that so long as the British government continued to maintain a helpless and depraved king upon the throne, it was morally responsible for the evils of the maladministration. In 1831 Lord William Bentinck threatened the king of Oude that the British government would take over the management of the country unless he reformed the administration. Subsequently the Court of Directors authorised the Governor-General to assume the government of Oude; but by this time Lord William Bentinck was about to leave India, and he contented himself with giving the king a parting warning.

Intervention: Coorg and Mysore.

In two other territories, Coorg and Mysore, Lord William Bentinck was compelled to interfere; but in order to apprehend the force of his measures it will be necessary to review the history of the two countries.

Isolation of Coorg.

Coorg is a little alpine region between Mysore and Malabar; a land of hills, forests, ravines, and heavy rains; abounding in wild elephants and different kinds of game, and enclosing valleys covered with cultivation. On three sides it is walled off from its neighbours by stupendous mountains; on the fourth side by dense and tangled jungles.

Warlike population.

The people of Coorg are hardy, athletic, and warlike; clinging to their homes of mist and mountain with the devotion of highlanders. One fourth of the population are Coorgs properly so-called—a warrior caste, the lords of the soil. The remaining three-fourths are low castes, who were serfs or slaves under Hindu rule, but have since become free labourers.

[1] See *ante*, p. 403, *note*.

A.D. 1828-1835

Religious origin of the Raj.

The Coorg Raj was founded in the sixteenth century by a holy man, who migrated from Ikkeri during the breaking up of the Hindu empire of Vijayanagar, and established a spiritual ascendency in Coorg which grew into a temporal sovereignty.[1] He collected shares of grain from the villages round about, and founded a dynasty known as the Vira Rajas.

Aggressions of Hyder Ali of Mysore.

For nearly two centuries nothing is known of the Vira Rajas. In the eighteenth century Hyder Ali became sovereign of Mysore, conquered Malabar, and demanded tribute from the reigning Vira Raja of Coorg. Payment was refused; Mysore troops marched into the country; mountains, ravines, and forests presented insurmountable difficulties; and the Coorgs offered a brave and bloody resistance. Hyder Ali achieved a partial success by capturing two or three fortresses; by deporting some of the inhabitants, and giving their lands to Muhammadans; and also by imprisoning and murdering several members of the reigning family.

Aggressions of Tippu: Coorg Raja joins the English.

After the death of Hyder Ali his son Tippu tried to destroy the independence of Coorg, and bring it under the Muhammadan yoke; but in every case the invaders were slaughtered or driven back; and whenever a Raja was slain, the Coorgs set up the eldest surviving prince as their Raja. The new Vira Raja was then carried away captive into Mysore; but after four years he escaped back to Coorg and renewed the old struggle. During the wars against Tippu he was the staunch ally of the English, but plundered the Mysore villages with much cruelty and barbarity. After the downfall of Seringapatam in 1799, he was relieved from tribute, but sent an elephant every year to the British authorities in acknowledgment of fealty.

Non-intervention.

For many years the British government abstained from all interference in Coorg. The country was remote, inaccessible, and uninviting. The Raja was loud in professions of loyalty and gratitude; anxious to stand well with the British authorities, and hospitable to the few officials who visited his country, entertaining them with field sports, animal fights, and other amusements of a like character.

[1] A picture of Ikkeri about this period is furnished by Della Valle. See *ante*, p. 112. The foundation of cities and kingdoms by holy men is a common incident in Hindu tradition.

A.D. 1828-1835

British interference in the succession.

In 1807 the Vira Raja lost his favourite wife. She left no son, but several daughters; and the Vira Raja was anxious that a daughter should succeed him on the throne of Coorg, to the exclusion of his two brothers. Accordingly he begged the British authorities to sanction the arrangement. The English at Madras had no objection; they cared nothing about the Coorg succession; they supposed that the Raja might do as he liked, and that he only asked their permission out of loyal subserviency to the British government. Accordingly the Madras government acquiesced as a matter of course. Years afterwards it was discovered that the succession of a daughter to the exclusion of a brother was contrary to the laws and usages of Coorg; and that the Vira Raja had requested the sanction of the British government in order that he might violate the long-established customs of his own country.

Madness of the Raja: wholesale executions.

Meanwhile the Raja had fits of insanity. He was suspicious, morose, and bloodthirsty. He was in constant dread of assassination, and ordered frequent executions during his furious outbreaks. He beheaded his elder brother to secure the succession of his daughter; and he would have beheaded his younger brother Lingaraja in like manner, but the latter abjured the throne, and devoted himself to a life of sanctity, and was generally regarded as stupid and imbecile.[1]

Reign of Lingaraja, 1811-20.

In 1809 the Vira Raja died, and was succeeded by his daughter, whilst her husband became minister. Subsequently his younger brother, Lingaraja, appeared upon the scene, and showed himself in his true colours. The dull-witted devotee turned out to be an extremely crafty and cruel individual. He forced the husband to retire from the post of minister, and took the government of Coorg into his hands; and he then placed his niece in prison, and gave out that she had abdicated the throne. There was no one to interfere, and Lingaraja became ruler of Coorg.

But Lingaraja was in morbid fear of the British authorities. He was guilty of the most cold-blooded cruelties, but took

[1] Sir Lewin Bowring, the late Chief Commissioner of Mysore, states that the Coorg Raja put hundreds of his subjects to death in his mad fits of passion. He expresses an opinion, in which most students in Asiatic history will concur, that a brave people, like the Coorgs, would never have submitted to the tyranny and barbarity of the Vira Rajas, but for a belief in their divine right or origin. Bowring's *Eastern Experiences*.

every precaution to prevent their getting wind. He allowed none of his subjects to leave Coorg; he surrounded every British officer who visited his territories with guards and spies; and constructed stockades and defences in the passes leading into his country in order to shut out any force that might be sent to coerce or dethrone him. He died in 1820, and was succeeded by a son named Chikka Vira Raja.

A.D. 1828-1835

Reign of Chikka Vira Raja, 1820-34: cruel butcheries.

For the space of fourteen years the reign of Chikka Vira Raja was a series of frightful barbarities. He murdered all who had offended him, including all his relatives, old and young, male and female. None were saved excepting his own wives and children, and a married sister who fled from his violence into British territory. Many were shot with his own hands in the courtyard of the palace. Others were dragged out of the palace at night and beheaded in the jungle. His depravity was worse than his butchery; but that was confined to the recesses of his zenana.

Warnings: declares war.

At last the atrocities of the Coorg Raja were noised abroad, and the Raja was told that the British government would no longer permit him to perpetrate such merciless massacres. In reply he asserted that he was an independent Raja, and demanded the surrender of his sister and her husband; and when this was refused he declared war against the British government.

Flight and surrender of the Coorg Raja.

In 1834 the career of Chikka Vira Raja was brought to a close. A British force was marched into Coorg. The country was difficult of access, and the Coorgs fought with all the valour of their race; but the Raja was as cowardly as he was cruel, and fled to the jungle and committed more murders. The dead body of his minister was found hanging from a tree; but whether he was hanged by the Raja, or hanged himself to escape punishment, is unknown to this day. The Raja surrendered to the British authorities, and laid all the murders at the door of his dead minister.

Preference of the people for British rule.

Lord William Bentinck, with his characteristic predilection for Hindu rulers, was anxious that the leading men of Coorg should choose a Raja for themselves. The people of Coorg, without a dissentient voice, declared their preference for the government of the East India Company; but they stipulated that the Raja should be sent away from Coorg, and never allowed to return, as otherwise they would

A.D. 1828-1835

feel bound to obey him.[1] Accordingly Chikka Víra Raja was removed to Benares, and afterwards allowed to visit England; and Lord William Bentinck was reluctantly obliged to annex the territory of Coorg to the British dominions, "in consideration of the unanimous wish of the people."

Mysore affairs: resuscitation of the extinct Raj.

Mysore was a more important country than Coorg. After the downfall of Tippu in 1799, a child of the extinct Hindu dynasty was placed on the throne of Mysore; whilst a Brahman, named Purnea, conducted the administration under the supervision of an English Resident.[2] The boy was named Krishnaraj. He was not heir to the Raj, but only a child of the family; and he owed his elevation entirely to the favour or policy of the British government. Accordingly, in order to give him a show of right, he was formally adopted by the widows of the last two Rajas of the dynasty.

Purnea, the Brahman minister, 1799-1811.

Purnea was a Brahman of experience and capacity. For years he had been the minister of Tippu, and he soon won the confidence of the English Resident at Mysore. He was courteous, dignified, industrious, and careful to keep everything unpleasant out of sight. Successive English Residents, —Barry Close, Mark Wilks, and John Malcolm,—were more orientalised than political officers of the modern school, more isolated from Europeans, and more dependent

[1] The people of Coorg insisted on another condition, namely, that no cows should be killed in Coorg. Indeed, all Hindus, whose feelings have not been blunted by association with Muhammadans or Europeans, regard the slaughter of a cow with the same horror that they would the murder of a mother. Some authorities have cavilled at this stipulation as a concession to Hindu prejudices; and Sir John Malcolm refused to concede it to Daulat Rao Sindia after the victories of Assaye and Argaum. But the two cases were altogether different. Sindia was not in a position to demand such a concession; and setting aside all other considerations, it would have been most impolitic to have admitted it. Moreover, the people of Hindustan had been subjected for ages to Muhammadan dominion. On the other hand the acquisition of Coorg by the English was of the nature of a compact. The concession was restricted to a little secluded territory sixty miles long and forty broad, which had never been conquered by the Muhammadans. Above all, the stipulation is no breach of morality or decency, although it may be inconvenient to Europeans. If the Hindus of Coorg had claimed the right to burn living widows, or to display obscene symbols on idol cars, the case would have been different.

[2] See *ante*, pp. 407, 414.

on natives. They were well versed in native character, and more considerate as regards native ways. They did not expect too much from Brahman administrators; judging them by oriental rather than by European standards; and content to let things alone so long as there were no outbreaks, no brigands, and a good surplus in the public treasury. Accordingly things went on smoothly between the Resident and the Brahman; and as Purnea accumulated large sums in the public treasury, he was lauded to the skies as a minister worthy of Akbar.

A.D. 1828-1835

Purnea aspires to be a Peishwa.

But Purnea was a Mahratta Brahman of the old Peishwa type, who considered that Brahmans should govern kingdoms whilst Rajas enjoyed themselves. He was willing that Krishnaraj should be a symbol of sovereignty, and show himself on state occasions to receive the homage of his subjects; but he was bent on making the Raja of Mysore a puppet like the first Maháraja of Satara, whilst he perpetuated his own power as minister and sole ruler.

Krishnara enthroned death of Purnea.

In 1811 Krishnaraj attained his sixteenth year, and proposed to undertake the government of Mysore. The British authorities had no objection; but Purnea was exasperated at the threatened loss of power, and so far forgot himself as to use strong language. Resistance however was out of the question. The Raja was placed at the head of affairs, and Purnea resigned himself to his fate, retired from his post, and died shortly afterwards.

Ruinous profligacy of the Raja.

The government of Mysore ought never to have been entrusted to a boy, without some controlling authority. Krishnaraj was a polished young prince of courtly manners, but he had less knowledge of the world than an English charity boy. He was imbued with a strong taste for oriental pleasures and vices, and there was no one to say him nay. From his infancy he had been surrounded by obsequious flatterers, who were his willing slaves. The result might have been foreseen. Within three years the English Resident reported that the accumulations of Purnea, estimated at seven millions sterling, had already been squandered on priests and parasites. Later on he reported that the finances were in utter disorder. The pay of the army was in arrears, and the Raja was raising money by the sale of offices and monopolies. Worst of all the public revenues were alienated; the lands were let to the highest bidders,

A.D. 1828-1835 — and the lessees were left to extort what they could from the cultivators, whilst the Raja continued his wasteful expenditure on vicious indulgences and riotous living.

Fruitless warnings. Had the Raja been seriously warned in time that he would be deposed from his sovereignty unless he mended his ways, he would probably have turned over a new leaf. But non-intervention proved his ruin. The English Resident advised him to reform his administration, but he used soft and conciliatory tones which were lost upon the Raja. Matters grew worse and rebukes became louder, until at last the Raja was case-hardened. The once famous Sir Thomas Munro, the governor of Madras, solemnly pointed out the coming danger to the Raja; but he might as well have preached to the winds. Nothing was done, and the warnings became a farce. The Raja promised everything whilst the Resident was present; but when the Resident's back was turned, he thrust his tongue into his cheek for the amusement of his courtiers.

Rebellion and deposition. In 1830 the people of Mysore broke out in rebellion, and the British government was compelled to send a force to suppress it. It would be tedious to dwell on the military operations, or the political controversies that followed. In the end the administration of Mysore was transferred to English officers under the supervision of the English Resident; whilst the Raja was removed from the government, and pensioned off, like the Tanjore Raja, on an annual stipend of thirty-five thousand pounds, and a fifth share of the net revenues of Mysore.

Vacillations of Lord William Bentinck. But Lord William Bentinck was still anxious to perpetuate Hindu rule in Mysore. He proposed to restore the government to the Raja under a new set of restrictions; but the home authorities negatived the proposal; and indeed it would probably have ended in the same kind of explosion as that which extinguished the Mahratta Peishwa. He also contemplated a restoration of the old status of an English Resident and a Brahman minister; but Purnea's administration would not bear investigation. It had been cruel and oppressive; and the native officials under him had exacted revenue by methods which were revolting to civilised ideas.[1] Accordingly Lord William Bentinck left matters to drift on;

[1] See *ante*, p. 414.

A.D. 1828-1835

and a few years afterwards the English Resident was turned into a Commissioner, and Mysore became a British province in everything except the name. Meanwhile Mysore rose to a high pitch of prosperity; the people were contented and happy; and the yearly revenues of the province rose from four hundred thousand pounds to more than a million sterling.

Renewal of the Company's charter, 1833.

In one other direction the administration of Lord William Bentinck is an epoch in the history of India. It saw the renewal of the charter of the late East India Company in 1833. Henceforth the Company withdrew from all commercial transactions; and the right of Europeans to reside in India, and acquire possession of lands, was established by law.

Political administration of Lord William Bentinck.

Lord William Bentinck retired from the post of Governor General, and embarked for England in March 1835, after having held the reins of government for nearly eight years. Whatever may have been his shortcomings in his dealing with native states, there can be no question as to the purity of his motives, his sincere anxiety for the welfare of the princes and people of India, and the general success of his administration of the British Indian empire. His financial and judicial reforms are forgotten now, although their results have largely contributed to the well-being of the masses; but in other respects, the material prosperity of the empire dates from the administration of Lord William Bentinck. The acquisition of Cachar and Aman, between Bengal and Burma, during the first Burmese war, was followed by the cultivation of tea, which has already assumed proportions which would have appeared incredible in a past generation, and ought to increase the domestic comfort of every cottage throughout the British dominion. But the most memorable act in his administration was the abolition of suttee. This horrible rite, which had been practised in India from a remote antiquity, and had been known to Europe ever since the days of Alexander, was prohibited by law throughout British territories in the teeth of dismal forebodings and prejudiced posterity; and not only has the abolition been carried out with comparative ease, but it has recommended itself to the moral sense of the whole Hindu community of India. In the present day, whilst the education of females is still looked upon with

A.D. 1828-1835

distrust, and the attempts to put an end to female infanticide are distasteful in many quarters, every Hindu of ordinary education and intelligence rejoices in his heart that the burning of living widows with their deceased husbands is an abomination that has passed away.

Sir Charles Metcalfe, Governor-General, 1835-36.

In 1835 Lord William Bentinck was succeeded by Sir Charles Metcalfe as Governor-General of India. Sir Charles, afterwards Lord Metcalfe, was one of the ablest and most experienced civil servants of the late Company; but his administration was only provisional, and, beyond repealing the regulations which fettered the liberty of the press, it occupies but a small space in history. It was brought to a close in March 1836 by the arrival of Lord Auckland.

Peace and war decades.

The present chapter brings a decade of peace to a close. It began at the end of the Burmese war in 1826, and ended in 1836, when dark clouds were beginning to gather on the north-west. The war decade begins with the outbreak of hostilities beyond the Indus in 1839, and ends with the conquest of the Sikhs and annexation of the Punjab in 1849.

Lord Auckland, 1836: Russian extension.

The administration of Lord Auckland opens up a new era in the history of India. In the beginning of the century the Marquis of Wellesley had deemed it a peremptory duty to guard India against the approaches of France and the first Napoleon. In the second quarter of the same century Lord Auckland's government took alarm at the extension of Russian power and influence in Central Asia; and this alarm found expression in the first Afghan war. Before, however, dealing with the preliminary operations in Kandahar and Kábul, it may be as well to devote a preliminary chapter to the current of events in Central Asia and the previous history of the Afghans.

CHAPTER XVIII.

CENTRAL ASIA: AFGHAN HISTORY.

A.D. 1747 TO 1838.

A.D. 1747-1838 — Central Asia.

DURING the eighteenth century and first quarter of the nineteenth, Central Asia was a neutral and little-known region; the homes of Usbegs and Afghans; isolated from the outer world by desert and mountain; but environed more and more closely, as time went on, by the four great Asiatic empires of Persia, Russia, China, and British India.

Usbeg states northward of the Oxus.

Roughly speaking, the country northward of the river Oxus is occupied by Usbegs; whilst that to the south is occupied by Afghans. The Usbegs to the northward of the Oxus may be divided into the dwellers in towns, or Usbegs proper, and the nomads of the desert, better known as Turkomans. In modern times the Usbeg dominion has been parcelled out into the three kingdoms of Khiva, Bokhara and Khokand, which may be described as three semi-civilised oases in the barbarous desert of Turkomans.

Russian advances towards the Usbegs.

Ever since the reign of Peter the Great in the beginning of the eighteenth century, Russia has been extending her empire southwards over the Kirghiz steppes which separate her from the Usbegs. These steppes are occupied by the three great tribes of nomads, known as the little horde, the middle horde, and the great horde. Gradually, by a policy of protection followed by that of incorporation, these rude hordes of nomads were brought under Russian subjection; and when Lord Auckland landed in India the tide of Russian influence appeared to be approaching the three Usbeg kingdoms of Khiva, Bokhara, and Khokand.

A.D. 1747-1838

Afghan dominion south of the Oxus.

Meanwhile the British government had not been unmindful of the progress of affairs in Afghanistan to the southward of the Oxus. This region is distributed into four provinces, each having a city of the same name, corresponding to the four points of the compass. Kábul is on the north, Kandahar on the south, Peshawar on the east, and Herát on the west. Sometimes, but very rarely, these provinces have been formed into a single empire having its capital at Kábul. At all other times they have been parcelled out under different rulers,—sons, brothers, or other kinsmen of the suzerain at Kábul, but often independent of his authority. In the centre is the ancient city of Ghazni, the half-way house between Kandahar and Kábul, and the frontier fortress to Kábul proper on the side of Kandahar.

Mountains and valleys of Afghanistan.

Afghanistan is a region of rugged mountains and elevated valleys. The Hindu Kúsh, which forms the western end of the Himalayas, throws off towards the south-west a series of mountain ranges, which bound Kábul on the north, and then run in a westerly direction towards Herát, under the names of Koh-i-Baba and Siah Koh. Indeed the whole region may be described as a star of valleys, radiating round the stupendous peaks of Koh-i-Baba in the centre of the Afghan country, which are clad with pines and capped with snow. The valleys and glens are watered by numberless mountain streams, and are profusely rich in vegetable productions, especially fruits and cereals.[1] The lower slopes throw out spurs which are bleak and bare, and have an outer margin of barren or desert territory.[2] The population of

[1] Afghanistan produces wheat, barley, maize, millet and rice; also cotton, tobacco, and castor-oil. It is famous for the culture of fruits, including apples, pears, almonds, apricots, quinces, plums, cherries, pomegranates, limes, citrons, grapes, figs and mulberries. All of these fruits, both fresh and dried, are exported to Hindustan in immense quantities, and are the main staple of the country. Horses and wool are also exported to Bombay.

[2] The heights of Koh-i-Baba bear traces of a remote antiquity. They include the rock fortress of Zohak, the demon king of Arabia, who is celebrated in the Shah Namah. They also include the valley of Bamean on the north of Kábul, with huge colossal statues and temple caves; the relics of the old Buddhist faith which was driven out of Kábul by the advance of Islam under the Khalifs of Damascus and Bagdad.

The Siah Koh includes the mountain fortress of Ghor, which gave its name to a dynasty of Afghan conquerors of Hindustan, which was

Afghanistan is about five millions, but only about half can be reckoned as Afghans. A.D. 1747-1838

In 1836 the Afghans were separated from British territories by the empire of Runjeet Singh in the Punjab; and also by the dominions of the Amírs of Sinde on the lower Indus. But Afghanistan had always been the highway for armies invading India; for Assyrian, Persian, and Greek in ancient times, and for Turk, Afghan, and Moghul in a later age. In the earlier years of the present century, as already related, missions were sent by the British government to form defensive alliances with the Amír of Kábul and the Shah of Persia against the supposed designs of the first Napoleon.

Punjab and Sinde.

The Afghans are Muhammadans of the Sunní faith; they reverence the first four Khalifs, and have no particular veneration for the prophet Ali. They are split up into tribes, clans, and families, each under its own head, commander, or Sirdar; and they are often at war or feud, and often engaged in conspiracies, rebellions, and assassinations. They are tall, burly, active men, with olive complexions, dark Jewish features, black eyes, and long black hair hanging down in curls. Their countenances are calm, and they affect a frankness and bon-hommie; they will sometimes indulge in a rude jocularity; but their expression is savage, and evil passions are often raging in their hearts like hidden fires. They are bloodthirsty, deceitful, and depraved; ready to sell their country, their honour, and their very souls for lucre. They care for nothing but fighting and loot; delighting in the din of arms, the turmoil of battle, and the plunder of the killed and wounded; without any relish for home life or domestic ties; without a sting of remorse or a sense of shame. There are no people on earth that have a finer physique or a viler morale. They are the relics of a nation who have played out their parts in history. In bygone ages they conquered Hindustan on the one side and Persia on the other; but the conquering instinct has died away amidst the incessant discord of family feuds and domestic broils.

The Afghan people.

In olden time there were fierce contentions between

founded in the twelfth century of the Christian era. The same name reappears in Gour, the ancient capital of Bengal, which is now a heap of ruins. See *ante*, pp. 77 to 80.

A.D. 1747-1838

Abdalis and Ghilzais.

Abdalis and Ghilzais. The Abdalis were descended from the sons of a wife, and the Ghilzais from the sons of a concubine. Accordingly the Abdalis declared that they alone were the true Afghans, and that the Ghilzais were an illegitimate offspring. It was a later version of the old feud between Sarah and Hagar, between the children of Isaac and the children of Ishmael. Ultimately the Abdalis got the uppermost, and the Ghilzais took refuge in the mountains.

Dúranís and Barukzais.

The Abdalis are pure Afghans: legitimate and orthodox. In ancient times there was a distinguished offshoot, known as the tribe of Barukzais. In modern times the Abdalis have been known as Dúranís; and a distinction has grown up between the Duranís and the Barukzais. The origin of this distinction is unknown, but the rivalry between the two is the key to Afghan history. The dynasty of Ahmad Shah Abdali was known as the Dúraní Shahs;[1] their hereditary ministers were heads of the Barukzai tribe; and Afghan history has culminated in modern times in the transfer of the sovereignty from the Shah to the minister, from the Dúraní to the Barukzai.[2]

Death of Nadir Shah, 1747: Afghans return to Kandahar.

The modern history of the Afghans begins with the assassination of Nadir Shah in 1747. This catastrophe convulsed Asia like the sudden death of Alexander the Great at Babylon twenty-two centuries ago. The overgrown Persian empire was broken up, and there were bloody wars for the fragments. The Afghan Sirdars and their several contingents left the Persian army, and went to Kandahar to choose a Shah for themselves, who should be a king in his own right, and owe no allegiance to the Persian or the Moghul.

The Afghans could not agree about a Shah. The Sirdars quarrelled and wrangled according to their wont. Some

[1] Ferrier says that the name of Dúraní was given to the Abdalis by Ahmad Shah Abdali on his accession to the throne in 1747; but the name may have had a still earlier origin. Both Dúranís and Barukzais were originally included under the name of Abdalis.

[2] There are more intricacies of clans and tribes, which would only bewilder general readers. Thus the hereditary ministers, described hereafter as Barukzais, were, properly speaking, Mohamedzais, the most distinguished branch of the Barukzais. The Mohamedzais comprised about four or five thousand families, whilst the Barukzais numbered fifty thousand families.

called out for Ahmad Khan, the chief of the Dúranís; others called out for Jemal Khan, the chief of the Barukzais; but in their hearts every Sirdar wanted to be the Shah. At last a holy Dervish called out amidst the uproar, "God has made Ahmad Khan the greatest man amongst you!" And he twisted barley stalks into a wreath and placed it on the head of Ahmad Khan. Then Jemal Khan hailed Ahmad Khan as Shah;[1] and the people carried Ahmad Khan to the great mosque at Kandahar; and the chief Múlla poured a measure of wheat upon his head, and proclaimed that he was the chosen of God and the Afghans. So Ahmad Khan Dúraní became Shah of Kandahar, and Jemal Khan Barukzai was the greatest man in the kingdom next the Shah.

A.D. 1747-1838

Election of Ahmad Shah: coronation at Kandahar.

All this while Kábul was held by certain Persian families, who were known as Kuzzilbashes, or "Red-caps;" for when Nadir Shah was alive he placed the Persian "Red-caps" in the fortress of Bala Hissar,[2] to hold the city of Kábul against the Afghans. The Kuzzilbashes are Shíahs, whilst the Afghans are Sunnís; nevertheless Ahmad Shah made a league with the "Red caps," and they opened their gates to him, and he became Shah of Kábul as well as of Kandahar. Henceforth Ahmad Khan spent the spring and summer at the city of Kábul, and the autumn and winter at the city of Kandahar.

Surrender of Kábul by the Kuzzilbashes.

Ahmad Shah treated his Sirdars as friends and equals, but he showed the greatest kindness to Jemal Khan. He kept the Afghans constantly at war, so that no one cared to conspire against him. He conquered all Afghanistan to the banks of the Oxus; all Herát and Khorassan; all Kashmír and the Punjab as far as the Himalayas; and all Sinde and Beluchistan to the shores of the Indian Ocean. He invaded Hindustan, captured Delhi, and re-established the sovereignty of the Great Moghul.[3] He gave his Sirdars governments and commands in the countries he conquered; and they lived in great wealth and honour, and were faithful

Glorious reign of Ahmad Shah Dúraní, 1747-73.

[1] Shah signifies "king," and Mirza signifies "prince," or son of the Shah.

[2] The Bala Hissar, or "palace of kings," has been the scene of many a revolution and massacre. At this moment (November, 1879,) it is being destroyed by the British army.

[3] See *ante*, pp. 338, 347.

A.D. 1747-1838

to him all his days. He died in 1773, being the year after Warren Hastings was made Governor of Bengal.

Flight of the first-born.

Ahmad Shah left eight sons, but he set aside his first-born, and named his second son Timúr Mirza to be his successor on the throne. The first-born was proclaimed Shah at Kandahar, but Timúr marched an army against him; and all the chief men on the side of the first-born deserted his cause and went over to Timúr, but Timúr beheaded them on the spot lest they should prove to be spies. Then the first-born fled into exile, and Timúr Shah sat on the throne of his father, Ahmad Shah.

Timúr Shah, 1773-93.

Timúr Shah gave commands and honours to his Sirdars, and heaped rewards on the head of Payendah Khan, the son of Jemal Khan, who succeeded his father as hereditary chief of the Barukzais. But the Sirdars thwarted the new Shah, and wanted to be his masters; and he abandoned himself to his pleasures and put his trust in the Kuzzilbashes.

Disaffection in Balkh.

At this time the people of Balkh to the northward of Kábul were insolent and unruly.[1] They affronted every governor that Timúr Shah put over them, and refused to pay taxes; and at last no Sirdar would accept the government. So the matter became a jest amongst the Afghans; and monkeys were taught to howl with grief, and throw dust upon their heads, whenever one of them was offered the government of Balkh.

Revolt at Peshawar: massacre of the inhabitants.

Meanwhile there were troubles in the Punjab and Sinde; and Timúr Shah went to Peshawar with his army of Kuzzilbashes to put them down. One afternoon the Shah was taking his siesta in the fortress at Peshawar, and the Kuzzilbashes were slumbering outside the walls, when a company of armed conspirators got in by treachery, and sought to murder him. Timúr Shah heard the tumult, and ran into a tower and barred the gateway. He then hastened to the top of the tower, and shouted to the Kuzzilbashes below, and unfolded his long Kashmír turban, and waved it from the battlements. The Red-caps awoke just in time. The conspirators were breaking into the tower when they were assailed and cut to pieces. The leader of the conspiracy

[1] Balkh is a fertile but little known territory to the northward of Kábul, between the so-called Himalayas (Koh-i-Baba) and the Oxus. It was the Baktria of Herodotus. The beautiful Roxana, whom Alexander loved and married, was a daughter of the king of Baktria.

escaped to the mountains, but was cajoled into surrender by solemn oaths of pardon and promises of reward, and was then put to death without scruple. Timúr Shah was so furious at the outbreak that he wreaked his vengeance upon the inhabitants of Peshawar, and put a third of the people to the sword. A.D. 1747-1838

After this massacre Timúr Shah was stricken with remorse and terror, and grew melancholy mad. He died in 1793, leaving twenty-three sons to fight against each other for the throne of Afghanistan. Remorse and madness.

The princes were preparing for war when Payendah Khan, the new chief of the Barukzais, averted the bloodshed. He had resolved that the fifth son of Timúr Shah, named Zemán, should succeed to the throne; but he called all the sons of Timúr Shah, and all the Sirdars, together in one building in order that they might choose a Shah. After long debate Zemán quietly left the assembly followed by Payendah Khan; and all those who remained behind found that the doors and windows were locked and barred, and that the place was surrounded by soldiers. For the space of five days no one could get out, and no one could break in. Every day a small morsel of bread was given to each prisoner, which sufficed to keep him alive; and when they were all reduced to skin and bone, they yielded to their fate, and swore allegiance to Zemán Shah. Imprisonment and starvation.

After this Zemán Shah resolved to cripple the power of the Sirdars. He would not seek to conciliate them as his father and grandfather had done; but he deprived them of their commands and emoluments. He grew jealous of Payendah Khan to whom he owed his throne, and removed him from his posts, and reduced him to poverty. The flames of discontent began to spread abroad amongst the Sirdars, but were quenched by treachery and massacre. Many were tempted to court by oaths and promises, and were then put to death. In this manner Zemán Shah established a reign of terror at Kábul. Oppressive reign of Zemán Shah, 1793-1800

At this time the brothers of Zemán Shah were dispersed over the provinces, and breaking out in plots and insurrections. The Sikhs were rebelling in the Punjab. Zemán Shah set out from Kábul to repress the revolt; but he was called back by the news that his eldest brother had been proclaimed Shah at Kandahar, and that another brother, Plots and insurrections.

A.D. 1747-1838 — named Mahmúd Mirza, had rebelled at Herát. After a while his eldest brother was taken prisoner and deprived of eyesight; and Mahmúd Mirza was bribed to quietness by being appointed governor of Herát.

Pacification of the Punjab; rise of Runjeet Singh. Zemán Shah next marched to Lahore, and quieted the Sikh rebels in like manner. He cajoled the head rebel, Runjeet Singh, into a show of obedience, and appointed him Viceroy of the Punjab; but from that day the Punjab was lost to the Afghans, and passed into the hands of the Sikhs. Runjeet Singh proved himself to be a warrior of mark, who laid the foundations of a Sikh empire. His later relations with the British government have already been told in dealing with the administration of Lord Minto.

Shah Shuja at Peshawar. When Zemán Shah had settled Lahore, he placed his brother Shah Shuja in the government of Peshawar, which was the gate of the Punjab, and then returned to Kábul.

Zemán Shah and Lord Wellesley, 1800. Whilst Zemán Shah was at Lahore, he threatened to invade Hindustan, and invited Lord Wellesley to join him in the conquest of the Mahrattas. Had Lord Wellesley been acquainted with the surroundings of Zemán Shah, he would have scoffed at the idea of an Afghan invasion.

Plottings at Kandahar: massacre of the Barukzais. No sooner had Zemán Shah returned to Kábul than tidings reached him that the Barukzais were plotting against him at Kandahar, to avenge the disgrace of Payendah Khan, the chief of their tribe. Accordingly Zemán Shah hurried away to Kandahar, and thought to crush the Barukzais by confiscating their wealth, and executing all who were disaffected. The Barukzais grew desperate, and plotted to set up Shah Shuja of Peshawar in the room of Zemán Shah; but the plot was betrayed by one of the conspirators. Accordingly Payendah Khan, and every Sirdar who had leagued with him, were summoned to the fortress at Kandahar under the pretence of being consulted by the Shah on public affairs. One by one they were conducted into the presence of Zemán Shah and butchered on the spot, and their bodies were exposed in the public square. In this way Zemán Shah established his authority at Kandahar, and then returned to Kábul.

Zemán Shah dethroned: asylum at Ludhiana. Payendah Khan, chief of the Barukzais, left nineteen sons by six different mothers, and the eldest was named Futih Khan. When the unfortunate father was murdered at Kandahar, Futih Khan fled to Herát, and began to plot with Mahmúd Mirza, the governor of Herát, to dethrone Zemán Shah, and set up Mahmúd in his room. When their plans were all ready, Futih Khan conducted Mahmúd to Kandahar, and raised an army of Barukzais, and marched towards Kábul. Zemán Shah came out against them, but was defeated utterly, and taken prisoner and deprived of sight. Mahmúd thus became Shah of Afghanistan, whilst his blinded brother Zemán fled through many countries, and suffered many pangs and privations, and at last found an asylum at Lúdhiana in British territory. Thus the once famous Afghan ruler, who threatened to conquer Hindustan, and excited the alarm of Lord Wellesley, was supported to the end of his days on a pension granted him by the East India Company. A.D. 1747-1838

Mahmúd was Shah only in name; the real sovereign was Futih Khan, the Vizier, who had succeeded his father as chief of the Barukzais. Mahmúd the Dúraní Shah was a puppet like the Mahratta Sahu; whilst Futih Khan, the Barukzai Vizier, was a Peishwa like Balaji Rao. Mahmúd Shah, 1800-3.

In 1801-2 there were risings of the Ghilzais, the children of the concubine, the Ishmaels of the Afghans; but Futih Khan attacked them in the mountains and routed them with great slaughter; and he then built up a pyramid with their heads and returned in triumph to Kábul. Risings of the Ghilzais.

After a while there was a bloody strife at Kábul between the Sunnís and the Shíahs; in other words, between the Afghans and the Red-caps. The Red-caps thought to spite the Sunnís by tormenting an Afghan boy; and the parents of the lad went to the palace for justice, and were told to go to the mosque.[1] The parents ran into the great mosque at Kábul whilst a Saiyid was preaching, and rent their clothes and filled the air with their cries. The Saiyid stopped the sermon to hear their story, and then issued a fatwa[2] for the slaughter of all the Shíahs in Kábul. The Sunní congregation armed themselves and rushed to the quarter of the Kuzzilbashes, slaughtered every Red-cap they met in the streets, and then broke into the Sunnís and Shíahs: slaughter of Kuzzilbashes.

[1] The Dúraní Shahs had always trimmed between the Afghans and the Kuzzilbashes, or Red-caps, and stood aloof from every conflict between the two. Accordingly both the Dúraní Shah and the Barukzai Vizier got rid of the petition of the parents by referring the complainants to a religious tribunal.

[2] A fatwa was a religious command bearing some resemblance to a papal bull.

A.D. 1747-1838 houses, carried off the plunder, and set the buildings on fire. The storm raged throughout four days. At last the Barukzai Vizier interposed with a troop of horsemen, and put a stop to the riot, but not before four hundred Kuzzilbashes had been slain.

Shah Shuja 1803-9. The Sunnís had been scattered by matchlock and sabre, but their wrath was not appeased, and they swore to be revenged on the friends of the Shíahs. In 1803, when the Barukzai Vizier was putting down revolts amongst the mountain tribes at a distance from Kábul, Shah Shuja was persuaded to come from Peshawar, and was hailed by the Sunni multitude at Kábul with shouts and acclamations. Mahmúd Shah fled in alarm to the Bala Hissar, but soon found himself a close prisoner in one of the dungeons. Shortly afterwards the Barukzai Vizier returned to Kábul and became minister to Shah Shuja.[1]

Flight of Shah Shuja to Lúdhiana, 1809. In 1809 there were other plots and other explosions. Shah Shuja had grown impatient of the dictation of his Barukzai Vizier and removed him from office; and then went to Peshawar to receive Mr. Elphinstone, and make an alliance with the English against France and Napoleon. Meanwhile the deposed Vizier leagued with the Kuzzilbashes, and delivered his old master, Mahmúd Shah, from his prison, and placed him on the throne at Kábul. Shah Shuja completed his negotiations with Mr. Elphinstone, and then turned back to go to Kábul, but was routed by the Barukzais and Kuzzilbashes; and he fled through the Punjab to British territory, and became a pensioner at Lúdhiana like his brother Zemán Shah.

Mahmúd Shah restored, 1809-16. Mahmúd Shah was thus restored to the throne of Afghanistan, but he was still feeble and effeminate, and a mere tool in the hands of his Barukzai Vizier, Futih Khan. He abandoned himself to his pleasures, and left the government to his Vizier. But Afghanistan prospered under the rule of the Barukzai. Futih Khan was a conqueror as well as an administrator. He reduced Sinde and Beluchistan to obedience, but he could do nothing in the Punjab, for he was constantly baffled and defeated by the Sikh ruler, Runjeet Singh.

[1] The Barukzai Vizier's acceptance of office under Shah Shuja, whilst his old master Mahmúd was pining in the dungeons of the Bala Hissar, is one of those typical data which serve to bring out the real character of the Afghans.

A.D. 1747-1838 — Quarrel between Persia and Afghanistan about Herát, 1816.

About this time Herát became a bone of contention between the Afghans and the Persians.[1] It has already been seen that when Zemán was Shah, his brother Mahmúd became governor of Herát. When Mahmúd became Shah, another brother, named Firuz, became governor of Herát. Firuz coined money in the name of Mahmúd Shah, and his son married a daughter of Mahmúd Shah; but Firuz ruled Herát as an independent sovereign, and refused to send any tribute to Kábul.

Herát seized by the Barukzai Vizier: plundering of the zenana, 1816.

In 1816 Firuz was between two fires. On one side Kábul demanded tribute; on the other side Persia demanded possession. At last Persia sent an army to take possession of Herát, and Firuz was forced to send for help to Kábul. The Barukzai Vizier rejoiced over the request. He marched an army to Herát before the Persians reached the place; and he entered the fortress and declared that Firuz was a rebel, and took him prisoner and sent him to Kábul. At the same time the Vizier's younger brother, Dost Muhammad Khan, broke into the zenana and robbed the ladies of their jewels, and carried away a girdle set with precious stones that was worn by the daughter of Mahmúd Shah. Futih Khan was angry at this outrage, and ordered his brother to restore the girdle; but Dost Muhammad Khan refused to give it back, and fled away to Kashmír.[2]

Blinding of Futih Khan.

All this while Kamran Mirza, the son of Mahmúd Shah, had been very jealous of the Vizier; and when he heard that his sister at Herát had been robbed of her girdle, he complained to his father very bitterly. So Mahmúd Shah was persuaded to avenge the insult by destroying the Vizier's eyesight, and Kamran hastened to Herát to carry out the sentence. Futih Khan was surprised and bound,

[1] The Shah of Persia claimed Herát on the ground that it had been conquered by Nadir Shah. The claim however was a mere sham. Persia might just as well have claimed Kábul and Kandahar, since both provinces had been conquered by Nadir Shah. The plain fact was that Ahmad Shah Dúraní had conquered Herát, but his successors could not hold it, as it was too remote from Kábul; and Herát became an independent sovereignty in the hands of any Afghan prince who obtained the government.

[2] This is the first appearance of Dost Muhammad Khan, the founder of the Barukzai dynasty, upon the page of history. At a later period he was a leading character in the Afghan war of 1839-42.

A.D. 1747-1838

and his eyes were pierced with red-hot needles in the presence of Kamran.[1]

Dost Muhammad Khan takes Kábul: murder of Futih Khan.

When Dost Muhammad Khan heard what had been done, he raised an army in Kashmír and marched against Kábul, to avenge the atrocity committed on his eldest brother. Mahmúd Shah was seized with terror at the approach of the avenging army, and fled away to Ghazni, the half-way fortress between Kábul and Kandahar. At Ghazni he was joined by his son, Kamran, and the blind Barukzai Vizier from Herát. But his kingdom had passed out of his hands, and his troops deserted him in large numbers, and went over to Dost Muhammad Khan. In his wrath he sent for the blind Vizier, and ordered his Sirdars to put him to death before his eyes. Kamran struck the first blow. All the Sirdars then began to torment the blind Vizier with their daggers; and after enduring excruciating agony, Futih Khan expired without a groan.

Dúraní puppets and Barukzai rulers, 1818-26.

The plots and broils which followed are tedious and bewildering. Mahmúd Shah and his son, Kamran, fled to Herát, and became independent rulers of that remote territory. The surviving sons of Payendah Shah, known as the Barukzai brothers, assumed different commands in Kábul, Kandahar, Kashmír, and Beluchistan. But Afghanistan was without a sovereign. Not one of the Barukzai brothers ventured at this period to usurp the Dúraní sovereignty. They were willing to set up Shah Shuja as a puppet and to rule Afghanistan in his name; but Shah Shuja refused to accept their terms, and insisted upon being absolute and uncontrolled sovereign of the Afghans. Under such circumstances the Barukzai brothers abandoned Shah Shuja, and he was forced to return to Lúdhiana. They then tried to set up another prince of the family; but soon found that their new Dúraní puppet was plotting against them with Shah Shuja on one side at Lúdhiana, and with Mahmúd

[1] The following table of Dúraní Shahs and Barukzai Viziers may be found a convenient aid to the memory :—

Ahmad Shah Dúraní . .	1747	Jemal Khan Barukzai . .	1747
Timúr Shah ,, . .	1773	Payendah Khan ,, . .	1773
Zemán Shah ,, . .	1793	Futih Khan ,, . .	1800
Mahmúd Shah ,, . .	1800	,, ,, . .	1803
Shah Shuja ,, . .	1803	Dost Muhammad Khan	
Mahmúd Shah (*restored*) .	1809	Barukzai, Amír of Kábul	1826

Shah on the other side at Herát. The result was that the puppet was dethroned, and the Barukzai brothers quarrelled amongst themselves, whilst Runjeet Singh occupied Peshawar and Persia threatened Herát.

A.D. 1747-1838

At last, in 1826, Dost Muhammad Khan became master of Kábul. Subsequently he was formally elected king by an assembly of Sirdars, and proclaimed Amír by the chief Múlla, with all the ceremonies that had been observed at the coronation of Ahmad Shah. But he was environed by dangers. On the north there were revolts in Balkh; on the south one of his brothers was holding out against him at Kandahar; on the east he was harassed by Runjeet Singh at Peshawar, with Shah Shuja and the British government in the background; on the west there was Mahmúd Shah and Kamran at Herát, with Persia plotting behind and Russia looming in the distance. Amidst such perplexities Dost Muhammad Khan was willing and anxious to conclude an alliance with the British government, provided only he could be assured that the English were not plotting to restore Shah Shuja, and would help him to recover Peshawar from Runjeet Singh.

Dost Muhammad Khan Amír of Kábul, 1826-36.

In the midst of these turmoils, Great Britain and Russia were at variance in Central Asia. The bone of contention was Herát. From a remote antiquity Herát has been the key to India; the first turnpike on the great highway from Persia to Hindustan.[1] In 1836 Russia was making a cat's paw of Persia and urging the Shah to seize Herát. Great Britain was anxious to keep Persia out of Herát, lest the place should become a gateway through which Russia might advance towards India. But the British government did not tell Persia plainly that war would be declared if she attempted to occupy Herát. Had this been done, Persia would never have besieged Herát, and an English army would never have invaded Afghanistan.

Contentions respecting Herát.

The result of all this underplotting and hesitation was that in 1837 the Shah of Persia marched an army against Herát. By this time the government of Herát had changed hands. Mahmúd Shah had been murdered in 1829, and

Herát under Yar Muhammad Khan, 1830-36.

[1] The fortified city of Herát is a quadrangle about four miles on each side. It was surrounded by a rampart of earth about ninety feet high, which appeared to environ the city like a long hill. The rampart was supported on the inside by buttresses of masonry; and was surmounted by a wall thirty feet high, flanked with round towers and loop-holed for musketry.

A.D. 1747-1838 — his son Kamran was sovereign of Herát; but Kamran was a slave to opium-eating and other enervating pleasures, and his Vizier, Yar Muhammad Khan, was the real ruler. Yar Muhammad Khan was a cruel and extortionate despot; he has been described as the most accomplished villain in Central Asia; but at this period he hated Persia with all his heart and soul. On one occasion he had been entrapped into a meeting with a Persian prince on the frontier, under pretence of settling all differences between Herát and Persia; and two of his teeth had been forcibly extracted to induce him to comply with the demands of the Shah.[1] Kamran would have submitted to the Shah of Persia at the first summons; but Yar Muhammad Khan swore that he would never surrender Herát until his teeth were restored to his gums; and that as long as he had a sabre to draw or a cartridge to fire, he would never bow his head to the Kajar Shah.

Persia besieges Herat, 1837-38.

The siege of Herát was one of the most memorable events of the time. It lasted from November, 1837, to September, 1838. The Afghans fought manfully, harassing the Persian army with repeated sorties. Even the women and children mounted the walls, and threw down bricks and stones on the Persian soldiers. But the canals which supplied the city with water were cut off by the enemy; the inhabitants were starving; and Kamran was treacherously plotting the surrender of the city to the Persians. Indeed, Herát would have been lost to the Afghans, but for the heroic exertions of a young lieutenant, named Eldred Pottinger, who was present in the city during the siege. Pottinger animated the Afghan soldiery by his gallant exploits, and cheered the drooping spirits of Yar Muhammad Khan by his energy and counsel. At last the siege was brought to a close by diplomacy. The British government threatened Persia with war, and the Shah raised the siege of Herat, and returned to his own dominions.

[1] The Persian prince was Abbas Mirza, eldest son of Futih Ali Shah, the second sovereign of the Kajar dynasty. Abbas Mirza died a few months afterwards, and Yar Muhammad Khan escaped to Herát. Futih Ali Shah died in 1834, and was succeeded on the throne of Persia by his son, Muhammad Shah, who besieged Herát in 1837. Futih Ali Shah, sovereign of Persia, must not be confounded with Futih Khan, the Barukzai minister at Kábul, who was murdered in the year 1817.

A.D. 1747-1838

All this while Dost Muhammad Khan was most anxious to recover Peshawar from Runjeet Singh. He implored Lord Auckland to call on Runjeet Singh to restore Peshawar. But the British government had no desire to pick a quarrel with Runjeet Singh, and declined to interfere. The result was that Dost Muhammad Khan made advances to Russia, and received a Russian mission at Kábul; and the British government in return resolved to dethrone Dost Muhammad Khan, and restore Shah Shuja to the throne of Kábul.

CHAPTER XIX.

AFGHAN WAR: LORDS AUCKLAND AND ELLENBOROUH.

A.D. 1839 TO 1842.

A.D. 1839-1842

British army advances to Quetta.

On the 1st of October, 1838, Lord Auckland published a declaration of war at Simla; and shortly afterwards the British forces were on the move for Kábul. They could not march through the Punjab, because Runjeet Singh refused permission. Accordingly they marched through Sinde to Quetta; and there the Bombay column joined the Bengal column. At Quetta Sir John Keane took the command of the united armies, and then set out for Kábul.

Capture of Kandahar, Ghazni, and Kábul, 1839.

Kandahar was captured in April, 1839. A British force was left at Kandahar under the command of General Nott; whilst Major (now Sir Henry) Rawlinson, was placed in political charge of the province in the name of Shah Shuja. In July, Ghazni was taken by storm,[1] and Dost Muhammad Khan fled over the Oxus into Bokhara. In August the British army entered Kábul, and Shah Shuja was restored to the throne of Afghanistan. Henceforth he was supposed to govern the country under the advice and help of the English minister and envoy, Sir William Macnaghten.

Russian expedition to Khiva: its failure.

In November, 1839, the Russian government sent a counter expedition from Orenberg towards Khiva, with the view of establishing Russian influence over the three Usbeg Khanates to the northward of the Oxus. The time of year, however, was most unfortunate. Winter snows and

[1] At the storming of Ghazni the late Sir Henry Durand distinguished himself as a young subaltern in the Engineers by blowing up the Kashmír gate.

A.D. 1839-1842

waterless wastes forbade the Russian force to reach Khiva; and after heroically fighting against the severest privations and disasters, it was compelled to return to Orenberg.

British occupation of Kábul, 1840.

Meanwhile the Afghans seemed perfectly satisfied with British occupation. Large subsidies were paid by the English envoy to Afghan chiefs, as well as to the mountain tribes who guarded the passes; whilst the presence of the English troops was a godsend to all the shop-keepers and provision-dealers in the bazars. The British army remained at Kábul during 1840. Towards the end of the year, Dost Muhammad Khan surrendered to the English envoy, and was sent to Calcutta, where he was detained as a prisoner, but treated as a guest. The old Barukzai warrior was indeed often entertained at Government House, where he is said to have played at chess with Miss Eden, the sister of the Governor-General.

Herát affairs, 1838-41; British gold.

Meanwhile there were complications at Herát. After the retreat of the Shah of Persia in 1838, the revenues of Herát were exhausted, the troops were without pay, the inhabitants were starving, and the Vizier, Yar Muhammad Khan, was trying to raise money and get rid of the surplus population, by selling the people as slaves to the Usbegs. The British government averted these evils by advancing large sums of money for the payment of the troops, the repair of the fortifications, and the relief of Kamran and his Vizier; no doubt with the view of establishing a permanent influence at Herát.

Withdrawal of Major Todd: wrath of Lord Auckland.

Kamran and his Vizier were in no way grateful for these subsidies. They suspected that the British government had sinister designs on Herát, and accordingly opened up a treacherous correspondence with the Shah of Persia. Major D'Arcy Todd, who had been appointed English envoy at Herát, withheld the money payments on his own authority, unless the Vizier agreed to receive a contingent of British troops into Herát. The result was that the Vizier grew furious at the stoppage of the subsidies, and called on Major Todd either to pay up the money or to leave Herát. Major Todd was so disgusted with the perfidy and greediness of the Herát rulers, that he threw up his post and returned to British territory. Lord Auckland was naturally exasperated at the abandonment of Herát. Matters had been squared with Persia, and the continued

A.D. 1839-1842

presence of Major Todd would have sufficed to maintain British influence at Herát. Major Todd was dismissed from political employ, but found a soldier's death four years afterwards on the field of Ferozeshahar.

Growing discontents.

The British occupation of Afghanistan continued through the year 1841, for it was not deemed safe to leave Shah Shuja unprotected at Kábul. Meanwhile, the double government satisfied no one. Shah Shuja was smarting under the dictation of Sir William Macnaghten. The English envoy and minister was in his turn impatient of Afghan ways and prejudices. The Afghan officials were disgusted with the order and regularity of English administration, which was introduced under the new régime. The Múllas refused to offer up public prayers for Shah Shuja, declaring that he was not an independent sovereign. Even the rise of prices, which filled the pockets of the bazar dealers, lessened the value of money and excited the discontent of the masses.

Economy and disaffection, 1841.

So long however as subsidies and money allowances were lavished amongst turbulent Sirdars and refractory mountain tribes, there was no lack of loyalty towards Shah Shuja and his English allies. But the flow of gold could not last for ever. The revenues of Afghanistan had been overrated. The British authorities had put their trust in the estimates of Shah Shuja when at Lúdhiana; forgetting the Machiavellian maxim that it is dangerous to rely upon the representations and hopes of exiles. The expenses of the British occupation were so enormous that economy was imperative. Accordingly Sir William Macnaghten began to cut down the subsidies and money allowances. From that moment the loyalty, which had sprung up in a single night like the prophet's gourd, began to sicken and die away. The Afghans grew weary of the English, and their puppet ruler, Shah Shuja. Conspiracies were formed; petty outbreaks became frequent; whilst the Ghilzais, and other mountain tribes at the passes, being no longer bribed into acquiescence, became most troublesome and disorderly.

Absence of alarm.

At this period there were no alarms for the safety of the British army in Kábul. On the contrary, English officers had been induced to bring up their wives and families from the depressing heats of Bengal to the cool climate of Kábul; and no precautions were taken against a possible rising of

A.D. 1839-1842

the whole people. The British cantonment was three miles from the city, with only a mud wall round it that could be easily ridden over. Sir William Macnaghten and his family lived in a house close by the cantonments; he had been appointed Governor of Bombay, and was about to be succeeded by Sir Alexander Burnes as envoy and minister at Kábul. Burnes himself was as much at home at Kábul as at Calcutta; he occupied a house near the centre of the city, surrounded by bazars, and above all by a turbulent population of Afghans and Kuzzilbashes, who were ever and anon endeavouring to settle the knotty disputes between Sunnís and Shíahs by force of arms.

General Elphinstone.

Meantime there had been some changes in the command of the British army of occupation. General Elphinstone, an aged and infirm officer, unfit for the post, had taken the place of Sir John Keane. Next to General Elphinstone were Sir Robert Sale and Brigadier Shelton.

Bala Hissar.

The British army of occupation was exposed to danger from another cause. It had been originally quartered in the fortress known as the Bala Hissar, which commanded the whole city and suburbs of Kábul. So long as the British kept possession of the Bala Hissar, they could hold out against any insurrection. But Shah Shuja quartered his harem in the Bala Hissar, and objected to the presence of the English soldiers; and Sir William Macnaghten was weak enough to remove the troops from the fortress, and quarter them in an unprotected cantonment about three miles from the city.

General Sale at Jellalabad.

The catastrophe that followed may be told in a few words. In October, 1841, Sir Robert Sale left Kábul with a brigade to re-open communications between Kábul and Jellalabad, which had been closed by the disaffected mountaineers. Sale effected his task after a long struggle and considerable loss. His subsequent defence of Jellalabad against the repeated assaults of a large Afghan army is one of the heroic events in the war.

Insurrection at Kábul: murder of Burnes, November, 1841.

On the 2nd of November, 1841, an insurrection broke out in the streets of Kábul. Sir Alexander Burnes thought of escaping to the English cantonment in the disguise of an Afghan; but he changed his mind, and resolved to hold out to the last in his English uniform. He barricaded his house, and sent to Macnaghten for a battalion of infantry

A.D. 1839-1842

and two field-pieces. Such a force at the beginning of the outbreak would have saved the life of Burnes. Its appearance in the streets of Kábul would have led the Kuzzilbashes to rally round Burnes, and raise the war-cry against the Sunnís. But Macnaghten was doubtful, and General Elphinstone was afraid that Shah Shuja might object, and the two together agreed to wait for further information. Meanwhile the mob of Kábul, the most dangerous in Central Asia, was surging round the house of the Englishman. Burnes held out with thirty-two others from eight o'clock in the morning until two in the afternoon, when the mob burned down the gate, and rushed in, and all was over. Burnes and twenty-three others were killed the remaining nine escaped by a miracle.

National uprising.

At three o'clock that same afternoon, Brigadier Shelton made a lame attempt to enter the city with a couple of battalions of infantry; but by this time the suburban population had joined the rioters. It was impossible to cut a way through the narrow streets and crowded bazars, and Shelton was compelled to return to the cantonment. Meanwhile the uproar was increasing in the city. Thousands of Afghans flocked to Kábul in hopes of plunder, and it soon appeared that the whole Afghan nation had risen against the rule of the foreigner.

Proposed retreat to Jellalabad.

At this crisis the British commanders appear to have been paralysed. General Elphinstone and Sir William Macnaghten were planning a retreat to Jellalabad, the half-way house between Kábul and Peshawar. Provisions were running short; the people of Kábul kept back all supplies from the British cantonment, and the army of occupation was becoming demoralised.

Negotiations with rebel leaders.

At last, Macnaghten began to negotiate with the leaders of the insurrection, and especially with Akbar Khan, the eldest son of Dost Muhammad Khan. This man had fled from Kábul about the same time that his father had made his way to Bokhara; but on hearing of the revolt, he had hastened back to Kábul, and was bent on seizing the government of the country. Shah Shuja was shut up in the Bala Hissar but could do nothing; he was already ignored, and his end was drawing nigh.

Akbar Khan and other Afghan Sirdars solemnly engaged to supply the British army with carriage and provisions. In return they received from Macnaghten promises of large sums of money, and hostages for the payment. But instead of keeping to their engagement, the Afghans demanded more money and more hostages. Winter had set in, and snow was falling; and it was even proposed that the British army should remain at Kábul till the spring. At length, after many delays and evasions, there was a final meeting between Macnaghten and the Afghan chiefs on the 23rd of December, 1841. But the English envoy had given mortal offence to the Afghans, and when he appeared at the meeting he was suddenly attacked and murdered by Akbar Khan.

A.D. 1839-1842 — Treachery and murder.

Subsequently the Afghan chiefs tried to explain away the murder. Akbar Khan vowed that he had acted on the mad impulse of the moment, and not with any deliberate intention of committing murder. Negotiations were renewed, and in January, 1842, the British forces began their retreat from Kábul, followed by Akbar Khan and a large army of Afghans. Then followed a horrible series of treacheries and massacres. Akbar Khan demanded more hostages, including English ladies and children. The Ghilzai mountaineers covered the heights on either side of the Khaiber Pass, and poured a murderous fire on the retreating force. Akbar Khan declared that he could not restrain the Ghilzais, but at the same time he permitted his own forces to share in the massacre and plunder. Thousands of British troops and camp-followers were carried off by successive volleys, or died of hunger and privations, or fell down in the snow from wounds or fatigue and were butchered by the Afghans. Thus perished a force which left Kábul with four thousand fighting men, and twelve thousand followers. Out of all this number, only a solitary individual, an English surgeon named Brydon, managed to escape to Jellalabad. He was brought in by Sale's garrison half dead from hunger and wounds; but he lived to tell the tale for more than thirty years afterwards.

Destruction of the British army in the Khaiber.

Such was the state of affairs in February, 1842, when Lord Ellenborough landed at Calcutta and succeeded Lord Auckland as Governor-General. Men's hearts were bursting with shame and indignation as they heard of the murder of the British envoy, and the destruction of sixteen thousand men. Englishmen in India were burning to retrieve the

Lord Ellenborough, 1842-44: conflicting feelings.

A.D. 1839-1842

disgrace which had befallen British arms, and to avenge the slaughter which cast a gloom over the whole country. But Lord Auckland had been too much oppressed by the disaster to respond to the call; whilst Lord Ellenborough, who succeeded him, was too much alarmed at the danger to which the British garrisons were exposed at Jellalabad and Kandahar to plan such a scheme of vengeance as should vindicate the honour of England, and restore the prestige of British arms.

Pollock's advance to Peshawar, 1842.

A force was assembled under General Pollock to march through the Punjab, and relieve Sale's garrison at Jellalabad. Runjeet Singh died in June, 1839, and the Sikh rulers who came after him did not resist the passage of British troops. In due course Pollock marched his army through the Punjab and reached Peshawar, but halted there for some weeks to reassure the sepoys, who were reluctant to enter the Khaiber Pass.

Advance to Jellalabad.

In April, 1842, Pollock crowned the heights of the Khaiber with British infantry, and engaged hotly with the mountaineers; and within a short space of time the white dresses of the Ghilzais were to be seen flying off in all directions He then pursued his victorious march through the Khaiber to Jellalabad, and reached the place at a critical moment. Sale had been closely beleaguered by a large army of Afghans under the command of Akbar Khan; and he had just inflicted a heavy defeat on the enemy, and compelled Akbar Khan to raise the siege and return to Kábul.

Distractions in Kábul: murder of Shah Shuja.

Meanwhile the city of Kábul was distracted by the struggle between the factions of Barukzais and Dúranís. A Barukzai chief, named Zemán Khan, had taken possession of the city;[1] whilst the Dúraní sovereign, Shah Shuja, shut himself up in the Bala Hissar. Indeed Shah Shuja was in sore peril and perplexity. He sent letters to Jellalabad, swearing eternal devotion to the British government; and he sent messages to the Barukzai leaders, swearing to drive the British out of Afghanistan. At last the Barukzais called upon him to lead the Afghan army against the British garrison at Jellalabad, and bound themselves by solemn oaths to protect him from all harm. The old Dúraní left the fortress of the Bala Hissar decked out in all his robes

[1] Zemán Khan was a nephew of Dost Muhammad Khan. He had been elected king by the Barukzais in the absence of Akbar Khan.

A.D. 1842

and jewels; and was then shot dead by an ambush of matchlock men, and rifled of all his precious things.

Barukzais *versus* Dúranís.

The Barukzais, however, failed for the moment to get the mastery. The Bala Hissar was still in the hands of the Dúranís, and a son of Shah Shuja was proclaimed sovereign within the walls of the fortress. The civil war continued to rage between the two parties. There was fighting in the streets from house to house, whilst the guns of the Bala Hissar were playing upon the city.

Abkar Khan, ruler of Kábul

At this juncture Akbar Khan returned from his defeat at Jellalabad. Both Barukzais and Dúranis were dreading the return of the English; and Akbar Khan commanded the respect of all parties of Afghans by declaring that he was negotiating with General Sale. But Akbar Khan had his own game to play. He joined the Barukzais and captured the Bala Hissar. Then he went over to the Dúranís, paid his homage to the son of Shah Shuja, and began to rule as minister. The boy sovereign however was in mortal fear of being murdered by his self-constituted minister; and he at last escaped to the British camp, and placed himself under the protection of General Pollock.

Negotiations for the restoration of the prisoners.

Akbar Khan thus became ruler of Kábul, and the fate of the prisoners and hostages was in his hands. He had not treated them unkindly, but he was determined to use them for his own purposes. He wrote to General Pollock offering to deliver them up, provided the English departed from Jellalabad and Kandahar without advancing to Kábul. Pollock rejected the proposals. Akbar Khan then sent the captives to a hill fortress far away to the northwards; and marched out of Kábul with a large army to prevent Pollock from advancing on the Afghan capital.

Question of retreat or advance.

Meanwhile Lord Ellenborough was hesitating whether to withdraw the garrisons from Jellalabad and Kandahar, or permit them to march to Kábul. Secret instructions were sent to the two generals to withdraw; but the secret got wind and raised a storm of indignation, as it was imagined that the captives were to be abandoned to the tender mercies of the Afghans. Accordingly Lord Ellenborough modified his instructions, and ordered the two generals to use their own discretion as regards an advance to Kábul.

General Nott was a hot-tempered officer, and when he received the orders to withdraw, he was furious with

A.D. 1842

Nott and Rawlinson at Kandahar, 1842.

rage. Both Nott and Rawlinson knew that a retreat from Kandahar would raise the whole country against them, and end in disaster like the retreat from Kábul. Rawlinson had already tried to stir up the neighbouring Dúrani chiefs to rally round Shah Shuja, but found that they were as bitterly opposed to the British occupation as the Barukzais. Accordingly there was no alternative but to wait for reinforcements; and for months the forc at Kandahar was exposed to desperate assaults, which were met by still more desperate repulses; whilst Nott and Rawlinson continued to hope for a change of orders.

Pollock and Sale at Jellalabad: advance to Kábul.

General Pollock was the mildest of men, but even he was moved with shame and anger at the order to withdraw. He wrote to Nott begging him not to leave Kandahar until he heard more; and reported to head-quarters that he could not leave Jellalabad for want of transport. Subsequently, he received the modified instructions; and in August 1842, he heard that Nott had set his face towards Kábul. Accordingly he left Jellalabad accompanied by Sale, and entered the Tezeen valley.

Defeat of Akbar Khan at Tezeen: occupation of Kábul.

At Tezeen the British soldiers beheld a sight which could never be forgotten. The valley was the scene of one of the bloodiest massacres during the ill-starred retreat from Kábul. The remains of their murdered comrades were still lying on the ground, and the sight exasperated the avenging army. At that moment the army of Akbar Khan appeared upon the scene; and the heights around bristled with matchlock men from Kábul. Pollock's force advanced in the face of a murderous fire, and gave no quarter. The enemy was utterly routed; indeed the victory at Tezeen was the crowning event of the war. Akbar Khan fled to the northern mountains, never to return until the English left Afghanistan; and in September 1842 the British flag was floating over the Bala Hissar.

Nott reaches Kábul with the gates of Somnáth.

Nott soon arrived at Kábul bringing with him the sandal wood gates of Somnáth, which Mahmúd of Ghazni had brought away from Guzerat in the eleventh century, and had since then adorned his tomb at Ghazni. This was a whim of Lord Ellenborough's, who had ordered the gates to be brought away as trophies of the war.[1]

[1] Sir Henry Rawlinson was of opinion that the gates were not genuine, but *facsimiles* of the originals, which must have perished long

A.D. 1842

All this while the probable fate of the prisoners and hostages caused the utmost anxiety. Suddenly all fears were allayed. The captives managed to bribe their keepers, and were brought into the British camp at Kábul amidst the general acclamation.

Recovery of the captives.

The glory of the avenging army was marred by acts of barbarity. The great bazar at Kábul was blown up by gunpowder. It was one of the finest stone buildings in Central Asia, but it was the place where Macnaghten's remains had been exposed, and it was destroyed as a fitting punishment for the crime. Amidst the confusion, the two armies broke into the city and perpetrated deeds in revenge for the slaughter of their comrades in the Khaiber, over which history would fain draw a veil.

Barbarous revenge.

The proceedings of Lord Ellenborough at the close of the Afghan war were much condemned by his contemporaries. He issued a bombastic proclamation respecting the gates of Somnáth which exposed him to much ridicule. The gates had been carried away from an idol temple by a follower of the prophet; consequently their recovery could not delight the Muhammadan princes of India. Again the gates had adorned the tomb of Mahmúd of Ghazni; consequently they were impure in the eyes of Hindus. Lord Ellenborough also received the avenging army on its return from Kábul, with a show of painted elephants, and other displays of oriental pomp, which jarred against English tastes. But these eccentricities are forgotten by the present generation, and can hardly be treated as history.

Bombast of Lord Ellenborough.

One episode in the history of the Afghan war conveys a useful lesson. In the heyday of success, when Afghanistan was first occupied by a British army, it was proposed to establish British influence in the Usbeg Khanates to the northward of the Oxus. Colonel Stoddart was sent to Bokhara to form friendly relations with the Amír; and Captain Conolly, who had been sent on a like mission to the ruler of Khokand, joined Colonel Stoddart at Bokhara. The Amír of Bokhara regarded both officers with suspicion, and kept them under close surveillance; but he hesitated to proceed to extremities; for aught he knew, the British army at Kábul might be moved across Balkh and the Oxus

Fate of Stoddart and Conolly at Bokhara, 1842.

ago. The author has seen the gates at Agra, and has no doubt of the correctness of Sir Henry Rawlinson's conclusions.

A.D. 1842

into Bokhara. But successive disasters in Kábul sealed the doom of the two officers. When the news of the insurrection at Kábul and murder of Sir Alexander Burnes reached Bokhara, both officers were imprisoned in loathsome dungeons; but when it was known that the British army had perished in the Khaiber pass, they were taken out of their dungeons and publicly beheaded in the market-place of Bokhara.

CHAPTER XX.

SINDE AND GWALIOR: LORD ELLENBOROUGH.

A.D. 1843 TO 1844.

A.D. 1843-1844

Conquest of Sinde, 1843.

THE first act of Lord Ellenborough after the Kábul war was the conquest of Sinde. This territory occupied the lower valley of the Indus. In the middle of the eighteenth century it formed a province of the Afghan empire of Ahmad Shah Abdali. Subsequently the Amírs or rulers of Sinde established a certain kind of independence, or only paid tribute to Kábul when compelled by force of arms.

Cause and conduct of the war.

During the early part of the British occupation of Afghanistan, the Sinde Amírs had rendered good service to the British government; but after the disastrous retreat from Kábul, some of the Amírs swerved from their treaty obligations. The result was a war which was triumphantly carried to a close by Sir Charles Napier. In February 1843 Napier won the battle of Meanee; and in the following March he won the battle of Hyderabad in the neighbourhood of the Sinde capital of that name. The war was brought to an end by the annexation of Sinde to the British empire.

The Sinde controversy: Napier *versus* Outram.

It would be useless in the present day to attempt to review the Sinde question. Sir Charles Napier, who commanded the army, considered that the Amírs were guilty of disaffection and deception; whilst Major Outram, who was political agent in Sinde, considered that their guilt was not sufficiently proved. One Amír, who professed the utmost loyalty to the British government, and who convinced Sir Charles Napier of the guilt of the others, was subsequently

A.D. 1843-1844

convicted of perjury and forgery, which was punished at the time, but since then has been more or less condoned. The difficulty of proof amongst a people, who cannot be bound by oaths, and who have always been accustomed to the forgery of seals and fabrication of documents, has often enabled the guilty to escape, and may sometimes have led to the punishment of the innocent. The question, however, of whether the Sinde Amírs were guilty or otherwise of treacherous designs against the British government has long since died out of political controversy.

Mahratta states: change of policy.

During the administration of Lord Ellenborough there was a change of policy in dealing with the Mahratta states of Sindia and Holkar. Lord Ellenborough remodelled the government of Gwalior, and contemplated the annexation of Indore. Such strong proceedings were direct violations of the non-intervention policy of Lord William Bentinck; but in order to decide how far they were expedient, it will be necessary to bring the following facts under review.

Gwalior affairs; Jankoji Rao Sindia, 1833-43.

The condition of Gwalior under Daulat Rao Sindia has already been indicated.[1] It will be remembered that at his death in 1827, his widow Baíza Baí became queen regent and adopted a boy to succeed her deceased husband as Maháraja. In 1833 the boy attained his majority, but disputes arose which ended in civil war. At last Lord William Bentinck was forced to interfere against his will, and the war was at an end. Baíza Baí retired from Gwalior, and Maháraja Jankoji Rao ascended the throne of Sindia.

Weak and distracted government.

Justice was satisfied by the elevation of the young Maháraja, but the queen regent was revenged. Baíza Baí had proved herself to be an able administrator; and as long as she was sole ruler, the government of Gwalior worked smoothly. On the other hand, Jankoji Rao Sindia was a do-nothing Maháraja. He was content with the pride and pomp of power; he was assured of the protection of the British government; and he cared nothing for his country or people. Accordingly the government was weak and distracted. The administration was carried on by a council of ministers, but there was a rankling rivalry for the post of premier between an uncle of the Maháraja, named Mama

[1] See *ante*, pages 527, 528.

Sahib, and the hereditary keeper of the crown jewels, named Dada Khasji. In the end the uncle of the Maháraja got the better of the jewel-keeper, and Mama Sahib became chief minister.

A.D. 1843-1844

Over-grown army.

Meanwhile the army of Gwalior had grown turbulent and disaffected. It numbered 30,000 infantry, 10,000 cavalry, and 200 guns. It was not required for defence, as Gwalior was protected against foreign invasion by the subsidiary alliance with the British government; but it absorbed two thirds of the revenues of Gwalior, and resisted all attempts at disbandment or reduction.

Sikh storm brewing in the Punjab.

The British government had no concern with the army of Gwalior so long as it kept within Sindia's territories. But the Punjab had become a political volcano. Ever since the death of Runjeet Singh in 1839, the Sikh army of the Khálsa, numbering 70,000 soldiers and 300 guns, had been a menace to Hindustan. Lord Ellenborough foresaw that sooner or later the Sikh army would cross the Sutlej into British territory. A spark would have kindled a flame in the army of Gwalior; and if its movements were combined with those of the Sikh army, they would have raised such a storm in Hindustan as had not been witnessed since the days of Nadir Shah.[1]

Adoption of Jyaji Rao Sindia, 1843.

Jankoji Rao Sindia died in February, 1843, leaving no children real or adopted. His widow, named Tara Bai, was a girl of twelve years of age. This girl adopted a boy, who was a distant relative of her husband's family. The boy was only eight years of age, but he was enthroned as Maháraja under the name of Jyaji Rao Sindia.[2] The adoption was approved by the durbar and the army, and was recognised by the British government.

Appointment of a regent.

The next question was the appointment of a regent. The Gwalior durbar wished the administration to be carried on as before by a council of ministers; but Lord Ellenborough urged the appointment of one individual as regent.

[1] It was this consideration which induced Lord Ellenborough to pause before sending the avenging army under General Pollock into Kábul. Meanwhile any attempt at explanation would have precipitated a Sikh invasion. Consequently Lord Ellenborough, whilst proving himself a statesman of forecast, was for some time one of the best abused Governors-General that ever landed in India.

[2] In the present year (1880) Jyaji Rao Sindia is still Maháraja of Gwalior.

A.D. 1843-1844

The girl queen was anxious that the Dada should be regent; but Lord Ellenborough was in favour of Mama Sahib. Accordingly the Gwalior durbar was told that the Governor-General preferred Mama Sahib, and Mama Sahib was appointed regent of Gwalior.

Fall of Mama Sahib.

Then followed a feminine intrigue. Tara Bai, in spite of her youth, set to work with the other palace ladies to thwart and harass Mama Sahib. The vexed and baffled regent sought to strengthen himself against this female confederacy, by betrothing the boy Maháraja to his own niece; but this step proved his ruin. Tara Bai feared that the marriage would ultimately destroy her own influence over the Maháraja; and in spite of the remonstrances of the British Resident, this young girl dismissed Mama Sahib on her own authority, and assumed the name of regent, leaving all real power in the hands of the Dada.

Wrath of Lord Ellenborough: recall of the Resident.

Lord Ellenborough was excessively angry at this movement, and well he might be. He had interfered in behalf of a minister, whom he would not support; and he had been defied by a Mahratta girl of twelve. The restoration of Mama Sahib was out of the question; the Governor-General could not reinstate a regent minister who had been outwitted by a girl. He could however insist on the removal of Dada Khasji; and accordingly he ordered the British Resident to withdraw from Gwalior, and not to return until the Dada had been dismissed from office. The Gwalior durbar was greatly alarmed, and entreated the Resident to return, but he was immovable.

Disturbances at Gwalior: advance of the British army.

Meanwhile the Dada had gained over the army of Gwalior by his largesses, and disturbances broke out in which fifty or sixty persons were killed. Accordingly Lord Ellenborough determined to take active measures for restoring tranquillity to Gwalior, and disbanding the army. In December, 1843, he arrived at Agra, but there were no signs of submission at Gwalior. He ordered the British army to advance to Gwalior under Sir Hugh Gough. The Dada now made his submission, but Lord Ellenborough was bent on the disbandment of the dangerous army.

Victories at Maharajpore and Punniar.

The chiefs and soldiers of Sindia saw that the independence of the state, and the existence of the army, were threatened by the British government. Accordingly they made common cause against the Governor-General, and were defeated in the battles of Maharajpore and Punniar, both of which were fought on the 29th of December, 1843. A.D. 1843-1844

Settlement of Gwalior affairs, 1844.

In January, 1844, a treaty was concluded at Gwalior which placed the future relations of the British government with that state on an improved footing. The administration was entrusted to a council of six nobles, which was called the council of regency, and was required to act implicitly on the advice of the Resident whenever he might think fit to offer it. The new government was required to cede enough territory to maintain a contingent trained and disciplined by British officers, henceforth known as the Gwalior Contingent. At the same time the overgrown army of Gwalior was reduced to 6,000 cavalry, 3,000 infantry, and 32 guns.

Lapsed condition of Holkar's state of Indore, 1844.

In February, 1844, there was a crisis in Holkar's state of Indore. Hari Rao Holkar died in 1843, and was succeeded by an adopted son, who died in 1844, leaving no son, real or adopted. There was not only no heir, but no person having the right to adopt an heir. The Indore state was of modern origin; it owed its existence to predatory conquest; and it was maintained for the sole benefit of the followers of the court. Lord Ellenborough ordered steps to be taken to ascertain the national feeling on the subject.

Irregular installation of Tukaji Rao Holkar.

Meanwhile the government of Indore was left under the regency of the mother of Hari Rao Holkar, who died in 1843; and this lady proposed to nominate a fitting successor to the boy who died in 1844. Before, however, Lord Ellenborough could decide the question, the British Resident at Indore declared, on his own authority, that the British government would perpetuate the state of Holkar; and he enthroned the nominee of the queen mother, with all the formality of a hereditary chieftain, under the name of Tukaji Rao Holkar.[1] Lord Ellenborough was exceedingly wroth at this unauthorised proceeding, and severely censured the Resident, but, under the circumstances, he declined to interfere with the succession of Tukaji Rao Holkar.

Recall of Lord Ellenborough, 1844.

In June, 1844, Lord Ellenborough was recalled from the post of Governor-General. This arbitrary measure took India by surprise. There had, however, been angry controversies between Lord Ellenborough and the Court of Directors, and the former had not been always discreet;

[1] In the present year (1880) Tukaji Rao Holkar is still Maháraja of Indore.

A.D. 1843-1844

but the ability, industry, and energy of the noble earl had deeply impressed the public mind, and there were many who regretted his recall.

Lord Hardinge, Governor-General, 1844.

Lord Ellenborough was succeeded by Sir Henry Hardinge in the post of Governor-General. During the remainder of 1844, and nearly the whole of 1845, the new Governor-General was chiefly occupied in watching the progress of events in the Punjab until the breaking out of the first Sikh war. Before, however, treating of those important transactions, it will be necessary to glance at the current of affairs in other quarters.

CHAPTER XXI.

WAR DECADE: BURMA AND NIPAL.

A.D. 1839 TO 1849.

A.D. 1839-1849

Ferment outside the frontier.

DURING the administration of Lords Auckland and Ellenborough, there were strange troubles in Burma, Nipal, and the Punjab. The native courts at Ava, Khatmandu, and Lahore, were in a state of ferment, more or less excited by the Kábul war; and the political workings are all the more important from the pictures which they present of oriental life outside the area of British suzerainty.

No disaffection within the frontier.

This ferment was not visible within the British pale. The Mahratta governments of Sindia and Holkar were too weak and distracted to indulge in hopes or fears as regards the possible downfall of the British empire. The Rajpút states were a prey to the maladministration of their rulers and the disaffection of their respective feudatories. In Marwar especially, the growing anarchy and disorder compelled the British government to send a force to keep the peace between the Maháraja and his Thakúrs during the very year that the columns from Bengal and Bombay were advancing on Kábul. Neither Rajpút nor Mahratta troubled about disasters in Central Asia, or imagined the possibility of a renewal of the old wars in Hindustan.

Threatening war-clouds, east, west, and north-west.

But public feeling was different in the three courts outside the frontier. Rumours were rife that the Governor-General had sent the flower of the British army into the remote regions of Central Asia to fight against the Amír, the Shah, and the Czar; and the air was clouded with predictions that British power would be shattered in the

A.D. 1839-1849 coming storm, and that Bráhma and Muhammad, Gótama Buddha and Guru Govind would be avenged on the followers of the Nazarene.

Hostile demonstrations. In Burma and Nipal there was marked hostility towards the British government. Indeed in 1840 it seemed likely that whilst one *corps d'armée* was occupying Kábul, and a second was keeping the peace in Rajpútana, a third would be threading the valley of the Irawadi, whilst a fourth would be climbing the slopes and shelves of the Himalayas. At Lahore there was less hostile display, but the war spirit was burning beneath the surface like the hidden fires of a volcano, and was destined at no distant period to burst into flames.

Political relations with Ava, 1830. Burma was essentially a weak government, and its army was beneath contempt; but the heavy cost of the Burmese war of 1824-1826, and the terrible loss of life from fever and malaria, had rendered the British government most anxious to keep on friendly terms with the Court of Ava. In 1830 Colonel Burney was sent as a permanent Resident to Ava, in accordance with the treaty of Yandabo; but he was treated by the barbarous court more as a spy to be watched and guarded, than as an envoy anxious only for the maintenance of friendly relations.

Revolution at Ava, 1837. In 1837 there was a revolution in the palace at Ava. The king, Phagyi-dau, had become hypochondriacal and insane, and was dethroned by his brother Tharawadi, and placed in confinement. Then followed the inevitable massacre. The sorceress queen, the heir-apparent, and the ministers of the deposed sovereign, were all put to death, together with their dependants. Tharawadi became king of Burma, and sought to blot out the memory of his predecessor by removing his capital from Ava to Amarapúra.

Retirement of the British Resident. Colonel Burney was alarmed at this revolution. He knew that Tharawadi was a bitter enemy of the English, and had heard him express contempt for the British government. Accordingly he deemed it prudent to retire from the scene, and thus escape an insult which might provoke a rupture.

Expulsion of the British Residency, 1840. Lord Auckland was angry at the withdrawal of Colonel Burney, and sent another Resident to take his place. But Tharawadi was intolerable; he was not only cruel and depraved, but arrogant and insolent to the last degree. No

English officer would remain long in the depressing climate of Upper Burma, to be treated with scorn and contumely by an ignorant barbarian. One Resident after another retired to Rangoon on the plea of ill-health. At last in 1840 Tharawadi drove the Residency out of the capital, in violation of the treaty of Yandabo. Lord Auckland's government ignored the outrage rather than resent it, and abstained from all further attempts to maintain a Resident at Amarapúra.

A.D. 1839-1849

Empty threats of king Tharawadi, 1841.

Tharawadi was puffed up beyond measure at the success of his efforts to throw off the English alliance. In 1841 he marched a large army to Rangoon, threatening to drive the English out of Arakan and Tenasserim. But his warlike ardour cooled down as he approached Rangoon, for he remembered how the Burmese fled from before the English in 1824. Accordingly he put aside all thoughts of war, and amused his subjects by casting a great bell for the golden pagoda at Rangoon. After a few months he returned to his remote capital in the upper valley of the Irawadi with all the barbaric pomp of gilded barges, whilst nothing more was heard of war.

Assassination of Tharawadi, 1845.

In 1845 the reign of Tharawadi was brought to a close. He had degenerated into a tyrant of the worst type; drinking himself into such paroxysms of fury, that it was dangerous to approach him. In these mad fits he would shoot a minister or stab a queen; and courtiers and ladies plotted together for their own protection. Suddenly Tharawadi passed away from the palace, and was never seen again. Whether strangled, smothered, or poisoned, is a palace mystery, like the suicide with scissors in the palace at Stamboul. It is sufficient to know that in 1845 Tharawadi ceased to reign, and his eldest son ascended the throne of Burma.

Pagán Meng, a mean and cruel king, 1845-52.

Pagán Meng, the new sovereign, was of a different stamp to his father. Tharawadi, with all his faults, had a majestic presence, and spoke and looked like a king. Pagán Meng, on the contrary, was a man of low tastes and vulgar pleasures. He moved his capital from Amarapúra to Ava, and there he devoted himself to cock-fighting, ram-fighting, gambling, and other mean pursuits. Meanwhile, like Macbeth, he was in constant terror. He would not trust his own Burmese courtiers, but preferred a Muhammadan for his minister. He condemned all suspected persons to the

A.D. 1839-1849

most horrible deaths; and stifled all complaints by throwing the blame upon the minister. Two of his own brothers were butchered in this horrid fashion, together with their wives, children, servants, and dependants of every kind.

Insurrection at Ava.

At last the people of Ava rose in revolt against such detestable cruelty. The minister was given up to the populace to secure the safety of the king. For three days this unfortunate Muhammadan was tortured by the mob, and was then beheaded at the place of execution with numbers of his creatures.

Petty oppressions at Rangoon.

All this while there was no British Resident at Ava to act as a check upon he king or his people. Rangoon was near the sea, and was consequently free from such atrocities; but petty acts of tyranny were practised by the local governor towards European and American strangers, who were fined, imprisoned, or put in the stocks on the most frivolous charges. No civilised man will endure such barbaric insolence without appealing to his government for redress; and no government can ignore such appeals without loss of prestige and national honour. It was not, however, until the Punjab had been brought under British administration, that Lord Dalhousie saw the necessity for remonstrating with the king of Burma. The sequel will be told hereafter in dealing with Lord Dalhousie's administration.

Political relations with Nipal.

The progress of affairs in Nipal during the war decade was more serious than in Burma. There was some bond of common interest between the Ghorka and British governments; whilst the court of Khatmandu was more respectable and intelligent than the court of Ava, and had a much better army at its command.

Benares, a centre of political refugees.

Here it should be explained that from a remote period in history the sacred city of Benares has been the resort, not only of pilgrims and devotees, but of Hindu political refugees of every class and kind. Dethroned sovereigns, childless queens, disgraced ministers, and forlorn princes and princesses, have taken up their abode at Benares, and generally to intrigue and plot, as well as to sacrifice and pray.

Ever since the rise of the Ghorka dynasty in Nipal, revolutions have been frequent in the court of Khatmandu.

A.D. 1839-1849

Frequent revolutions in Nipal.

Sometimes an able minister of the stamp of Bhím Sein Thapa and Jung Bahadur has kept the peace for a number of years; but such intervals of tranquillity are always sooner or later brought to a close by revolutions. Such revolutions were common enough in every Hindu court in India before the British government became the paramount power; and one and all have been accompanied by a massacre, together with a stampede to Benares of all the survivors of a fallen dynasty or ministry. Consequently throughout the present century Benares has been a hot-bed of intrigues and plots for restoring some royal exile to Nipal.

Bhím Sein Thapa, premier and paramour.

From 1804 to 1837 Bhím Sein Thapa was the sole ruler of Nipal; not only as prime minister, but for a long period as the paramour of the regent-mother; and for thirty-three years he filled up all superior posts and commands at the annual Panjani with members of the Thapa clan; and rigidly excluded all others, whether Bharadars or Brahmans, from office or power.

Infant Maháraja, 1816-32.

The Nipal war of 1814-16 did not weaken the authority of Bhím Sein Thapa. The young Maháraja attained his majority in 1816, but died shortly afterwards, and was succeeded in his turn by an infant son. In 1832 the old regent-mother died, but Bhím Sein Thapa was still supreme. The infant attained his majority, and was placed upon the throne; but he proved a weak and vacillating prince, and for a long time was a mere puppet in the hands of Bhím Sein Thapa.

An ambitious queen.

But Bhím Sein Thapa was thwarted by an unexpected enemy. He had selected the daughter of a Hindu farmer in British territory to be the bride of the young Maháraja.[1] The girl grew into an ambitious and scheming woman, and was constantly stirring up her husband to throw off the yoke of the minister. Bhím Sein Thapa thought to neutralise or divide her influence by introducing a second bride into the palace. The step, however, proved fatal to his power. The elder queen became more bitter than ever; she soon behaved like a female fiend bent on the destruction of Bhím Sein Thapa and his family.

The restless activity of this extraordinary woman is a

[1] The duty of the minister to choose a bride for the boy Maháraja is as old as the Mahá Bhárata. It will be remembered that Bhíshma provided wives for his half-brother and nephews.

A.D. 1839-1849

Feminine intrigues.

remarkable feature in Nipal history. She formed a close intimacy with Runjung Pandey, the son of the prime minister who had been disgraced and ruined in 1803. She persuaded the Maháraja to restore the estates of the Pandey family, which had been confiscated on that occasion. She won over the Guru, or spiritual teacher of the Maháraja, known as the Misr Guru;[1] and this religious intriguer soon proved a most formidable opponent to the British government as well as to the Thapa ministry.

Entanglement of the British Resident.

Mr. Hodgson, the British Resident at Khatmandu, was in danger of being entangled in this web of intrigue. Ever since the war of 1814-16, Bhím Sein Thapa had been as friendly towards the English, as a Ghorka nobleman of those times could allow himself to be. At the conclusion of the war the enemies of the prime minister wanted the British government to deliver the young Maháraja out of his hands; but the predecessor of Mr. Hodgson had declared emphatically that the British government would not interfere in the affairs of Nípal. This very refusal to interfere led the whole court to regard that British Resident as the friend of Bhím Sein Thapa; and Mr. Hodgson was thus hated by all the enemies of the prime minister; by the elder queen, the Pandeys, and the Misr Guru.

Fall of Bhím Sein Thapa, 1837.

In 1837 there was an explosion. The youngest son of the elder queen died suddenly. It was widely rumoured that the infant had taken poison intended for the mother; and Bhím Sein Thapa was charged with having instigated the court physicians to administer poison to the elder queen. Amidst the commotion, Runjung Pandey, the head of the Pandey clan, was appointed prime minister by the Maháraja, Bhím Sein Thapa was arrested, put in irons, and thrown into prison, together with a nephew named Matabar Singh. The family of Bhím Sein Thapa was placed under a guard, and all the family property was confiscated. The physician, who attended the child, was put to the torture until he implicated Bhím Sein Thapa, and then he was put to death.

Ministerial complications.

This revolution, however, only went half way, and was then met by a reaction. There was a moderate party at Khatmandu, represented by a Brahman named Rughonath Pundit,[1] and a Bharadar named Futteh Jung Chountria.

[1] If a Brahman is addressed as a learned man he is called Pundit; if otherwise he is called Misr, or Mitter, *i.e.* Mithra, or the sun.

A.D. 1839-1849

This moderate party was willing that Bhím Sein should be brought under some control, but was opposed to the destruction of the Thapas and elevation of the Pandeys. Again the younger queen was a staunch friend of Bhím Sein Thapa: she had been given in marriage to the Maháraja in order that she might act as a counterpoise to the elder queen; and she perpetually urged the Maháraja to restore Bhím Sein Thapa to the post of prime minister.

Political compromise.

The working of these jarring influences ended in a political compromise. The Pandeys were removed from the ministry, Rughonath Pundit, the leader of the moderate party, was made premier, and moderate councils prevailed. The Thapas were not restored to power, but Bhím Sein and his nephew, Matabar Singh, were released, pardoned, and received by the Maháraja in public durbar. They were then each presented with a dress of honour and a caparisoned horse, and returned to their respective homes amidst the cheers and acclamations of soldiers and citizens. The family estates were still under confiscation, but a garden house was restored to Bhím Sein Thapa, and a yearly pension was assigned for his support. Thus for a brief space matters seemed to quiet down at Khatmandu.

Quarrel between queens: flight of the elder queen, 1838.

These moderate measures would not satisfy either of the two queens. In 1838 there were violent dissensions in the palace. The elder queen insisted on the restoration of the Pandeys to the ministry, whilst the younger queen insisted on the restoration of the Thapas. Suddenly the elder queen left the palace in a fury, and proceeded to the temple of Pusput Nath, accompanied by Runjung Pandey, declaring that she would never return to the palace until the Maháraja appointed her favourite to be prime minister.

Great temple of Pusput Nath.

The temple of Pusput Nath is about three miles from Khatmandu. It is well worthy of description, for it is the most celebrated fane in all Nipal. It is approached by a road through the suburbs of the city, beautifully paved with brick and granite. Hard by the temple precinct are the houses of priests, three or four stories high, built of bricks, which are hidden by woodwork curiously carved; with wooden balconies supported by carved rafters, and railed in by wood carvings. Intricate tracery hangs down from the balconies in broad wooden fringes; whilst other tracery surrounds the grotesque windows. The temple precinct is

A.D. 1839-1849

inclosed by a wall. Massive folding doors open into a handsome courtyard, filled with images, shrines, a kneeling figure of Siva, a huge bell, and other sacred objects in picturesque confusion. The temple building stands in the centre of the court facing the folding doors. It is a quaint structure roofed with lead, with silver doors, carved windows, and large eaves covered with gilding. It is ascended by a double flight of steps, guarded by four sculptured lions, and a large copper figure of a bull kneeling, superbly covered with gilding.

Triumph of the elder queen: the Pandey ministry.

In this sacred place the elder queen took up her abode; and during her stay there the Maháraja attended on her daily with all his court. This flight to Pusput Nath was the first of a series of vagaries by which the elder queen tormented the whole court, and forced the Maháraja to do her bidding. In the present case she was appeased by the retirement of Rughonath Pundit, and the appointment of Runjung Pandey to the post of premier.

Tragedies at Khatmandu, 1839: non-intervention.

In 1839 the elder queen succeeded in wreaking her vengeance on the Thapa family. The charge of poisoning was revived. The execution of the physician who attended her infant son would not satisfy her thirst for vengeance. The other court physicians were thrown into prison, and only escaped torture by committing suicide. The brother of Bhím Sein, named Runbír Singh, turned fakír. Bhím Sein saw that he was doomed, and appealed to the Resident for protection; but the Resident could do nothing, for he had been strictly forbidden to interfere in the affairs of Nipal.

Condemnation of Bhím Sein Thapa.

At last Bhím Sein Thapa was brought before the durbar, and the so-called confessions of the dead physicians were produced against him, charging him with wholesale poisonings at intervals, during a long series of years. He manfully defended himself, denounced the confessions as forgeries, and demanded to be confronted with his accusers. Not a single chieftain, however, dared to say a word in his behalf. The Maháraja gave way to a burst of indignation, real or feigned, and ordered him to be chained and imprisoned as a traitor.

Doom of the Thapas.

The fate of Bhím Sein Thapa has many parallels in oriental history. He was threatened with torture, with dishonour in his zenana, with torment and shame unknown to Europe,

A.D. 1839-1849

until he killed himself in despair. His remains were dismembered and thrown to the dogs and vultures. His family was reduced to penury, and banished to the snows of the Himalayas; and a decree was issued declaring that the Thapas were outcasts, and that no one of the Thapa clan should be employed in the public service for the space of seven generations.

Intrigues of the elder Ránı́ and Pandey ministry against the British.

All this while the elder queen and the Pandey ministry had been intriguing against the British government. Matabar Singh had been sent to the court of Runjeet Singh at Lahore, and thus escaped the doom which had befallen his uncle. A second emissary was sent to Burma to report on the growing rupture between the Burmese court and the British government. A third had gone to Lhassa to persuade the Chinese authorities that some recent conquests of the Sikhs in Ladakh had been made at the instigation of the British government. A fourth had been sent to Herát to report on the prospects of a war between the English and Persia. Meanwhile prophecies were disseminated through British provinces predicting the speedy downfall of the British supremacy, and preparations were being made for war throughout Nipal. It was thus evident that the Ghorka court was only waiting for some disaster to the British arms to declare war against the British government.

Measures of Lord Auckland: change of ministry.

In 1840 Lord Auckland addressed a letter of remonstrance to the Maháraja, and moved a corps of observation to the frontier. This measure had a wholesome effect upon the Maháraja. He dismissed the Pandey ministry in a panic, and appointed Futteh Jung Chountria to be premier. This latter chieftain belonged to the moderate party, and was well disposed towards the British government. In 1841 the Maháraja dismissed the Misr Guru, and the latter was forced to go on pilgrimage to Benares.

Violence of the elder queen.

The elder queen was driven frantic by this reversal of her designs. She was not content with leaving the palace and going to Pusput Nath; she separated herself altogether from the Maháraja, assumed the dress of a female ascetic, and threatened to go on pilgrimage to Benares. She tried to terrify the Maháraja into abdicating the throne in favour of her eldest son, the heir-apparent. On one occasion she induced the soldiery at Khatmandu to break out in mutiny. She encouraged the heir-apparent to commit the most

A.D. 1839-1849

extravagant and cruel acts in order to alarm the Maháraja. All this while she was constantly urging the Maháraja to reinstate the Pandeys, dismiss the British Resident, and declare war against the British government.

A vacillating Maháraja.

The weak and vacillating Maháraja was moved to and fro like a pendulum by alternate hopes and fears. At one time he expatiated in durbar on the rumoured disasters of the English in Burma and China. At another time he was assuring the Resident of his friendship towards the British government, and offering to send his forces in support of the British army in Afghanistan.

Death of the elder queen, 1841: general reconciliation.

In 1841 the elder queen was indisposed, and the Maháraja was anxious for a reconciliation. She became softened by her sickness, and threw off her ascetic dress, and talked of restoring the Thapas to their caste and estates. Towards the end of the year she died suddenly, not without suspicions of poison. After her death there was no more talk of hostility with the British government, and the corps of observation was soon withdrawn from the frontier. All difficulties in the relations between the two states were thus removed; and all signs of secret agents from other native states passed away from Khatmandu.

Wrath of the Maháraja at English newspapers, 1842.

In 1842 a curious incident occurred which reveals something of the working of English journalism on oriental minds. A report appeared in a Calcutta newspaper that the elder queen had been poisoned. The Maháraja was wild with rage, and called on the British Resident to surrender the editor. He was determined, he said, to flay the journalist alive, and rub him to death with salt and lemon-juice; and he threatened to declare war if the Governor-General refused to accede to his demand. After a suitable explanation of British law and usage, the Maháraja cooled down, and subsequently sent an apology to the Resident for the warmth of his language.

Mad freaks of the heir-apparent.

At this period the mad freaks of the heir-apparent caused great excitement in Nipal. He engaged elephants to fight in the streets of Khatmandu, and caused the death of several persons. He wounded Bharadars and their sons with a sword or knife. He was only a boy of twelve, but he would often beat his wives who were girls of nine or ten. Sometimes he threw them into the river; and he kept one poor girl so long in a tank that she died in consequence. A female attendant interfered and he set her clothes on fire. He was brutally jealous of his step-mother, the younger queen and her two sons, and they ultimately fled from his cruelty into the plains.[1] In these acts of insane violence he had been originally encouraged by his deceased mother in the hope of terrifying his father into abdication; and after her death they became more frequent than ever.

A.D. 1839-1849

Dangerous freaks.

When the news of the destruction of the British army in the Khaiber Pass reached Khatmandu, the heir-apparent indulged in still more dangerous freaks. He threatened to murder the British Resident, or drive him out of the country. He displayed a special spite against Jung Bahadur, the same chief who afterwards became celebrated in Europe. He commanded Jung Bahadur and other chiefs at court to jump down wells at the hazard of their lives; and no one seems to have ventured to disobey him.[2] Many of the common soldiers were maimed for life by being compelled at his orders to jump down wells, or off the roofs of houses. Strange to say the Maháraja made no attempt to restrain his son in these eccentric cruelties, because the astrologers had declared that the young prince was an incarnation of deity, and foretold that at no distant period he would extirpate the English foreigners. The consequence was that on more than one occasion the prince assaulted his own father, and once inflicted severe wounds.

Kábul disaster: reaction against the British government.

Meanwhile the disasters in Kábul induced the Maháraja to recall the Pandeys to court, and the Misr Guru from Benares. One of the Pandeys, named Kubraj, amused the heir-apparent by getting up mock fights between Ghorkas and English. The English were represented by natives of low caste painted white, and dressed in British uniforms; and they were of course defeated, and dragged about the streets in most ignominious fashion.

At this juncture, however, the Pandeys made a false step. A number of libels, reviving the old scandal that the elder

[1] Major, afterwards Sir Henry Lawrence, succeeded Hodgson as Resident at Khatmandu. He refers to these strange scenes, and gives the leading actors the names of Mr. Nipal, Mrs. Nipal, and Master Nipal. See *Memoirs of Lawrence*, by Edwardes and Merivale.

[2] In after years Jung Bahadur boasted that he had practised the art of jumping down wells as the best means of saving his life on these occasions. See Oliphant's *Journey to Khatmandu*.

A.D. 1839-1849

Great state trial at Khatmandu.

queen had died from poison, were traced to Kubraj Pandey, and he and other Pandeys were arrested and put in irons. A State trial was held by the Bharada Sobah, or council of chieftains, at which the Maháraja sat as President. The trial lasted several days, during which there was a general stoppage of business. At last Kubraj Pandey was convicted: his right hand was cut off, his property was confiscated, and he was sent into banishment.

National movement against the heir-apparent.

Towards the close of 1842 the cruelties and insults of the heir-apparent towards all classes, and the cowardly apathy of the Maháraja, brought Nipal to the brink of a revolution. The chiefs and people complained that they did not know who was the Maháraja, the son or the father. The ferment spread through the whole valley; public meetings were held on the parade ground at Khatmandu; and at one large meeting, said to number eight thousand people, a committee was appointed for drawing up a petition of advice and remonstrance to the Maháraja. Finally the soldiery made common cause with the chiefs and people. They demanded that the Misr Guru should be sent back to Benares, and that the surviving queen should be recalled from her voluntary exile in the plains, and appointed regent of Nipal.

Maháraja faces the revolutionary body.

On the 2nd of December, 1842, there was a meeting of the chiefs and officers, at which the Maháraja unexpectedly made his appearance. His presence prevented any allusion to the regency of the queen. He sought by arguments, entreaties, and threats, to induce the assembly to let things remain as they were. In reply, he was told that the people could not obey two masters; that he must either keep his son under control, or abdicate the throne in his son's favour. Many instances were quoted in which the soldiers had been punished by the heir-apparent for obeying the commands of the Maháraja. The Maháraja promised to abdicate by and by, and begged that during the interval his son might be addressed by his title; but the assembly raised a groan of dissent. The Maháraja ordered the officers of the army to leave the meeting, but they refused. Next he ordered the Bharadars to leave, but they also refused. He then retired, and the assembly broke up, convinced that the Maháraja and his son were infatuated beyond redemption.

There was evidently something behind the scenes. It

A.D. 1839-1849

Behind the scenes.

was said that the Maháraja had solemnly promised the deceased queen that he would abdicate the throne in favour of her son, and that he was equally afraid of breaking his oath and retiring from the sovereignty. The Chountria ministry vacillated between father and son. They were anxious to know who was to be Maháraja, but they were jealous of the movement for the regency of the surviving queen.

Petition of advice and remonstrance

On the 5th of December the draft petition was submitted by the committee to a vast assembly of all the Bharadars, municipal authorities, merchants, and officers and soldiers of every grade. It was unanimously approved and ordered for presentation on the 7th, as the intermediate day was unlucky. The Maháraja was present with the heir-apparent, and tried to browbeat the assembly, but all his wrath was expended in vain.

Attempted arrest of revolutionary leaders: Maháraja submits.

On the night of the intermediate day there was an outbreak in the city of Khatmandu. The bugles were sounded, and three hundred soldiers tried to arrest the Bharadars under the orders of the Maháraja. The attempt failed, and kindled the popular indignation to the highest pitch. Next day the Maháraja yielded to the petition, and a deputation was despatched to bring in the young queen.

Queen appointed regent.

Next day the queen was conducted into Khatmandu, and invested with the authority of regent. The Bharadars and officers presented their honorary gifts and congratulations. But the ferment soon died out, and her authority ebbed away. The Chountrias vacillated between the Maháraja, the heir-apparent, and the regent queen; and the counsels and commands of the queen were unheeded by the durbar.

Plots of the queen.

In 1843 the Chountria ministers were again in trouble. They implored the queen to stand forth as the head of the country, to insist on the December pact, or to retire to the plains; and they promised to accompany her with all the leaders of her party. But she said that they had let the occasion slip, and the country was not ripe for another revolution. In reality she was plotting to set aside the heir-apparent on the plea of insanity, and to set up the elder of her two sons in his room; and she suspected that the Chountrias were secret supporters of the heir-apparent.

Matabar Singh.

About this time all parties at Khatmandu were inviting Matabar Singh to return to Nipal. This man was as able

A.D. 1839-1849

and brave as his famous uncle Bhím Sein Thapa. He spent some time feeling his way, but at last entered Khatmandu, and had an interview with the Maháraja.

Destruction of the Pandeys: the Thapas revenged.

A few days afterwards there was a council of Bharadars at the palace. The written confessions of the Pandeys were produced, admitting that the charges of poisoning originally brought against the Thapas were all false. Five Pandeys were then beheaded. Kubraj Pandey was dragged to the place of execution with a hook through his breast. Others were flogged and their noses cut off. Runjung Pandey, the head of the family, was on his death-bed, and was mercifully permitted to die in peace. In this way Matabar Singh wreaked his vengeance on the murderers of Bhím Sein Thapa.

Matabar Singh premier: excites the enmity of the queen.

Before the end of 1843, the decree against the Thapas was annulled, and Matabar Singh was appointed premier in the room of Futteh Jung Chountria; but he soon found that it was impossible to please the conflicting parties. He tried to support the heir-apparent in the hope of procuring the restoration of the confiscated estates of his family; but by so doing he excited the bitter resentment of the queen; and from this time she was apparently bent upon working his destruction.

Threatened massacre prevented by Major Lawrence.

In 1844, Nipal seemed to be again on the eve of a revolution. The violent acts of the heir-apparent, the vacillations of the Maháraja, the rash and overbearing conduct of Matabar Singh, and the absurd and contradictory orders which daily issued from the palace, were exhausting the patience of the Bharadars. These chiefs were anxious that there should be but one ruler in Nipal, but they were unwilling that Matabar Singh should be that ruler. Matabar Singh would probably have cut his way to supreme power by a wholesale massacre of Bharadars, as his uncle, Bhím Sein had done at the beginning of the century; but he was restrained by the wholesome counsels of Major, afterwards Sir Henry Lawrence, who about this time succeeded Mr. Hodgson as British Resident at Khatmandu.

More plots.

All this while Matabar Singh was plotting to drive the Maháraja to abdicate the throne in favour of the heir-apparent; whilst the Maháraja and the queen were secretly plotting to destroy Matabar Singh. The Maháraja, however, continued to heap honours on the head of the minister he had resolved to destroy. In the beginning of 1845, Matabar Singh was appointed premier for life. Later on the Maháraja bestowed other marks of favour on the premier. At last, on the night of the 18th of May, 1845, Matabar Singh was murdered in the palace.

Horrible murder of Matabar Singh, 1845.

The story was horrible. Late at night the minister had been summoned to the palace, under the pretence that the queen had seriously hurt herself. He hurried off unarmed to obey the summons, accompanied by two kinsmen. The kinsmen were stopped at the foot of the palace stairs, and Matabar Singh was conducted alone to a room next the queen's where the Maháraja was standing. As he advanced towards the Maháraja a rapid fire was opened upon him from behind the trellised screen. He begged for mercy for his wife and children, and then expired. His mangled remains were lowered into the street, and carried off for cremation to the temple of Pusput Nath; and the paved road to the sanctuary was trickled with his blood. Many chiefs were suspected of being implicated in the murder. Jung Bahadur boasted that he had fired the fatal shot; but the prime mover in the plot is said to have been Guggun Singh, the paramour of the relentless queen.

Sikh invasion of Hindustan, November, 1845.

The murder of Matabar Singh was followed by a ministerial crisis which lasted many months. Meanwhile all India was watching the Sikh war on the north-west. The war was brought to a close early in 1846, and the year was approaching its fourth quarter, when Khatmandu was aroused by a story of a massacre which sent a thrill of horror through Hindustan.

New ministry at Khatmandu.

Ever since the murder of Matabar Singh, there had been bitter quarrels in the palace. A ministry had been formed by Futteh Jung Chountria; and the queen had procured the appointment of her favourite Guggun Singh, as a member of the ministry.[1] At this period the queen exercised a commanding influence in the government of Nipal, and plotted to secure the succession of her elder son to the throne in the room of the heir-apparent.

The heir-apparent was filled with wrath at the aspect of affairs. He swore to be revenged on the murderers of

[1] The ministry comprised Futteh Jung Chountria as premier, three other members as his colleagues and deputies, and Jung Bahadur as military member.

A.D. 1839-1849

Threats of the heir-apparent.

Matabar Singh, and he publicly threatened Guggun Singh. He abused his father for not abdicating the throne in his favour, and declared that he would seize the government; whilst the Maháraja vacillated as usual, or played one party against another to suit his own purposes.

Assassination and massacre.

On the night of the 14th of September, 1846, Guggun Singh was murdered in his own house. The queen heard of the catastrophe, and hastened to the place on foot, and filled the air with her lamentations. She despatched a messenger to tell the Maháraja of the murder; and she summoned all the civil and military officers to the spot. The council assembled in such hot haste that many appeared without arms. The queen demanded the immediate execution of one of the Pandeys, whom she charged with the murder; but the Maháraja refused to have the man put to death unless it was proved that he was guilty. Altercations arose; shots were fired; and the premier and others fell dead. A party of soldiers, armed with double-barrelled rifles, poured in a murderous fire, and more than thirty chiefs were slaughtered.[1] Jung Bahadur was appointed premier on the spot, and undertook the sole management of affairs.

Jung Bahadur all powerful.

The queen next called on Jung Bahadur to destroy the heir-apparent and his brother; but the new premier declared for the heir-apparent, and carried out more executions. Subsequently, the Maháraja proceeded on pilgrimage to Benares, accompanied by the queen, leaving the heir-apparent to carry on the government until his return to Khatmandu.

Installation of the heir-apparent.

In 1847 the Maháraja left Benares to return to his capital, but he loitered so long on the way, and displayed so many aberrations of mind, that the Bharadars installed the heir-apparent on the throne, and declared that the Maháraja had abdicated the sovereignty.

Conclusion.

Meanwhile, Jung Bahadur was appointed prime minister for life, and tranquillity returned to the court of Nipal. In 1850 Jung Bahadur paid a visit to England, and after his return in 1851 an abortive plot was formed to destroy him. Since then the Ghorkas have engaged in wars on the side of Thibet, but nothing of permanent interest has transpired in Nipal. Jung Bahadur died early in 1877.

[1] It is impossible to say how many persons fell in this horrible butchery. Reports vary from thirty to a hundred and twenty.

CHAPTER XXII.

SIKH HISTORY: RUNJEET SINGH, ETC.

Ante 1845.

THE history of the Punjab is one of the most important episodes in Indian history. The Sikh government was a theocratic commonwealth, like that of the Hebrews under the Judges; but they were a sect rather than a nationality, animated with a stern military enthusiasm like Cromwell's Ironsides. Nanuk Guru founded the Sikh community in the fifteenth century, but great reforms were carried out in the seventeenth century by Guru Govind. The essence of the Sikh faith was that there was only one God; that the Guru for the time being was his prophet; that all Sikhs were equal in the eyes of God and the Guru; and that all were bound together in a holy brotherhood known as the Khálsa. Guru Govind abolished all social distinctions amongst the Khálsa. He sprinkled holy water upon five faithful disciples, namely, a Brahman, a Kshatriya, and three Súdras. He hailed them as Singhs or lion warriors; he declared that they were the Khálsa,[1] or brotherhood of faith in God and the Guru;[2] and he promised that whenever five Sikhs were gathered together, he would be in the midst of them. This idea of five Sikhs forming a Khálsa, will be found to have a strange meaning in the later history.

A.D. *Ante* 1845 — Rise of the Sikh commonwealth in the Punjab

[1] According to Cunningham, the Khálsa signifies "the saved or liberated."

[2] God, as taught by Guru Govind, was a spirit invisible to ordinary eyes, and only to be seen by the eye faith in the general body of the Khálsa.

A.D. *Ante* 1845

The Gurus and yearly assemblies.

Henceforth a representative of Nanuk Guru and Guru Govind was the spiritual teacher of the Sikhs. He was emphatically known as the Guru, and the watchword of the Sikhs was "Hail, Guru!"[1] He combined the functions of a prince with those of a prophet. The city of Umritsir, the "pool of immortality," became the religious centre of the Sikhs; and every year there was a grand gathering at the sacred city, like the Hebrew gatherings at Shiloh.

The Khálsa: the twelve Misls or fraternities.

The Sikhs originally had no nationality. They were a close religious community formed out of Hindus, Muhammadans, and others. They were all soldiers of the Khálsa. They were divided into twelve fraternities, known as Misls, or "equals." The Misls were not tribes in the Hebrew sense of the word. They were not descended from the twelve sons of a common ancestor; there was no division of the land amongst the twelve Misls as there was amongst the twelve tribes. The Misls were fraternities, increasing and diminishing according to circumstances. Indeed, the number "twelve" was more traditional than real; some gave birth to other Misls, whilst some died out altogether.

Sirdars, or leaders of Misls.

The leader of a Misl was known as the Sirdar; he was the arbiter in time of peace, and the leader in time of war. The Sirdar might be fervent in his devotion to God and the Guru, and at the same time he might be nothing more than a freebooter. Irrespective of the Misls, any Sikh warrior who gained distinction by killing a tiger, or shooting an arrow through a tree, would soon be joined by a band of lawless followers, and call himself a Sirdar. There was no question of pay. Every man provided himself with a horse and matchlock, and perhaps other weapons, and then fought and plundered under the banner of his chosen Sirdar, in the name of God and the Guru.

Types of Sirdars, Puritan and Pindhari.

The Sirdars were warriors and judges, like Joshua or Jephthah, and they differed just as widely. There were Sirdars of the Puritan type, who took the field at the head of their sons and vassals; tall wiry men, with eagle eye, soldier-like bearing, unshorn locks, and flowing beards; armed to the teeth with matchlock, pistol, blunderbuss, sword, and spear; and attended with all the showy accompaniments of stately camels, prancing steeds, and tinkling

[1] The cry "Hail, Guru!" implies "Hail to the state or church of the Guru!"

A.D. *Ante* 1845

bells. There were also Sirdars of the Pindhari type, whose followers were low caste men, turned into Sikhs by twisting up the hair, combing out the beard, assuming a tall turban and yellow girdle, and mounting a strong bony horse with a sword at their side, and a spear in their hand.

Akális, or Sikh zealots.

Besides these regular and irregular Sikhs, there were a set of fierce fanatics known as Akális. They were a stern and sombre brotherhood of military devotees,—soldiers of God, —instituted by Guru Govind, and distinguished by steel bracelets and blue dresses and turbans. The Akális were not lazy drones like Fakírs, for when not engaged in arms, they would find other work to do for the good of the community at large.[1]

Decay of the Misls.

Towards the close of the eighteenth century, the Sikh Misls were dying out. The fraternities had been broken up by assaults from Afghan and Moghul, by internal feuds, and by the freebooting habits of irregular Sirdars. The old religious fervour was still burning in the breasts of the Khálsa, but there was no one to direct it or control it.

Rise of Runjeet Singh, 1800.

About 1800 the young warrior Runjeet Singh came to the front. Born in 1780, he was appointed viceroy of Lahore by the Afghan sovereign at Kábul before he was twenty. His career was now before him. He stirred up the enthusiasm of the Khálsa to throw off the yoke of the Afghans. He engaged in conquests on all sides, and brought new countries and peoples under the dominion of the Khálsa. He never suffered the Khálsa to be at rest; and he thus prevented the Sirdars from revolting against his authority, or fighting one another. His ambition was boundless except on the side of the Sutlej. Had he flourished a generation earlier he might have conquered Hindustan; but whilst he was still a young man, the British empire in India was an established fact; and the victories of Lord Lake had inspired him with a wholesome respect for the British power. He refused to protect Jaswant Rao Holkar in 1805; and

[1] The late Captain Cunningham states in his *History of the Sikhs*, that he once found an Akáli repairing, or rather making, a road among precipitous ravines. On the other hand a Sikh fakír has been lying on a large stone outside Allahabad for the last thirty or forty years, absorbed in religious contemplations, and supported by voluntary subscriptions. He is said to have lain there during the mutiny, regardless of shot or shell. The author saw him in 1878, when he appeared to be a robust devotee of seventy, or perhaps older.

A.D. Ante 1845 — he yielded to the demands of the British government in 1809 as regards the Ciz-Sutlej states. Henceforth he proved as faithful to his alliance with the British government, as Herod, king of the Jews, was faithful to his alliance with Rome.

Politic dealings with the Sikh Khálsa. Meanwhile Runjeet Singh knew how to deal with the Khálsa. The Sikh army was drilled by successive French adventurers, named Allard, Ventura, Avitable and Court; but Runjeet Singh would not needlessly excite the jealousy of the Sirdars by treating the Europeans as trusted advisers. Again, Runjeet Singh was known as the Maháraja of the Punjab, but he only styled himself the commander of the army of the Khálsa, and he ascribed all the glory of his victories to God and the Guru Govind.

Characteristics of Runjeet Singh. Runjeet Singh was short in stature, and disfigured with small-pox which had deprived him of his left eye. He could neither read nor write. Yet this stunted and illiterate being was gifted with a genius, tact, and audacity, which enabled him to keep both the Punjab and army of the Khálsa under perfect control. He shrank from inflicting capital punishments, but he was remorseless in cutting off noses, ears, and hands; and for years after his death there were many poor wretches at Lahore, who complained of the mutilations they had suffered under the iron rule of Runjeet Singh.

Sikh morals. The religion of Guru Govind may have purified the forms of public worship, and reformed the morals of the lower classes, but many abominations lingered in the land down to the end of the Sikh government. Widows were burnt alive with their deceased husbands. Murders were frequent in the provinces. The court of Lahore was a sink of iniquity; rampant with all the vices that brought down fire and brimstone on the cities of the plain.

Death of Runjeet Singh, 1839. Runjeet Singh died in 1839, and five favourite queens and seven female slaves were burnt alive with his remains. Then began a series of revolutions which shook the Sikh dominion to its foundations, and left it prostrate at the feet of the British power.

Sikh and Rajpút factions. At this period the court of Lahore was split into two factions, the Sikhs and the Rajpúts. The Sikhs had been jealous at the rapid rise of two Rajpút brothers in the favour of Runjeet Singh. The brothers were originally common soldiers, but had been raised to the rank of Rajas, and were known as the Jamu Rajas. Gholab Singh, the elder, was appointed viceroy of Jamu, between Lahore and Kashmír. Dhián Singh, the younger, was prime-minister at Lahore.

A.D. *Ante* 1845

Kharak Singh, 1839-40.

In 1839, Kharak Singh, eldest son of Runjeet Singh, succeeded to the throne of Lahore. He was an imbecile, but he had a son of great promise, named Nao Nihal Singh. Both father and son were bent on the destruction of the Jamu Rajas. They began by the removal of Dhián Singh, the younger of the two Rajas, from his post as head of the administration at Lahore; and they appointed a wretched parasite in his room, who was regarded with contempt by the whole court. But the Rajpút blood of Dhián Singh boiled at the indignity, and he cut his successor to pieces in the presence of his royal master. Kharak Singh took fright at the murder, and shut himself up in his palace where he perished within a year of his accession.

Nao Nihal Singh, 1840.

In 1840, Nao Nihal Singh became Maháraja, but was killed at his father's funeral by the fall of an archway.[1] This sudden and tragic event led to the general belief that both father and son were murdered by the exasperated ex-minister.

A queen regent.

Dhián Singh was an intriguer of the common Asiatic type. He thought to set up a son of Runjeet Singh as a puppet Maháraja, and to rule in his name under the title of minister. But he was checkmated for a while by the old dowager queen, the widow of Kharak Singh. This lady declared that the widowed queen of the young Nao Nihal Singh was about to become a mother; and on the strength of this assertion, she assumed the post of queen regent in behalf of the unborn infant. The story was a farce, for the alleged mother was a girl of eight; but the Sikh court at Lahore held Dhián Singh in such hatred that all the chief Sirdars affected to believe the story, and recognised the regency of the dowager queen.

In 1841, the Sirdars were disgusted with the queen regent.

[1] Strange to say, there is a plot in an ancient Hindu drama for the destruction of Chandragupta, the Sandrokottos of the Greeks, by the very same artifice of a falling archway. The drama is known as "Mudra Rakshasa," or the "Signet of the Minister." An English translation will be found in Wilson's *Theatre of the Hindus*. For the story of Chandragupta, see *ante*, page 50.

A.D. *Ante* 1846.

Exile and murder, 1841.

Her private life was detestable; and she was compelled to resign the regency and retire into the country. Subsequently, she was beaten to death at the instigation of Dhián Singh, by four of her own slave girls, who dashed out her brains with a heavy stone whilst engaged in dressing her hair.

Sher Singh and his Rajpút minister, 1841-43.

Meanwhile Dhián Singh was triumphant. He placed Sher Singh, a reputed son of Runjeet Singh, on the throne at Lahore, and ruled the kingdom as minister. But a new power had risen in the body politic, which within a few short years was destined to work the ruin of the dynasty.

Dangerous power of the Sikh army.

Ever since the death of Runjeet Singh in 1839, the army of the Khálsa had grown more and more turbulent and unruly. They rose against their French generals, and compelled them to fly for their lives.[1] They clamoured for increase of pay, and committed the most frightful excesses and outrages. Sher Singh and his minister were compelled to yield to the demands of the troops; and henceforth the army of the Khálsa was absolute master of the state. The soldiers continued to obey their own officers, but the officers themselves were subject to the dictation of punchayets, or committees of five, which were elected from the ranks. Guru Govind had promised that whenever five Sikhs were assembled in his name, he would be in the midst of them. Accordingly, punchayets were formed in every regiment, and were supposed to be under the guidance of the unseen Guru; and their united action controlled the whole army. Sher Singh and his minister saw that no power, save that of the English, could deliver the Sikh government from the dictation of the Khálsa. In 1841, they opened the Punjab to troops passing between British territory and Kábul, and they begged the British government to interfere and suppress the growing disorders of the Khálsa.

Assassinations at Lahore, 1843.

In 1843 there was an explosion at Lahore. Maharaja Sher Singh had been plotting the murder of the minister, and the minister had been plotting the murder of the Mahâraja. Both plots were successful, and recoiled on the heads of the authors. One morning Sher Singh was shot dead on parade, and his son was assassinated, whilst Dhián Singh was murdered about the same hour.

[1] At this period there were only two French generals in the Sikh army, Avitable and Court.

Amidst these commotions, a son of Dhián Singh, named Híra Singh, appealed to the army of the Khálsa, and promised large money rewards. With the aid of these Prætorian bands, he placed an infant son of Runjeet Singh upon the throne, under the name of Maháraja Dhulíp Singh. The mother of the boy was then appointed queen regent, and Híra Singh succeeded his murdered father in the post of minister. It was at this crisis that Lord Ellenborough foresaw that the army of the Khálsa would one day threaten Hindustan; and he marched a British force towards Gwalior with the view of disbanding Sindia's unruly army as described in a previous chapter.

A.D. *Ante* 1845.

Dhulíp Singh and the regent-mother.

During 1844 affairs at Lahore reached a crisis. The new minister tried in vain to break up the army of the Khálsa; the punchayets were all-powerful, and would not allow a company to be disbanded, or even removed from Lahore, without their consent. The result was that Híra Singh was murdered, and the government of Lahore was left in the hands of a boy Maháraja, a regent-mother, and a disaffected army.

Crisis of 1844.

The regent-mother was as depraved as the widow of Kharak Singh, who was deposed in 1841. She appointed two ministers; one was her own brother, and the other was a paramour, named Lal Singh. The army of the Khálsa grew more and more clamorous for largesses and increase of pay; and were only prevented from plundering Lahore by being moved away under the sanction of the punchayets to exact money contributions from the viceroys of outlying provinces, such as Kashmír and Múltan. At the same time the two ministers, the brother and the paramour, were intriguing against each other. The brother gave mortal offence to the army of the Khálsa, and was tried and condemned by the punchayets as a traitor to the commonwealth, and was finally shot dead by a party of soldiers outside Lahore.

Rivalry of the brother and paramour.

The regent-mother and her paramour were now in sore peril. The paramour Lal Singh became sole minister, but another Sirdar, named Tej Singh, was appointed to the nominal command of the army of the Khálsa. But Tej Singh was the slave as well as the commander-in-chief of the army of the Khálsa; and was compelled to act according

Sikh army invades British territory, 1845.

A.D. Ante 1845

to the dictation of the punchayets. In a word, the new government was at the mercy of the army, and saw no way of saving themselves, except by launching the Sikh battalions on British territories, and no way of averting the sack of Lahore, except by sending the Sikh soldiery to sack Delhi and Benares

CHAPTER XXIII.

TWO SIKH WARS: LORDS HARDINGE AND DALHOUSIE.

A.D. 1845 TO 1849.

In November 1845, the Sikh army of the Khálsa crossed the Sutlej, to the number of 60,000 soldiers, 40,000 armed followers, and 150 large guns. The Sikh army had been strangely underrated by the British government. It was as superior to all other native armies, excepting perhaps the Ghorkas, as Cromwell's Ironsides were to the rabble following of the other parliamentary leaders. Its marked strength however was neutralised by the duplicity of its leaders—Lal Singh, the paramour, and Tej Singh, the nominal commander-in-chief. Both men were traitors of the deepest dye; both at heart were willing to see the Sikh battalions mowed down by British artillery in order that they might secure their own personal safety, and the continuance of their own government at Lahore. All this crafty and unscrupulous villany was conspicuous throughout the subsequent war.

A.D. 1845-1846 — Treachery of the Sikh generals.

The British government, under Sir Henry Hardinge, the new Governor-General, was scarcely prepared for the storm that was gathering on the line of the Sutlej. Sir John Littler held the fortress of Ferozepore with 10,000 troops and 31 guns; but if the Sikh generals had only been true to the Khálsa, they might have environed Ferozepore, overwhelmed Littler's force, and pushed on to the heart of Hindustan. As it was, Littler marched out of Ferozepore and offered the enemy battle; but the Sikh generals declined it, and divided their forces. Lal Singh moved with one *corps d'armée* towards Ferozeshahar, about ten miles off, and

Position of Littler at Ferozepore.

A.D. 1845-1846 began to build formidable entrenchments, leaving Tej Singh to watch Littler at Ferozepore.

Battle of Moodkee, December, 1845. Meanwhile Sir Hugh Gough, Commander-in-Chief, and Sir Henry Hardinge, the new Governor-General, were hurrying towards the frontier with a large force to relieve Littler. On the 18th of December they met the army of Lal Singh at Moodkee, and gained a doubtful victory. The British sepoys reeled before the Khálsa battalions, and even a European regiment was staggered for a few moments by the rapidity and precision of the Sikh fire. But Lal Singh fled at the beginning of the action, and thus brought about the defeat of the Sikh army.

Assault of Ferozeshahar. Two days after the battle of Moodkee, the British army advanced against the Sikh entrenchment at Ferozeshahar, and was joined there by the force under Littler. The assault was made on the 21st of December, but the Sikhs defended their position with the obstinacy and desperation of fanatics. Such resistance was terrific and unexpected. Gough charged up to the muzzle of the Sikh guns, and carried the batteries by cold steel; but it was in the face of an overwhelming fire. British cannon were dismounted and the ammunition blown into the air. Squadrons were checked in mid career; battalion after battalion was hurled back with shattered ranks; and it was not until after sunset that portions of the enemy's positions were finally carried by the British army.[1]

Flight of Lal Singh and Tej Singh. After a night of horrors the battle was renewed, but meanwhile there had been mutiny and desertion in the enemy's camp. The treasury of Lal Singh had been plundered by his own soldiers. The British troops met with feeble opposition; and it was soon discovered that, owing to the cowardice or treachery of Lal Singh, the Sikh army was in full flight to the Sutlej. Tej Singh marched up at this crisis, and found the entrenchments at Ferozeshahar in the hands of the British. Accordingly after a brief cannonade, he fled precipitately to the Sutlej, leaving his forces without orders, to fight or follow at their pleasure.

Battle of Aliwal, January, 1846. In January, 1846, both sides were reinforced; the Sikhs recrossed the Sutlej into British territory, and hostilities were renewed. On the 26th of the month, Sir Harry Smith defeated a Sikh force at Aliwal.

[1] Cunningham's *History of the Sikhs*.

A.D. 1846

Fruitless negotiations.

At this time Gholab Singh of Jamu had arrived at Lahore, and offered to make terms with the Governor-General. Sir Henry Hardinge replied that he was ready to acknowledge a Sikh sovereignty at Lahore, but not until the army of the Khálsa had been disbanded. The Sikh generals were utterly unable to fulfil such a condition; they were literally at the mercy of the Khálsa army. It is said, however, that they offered to abandon the Khálsa army to its fate, and to leave the road open to the march of the British army to Lahore, provided the Governor-General acknowledged the sovereignty of Maháraja Dhulíp Singh, and accepted the government of the regency.

Sikh entrenchments at Sobraón.

Meanwhile the main body of the Khálsa army had thrown up a formidable series of entrenchments at Sobraón. Early in February, 1846, the British army advanced to the attack under Gough and Hardinge. Sobraón proved to be the hardest fought battle in the history of British India. The Sikh soldiers, unlike their treacherous commander Tej Singh, were prepared to conquer or die for the glory of the Khálsa. The British brought up their heavy guns, and prepared to pour in a continuous storm of shot and shell, and then to carry the entrenchments by storm.

Bloody victory at Sobraón, February, 1846.

Shortly after midnight on the 10th of February, the British planted their guns in the desired positions. At early morning, amidst darkness and fog, the English batteries opened upon the enemy. At seven o'clock the fog rolled up like a curtain, and the soldiers of the Khálsa, nothing daunted, returned flash for flash, and fire for fire. As the sun rose higher, two British divisions of infantry in close order prepared for the assault. The left division advanced in line instead of column, and the greater part was driven back by the deadly fire of muskets and swivels and enfilading artillery. The right division formed instinctively into wedges and masses, and rushed forward in wrath, leaped the ditch with a shout, and then mounted the rampart and stood victorious amidst captured cannon. Tej Singh fled to the Sutlej at the first assault, and broke the bridge over the river; but whether this was done by accident or treachery is a problem to this day. Meanwhile the soldiers of the Khálsa fought with the valour of heroes, the enthusiasm of crusaders, and the desperation of zealots sworn to conquer the enemy or die sword in hand. At last they gave way;

A.D. 1846 they were driven by the fire of batteries and battalions into the waters of the Sutlej, and the battle of Sobraón was won. But the victory was dearly purchased. More than two thousand British troops were killed or wounded before the day was brought to a close; but the Sikhs are said to have lost eight thousand men.

Close of the first Sikh war. Thus ended the first Sikh war. The British army crossed the Sutlej in a bridge of boats, and pushed on to Lahore, and dictated their own terms at the old capital of Runjeet Singh. The reduction of the Sikh army of the Khálsa was carried out without further parley, and its numbers were limited for the future to 20,000 infantry and 12,000 cavalry. The Jullunder Doab was taken over by the British government, and the British frontier was extended from the Sutlej to the Raví. Meanwhile Sir Henry Hardinge was raised to the peerage.

Sale of Kashmír to Gholab Singh. Lord Hardinge called on the Lahore government to pay one million and a half sterling towards the expenses of the war. But the treasures of Runjeet Singh, estimated at the time of his death at twelve millions sterling, had been squandered during the anarchy which followed his decease, and only half a million remained to meet the demands of the British government at this crisis. Gholab Singh, viceroy of Kashmír and Jamu, offered to pay the million to the British government, provided he was recognised as Maháraja of those territories. The bargain was concluded, and henceforth Gholab Singh was an ally of the British government, and independent of the Sikh government of Lahore.

Settlement of the Punjab: no subsidiary force. Lord Hardinge was next called upon to decide on the future settlement of the Punjab. He would not annex the country, or take over the internal administration. He preferred accepting the existing government of the infant Maháraja, Dhulíp Singh, and the regency of the queen mother and her paramour. But he would not create a subsidiary army for the protection of the native government, as had been done in the case of the Nizam of Hyderabad and the Mahrattas. On the contrary he was resolved to withdraw the British troops from the Punjab at the earliest possible opportunity; for experience had taught the bitter lesson that a subsidiary force only demoralised native rulers, and rendered the British government responsible for the maintenance of oppression and misrule.

A.D. 1846

Temporary British occupation.

But Lord Hardinge was thwarted by circumstances. The Lahore durbar loudly declared that unless a British force remained to keep the peace in the Punjab, the army of the Khálsa would recover its strength and overturn the regency. Accordingly, much against his inclination, Lord Hardinge deferred withdrawing the British force until the close of the year; but he solemnly assured the Lahore durbar that at the end of 1846 every British soldier and sepoy must return to British territory. The Sirdars bent to their fate, but many declared that annexation had become a necessity; and that so long as a Sikh government was maintained at Lahore, with or without British troops, so long the disbanded army of the Khálsa would cherish hopes of a return to independent power.

Treachery and downfall of Lal Singh.

Major Henry Lawrence was appointed British Resident at Lahore, and Lal Singh, the paramour of the queen mother, filled the post of prime minister.[1] Shortly afterwards a flagrant act of treachery was proved against Lal Singh. A rebellion broke out in Kashmír and Jamu against the sovereign authority of Maháraja Gholab Singh. Major Lawrence hastened to the spot with a body of Sikh troops, and effectually suppressed it; and the leader of the rebellion then produced the written orders of Lal Singh, urging him to resist Gholab Singh by every means in his power. Such a breach of faith was unpardonable. Lal Singh was removed from his office, and deported to British territory, where he passed the remainder of his days in confinement.

British Resident and Sikh council of regency.

The year 1846 drew to a close. Again the Lahore durbar assured Lord Hardinge that the Khálsa army would regain its old ascendancy if the British force was withdrawn. Accordingly a compromise was effected. Eight leading Sirdars were formed into a council of regency under the express stipulation that the entire control and guidance of affairs should be vested in the British Resident. Having thus guarded against oppression or misrule, Lord Hardinge

[1] In dealing with the modern history of British India, the distinction between the three Lawrence brothers must always be borne in mind. George was one of the hostages in the first Afghan war, and had a narrow escape with his life at the time when Macnaghten was murdered. Henry had been Resident in Nipal, and was now transferred to Lahore. John was Commissioner of the Jullunder Doab, and afterwards became successively Chief Commissioner and Lieutenant-Governor of the Punjab, and finally Governor-General and Viceroy of India.

A.D. 1848-1849

decided that the British force should remain in the Punjab for a period of eight years, by which time Maháraja Dhulíp Singh would attain his majority, and might be intrusted with the supreme authority.

Lord Hardinge returns to England, 1848.

This settlement of the Punjab continued, without material change, until the departure of Lord Hardinge from India in 1848. During the interval many useful measures were carried out. The British army in India was reorganised; the finances were restored; and efforts were made to induce the native states to follow the example of the British government, in forbidding widow burning, female infanticide, slavery, and other abominations, throughout their respective territories. In 1848 Lord Hardinge returned to England with the pleasant conviction that he had secured the peace of India for some years to come.

Lord Dalhousie Governor-General, 1848.

Lord Dalhousie, the new Governor-General, landed at Calcutta in January, 1848. The history of his administration will be told in the next chapter, but it may be as well in the present place to review the current of Punjab affairs, which ended in the second Sikh war, and permanent annexation of the kingdom of Runjeet Singh.

Lawrence succeeded by Currie at Lahore.

Major Henry Lawrence, the Resident at Lahore, was an officer in the Bengal artillery, of large political experience. About this time he was obliged to proceed to England on account of his health, and was succeeded by Sir Frederic Currie, a Bengal civilian. New systems of finance and revenue were subsequently introduced into the Punjab, which guarded against undue exactions, and secured a greater regularity in the collection of revenue, but gave great umbrage to Sikh Sirdars. Discontent and disaffection began to seethe beneath the surface, and it was soon evident that the spirit of the Khálsa was still burning in the breasts of the disbanded soldiery.

Grievance of Múlraj, viceroy of Múltan.

A spark sufficed to set the Punjab in a conflagration. Múlraj, viceroy of Múltan, had succeeded his father in the government of the province as far back as 1844; but the Lahore durbar had required him to pay a million sterling as a fine on succession. He took advantage of the struggles between the regency and the soldiery to delay payment. He then managed to get his claim reduced to less than one-fifth, and finally refused to pay the fraction. When, however, the

A.D. 1848-1849

Sikh war was over, and a British Resident was posted to Lahore, Múlraj found that further resistance was useless, and that he must pay up. But he was irritated at the new order of things. He complained that the new system of finance and revenue about to be introduced by the British Resident would diminish his income. Finally he resigned the government of Múltan on the plea that there were dissensions in his family.

Feigned resignation of Múlraj.

Sir Frederic Currie and the council of regency took Múlraj at his word. A successor, named Khan Singh, was appointed to the government of Múltan. Mr. Vans Agnew, a Bengal civilian, was appointed to accompany Khan Singh, and introduce the new fiscal system into Múltan. In April, 1848. Khan Singh, Mr. Vans Agnew, and Lieutenant Anderson, arrived at Múltan with an escort of 350 Sikh troops and a few guns, and encamped at a fortified mosque in the suburbs, known as the Edgah.

Treachery and murder.

Múlraj paid a visit to Mr. Vans Agnew at the Edgah, and declared himself ready to deliver up the town and citadel. He then produced the accounts of the previous year, and asked for a deed of acquittance. Mr. Vans Agnew, however, called for the accounts of the previous six years. Múlraj was affronted at the demand, but nevertheless agreed to furnish the documents. Mr. Vans Agnew and Lieutenant Anderson next proceeded with Múlraj to inspect the establishments in the citadel, and at his request they dismissed a portion of their escort. On leaving the citadel the two Englishmen were felled from their horses and dangerously wounded. Múlraj was riding by the side of Mr. Vans Agnew, but at once galloped off to his country residence. The wounded officers were carried off by their attendants to the Edgah, but the guns of the citadel began to open fire upon the mosque. In spite however of their wounds, the two officers made a manful resistance, and returned the fire with the guns of the Sikh escort; but the escort proved treacherous, and went over to the enemy; and a mob of savages rushed into the mosque, and cut the two Englishmen to pieces. Immediately afterwards Múlraj removed his family and treasure into the citadel, and issued a proclamation calling upon the people of every creed to rise against the English.

These atrocious murders were committed after the setting

A.D. 1848-1849

Successes of Herbert Edwardes.

in of the hot weather. Lord Gough was anxious to postpone military operations for some months until the beginning of the cold weather; and there was consequently much delay in putting down the revolt. A young lieutenant, named Herbert Edwardes, who was employed in the revenue settlement of Bunnu, beyond the Indus, marched a force to Múltan on his own responsibility; and being joined by other levies, he defeated Múlraj on the 18th of June, and ultimately shut him up in the citadel at Múltan.

Queen mother removed to Benares.

Meanwhile there was treachery in the Sikh government at Lahore. The queen mother of Dhulíp Singh was exasperated at the loss of her paramour, and was secretly corrupting the troops. At the same time she was organising a confederacy of Sirdars against the British government, and carrying on intrigues with the Amír of Kábul, the Maháraja of Kashmír, and the princes of Rajpútana. Fortunately these proceedings were discovered in time, and the dangerous lady was removed from Lahore to the sacred city of Benares, and provided with a suitable pension.

Revolt of Sher Singh: general disaffection.

Subsequently, an influential Sirdar, named Sher Singh, was sent at the head of a Sikh force to co-operate with Lieutenant Edwardes against Múlraj. But Sher Singh played a double game. Whilst swearing eternal fidelity to the British government he was secretly corresponding with the rebels. A force of 7,000 British troops under General Whish was sent against Múltan, and it was confidently expected that the town and fortress would be speedily taken, and that Múlraj would then receive the just punishment of his crimes. The guns had already begun to open on Múltan, when Sher Singh ordered the drums of religion to be beaten, and went over to the enemy with 5,000 Sikhs, and proclaimed a religious war against the English. General Whish was obliged to retire from Múltan and throw up entrenchments. It was soon evident that the whole of the Punjab was in a state of revolt; and that the veterans of Runjeet Singh's army were assembling to renew the contest with the British government, retrieve their lost honour, and revive the glory and supremacy of the army of the Khálsa. In a word, the delay in crushing the paltry outbreak of Múlraj had aroused the military enthusiasm of the Sikhs throughout the Punjab, and necessitated a second Sikh war.

Lord Dalhousie rose to the occasion. Being new to

A.D. 1848-1849

Energy and resolution of Lord Dalhousie.

India he had deferred to the opinion of the Commander-in-Chief as regards the postponement of military operations, but he soon apprehended the dangerous significance of the revolt. He saw that the work of his predecessor had to be done over again; and he was resolved that this time there should be no half measures; no bolstering up of an effete and treacherous government, but a restoration of order and law under British administration. In October, 1848, he proceeded from Bengal to the Punjab. Before he went he made a declaration in a public speech, which is at once characteristic and historical:—"Unwarned by precedent, uninfluenced by example, the Sikh nation has called for war, and on my word, Sirs, they shall have it with a vengeance."

Sikhs joined by Afghans.

All this while Sher Singh had been coldly and suspiciously received by Múlraj. Both had revolted against a common enemy, but each one was jealous of the other, and had his own ends to pursue. Accordingly, Sher Singh left Múltan, and marched boldly towards Lahore. About the same time his father, Chutter Singh, had been tempting Dost Muhammad Khan, Amír of Kábul, to join in the general rising against the British government, by promising to make over the coveted province of Peshawar. Major George Lawrence, a brother of Henry, was in charge of Peshawar, which was held by a garrison of 8,000 Sikhs; but the Sikh garrison went over to the Afghans and attacked the Residency, and George Lawrence and others were carried off prisoners. Captain Herbert held out for a while in the fort of Attock, near the junction of the Kábul river and the Indus to the eastward of Peshawar, but was forced in like manner to succumb to the Afghans.

Battle of Chilianwallah, January, 1849.

In October 1848 the British army under Lord Gough was assembled at Ferozepore. In November it crossed the Raví, and engaged Sher Singh in an indecisive action at Ramnuggur. On the 13th of January, 1849, Lord Gough approached Sher Singh's entrenchments at Chilianwallah, which were held by 30,000 Sikhs and 60 guns. Nothing was known of the disposition of the Sikhs, for their camp was covered by a thick jungle, and Lord Gough resolved to defer the attack till the following morning. At that moment the Sikhs opened fire with some guns in advance. The indignation of Lord Gough was kindled at the challenge, and he rashly ordered a general charge. Then followed the

A.D. 1848-1849

most sanguinary encounter in the history of British India, which ended in a doubtful victory on the part of the English. The Sikhs were driven from their position, but they took up another three miles off. Both sides fired salutes in honour of victory, but the English had lost more than 2,400 officers and men.

Sir Charles Napier sent to India; surrender of Múltan.

The fatal field of Chilianwallah is already half forgotten, but the tidings of the disaster were received in England with an outburst of alarm and indignation. Sir Charles Napier was hastily sent to India to supersede Lord Gough as Commander-in-Chief. Meanwhile General Whish captured the town of Múltan and opened a terrible cannonade on the citadel. Múlraj offered a desperate resistance, but was at last compelled to surrender the fortress, and gave himself up to the English. General Whish then left Múltan in charge of Lieutenant Edwardes, and proceeded to join Lord Gough in a final struggle with Sher Singh.

Crowning victory at Guzerat, February, 1849.

The crowning victory at Guzerat was gained by Lord Gough on the 22nd of February, 1849. It was essentially an artillery action, and is known as the battle of the guns. The Sikhs opened a cannonade with sixty guns and fired with singular rapidity, but their resistance was in vain. For two hours and a half they were exposed to a storm of shot and shell, which was eventually followed by a charge of bayonets, and rush of cavalry. The Sikh army became literally a wreck; its camp, its standards, and nearly all its cannon, fell into the hands of the conquerors. The battle of Guzerat decided the fate of the Punjab, and the hopes of the Khalsa were quenched for ever.

Annexation of the Punjab.

Lord Dalhousie was fully prepared for this result. He had resolved on the annexation of the Punjab, and had already drawn up a programme for the civil administration of the province, and the appointment of British officials to the several grades. All old errors in former settlements were rectified in dealing with the Punjab; all known abuses were guarded against; and the government of the Punjab, instead of struggling into existence like the government of Bengal, seemed to spring like another Minerva, full armed from the brain of Zeus. To this day the administration of the Punjab is one of the greatest triumphs of British rule, and a model for Asiatic statesmen throughout all time.

The minor details connected with the conclusion of the

war may be dismissed in a few words. Dost Muhammad Khan and his Afghans were driven out of Peshawar, and narrowly escaped to Kábul. Múlraj was imprisoned for life on account of the part he played in the murder of the two Englishmen. The young Maháraja Dhulíp Singh was provided with a yearly annuity of fifty thousand pounds, and ultimately settled in England. Within a few short years the memory of Runjeet Singh died away from the land. The soldiers of the Khálsa enlisted under British banners, and during the sepoy revolt of 1857 were the foremost amongst those who wrested Delhi from the sepoy mutineers, and avenged the insulted sovereignty of British rule.

A.D. 1848-1849

Final settlement.

CHAPTER XXIV.

MATERIAL PROGRESS: LORD DALHOUSIE.

A.D. 1848 TO 1856.

A.D. 1848-1856

Genius of Lord Dalhousie.

LORD DALHOUSIE was a man of energy and power. Short in stature, like the once famous Marquis of Wellesley, there was a fire and determination in his eye which revealed a genius for command.[1] So long as he held the reins of government his administrative ability and intellectual vigour commanded general respect and admiration; but his imperious temper, impatience of opposition, and alleged lack of sympathy for native rulers stirred up an antagonism to his policy which is only slowly fading away.

Administrative culture.

Lord Dalhousie was Governor-General of India at the age of thirty-six. He was a staunch believer in moral and material progress, and he had already served an apprenticeship to the work as President of the Board of Trade under the premiership of Sir Robert Peel. Within two years of his arrival in India he had perfected his knowledge of the country and people. The Sikh uprising of 1848 familiarised him with those convulsions on the frontier to which Hindustan has always been exposed; whilst the newly conquered territory of the Punjab opened out a virgin field to his administrative energies.

Creation of a government in the Punjab.

The Punjab is nearly as large as England. It covers fifty thousand square miles, and contains a population of four millions. One-fourth of the people are Sikhs: the

[1] De Quincey talks of the foppery of the eye, and quotes the cases of Lord Wellesley, Dr. Parr, and Augustus Cæsar; but there was no foppery about the eye of Lord Dalhousie.

A.D. 1848-1856

remainder are Hindus and Muhammadans. The Sikh government and the army of the Khálsa had been scattered to the winds. Accordingly Lord Dalhousie was called upon to create a new administration out of chaos, which should adapt itself to a mixed population who knew nothing of order or law; and he brought to bear upon his task the experiences which had been gained during a century of British rule in India, and which enabled him to avoid the mistakes which had been committed by his predecessors in Bengal and elsewhere.

Divisional and district officers.

The new province was divided by Lord Dalhousie into seven divisions, and each division into as many districts as were necessary. Each division was placed under a commissioner, and each district under a deputy-commissioner. Fifty-six officers were employed in these two grades; one half being selected from the civil service, and the other half from the army. Below these were the subordinate grades of assistant and extra-assistant commissioners, who were selected from what is known as the uncovenanted service and comprised Europeans, East Indians, and natives.

Board of Administration.

The management of the new administration was entrusted to a Board of Administration, consisting of three members, namely, Henry Lawrence, John Lawrence, and Robert Montgomery.[1] Henry Lawrence presided at the Board, and carried on the political work, namely, the disarming of the country, the negotiations with Sikh Sirdars, and the organisation of new Punjabi regiments. John Lawrence took charge of the civil administration, especially the settlement of the land revenue. Robert Montgomery superintended the administration of justice throughout the province, and compiled a short manual for the guidance of the officials and people, which contained all that was necessary in a few pages.

John Lawrence first Chief Commissioner.

The working of the Board of Administration was not satisfactory. The sympathies of Henry Lawrence were all on the side of the Sikh Sirdars, who were regarded with

[1] Colonel, afterwards Sir Henry, Lawrence, belonged to the Bengal Artillery. John Lawrence, afterwards Viceroy of India and a peer of the realm, belonged to the Civil Service. Mr. Charles Grenville Mansel was originally third member of the Board, but he was subsequently succeeded by Sir Robert Montgomery. Both Mansel and Montgomery belonged to the Civil Service.

A.D. 1848-1856

disfavour by Lord Dalhousie, and whose antecedents were certainly as bad as they well could be. The result was that in 1853 the Board of Administration was broken up, and John Lawrence was placed in the sole charge of the government as Chief Commissioner.

Administration under Runjeet Singh.

The British administration of the Punjab was in every way a new creation. The government of Runjeet Singh had been the rude work of an unlettered warrior, without constitutional forms of any sort or kind, and without any law except the will of the one great despot at the head. The only officers of state were soldiers and tax-collectors; the only punishments were fines and mutilations; and there was not a single civil court in the Punjab excepting at Lahore. The local authorities were little despots who oppressed the people and defrauded the state, like the underlings of Tippu Sultan in Mysore; but sooner or later the majority were compelled to disgorge their ill-gotten wealth, and were often condemned to poverty and mutilation at the arbitrary will of Runjeet Singh.

Duties of British officials.

The officers of the new Punjab commission were required to fulfil every kind of administrative duty. They were magistrates and judges, revenue collectors and head policemen, diplomatists and conservancy officers. For many months of the year their homes were in camp, with their tents open to all comers, from the lowest class of petitioners to the wealthiest Sirdars.[1]

Defence of the frontier westward of the Indus.

One of the first measures of Lord Dalhousie was to provide for the military defence of the province. The British frontier had been advanced from the Sutlej westward to the range of mountains beyond the Indus. The mountains were inhabited by brave and lawless tribes, who numbered a hundred thousand men at arms, and had been the pest of the plains ever since the days of Akbar. Lord Dalhousie tried to bar out these barbarians by a series of fortifications, connected by a line of roads, along the whole frontier; and he organised a special force of five regiments of infantry and

[1] The general confidence of the natives of the Punjab in British officers was sometimes carried to an amusing excess. On one occasion, when the late Lord Lawrence was Viceroy of India, a number of Punjab people travelled to Calcutta, a distance of some fifteen hundred miles, to speak to "Jan Larrens Sahib" about a cow. The writer saw the men himself. Unfortunately "Jan Larrens Sahib" was at Simla.

A.D. 1848-1856

four of cavalry for the protection of the marches.[1] Meanwhile he disarmed the whole of the population of the Punjab, excepting the inhabitants on the British side of the border. A hundred and twenty thousand weapons were surrendered to British officers; and the manufacture, sale, or possession of arms was strictly prohibited.

Land revenue reduced.

The land revenue was settled on easy terms. Runjeet Singh had collected half the produce. Lord Dalhousie reduced it to an average of one fourth, and ordered a further reduction of ten per cent., to reconcile the renters to the payment of coin instead of kind. The consequence was that cultivation largely increased, and thirty thousand of the old Khálsa soldiery exchanged the sword for the plough.

Transit duties abolished.

Transit duties were abolished altogether. Runjeet Singh had covered the Punjab with a network of custom-houses for the collection of these duties on goods and merchandise; but all were swept away by a stroke of the pen from Lord Dalhousie.

Miscellaneous measures.

Meanwhile slavery and thuggee were rooted out of the Punjab; and infanticide, that bane of oriental life, was suppressed as far as might be. Bands of outlaws and dacoits, who had been accustomed under Sikh rule to plunder villages and travellers with impunity, were attacked, captured and punished by sheer force of arms. The Punjab was intersected with roads as if it had been a Roman province.[2] In a word, within seven years of the battle of Guzerat, the Punjab presented more traces of British civilisation and dominion than any other province in British India.

[1] This is the line of frontier which has recently been abandoned (1880). Further particulars respecting it will be found in the story of the Sitana campaign of 1863, which is told in the concluding chapter of the present volume.

[2] The most important road constructed in the Punjab was that which united Lahore with Peshawar. It extended very nearly 300 miles, passed over 100 great bridges and 450 smaller ones, penetrated six mountain chains, and was carried by embankments over the marshes of two great rivers. Every obstacle was overcome by Colonel Robert Napier, of the Bengal Engineers, whose work in the Punjab would have won him the highest honours in Europe, and who has become famous in later days as Lord Napier of Magdala. Canals and irrigation works were not forgotten. Amongst others the great canal of the Bari Doab was constructed between the Ravi and the Chenab, under the direction of Colonel Napier. It was equal to the noblest canal in Europe, and extended with its three branches to the length of 465 miles.

A.D. 1848-1856

Second Burmese war, 1852: reluctance of the British government.

Three years after the conquest of the Punjab the British government was drawn into a second war with the King of Burma. Never was a war began with greater reluctance. To all appearance there was nothing to gain; for the territories of Arakan and Tenasserim, which had been acquired after the first war, had never paid their expenses. But Lord Dalhousie had no alternative. By the treaty of Yandabo both the British and Burmese governments were pledged to afford protection and security to all merchants trading at their respective ports or residing within their respective territories. This treaty however had been repeatedly broken; and Englishmen trading at Rangoon were oppressed and maltreated by the Burmese officials, whilst every effort to obtain redress was treated with contempt and scorn.

Oppression of British subjects at Rangoon.

In 1851 the European merchants at Rangoon laid their complaints before the British government at Calcutta. English sea captains had been condemned on false charges to pay heavy fines, and were then subjected to imprisonment and insult. British merchants, who had been living at Rangoon under the provisions of the treaty of Yandabo, were driven to declare that unless they were protected by their own government they must abandon their property and leave Burmese territory.

Mission of Commodore Lambert.

Ever since 1840 the British government had ceased to maintain an accredited agent at Ava. Accordingly Lord Dalhousie sent Commodore Lambert to Rangoon in Her Majesty's ship the *Fox*, to investigate the complaints; and also entrusted him with a letter of remonstrance to the king of Burma, which he was to forward to Ava or withhold as might seem expedient. When the *Fox* reached Rangoon, the Burmese governor threatened to put any one to death who dared to communicate with the ship. Some Europeans however escaped to the frigate, and the Commodore sent on the letter from Lord Dalhousie to the king at Ava. After some weeks a reply was received to the effect that the offending governor would be removed from Rangoon, and that strict inquiries would be made into the complaints brought against him.

Deceit and arrogance.

Commodore Lambert was delighted with the letter from Ava. He thought everything was settled, but he was soon undeceived. The governor was certainly recalled from Rangoon, but he went away in triumph, with all the pomp of music and war boats. A new governor arrived, but he was bent on treating the English with the same contempt and arrogance as had been displayed by his predecessor. He took no notice whatever of the Commodore. At last he was asked to fix a day for receiving a deputation of English officers, and he replied that any day would do. Accordingly early one morning he was told that a deputation would wait upon him at noon. At the time appointed the English officers reached the governor's house, but were not allowed to enter. They were kept out in the sun by the menial servants, and told that the governor was asleep; whilst the governor himself was looking insolently out of the window, and seeing them exposed to the insults and jeers of the mob. At last the patience of the officers was exhausted, and they returned to the frigate.

Beginning of the war.

Commodore Lambert then took possession of one of the king's ships lying in the river, but promised to restore it, and to salute the Burmese flag, on receipt of ten thousand rupees, as compensation for the injured merchants, and a suitable apology from the governor of Rangoon. In reply, the Burmese opened fire on the *Fox* from some stockades on both sides of the river; but the guns of the *Fox* soon demolished the stockades, and the Burmese ports were declared in a state of blockade.

Expedition to Rangoon under General Godwin.

Lord Dalhousie made another appeal to the king of Burma, and meanwhile prepared for war. A land force of 5,800 men was sent to Rangoon under General Godwin, together with nineteen steamers manned with 2,300 sailors and marines. A steamer was sent up the river Irawadi with a flag of truce to receive a reply from the king, but it was fired upon by the Burmese. Accordingly the troops were landed; Rangoon was captured in the face of a heavy cannonade, the three terraces of the great Shivé Dagon pagoda were carried by storm, and the British ensign was fixed on the golden dome.

Conquest of Pegu.

The capture of Rangoon was followed by that of Bassein and Prome.[1] The Burmese soldiery fled to Upper Burma, and the people flocked to Rangoon and hailed the British

[1] There are two places named Bassein. There is Bassein, near Bombay, where the Peishwa concluded a treaty with Lord Wellesley; and the Bassein named in the text, which is situated on the south-west corner of the delta of the Irawadi.

A.D. 1848-1856

as their deliverers. Meanwhile there had been a revolution in Ava. The Pagan Meng had been deposed, and his half-brother, the Meng-don Meng, was taken from a Buddhist monastery and placed upon the throne. The new sovereign was anxious for peace, but refused to conclude any treaty. Lord Dalhousie steamed to Rangoon the following September, and decided on annexing Pegu to the British empire, and leaving the king in possession of Upper Burma.

Prosperity of British Burma.

The same administrative changes were carried out at Pegu as had been begun in the Punjab, but with limited resources and on a less brilliant scale. Major, the present Sir Arthur Phayre, was appointed Commissioner of Pegu, and introduced British administration with a strong substratum of Burmese officials. With the assistance of Captain, now General Fytche, and other distinguished officers, Major Phayre succeeded in clearing the new province of robbers and outlaws and establishing order and law. Ultimately in 1862 the three territories of Arakan, Pegu, and Tenasserim were formed into the province of British Burma, with Major Phayre as Chief Commissioner. The consequence has been that British Burma not only pays the whole expense of the local administration, but contributes a large yearly surplus to the imperial treasury. Since 1852 the population of Rangoon alone has increased tenfold, and promises to become another Calcutta; and when the population of Pegu has increased in a like ratio, the province will prove as productive as Bengal. Already the Irawadi is beginning to pour down as much wealth to the sea as the Ganges and Jumna before the introduction of the railways; and within another generation, when existing obstructions are removed, new fields of commerce will be opened out in Western China, and restore the fabled glories of the Golden Chersonese to the Malacca peninsula.[1]

The Punjab and Pegu were the favourite, but not the only fields of Lord Dalhousie's labours. His influence was felt in every province of the empire, every department

[1] Should the frontier of British India ever be conterminous with Persia, Russia, and China, new markets will be opened to British manufactures of which the present generation can form no conception, whilst the resources of the new countries, which at present are undeveloped, will serve to enrich half Asia.

A.D. 1848-1856

Energy and capacity of Lord Dalhousie.

of government, and every native state under British protection. His reforms extended to every branch of the administration,—army, public works, education, revenue, finance, justice, and general legislation. He promoted canals and steam navigation, and he introduced railways and cheap postage. He constructed four thousand miles of electric telegraph wires, and two thousand miles of road, bridged and metalled. He opened the Ganges canal, the longest in the world. In a word, Lord Dalhousie was emphatically the pioneer of western civilisation in India; the first of that modern dynasty of rulers, under whom India has ceased to be a remote and outlying region, and has become part and parcel of the British empire, sharing in all the blessings of European science and culture.

Suppression of barbarous usages in native states.

The administrative successes of Lord Dalhousie naturally impressed him with a strong sense of the vast superiority of British administration over oriental rule. He would not interfere with the treaty rights of native allies, but he was resolute in putting down widow burning, witch torturing, self immolation, mutilation, and other barbarous usages, in the territories of native princes, as much as in those under British administration. Any prince, Rajpút or Mahratta, who hesitated to punish such atrocities within his own territories to the entire satisfaction of the British government, was visited with the marked displeasure of Lord Dalhousie, threatened with the loss of his salute, refused admittance to the Governor-General's durbar, or deprived of one or other of those tokens of the consideration of the British government which are valued by the princes and nobles of India. At the same time Lord Dalhousie was never wanting in paternal regard for native states during a minority. He duly provided for the education and administrative training of Sindia and Holkar; and was anxious that they should be fitted for the duties of government before they attained their majority and were placed in charge of their respective territories.

Political dictum of Lord Dalhousie.

The administration of native states was no doubt wretched in the extreme. Indeed it is only of late years that native officials have received an English education, and profited by the example set in British territories, to carry out some measures of reform. Both Lord Dalhousie, and his predecessor, Lord Hardinge, were deeply impressed with the

A.D. 1848-1856

responsibility incurred by the British government in perpetuating native misrule. Both agreed that no rightful opportunity should be lost of acquiring territory and revenue; in other words, of bringing native territory under British administration. The motives of both rulers were unquestionably pure; neither Hardinge nor Dalhousie could have any personal object in adding to the territories of the late East India Company beyond the promotion of the moral and material welfare of the native populations. But their sentiments were open to misconstruction, and might be interpreted to mean that the appropriation of native territory would be always justifiable, provided a decent excuse could be found for the transfer.

Obligations of the British government towards native states.

No one seems to have doubted that the British government was bound to maintain the integrity of native states so long as a native ruler did not forfeit his rights by some public crime. Again, no one doubted the right of a son, or other male heir, to inherit a Raj. But a question was raised as to the rights of an adopted son; and as this question has been much distorted by controversy, it may be as well to explain it from a Hindu point of view. Practically, the law of adoption has ceased to have any political importance. The British government has conceded the right of adopting an heir to the Raj to native princes in general. But a right understanding of the law of adoption is absolutely necessary to a right understanding of the policy of Lord Dalhousie.

Hindu belief in the necessity for a son.

Amongst all orthodox Hindus a son is regarded as a religious necessity. A son is required to offer cakes and water to the soul of a deceased father, and indeed to the souls of all deceased ancestors up to a certain generation. Moreover, in the belief of modern Hindus, the world of shades is a kind of temporary hell or purgatory, where the soul of the father is supposed to dwell until all its sins have been wiped away by the sacrifices and other good works of the son. When this end has been attained, the soul either returns to earth to resume its existence through successive transmigrations, or it ascends to eternal life in some superior heaven, or is absorbed in the Supreme Spirit—Vishnu, Siva, or Brahma.

It is this religious necessity which has brought about the early marriage of Hindu boys. Should however the husband fail to become the father of a son, he may either marry a second wife, or he may adopt a son; and a son in either case, whether natural or adopted, inherits the property at the father's death, and becomes the head of the household.

A.D. 1848-1856

Adoption a religious rite.

The question of adoption in the case of a Hindu principality stands on a different footing. The adopted son may succeed to the property of his nominal father, and perform all his religious duties; but the question of inheriting a Raj is of a political character, and depends on the will of the paramount power. In either case, whether the inheritance to a Raj is granted or refused, the adopted son is still expected to perform all the religious duties necessary for the well-being of the deceased father.[1]

Political aspect of the question.

The question of the right of adoption in the case of a Hindu principality was never raised in India before the rise of British power. There was no public law in the matter; the question of might alone made the right. If a Hindu principality was conveniently near, it was brought under Moghul rule by treachery, chicanery, or force of arms, without the slightest regard to the rights of a reigning Raja, or the rights of his heirs or representatives.[2] If a principality was remote and strong, every effort was made to seduce or threaten the native ruler into paying tribute; or at any rate into rendering homage and presenting nuzzers, or honorary gifts, as an acknowledgment of the suzerainty of the Moghul. Whatever, however, might be the circumstances of the case, no succession was deemed valid unless it received the formal approval and sanction of the paramount power; and this end could only be obtained by a Hindu prince in the same way that a Muhammadan officer obtained the government of a province, namely, by sending presents

Abeyance under Moghul rule: might making right.

[1] The present Maháraja Holkar has more than once taken over the estate of a feudatory on the ground that he had left no natural heirs, and that the adopted son had no claim to inherit landed property.

[2] Akbar was anxious to maintain the Rajpút principalities as a counterpoise against Afghans and Moghuls, and his policy was to give a daughter in marriage to a Rajpút prince, and insist upon her son being the heir to the principality. But Aurangzeb was only anxious to convert the Hindus to Islam, and a Rajpút prince who turned Muhammadan would have been recognised as heir to the principality in the same way that an Irishman of a Roman Catholic family secured the family estate in the last century by becoming a Protestant. Neither Akbar nor Aurangzeb were likely to trouble themselves about the law of adoption.

A.D. 1848-1856

and tribute to the Moghul court, and receiving letters and insignia of investiture in return.

Adoption recognised by the British government.

The British government, however, professed from the very first to adhere to the policy of non-intervention, and cared not who succeeded to the throne so long as there were no civil wars.[1] Accordingly in the case of Sindia, as already seen, the dying ruler was advised by the British government to adopt a son in order to prevent any broils as regards a successor. At the same time the queen or minister was generally anxious for an adoption, as if it could be established it might set aside the claim of a brother or other collateral heir, and would enable the queen or minister to exercise sovereign authority during the minority. It thus became customary for a native prince to apply for the consent of the British government before adopting a son who should be heir to the Raj; and at every succession, whether the son was natural or adopted, the recognition of the British government was deemed necessary to its validity. The youthful heir was formally invested with a dress of honour by the British representative, and in return he publicly acknowledged his fealty to the British government.

Raj of Satara: resuscitated 1818.

The policy of Lord Dalhousie will be rendered intelligible by dealing with matters of fact. The first native principality brought to his notice was that of Satara. The story of Satara has already been told. The representative of Sivaji reigned as a puppet Raja in a state prison at Satara, whilst successive Peishwas, or ministers, reigned as real sovereigns at Poona. After the extinction of the Peishwas in 1818, Lord Hastings resuscitated the Raja of Satara for reasons of state; took him out of a prison, and invested him with a small principality. He thought by so doing to reconcile Sindia and Holkar to the extinction of the Peishwas. But the generosity, whether real or apparent, was thrown away. The Mahrattas had long forgotten to care for the Raja of Satara, and they soon forgot the ex-Peishwa.

Extravagant pretensions of the Raja.

But the elevation of the Raja of Satara from a prison to a principality turned the young man's head. Instead of being grateful for his change of fortune, he was incensed with his benefactors for not restoring him to the throne and empire of Sivaji. He fondly imagined that if he could

[1] See *ante*, page 523.

A.D. 1848-1856

only get rid of the British government, he might recover the old Mahratta sovereignty which had been usurped by the Peishwas for more than seventy years, and which, as far as Satara was concerned, had never been anything more than a shadow and a sham. Accordingly, in spite of his treaty obligations to abstain from all correspondence with states or individuals outside his jurisdiction, the Raja of Satara opened up communications with the Portuguese authorities at Goa, and even with the exiled Appa Sahib of Nagpore; and to crown his misdoings, he employed certain Brahmans to tamper with some sepoy officers in the Bombay army.

Dethronement of the Raja, 1839.

It was impossible to overlook these proceedings, and there was some talk of punishing the Raja; but Sir James Carnac, the Governor of Bombay, took a lenient view of the case, and told the Raja that all would be forgiven if he would only promise to keep the treaty more faithfully for the future. But by this time the Raja was too far gone to listen to reason. He spurned all interference, asserted his sovereignty, and was accordingly deposed, and sent to Benares, and his brother was enthroned in his room.

Adoption refused to his successor.

The new Raja of Satara took warning by the fate of his predecessor, and gave no trouble to the British authorities. But he had no son or male heir, and he repeatedly requested the British government to permit him to adopt a son who should inherit the Raj. Every application however was refused. Under such circumstances he might possibly have adopted a son who would have inherited his private property, and performed all the religious ceremonies necessary for delivering his soul from a Hindu purgatory. But he appears to have hoped on to the last; and in 1848, two hours before his death, he adopted an heir on his own responsibility, and left the result in the hands of the British government.

Lapse of Satara.

Lord Dalhousie decided that the adopted son might inherit the private property of the deceased Raja, but that the principality of Satara had lapsed to the British government. This decision was confirmed by the Court of Directors. The result was that the Raj of Satara was incorporated with the Bombay Presidency, and brought under British administration.

Kerauli a Rajpút principality.

Shortly afterwards the Kerauli succession was taken into consideration. Kerauli was a Rajpút principality, which had paid a yearly tribute to the Peishwa; but it was taken under

A.D. 1848-1856

British protection in 1818, and relieved from the further payment of tribute. The Raja showed his gratitude by joining in the outbreak of Dúrjan Sál of Bhurtpore in 1826; but he subsequently expressed his attachment to the British government, and his offence was condoned.

Adoption recognised.

The Raja of Kerauli died in 1848 without a natural heir, but, like the Satara Raja, he adopted a son just before his death. Lord Dalhousie was inclined to think that Kerauli, like Satara, had lapsed to the British government; but the Court of Directors decided that Kerauli was a "protected ally," and not a "dependent principality," and accordingly the government of Lord Dalhousie recognised the adopted son as the heir to the Raj.

Nagpore a Mahratta Raj.

In 1853 the Nagpore succession was brought under discussion. The fortunes of this Raj are of peculiar interest. The story begins with Lord Hastings and ends with Lord Dalhousie; but it may be told in the present place as an episode.

British management, 1818-26.

In 1818 the territory of the Bhonsla Rajas was placed at the disposal of the British government. The treacherous Appa Sahib had fled into exile, leaving no son, real or adopted, to succeed him on the throne of Nagpore. Accordingly the ladies of the family were permitted to adopt a boy, who assumed the name of Bhonsla, and was accepted as an infant Raja; and Mr. Richard Jenkins, the Resident at Nagpore, was entrusted with the management of affairs during the minority, and exercised something like uncontrolled powers.

Prosperity of Nagpore.

The management of Mr. Jenkins was denounced in England as a departure from the ruling doctrine of non-intervention; but nevertheless it was attended with singular success. Mr. Jenkins organised a native administration under British management, and did not commit the fatal error of expecting too much.[1] The consequence was that in Nagpore, and in Nagpore alone, outside British territory, disorders were repressed, vexatious taxes abolished, debts liquidated, and expenditure reduced; whilst crime diminished,

[1] There is a well-known couplet by Mat Prior, which English officials in high position would do well to bear in mind in dealing with native subordinates:—

"Be to their virtues very kind,
Be to their faults a little blind."

revenue improved, and a large surplus accumulated in the public treasury.[1] A.D. 1848-1856

Deterioration under native rule, 1826-37.

In 1826 the young Raja attained his majority, and the British management was withdrawn from Nagpore. In 1837 the Raja had grown utterly demoralised; he cared nothing for his people, but spent his whole time, like a little Sardanapalus, in the female apartments of his palace. In spite of this adverse circumstance, the people of Nagpore were less oppressed than those of any other native state in India. The system organised by Mr. Jenkins was much deteriorated, especially in the administration of justice. But the people spoke of "Dunkin Sahib" with affection, and all the middle and lower classes were heartily desirous of British rule.

Annexation of Nagpore, 1853.

In 1853 the Raja of Nagpore died, leaving no son or heir, natural or adopted. Nagpore had been a "dependent principality" ever since 1818, and Lord Dalhousie had to determine whether to permit the widows to adopt a son, and thus make over Nagpore to a Mahratta lad who might have turned out no better than his successor;[2] or to bring

[1] The exponents of the policy of non-intervention had much to say in its favour. The subsidiary system which secured native princes on their thrones, was supposed to have aggravated the evils of native rule by stripping the state of all responsibility, and thus stifling all desire for the improvement of the country and people. The princes of India lost their accustomed stimulants of war and plunder, and sank into apathy, or sought consolation in vicious self-indulgence. Under such circumstances there were grounds for hoping that non-intervention would revive the sense of responsibility, and enable every native principality to recover its lost vitality.

But this lost vitality is a myth. It may have existed in some remote era, some golden age of Rajpút romance; but it is as unknown to history as the exploits of King Arthur and the Knights of the Round Table. It was the dream of the Brahmanical compilers of the Hindu epics, and is as unreal as the fabled stories in the Arabian Nights of the golden reign of Haroun Alraschid. Ever since Europeans became acquainted with India the vitality of native rule has only found expression in predatory wars and administrative extortions; and when at last the princes of India were bound over by the subsidiary alliances to keep the peace, the native states were moribund, and nothing but new blood would impart life or energy to native administrations.

What was really wanted was a guiding influence to open the eyes of native rulers to their duties towards their subjects, and to inspire them with that spirit of emulation which is necessary to awaken them to a higher ambition and loftier aims. After the wars of 1817-18 the princes of India were peculiarly amenable to such influences, and hence the administrative successes of Mr. Jenkins in Nagpore.

[2] The widows of the deceased Raja are said to have adopted a son immediately after his demise, but this was a religious ceremony having

A.D. 1848-1856

Nagpore under a similar administration to that which had proved so successful in the Punjaub. Lord Dalhousie decided on the latter course, and his view was accepted by the Court of Directors. Accordingly Nagpore was incorporated with British territory, and now forms a part of the Central Provinces.

Dealings with the Carnatic and Tanjore families.

Besides the annexation of territories, Lord Dalhousie abolished certain expensive pageants, which had long ceased to exercise any authority or influence, and only proved a dead weight on the public treasury. In 1853 the titular Nawab of the Carnatic died without an heir; and Lord Dalhousie declared the dignity extinct, and withdrew the heavy share of the revenue which had been made over by Lord Wellesley for the maintenance of the pageantry. At the same time pensions were assigned to the different members of the Carnatic family. Shortly afterwards the titular Raja of Tanjore died without heirs, and the family were treated in like fashion. Since then the home government have placed the different pensions on a more liberal footing.

Death of Baji Rao, the last of the Peishwas, 1853.

In 1853, Baji Rao, the ex-Peishwa, was gathered to his fathers. He was the last relic of the old Mahratta empire. He was born in 1775, when Warren Hastings was being dragged into the first Mahratta war. In 1795, at the age of twenty, he became Peishwa of Poona. In 1802 he ran away from Jaswant Rao Holkar, and threw himself into the arms of the English at Bassein, near Bombay. He was restored to Poona by the British army, but forfeited his throne in 1817 by his treacherous outbreak against the British government. From 1818 to 1853, from the age of forty-three to that of seventy-seven, he dreamed away his life in oriental indulgences at Bit' ɔor, on the liberal pension of eighty thousand pounds a year.

Baji Rao left no natural heir. He had adopted a son, who was afterwards known as Nana Sahib. He must have saved a large sum out of his yearly allowance. Nana Sahib

nothing to do with the Raj. Indeed the widows were aware at the time that such an adoption was invalid as regards the Raj without the previous sanction of the British government.

[1] Besides the foregoing annexations the little principality of Jhansi, in Bundelkund, lapsed to the British government in like manner from want of natural heirs. The matter is only of moment from the terrible revenge exacted by the ex-queen during the Sepoy revolt of 1857.

A.D. 1848-1856

Pretensions of Nana Sahib rejected.

acknowledged that the accumulations amounted to nearly three hundred thousand pounds sterling; but it was subsequently discovered that they aggregated half a million. Nevertheless, Nana Sahib prayed for the continuation of the pension, and pretended that it had been granted, not by way of grace or favour, but as compensation to the ex-Peishwa for his loss of territory. Such a preposterous claim was beneath discussion; but it was taken into consideration by Lord Dalhousie and the Court of Directors, and was only rejected after the fullest inquiry.

Hyderabad: origin of the Nizam's Contingent.

The dealings of Lord Dalhousie with the Nizam of Hyderabad demand a passing notice. By the treaty of 1801 the Nizam was bound to furnish a military contingent in time of war of 6,000 infantry and 9,000 horse. But the rabble soldiery which he supplied during the subsequent wars proved to be worse than useless in the field. Accordingly it was agreed by mutual consent that a permanent force should be maintained by the Nizam, reduced to half the number of native troops, but to be disciplined and commanded by British officers. This new body of troops was known as the Nizam's Contingent, as distinguished from the Hyderabad Subsidiary Force.[1]

Accumulated debt of the Nizam.

From a very early period the Nizam had failed to provide the necessary funds for the maintenance of the Contingent. From time to time large advances were made by the British government to meet the current expenditure, until a debt accumulated of half a million sterling. The Nizam might have escaped this obligation by disbanding the Contingent; but this he repeatedly and obstinately refused to do, and indeed the force was necessary for the maintenance of peace and order in his own territories. Again, he might have disbanded the hordes of foreign mercenaries, Arabs and Rohillas, which he kept up under the name of an army, and which were a burden upon his treasury, a terror to his subjects, and useless for all military purposes. But he was as obstinate upon this point as upon the other. At last, in 1843, he was told by Lord Ellenborough that unless the debt was liquidated and the necessary funds were provided regularly for the future, the British government would take over territory and revenue as security for the payment.

[1] The Nizam's Contingent on the new footing consisted of 5,000 infantry, 2,000 cavalry, and four field batteries.

A.D. 1848-1856

Drift.

This threat seems to have created some alarm in Hyderabad. Chandu Lal resigned the post of minister, and the Nizam attempted to carry on the administration alone, but his efforts were fitful and desultory. Meanwhile mere dribblets of the debt were paid off, and the Resident was amused with excuses and promises; and in this fashion matters drifted on.

Cession of Berar, 1853

At last Lord Dalhousie insisted on a cession of sufficient territory to provide for the maintenance of the Nizam's Contingent. He would not touch the hereditary dominions of the Nizam; he merely took over the territory of Berar, which Lord Wellesley had given to the Nizam in 1803, after the conquest of the Raja of Nagpore. Accordingly Berar was brought under British administration; and since then all surplus revenue accruing from the improvements in the revenue system has been made over to the Nizam's treasury.

Oude: oppression and anarchy, 1801-1847.

The last important measure in the career of Lord Dalhousie was the annexation of Oude. The story of Oude is an unpleasant episode in the history of British India. In 1764 the English conquered Oude, but Lord Clive gave it back to the Nawab Vizier. In 1801 Lord Wellesley took over one half of the territory to provide for the defence of Hindustan against Afghans, French, and Mahrattas. From the days of Lord Wellesley to those of Lord Dalhousie Oude was a millstone round the neck of the British government. Every Governor-General in turn condemned the administration of Oude as tyrannical, extortionate, and corrupt to the last degree; each in turn denounced the reigning Nawab Vizier, and yet shrank from the distasteful task of taking the necessary steps for carrying out a radical reform. Lord Hastings tried polite remonstrance; he wished, he said, to treat the Nawab Vizier like a gentleman; and the result was that the Nawab Vizier assumed the title of "king," in order to place himself on a par with the so-called king of Delhi. In 1831 Lord William Bentinck, the friend of native princes, threatened to assume the direct administration of Oude, but ultimately left India without doing it. From the day of his departure the introduction of British rule in Oude was a mere question of time. It was one of those painful operations which no Governor-General liked to perform; but it was absolutely necessary to the well-being, not only of the people of Oude, but of the British empire in India. In 1847 Lord Hardinge, who had laboured to save the Sikh government in the Punjab, was so aghast at the desolation of Oude, that he solemnly warned the king that the British government would assume the management of his country within two years unless he employed the interval in carrying out a complete reform in his administration. A.D. 1848-1856

Sleeman's report, 1851.

In 1851 Colonel Sleeman, the British Resident at Lucknow, made a tour through Oude, and reported on the state of the country. The people were at the mercy of the soldiery and landholders. Whilst Oude was protected by British troops from every possible foe, a standing army of seventy thousand men was kept up by the king; and as the pay of the troops was very small, and nearly always in arrears, they were driven to prey upon the helpless villagers. It is needless to dwell on the plunder, outrage and crime that were the natural consequence. The wretched inhabitants complained that brigands and outlaws were sometimes merciful; but that the king's troops never knew how to pity or how to spare. The Talúkdars, or landholders, built forts throughout the country, and levied revenue and black mail, like the Afghan chiefs who preyed on Hindustan before the days of Akbar. All this while the king was shut up in his palace; he was seen by no one except women, musicians, and buffoons. The government was a monstrous system of corruption, under which every office was bought with money, and every official was left to reimburse himself as fast as he could by oppression and extortion. Reform was out of the question; every evil had been festering in the body politic for the greater part of a century, and nothing but new blood could save the country from destruction.

Annexation of Oude, 1856.

Lord Dalhousie was anxious to deal gently with the king of Oude. The family had always been loyal to the British government, and had always done their best to help it in the hour of need. Lord Dalhousie would have left the king in the possession of the sovereignty whilst taking over the direct management of his territories. But the patience of the Court of Directors was worn out; they were determined to annex the country and abolish the throne; and in 1856, being the last year of Lord Dalhousie's administration, the sovereignty of the kings of Oude was brought to a close.

During the administration of Lord Dalhousie the hill tribes of Bengal forced themselves on the attention of the British government. As far back as 1832 there had been a

A.D. 1848-1856

Outbreak of hill-tribes: Koles and Santáls.

strange rising of the Koles, an aboriginal tribe of Western Bengal, who at some remote period had been driven into the hills by the Hindu settlers, and there maintained their primitive language, habits, and superstitions, down to modern times. The Koles had been troubled by British laws and exasperated by encroaching Zemindárs. Accordingly they broke out in rebellion, and committed many outrages before they were repressed. Lord William Bentinck withdrew the Koles from the operation of the ordinary laws, and placed their country in charge of a special commissioner. Since then the Koles had advanced in civilisation and prosperity, and large numbers had been converted to Christianity. In 1855 there was an insurrection of another aboriginal tribe, known as the Santáls, who inhabit the hill ranges of Rajmahal on the north-west frontier of Bengal proper. They had been harassed by the civil suits of Bengali money-lenders, and they advanced into the plains, to the number of thirty thousand men, to make war upon the British government with pickaxes and poisoned arrows. The British authorities were taken by surprise. The Santáls began the work of pillage and murder, and spread abroad a wild alarm before a British force could be marched against them. The outbreak, however, was soon suppressed, and Lord Dalhousie dealt with the Santáls in the same way that Lord William Bentinck had dealt with the Koles, namely, by placing them in charge of a special commissioner.

CHAPTER XXV.

SEPOY MUTINIES: LORD CANNING.

A.D. 1856 TO 1858.

LORD CANNING was forty-four years of age when he succeeded Lord Dalhousie as Governor-General of India. He had seen something of official life; he had been Under-Secretary for Foreign Affairs under Sir Robert Peel, and Postmaster-General under Lord Aberdeen and Lord Palmerston. He was a good administrator—moderate, cautious, conscientious, and "safe"; and as such he was well fitted to carry on, slowly but surely, the great work of moral and material progress begun by Lord Dalhousie.

A.D. 1856

Lord Canning, Governor-General, 1856-62.

In 1856 the political atmosphere of India was without a cloud. A few events occurred, but they were of small historical interest, and cannot be regarded as in any way foreshadowing the storm which was about to burst upon the plains of Hindustan.

Cloudless sky, 1856.

The annexation of Oude had been carried out with more harshness than Lord Dalhousie had intended. The king removed from Lukhnow to Calcutta, and settled down with his women and dependants in the suburbs at Garden Reach, whilst the queen-mother and heir apparent went on a bootless mission to England. Meanwhile an administration, like that which had proved so successful in the Punjab, was introduced into Oude; but it did not work smoothly. The new rulers forgot that Oude was not a conquered country like the Punjab; and that the Oude Talúkdars, bad as they may have been, were not rebels and traitors against the British government. Consequently the leading officers

English administration in Oude: Henry Lawrence.

A.D. 1856-1857

disputed amongst themselves; and there were many complaints of severity towards native officials and landholders. At last, early in 1857, Sir Henry Lawrence was appointed Chief Commissioner of Oude, and it was believed that all would soon be well.

Moghul kings of Delhi. 1803-56.

The status of the so-called kings of Delhi was placed upon a new footing. Ever since 1803, when Shah Alam was taken under British protection by Lord Wellesley, the kings had been without a history. The family dwelt in the old Moghul palace at Delhi, and multiplied in Muhammadan fashion. Palace life was made up of vain attempts to revive the dignity and pomp of a bygone age, or to obtain an increase of pension from the British government. All political vitality had died out of the family. Deaths, marriages, and births followed in dreary monotony, varied by quarrels and intrigues, which had little meaning or interest outside the palace walls.

Mischievous influences at Delhi.

The continued residence of the Moghul family at Delhi infected the whole capital. The Muhammadan population was more disaffected towards the British rule than in any other city in India. Lord Wellesley would have removed the family to Bengal at the beginning of the century; but the poor old pageant of that day clung to Delhi with the pertinacity of second childhood, and it seemed cruel to remove him in his old age. Since then two generations had passed away; the Moghul court had become an antiquated nuisance, and Lord Dalhousie determined to banish it for ever.

Proposed removal to the Kútub.

The reigning king at Delhi was an infirm old man named Bahadur Shah. The heir apparent was his grandson; and Lord Dalhousie agreed to recognise the grandson as the successor to the pageant throne, and to make some addition to his pension, on the condition that he should clear out of Delhi on the death of his grandfather, and take up his abode at the Kútub—an old royal residence near Delhi, which had been founded in the thirteenth century.[1] But Bahadur Shah married a young wife in his old age, and she gave birth to a son; and henceforth the young queen strained every nerve to secure the pageant throne for her boy, after the manner of younger wives since patriarchal times.

In July, 1856, the heir apparent died suddenly in the palace.

[1] See *ante*, page 79.

There is no moral doubt that he was poisoned, and that the young queen was implicated in the crime. The catastrophe was suspiciously followed by applications from old Bahadur Shah that the son of his favourite wife might be recognised by the Governor-General as the heir and successor to the throne. But the request was refused. An elder brother stood in the way, and Lord Canning recognised this elder brother as heir apparent, but without any bargaining or agreement. When Bahadur Shah died the new king was to remove to the Kútub by the simple decree of the British government.

A.D. 1856-1857

Plots and intrigues at Delhi.

Wrath of the young queen.

The wrath of the favourite queen may be left to the imagination. She is said to have been a daughter of the house of Nadir Shah, and the hereditary ambition of the family was burning in her brain. She intrigued in all directions against the British government; possibly with the Shah of Persia, with whom Great Britain was at war; possibly with Kuzzilbash chiefs at Kábul; but the extent and character of her plots must be left to conjecture. No one dreamt that the mortified princess could in any way work mischief to the British government; and to this day it is difficult to believe that she was in any way the originator of the sepoy mutiny.

Persian war, 1856-57.

Meantime there were more difficulties with Persia respecting Herát. The death of Yar Muhammad Khan, in 1852, was followed by troubles in Herát; and the province became a bone of contention between the Shah of Persia and old Dost Muhammad Khan, of Kábul. At last the Shah moved an army to Herát and captured the fortress, contrary to his treaty with the British government. Accordingly England declared war against Persia. An expedition was sent from Bombay to the Persian Gulf under the command of Sir James Outram. The alliance with Kábul was strengthened;[1] four thousand stand of arms were presented to Dost Muhammad Khan, and he was promised a subsidy of ten thousand pounds a month so long as the Persian war lasted. The capture of Bushire by the English and the victory at Mohamrah brought the Shah to his senses. He withdrew from Afghanistan, and renounced all pretensions

[1] The hostility of Dost Muhammad Khan during the second Sikh war had been condoned; and a treaty of friendship was concluded by Lord Dalhousie with the Kábul ruler in 1855.

A.D. 1856-1857

to Herát; and in March, 1857, peace was concluded between Great Britain and Persia.

Evil rumours and prophecies.

About this time there is said to have been rumours of a coming danger to British rule in India. In some parts of the country chupaties, or cakes, were circulated in a mysterious manner from village to village. Prophecies were also rife that in 1857 the Company's Raj would come to an end. Lord Canning has been blamed for not taking alarm at these proceedings; but something of the kind has always been going on in India.[1] Cakes or cocoa-nuts are given away in solemn fashion; and as the villagers are afraid to keep them or eat them, the circulation goes on to the end of the chapter. Then again holy men and prophets have always been common in India. They foretell pestilence and famine, the downfall of British rule, or the destruction of the whole world. They are often supposed to be endowed with supernatural powers, and to be impervious to bullets; but these phenomena invariably disappear whenever they come in contact with Europeans, especially as all such characters are liable to be treated as vagrants without visible means of subsistence.[2]

[1] A great deal of alarm has been written and spoken as regards native intrigues. As a matter of fact, plots and intrigues of one sort or another are the daily life of the natives of India. There are more plots and intrigues in a single establishment of native servants than in a hundred English households. An Englishman in India, who chooses to study the character of his servants, will know more in a few months of native thoughts and ways than he can learn in books from the study of a lifetime. A still better insight into native character may be obtained in government schools. The author is conscious that during the three or four years that he held the post of Professor of Moral Philosophy and Logic in the Madras Presidency College, he gained a larger knowledge of Hindu life, and a greater respect for Hindu character, than during the many years he has since spent in official and literary duties. The warm friendships amongst young Hindus, their devotion to the wishes of their parents, and the unreserved trust which they place in their English instructors who take the trouble to win their confidence, have never perhaps been sufficiently appreciated.

[2] There are few human beings so helpless or so ignorant that they cannot prophesy the end of all things. Prophecies however are not confined to orientals. The great German traveller, Carsten Niebuhr, who visited Bombay in 1763, two years after the battle of Paniput, was guilty of the following oracular utterance, which reads somewhat strangely by the light of later history:—"The power of the Muhammadans indeed becomes daily less; and there are at present some

A.D. 1857

Greased cartridges.

One dangerous story, however, got abroad in the early part of 1857, which ought to have been stopped at once, and for which the military authorities were wholly and solely to blame. The Enfield rifle was being introduced; it required new cartridges, which in England were greased with the fat of beef or pork. The military authorities in India, with strange indifference to the prejudices of sepoys, ordered the cartridges to be prepared at Calcutta in like manner; forgetting that the fat of pigs was hateful to the Muhammadans, whilst the fat of cows was still more horrible in the eyes of the Hindus.

Panic at Barrackpore.

The excitement began at Barrackpore, sixteen miles from Calcutta At this station there were four regiments of sepoys, and no Europeans except the regimental officers.[1] One day a low caste native, known as a Laskar, asked a Brahman sepoy for a drink of water from his brass pot. The Brahman refused, as it would defile his pot. The Laskar retorted that the Brahman was already defiled by biting cartridges which had been greased with cow's fat. This vindictive taunt was based on truth. Laskars had been employed at Calcutta in preparing the new cartridges, and the man was possibly one of them. The taunt created a wild panic at Barrackpore. Strange, however, to say, none of the new cartridges had been issued to the sepoys; and had this been promptly explained to the men, and the sepoys left to grease their own cartridges, the alarm might have died out. But the explanation was delayed until the

Hindu princes who may restore the nation to its ancient splendour. The Mahrattas have successfully begun a project which has this aspect. It is the exorbitant power of the English that at present retards the progressive improvement of the Hindus. But when this colossal statue, whose feet are of clay, and which has been raised by conquering merchants, shall be broken in pieces, an event which may fall out sooner than is supposed, then shall Hindustan become again a flourishing country." The learned German must have been utterly ignorant of Mahratta rule, and seems to have formed an idea out of his moral consciousness.

[1] A sepoy regiment of infantry in the Bengal army was at this time composed of 1,000 privates, 120 non-commissioned officers, and 20 commissioned officers, all natives. It was divided into ten companies, each containing 100 privates, 12 non-commissioned officers, and 2 commissioned officers. The non-commissioned officers were known as naiks and havildars, corresponding to corporals and sergeants. The commissioned officers were known as jemadars and subahdars, corresponding

A.D. 1857 — whole of the Bengal army was smitten with the groundless fear; and then, when it was too late, the authorities protested too much, and the terror-stricken sepoys refused to believe them.[1]

Credulity of sepoys. The sepoys have proved themselves brave under fire, and loyal to their salt in sharp extremities; but they are the most credulous and excitable soldiery in the world. They regarded steam and electricity as so much magic;[2] and they fondly believed that the British government was binding India with chains, when it was only laying down railway lines and telegraph wires. The Enfield rifle was a new mystery; and the busy brains of the sepoys were soon at work to divine the motive of the English in greasing cartridges with cow's fat. They had always taken to themselves the sole credit of having conquered India for the Company; and they now imagined that the English wanted them to conquer Persia and China. Accordingly, they suspected that Lord Canning was going to make them as strong as Europeans by destroying caste, forcing them to

to lieutenants and captains. The European officers corresponded to those in English regiments.

The sepoy regiment was never quartered in barracks, but in lines. Every regiment occupied ten rows of thatched huts, a company to each row. In front of each row was a small circular building for storing arms and accoutrements after they had been cleaned.

The European officers lived in bungalows, or thatched houses near the lines, but too far off to control the movements of the men during the heat of the day. In order however to maintain continuous European supervision, two European sergeants were allowed to every regiment to live within the lines, and report day by day all that was going on to the European adjutant.

[1] There is however some excuse for the military authorities even in the matter of greased cartridges. Bazar rumours are often flying about in India, and causing the utmost alarm, whilst any attempt at authoritative contradiction on the part of government only gives further currency to the fable, and increases the panic. If a bridge is about to be built, it is noised abroad that children's heads are wanted for the foundations, and then not a child is to be seen in the streets for weeks. This has been of common occurrence, even within the last twenty years. Again, in Lord Auckland's time, a rumour got abroad that the blood of hill-men was required to restore the Governor-General to pristine youth; and all the coolies and hill-men at Simla suddenly ran away. Contradiction would have been useless in such extreme cases; but still, if undertaken in time, it might have quieted the minds of the sepoys.

[2] To this day the Asiatic Museum at Calcutta is only known to natives as the "magic house."

become Christians, and making them eat beef and drink beer. A.D. 1857

The story of the greased cartridges, with all its absurd embellishments, ran up the Ganges and Jumna to Benares, Allahabad, Agra, Delhi, and the great cantonment at Meerut; whilst another current of lies ran back again from Meerut to Barrackpore. It was noised abroad that the bones of cows and pigs had been ground into powder, and thrown into wells and mingled with flour and butter, in order to destroy the caste of the masses and convert them to Christianity.[1]

Sepoy grievances.

The stories of sinister designs on the part of the English were sharpened by sepoy grievances. Very much had been done for the well-being of the native army; the sepoys had become puffed up and unmanageable; and they complained of wrongs, or what appeared in their eyes to be wrongs, which Englishmen cannot easily understand. When quartered in foreign countries, such as Sinde and the Punjab, they had been granted an extra allowance, known as batta; but when Sinde and the Punjab became British territory the batta was withdrawn. Numbers, again, had been recruited in Oude, and they had another secret grievance. So long as Oude was under Muhammadan rule, every complaint from an Oude sepoy, that his family or kindred were oppressed, was forwarded to the British Resident at Lukhnow, and promptly redressed. When, however, the country was brought under British administration the complainants were referred to the civil courts. This was resented by the sepoy as a grave indignity. He was no longer the great man of the family or village; he could no longer demand the special interference of the British Resident in their behalf. Accordingly he was exasperated at the introduction of British rule in Oude; at the same time he never manifested the slightest desire for the restoration of the ex-king.

[1] There was some excuse for this credulity. Forced conversions had been common enough under Muhammadan rule. Aurangzeb destroyed pagodas and idols, and compelled all servants of government to become Muhammadans. Tippu Sultan converted crowds of Brahmans to Islam by compelling them to swallow cow's flesh. The Hindu sepoys, who had been taken prisoners by the Afghans during the Kábul war, were forced to become Muhammadans.

A.D. 1857

Incendiary fires at Barrackpore.

In January, 1857, there were incendiary fires at Barrackpore. In February, General Hearsey, who commanded the Presidency division, expostulated with the sepoys on the absurdity of their fears as regarded their religion; but his words were without authority, and no one heeded them.

Mutiny at Barrackpore.

Towards the end of February a detachment of the 34th Native Infantry at Barrackpore arrived at Berhampore, a hundred and twenty miles up country, near Murshedabad. Accordingly the sepoys from Barrackpore told the story of the cartridges to their comrades of the 19th Native Infantry, which was stationed at Berhampore. A day or two afterwards the sepoys of the 19th refused to receive the cartridges that were served out to them; and at night-time they seized their arms, shouted defiance, and created a disturbance. Unfortunately there were no European soldiers at Berhampore; indeed there was only one European regiment in the whole line of country from Barrackpore to Patna, a distance of four hundred miles; and half of that was quartered at Fort William at Calcutta, and the other half at Dumdum, six miles from Calcutta.[1] Colonel Mitchell, the officer in command at Berhampore, had no force to bring to bear upon the mutinous infantry except a detachment of native cavalry and a battery of native artillery; and it was exceedingly doubtful whether they would act against their fellow-countrymen. However, the 19th was not ripe for revolt; and after some remonstrances the sepoys laid down their arms and returned to the lines.

Outbreak of Mungal Pandy at Barrackpore.

In March the 84th Europeans was brought away from Rangoon to the river Hughli. With this additional strength, Lord Canning resolved to take action. Accordingly the 19th was marched from Berhampore to Barrackpore to be disbanded. Before it reached its destination there was much excitement in the lines of the 34th, which probably originated in the sympathies of the sepoys for their comrades who were coming from Berhampore. A sepoy, named Mungal Pandy, walked about the lines with a loaded pistol, calling upon his comrades to rise, and threatening to shoot the first European

[1] There was also one European regiment at Dinapore, near Patna, and another at Agra. Beyond these there was nothing but a handful of European artillerymen and a few invalided soldiers of the Company's European army. The largest European force in Hindustan was stationed at Meerut, forty miles from Delhi.

that appeared. Lieutenant Baugh, the adjutant of the regiment, rode to the parade-ground, followed by the European sergeant and a Muhammadan orderly. Mungal Pandy fired at him, wounded his horse, and brought Lieutenant Baugh to the ground. A scuffle ensued; Baugh received a severe blow from a sword; whilst a guard of sepoys under a jemadar stood by and did nothing. The sergeant came up breathless, called on the jemadar for help, and tried to seize Mungal Pandy; but he too was struck down. To crown all, the jemadar came up with his twenty sepoys and began to beat the heads of the two Europeans with the butt ends of their muskets. At this moment Mungal Pandy was arrested by the Muhammadan orderly; and General Hearsey galloped up, pistol in hand, and ordered the sepoy guard back to their posts, threatening to shoot the first man who disobeyed orders. The sepoys were overawed by the general, and the disaffection was stayed. Mungal Pandy saw that his game was up, and tried to shoot himself, but failed. A day or two afterwards the European regiment from Rangoon was marched to Barrackpore; and the 19th Native Infantry arrived from Berhampore, and was disbanded without further trouble. In the following April Mungal Pandy and the mutinous jemadar were brought to trial, convicted, and hanged.

Gathering of the storm, April, 1857.

For a brief interval it was hoped that the disaffection was suppressed. Excitement manifested itself in various ways at different stations throughout the length of Hindustan and the Punjab—at Benares, Lukhnow, Agra, Umballa, and Sealkote. In some stations there were incendiary fires; in others the sepoys were wanting in their usual respect to their European officers. But it was believed that the storm was spending itself, and that the dark clouds were passing away.

Explosion at Lukhnow, 3rd May: prompt suppression by Henry Lawrence.

Suddenly, on the 3rd of May, there was an explosion at Lukhnow. A regiment of Oude Irregular Infantry, previously in the service of the king, broke out in mutiny, and began to threaten their European officers. Sir Henry Lawrence, the new Chief Commissioner, had a European regiment at his disposal, namely the 32nd Foot. That same evening he ordered out the regiment, and a battery of eight guns manned by Europeans, together with four sepoy regiments, three of infantry and one of cavalry. With

A.D. 1857

this force he proceeded to the lines of the mutineers, about seven miles off. The Oude Irregulars were taken by surprise; they saw infantry and cavalry on either side, and the European guns in front. They were ordered to lay down their arms, and they obeyed. At this moment the artillery lighted their port fires. The mutineers were seized with a panic, and rushed away in the darkness; but the ringleaders and most of their followers were pursued and arrested by the native infantry and cavalry, and confined pending trial. Subsequently it transpired that the native regiments sympathised with the mutineers, and would have shown it but for their dread of Henry Lawrence and the Europeans. The energetic action of Lawrence sufficed to maintain order for another month in Oude. Meanwhile the 34th Native Infantry was disbanded at Barrackpore, and again it was hoped that the disaffection was stayed.

Meerut: superior European force.

The demon of mutiny was only scotched. Within a week of the outbreak at Lukhnow, the great military station of Meerut was in a blaze. Meerut was only forty miles from Delhi, and the largest cantonment in India. There were three regiments of sepoys,—two of infantry and one of cavalry; but there were enough Europeans to scatter four times the number; namely, a battalion of the 60th Rifles, a regiment of Dragoon Guards known as the Carabineers, two troops of horse artillery, and a light field battery.

Disaffection.

In spite of the presence of Europeans there were more indications of excitement at Meerut than at any other station in the north-west. At Meerut the story of the greased cartridges had been capped by the story of the bone-dust; and there were the same kind of incendiary fires, the same lack of respect towards European officers, and the same whispered resolve not to touch the cartridges, as at Barrackpore. The station was commanded by General Hewitt, whose advancing years unfitted him to cope with the storm which was bursting upon Hindustan.

Mutiny at Meerut: imprisonment of the mutineers.

The regiment of sepoy cavalry at Meerut was strongly suspected of disaffection; accordingly it was resolved to put the men to the test. On the 6th of May it was paraded in the presence of the European force, and cartridges were served out; not the greased abominations from Calcutta, but the old ones which had been used times innumerable by the sepoys and their fathers. But the men were terrified and obstinate, and eighty-five stood out and refused to take the cartridges. The offenders were at once arrested, and tried by a court-martial of native officers; they were found guilty, and sentenced to various periods of imprisonment, but recommended for mercy. General Hewitt saw no grounds for mercy, excepting in the case of eleven young troopers; and on Saturday, the 9th of May, the sentences were carried out. The men were brought on parade, stripped of their uniforms, and loaded with irons. They implored the general for mercy, and finding it hopeless, began to reproach their comrades; but no one dared to strike a blow in the presence of loaded cannon and rifles. At last the prisoners were carried off and placed in a jail, not in charge of European soldiers, but under a native guard.

A.D. 1857

Terrible rising at Meerut; Sunday, 10th May.

The military authorities at Meerut seem to have been under a spell. The next day was Sunday, the 10th of May, and the hot sun rose with its usual glare in the Indian sky. The European barracks were at a considerable distance from the native lines, and the intervening space was covered with shops and houses surrounded by trees and gardens. Consequently the Europeans in the barracks knew nothing of what was going on in the native quarter. Meanwhile there were commotions in the sepoy lines and neighbouring bazaars. The sepoys were taunted by the loose women of the place with permitting their comrades to be imprisoned and fettered. At the same time they were smitten with a mad fear that the European soldiers were to be let loose upon them. The Europeans at Meerut saw nothing and heard nothing. Nothing was noted on that Sunday morning, excepting the absence of native servants from many of the houses, and that was supposed to be accidental. Morning service was followed by the midday heats, and at five o'clock in the afternoon the Europeans were again preparing for church. Suddenly there was an alarm of fire, followed by a volley of musketry, discordant yells, the clattering of cavalry, and the bugle sounding an alarm. The sepoys had worked themselves up to a frenzy of excitement; the prisoners were released with a host of jail birds; the native infantry joined the native cavalry, and the colonel of one of the regiments was shot by the sepoys of the other. Inspired by a wild fear and fury, the sepoys ran about murdering or wounding

A.D. 1857

every European they met, and setting houses on fire, amidst deafening shouts and uproar.

Fatal delays.

Meanwhile there were fatal delays in turning out the Europeans. The Rifles were paraded for church, and time was lost in getting arms and serving out ball cartridges. The Carabineers were absurdly put through a roll call, and then lost their way amongst the shops and gardens. Meanwhile European officers were being butchered by the infuriated sepoys. Gentlemen and ladies were fired at or sabred whilst hurrying back in a panic from church. Flaming houses and crashing timbers were filling all hearts with terror, and the shades of evening were falling upon the general havoc and turmoil, when the Europeans reached the native lines and found that the sepoys had gone, no one knew whither.

Flight of the sepoys to Delhi: mutiny turned to revolt.

The truth was soon told. The mutiny had become a revolt: the sepoys were on the way to Delhi to proclaim the old Moghul as sovereign of Hindustan; and there was no Gillespie to gallop after them and crush the revolt at its outset, as had been done at Vellore half a century before. One thing, however, was done. There were no European regiments at Delhi; nothing but three regiments of sepoy infantry, and a battery of native artillery. The station was commanded by Brigadier Graves; and there were no Europeans under his orders excepting the officers and sergeants attached to the three native corps. Accordingly telegrams were sent to Brigadier Graves to tell him that the mutineers were on their way to Delhi.

Monday morning at Delhi.

Monday at Delhi was worse than the Sunday at Meerut. The British cantonment was situated on a rising ground about two miles from the city, which was known as the Ridge. The great magazine, containing immense stores of ammunition, was situated in the heart of the city. One of the three sepoy regiments was on duty in the city; the other two remained in the cantonment on the Ridge.

Approach of the rebels.

The approach to Delhi from Meerut was defended by the little river Hindun, which was traversed by a small bridge. It was proposed to procure a couple of cannon from the magazine and place them on the bridge; but before this could be done the rebel cavalry from Meerut were seen crossing the river, and were subsequently followed by the rebel infantry. The magazine remained in charge of

Lieutenant Willoughby of the Bengal Artillery. He was associated with two other officers, and six conductors and sergeants; the rest of the establishment was composed entirely of natives. A.D. 1857

Preparations for defence.

Brigadier Graves did his best to protect the city and cantonment until the arrival of the expected Europeans from Meerut. Indeed, throughout the morning and greater part of the afternoon every one in Delhi was expecting the arrival of the Europeans. Brigadier Graves ordered all the non-military residents, including ladies and children, to repair to Flagstaff Tower,—a round building of solid brickwork at some distance from the city. Large detachments of sepoys were sent from the Ridge to the Kashmír gate, under the command of their European officers, to help the sepoy regiment on duty to maintain order in the city.

Sepoy regiments join the rebels.

Presently the rebel troops from Meerut came up, accompanied by the insurgent rabble of Delhi. The English officers prepared to charge them, and gave the order to fire, but some of the sepoys refused to obey, or only fired into the air. The English officers held on, expecting the European soldiers from Meerut. The sepoys hesitated to join the rebels, out of dread of the coming Europeans. At last the Delhi sepoys threw in their lot with the rebels, and shot down their own officers. The revolt spread throughout the whole city; and the suspense of the English on the Ridge, and at Flagstaff Tower, began to give way to the agony of despair.

Explosion of the magazine.

Suddenly, at four o'clock in the afternoon, a column of white smoke arose from the city, and an explosion was heard far and wide. Willoughby and his eight associates had held out to the last, waiting and hoping for the coming of the Europeans. They had closed and barricaded the gates of the magazine; and they had posted six-pounders at the gates, loaded with double charges of grape, and laid a train to the powder magazine. Messengers came in the name of Bahadur Shah to demand the surrender of the magazine, but no answer was returned. The enemy approached, and raised ladders against the walls; whilst the native establishment escaped over some sheds and joined the rebels. At this crisis the guns opened fire. Round after round of grape made fearful havoc on the mass of humanity that was heaving and surging round the gates. At last the ammunition

A.D. 1857

was exhausted. No one could leave the guns to bring up more shot. The mutineers were pouring in on all sides. Lieutenant Willoughby gave the signal; Conductor Scully fired the train; and with one tremendous upheaval the magazine was blown into the air, together with fifteen hundred rebels. Not one of the gallant nine had expected to escape. Willoughby and three others got away, scorched, maimed, bruised, and nearly insensible; but Scully and his comrades were never seen again. Willoughby died of his injuries six weeks afterwards, whilst India and Europe were ringing with his name.

Tragedies within the palace.

All this while bloody tragedies were taking place within the palace at Delhi. The rebels from Meerut were quartering themselves in the royal precincts, and murdering every European they could find. Mr. Fraser the commissioner, Mr. Hutchinson the collector, and Captain Douglas, who commanded the palace guards, were all slaughtered within the palace walls. So was an English chaplain, with his wife, daughter, and another young lady, all of whom had been residing as guests with Captain Douglas. Fifty Christian people—men, women, and children—who had been captured by the rebels and thrown as prisoners in the palace dungeons, were butchered in cold blood by the order of the king.[1]

Flight of the English from Delhi.

On the evening of that terrible Monday all was lost. The city of Delhi was in the hands of the rebels. The so-called royal family, which had been maintained by the generosity of the British government for more than half a century, had joined the rebel sepoys. Brigadier Graves and the surviving officers on the Ridge, and all the anxious fugitives in Flagstaff Tower, were compelled to fly for their lives. Their subsequent trials and sufferings were amongst the most touching episodes in the story of the great convulsion. Meanwhile the European regiments which might have saved them, and saved Delhi, were kept at Meerut to guard the barracks and treasury. The greased cartridges had created the panic and brought about the mutiny; but it was the incapacity of the military authorities at Meerut that raised the revolt in Hindustan.

[1] The old king, Bahadur Shah, has been held responsible for these murders, but his vindictive queen was probably more to blame. Her son, a mere lad at the time, was appointed vizier to his father.

A.D. 1857

The revolution at Delhi opened the eyes of Lord Canning to the gravity of the crisis. Hitherto his sympathies had been with the sepoys. An ignorant and credulous soldiery had been thrown into a panic, and had been worked into a state of perilous excitement by intriguing Brahmans and fanatical Múllas, as well as by secret agents and alarmists of all kinds. But now the excitement had culminated in intoxication and madness; the sepoys were thirsting for the blood of Europeans; and pity was changed to indignation and horror. Accordingly Lord Canning telegraphed for European regiments from every quarter—from Bombay and Burma, from Madras and Ceylon—to crush a rebellion which was establishing a reign of terror in Hindustan.

Change in Lord Canning.

The sepoy mutiny at Barrackpore might possibly have been crushed at the outset by physical force. In 1824, at the beginning of the Burmese war, there was a similar mutiny at the same cantonment. Three sepoy regiments had been ordered to Chittagong, but refused to march. They had been frightened by rumours of the bad climate of Burma, and the magical arts which were said to be practised by the Burmese. There had also been some difficulties about transport, and they demanded an extra allowance, known as double batta. Sir Edward Paget was Commander-in-chief in Bengal. He marched to Barrackpore with two regiments of Europeans and a detachment of artillery. He paraded the disaffected regiments in the presence of the Europeans, and loaded his guns with grape. The sepoys were told that they must either begin the march or ground their arms. They replied with defiant shouts. Then the fatal order was given, and the guns opened fire on the disaffected soldiery. Eleven sepoys only were killed, but the remainder broke up and fled in a panic of terror. Sir Edward Paget was much censured, but a generation passed away before there was another mutiny.

Mutiny of 1824 stopped by grape-shot.

Whether Paget was right or wrong, it would have been a blunder and a crime to have taken such an extreme measure at the outset of the disaffection in 1857. Indeed, Lord Canning indignantly refused to contemplate such measures; and by so doing he saved the reputation of the British nation. But when the sepoy rebels set up the Moghul at Delhi as their nominal sovereign, the security of the population of India was at stake. In other words, the

Empire and people at stake in 1857.

A.D. 1857 — establishment of the supremacy of the British government at the earliest possible date was necessary, not only for the safety of the British empire in India, but for the salvation of the masses.

Revolt of the Bengal army. The progress of the revolt throws no further light on its origin or character. Station after station followed the example of Meerut. The sepoys seem to have all been infected by the same delirious fever; they rose in mutiny, shot down their officers in most cases, set the buildings on fire, plundered the treasury, and then rushed off to Delhi. Wherever, however, the Europeans were in any force, and were brought directly to bear upon the mutineers regardless of red tape and routine, the station was either saved from destruction, or the mischief was reduced to a minimum.

Political element. It would be tedious and needless to tell the story of the sepoy revolt so far as it was a mere military mutiny, with Delhi for its head-quarters. But at three stations the mutiny was more or less of a political character, which imparts an individuality to the history: namely, at Lukhnow, at Jhansi, and at Cawnpore.

Lukhnow: the Residency and Muchi Bawun. The city of Lukhnow, the capital of Oude, extends four miles along the right bank of the river Goomti. All the principal buildings, including the British Residency, were situated between the city and the river. The Residency was a large walled inclosure, comprising not only the mansion of the Chief Commissioner, but several houses and underground buildings on a large scale. Near it was a strong turreted, castellated structure known as the Muchi Bawun.

The city and cantonment. Ever since the explosion at Lukhnow on the 3rd of May, Sir Henry Lawrence had been incessantly occupied in taking precautionary measures against an outbreak which he knew to be inevitable. On one side of the Residency was a disaffected city, the homes of palace parasites, who had been deprived of their means of subsistence by the breaking up of the native court and departure of the royal family to Calcutta. On the opposite bank of the river Goomti was the native cantonment, occupied by British sepoys as evilly disposed towards the English as the disaffected rabble of Lukhnow. Accordingly Sir Henry Lawrence saw that the work before him was to prevent mutiny in the cantonment and rebellion in the city; and to make every preparation

A.D. 1857

for a successful defence in the event of a general insurrection.

Sepoys and Europeans.

The native force at Lukhnow consisted of the three sepoy regiments of infantry, and one of cavalry; there was also a native battery of artillery. The whole numbered 3,500 men. The European force consisted of the 32nd Foot, numbering 570 strong, and sixty artillerymen.

Preparations of Henry Lawrence.

The communication between the cantonment and the city was by two bridges; one near the Residency, and the other at the Muchi Bawun. Sir Henry Lawrence brought all the European non-combatants with their families within the Residency walls; and took steps to prevent any combined movements on the part of the cantonment and city. He disposed his troops, European and native, in such a way as to bear directly on the sepoys in the event of a rising; and he established a strong post between the Residency and the Muchi Bawun to command the two bridges leading to cantonments.

Mutiny of the Sepoys, 30th May: flight to Delhi.

At nine o'clock on the night of the 30th of May, the outbreak began at the native cantonment. Shots were fired as a signal, and parties of sepoys began to burn down the bungalows and shoot their European officers. Presently the insurgents rushed to the bridges, infuriated with bhang and excitement, but were received with such a volley of grape, that they retreated towards their lines hotly pursued by Sir Henry Lawrence and his Europeans. They attempted to return to the cantonment, but found it hopeless, and made off to Delhi. Sir Henry Lawrence dared not pursue them with a disaffected city in his rear, which was already surging with excitement. Accordingly, he left a detachment of Europeans to guard the cantonment, and then returned to Lukhnow. Of all the 3,500 sepoys, scarcely a fourth remained true to their colours, and these gradually dropped off during the progress of the rebellion.

Mutiny at Jhansi, 4th June.

On the 4th of June there was a mutiny at Jhansi,—a little chiefship of Bundelkund, which had lapsed to the British government in 1853 from want of natural heirs. The town was situated about a hundred and forty miles to the south of Agra. It was garrisoned entirely by sepoys, and the mutiny was of the usual type. The sepoys went about burning and murdering; whilst the Europeans, including women and children, and numbering fifty-five in all, took refuge in the fort.

A.D. 1857

Ráni of Jhansi.

At this moment, the Ráni of Jhansi the widow of the deceased chief, sent guns and elephants to help the mutineers. She was a vindictive woman, inflamed with the blind ferocity of an oriental, and burning to be revenged on the English for not having been entrusted with the adoption of a son, and the management of the little principality.

Treacherous massacre of Europeans.

The fugitives in the fort were short of provisions; they could not have held out for twenty-four hours longer. The Ráni solemnly swore that if they surrendered the fort without further fighting, their lives should be spared, and they should be conducted in safety to some other station. The rebel sepoys took the same oath, and the little garrison were tempted to accept the terms, and leave the fort two by two. With fiendish treachery the whole fifty-five,—men, women, and children,—were seized and bound, and butchered in cold blood, by the orders of the Ráni.

Cawnpore: its history.

Still more terrible and treacherous were the tragedies enacted at Cawnpore, a city situated on the Ganges about fifty-five miles to the south-west of Lukhnow. Cawnpore had been in the possession of the English ever since the beginning of the century, and for many years was one of the most important military stations in India; but the extension of the British empire over the Punjab had diminished the importance of Cawnpore; and the last European regiment quartered there had been removed to the north-west at the close of the previous year.

Paucity of European soldiers.

In May 1857, there were four native regiments at Cawnpore, numbering 3,500 sepoys. There were no Europeans whatever, excepting the regimental officers, and sixty-one artillerymen. To these were added small detachments of European soldiers, which had been sent in the hour of peril from Lukhnow and Benares during the month of May.

Sir Hugh Wheeler.

The station of Cawnpore was commanded by Sir Hugh Wheeler, a distinguished general in the Company's service, who was verging on his seventieth year. He had spent fifty-four years in India, and had served only with native troops. He must have known the sepoys better than any other European in India. He had led them against their own countrymen under Lord Lake; against foreigners during the Afghan war; and against Sikhs during both campaigns in the Punjab.

A.D. 1857

The news of the revolt at Meerut threw the sepoys into a ferment at every military station in Hindustan. Rumours of mutiny, or coming mutiny, formed almost the only topic of conversation; yet in nearly every sepoy regiment the European officers put faith in their men, and fondly believed that though the rest of the army might revolt, yet their own corps would prove faithful. Such was eminently the case at Cawnpore, yet General Wheeler seems to have known better. Whilst the European officers continued to sleep every night in the sepoy lines, the old veteran made his preparations for meeting the coming storm.

Faith of European officers in sepoys.

European combatants were very few at Cawnpore, but European impedimenta were very heavy. Besides the wives and families of the regimental officers of the sepoy regiments, there was a large European mercantile community. Moreover, whilst the 32nd Foot was quartered at Lukhnow, the wives, families, and invalids of the regiment were residing at Cawnpore. It was thus necessary to secure a place of refuge for this miscellaneous multitude of Europeans in the event of a rising of the sepoys. Accordingly General Wheeler pitched upon some old barracks which had once belonged to a European regiment; and he ordered earthworks to be thrown up, and supplies of all kinds to be stored up, in order to stand a siege. Unfortunately there was fatal neglect somewhere; for when the crisis came the defences were found to be worthless, whilst the supplies were insufficient for the besieged.

European non-combatants at Cawnpore: the place of refuge.

All this while the adopted son of the ex-Peishwa was residing at Bithoor, about six miles from Cawnpore. His real name was Dhundu Punt, but he is better known as Nana Sahib. The British government had refused to award him the absurd life pension of eighty thousand pounds sterling, which had been granted to his nominal father; but he had inherited at least half a million from the ex-Peishwa; and he was allowed to keep six guns, to entertain as many followers as he pleased, and to live in half royal state in a castellated palace at Bithoor. He continued to nurse his grievance with all the pertinacity of a Mahratta; but at the same time he professed a great love for European society, and was profuse in his hospitalities to English officers, and was popularly known as the Raja of Bithoor.

Nana Sahib, *alias* Dhundu Punt, Raja of Bithoor.

A.D. 1857

Deceitful professions of the Nana.

When the news arrived of the revolt at Meerut on the 10th of May, the Nana was loud in his professions of attachment to the English. He engaged to organise 1,500 fighting men to act against the sepoys in the event of an outbreak. On the 21st of May there was an alarm. European ladies and families, with all European non-combatants, were removed into the barracks; and General Wheeler actually accepted from the Nana the help of two hundred Mahrattas and a couple of guns to guard the treasury. The alarm, however, soon blew over, and the Nana took up his abode at the civil station at Cawnpore, as a proof of the sincerity of his professions.

Mutiny at Cawnpore, 4th June.

At last, on the night of the 4th of June, the sepoy regiments at Cawnpore broke out in mutiny. They were driven to action by the same mad terror which had been manifested elsewhere. They cared nothing for the Moghul, nothing for the pageant king at Delhi; but they had been panic-stricken by extravagant stories of coming destruction. It was whispered amongst them that the parade ground was undermined with powder, and that Hindus and Muhammadans were to be assembled on a given day and blown into the air. Intoxicated, with fear and bhang, they rushed out in the darkness,—yelling, shooting, and burning according to their wont; and when their excitement was somewhat spent, they marched off towards Delhi. Sir Hugh Wheeler could do nothing. He might have retreated with the whole body of Europeans from Cawnpore to Allahabad; but there had been a mutiny at Allahabad, and moreover he had no means of transport. Subsequently he heard that the mutineers had reached the first stage on the road to Delhi, and consequently he saw no ground for alarm.

Wild dreams of Nana Sahib.

Meanwhile the brain of Nana Sahib had been turned by wild dreams of vengeance and sovereignty. He thought not only to wreak his malice upon the English, but to restore the extinct Mahratta empire, and reign over Hindustan as the representative of the forgotten Peishwas. The stampede of the sepoys to Delhi was fatal to his mad ambition. He overtook the mutineers, dazzled them with fables of the treasures in Wheeler's entrenchment, and brought them back to Cawnpore to carry out his vindictive and visionary schemes.

At early morning on Saturday, the 6th of June, General Wheeler received a letter from the Nana, announcing that

A.D. 1857

Threatening letter to General Wheeler.

he was about to attack the entrenchment. The veteran was taken by surprise, but at once ordered all the European officers to join the party in the barracks, and prepare for the defence. But the mutineers were in no hurry for the advance. They preferred booty to battle, and turned aside to plunder the cantonment and city, murdering every Christian that came in their way, and not sparing the houses of their own countrymen. They appropriated all the cannon and ammunition in the magazine by way of preparation for the siege; but some were wise enough to desert the rebel army, and steal away to their homes with their ill-gotten spoil.

Siege of Cawnpore, 6th to 25th June.

About noon the main body of the mutineers, swelled by the numerous retainers of the Nana, got their guns into position, and opened fire on the entrenchment. For nineteen days—from the 6th to the 25th of June—the garrison struggled manfully against a raking fire and fearful odds, amidst scenes of suffering and bloodshed which cannot be recalled without a shudder. It was the height of the hot weather in Hindustan. A blazing sun was burning over the heads of the besieged; and to add to their misery, one of the barracks containing the sick and wounded was destroyed by fire. The besiegers, however, in spite of their overwhelming numbers, were utterly unable to carry the entrenchment by storm, but continued to pour in a raking fire. Meanwhile the garrison was starving from want of provisions, and hampered by a multitude of helpless women and children. Indeed, but for the latter contingency, the gallant band would have rushed out of the entrenchment, and cut a way through the mob of sepoys, or perished in the attempt. As it was, they could only fight on, waiting for reinforcements that never came, until fever, sunstroke, hunger, madness, or the enemy's fire, delivered them from their suffering and despair.

On the 25th June a woman brought a slip of writing from the Nana, promising to give a safe passage to Allahabad to all who were willing to lay down their arms.[1] Had there been no women or children the European garrison would never have dreamt of surrender. The massacre at

[1] Nana Sahib pretended to grant this boon only to those who were not connected with the acts of Lord Dalhousie. Subsequent events prove that this was sheer hypocrisy.

A.D. 1857

Treacherous proposals of Nana Sahib.

Patna a century before had taught a lesson to Englishmen which ought never to have been forgotten. As it was there were some who wanted to fight on till the bitter end. But the majority saw that there was no hope for the women or the children, the sick or the wounded, except by accepting the proffered terms. Accordingly the pride of Englishmen gave way, and an armistice was proclaimed.

Negotiations for a surrender, 26th June.

Next morning the terms were negotiated. The English garrison were to surrender their position, their guns, and their treasure, but to march out with their arms, and with sixty rounds of ammunition in the pouch of every man. Nana Sahib on his part was to afford a safe conduct to the river bank, about a mile off; to provide carriage for the conveyance of the women and children, the sick and the wounded; and to furnish boats for carrying the whole party, numbering some four hundred and fifty individuals, down the river Ganges to Allahabad. The Nana accepted the terms, but demanded the evacuation of the entrenchment that very night. General Wheeler protested against this proviso. The Nana began to bully, and to threaten that he would open fire. He was told that he might carry the entrenchment if he could, but that the English had enough powder left to blow both armies into the air. Accordingly the Nana agreed to wait till the morrow.

Embarkation on the Ganges, 27th June.

At early morning on the 27th of June the garrison began to move from the entrenchment to the place of embarkation. The men marched on foot; the women and children were carried on elephants and bullock-carts, whilst the wounded were mostly conveyed in palanquins. Forty boats with thatched roofs, known as budgerows, were moored in shallow water at a little distance from the bank; and the crowd of fugitives were forced to wade through the river to the boats. By nine o'clock the whole four hundred and fifty were huddled on board, and the boats prepared to leave Cawnpore.

The massacre in the river.

Suddenly a bugle was sounded, and a murderous fire of grape shot and musketry was opened upon the wretched passengers from both sides of the river. At the same time the thatching of many of the budgerows was found to be on fire, and the flames began to spread from boat to boat. Numbers were murdered in the river, but at last the firing ceased. A few escaped down the river, but only four men survived to tell the story of the massacre.[1] A mass of fugitives were dragged ashore; the women and children, to the number of a hundred and twenty-five, were carried off and lodged in a house near the head-quarters of the Nana. The men were ordered to immediate execution. One of them had preserved a prayer-book, and was permitted to read a few sentences of the liturgy to his doomed companions. Then the fatal order was given; the sepoys poured in a volley of musketry, and all was over. A.D. 1857

Coronation of the Nana as Peishwa.

On the 1st of July Nana Sahib went off to his palace at Bithoor, and was proclaimed Peishwa. He took his seat upon the throne, and was installed with all the ceremonies of sovereignty, whilst the cannon roared out a salute in his honour. At night the whole place was illuminated, and the hours of darkness were whiled away with feasting and fireworks. But his triumph was short-lived. The Muhammadans were plotting against him at Cawnpore. The people were leaving the city to escape the coming storm, and were taking refuge in the villages. English reinforcements were at last coming up from Allahabad, whilst the greedy sepoys were clamouring for money and gold bangles. Accordingly the Nana hastened back to Cawnpore, and scattered wealth with a lavish hand; and sought to hide his fears by boastful proclamations, and to drown his anxieties in drink and debauchery.

Massacre of fugitives from Futtehgurh.

Within a few days more the number of helpless prisoners was increased to two hundred. There had been a mutiny at Futtehgurh, higher up the river, and the fugitives had fled in boats to Cawnpore, a distance of eighty miles. They knew nothing of what had transpired, and were all taken prisoners by the rebels, and brought on shore. The men were all butchered in the presence of the Nana; the women and children, eighty in number, were sent to join the wretched sufferers in the house near the Nana.

Advance of Neill to Allahabad.

Meanwhile Colonel Neill, commanding the Madras Fusiliers,[2] was pushing up from Calcutta. He was bent on the

[1] The survivors were Lieutenants Mowbray-Thomson, and Delafosse; and Privates Murphy and Sullivan.

[2] The Madras Fusiliers was a European regiment which had been raised by the East India Company for local service. It fought under Clive at Arcot and Plassy. At the amalgamation of the army of the Company with that of the Queen it became the 102nd Foot.

A.D. 1857

relief of Cawnpore and Lukhnow, but was delayed on the way by the mutinies at Benares and Allahabad. In July he was joined at Allahabad by a column under General Havelock, who was destined within a few short weeks to win a lasting name in history.

General Havelock: his specialities.

General Havelock was a Queen's officer of forty years standing; but he had seen more service in India than perhaps any other officer in Her Majesty's army. He had fought in the first Burma war, the Kábul war, the Gwalior campaign of 1843, and the Punjab campaign of 1845-6. He was a pale, thin, thoughtful man; small in stature, but burning with the aspirations of a puritan hero. Religion was the ruling principle of his life, and military glory was his master passion. He had just returned to India after commanding a division in the Persian war. Abstemious to a fault, he was able, in spite of his advancing years, to bear up against the heat and rain of Hindustan during the deadliest season of the year.

Advance of Havelock towards Cawnpore, 7th to 16th July.

On the 7th of July General Havelock left Allahabad for Cawnpore. The force at his disposal did not exceed 2,000 men, Europeans and Sikhs. He had heard of the massacre at Cawnpore on the 27th of June, and burned to avenge it. On the 12th of July he defeated a large force of mutineers and Mahrattas at Futtehpore. On the 15th he inflicted two more defeats on the enemy. Havelock was now within twenty-two miles of Cawnpore, and he halted his men to rest for the night. But news arrived that the women and children were still alive at Cawnpore, and that the Nana had taken the field with a large force to oppose his advance. Accordingly Havelock marched fourteen miles that same night, and on the following morning, within eight miles of Cawnpore, the troops bivouacked beneath some trees.

Massacre of women and children at Cawnpore, 15th July.

On that same night, the 15th of July, the crowning atrocity was committed at Cawnpore. The rebels, who had been defeated by Havelock, returned to the Nana with the tidings of their disaster. In revenge the Nana ordered the slaughter of the two hundred women and children. The poor victims were literally hacked to death, or almost to death, with swords, bayonets, knives, and axes. Next morning the bleeding remains of dead and dying were dragged to a neighbouring well and thrown in.

At two o'clock in the afternoon after the massacre, the

force under Havelock was again upon the march for Cawnpore. The heat was fearful; many of the troops were struck down by the sun, and the cries for water were continuous. But for two miles the column toiled on, and then came in sight of the enemy. Havelock had only 1,000 Europeans and 300 Sikhs; he had no cavalry, and his artillery was inferior. The enemy numbered 5,000 men, armed and trained by British officers, strongly entrenched, with two batteries of guns of heavy calibre. Havelock's artillery failed to silence the batteries, and he ordered the Europeans to charge with the bayonet. On they went in the face of a shower of grape, but the bayonet charge was as irresistible at Cawnpore as at Assaye. The enemy fought for a while like men in a death struggle. Nana Sahib was with them, but nothing is known of his exploits. At last they broke and fled, and there was no cavalry to pursue them.

A.D. 1857

Battle of Cawnpore, 16th July.

As yet nothing was known of the butchery of the women and children. Havelock halted for the night, and next morning marched his force into the station at Cawnpore. The men beheld the scene of the massacre, and saw the bleeding remains in the well. But the murderers had vanished, no one knew whither. Havelock advanced to Bithoor, and destroyed the palace of the Mahratta. Subsequently he was joined by General Neill, with reinforcements from Allahabad; and on the 20th of July he set out for the relief of Lukhnow, leaving Cawnpore in charge of General Neill.

Advance of Havelock to Cawnpore and Bithoor, 17th July.

The defence of Lukhnow against fifty thousand rebels was, next to the siege of Delhi, the greatest event in the mutiny. The whole province of Oude was in a blaze of insurrection. The Talúkdars were exasperated at the hard measure dealt out to them before the appointment of Sir Henry Lawrence as Chief Commissioner. Disbanded sepoys, returning to their homes in Oude, swelled the tide of disaffection. Bandits that had been suppressed under British administration returned to their old work of robbery and brigandage. All classes took advantage of the anarchy to murder the money lenders.[1] Meanwhile the country was bristling with the fortresses of the Talúkdars; and the

Oude: general insurrection.

[1] Money lenders in India are a special institution. The masses are in a normal state of debt. They are compelled by custom to incur large expenses at every marriage and festival, and in consequence

A.D. 1857

cultivators, deprived of the protection of the English, naturally flocked for refuge to the strongholds of their old masters.

Defence of the Residency at Lukhnow: death of Sir Henry Lawrence, 4th July.

The English, who had been lords of Hindustan ever since the beginning of the century, had been closely besieged in the Residency at Lukhnow ever since the final outbreak of the 30th of May. For nearly two months the garrison had held out with a dauntless intrepidity, whilst confidently waiting for reinforcements that seemed never to come. "Never surrender" had been from the first the passionate conviction of Sir Henry Lawrence; and the massacre at Cawnpore on the 27th of June impressed every soldier in the garrison with a like resolution. On the 2nd of July the Muchi Bawun was abandoned, and the garrison and stores removed to the Residency. On the 4th of July Sir Henry Lawrence was killed by the bursting of a shell in a room where he lay wounded; and his dying counsel to those around him was "Never surrender!"

Assault of the 20th July.

On the 20th of July the rebel force round Lukhnow heard of the advance of General Havelock to Cawnpore, and attacked the Residency in overwhelming force. They kept up a continual fire of musketry whilst pounding away with their heavy guns; but the garrison held their ground against shot and shell, and before the day was over the dense masses of assailants were forced to retire from the walls.

Between the 20th and 25th of July General Havelock

are driven to borrow of money lenders. An enormous rate of interest is charged, and a son becomes responsible for the debts of his father.

Under native rule loans were regarded as debts of honour, or rather of piety. They might possibly be recovered in a civil tribunal, but native courts were hopelessly corrupt, and the judge always appropriated a fourth of the claim as his rightful fee. Accordingly the payment was regarded not so much a legal obligation as an act of piety, except in cases of forgery or cheating.

The introduction of British administration put all such debts on a new footing. A money lender could enforce the payment of a decree in the civil court; and lands and personal property were alike treated as available assets. Accordingly soon after the annexation of Oude the people became very bitter against the English courts. When the courts were closed in consequence of the mutiny, the people wreaked their vengeance upon the money lenders.

A law against usury would scarcely remedy the evil. The people have been so long accustomed to high rates of interest, that they would continue to pay them in spite of the law, from a sense of religious obligation.

A.D. 1857

began to cross the Ganges, and make his way into Oude territory; but he was unable to relieve Lukhnow. His small force was weakened by heat and fever, and reduced by cholera and dysentery; whilst the enemy occupied strong positions on both flanks. In the middle of August he fell back upon Cawnpore. Meanwhile General Neill was threatened on his right by the Nana, who re-occupied Bithoor in great strength; and on his left by a large force of rebel sepoys; and he could not attack either without leaving his entrenchment exposed to the other.

Havelock's campaign in Oude: its failure.

On the 16th of August Havelock left a detachment at Cawnpore, and advanced towards Bithoor with 1,500 men. He found the enemy drawn up in a position which revealed the handiwork of a born general. The infantry were posted in front of an entrenched battery, which was nearly masked with sugar canes, and defended with thick ramparts of mud. This position was flanked on both sides by entrenched quadrangles filled with sepoys, and sheltered by plantations of sugar cane.[1] Havelock brought up his guns and opened fire; but the infantry had only been posted in front of the enemy's entrenchment to draw the English on. The moment Havelock's guns began to fire, the infantry retreated into their defences, whilst the batteries poured a storm of shot and shell upon the advancing line of the British army. After twenty minutes Havelock saw that his guns made no impression on the enemy's fire, and ordered a charge with the bayonet. Again the English bayonets prevailed against native batteries, and the enemy fled in all directions. Havelock, however, had no cavalry for the pursuit, and was compelled once more to fall back on Cawnpore. Thus ended Havelock's first campaign for the relief of Lukhnow.

Victory at Bithoor, 16th August: return to Cawnpore.

All this while the Mahratta and Rajpút princes remained loyal to the British government. They had nothing to do with the sepoy mutiny, for they were evidently taken by surprise and could not understand it; and if some held aloof, and appeared to await events, there were others who made common cause with the British government at the

Rajpúts and Mahrattas: Sindia and Holkar.

[1] The only rebel leader who showed a real genius for war throughout the mutinies was a Mahratta Brahman, in the service of the Nana, known as Tantia Topi. No doubt it was Tantia Topi who drew up the rebel army at Bithoor.

A. D. 1857

outset. But the sepoys in the subsidiary armies, who were commanded by British officers, were as much terrified and troubled by the greased cartridges as those in the Bengal regiments; and the revolt at Delhi on the 11th of May acted upon them in the same way as it acted upon the sepoys in British territories. The Gwalior contingent, which was largely composed of Oude soldiery, was more than once inclined to mutiny; but Maháraja Sindia managed to temporise with them; and they did not finally break away from Gwalior until the following October. At Indore the army of Holkar broke out in mutiny and attacked the British Residency, and then went off through Gwalior territory to join the rebels near Agra; but at that time the Gwalior soldiery were tolerably staunch, and refused to accompany them.[1]

Delhi, the head-centre of revolt.

During the four months that followed the revolt at Delhi on the 11th of May, all political interest was centred at the ancient capital of the sovereigns of Hindustan. The public mind was occasionally distracted by the current of events at Cawnpore and Lukhnow, as well as at other stations which need not be particularised; but so long as Delhi remained in the hands of the rebels, the native princes were bewildered and alarmed; and its prompt recapture was deemed of vital importance to the prestige of the British government, and the re-establishment of British sovereignty in Hindustan. The Great Moghul had been little better than a mummy for more than half a century; and Bahadur Shah was a mere tool and puppet in the hands of rebel sepoys; but nevertheless the British government had to deal with the astounding fact that the rebels were fighting under his name and standard, just as Afghans and Mahrattas had done in the days of Ahmad Shah Durani and Mahadaji Sindia. To make matters worse, the roads to Delhi were open from the

[1] Major, afterwards, General Sir Henry Durand, who had served for eight years as political agent at Bhopal, was residing at Indore at this crisis, as agent to the Governor-General in Central India. The Residency at Indore held out until the safety of the ladies and their families was secured; and the subsequent hospitable reception of the refugees by the late Begum of Bhopal is a touching illustration of the loyalty of a native princess towards the British government.

Sir John Kaye, in the first edition of his history of the sepoy revolt, was unfortunately led to give currency to an untrue statement about Major Durand's conduct at Indore. It is gratifying to know that before he died he publicly retracted the insinuation.

south and east; and nearly every outbreak in Hindustan was followed by a stampede of mutineers to the old capital of the Moghuls. A.D. 1857

The Punjab under John Lawrence, the salvation of India.

Meanwhile, in the absence of railways, there were unfortunate delays in bringing up troops and guns to stamp out the fires of rebellion at the head centre.[1] The highway from Calcutta to Delhi was blocked up by mutiny and insurrection; and every European soldier sent up from Calçutta was stopped for the relief of Benares, Allahabad, Cawnpore, or Lukhnow. But the possession of the Punjab at this crisis proved to be the salvation of the empire. Sir John Lawrence, the Chief Commissioner, was called upon to perform almost superhuman work:—to maintain order in a newly conquered province; to suppress mutiny and disaffection amongst the very sepoy regiments from Bengal who were supposed to garrison the country; and to send reinforcements of troops and guns, and supplies of all descriptions, to the siege of Delhi. Fortunately the Sikhs had been only a few short years under British administration; they had not forgotten the miseries that prevailed under the native government, and could appreciate the many blessings they enjoyed under British rule. They were staunch to the British government, and eager to be led against the rebels. In some cases terrible punishment was meted out to mutinous Bengal sepoys within the Punjab;[2] but the imperial interests at stake were sufficient to justify every severity, although all must regret the painful necessity that called for such extreme measures.

Barnard's advance to Delhi, 8th June.

On the 8th of June, about a month after the revolt at Delhi, Sir Henry Barnard took the field at Alipore, about ten miles from the rebel capital. He defeated an advance division of the enemy; and then marched to the Ridge,

[1] The deaths of succesive Commanders-in-chief led to other delays. The news of the revolt at Delhi brought General Anson down from Simla to undertake the siege of Delhi; but he died at Kurnál on the 27th of May. Sir Henry Barnard who succeeded him as Commander-in-chief, died on the 5th July. General Reed succeeded Barnard, but was compelled by ill health to resign the appointment on the 17th July. General Wilson of the Bengal artillery then took the command, whilst Colonel Baird Smith was chief engineer.

[2] The wholesale executions in the 26th regiment of native infantry, which were carried out by the late Mr. Cooper, can only be justified by stern necessity.

A.D. 1857 and re-occupied the old cantonment which had been abandoned on the 11th of May. So far it was clear that the rebels were unable to do anything in the open field, although they might fight bravely under cover. They numbered about thirty thousand strong; they had a very powerful artillery, and ample stores of ammunition; whilst there was an abundance of provisions within the city throughout the siege.

Defences of Delhi. The defences of Delhi covered an area of three square miles. The walls consisted of a series of bastions, about sixteen feet high, connected by long curtains, with occasional martello towers to aid the flanking fire. Every bastion was mounted with eleven guns; namely, one on the salient, three on each face, and two on each flank. Both bastions and curtains were built of masonry about twelve feet thick. Running round the base of these bastions and curtains was a berm or terrace varying in width from fifteen to thirty feet, having on its exterior edge a wall loop-holed for musketry. The whole was surrounded by a ditch twenty feet deep and twenty-five feet wide.[1] On the eastern side of the city the river Jumna ran past the palace of the king and the old state prison of Selimgurh. The bridge of boats leading to Meerut was in front of Selimgurh.

City gates. There were seven gates to the city, namely, Lahore gate, Ajmir gate, Turkoman gate, Delhi gate, Mori gate, Kábul gate, and Kashmir gate. The principal street was the Chandni Chouk, which ran in a direct line from the Delhi gate to the palace of the Moghuls. The great mosque, known as the Juma Musjid, stands on a rocky eminence at the back of the Chandni Chouk.

British camp on the Ridge. The British camp on the Ridge presented a picture at once varied and striking;—long lines of European tents, thatched hovels of the native servants, rows of horses, parks of artillery, English soldiers in their grey linen coats and trousers, Sikhs with their red and blue turbans, Afghans with their gay head-dresses and coloured saddle-cloths, and the Ghorkas in Kilmarnock hats and woollen coats. There

[1] *Meeting of the Bengal Army*, London, 1858. *Bacon's First Impressions of Hindustan*, London, 1837. The loop-holed wall was a continuation of the escarp or inner wall of the ditch. The counterscarp, or outer wall of the ditch, was not of masonry, but was a mere earthen slope of easy incline.

A.D. 1857

were but few Hindu sepoys in the British ranks, but the native servants were very numerous. In the rear were the booths of the native bazars; and further out in the plain were thousands of camels, bullocks and baggage horses. Still further to the rear was a small river crossed by two bridges; but the bridges were subsequently blown up. On the extreme right of the camp, on a spot nearest the city walls, was a battery on an eminence, known as the Mound battery, which faced the Mori gate. Hard by was Hindu Rao's[1] house, the head-quarters of the army during the siege. From the summit of the Ridge was to be seen the river Jumna winding along to the left of the city;—the bridge of boats, the towers of the palace, the minarets of the great mosque of the Juma Musjid, the house roofs and gardens of the doomed city, and the picturesque walls, with batteries here and there sending forth white clouds of smoke among the green foliage that clustered round the ramparts.

Old suburbs.

To the right of the Mound battery was the old suburb known as the Subzi Mundi. It was the vegetable bazar which figures in the scandalous stories of the later Moghul princes as the scene of their frolics and debaucheries. It was occupied by old houses, gardens with high walls, and narrow streets and lanes; and thus it furnished the very cover which makes Asiatics brave.[2] Similar suburbs intervened between the actual defences of Delhi and the whole line of the English position.

Delay of siege operations.

For many weeks the British army on the Ridge was unable to attempt siege operations. It was, in fact, the besieged, rather than the besiegers; for although the bridges in the rear were blown up, the camp was exposed to continual assaults from all the other sides.

On the 23rd of June, the hundredth anniversary of the battle of Plassy, the enemy made a greater effort than ever

[1] Hindu Rao is one of the forgotten celebrities who flourished about fifty years ago. He was a brother of Baiza Bai, the ambitious widow of Daulat Rao Sindia, who worried Lord William Bentinck. Hindu Rao had a claim to the throne of Gwalior, but was outwitted by his strong-minded sister, and sent to live at Delhi on a lakh of rupees per annum, *i.e.*, ten thousand pounds a year. Like the great Jaswant Rao Holkar, he was a victim to cherry brandy.

[2] The Subzi Mundi was subsequently cleared from all the rubbish and *débris*. At the Imperial Assemblage at Delhi, on the 1st of January, 1877, it formed the site of part of the Vice-Regal encampment.

A.D. 1857

General assault on the British camp, 23rd June.

to carry the British position. The attack began on the right from the Subzi Mundi, its object being to capture the Mound battery. Finding it impossible to carry the battery, the rebels confined themselves to a hand to hand conflict in the Subzi Mundi. The deadly struggle continued for many hours; and as the rebels came up in overwhelming numbers, it was fortunate that the two bridges in the rear had been blown up the night before, or the assault might have had a different termination. It was not until after sunset that the enemy was compelled to retire with the loss of a thousand men. Similar actions were frequent during the month of August; but meanwhile reinforcements were coming up, and the end was drawing nigh.

Preparations for storming Delhi, August and September.

In the middle of August, Brigadier John Nicholson, one of the most distinguished officers of the time, came up from the Punjab with a brigade and siege train. On the 4th of September a heavy train of artillery was brought in from Ferozepore. The British force on the Ridge now exceeded 8,000 men. Hitherto the artillery had been too weak to attempt to breach the city walls; but now fifty-four heavy guns were brought into position and the siege began in earnest. From the 8th to the 12th of September four batteries poured in a constant storm of shot and shell; number one was directed against the Kashmír bastion, number two against the right flank of the Kashmír bastion, number three against the Water bastion, and number four against the Kashmír and Water gates and bastions. On the 13th of September the breaches were declared to be practicable, and the following morning was fixed for the final assault upon the doomed city.

Final assault, 14th September.

At three o'clock in the morning of the 14th September, three assaulting columns were formed in the trenches, whilst a fourth was kept in reserve. The first column was led by Brigadier Nicholson; the second by Brigadier Jones; the third by Colonel Campbell; and the fourth, or reserve, by Brigadier Longfield.

Fighting inside Delhi, 14th to 20th.

The powder bags were laid at the Kashmír gate by Lieutenants Home and Salkeld. The explosion followed, and the third column rushed in, and pushed towards the Juma Musjid. Meanwhile the first column under Nicholson escaladed the breaches near the Kashmír gate, and pushed along the ramparts towards the Kábul gate, carrying the

A.D. 1857

several bastions in the way. Here it was met by the second column under Brigadier Jones, who had escaladed the breach at the Water bastion. The advancing columns were met by a ceaseless fire from terraced houses, mosques, and other buildings; and John Nicholson, the hero of the day, whilst attempting to storm a narrow street near the Kábul gate, was struck down by a shot and mortally wounded. Then followed six days of desperate warfare. No quarter was given to men with arms in their hands; but women and children were spared, and only a few of the peaceable inhabitants were sacrificed during the storm.

Capture of the palace: flight of the king to Humáyun's tomb.

On the 20th of September the gates of the old fortified palace of the Moghuls were broken open, but the royal inmates had fled. No one was left but a few wounded sepoys and fugitive fanatics. The old king, Bahadur Shah, had gone off to the great mausoleum without the city, known as the tomb of Humáyun. It was a vast quadrangle raised on terraces and inclosed with walls. It contained towers, buildings, and monumental marbles, in memory of different members of the once distinguished family; as well as extensive gardens, surrounded with cloistered cells for the accommodation of pilgrims.

Hodson's arrest of the king: shooting two princes.

On the 21st of September Captain Hodson rode to the tomb, arrested the king and brought him back to Delhi with other members of the family, and lodged them in the palace. The next day he went again with a hundred horsemen, and arrested two sons of the king in the midst of a crowd of armed retainers, and brought them away in a native carriage. Near the city the carriage was surrounded by a tumultuous crowd; and Hodson, who was afraid of a rescue, shot both princes with his pistol, and placed their bodies in a public place on the walls for all men to see.

Re-occupation of Delhi: losses.

Thus fell the imperial city; captured by the army under Brigadier Wilson before the arrival of any of the reinforcements from England. The losses were heavy. From the beginning of the siege to the close the British army at Delhi had nearly 4,000 killed and wounded. The casualties on the side of the rebels were never estimated. Two bodies of sepoys broke away from the city, and fled down the valleys of the Jumna and Ganges, followed by two flying columns under Brigadiers Greathed and Showers. But the great mutiny and revolt at Delhi had been stamped out; and the flag

A.D. 1857

of England waved triumphantly over the capital of Hindustan.

Rebellion still rampant in Oude.

The capture of Delhi, in September 1857, was the turning point in the sepoy mutinies. The revolt was crushed beyond redemption; the rebels were deprived of their head centre; and the Moghul king was a prisoner at the mercy of the power whom he had defied. But there were still troubles in India. Lukhnow was still beleagured by a rebel army, and insurrection still ran riot in Oude and Rohilkund.

Havelock joined by Outram at Cawnpore.

In the middle of August General Havelock had fallen back on Cawnpore, after the failure of his first campaign for the relief of Lukhnow. Five weeks afterwards Havelock made a second attempt under better auspices. Sir Colin Campbell had arrived at Calcutta as Commander-in-chief. Sir James Outram had come up to Allahabad. On the 16th of September, whilst the British troops were storming the streets of Delhi, Outram joined Havelock and Neill at Cawnpore with 1,400 men. As senior officer he might have assumed the command; but with generous chivalry, the "Bayard of India" waived his rank in honour of Havelock.

Advance to Lukhnow, September 25th.

On the 20th of September General Havelock crossed the Ganges into Oude at the head of 2,500 men. The next day he defeated a rebel army, and put it to flight, whilst four of the enemy's guns were captured by Outram at the head of a body of volunteer cavalry. On the 23rd Havelock routed a still larger rebel force which was strongly posted at a garden in the suburbs of Lukhnow, known as the Alumbagh. He then halted to give his soldiers a day's rest. On the 25th he was cutting his way through the streets and lanes of the city of Lukhnow;—running the gauntlet of a deadly and unremitting fire from the houses on both sides of the streets, and also from guns which commanded them. On the evening of the same day he entered the British entrenchments; but in the moment of victory a chance shot carried off the gallant Neill.

Heroism of the besieged.

The defence of the British Residency at Lukhnow is a glorious episode in the national annals. The fortitude of the beleaguered garrison was the admiration of the world. The ladies nursed the wounded, and performed every womanly duty, with self-sacrificing heroism; and when the fight was over they received the well-merited thanks of Her Majesty Queen Victoria.

A.D. 1857.

Story of the relief of Lukhnow.

During four long months the garrison had known nothing of what was going on in the outer world. They were aware of the advance and retreat of Havelock, and that was all. At last, on the 23rd of September, they heard the booming of the guns at the Alumbagh. On the morning of the 25th they could see something of the growing excitement in the city; the people abandoning their houses and flying across the river. Still the guns of the rebels kept up a heavy cannonade upon the Residency, and volleys of musketry continued to pour upon the besieged from the loopholes of the besiegers. But soon the firing was heard from the city; the welcome sounds came nearer and nearer. The excitement of the garrison grew beyond control. Presently the relieving force was seen fighting its way towards the Residency. Then the pent up feelings of the garrison burst forth in deafening cheers; and wounded men in hospital crawled out to join in the chorus of welcome. Then followed personal greetings as officers and men came pouring in. Hands were frantically shaken on all sides. Rough bearded soldiers took the children from their mothers' arms, kissed them with tears rolling down their cheeks, and thanked God that they had come in time to save them from the fate that had befallen the sufferers at Cawnpore.

Second relief by Sir Colin Campbell, November.

Thus after a siege of nearly four months Havelock succeeded in relieving Lukhnow. But it was a reinforcement rather than a relief, and was confined to the British Residency. The siege was not raised; and the city of Lukhnow remained two months longer in the hands of the rebels. Sir James Outram assumed the command, but was compelled to keep on the defensive. Meanwhile reinforcements were arriving from England. In November Sir Colin Campbell reached Cawnpore at the head of a considerable army. He left General Windham with 2,000 men to take charge of the entrenchment at Cawnpore; and then advanced against Lukhnow with 5,000 men and thirty guns. He carried several of the enemy's positions, cut his way to the Residency, and at last brought away the beleaguered garrison, with all the ladies and children. But not even then could he disperse the rebels and re-occupy the city. Accordingly he left Outram at the head of 4,000 men in the neighbourhood of Lukhnow, and then returned to Cawnpore.

On the 24th of November, the day after leaving Lukhnow,

A.D. 1857

Death of Havelock, 24th of November.

General Havelock was carried off by dysentery, and buried in the Alumbagh. His death spread a gloom over India, but by this time his name had become a household word wherever the English language was spoken. In the hour of surprise and panic, as successive stories of mutiny and rebellion reached England, and culminated in the revolt at Delhi and massacre at Cawnpore, the victories of Havelock revived the drooping spirits of the British nation, and stirred up all hearts to glorify the hero who had stemmed the tide of disaffection and disaster. The death of Havelock, following the story of the capture of Delhi, and told with the same breath that proclaimed the deliverance at Lukhnow, was received in England with a universal sorrow that will never be forgotten, so long as men are living who can recall the memory of the mutinies of Fifty-seven.

Revolt of the Gwalior contingent: retreat of General Windham.

Sir Colin Campbell was approaching Cawnpore, when he heard the roll of a distant cannonade. There was another surprise, and unfortunately another disaster. Tantia Topi had come once more to the front. That wonderful Mahratta Brahman had made his way from the side of Nana Sahib to the capital of Sindia; and had persuaded the Gwalior contingent to break out in open revolt, and march against Cawnpore. General Windham was an officer of distinction. He had earned his laurels in the Crimean campaign, but he was unfamiliar with Asiatic warfare. He went out to meet the rebels, and routed the advanced body; but he was outwitted by the consummate genius of Tantia Topi. He found himself outflanked, and took alarm, and fell back upon the entrenchment; leaving not only his camp equipage and stores, but the whole city of Cawnpore in the hands of the rebel sepoys.[1] To crown all, the bridge of boats over the Ganges, by which Sir Colin Campbell was expected to cross the river on his way to Cawnpore, was in imminent danger of being destroyed by the rebels.

Fortunately the bridge escaped the vigilance of Tantia

[1] Major Adye of the Royal Artillery was present at the engagement and lost two of his guns. In sheer desperation he went out at night with a small party, and succeeded in finding his guns and bringing them back in triumph. It thus appeared that not even Tantia Topi could persuade Asiatics to keep on guard against a night attack; and had Windham beaten up the enemy's quarters at midnight he might possibly have retrieved his disaster. Major Adye is now General Sir John Adye, Governor of the Royal Military Academy at Woolwich.

A.D. 1857

Sir Colin Campbell at Cawnpore: defeat of the Gwalior rebels.

Topi, and Sir Colin Campbell reached the entrenchment in safety. His first act was to despatch the garrison from Lukhnow, together with his sick and wounded, down the river to Allahabad. He then took the field and routed the Gwalior rebels that repulsed General Windham, and drove them out of Cawnpore. The naval brigade under Sir William Peel gained great renown during these operations, handling their 24-pounders like playthings; whilst Generals Little and Mansfield and Brigadier Hope Grant distinguished themselves in the pursuit of the rebels.

Trial and transportation of the ex-king of Delhi.

In January, 1858, the ex-king Bahadur Shah was tried by a military commission at Delhi, and found guilty of ordering the massacre of Christians, and of waging war against the British government. Sentence of death was recorded against him; but ultimately he was sent to Rangoon, with his favourite wife and her son, and kept under surveillance as a state prisoner until his death five years afterwards.

Lord Clyde's campaign in Oude and Rohilkund: Outram's capture of Lukhnow.

The subsequent history of the sepoy revolt is little more than a detail of the military operations of British troops for the dispersion of the rebels and restoration of order and law. Sir Colin Campbell, now Lord Clyde, undertook a general campaign against the rebels in Oude and Rohilkund, and restored order and law throughout those disaffected provinces; whilst Sir James Outram drove the rebels out of Lukhnow, and re-established British sovereignty in the capital of Oude.

Brilliant campaign of Sir Hugh Rose in Central India.

At the same time a column from Bombay under Sir Hugh Rose, and another from Madras under General Whitlock, carried out a similar work in Central India and Bundelkund. History has scarcely done justice to the brilliant campaign of Sir Hugh Rose in Central India from the borders of the Bombay Presidency to the banks of the Jumna. The military operations of Lord Clyde, were on a far larger scale, but they were conducted in an open and well-peopled country. The campaign of Sir Hugh Rose was carried out amidst the jungles, ravines, and broken ground of the Vindhya mountains, and the equally secluded region of Bundelkund, which for centuries had set the Muhammadan power at defiance. With a small but well appointed force, a tithe of that under Lord Clyde's command, Sir Hugh Rose captured fortresses and walled towns, fought battles against enormous odds, and never for a moment gave the enemy time to

A.D. 1857

breathe. He besieged and captured the rebel fortress of Jhansi, where Tantia Topi had come to the help of the Rání. The bloody-minded Rání fled to the jungles; and Tantia Topi escaped to the north-east, and concentrated a rebel army of 20,000 men near Kalpí on the Jumna. After some desperate actions, Sir Hugh Rose utterly routed Tantia Topi, and scattered his forces in all directions. Sir Hugh Rose considered that he had now brought his campaign in Central India to a glorious close; and he congratulated the troops under his command at having marched a thousand miles and captured a hundred guns.

Intrigues of Tantia Topi at Gwalior.

But Sir Hugh Rose had reckoned without his host. At this very time the irrepressible Mahratta Brahman, Tantia Topi, had secretly proceeded to Gwalior, the capital of Maháraja Sindia. He had made Gwalior the rallying point for all the scattered troops of the rebel army; and organised a conspiracy against Sindia to be supported by the rebels as fast as they arrived. The plot was discovered in time by the Maháraja and his minister, Dinkur Rao; and it was plain that neither the one nor the other could have felt the slightest sympathy in a movement for upsetting the British government and restoring a dynasty of Peishwas.

Defeat and flight of Sindia.

Dinkur Rao counselled the Maháraja to adopt a defensive policy until a British force arrived from Agra. But Sindia was young and enthusiastic, and anxious to show his loyalty to the British government. Accordingly he marched out with 8,000 men and twenty-five guns to attack the rebel army. The result was one of those surprises and disasters which characterised different epochs of the mutiny. Sindia's army deserted him, and either joined the rebels or returned to Gwalior. His own body-guard remained with him, and fought against the rebels with the old Mahratta spirit, but they suffered heavily in the action. Sindia was thus compelled to fly to Dholepore on the road to Agra, where he was joined by Dinkur Rao.

New rebel army under Tantia Topi.

The city of Gwalior, with all its guns, stores, and treasure, was thus abandoned to the rebels. Nana Sahib was proclaimed Peishwa; and a revolution was beginning of which no one at Gwalior could see the ending. In the beginning of June, 1858, in the height of the hot weather, a new rebel army, numbering 18,000 men, had sprung into existence in

A.D. 1857

Central India under the command of Tantia Topia, with all the famous artillery of Sindia at his disposal.

Routed by Sir Hugh Rose.

This astounding state of affairs soon called Sir Hugh Rose to the front. On the 16th of June he defeated a rebel force which was posted in the cantonment at Morar. The next day he was joined by a column under Brigadier Smith; and on the 18th all the rebel entrenchments and positions were stormed and captured. During these operations the Rání of Jhansi fought on the side of the rebels in male attire. She was killed by a trooper before her sex was discovered; and is said to have courted her fate to escape the punishment of her crimes.

Dashing charge of Brigadier Napier.

Tantia Topi, however, was a born general, and his genius never deserted him. He made good his retreat from Gwalior with 6,000 men, and carried away thirty field-pieces. But his case was hopeless. Two days afterwards, Brigadier Robert Napier, the present Lord Napier of Magdala, dashed amongst the retreating force with 600 horsemen and six field guns, and put them to flight, whilst recovering nearly all the artillery they had carried away. This successful action was regarded as one of the most brilliant exploits in the campaign.

Pursuit of Tantia Topi, 1858–59.

In spite of these crushing defeats, Tantia Topi evaded all pursuit for ten months longer. Different columns strove to hem him in; but the active Mahratta, with all the spirit and pertinacity of his race, made his way to the banks of the Nerbudda with a large body of fugitives, mounted on the small hardy ponies of India. With all the pertinacity of a Mahratta, he still clung to the wild hope of reaching the western Dekhan, and creating a new Mahratta empire in the dominions of the ex-Peishwa, which had been British territory for more than forty years. Whether it was possible for him to have raised a Mahratta insurrection is a problem he was never destined to solve.

Capture and execution.

Tantia Topi was driven back by the Bombay troops, and never crossed the Nerbudda. From that time Tantia Topi and the British troops appeared to be playing at hunting the hare all over Central India. He and his men rode incredible distances, and often appeared to be in several places at once. At last a cordon of hunters surrounded him. He was driven into the western deserts of Rajpútana, but compelled, from want of supplies, to double back on

A.D. 1857

Bundelkund. In April, 1859, his hiding-place in the jungles was betrayed by one of his own rebel generals; and he was arrested by Major Meade, and tried, convicted, and hanged, to the general satisfaction of all concerned.

Tantia Topi a type of the old Peishwa.

Tantia Topi was a cruel and crafty villain, with a cleverness that calls to mind the genius and audacity of the old Mahratta Peishwas. He was no doubt the originator of the rebellion of the Nana Sahib, and the prime mover in the massacres at Cawnpore; whilst the Nana was a mere tool and puppet in his hands, like Maháraja Sahu in the hands of the Peishwas. Could the Nana have succeeded in gaining a throne, he would most probably have been imprisoned or murdered by Tantia Topi; and Tantia Topi would have founded one of those dynasties of ministerial sovereigns which so often sprung into existence in the palmy days of Brahmanical rule.[1]

[1] The death of Tantia Topi has carried the reader beyond the mutinies into the year 1859. In the next chapter it will be necessary to revert to the close of the mutinies in 1858.

CHAPTER XXVI.

IMPERIAL RULE: CANNING: ELGIN: LAWRENCE: MAYO: NORTHBROOK AND LYTTON.

1858 TO 1880.

A.D. 1858-1859

The Queen's proclamation, 1st November, 1858.

ON the 1st of November 1858, the proclamation of Her Majesty Queen Victoria brought the sepoy revolt to a close. It was the Magna Charta of India, and was translated into all the languages of the country. It announced the transfer of the direct government of India from the Company to the Crown. It confirmed all existing dignities, rights, usages, and treaties.[1] It assured the people of India that the British government had neither the right nor the desire to tamper with their religion or caste. It granted a general amnesty to all mutineers and rebels, excepting only those who had been directly implicated in the murders.

Rebellion ended, 1859.

In January, 1859, Lord Canning published a despatch from Lord Clyde, declaring that rebellion no longer existed in Oude.[2] The campaign was at an end, for no organised

[1] The administrative results of the transfer of the government of India from the East India Company to the Crown may be summed up in a few words. The Governor-General became a Viceroy. Non-officials, natives and Europeans, were introduced into the so-called legislative councils at the different Presidencies, and into the legislative council of the Viceroy. The Company's army was amalgamated with the Queen's army. The Company's Courts of Appeal at the different Presidencies, known as the Suddar Courts, in which the judges were selected from the Civil Service, were amalgamated with the Supreme Courts, in which the judges were sent out from England under the nomination of the Crown. The new Courts are now known as High Courts.

[2] Oude was disarmed after the rebellion, just as the Punjab had been disarmed after the annexation. The number of arms collected was very large; there were 684 cannon, 186,000 fire-arms, 560,000

A.D. 1859-1862

armies of rebels remained in the field; but hordes of armed men, of whom Tantia Topi was a type, were still fighting as it were with halters round their necks. But brigades and detachments were in motion from the Nerbudda river to the north-east frontier of Oude; and the work of trampling out the last embers of the great conflagration was gradually brought to a close.

Lord Canning's durbar at Agra: right of adoption conceded.

During the cold weather of 1859 Lord Canning left Calcutta for a tour in the upper provinces. In November he held a grand durbar at Agra, at which his dignified presence created an impression amongst the native princes which was never forgotten. He acknowledged the services rendered to the British government during the mutinies by Maháraja Sindia, the Raja of Jaipur, and others. At the same time, as the representative of Her Majesty, he publicly announced the concession to native rulers of the right of adopting a son, who should succeed to the government of their several principalities in the event of a failure of natural heirs.

Departure and death of Lord Canning, 1862.

In March, 1862, Lord Canning left India for ever. The leading event of his administration was the sepoy revolt; but it was followed by measures of economy and reform which proved him to be one of the most conscientious and hard-working statesmen that ever governed India. Unfortunately his career was rapidly brought to a close. He died the following June, and was buried in Westminster Abbey.

Lord Elgin, Viceroy, 1862-63.

Lord Elgin succeeded Lord Canning as Viceroy of India. His administration was short, but was marked by two events which will always find a place in history; namely, a little mountain expedition on the north-west frontier which led to an expensive campaign, and a mission to Bhutan which led to a still more disastrous war.

North-western frontier of India: the Sulaiman range.

The frontier of British India westward of the river Indus, was formed in 1849 by a chain of mountains, which ran southward from the Hindu Kúsh into Sinde, and served as a natural wall between the Punjab and Afghanistan.[1] These

swords, 50,000 spears, and more than 600,000 weapons of other descriptions; whilst more than 1,500 fortresses, great and small, were demolished or dismantled.

[1] The wall is not continuous. It is pierced by the Khaiber Pass which leads to Kábul, and the Bolan Pass which leads to Quetta and Kandahar. Other passes were discovered during the campaigns of 1878–79.

A.D. 1862-1863

mountains are known as the Sulaiman range. They are inhabited by tribes who are closely akin to the Afghans; equally bloodthirsty and treacherous, and still more ignorant and barbarous. They have no government, but each tribe has its own council of elders, known as the Jirgah. They are Muhammadans of the worst type; intolerant and priest-ridden. They always carry arms, such as matchlocks and short swords, whether grazing cattle, tilling the soil, or driving beasts of burden; for every tribe has its internecine war, every family its hereditary blood feud, and every man his personal enemy. At the same time, whenever they are exposed to the assaults of an invader, they forget all their feuds and quarrels, and make common cause against the foreigner.[1]

Changes under British rule.

In the old days of Runjeet Singh and his successors, the mountain tribes were always ready to carry fire and sword into the bordering villages of Sikhs and Hindus, on the side of the Punjab. They plundered homesteads, slaughtered all who opposed them, and carried off women, children, and cattle. Since the British conquest of the Punjab there has been a vast improvement in the state of affairs on the frontier; and the mountain tribes have been kept out of the plains by the Punjab Irregular Force organised by Lord Dalhousie.

Peshawar.

The most important British district on the line of frontier is that of Peshawar. It is the key of the whole position. It extends from the fort of Attock, at the junction of the Kábul and Indus rivers, westward as far as the mouth of the Khaibar Pass, which leads to Kábul. Accordingly the British cantonment at Peshawar has always been held by a large force of the regular army.

Forty miles to the north of Attock is a village, or group of villages, called Sitana. The settlement is situated outside the frontier, on the eastern face of a square mass of rock, eight thousand feet high, known as the Mahabun mountain.[2] It

[1] The data respecting the population of the Sulaiman range, is condensed from a Report on the independent tribes of the north-west frontier, drawn up many years ago by Sir Richard Temple. The original extract will be found in page 27 of the Blue Book on Afghanistan, published in 1878.

[2] The whole region is classic ground, the scene of Alexander's invasion of India. The Mahabun mountain has been identified with the

A.D. 1862-1863

Hindustani fanatics at Sitana and Mulka on the Mahabun mountain.

had been occupied ever since 1831, or thereabouts, by a colony of Hindustani fanatics from Bengal. These men were a sect of Muhammadan puritans, known as Wahabis, who affect a strict and ascetic way of life, such as prevailed in the time of the Prophet, and denounce all commentaries on the Koran, and all such modern innovations as the worship of relics. The Hindustani fanatics at Sitana were dangerous neighbours. They were brigands as well as bigots, like the zealots described by Josephus. They committed frequent raids on British territory, being inspired by religious hatred as well as love of plunder; and strange to say, they were recruited from time to time with men and money from disaffected Muhammadans in Patna and other localities in Bengal, at least twelve hundred miles off. In 1858 they were driven out of Sitana by General Sir Sydney Cotton, who commanded at Peshawar; but they only retired to Mulka, on the further slope of the Mahabun mountain; and in 1862 they returned to Sitana and renewed their depredations.

British expedition under General Chamberlain: Umbeyla pass.

In 1863 a British force of 5,000 men, under General Sir Neville Chamberlain, was sent to root out the Hindustani fanatics from Mulka as well as Sitana. It would however have proved a difficult operation to march a column up the side of a steep mountain in the face of swarms of mountaineers and fanatics; and then after capturing Sitana, to march over a crest 8,000 feet high, in order to attack a strong force at Mulka on the further slope. Accordingly it was resolved to reach the slope in question by a narrow gorge that ran along the western face of the Mahabun mountain, and was known as the Umbeyla pass; and thus to take Mulka, as it were, in the rear.[1]

natural fortress of Aornos, which was captured by the Macedonians. Attock has been identified with Taxila, the first city entered by the great conqueror after the passage of the Indus.

[1] See *Sitana: a Mountain Campaign on the Borders of Afghanistan.* By Colonel John Adye, R.A. The author is largely indebted to this valuable contribution to military history. Colonel, now General Sir John Adye, maintains that the Hindu Kúsh and not the Sulaiman range is the true frontier of our British Indian empire. The author would add that if we accept the Hindu Kúsh as our mountain fortress, then, to use a technical phrase, Afghan-Turkistan is our berm and the Oxus our ditch. Russia already holds the glacis as represented by Bokhara and Khiva.

A.D. 1863

Neighbouring tribes: Akhoond of Swat.

Whilst however one side of the Umbeyla Pass was formed by the Mahabun mountain, the other side was formed by another steep height, known as the Guru mountain; and beyond the Guru mountain were many strong tribes, known as Bonairs and Swatis; and above all there was a certain warrior priest, known as the Akhoond of Swat, who exercised a powerful influence as prince and pontiff over many of the tribes far and wide. Then again the Umbeyla Pass was outside the British frontier, and really belonged to the Bonairs. It was, however, imagined that the Afghan mountaineers could have no sympathy with the Hindustani fanatics; especially as the Akhoond of Swat had fulminated his spiritual thunder against the Hindustani fanatics at Mulka and Sitana, in a way which betokened a deadly sectarian hostility. Moreover, as the Umbeyla pass was only nine miles long, it was possible to reach Mulka and destroy the village before Bonairs or Swatis could know what was going on.

British authorities outwitted.

Unfortunately the Hindustani fanatics were too sharp for the British authorities. They got an inkling of the coming expedition, and sent out letters to all the neighbouring tribes. They declared that the English infidels were coming to devastate the mountains and subvert the religion of the tribes. It was cunningly added that in the first instance the infidels would say that they only came to destroy the Hindustanis; but if once they got into the mountain, every one of the tribes would share the fate of the Hindustanis.

Advance through the Umbeyla pass.

Unconsciously General Chamberlain played into the hands of the Hindustanis. He told the neighbouring tribes that he was going to destroy Mulka, but that he had no intention whatever of interfering with any one but the Hindustanis. He entered the Umbeyla pass before he could receive any reply; but on getting three parts of the way, he was compelled to halt for the baggage. He sent on a party to reconnoitre the Chumla valley, which intervened between the pass and Mulka, and then it was found that the Guru mountain was swarming with armed men. Accordingly the reconnoitring party had much difficulty in returning to the camp; and it was soon evident that the British force had been drawn into a defile; and that it would be impossible to advance without reinforcements, and almost equally impossible to return to British territory.

A.D. 1863

General uprising of the tribes: British force blocked up.

The movements of the British force had excited the suspicions of the tribes by confirming all that the Hindustanis had said. The Bonairs were exasperated at the violation of their territory, without any previous reference to their council of elders. Fear and alarm spread far and wide, and the tribes flocked to the Guru mountain from all quarters. The Akhoond of Swat came in person with 15,000 men. The mountain tribes on the Mahabun made common cause with the Hindustanis in resisting the invaders. In a word, General Chamberlain was threatened by swarms of matchlock men on his two flanks, whilst his rear was blocked up by mules, camels, and other impedimenta. Under such circumstances he was compelled to keep off the enemy as he best could, and wait for reinforcements, or for orders to retire. To make matters worse, he himself was wounded; whilst Lord Elgin was dying at Dhurmsala in the Himalayas.

Action of Sir Hugh Rose.

At this crisis Sir Hugh Rose, who had succeeded Lord Clyde as Commander-in-chief, solved the difficulty. He protested against any retirement, as it would only necessitate an expensive campaign in the following spring; and he ordered up reinforcements with all speed from Lahore.

Sir William Denison, provisional Viceroy, 1863.

Lord Elgin died in November, 1863. Sir William Denison, Governor of Madras, came up to Calcutta to act as his successor until a Viceroy could be appointed by the home government; and he at once sanctioned the steps taken by Sir Hugh Rose. General Garvock assumed the command in the room of General Chamberlain, and found himself at the head of nearly 9,000 men all eager for the fray. The mountain tribes were soon brought to reason; and a brilliant campaign ended in a political triumph. The Bonairs were so satisfied of the good faith of the British authorities, that they went themselves to Mulka, and burnt down the village; and for a while nothing more was heard of the Hindustanis.[1]

Sir John Lawrence, Viceroy, 1864–69.

The idea of a Muhammadan conspiracy, running along a line of 1,200 miles between Patna and Sitana, created undue alarm in England. The result was that Sir John Lawrence, whose administration of the Punjab during the sepoy mutinies

[1] In 1868 an expedition under the command of General Wylde was sent against the Afghan tribes on the Black Mountain, immediately to the north of the Mahabun. The military operations were successful, and sufficed for the suppression of disturbances and restoration of peace.

had excited general admiration, was appointed to succeed Lord Elgin as Viceroy of India. The appointment was contrary to established usage; for it had been ruled in the case of Sir Charles Metcalfe that no servant of the Company could fill the substantive post of Governor-general. The elevation of Sir John Lawrence however was regarded with universal satisfaction. He arrived at Calcutta in January, 1864; but by this time the Sitana campaign had been brought to a close. A.D. 1864

Mission to Bhutan, 1863-64.

Shortly after Sir John Lawrence had taken over the government of India, a mission which had been sent to Bhutan by Lord Elgin was brought to an unfortunate close. Before, however, describing the progress of events, it will be necessary to glance at the country and people of Bhutan, and review the circumstances which led to the despatch of the mission.

Description of Bhutan.

Bhutan is a mountain region in the Himalayas, having Thibet on the north and Bengal and Assam on the south. It also lies between Nipal on the west and another portion of Thibet on the east.[1] Like Nipal, it forms a fringe of mountain territory to the south of the great Thibetan tableland. Originally it belonged to Thibet, but became independent from the inability of the Thibetan government to keep the mountaineers in subjection.

The people.

The people of Bhutan are rude, robust, and dirty; with flat faces of the Tartar type, and high cheek bones narrowing down to the chin. They have ruddy brown complexions; black hair cut close to the head; small black almond-shaped eyes; very thin eyelashes; and little or no eyebrows or beards. They are coarse and filthy in their manners, and leave all the field work to the women, who are as coarse as the men.

Corrupt Buddhism.

This repulsive barbarism is the outcome of a corrupt form of Buddhism. Thousands of Buddhist monks lead lives of religion and laziness in their secluded monasteries; leaving the laity to grovel away their existence in gross and undisguised debaucheries.

Dharma and Deva Rajas.

The government of Bhutan is half clerical and half secular; including a pontiff as well as a prince. The pontiff is known as the Dharma Raja; he is supposed to be an

[1] Bhutan is separated from Nipal by the little principality of Sikhim and the hill station of Darjeeling.

A.D. 1863

incarnation, not of deity, but of that exalted virtue and goodness which are summed up by Buddhists in the single term—Dharma;[1] and the Bhutanese believe that the Dharma Raja has the power of raising evil spirits, or demons, for the destruction of their enemies. The temporal prince is known as the Deb or Deva Raja, and is subordinate to the Dharma Raja. He represents the hero Rajas,—the Devas or Devatas of Hindu traditions,—who figured as heroes and were worshipped as gods until the old mythology was submerged in the metaphysical atheism of Buddhism.[2]

Three classes of officials,—Penlows, Jungpens, and Zingaffs.

Bhutan is separated into three provinces, each of which is in charge of a governor known as a Penlow. The governor of western Bhutan is called the Paro Penlow; that of central Bhutan is the Daka Penlow; and that of eastern Bhutan is the Tongso Penlow. Subordinate to the three Penlows are the commandants of fortresses, known as Jungpens. Below these is an inferior class of officials, who serve as messengers, and are known as Zingaffs.

Constitutional element: supreme council.

There is, however, a constitutional element in the Bhutan government. The Dharma and Deva Rajas are assisted by a council composed of the chief secretary to the Dharma Raja, the prime minister, the chief justice, the three Penlows when present at the capital, and three of the principal Jungpens.

Border aggressions.

The disputes between the British government and the tribes and states beyond the border are of the same mixed character along the whole line of frontier from Afghanistan to Arakan. Sometimes British villages are harried by mountain tribes; sometimes they have been silently and systematically annexed, as in the case of Nipal. Bhutan was guilty of both offences. Abortive attempts were made by the British government to keep the peace by paying yearly rent for disputed tracts; but nothing would stop the raids and kidnapping; and at last Lord Elgin sanctioned a proposition of the Bengal government to send an English mission to Punakha, the capital of Bhutan, to lay the complaints of the British authorities before the Bhutanese government.

[1] Dharma was the religion of the edicts of Asoka. See *ante*, page 52.

[2] In the ancient Sanskrit religion, Indra was the hero of the Aryan race and the Vaidik god of the firmament; as such he was worshipped as the king of the Devas or Devatas. See *ante*, page 62.

The story of the mission to Bhutan is only historical so far as it brings out the national characteristics of the Bhutanese. In the first instance a native messenger was sent to the Deva Raja to announce the coming of the mission. The Deva Raja replied that the complaints were too trival to be referred to the Dharma Raja, and that the British government ought not to have listened to them; but he promised to send some of the lowest officials, known as Zingaffs, to settle all disputes. The Zingaffs never came, and at last the English mission left Darjeeling for Punakha.

A.D. 1864

Historical importance of the mission to Bhutan.

At this very moment there was a revolution in Bhutan. The Deva Raja lost his throne and retired to a monastery; but civil war was still at work in western Bhutan, the very country through which the mission was about to pass on its way to Punakha. The Paro Penlow was staunch to the ex-Deva Raja; but his subordinate, the Jungpen of the frontier fortress of Dhalimkote, had joined the revolutionary party. The troops of the Paro Penlow were besieging the fortress of Dhalimkote, but retired on the approach of the English mission.

Civil war in Bhutan: flight of the ex-Deva Raja.

Under such cirumstances the Jungpen of Dhalimkote welcomed the approach of the English mission with warm professions of attachment to the British government. But the selfish craft of the Bhutanese barbarian was soon manifest. He sent musicians and ponies to conduct the Envoy to Dhalimkote; but he charged exorbitant prices for every article he supplied; and paid long complimentary visits to the different members of the mission, during which he drank spirits until he was permitted to retire, or, properly speaking, was turned out. Meanwhile the Envoy received a letter from the new Deva Raja, telling him to acquaint the Jungpen with the object of his mission. The Envoy replied that he could only negotiate with the head of the Bhutanese government. Accordingly, after many delays, he at last set out for Punakha.

Low cunning of the Jungpen at Dhalimkote.

It was obviously unwise to send a mission into a barbarous country like Bhutan without some knowledge of the state of parties. It was still more unwise for the British government to appear to side with either party. Yet Sir William Denison, the provisional Governor-General from Madras, ordered the mission to proceed on the ground that

Error of the provisional government at Calcutta.

A.D. 1864 — as the revolutionary party had got the uppermost, it would be politic to secure the help of the Jungpen who had espoused its cause. Thus a mission was sent to a new ruler, whose predecessor had only just been ousted from the throne, not with a formal recognition of his usurpation, but to complain of cattle lifting and kidnapping, and to settle all disputes respecting the border territory.

Opposition of the Bhutanese. In reality the Bhutanese authorities did not want to receive a mission at all; or to conclude a treaty which would only tie their hands. Accordingly they threw every obstacle in the way of the Envoy, and exhausted every possible means of inducing him to return short of main force. Of course it would have been more dignified to retire; but the Envoy was naturally anxious to carry out the instructions of his own government, and to lose no opportunity which would enable him to realise the object of his mission; and he would probably have been open to as much blame for a premature return to British territory as for a rash advance to the capital of Bhutan.

Letters from the Deva Raja. After leaving Dhalimkote an incident occurred which brings out the peculiar temper of the Bhutanese. Some messengers appeared carrying two letters to the Jungpen of Dhalimkote. They took upon themselves to tell the Envoy that the letters contained the orders of the new Deva Raja for the return of the mission; and then, as the Envoy was the party concerned, they made over to him the letters which were intended for the Jungpen. Accordingly the letters were opened and read. In one the new Deva Raja expressed a warm attachment to the British government, and directed the Jungpen to satisfy the Envoy on every point, and to settle every dispute. The other letter ought certainly to have been marked "private." It threatened the Jungpen with death for having permitted the mission to cross the frontier, and ordered him to make every effort to induce the Envoy to go back. Should, however, the Envoy still persist in going to Punakha, he was to be sent by another road, and to be furnished with all necessary supplies.

Failure of the mission. Such were the unpromising circumstances under which the Envoy pushed on to the capital. At Punakha the barbarian government gave vent to its coarseness. The Envoy was treated with rudeness and insult, and forced to sign a treaty "under compulsion," engaging to restore the territory in

A.D. 1864-1865

dispute to Bhutan.[1] No redress was offered for the outrages committed on British subjects, and none of the kidnapped persons were surrendered. On the contrary, the Bhutanese authorities set the British government at defiance; and the great Dharma Raja, the living incarnation of goodness, threatened to raise a score of demons of enormous magnitude for the destruction of the British empire, unless the territories signed away by the Envoy were promptly made over.

Bhutan war, 1864-65: its results.

Under these circumstances the treaty was nullified by a declaration of war. A campaign was begun in a difficult country of passes and precipices, reeking with a deadly malaria, and defended by a contemptible enemy, armed with matchlocks and poisoned arrows. It is needless to dwell upon military operations which reflect no glory on British arms or diplomacy. In the end the Bhutanese were brought to their senses, and compelled to restore the British subjects that had been carried away into slavery, and to make other restitutions which were necessary to satisfy the insulted honour of the British government. Arrangements were subsequently concluded as regards the disputed territory, and the payment of a yearly rent, which have proved satisfactory. Since then the Bhutanese authorities have profited by the lessons of 1864-65, and have proved better neighbours than at any previous period.

Central Asia: Russian advances and Afghan distractions.

Meanwhile the progress of events in Central Asia was forced upon the attention of the British government. Russia had reached the Jaxartes, and was supposed to be threatening the Usbeg States between the Jaxartes and the Oxus. Great Britain still maintained the Sulaiman range as her frontier against Afghanistan; but could not shut her eyes to the approaches of Russia towards the Oxus. At this crisis Dost Muhammad Khan was gathered to his fathers, and Afghanistan was distracted by a war between his sons for the succession to the throne.

Dost Muhammad Khan died in June, 1863. Ever since the treaties of 1855 and 1857 he had proved staunch to the

[1] The real offender on this occasion was the Tongso Penlow, the governor of Eastern Bhutan, and prime head of the revolutionary party, who was trying to usurp the government. The Deva Raja, and other members of the council, attempted to apologise for the rudeness of the Tongso Penlow, by pretending that it was all done in the way of friendly jocularity.

A.D. 1864-1865

Death of Dost Muhammad Khan, 1863.

English alliance. His anxiety to recover Peshawar was as strong as in the days of Runjeet Singh; but he held out against the temptations offered by the sepoy mutinies of 1857-58, and continued to respect the British frontier. Meanwhile, however, he established his suzerainty over Afghan-Turkistan,[1] as well as over Kábul and Kandahar; and shortly before his death he wrested Herát from the government of a disaffected son-in-law, and thus became the undisputed sovereign of a united Afghan empire.

Rivalry between Sher Ali Khan and Afzal Khan: recognition of Sher Ali by the British government.

Dost Muhammad Khan had fallen into the patriarchal error of nominating Sher Ali Khan, a younger son by a favourite wife, to be his successor to the throne, to the exclusion of Muhammad Afzal Khan, his eldest son by a more elderly partner. Accordingly a fratricidal war seemed inevitable. Afzal Khan was governor of Afghan-Turkistan; a post which he had held for many years during the lifetime of his father; and he began to prepare for a deadly struggle with his younger brother. Under such circumstances Sher Ali Khan was anxious for the recognition of the British government to his succession to the throne; and after some delay this was formally granted in December, 1863, by Sir William Denison, the provisional Viceroy.

Treacherous imprisonment of Afzal Khan by Sher Ali, 1864-66.

The bare recognition of Sher Ali Khan by the British government could not avert the fratricidal war. In June 1864 there was an indecisive battle between Sher Ali Khan and his elder brother, which was followed by a sham reconciliation. Each in turn swore on the Koran to abandon all designs against the other; and then, with the customary faithlessness of an Afghan, Sher Ali Khan suddenly ordered the arrest of Muhammad Afzal Khan, bound him with chains, and kept him in close confinement until the iron entered his soul.

Murder of Sher Ali's firstborn son: madness of the Amír.

This act of treachery was followed by a fearful retribution in the Amír's own family. Sher Ali Khan was warmly attached to his eldest son, and had appointed him heir apparent. The son was killed by an uncle in a fit of jealousy; and the uncle was in his turn cut to pieces by the soldiery. The murder of his eldest son drove Sher Ali Khan into a state of

[1] Afghan-Turkistan is the geographical term for the region northward of Kábul, lying between the Hindu Kúsh and the river Oxus. It comprises the districts of Maemana, Andkui, Saripul, Shibrghan, Balkh, Khulm, Kunduz and Badakhshan.

A.D. 1866-1867

temporary insanity; and to the end of his days he was often morose, melancholy and mad, like another Saul.

Flight of Sher Ali to Kandahar: Afzal Khan proclaimed Amír, 1866.

All this while Afzal Khan was in prison at Kábul; but his brother, Azim Khan, and his son, Abdul Rahman Khan, remained in possession of Afghan-Turkistan, and prepared for a renewal of the war. In May 1866 the uncle and nephew marched an army towards Kábul. A battle was fought in Afghan fashion. There was a brisk cannonade which did no execution, and then the bulk of Sher Ali Khan's troops suddenly deserted him and went over to the rebel army. The result was that Sher Ali Khan fled with a few horsemen to Kandahar, whilst Muhammad Afzal Khan was released from prison and proclaimed Amír of Afghanistan amidst general illuminations and a salute of a hundred guns.

Partition of Afghanistan.

In June, 1866, Afghanistan was distributed as follows: Kábul and Afghan-Turkistan were in the possession of Muhammad Afzal Khan. Kandahar remained in the hands of Sher Ali Khan; whilst his son, Yakúb Khan held the government of Herát, and retained it throughout the war.

Recognition of Afzal Khan and Sher Ali Khan by Sir John Lawrence.

The British government was in a dilemma. It had recognised Sher Ali as Amír of Afghanistan, on the plea that he was *de facto* Amír; but it was not prepared to give the Amír material help in the contest with his eldest brother. The fortunes of war however had placed Muhammad Afzal Khan in the position of *de facto* Amír. Sir John Lawrence tried to solve the problem by recognising Afzal Khan as ruler of Kábul and Afghan-Turkistan, and Sher Ali Khan as ruler of Kandahar.

Drunkenness of Afzal Khan: oppressions of Azim Khan.

Imprisonment however had exercised an evil influence on Afzal Khan, and he was no longer fitted to rule. He left the administration of affairs in the hands of his brother Azim Khan, and took to hard drinking. The government of Azim Khan was fearfully oppressive, owing to the pressing want of money. Caravans were stopped and plundered until all trade was at a standstill. Loans and contributions were mercilessly exacted from the people. Every sign of disaffection was stamped out by murder and confiscation; whilst the women and children of the offenders were condemned to beggary or starvation.

In January, 1867, Sher Ali Khan made an effort for the recovery of his throne. He raised an army at Kandahar and then marched towards Kábul. Azim Khan tempted

A.D. 1867-1868

Flight of Sher Ali from Kandahar to Herát, 1867.

him to a premature advance by feigning to retreat; and then suddenly opened a fire from his guns, which cut up the army from Kandahar. Sher Ali Khan managed to escape with a small body of horsemen to his son, Yakúb Khan, at Herát; but by so doing he left Kandahar in the hands of his brothers. To all appearance he had been deprived of his kingdom for ever, and was condemned to pass the remainder of his days in exile.

Death of Afzal Khan: accession of Azim Khan.

In October, 1867, Muhammad Afzal Khan perished of intemperance and disease. His death was followed by a fierce contest between his brother Azim Khan and his son, Abdul Rahman Khan. But the widow of Afzal Khan forced Abdul Rahman Khan to submit to his uncle, by pointing out that any rivalry between them would only serve to strengthen the hands of Sher Ali Khan.

Sher Ali Khan recovers the throne of Afghanistan, 1868.

Azim Khan reigned as Amír of Afghanistan from October, 1867, until August, 1868, when another revolution drove him from the throne. Yakúb Khan marched an army from Herát to Kandahar, and began an unexpected career of victory which ended in the restoration of his father, Sher Ali Khan, to the throne of Afghanistan. Azim Khan and his nephew, Abdul Rahman Khan, fled away to the northward, into Afghan-Turkistan; but were driven out the following year, and compelled to seek a refuge in Persian territory.[1]

Policy of Sir John Lawrence: gift of money and arms to the Amír.

During the fratricidal war in Afghanistan, the advances of Russia towards the Usbeg states of Khokand and Bokhara continued to excite attention. Sir John Lawrence however was of opinion that all difficulties might be removed by a friendly understanding with Russia. He was averse to any change of frontier, or to any interference whatever in the affairs of Afghanistan. But Sher Ali Khan was complaining and with some show of reason, that whilst he had shown his attachment to the British government in a variety of ways, he had received but few tokens of friendship or kindness in return. Accordingly it was proposed to strengthen the

[1] The writer was of opinion at the time, and freely ventilated it in an Indian journal, that the progress of the fratricidal war ought to have been stopped by the partition of Afghanistan between two or more chiefs; whilst the British government assumed the paramount power, and threatened to interfere unless the rival parties kept the peace. Later events have not induced him to change that opinion.

friendship between Great Britain and Afghanistan by a free gift of money and arms to the restored Amír.[1]

A.D. 1869-1870

Retirement of Sir John Lawrence.

Early in 1869 Sir John Lawrence was succeeded by Lord Mayo as Viceroy of India. He returned to England, and was raised to the peerage; and lived ten years longer, doing all the good work that fell in his way. He died in 1879 and was buried in Westminster Abbey. Few men of modern times have approached him in energy and capacity, and none have rendered greater services to the empire of British India.

Lord Mayo, Viceroy, 1869-72

Lord Mayo was a Viceroy of a different stamp from the famous Indian civilian. He was naturally wanting in a thorough familiarity with the details of Indian administration, but he had a wider knowledge of humanity, and a larger experience in European statesmanship. Courtly as well as dignified and imposing, there was a charm in his manner which ensured him a larger share of personal popularity than often falls to the lot of a Governor-General of India.

Conference with Sher Ali Khan at Umballa, 1869.

Shortly after the arrival of Lord Mayo at Calcutta, preparations were made for a meeting between the new Viceroy and Sher Ali Khan. In March, 1869, the conference took place at Umballa, about a hundred and twenty miles to the north-west of Delhi. It was attended with the best possible results. Sher Ali Khan had been chilled by the icy friendship of Sir John Lawrence, but he threw off all reserve and suspicion in the presence of Lord Mayo. The English nobleman won the heart of the Afghan, and established a personal influence which brightened for a while the political relations between the British government and the Amír.

Political difficulties.

But difficulties always crop up between a civilised power like Great Britian and a semi-barbarous government like that of Afghanistan, whenever attempts are made on either

[1] The policy of recognising a *de facto* ruler, and refusing to help him in times of difficulty and danger, may appear to be wise and prudent from an English point of view, but must seem cold and selfish to oriental eyes. When Sher Ali Khan was in danger of his throne and life, the English not only refused to help him, but recognised Muhammad Afzal Khan as Amír of Kábul and Afghan-Turkistan. When, however, Sher Ali Khan recovered his territory and throne, the British government was willing to help him with money and arms. Such friendship, so easily transferred from one prince to another, (with perhaps for decency's sake an expression of pity for the prince who has been worsted,) may be the outcome of masterly inactivity, but it has the disadvantage of appearing hollow and insincere.

A.D. 1870-1871

side to place political relations on a footing of equality. Sher Ali Khan naturally scrutinised the existing treaty with a jealous and jaundiced eye. It had been negotiated in 1855 by Sir John Lawrence with Dost Muhammad Khan.[1] It bound the Amír to consider the friends and enemies of the British government as his friends and enemies; but it did not bind the British government to like conditions as regards the friends and enemies of the Amír. Sher Ali Khan declared that this was a one-sided arrangement, and so in truth it was; but the British government was the protecting power, and had the right to insist on its conditions; and this was still more emphatically the case when it appeared as the giver of arms and money. Moreover, if the British government committed itself to the obligations proposed, it might have found itself compelled to interfere in civil broils, or take a part in foreign wars, in which it had no concern, and in which Sher Ali Khan might have been obviously in the wrong.

Conciliatory policy of Lord Mayo.

Accordingly Lord Mayo tried to reassure the Amír by telling him that the British government regarded him as the rightful as well as the *de facto* ruler of Afghanistan; and would view with severe displeasure any attempt on the part of his rivals to oust him from his throne. He added that the British government would not interfere with the internal affairs of Afghanistan, and would not, under any circumstances, employ its troops beyond the frontier to quell civil dissensions or family broils. The home government subsequently directed that Sher Ali Khan should be further informed that the British government would still be free to withhold the promised help should his government become notoriously cruel and oppressive. This however never seems to have been done.[2]

[1] The subsequent treaty of 1857 was also concluded by Sir John Lawrence, but was confined to arrangements consequent on the war which had broken out between Great Britain and Persia, and in no way superseded the treaty of 1855.

[2] All conditions as regards cruelty and oppression should be understood rather than expressed in dealing with foreign states. No diplomatic language can prevent its being regarded as a direct insult by any ruler, European or Asiatic. Moreover, it is wholly unnecessary. It is always competent for a state to threaten to break off all political relations in the case of notorious cruelty and oppression, or to carry its threats into execution in the event of a persistence in such a line of conduct. Similar conditions are understood in all societies, whenever a gross outrage is committed by any one of its members.

A.D. 1872-1880

Burma affairs.

Lord Mayo was the first Indian Viceroy since Lord Dalhousie who took a special interest in the affairs of British Burma. In 1862 Sir Arthur Phayre had been appointed Chief Commissioner of the united provinces of Arakan, Pegu and Tenasserim; and had proceeded to Mandalay the same year, and concluded a friendly treaty with the King of Burma. In 1867 his successor, General Fytche, proceeded in like manner to Mandalay, and concluded a second treaty, which led to a large extension of trade with Upper Burma, and the establishment of a line of steamers to Mandalay and Bhamo. No Viceroy, however, had landed at Burma since the visit of Lord Dalhousie in 1852. Accordingly when it was known in 1871 that Lord Mayo proposed making a trip to the province, the susceptible Burmese population were thrown into excitement by his expected arrival.

Visit of Lord Mayo to Rangoon and Maulmain: assassination at Port Blair. 1872.

The career of Lord Mayo was however destined to end in a tragedy. He landed at Rangoon in February 1872, with his personal staff and a brilliant party of guests, and was welcomed with the acclamations of thousands. Crowds of native ladies, a sight unknown in India, were present at the wharf to welcome Lord and Lady Mayo with offerings of flowers. Nearly an entire week was spent by Lord Mayo in receiving deputations from all classes of the community, and in surveying the vast strides which western civilisation had made in that remote territory during the brief period of twenty years. From Rangoon he paid a flying visit to Maulmain, and then steamed to the Andaman Islands to inspect the penal settlement at Port Blair. There in the dusk of the evening he was suddenly stabbed to death by an Afghan, who had been condemned to penal servitude for life on account of a murder he had committed on the British side of the north-west frontier, and who had taken the opportunity of wreaking his blind vengeance on the most popular of modern Viceroys.

Lord Northbrook, 1872-76: Lord Lytton, 1876-80.

With the death of Lord Mayo in 1872 the modern history of India is brought to a natural close. Lord Northbrook succeeded Lord Mayo as Viceroy, but resigned the post in 1876, and was succeeded in his turn by Lord Lytton. The details of their respective administrations are as yet too recent to be brought under review as matters of history. Two events however have occurred since 1872,

A.D. 1872-1880

which may be mentioned in the present place as likely to become landmarks in Indian annals.

Imperial Assemblage at Delhi, 1st January, 1877.

On the 1st of January 1877 Her Majesty Queen Victoria was proclaimed Empress of India in the old imperial capital at Delhi. The visit of His Royal Highness the Duke of Edinburgh to India in 1869, and the subsequent visit of His Royal Highness the Prince of Wales in 1875-76, had prepared the way for a closer association of the princes and people of India with the British Crown; and the celebration of an Imperial Assemblage at Delhi for the proclamation of the Empress will prove to all future ages an epoch in the annals of British India. It swept away the memory of the sepoy revolt of 1857, and associated Delhi with the might and majesty of the sovereign of the British empire. At the same time it brought all the princes and chiefs of India into personal intercourse in the same camp under the shadow of the British sovereignty. Old feuds were forgotten; new friendships were formed; and for the first time in history the Queen of the British Isles was publicly and formally installed in the presence of the princes and people as the Empress of India.

Estrangement of Sher Ali Khan: dealings with Russia.

Meanwhile, at the very moment that Delhi was the scene of festivity and rejoicing, black clouds were gathering beyond the north-western frontier. Sher Ali Khan had become estranged from the British government. He had placed his eldest son, Yakúb Khan, in close confinement on charges of disloyalty and rebellion; and he resented an attempt made by the British government to bring about a reconciliation. He considered himself ill-used in the settlement of his frontier on the side of Seistan with the Persian government. He was also mortified at the refusal of the British government to conclude a defensive alliance on equal terms, which had proved so disastrous in our dealings with Hyder Ali a century before.[1] In an evil hour he refused to receive a British mission at Kábul; whilst he made overtures to Russia, and received a Russian mission at his capital at a time when British relations with Russia were known to be unsatisfactory.

Second Afghan war.

Under such circumstances Sher Ali Khan was doomed to share the fate which befell his father, Dost Muhammad Khan, in 1839-40. In 1878 the British government made

[1] See *ante*, page 345.

a final effort to save him by sending a mission to his court; but it was driven back with threats and contumely. Accordingly the British government declared war, and a British force entered Afghanistan. Sher Ali Khan made a futile attempt at resistance, and then fled northward into Russian territory, where he died shortly afterwards.

A.D. 1878-1880

Flight and death of Sher Ali Khan, 1878-79.

Yakúb Khan came to terms with the British government. He was accepted as successor to his deceased father on the throne of Afghanistan; and he agreed to receive a British Resident, who should permanently remain at his capital. The treacherous attack on the Residency in September 1879, and massacre of Sir Louis Cavagnari and other officers, has led to the abdication of Yakúb Khan and British occupation of Afghanistan. What the result will be is one of the political problems of the day.[1]

Accession of Yakúb Khan: murder, and British occupation.

[1] The probable destiny of the Afghan people may possibly be gathered from an historical parallel in Jewish history, which the controverted question of Afghan ethnology renders none the less striking. The parallel is helped out by the fact which is beyond controversy; namely, that in physical characteristics and national instincts the Afghans closely resemble, if they are not akin to, the Jews (See *ante*, page 121). The old Assyrian kings tried hard to maintain Palestine as a buffer against Egypt; but they were ultimately compelled to transplant the Ten Tribes of Israel to the cities of the Medes; whilst the only king of Judah who was actively loyal to the Crown of Assyria was the unfortunate Josiah, who was slain by Pharaoh Necho in the battle of Megiddo. Four centuries later the Greek kings of Syria endeavoured to convert Palestine into a similar buffer; but after trying in vain to crush out the spirit of the nation by military despotism and massacre, they were compelled to succumb to the revolt of the Maccabees. Two centuries later the Romans made every effort to maintain order and law amongst the turbulent populations of Palestine; but after the death of Herod the Great,—a Dost Muhammad in his way,—the princes of his family dared not govern mildly lest their subjects should rebel, nor severely lest they should be deposed by Cæsar. Their régime proved a failure. No rulers, except Roman procurators of the stamp of Pilate and Festus, could succeed in keeping the peace. In the end, the grinding tyranny and rapacity of procurators of the stamp of Florus drove the nation frantic; and the struggle ended in the destruction of Jerusalem by Titus and final scattering of the Jewish nation.

From the sixteenth century to the nineteenth the political situation of Afghanistan has tallied with that of Palestine. The Moghuls tried to make Kábul a buffer against Persia, and Persia tried to make Kandahar a buffer against the Moghul. In the eighteenth century the Afghans rose against their conquerors; those of Kandahar overran Persia, and those of Kábul and Kandahar overran Hindustan. A new Afghan empire was subsequently founded by Ahmad Shah Dúraní, who bears a strange resemblance to king David; for in spite of his

A.D. 1878-1880 predatory wars and conquests, he gave utterance to strains of psalmody of which the following lines are a specimen :—

"I cry unto thee, O God! for I am of my sins and wickedness ashamed ;
But hopeless of thy mercy, no one hath ever from thy threshold departed.
Thy goodness and mercy are boundless, and I am of my evil acts ashamed ;
'Tis hopeless that any good deeds of mine will avail, but thy name I'll every refuge make.
O Ahmad ! seek thou help from the Almighty, but not from pomp and grandeur's aid."

It will also be seen that the reign of his grandson Zemán Shah bears some resemblances to that of Rehoboam ; whilst the revolt of the Barukzais, the viziers of the Dúranís, is not unlike the revolt of Jeroboam, the minister of Solomon. How far Afghanistan is likely to prove a buffer between British India and Russia, with or without British procurators, remains to be seen.

CHRONOLOGICAL TABLES OF INDIAN HISTORY.

CHRONOLOGICAL TABLES OF INDIAN HISTORY.

I. HINDU INDIA.

1500 B.C.—1400 B.C. Probable period of the Mahá Bhárata.
1000 „ Probable period of the Rámáyana.
500 „ Probable period of Sákya Muni, or Gótama Buddha.
327 „ Alexander invades the Punjab.
Passage of the Jhelum.
Defeat of Porus the Elder.
Alexander's retreat.
320 „ Empire of Magadha (Behar).
Chandra-gupta (Sandrokottos).
Asoka: Edicts of Asoka.
280 „ Græko-Baktrian supremacy.
100 „ Indo-Scythian supremacy.
56 „ Kanishka (Kanerke).
78 A.D.—Battle of Kahror.
Gupta supremacy.
319 „ Vallabhi Rajas.
Kingdoms of Andhra and Pandya.
400 „ Pilgrimage of Fah-Hian.
640 „ Travels of Hiouen-Thsang.
Empire of Kanouj: Maháraja Síláditya.
Buddhist-Brahman controversies.
1001 „ Muhammadan invasion.

II. MUHAMMADAN INDIA.

997 A.D.—Mahmúd of Ghazni.
1001 „ Mahmúd at Peshawar.
Turkish conquest of the Punjab.
Twelve Turkish invasions of Hindustan.
1001 A.D.—Battle of Somnáth.
1030 „ Death of Mahmúd.
1180 „ Afghan supremacy at Delhi: Muhammad Ghori (d. 1206).
1194 „ Mussulman advance to Benares.
Foundation of principalities in Rajpútana.
1206 „ Dynasty of Afghan Slave-kings: Kútub-ud-dín, Sultan of Delhi (d. 1210).
1290 „ Death of Jelál-ud-dín the last of the Slave-kings.
Alá-ud-dín, Sultan of Delhi (d. 1316).
Conquest of Guzerat.
Siege of Chitór.
1316 „ Tughlak, founder of the Tughlak Sultans of Delhi.
1325 „ Muhammad Tughlak (d. 1350).
1350 „ Firuz Shah (d. 1388).
Bahmani Sultans in the Dekhan.
1398 „ Timúr the Tartar invades Hindustan.
1400 „ Deva Rai, Maháraja of Narsinga.
1450 „ Lodi dynasty of Afghan Sultans at Delhi.
1498 „ Portuguese arrival in Malabar.
1500 „ Five Muhammadan kingdoms in the Dekhan.
Nanuk Guru founds the Sikh brotherhood in the Punjab.
1509 „ Albuquerque, Viceroy of Portuguese India (d. 1519).

1526 A.D.—Afghan Sultans at Delhi overthrown by Báber the Moghul (d. 1530).
Foundation of the Moghul empire.

1530 „ Báber succeeded by Humáyun (d. 1556).

1538 „ Portuguese mission to Bengal.
Turkish attack on the Portuguese at Diú.

1540 „ Humáyun defeated by Sher Khan.
Afghan rule in Hindustan.

1555 „ Return of Humáyun.

1556 „ Akbar, Padishah (d. 1605).
Akbar defeats the Afghans.

1565 „ Battle of Talikota.

1567 „ Destruction of Chitór.
Moghul conquest of Ahmadnagar and Berar.

1575 „ Rise of Abul Fazl.
Rebellion of Selim (Jehangír).

1599 „ Formation of the East India Company.

1605 „ Jehangír, Padishah (d. 1627).

1608 „ Mission of Captain Hawkins to Agra.

1615 „ Embassy of Sir T. Roe.

1623 „ Travels of Pietro della Valle.

1625 „ Venk-tapa Naik, Raja of Kanara.

1627 „ Shah Jehan, Padishah (d. 1665).

1632 „ Moghul capture of the Portuguese settlement at Húghli.

1639 „ English settlement at Madras.

1640 „ English settlements in Bengal at Húghli, Patna, and Dacca.

1658 „ Aurangzeb, Padishah (d. 1707).

1664 „ Sivaji the Mahratta captures Surat.

1666 „ War between Mahrattas and Moghuls.
Aurangzeb threatened by Persia.
Afghan massacre of Moghuls in the Khaiber Pass.

1673 „ Travels of Dr. Fryer.

1674 „ Sivaji Maháraja of the Mahrattas (d. 1680).

1677 „ Mahratta conquest in the Lower Carnatic.

1682 „ Moghul rebuffs in Rajpútana.

1685 „ War between the English and Moghuls.

1687 „ Moghul conquest of Bíjápur and Golkonda.

1689 „ Foundation of Calcutta.

1701 „ Dáúd Khan besieges Madras.

1707 „ Bahadur Shah, Padishah (d. 1712).

1707 A.D.—Sahu Rao, Maháraja of the Mahrattas (d. 1748).
Balaji Visvanath, first Peishwa (d. 1720).

1712 „ Jehandar Shah, Padishah.

1713 „ Farrukh Siyar, Padishah (d. 1719).

1715 „ English mission from Calcutta to Delhi.

1719 „ Muhammad Shah, Padishah (d. 1748).

1720 „ Baji Rao, second Peishwa (d. 1740).

1736 „ Mahratta advance on Agra and Delhi.
Nizam-ul-mulk, Nizam of the Dekhan; defeated by Baji Rao.

1738 „ Invasion of Nadir Shah.

1739 „ Battle of Kurnal.
Nadir Shah enters Delhi.

1740 „ Balaji Rao, third Peishwa (d. 1761).

1748 „ Raja Ram, the puppet Mahárája of the Mahrattas, a state prisoner at Satara.
Afghan invasion of India under Ahmad Shah Abdali.

III. BRITISH INDIA.

1736 A.D.—Civil war in Trichinopoly.

1739 „ Sarfaráz Khan, Nawab of Bengal (d. 1742).

1740 „ Mahrattas invade the Carnatic.

1742 „ Alivardi Khan, Nawab of Bengal.
Mahratta invasions of Bengal.

1743 „ English mission to Nizam-ul-mulk at Trichinopoly.

1745 „ War between England and France.

1746 „ Labourdonnais captures Madras.

1747 „ Rise of Ahmad Shah Dúrání, founder of the Afghan empire (d. 1773); Jemal Khan Barukzai.

1748 „ Stringer Lawrence fails to take Pondicherry.
Death of Muhammad Shah: Ahmad Shah, Padishah.
Death of Nizam-ul-mulk.
Death of Maháraja Sahu.
Peishwa sovereignty begins.
First appearance of Clive.

1749 „ English aggressions on Tanjore.

1750 „ Nasir Jung at Arcot; appoints Muhammad Ali Nawab.
Victories of Dupleix.

1750 A.D.—Bussy captures Jingi.
French capture of Masulipatam.

1750 „ Peace between Alivardi Khan and the Mahrattas.
Alom Phra the hunter founds a dynasty in Burma.

1751 „ Ascendancy of Dupleix.
Clive's expedition to Arcot.
Siege of Arcot.

1752 „ Clive's victories in the Carnatic.
French surrender Trichinopoly.

1753 „ Clive goes to England.

1754 „ Janoji Bhonsla succeeds Rhughoji Bhonsla as Raja of Berar.

1755 „ Anglo-French treaty at Pondicherry.
Removal of Dupleix.
Return of Clive.

1756 „ Destruction of Gheriah by Watson and Clive.
Suraj-ud-daula, Nawab of Bengal.
Suraj-ud-daula captures Calcutta.
The Black Hole.

1757 „ Clive and Watson recapture Calcutta.
English capture of Chandernagore.
Battle of Plassy.
Mír Jafir, Nawab of Bengal.
Mahrattas claim chout for Bengal and Behar.
Ahmad Shah Abdali at Delhi; drives out Ghazi-ud-dín.
Bussy's war against the Hindu Poligars; self-sacrifice of Bobili Rajpúts.
Bussy captures Vizagapatam.

1758 „ Advance of the Shahzada, eldest son of Ahmad Shah Padishah, towards Behar: defeated by Clive.
Lally at Pondicherry.
Lally captures Fort St. David.
Forde's successes in the Northern Circars.
Siege of Madras by Lally.
Clive governor of the English settlements in Bengal.

1759 „ Alamghir, Padishah, murdered at Delhi by Ghazi-ud-dín.
Second invasion of Ahmad Shah Abdali.
Lally raises the siege of Madras.
Battle of Wandiwash.

1760 „ Coote besieges Pondicherry.

1760 A.D.—Clive departs for England; succeeded by Holwell.

1761 „ Madhu Rao, fourth Mahratta Peishwa (d. 1772).
Nizam Ali, Nizam of the Dekhan.
Coote captures Pondicherry.
Battle of Paniput.
Ahmad Shah Abdali appoints Jewan Bakh (son of the Shahzada) deputy Padishah.
Regency of Najib-ud-daula (d. 1770).
Return of the Shahzada to Behar: proclaimed Padishah under the name of Shah Alam.
Shuja-ud-daula, Nawab of Oude (d. 1775), appointed Vizier to Shah Alam.
Vansittart, governor at Calcutta.
Deposition of Mír Jafir.
Mír Kasim, Nawab of Bengal; defeats the Nawab Vizier of Oude.
Installation of the Great Moghul at Patna.

1762 „ Disputes about private trade.
Warren Hastings in the Calcutta council.

1763 „ General abolition of duties by Mír Kasim.
Patna captured by the English, and recaptured by the Nawab's troops.
Capture of Cossimbazar by the Nawab's troops.
Mír Jafir proclaimed Nawab.
English capture Monghyr.
Massacre of English at Patna.
English storm Patna.
Delhi threatened by the Játs.

1764 „ The Nawab Vizier repulsed by the English at Patna.
Hector Munro stops a sepoy mutiny.
Battle of Buxar.
Rise of Shitab Rai.
Surrender of the Nawab Vizier.
Suraj Mal, the Ját hero, slain at Delhi.

1765 „ Death of Mír Jafir.
Governor Spencer sells Bengal and Behar to Muhammad Reza Khan.
Return of Clive to India: foundation of the double government.

1766 „ English treaty with Nizam Ali.

1767 „ Final departure of Clive.
Verelst, governor of Bengal.

1767 A.D.—Rise of Hyder Ali of Mysore.
Hyder Ali and Nizam Ali invade the Carnatic.
Death of Mulhar Rao Holkar: accession of Ailah Bai (d. 1795), and Tukaji Holkar (d. 1797.)
Last invasion of Ahmad Shah Abdali.
Ghorka conquest of Nipal: Prithi Narain, the Ghorka hero (d. 1771).

1768 " Second English treaty with Nizam Ali.
Hostile advance of Hyder Ali against the English.

1769 " English treaty with Hyder Ali at Madras.
Cartier, governor of Bengal.
Mahratta aggressions in Hindustan.

1770 " Famine in Bengal.

1771 " Mahadaji Sindia restores Shah Alam to the throne of Delhi.

1772 " Warren Hastings, governor of Bengal.
Narain Rao, fifth Peishwa.

1773 " Warren Hastings holds a secret conference with Shuja-ud-daula at Benares.
Narain Rao murdered.
Rughonath Rao, sixth Peishwa.
Rughoji Bhonsla, Raja of Berar.
Tanjore made over to Muhammad Ali.
Timúr Shah on the throne of Kandahar (d. 1793): Payendah Khan Barukzai.

1774 " Rohilla war.
Warren Hastings, first Governor-General.
The Calcutta Council; Francis, Clavering, Monson, and Barwell.
Creation of a Supreme Court of Judicature at Calcutta.
Revolution at Poona.

1775 " Asof-ud-daula, Nawab Vizier of Oude (d. 1797).
Charge of corruption against Warren Hastings.
Execution of Nund-komar.
Treaty between the English at Bombay and Rughonath Rao.
Rebellion of Cheit Singh, Raja of Benares.
Run Bahadur, Maháraja of Nipal.

1776 " Treaty of Purundhur.
Tanjore restored to the Raja by Lord Pigot.

1778 A.D.—Rumbold, governor of Madras.
English capture of Pondicherry.
Bombay expedition to Poona, 1778.

1779 " Convention of Wurgaum.
First Mahratta war.
Bhodau Phra, King of Burma (d. 1819).

1780 " English capture of Gwalior.
Whitehill, governor of Madras.
Hyder Ali invades the Carnatic.
Battle of Porto Novo.
Runjeet Singh, Viceroy of Lahore.

1781 " Lord Macartney, governor of Madras.
War between English and Dutch; capture of Pulicat and Sadras.

1782 " Close of the first Mahratta war.
Nana Farnavese ratifies the Treaty of Salbai.
Madhu Rao II., seventh Peishwa (d. 1795).
Death of Hyder Ali.

1784 " Treaty of Mangalore.
Mr. Pitt's Bill; the Board of Control.

1785 " Warren Hastings leaves India.
Macpherson, Mr., provisional Governor-General.

1786 " Lord Cornwallis, Governor-General.

1787 " Tippu Sultan attacks Travancore.

1788 " Gholam Kadir at Delhi.

1790 " Mysore war.

1792 " Submission of Tippu Sultan.
Mahadaji Sindia at Poona.
Chinese invasion of Nipal.
Ghorka treaty with the English.
Permanent land settlement in Bengal.

1793 " Sir John Shore (Lord Teignmouth), Governor-General.
Zemán Shah succeeds Timúr Shah at Kandahar.

1794 " Mahadaji Sindia succeeded by Daulat Rao Sindia.

1795 " Battle of Kurdla.
Umdut-ul-Umra, Nawab of Arcot (d. 1801).
Baji Rao II., eighth Peishwa (d. 1853).
Revolution at Khatmandu.
Threatened invasion of Zeman Shah.

1797 " Saádut Ali, Nawab Vizier of Oude.

1797 A.D.—Rise of Jaswant Rao Holkar.

1798 „ Lord Mornington (Marquis of Wellesley), Governor-General.
English alliance with Nizam Ali against Tippu.

1799 „ Last Mysore war.
Storming of Seringapatam.
Death of Tippu.
Purnea, minister at Mysore (d. 1811).

1800 „ Buchanan's travels in Mysore.
Malcolm's mission to Persia.
Death of Nana Farnavese.
Pandey conspiracy at Khatmandu: flight of Run Bahadur.
Mahmúd, Shah of Afghanistan (d. 1829).

1801 „ Assumption of the government of the Carnatic.
Risings of the Ghilzais in Kábul; suppressed by Futih Khan.

1802 „ Baji Rao and Sindia defeated by Jaswant Rao Holkar.
Treaty of Bassein.
Mission of Captain Knox to Khatmandu.

1803 „ Baji Rao restored to Poona.
Second Mahratta war.
Battles of Assaye and Argaum.
Battles of Alighur and Delhi.
Revolution at Khatmandu.
Moghul kings of Delhi become the pensioners of the British government.
Shah Shuja, Shah of Afghanistan.

1804 „ War between the English and Jaswant Rao Holkar.
Col. Monson's retreat.
Return of Run Bahadur to Khatmandu.
Downfall of the Pandeys.
Murder of Run Bahadur.
Massacre at Khatmandu of the enemies of the Thapas.
Ascendency of Bhím Sein Thapa.

1805 „ Lake defeats Holkar and besieges Bhurtpore.
Lord Cornwallis, Governor-General a second time.
Sir George Barlow, Governor-General.
Submission of Jaswant Rao Holkar.

1806 „ Mutiny at Vellore.

1807 „ Lord Minto, Governor-General.
Runjeet Singh's aggressions on the Cis-Sutlej states.

1808 A.D.—Metcalfe's mission to Runjeet Singh.

1809 „ Restoration of Mahmúd Shah to the throne of Kábul by the Barukzais.

1810 „ British occupation of the Mauritius and Java.

1811 „ Mulhar Rao Holkar succeeds to the throne of Indore.
Depredations of Amír Khan and of the Pindharies.
Lingaraja, ruler of Coorg, (d. 1820).
Krishnaraj assumes the government of Mysore.

1813 „ Lord Moira (Marquis of Hastings), Governor-General.
Ghorka aggressions on British territory.
Nipalese occupation of British districts.
Ghorka slaughter of British police.

1814 „ Nipal war.

1815 „ The Gaekwar of Baroda sends Gungadhur Shastri to Poona.
Murder of Gungadhur Shastri.
Imprisonment of Trimbukji Dainglia.

1816 „ Treaty of Segowlie.
Pindhari raids on British territories.
Quarrels between Persia and Afghanistan respecting Herát.
Escape of Trimbukji Dainglia.

1817 „ Treaty of Poona.
Pindhari War.
Baji Rao repulsed by the English at Khirkí.
Flight of the Peishwa from Poona.
Battle of Sitabuldí.
Battle of Mehidpore.

1818 „ Defence of Korygaum.
Extinction of the Peishwa.
Settlement of the Holkar state.
Resuscitation of the Raj of Satara.
Early Burmese history.
Portuguese adventurers.
Byeen-noung conquers Pegu.
Siege and capture of Martaban by Byeen-noung.

1820 „ Metcalfe, Resident at Hyderabad, condemns the bank of Palmer and Co.
Chikka Vira Raja succeeds Lingaraja at Coorg.

1823 A.D.—Mr. Adam, provisional Governor-General.
Lord Amherst, Governor-General.
1824 „ First Burmese war: British expedition to Rangoon.
„ Phagyi-dau, King of Burma.
1825 „ British advance to Prome.
Outbreak at Bhurtpore.
1826 „ Treaty of Yandabo.
Crawfurd's mission to Ava.
Capture of Bhurtpore.
Dost Muhammad Khan, Amír of Kabul.
1827 „ Daulat Rao Sindia succeeded by Jankoji Rao Sindia (d. 1843).
1828 „ Lord William Bentinck, Governor-General.
1833 „ Rebellion in Mysore: deposition of Krishnaraj by the British government.
1832 „ Disturbances in Jaipur.
1833 „ Civil wars stopped at Gwalior and Indore by British intervention.
Hari Rao Holkar on the throne of Indore.
Renewal of the East India Company's charter.
1834 „ The Maháraja of Jaipur poisoned.
British campaign in Coorg.
Annexation of Coorg.
1835 „ Murder of Mr. Blake in Jaipur.
Sir Charles Metcalfe, provisional Governor-General.
1836 „ Lord Auckland, Governor-General.
1837 „ The Shah of Persia marches against Herát.
Siege of Herát.
Revolution at Ava.
Tharawadi, king of Burma.
Fall of Bhím Sein Thapa at Khatmandu.
1838 „ The Shah of Persia raises the siege of Herát.
Lord Auckland declares war against Afghanistan.
British advance to Quetta.
1839 „ British capture of Kandahar, Ghazni and Kábul.
Russian expedition to Khiva.
Death of Runjeet Singh.
Tragedies at Khatmandu.
Death of Bhím Sein Thapa.
Kharak, Maháraja of Lahore, (d. 1840).
Dethronement of the Raja of Satara.
1840 „ British occupation of Kábul.
The British Residency expelled from Ava.
1840 A.D.—Lord Auckland remonstrates with the Maháraja of Nipal.
Nao Nihal Singh, Maháraja of Lahore.
1841 „ Withdrawal of Major Todd, the British Resident, from Herát.
Insurrection at Kábul: murder of Sir Alexander Burnes.
General reconciliation at Khatmandu.
Dhián Singh places Sher Singh on the throne of Lahore.
1842 „ Destruction of the British army in the Khaiber Pass.
Sale's defence of Jellalabad.
Lord Ellenborough, Governor-General.
Pollock's advance to Jellalabad.
British advance on Kábul.
Battle of Tezeen.
Murder of Stoddart and Conolly at Bokhara.
Disturbances at Khatmandu.
1843 „ Jyaji Rao Sindia, Maháraja of Gwalior.
Disturbances at Gwalior.
Battles of Maharajpore and Punniar.
Matabar Singh overthrows the Pandeys at Khatmandu.
Assassination of Dhián Singh and Sher Singh at Lahore; Dhulíp Singh, Maharaja.
1844 „ Settlement of Gwalior affairs.
Irregular installation of Tukaji Rao Holkar at Indore.
Lord Hardinge, Governor-General.
Crisis at Lahore.
1845 „ Pagán Meng, king of Burma.
Murder of Matabar Singh.
Sikh army of the Khálsa invades British territory: first Sikh war.
Battles of Moodkee and Ferozeshahar.
1846 „ Massacre at Khatmandu.
Jung Bahadur, prime minister.
Battle of Sobraón.
Close of the first Sikh war.
Jamu and Kashmír sold to Gholab Singh.
Temporary British occupation of the Punjab.
1848 „ Lord Dalhousie, Governor General.
Disaffection of Múlraj, Viceroy of Múltan.

1848 A D.—Treachery and murder at Múltan.

Successes of Herbert Edwardes.

Second Sikh war.

Revolt of Sher Singh.

The Sikhs joined by Afghans.

Lapse of Satara to the British government.

1849 „ Battle of Chillianwallah.

Battle of Guzerat.

Annexation of the Punjab.

1851 „ Mission of Commodore Lambert to Rangoon.

Second Burmese War.

Meng-don Meng, king of Burma.

Annexation of Pegu.

1853 „ Sir John Lawrence, Chief Commissioner of the Punjab.

Annexation of Nagpore.

Cession of Berar to the British government.

1855 „ Outbreak of hill-tribes, Koles and Santáls.

English alliance with Dost Muhammad Khan.

1856 „ Annexation of Oude.

Lord Canning, Governor-General.

Persian war.

Capture of Bushire and battle of Mohamrah.

1857 „ Sepoy mutiny.

Mutiny at Barrackpore.

March 29th Outbreak of Mungal Pandy.

May 3rd Explosion at Lukhnow.

„ 10th Mutiny at Meerut.

„ 11th The rebels at Delhi.

„ 30th Mutiny at Lukhnow.

June 4th Mutiny at Jhansi.

Mutiny at Cawnpore.

„ 6th Siege of Cawnpore by Nana Sahib.

„ 27th The massacre on the Ganges.

July 1st Coronation of Nana Sahib as Peishwa.

„ 7th Advance of Havelock towards Cawnpore.

„ 15th Massacre of women and children at Cawnpore.

„ „ Battle of Cawnpore.

„ 17th Havelock's advance to Bithoor.

General insurrection in Oude.

Defence of the Residency at Lukhnow; death of Sir Henry Lawrence.

Havelock's victory at Bithoor.

Barnard's advance to Delhi.

Sept. 14th Storming of Delhi.

„ 21st Arrest of the king; the two princes shot.

Sept. 25th Relief of the Residency at Lukhnow by Havelock and Outram.

Nov. 23rd Second relief by Sir Colin Campbell.

„ 24th Death of Havelock.

Defeat of the Gwalior rebels.

1858 „ Trial and transportation of Bahadur Shah.

Lord Clyde's campaign in Oude and Rohilkund.

Outram captures Lukhnow.

Sir Hugh Rose's campaign in Central India.

Sindia defeated by the Gwalior rebels.

Tantia Topi and the Gwalior rebels routed by Sir Hugh Rose.

1858 „ The Queen's proclamation.

Hindustani fanatics driven out of Sitana.

1859 „ Trial and execution of Tantia Topi.

End of the Oude rebellion.

Lord Canning's durbar at Agra.

1862 „ Lord Elgin, Viceroy.

Sir Arthur Phayre, Chief Commissioner of British Burma, concludes a treaty with the king of Burma.

1863 „ The Sitana campaign.

Sir William Denison, provisional Viceroy.

The Bhutan mission.

Death of Dost Muhammad Khan.

Sher Ali Khan recognised by the British government.

1864 „ Sir John Lawrence, Viceroy.

Bhutan war.

Sher Ali treacherously imprisons his brother, Afzal Khan.

1866 „ Flight of Sher Ali to Kandahar: Afzal Khan proclaimed Amír.

Partition of Afghanistan.

Sir John Lawrence's recognition of Afzal Khan and Sher Ali Khan.

1867 „ Sher Ali defeated by Azím Khan; his flight from Kandahar to Herát.

Death of Afzal Khan: accession of Azim Khan.

General Fytche, Chief Commissioner of British Burma, concludes a treaty with the king of Burma

1868 „ Sher Ali recovers the throne of Afghanistan.

1869 „ Lord Mayo, Viceroy.

The Umballa conference.

1869 A.D.—Visit of H.R.H. the Duke of Edinburgh to India.

1872 ,, Lord Mayo visits Rangoon; assassinated at Port Blair.

Lord Northbrook, Viceroy.

1875 ,, Visit of H.R.H. the Prince of Wales to India.

1876 ,, Lord Lytton, Viceroy.

1877 ,, The Imperial Assemblage at Delhi on the 1st of January 1877: proclamation of Her Majesty Queen Victoria as Empress of India.

1877 A.D.—Death of Jung Bahadur.

1878 ,, Sher Ali's rejection of a British mission.

Declaration of war against Afghanistan.

1879 ,, Death of Sher Ali.

Accession of Yakúb Khan.

Attack on the British Residency at Kábul; massacre of the English mission.

British occupation of Afghanistan.

INDEX.

INDEX.

A.

C.

D.

E.

H.

I

L.

M.

N.

O.

P.

R.

S.

T.

U.

V.

W.

Y.

Z.

THE END.